Football

An Encyclopedia of Popular Culture

EDWARD J. RIELLY

UNIVERSITY OF NEBRASKA PRESS • LINCOLN & LONDON

© 2009 by the Board of Regents of the
University of Nebraska
All rights reserved
Manufactured in the United States of America

∞

Library of Congress Cataloging-
in-Publication Data

Rielly, Edward J.
Football : an encyclopedia of popular culture /
Edward J. Rielly.
    p. cm.
Includes bibliographical references and index.
ISBN 978-0-8032-9012-9 (pbk. : alk. paper)
1. Football—United States—Encyclopedias.
2. Football—Social aspects—United States.
I. Title.
GV948.85.R54 2009
796.332—dc22
2009005245

Set in Minion by Kimberly Essman.

For Jeanne, whose support is always super

Contents

Preface

Football: An Encyclopedia of Popular Culture is a book, as the title indicates, about football and about popular culture, but especially about many of the points of intersection between the two. Football is not known as America's national pastime, a name that baseball has locked away securely in its diamond-shaped vault. Yet football, like baseball, reflects much of what we find in American society and in this nation's popular culture.

"Popular culture" has increasingly become a subject of academic study in recent decades. At the same time, it has achieved considerable respectability, no longer the inferior cousin to "high culture." This rise in esteem has come from a greater understanding of what the concept means. "Culture" is usually taken as the sum of those activities, interests, and values that members of a group (or at least a significant percentage of the members), in a certain place at a certain time, share and that therefore define the group. Adding the term "popular" to "culture" means that the group is not a small, elite coterie but the masses. There are those who decry anything smacking of mass consumption, but in a democracy that claims to place great value on both the individual and the collective citizenry, an elitist (which is to say "high") approach to culture appears contradictory.

Football is of the masses. As such, it is in itself part of America's popular culture. At the same time, football has become wedded to many other dimensions of American popular culture, and explaining those points of wedded bliss (or lack of bliss) is the point of this book. Subjects have been included that meet two criteria, rather broadly conceived. First, the item must have some intrinsic significance to football. Second, it must have some significance off the gridiron as well. So let us turn to some of those meetings of football and other areas of American culture.

Football has joined forces with film, literature, television, music, magazines, newspapers, and other avenues of expression. It is home to the most widely watched sports spectacle of the year, the Super Bowl. Saints (or at least very good people) and sinners (including some despicable criminals) have taken up residence within the sport.

Many of the men who have played or coached the game have become household names. Women also have found roles within football, although those roles have been generally limited and limiting. As with other areas of American society, football resisted admitting members of minorities, but ultimately African Americans integrated the sport as they did baseball and other American professions and pastimes. American Indians have been part of the history of football for a long time, yet today the struggle continues to remove pejorative mascots and team nicknames (even, in the case of the National Football League's Washington franchise, the official name of the club).

Military conflicts from World War I to the war in Afghanistan have had their impact on the game, and no element of American society, including football, remained untouched by the terrorist attacks of September 11, 2001.

Football players may become celebrities, but they have the same needs as other people, including a meaningful role in workplace governance and a retirement free from poverty and untreated illness. They also have the same responsibilities to abide by the law of the land and the norms of fair competition regarding dangerous or illegal substances. This book also explores these matters.

Stories of heroism and tragedy affect football players as they do others. Players overcome great odds to snatch victory from defeat on the gridiron, and more heroically give their lives on the field of battle. They also sometimes die young apart from warfare. Legends grow up about them, such as a young man on his deathbed urging his coach sometime when things are really tough to ask his players to win a game for him.

Fans of football include men and women, young and old, everyday folks and the rich and powerful. They even include presidents of the United States, some of whom played the game in earlier days.

These and many other matters provide the scope of this book. This is not a history of football, but it does include much history of the sport. There is no separate entry for the National Football League, but so many of the entries delineate the history of the league that a separate entry would have involved excessive repetition. Nor is the volume a compilation of all the great players past and present or even of all those who have earned admittance into a college or professional hall of fame. Many great players, and some that were not so great, appear within these pages, but usually because they connected with some aspect of society beyond the football field. Every reader will take issue with certain choices that were made about which players to include and which to exclude. In truth, this book could have gone on and on, until it became too heavy to carry.

Finally, the author had to say, "Enough is enough. It is time to turn off the computer and move on." In a strict sense, there is no true completion to this book, as there is no end to the game of football, no final moment in the life of the nation. But for now, this book, the author hopes, will be found to reflect many ways in which American society has affected football and in turn been affected by the sport. Like the fan who leaves the game for a moment to grab a sandwich from the refrigerator and returns to find a touchdown scored or a pass intercepted, the reader who comes to this book will look in vain for some important moments that transpired between the writing and the publishing or between the publishing and the reading. That is as it should be. The game really does go on.

Entries vary in length within this book. The length usually was determined by the complexity of the relationship between the subject and American society or by the magnitude of the subject itself. It is also true, the author readily admits, that some subjectivity on occasion probably impacted the length.

A word about voice. Most encyclopedias are written in a sort of bloodless, disembodied tone. Here the author speaks as the author, although he hopes with reason and emotion, and with attention to balance and fairness. But opinions are expressed and judgments made. The entries have been envisioned as essays, and essays usually have a point of view.

Finally, the author has drawn upon a great many helpful sources in writing this book. Entries include both cross-references and a short list for additional reading. These readings are also a way to acknowledge the author's gratitude for those many works that have provided information and insights. Certain sources, however, deserve special acknowledgment, such as the outstanding Web sites offered by the Pro Football Hall of Fame and the National Football Foundation's College Football Hall of Fame. In addition, a treasure trove of information is contained within the pages of *Total Football II: The Official Encyclopedia of the National Football League*, *ESPN College Football Encyclopedia*, and *The ESPN Pro Football Encyclopedia*.

The author also expresses his gratitude to the many thousands of individuals who over the years built the sport that has provided not only the basis for this book but so much personal entertainment. Finally, he is enormously appreciative of the assistance provided by his institution, Saint Joseph's College of Maine, and deeply grateful to his wife, Jeanne, for her unwavering support.

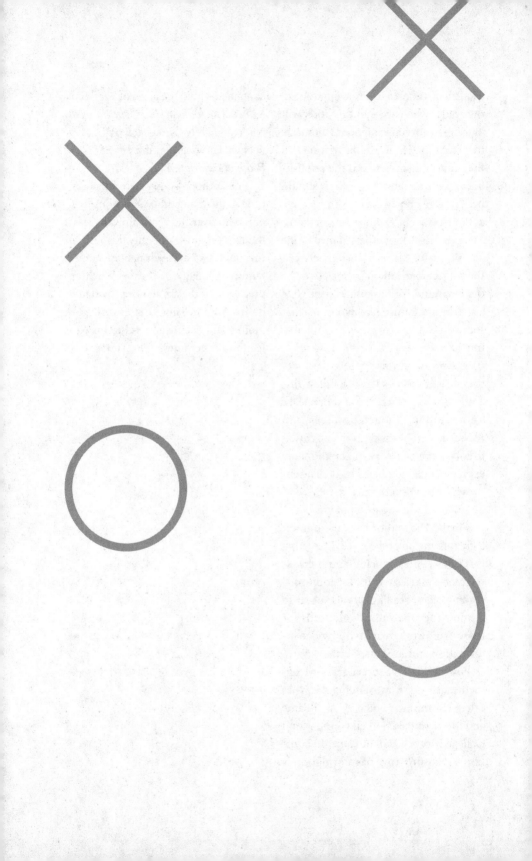

Football

African Americans (College)

College football in the North was at least moderately open to African Americans from its early days in the nineteenth century, although in the South integration, as in the broader society, would be much longer coming. When integration finally was achieved in southern football, more than halfway through the twentieth century, both the sport itself and the country would be much richer for it.

The first African American player in a major college football game is usually identified as William Henry Lewis, who played center for Amherst College in Massachusetts starting in 1889. Lewis later played for Harvard while attending law school there, coached the Harvard team (becoming the first salaried coach in the university's history), wrote A Primer of College Football (1896), and became a friend of Pres. Theodore Roosevelt. Roosevelt appointed Lewis assistant U.S. attorney for Boston, and Pres. William Howard Taft named him assistant attorney general of the United States (both firsts for an African American). At a time when President Roosevelt was demanding that football be made a less dangerous sport, Lewis rose to the occasion, suggesting a neutral zone between the offense and defense. That neutral zone at the line of scrimmage became a rule in college (and subsequently professional) football in 1906.

Another early African American player was George Jewitt, the starting fullback at the University of Michigan in 1890. Halfback Frederick "Fritz" Pollard played at Brown University in 1915 and 1916. After the 1915 season he became the first African American to play in the Rose Bowl as Brown lost to Washington State. The following season saw Pollard earn All-America honors. He later starred in professional football and became the first National Football League head coach when he co-coached the Akron Pros in 1921. Pollard was inducted into the College Football Hall of Fame in 1954.

Paul Robeson was a two-time All-American end during his collegiate days at Rutgers. After graduating as valedictorian of his class in 1919, he played professional football and achieved fame as an actor and singer while becoming a highly controversial political activist. Robeson was inducted into the College Hall of Fame in 1995.

Oze "Ozzie" Simmons, an all-state high school quarterback in Texas, showed up at the University of Iowa in 1933 along with his brother, Don, wanting to play football. After Ozzie returned two punts for touchdowns in a punting drill, Coach Ossie Solem added both brothers to his team.

Ozzie, nicknamed "the Ebony Eel" for his slipperiness as a runner and, of course, also for the color of his skin, went on to become a second-team Associated Press All-American as a halfback in 1935. His brother, although not Ozzie's equal as a football player, was a productive end for Iowa. Ozzie was expected to be named captain of the Iowa team in 1936, but the players, apparently not wanting him as captain and not wanting to vote against him, dropped the honorary position for the season.

George Halas apparently was inclined to sign Ozzie to a Chicago Bears contract in 1936, three years into a twelve-year period during which African Americans were excluded from the NFL, but could not get other owners to agree. Simmons instead played in an all-black league with the Patterson Panthers and for a largely white semipro team, the Patterson New Jersey Sox, through the 1930s.

The most tragic story of early African American college players is probably that of Jack Trice, the first African American athlete to attend Iowa State University. Primarily a tackle, Trice looked forward to his first game, an October 6, 1923, contest against the University of Minnesota in Minneapolis.

Trice's position as a pioneer and representative of his race weighed heavily on him, but he thoroughly accepted the responsibility. The night before the game, he wrote a letter later found in his suit. In the letter, he reflected on his responsibilities to his race, family, and, of course,

himself as he prepared to play Minnesota. The letter included details relating to how he intended to play and an assurance that he would do well. Unfortunately, he never had a real chance.

Trice broke his collarbone on the second play of the game but insisted he was all right. In the third quarter, Minnesota ran a wedge play, and Trice took on three players to try to disrupt the formation. The players hit him so hard that he was removed from the game despite his continued insistence that he was fine. Two days later, the young man who had been so determined to excel, for himself and for others, his lungs hemorrhaging, died from internal bleeding.

Four thousand students and faculty attended Trice's funeral on the Iowa State campus. Fifty years later, when a new football stadium was constructed at Iowa State University, the playing field was named Jack Trice Field, although the student government strongly favored naming the entire stadium after him. The student government, however, did not let the matter drop and in 1987 raised enough money to erect a statue of the former Iowa State student-athlete. The effort to rename the entire stadium after him continued, and finally, in 1997, it was renamed Jack Trice Stadium.

Countless African American athletes played football in northern colleges and universities in the following decades, but in the South segregation kept them out of most football programs except those at all-black institutions. The first football game between all-black schools took place in North Carolina in 1892, with Biddle College defeating Livingston College. Throughout the early twentieth century, strong football programs arose in many historically black colleges and universities.

The most powerful football program at a black college in the 1920s was at Tuskegee Institute (now University) in Alabama. Later, dominant football programs developed at, among other places, Morgan College (now Morgan State University) in Maryland and Grambling College (now Grambling State University) in Louisiana. Grambling's football program has achieved the most renown among all historically black colleges, thanks to the lengthy tenure of coaching legend Eddie Robinson.

As the civil rights movement spread throughout the South in the 1950s and 1960s, it affected football as well as the rest of society. Perhaps the two most pivotal games involving the issue of integration were the contests between the University of Pittsburgh and Georgia Tech at the Sugar Bowl in New Orleans on January 2, 1956; and the University of Southern California and the University of Alabama at Birmingham on September 12, 1970.

The Pittsburgh team in 1955 included an African American, Bobby Grier, who played fullback and linebacker. It had become common practice when an integrated team played a southern all-white squad to be ruled by which team was at home. If in the North, the black players would play; if in the South, the black players would stay home. Never had an African American played in the Sugar Bowl.

Pittsburgh, however, was not about to leave Bobby Grier home, and the thought of Georgia Tech playing an integrated team outraged Georgia Gov. Marvin Griffin. In December, just one day after Rosa Parks had refused to give up her seat on a bus in Montgomery, Alabama, Griffin railed against the game. "The South stands at Armageddon," he wrote in a telegram to Georgia's Board of Regents. Pittsburgh held firm, even demanding that the Sugar Bowl abandon its segregated seating for Pittsburgh fans who attended the game.

Opposition to Griffin came from many quarters: Georgia Tech students (who burned him in effigy), the press, and even at least one member of the Regents (David Rice). The Tech players seemed quite willing to play against Grier and had, in fact, played against black players before, including members of the University of Notre Dame team. Tech quarterback Wade Mitchell publicly announced that he had no objection to playing against an integrated team. Faced with such opposition, Griffin backed down. Pittsburgh's determination to bring its entire team or nobody at all helped to break down the ban on black players journeying south with their teams. Ironically, however, the game turned on an apparent mistake by Grier.

Grier played well for most of the game, breaking off a gain of 28 yards for the longest run of the Sugar Bowl contest. However, in the first quarter, with Tech in possession on the Pittsburgh 33-yard line, Grier was called for pass interference. The penalty put the ball on the 1, and Mitchell scored two plays later. The final score was Georgia Tech 7, Pittsburgh 0. Grier always claimed that receiver Don Ellis had pushed him and that offensive interference should have been called, but what mattered more than the penalty or even the final score was the fact that Bobby Grier had played. The football world was changing.

It still would be years, however, before some of the southern universities and their football programs would be integrated. The Southern Cal–Alabama game helped to move that process forward.

Only seven years before these teams met, Alabama Gov. George Wallace had stood in a doorway of the University of Alabama to prevent black students from entering the university. Yet here was African American Sam Cunningham, a sophomore and the starting fullback, playing his first varsity college game and doing it in one of the cities most associated with segregation. Several other African Americans were also on the Southern Cal squad, including tailback Clarence Davis, a Birmingham native.

The game proved not to be much of a contest. Southern Cal won 42–21 as Cunningham rushed for 135 years on just twelve tries and scored twice. After the game, Alabama coach Paul "Bear" Bryant took Cunningham into the Alabama locker room. "Gentlemen," he said to his own players, "this is what a football player looks like." Each of the Alabama players then rose and shook Cunningham's hand.

Bear Bryant's statement surely had two meanings, referring to Cunningham's status as an outstanding player who had just helped defeat his Alabama team, but also to his color. Bryant was making a point and justifying a decision that he had already made. Above all, Bryant wanted to win, and he was willing to accept black players on his own team in order to remain competitive. He knew how the winds of change were blowing and that all football teams would soon be recruiting black players. In fact, Bryant already had recruited his first African American, a speedy running back named Wilbur Jackson. Jackson, however, was only a freshman, and freshmen were not yet eligible to play on the varsity. Next year he would be truly a member of the Crimson Tide, and Bryant wanted his decision accepted. It would be, of course, in a state where Bear Bryant could do no wrong. Jackson would go on to star for Alabama, lead the team in rushing in 1973, be a first-round draft pick of the San Francisco 49ers in 1974, and have a successful professional career.

The following years would see African Americans play important roles within every major football program in the country, North or South. Progress in the coaching ranks, though, would be far slower. As of March 2007 only 6 of the 119

FBS football programs had a black head coach. The numbers were even worse in the lower levels: excluding historically black schools, just 5 in the FCS subdivision, 2 in Division II, 1 in Division III. In addition, just 12 African Americans held the position of athletics director in FBS institutions, and not a single African American served as commissioner of a major conference. By December 2008 the situation had improved only marginally, with eight black FBS head coaches. Much had changed since the days of William Henry Lewis, but some things had stayed too much the same.

See also: African Americans (Professional); Black College Football; Brown, Paul Eugene; Bryant, Paul William; Davis, Ernie; Grambling State University; Hudson, Donald Edward; Little Rock Central Tigers; Pollard, Frederick Douglass; Robeson, Paul Leroy Bustill; Robinson, Eddie Gay.

Additional Reading:
MacCambridge, Michael, ed. ESPN *College Football Encyclopedia: The Complete History of the Game.* New York: ESPN Books, 2005.
Oriard, Michael. *King Football: Sport and Spectacle in the Golden Age of Radio and Newsreels, Movies and Magazines, the Weekly and the Daily Press.* Chapel Hill: University of North Carolina Press, 2001.

African Americans (Professional)

African Americans experienced a period of exclusion from professional football, although it was much shorter in duration than the lengthy stretch from the late nineteenth century to 1947 in which African Americans were banned from Major League Baseball. In professional football, the color barrier stretched across twelve years, from the 1933 season to 1946. It would take years following World War II, however, for the National Football League to be thoroughly integrated with players, and much longer for African Americans to make their way in any significant numbers into the front office or the head coaching ranks.

Charles Follis is usually credited with being the first African American professional football player while with the Shelby Steamfitters team in the Ohio League. Follis actually joined Shelby in 1902, but there is no evidence of his being paid until the 1904 season. An outstanding running back, Follis ripped off an 83-yard touchdown run against Marion in the season's opening game. He continued to star through the 1905 season but retired in 1906 after a string of injuries.

One of Follis's teammates for Shelby was Branch Rickey, who while serving as football coach of the Ohio Wesleyan second team sometimes played for Shelby. Some sports historians conjecture that Rickey's observations of Follis may have played a role in his decision to bring Jackie Robinson into major league baseball. Rickey also had witnessed Follis from the other side, especially his four touchdowns for Wooster College against Ohio Wesleyan in 1903 at a time when Follis was playing for both his college team and Shelby.

Other African American pioneers who predated the National Football League included Charles "Doc" Baker, a onetime physician's assistant (hence his nickname) who played halfback for the Akron Indians; Henry McDonald, a halfback for the Rochester Jeffersons; and Gideon "Charlie" Smith, a tackle with the Canton Bulldogs. McDonald played seven seasons, more than any other early black players, becoming well known in the process. Smith had the shortest career, just one game with Canton in 1915. In that sole appearance, however, he recovered a fumble to preserve a 6–0 win over the Massillon Tigers.

The American Professional Football Association (soon to be known as the National Football League) began play in 1920. During its first fourteen seasons, thirteen African Americans played in the league, a small number but at least a presence. The 1923 season included the largest number of black players, six. While racism certainly was a major factor in limiting the number, it was also true that the black community in America much preferred baseball over football despite MLB's racial ban. Baseball, through the Negro Leagues, became a huge black industry until, ironically, integration in the 1940s began to destroy the Negro Leagues as top black players increasingly opted for trying to reach the majors rather than play in the Negro Leagues.

The most prominent of the thirteen African Americans in the early NFL was Frederick "Fritz" Pollard, a star at Brown University who played for several teams in the NFL between 1920 and 1926. An outstanding halfback, Pollard also became the first African American coach in NFL history when he served as co-coach for the Akron Pros in 1921.

Among the thirteen were end Jay "Ink" Williams, who played in the NFL from 1921 to 1926, primarily for the Hammond Pros; Fred "Duke" Slater, a tackle for a decade in the NFL (1922–31), the final six years with the Chicago Cardinals; and Sol Butler, a back who played from 1923 until 1926, closing out his career with the Canton Bulldogs. Paul Robeson played two years in the NFL, 1921 with the Akron Pros (for Fritz Pollard) and in 1922 when he followed Pollard to the Milwaukee Badgers. Robeson had been a first-team All-American at Rutgers but had a short professional career. His greatest fame came after football when he became a widely known singer and actor as well as a social activist.

The final African American players in the National Football League until 1946 were Ray Kemp and Joe Lillard. Kemp had limited impact while playing tackle for the Pittsburgh Pirates in his lone season. Lillard, however, was a multitalented player who excelled at running, passing, and kicking. His college career at the University of Oregon came to a premature end in 1931 when he was charged with playing semipro baseball. In 1932 Lillard joined the Chicago Cardinals, where he kicked and returned punts as well as rushing and passing. However, again Lillard ran into trouble; this time, his coach, Jack Chevigny, suspended Lillard for the final two games of the season after accusing him of missing practices, disobeying team rules, and failing his blocking assignments. Lillard was reinstated for the following season and, against the Chicago Bears, outran the great Red Grange to return a punt 53 yards for a touchdown. Although he led his team in scoring that year, his playing time was reduced as the season progressed and he was released after the final game.

The end of African American players in the NFL did not come overnight. It was a gradual development, with the number of players dropping until there were just two in 1933. Even then, the prohibition against blacks appeared not to be instantly absolute. Pittsburgh offered Kemp a contract for 1934, but he declined it to return to college. George Halas apparently wanted to employ halfbacks Ozzie Simmons and Kenny Washington in 1939, the latter being one of the greatest college football players of his time, but Halas could not get permission from other owners.

Charles K. Ross, author of *Outside the Lines: African Americans and the Integration of the National Football League*, argues that Washington Redskins owner George Preston Marshall was the primary agent behind establishing the color barrier. Whether or not that was the case, his Washington club was the last NFL team to integrate once the color barrier began to fall after World War II.

In the meantime, some all-black football teams and leagues formed, although nowhere near the level of the baseball Negro Leagues. Fritz Pollard organized an all-star black team as early as 1928 that later became the Chicago Black Hawks. In 1935 he moved to the Brown Bombers, a Harlem team named after boxing champion Joe Louis. Among his players was Joe Lillard. Pollard permitted his players to sing spirituals and "truck" from the huddle up to the line, somewhat along the entertainment lines of the Cincinnati Clowns baseball team or the Harlem Globetrotters, but without any antics during plays.

Other black teams included the Chicago American Giants, owned by H. G. Hall, who also owned the Negro League team of the same name, and the Chicago Comets (later the Chicago Panthers). Some teams joined together to form the Virginia Negro League, an all-black football league. African American players also played for white semipro teams, Joe Lillard, for example, with the Union City Rams in New Jersey. Ozzie Simmons, whom George Halas had once wanted to sign, played for the Patterson, New Jersey, Sox. Some also played for service teams during the war.

A major development that helped to open the professional football doors to African Americans began in a meeting in St. Louis, held on June 4, 1944, two days before D-Day, another, obviously much larger, pivotal event in American history. The St. Louis meeting, chaired by Arch Ward, sports editor of the *Chicago Tribune* and founder of the major league baseball and professional football all-star games (the latter between college all-stars and the NFL champion), produced an agreement to start a new professional football league, the All-America Football Conference.

As the All-America Football Conference moved toward its first season in 1946, the new league's Los Angeles Dons and the NFL's Los Angeles Rams (which had just moved from Cleveland) sought permission to play in the Los Angeles Municipal Coliseum. The Coliseum Commission, however, urged on by black sportswriters, expressed opposition to teams that practiced racial discrimination using the publicly owned stadium. Both teams yielded, promising to sign black players.

The Rams followed through, signing Kenny Washington, one of the best-known African American football players in the country. Washington had starred at UCLA, leading the nation in total yards in 1939. In that same year, Washington had teamed with end Woody Strode and halfback Jackie Robinson to help UCLA go undefeated, although they did have four ties. The Rams then brought in another African American player, Washington's college teammate, Strode. As other NFL teams integrated, they tended to follow the pattern of hiring black players in pairs, partly so that a player would have a supportive teammate of the same race but also so that black and white players would not have to room together.

The Dons, despite their pledge, did not sign a black player until 1947, but another All-America Football Conference team, the Paul Brown–led Cleveland Browns, did. Brown brought in two great players, both of whom would make the Pro Football Hall of Fame—tackle Bill Willis and fullback Marion Motley. Both also had played under Brown previously, Willis at Ohio State and Motley during the war at the Great Lakes Naval Training Center. Both would help the Cleveland Browns win their league championship in each of the four years of the league's existence.

Slowly, haltingly, the professional teams moved toward integration. Prior to the 1950 season the new league dissolved, most of the teams either shifting into the NFL or merging with existing NFL teams. Meanwhile, integration continued to inch forward.

The last holdout was the Washington Redskins. Finally, Secretary of the Interior Stewart Udall, a member of Pres. John F. Kennedy's cabinet, found the lever that would lift the Redskins into compliance, ending the embarrassing segregated status of the lone NFL team located in the nation's capital. George Preston Marshall had signed a lease to play home games at DC Stadium. However, the stadium, paid for with public funds, was located on land that was part of the National Capital Parks system. What that meant was that the Interior Department was the team's landlord and could demand that any organization doing business on park land not discriminate on the basis of race.

Udall issued an ultimatum, and Marshall tried to resist. However, he was going up against the United States government, and when other owners began to feel considerable embarrassment over the standoff, they asked Commissioner Pete Rozelle to meet with Marshall and urge compliance. Finally, on December 4, 1961, the NFL draft occurred. With the first pick, Washington selected Ernie Davis, an African American running back from Syracuse who had won the Heisman Trophy. Washington also drafted two other black players. The Redskins traded Davis to the Cleveland Browns but in return received two other African Americans, including running back Bobby Mitchell. The team also traded for Pittsburgh's John Nisby, an African American guard. Nisby and Mitchell starred for Washington, with Mitchell ultimately moving into Washington's front office as assistant general manager after retirement and being elected to the Pro Football Hall of Fame.

The process of integration was far from over when the new Redskins players took the field in 1962, but it continued. Certain positions, such as quarterback and middle linebacker, were largely closed to black players for years, and all head coaches and most assistant coaches remained white for decades.

By 2007, however, close to 70 percent of NFL players were African Americans. Several black quarterbacks were starting for their teams, and a black NFL quarterback, Warren Moon, had been inducted into the Hall of Fame. Art Shell became the first African American head coach in modern times when Al Davis, owner of the Oakland Raiders, hired him in 1989. Davis fired Shell in 1994, rehired him, and fired him again. The two head coaches in the 2007 Super Bowl for the first time in Super Bowl history were both black: Tony Dungy of the victorious Indianapolis Colts and Lovie Smith of the losing Chicago Bears. In all, six African Americans were head coaches at the beginning of the 2008 season, a significant improvement although well below what the number should be given the percentage of black players in the league. Especially discouraging was the small number of African American general managers, with only three holding that position. As with American society at large, much had been accomplished, but much still remained to do.

See also: African Americans (College); Black College Football; Brown, Paul Eugene; Davis, Allen; Davis, Ernie; Grambling State University; Pollard, Frederick Douglass; Robeson, Paul Leroy Bustill; Robinson, Eddie Gay; Rooney Rule.

Additional Reading:

African American Pioneers in Pro Football. Canton OH: Pro Football Hall of Fame, n.d.

Levy, Alan H. *Tackling Jim Crow: Racial Segregation in Professional Football.* Jefferson NC: McFarland, 2003.

Ross, Charles K. *Outside the Lines: African Americans and the Integration of the National Football League.* New York: New York University Press, 1999.

Agents

Football players share with actors, writers, and other professional athletes the practice of employing agents to help them find work and negotiate contracts. This can be good if the agent is honorable and knowledgeable, or lead to disaster if the agent is dishonest or incompetent.

Some 1,600 agents seek to represent the 1,900 football players who annually make up NFL rosters. That comes out to just over one player for each agent. The reality, however, is quite different. A survey conducted by the National Football League Players Association for the 2003 season found that 57 percent of agents had no football clients at all while seventy-seven agents had more than eleven clients. Two percent of the agents represented approximately 20 percent of the football players.

An agent usually receives 3 to 5 percent of the player's salary but 10 to 20 percent of endorsement contracts. Some of the agents also are lawyers, and most offer what is called "full-service" representation. In other words, the agent will negotiate the contract, handle the player's business affairs, decide on investments, serve as marketing consultant, and even arrange personal details of the player's life. That may sound good, but as Tim Green, a player turned author, points out in *The Dark Side of the Game*, few agents, even if honest and well intentioned, are qualified in all of these areas. Green also points out that some agents have been known to offer inducements, even sex and drugs, to persuade a player to sign with them.

Steps have been taken to protect players. The Players Association certifies agents but cannot compel players to use certified agents. The NFLPA also prohibits agents from offering anything of substantive value as an inducement, but that is a rule impossible to enforce completely. A majority of states have enacted legislation requiring agents to register, but registering, while a useful step, does not guarantee ethical behavior by each registered agent.

With players making big money, and top players suddenly finding themselves millionaires while still in their early twenties, there is a great deal of money to be made by agents. Honest effort can do a lot for players, and certainly many if not most agents try to act in an ethical manner. Yet there also is strong motivation to bend the rules and seek a quick killing even if the player suffers down the road. Players, especially young men just out of college and seeing big money for the first time, before signing on with an agent should heed that old caution, "Caveat emptor," or for those who never made it into the Latin end zone, let the buyer beware.

See also: Scouts.

Additional Reading:

Green, Tim. *The Dark Side of the Game: My Life in the NFL*. New York: Warner Books, 1997.

Rosenhaus, Drew. *A Shark Never Sleeps: Wheeling and Dealing with the NFL's Most Ruthless Agent*. With Don Yaeger and Jason Rosenhaus. New York: Pocket Books, 1997.

Shropshire, Kenneth L. *Agents of Opportunity: Sports Agents and Corruption in Collegiate Sports*. Philadelphia: University of Pennsylvania Press, 1990.

———, and Timothy Davis. *The Business of Sports Agents*. Philadelphia: University of Pennsylvania Press, 2003.

All-America Football Conference

The All-America Football Conference, the first professional league to compete with significant success against the National Football League, made three important contributions to American society. It helped to integrate professional football, it spread professional football to the West Coast, and it brought to American consciousness some of the most popular teams and players in the history of professional football.

The league to a great extent was the offspring of the influential *Chicago Tribune* sports editor Arch Ward, who previously had helped create the major league baseball All-Star Game and the College Football All-Star Game. Ward met with prospective owners in St. Louis on June 4, 1944, just two days before the Allied invasion of western Europe would begin to turn the tide of World War II. Out of that meeting came considerable interest in a new league and a name, the All-America Football Conference. Ward's rationale for another professional football league was the structure of major league baseball, which included two leagues. So why not professional football as well?

The league began play in 1946 and lasted as a separate entity for four years, but its impact would continue down to the present day. The new league's commitment to be taken seriously as an equal to the NFL was emphasized by the selection of its commissioner: Jim Crowley, former Notre Dame Four Horsemen teammate of the NFL's commissioner, Elmer Layden.

Adding to the name recognition of the new organization was the secretary-treasurer, Eleanor Gehrig, widow of the great Yankees star.

Unlike some of the earlier NFL competitors, these owners for the most part had plenty of money, so much so that their meetings were often referred to as "the millionaires' coffee klatch." Actor Don Ameche headed up the ownership team of the Los Angeles Dons. His ownership group included film producer Louis B. Mayer, comedian Bob Hope, and singer Bing Crosby. Lumber tycoon Anthony Morabito was a willing sponsor of the San Francisco 49ers. Dan Topping abandoned the Brooklyn Dodgers of the NFL to join the All-America Football Conference as owner of the (what else?) New York Yankees. These football Yankees came by their name more appropriately than their predecessors because Topping also was co-owner of the baseball Yankees. He was later joined as co-owners of the AAFC team by fellow baseball Yankees owners Larry MacPhail and Del Webb.

Eight teams organized in two divisions opened the 1946 season. Coaching the Cleveland Browns was Paul Brown, already famous in Ohio for his work at Massillon High School, Ohio State University, and, during the war, the Great Lakes Naval Training Center. Brown put on the field that first year two African American players who would eventually make the Pro Football Hall of Fame: fullback Marion Motley, who had played under Brown at the Great Lakes Training Center; and linebacker Bill Willis, a star for Brown at Ohio State.

With Los Angeles and San Francisco playing in California, the All-America Football Conference truly did stretch across the country from East to West, as well as from North to South (with the Miami Seahawks, although the Miami team lasted just one year). Rising to the challenge, the NFL also moved west in 1946, the Cleveland Rams shifting to Los Angeles. The Rams also began competing in a second major way, by signing African American players. The Rams, denied access to the Los Angeles Memorial Coliseum unless they integrated, signed former UCLA great Kenny Washington and his Bruins teammate, Woody Strode. In both leagues, the door was now open, and increasing numbers of African Americans would play their way through it. With the improvement in air travel, professional football also was on the West Coast to stay, and it would spread more fully throughout the rest of the country in the coming decades.

The All-America Football Conference brought names before the general public as well as the sports fan that would endure well beyond the careers of individual players and coaches. Two of the original AAFC teams—the Cleveland Browns and San Francisco 49ers—and a team added in the league's second year to replace Miami—the Baltimore Colts—would help to rewrite NFL history after joining that league in 1950. Paul Brown would ensure his place in coaching history as one of the greatest of coaching innovators, and a long stream of players would achieve lasting fame in the AAFC and later in the NFL, among them Otto Graham, Y. A. Tittle, and Elroy "Crazylegs" Hirsch.

The greatest AAFC team was Cleveland, coached by Brown and featuring Graham at quarterback, Motley at fullback, the great receivers Dante Lavelli and Mac Speedie, tackle and place-kicker Lou "the Toe" Groza, and linebacker Willis. The Browns won the league championship each year, suffering only four losses during the league's history and going through the 1948 season undefeated. Proving they were not just a big fish in a little pond, the Browns made it to the NFL Championship Game during each of their first six years after the merger, winning three times (1950, 1954, 1955).

The AAFC at its best was very good. The Browns certainly demonstrated that to everyone after joining the NFL, but the league overall proved able to attract talent as no other league, except the NFL, had been able to do. Forty of the sixty-six players in the College All-Star Game that followed the 1945 season signed with the new league, as did many of the returning war veterans. The Browns, Dons, and Yankees consistently drew large crowds to their games, with the Los Angeles and New York teams outdrawing their NFL competitors in those cities.

Overall, however, both the old and new leagues were losing money, a condition that along with the popularity enjoyed by some of the AAFC teams, led to the merger. The Colts had not been one of the league's successful teams, winning only one game in its final season. Nonetheless, the Colts entered the NFL along with the Browns and 49ers because Washington Redskins owner George Preston Marshall thought that a Baltimore team would create a natural rival for his club. Within a few years, a quarterback named Johnny Unitas would help make the decision to admit Baltimore look very good indeed.

Many players joined various NFL teams, including a defensive back from Brooklyn–New York (the Brooklyn Dodgers having merged with the Yankees in 1949) named Tom Landry, who would become one of the great NFL coaches. In a variety of ways, the AAFC thus remained alive even after its cessation as an independent league, including the current printing of its players' statistics alongside those of NFL players in *Total Football*, the reference bible of professional football.

See also: Brown, Paul Eugene; Four Horsemen of Notre Dame; Graham, Otto Everett, Jr.; Landry, Thomas Wade; Tittle, Yelberton Abraham; Ward, Arch.

Additional Reading:

Brown, Paul. *PB: The Paul Brown Story*. With Jack Clary. New York: Atheneum, 1979.

Carroll, Bob, et al., eds. *Total Football II: The Official Encyclopedia of the National Football League*. New York: HarperCollins, 1999.

Graham, Otto, and Duey Graham. *OttoMatic: The Remarkable Story of Otto Graham*. Wayne MI: Immortal Investments Publishing, 2004.

American Football League (I, II, III)

Few names for a league would seem to offer more marketing appeal than "American Football League," conveying as it does a nationalistic sense of connection, yet only the fourth league by that name achieved significant success. The first AFL lasted just one year and was largely a showcase for professional football's first superstar attraction, Red Grange.

Grange joined the Chicago Bears out of the University of Illinois in 1925. After the regular season concluded, the Bears embarked on a barnstorming tour that lasted until late January. Not only was Grange the first superstar of the National Football League, but also he was a pioneer in hiring an agent, C. C. Pyle (known commonly as "Cash and Carry" Pyle because of his focus, generally successful, on money). Pyle made a contract offer to the Bears for Grange's continued services in 1926 that included part ownership of the team. Turned down, he requested an NFL team in New York for Grange and himself. At the urging of Tim Mara, owner of the New York Giants, who wanted no competition in the city, the NFL gave Pyle another rejection.

Pyle then started his own league. It included nine teams, one of them the New York Yankees, owned by Pyle and featuring Red Grange. Pyle also had a financial stake in Los Angeles and Chicago teams. Some NFL players joined the new league, as did an occasional former college star, such as Harry Stuhldreher, one of the Four Horsemen of Notre Dame.

The league immediately ran into trouble with inadequate attendance, teams started folding within a month of the opening of the season, and only four teams survived the complete schedule, including the three clubs with which Pyle was personally involved.

The Yankees were probably the best team in the AFL but actually finished second to the Philadelphia Quakers with a 10-5 record to the Quakers' 8-2. Although the Grange-led Yankees demonstrated a good offense, overall the league managed just forty-two touchdowns in forty-one games. The tedium of watching teams battling unsuccessfully to reach a goal line proved less than inspiring to football fans.

The Yankees with Red Grange followed up the season, as the Bears had done the previous year, with a barnstorming tour to capitalize on Grange's fame, but the league could not survive its generally inauspicious first (and last) season.

A decade later, another AFL jumped into the professional football world. The guiding spirit behind this league was Dr. Harry March, personnel director of the New York Giants.

The second AFL was organized as a players' league, which seemed promising. Players would no longer be mere labor but management as well. Eight teams began play in 1936, but organizations quickly ran into financial trouble, some folding or relocating. March resigned, replaced by James Bush, president of the New York Yankees (again a New York team tried to piggyback on the name that the baseball club made famous). Five teams made it to the end, with the Boston Shamrocks winning the championship.

The league lasted one more year, with two new teams, one former member (the Cleveland Rams) accepted into the NFL, and yet another league president, J. J. Schafer. The advisory board for the AFL included boxing great Jack Dempsey and crooning great Bing Crosby. Again there was attrition during the season, with the winless Pittsburgh Americans dropping out. The Los Angeles Bulldogs swept through the campaign winning all nine of its games. No other team finished with a winning record, the lack of competition contributing to the demise of AFL II, although some of the teams continued as independents and a minor league AFL played for the remainder of the decade.

During the 1940s, for the third decade in a row, an American Football League emerged to challenge the NFL as a major football league. As with its predecessor, this one also would survive for just two years.

Six teams began play in 1940, with William D. Griffith as league president. Between the first and second seasons, there was considerable turnover in teams, and only five were around for the beginning of play. A draft experiment failed utterly, as the AFL introduced a plan to draft fifty top college players and then let the players choose their teams, but no top players bit.

The Yankees (with football folks refusing to give up on the name) signed John Kimbrough, an All-American fullback from Texas A&M. However, the AFL removed the Yankees owner, Douglas Hertz, and transferred the franchise to a group of new owners, who renamed the team the Americans. The newly revamped New York team then signed another All-American, Tom Harmon of Michigan.

Harmon, however, played just one game before entering military service. With the United States entering World War II after the attack on Pearl Harbor on December 7, 1941, the AFL canceled its plans for the 1942 season and never resumed play.

See also: American Football League (IV); Grange, Harold Edward.

Additional Reading:

Gill, Bob, and Tod Maher. *The Outsiders: The Three American Football Leagues of 1936–1941*. North Huntingdon PA: Professional Football Researchers Association, 1989.

Korch, Rick. "The Early AFLs." In *Total Football II: The Official Encyclopedia of the National Football League*. Ed. Bob Carroll et al., 523–26. New York: HarperCollins, 1999.

American Football League (IV)

By the 1960s many leagues had attempted to compete with the National Football League, but all finally had succumbed to the greater power and popularity of the NFL, although the All-America Football Conference in the 1940s had made the strongest case for an alternate league, ultimately merging with the NFL.

In the 1960s, however, the fourth league to take unto itself the appealingly nationalistic, if previously unsuccessful, name of "American Football League" began play. The league had some extremely wealthy men behind it, including Lamar Hunt, who had failed in his attempt to buy the NFL Chicago Cardinals and move the franchise to Dallas, Texas. Other owners included Bud Adams, a Houston oilman, and the automobile executive Ralph Wilson.

The NFL tried to thwart efforts to start a rival league by offering to expand into Dallas and Houston with new clubs, but the suggestion did not lure Adams and Hunt away from their fellow AFL owners. Max Winter of Minneapolis, former owner of the basketball Lakers, did prove susceptible, abandoning the AFL to accept, along with his partners, an expansion NFL team, the Minnesota Vikings. The first NFL team named for a state, the Vikings entered the league in 1961.

The American Football League, with Joe Foss, a former World War II pilot and South Dakota governor, as commissioner, began play in 1960 with eight teams in two divisions. The Los Angeles Chargers won the Western Division that first year and, after losing in the title game to the Eastern champion Houston Oilers (now the Tennessee Titans), moved to San Diego. The Chargers, a powerhouse during the first half of the 1960s, played in the championship game five times in the first six years of the league, although they won only once.

Another major move occurred prior to the 1963 season, when Hunt moved his

Texans from Dallas to Kansas City and renamed them the Chiefs. With Hank Stram as coach, the franchise won the AFL championship as the Texans in 1962 and as the Chiefs in 1966. After the latter season, the Chiefs met Vince Lombardi's Green Bay Packers in the first Super Bowl, losing 35–10. The Chiefs repeated as AFL champions in 1969, this time defeating the Minnesota Vikings 23–7 in Super Bowl IV.

Most AFL players at first were NFL veterans, such as quarterback and placekicker George Blanda, who resurrected their careers in the new league; or players who had failed to make it in the NFL, such as Jack Kemp, who became a star AFL quarterback and later a prominent political figure. The league also looked north to the Canadian Football League, from whence came Cookie Gilchrist, who rushed for more than 1,000 yards in 1962. From the start, however, the AFL also moved aggressively to compete for college stars, winning the bidding war for 1959 Heisman winner Billy Cannon.

Three key figures in helping the AFL succeed were David "Sonny" Werblin, Joe Namath, and Al Davis. Werblin purchased the New York Titans in 1963, renamed the team the Jets (a much more modern-sounding name), moved into an impressive new stadium in 1964, and signed quarterback Joe Namath in 1965. That same year he drafted Heisman quarterback John Huarte out of Notre Dame. The following year Huarte moved on to the Boston Patriots, but Namath became

an instant star, his skill and personality earning him the nickname "Broadway Joe." Werblin's quick splash as Jets owner in the nation's media capital certainly played a role in the AFL's obtaining a five-year contract with NBC in 1965 worth $36 million. Namath's prediction of victory in Super Bowl III came true as the Jets defeated the Baltimore Colts, 16–7, on January 12, 1969. The stunning upset demonstrated that the upstart league had achieved parity with the long-established NFL.

Al Davis was an assistant coach with the Chargers when the Oakland Raiders hired him as head coach and general manager in 1963. He left to become AFL commissioner in 1966 but returned as managing general partner and finished building the team that won the AFL championship in 1967 and played in Super Bowl II, losing to the Packers 33–14.

By 1965 discussions were occurring between the rival leagues concerning a merger. The talks were kept as secret as possible. Initially, Colts owner Carroll Rosenbloom and Bills owner Ralph Wilson conducted the meetings, before turning the process over to Chiefs owner Lamar Hunt and Tex Schramm, general manager of the Dallas Cowboys, to work out the details. Pete Rozelle, who had become NFL commissioner in 1960, announced the merger on June 8, 1966. The agreement included a common draft starting in 1967, a postseason game (soon known as the Super Bowl) to start with the 1966 season, and consolidation into one league by 1970.

Two new franchises were added to the AFL in these years, the Miami Dolphins in 1966 and the Cincinnati Bengals in 1968, the latter headed by Paul Brown, legendary former coach of the Cleveland Browns. Brown had wanted an NFL franchise but settled for one in the new league with the understanding that the merger would occur as previously announced.

After the second consecutive Super Bowl victory by the AFL, some owners decided that they truly had achieved equality and should continue as a separate league, playing the NFL champion in the postseason, in other words, maintaining the status quo. Brown, outraged and feeling betrayed, set out to convince the owners to abide by the earlier agreement.

Rozelle also stepped in, summoning all NFL and AFL owners to NFL headquarters in New York City and placing them in a room together to work out the merger. Davis, even then a brilliant but also unpredictable figure, came up with a workable compromise. Three of the sixteen NFL teams would switch to the AFL to give each league thirteen teams, with the owners of the three relocated franchises receiving $3 million each. The two leagues would then become the National and American Football Conferences, each further subdivided into three divisions, with the teams engaging in interconference play.

All owners had to vote for the plan for it to be accepted. Only one did not—Al Davis. The architect of the compromise refused to approve his own plan unless he were given veto power over the realignment of teams. Wayne Valley, majority owner of the Raiders, stepped in, however, and gave his approval, permitting the merger to go through.

All that remained was to finalize the divisional realignment. To make that decision, Rozelle had several scenarios written on slips of paper. Rozelle's secretary then drew one out of a hat, a remarkably basic way to make a decision with such high financial stakes. It worked, though, and the AFL, all of its teams intact, moved into the National Football League.

See also: Brown, Paul Eugene; Commissioners; Davis, Allen; Lombardi, Vincent Thomas; Namath, Joseph William; Super Bowl.

Additional Reading:

Clary, Jack. "The History of the National Football League." In *Total Football II: The Official Encyclopedia of the National Football League.* Ed. Bob Carroll et al., 14–33. New York: HarperCollins, 1999.

Gruver, Ed. *The American Football League: A Year-by-Year History, 1960–1969.* Jefferson NC: McFarland, 1997.

Horrigan, Jack, and Mike Rathet. *The Other League: The Fabulous Story of the American Football League.* Chicago: Distributed by Follett Publishing, 1970.

Miller, Jeff. *Going Long: The Wild Ten-Year Saga of the Renegade American Football League in the Words of Those Who Lived It.* Chicago: Contemporary Books, 2003.

American Indians

American Indians have contributed much to football in a variety of ways. The boarding schools established in the nineteenth century to assimilate Indian boys and girls into Euro-American culture, while seriously harming traditional Indian values, emphasized a variety of sports, including football. The football team at the Carlisle Indian Industrial School in Carlisle, Pennsylvania, coached by Pop Warner, was a national football powerhouse during the first two decades of the twentieth century. Jim Thorpe, of Sac and Fox heritage on his father's side and primarily Potawatomi from his mother's family, and many other great athletes helped Carlisle defeat some of the strongest football teams in the country.

The Haskell Institute, founded in 1884 in Lawrence, Kansas, reached its peak as a football power in the 1920s, competing against the likes of Notre Dame, Michigan State, Nebraska, and Army. Its 1926 squad went undefeated. Like Carlisle, Haskell also boasted many great football players, perhaps its most famous being fullback John Levi, an Arapaho who in 1923 earned first-team All-American honors on a squad named by *Athletic World.*

The next step for American Indian football players was professional competition. Thorpe, of course, shone more brightly than almost any other professional football player of his time, Indian or non-Indian. He starred for the Canton Bulldogs twice, first from 1915 to 1920, and again in 1926. In between he played for several other teams, including the Oorang Indians, closing out his career in 1928 with the New York Giants. He also served as the first president of the new American Professional Football Association (later renamed the National Football League) in 1920. His many honors included induction into both the college and professional football halls of fame.

Joe Guyon, of the White Earth Chippewas in Minnesota, was a star tackle on the Carlisle team in 1912, and after Thorpe departed, Guyon moved to halfback. After the 1913 season he was named to the second team on both Walter Camp's and Frank Menke's All-America teams. Guyon later played for John Heisman at Georgia Tech, where he was a member of the national championship team in 1917. He also starred for Georgia Tech in 1918, earning first-team All-America honors both years after switching at Georgia Tech from halfback to tackle. He later played professionally from 1919 through 1927, beginning his career with the Canton Bulldogs (the first of several years he teamed with Thorpe) and concluding his career with the championship New York Giants. Like Thorpe, Guyon was named to both the College Football Hall of Fame and the Pro Football Hall of Fame.

Guyon also shared with Thorpe another football chapter, as both were involved with the all-Indian Oorang Indians (1922–23). Thorpe was player-coach of the team, which operated out of the small town of LaRue, Ohio, and Guyon was one of his teammates.

A more successful all-Indian football team was the Hominy Indians. The team was the brainchild of Ira Hamilton, an Osage from Hominy, Oklahoma. The team reached its peak around

1925, with a powerful squad that featured many Haskell Institute graduates and players from more than a dozen tribal nations. John Levi, an Arapaho from Oklahoma, served as player-coach, with the team winning twenty-eight consecutive games before challenging the NFL champion New York Giants, who were barnstorming. When the teams met on December 26, 1927, John Levi threw a 60-yard touchdown pass to lead the Hominy Indians to a stunning upset of the Giants, 13–6. Caught in the financial woes of the Great Depression, the Hominy Indians played their final season in 1932.

Those early years of American football saw many other American Indians also star on the gridiron. Pete Calac, a Luiseño from California, was an important member of the Carlisle team from 1912 to 1916. He then fought in World War I in France and Belgium before returning to college football at West Virginia Wesleyan, at which time he also played under an assumed name for the Canton Bulldogs. In the early decades of professional football, it was not unusual for college players to assume another identity to preserve their college eligibility while earning some money playing for a pro team. After college Calac continued with Canton, joined Jim Thorpe with the Oorang Indians, played for the Buffalo All-Americans, and completed his playing career back with Canton in 1926.

Mayes Watt McLain, who was part Cherokee, scored thirty-eight touchdowns for the great 1926 Haskell team,

a college record that would stand until 1988. He transferred to the University of Iowa the next year and in 1928 was named to the second team of several All–Big 10 squads. Unfortunately, the uncovering of what became known as the Iowa Slush Fund scandal revealed that McLain and other Iowa athletes had been given illegal financial assistance. McLain played professional football briefly in the early 1930s before turning to professional wrestling and working as a stuntman in Hollywood films. He won the heavyweight championship of the American Wrestling Association in 1938, and in the year of his death, 1983, he was named to the Pro Wrestling Hall of Fame.

Several Indian football players, in addition to Jim Thorpe and John Levi, went into coaching. Albert Exendine, a Delaware (although the College Football Hall of Fame lists him as Arapaho), was captain of the Carlisle team in 1906, earned selection as an All-American end the following year, and had a long coaching career from 1909 to 1935, including stops at Georgetown, Washington State, and Oklahoma A&M. He was inducted into the College Football Hall of Fame in 1970. Exendine completed a law degree at Dickinson College in 1912 and practiced law in the off-seasons; after his retirement from football, he combined his law practice with work as a field agent for the Bureau of Indian Affairs.

Egbert Ward was born on the Yakima reservation in Washington State and went on to play quarterback for Haskell from 1923 to 1926. He served as an assistant coach at Haskell after graduation and later coached Navajo players at the Fort Wingate Vocational High School in New Mexico. Tommy Yarr, a Snohomish Indian, grew up in the state of Washington and played center for the University of Notre Dame from 1929 to 1931. He helped the Fighting Irish win national championships in his first two seasons and was elected team captain for 1931. Before his final season, his coach, the legendary Knute Rockne, died in a plane crash. At the funeral Yarr served as one of the pallbearers. In 1932 he was an assistant coach at Notre Dame under Hunk Anderson. Yarr later played professionally for the Chicago Cardinals and coached football at John Carroll University for two years before retiring from football in 1936 to go to work for a loan company in Chicago. On Christmas Eve 1941, at the young age of thirty-one, Tommy Yarr died of a heart attack. Almost a century later, in 1987, he was inducted into the College Football Hall of Fame.

William "Lone Star" Dietz attended Carlisle in 1907 and began playing football in 1909, later serving as an assistant coach at Carlisle under Pop Warner. Dietz was also an excellent artist and taught design at the School of Applied Art in Philadelphia. He coached Washington State College (later University) from 1915 to 1917, winning the Rose Bowl on January 1, 1916, over Brown University, 14–0. His Washington State team that year went undefeated, outscoring its regular-season opponents 190–10. He later coached at Purdue, Louisiana Polytechnic Institution, the University of Wyoming, Stanford, the Haskell Institute, Temple, and Albright College in Pennsylvania.

Dietz's college coaching was interrupted by his tenure as coach of the Boston team in the National Football League. The team had been known as the Braves, but owner George Preston Marshall renamed it the Redskins, moved the team from Braves Field to Fenway Park in Boston, and hired Dietz, who coached the team for two years (1933–34). The hiring of the Indian Dietz seemed to have been at least partly a publicity move in conjunction with Marshall's renaming of the team the "Redskins," although the club, which Marshall moved to Washington after the 1936 season, has argued that the nickname was chosen to honor the coach.

Life got difficult for Dietz after he left football. He incurred great criticism during World War I for registering as a "noncitizen Indian," which some saw as a way of avoiding military service, although he coached football for the Marines. Dietz was brought to trial twice for alleged draft evasion. The first trial resulted in a hung jury; during the second, Dietz, with no money to mount a defense, pleaded no contest (*nolo contendere*) and received a one-month jail sentence. Considerable controversy also arose over whether Dietz was indeed of Indian heritage (he claimed to be Oglala), or whether he made up his Indian background. A recent biography of Dietz by Tom Benjey, *Keep*

A-goin', suggests that his claim to being Indian was most likely true.

More recent American Indians who excelled in football include quarterback Jim Plunkett (Mexican American and American Indian), a Heisman Trophy winner at Stanford (1970) who quarterbacked the Oakland Raiders to Super Bowl victories after the 1980 and 1983 seasons. Plunkett was inducted into the College Football Hall of Fame in 1990. Another outstanding quarterback, Sonny Sixkiller, a Cherokee, starred with the University of Washington from 1970 to 1973. His exploits earned an appearance on the cover of *Sports Illustrated* in 1971 and a song about him, "The Ballad of Sonny Sixkiller." He played professionally in the World Football League during the mid-1970s and appeared in the film *The Longest Yard* (1974) with Burt Reynolds. Reynolds, part Cherokee, had himself been an outstanding running back at Florida State before leaving school in 1955 to embark on an acting career.

Jack Jacobs, a Creek, set a college record by averaging 47.8 yards per punt for the University of Oklahoma in 1940. He also was the team's quarterback. He later played in the NFL as a punter and quarterback for several teams between 1942 and 1949, with time out to serve in the army in 1943 and 1944. He then joined the Winnipeg Blue Bombers of the Canadian Football League and enjoyed great success as a quarterback during the 1950s, earning induction into the Canadian National Football League Hall of Fame in 1973.

Edward McDaniel, a Chickasaw, was often referred to as "Wahoo" McDaniel at a time when nicknames still routinely denigrated players' native heritage. McDaniel excelled as a linebacker and punter for the University of Oklahoma during the 1957–59 seasons and played nine years for the Houston Oilers, Denver Broncos, New York Jets, and Miami Dolphins. He also wrestled professionally, winning several championships during the 1960s and 1970s. He regularly wore a feather headdress into the ring as his personal signature and maintained a wrestling persona of the noble and honorable Indian facing evil villains.

Although American Indians did not face the same level of exclusion from sports that African Americans suffered, they did encounter much stereotyping. They also found themselves at times presented as showpieces as much as athletes. Nonetheless, many won lasting fame on the gridiron; overall, football would be much poorer without the contributions of American Indians since the early years of the game.

See also: Carlisle Indian Industrial School; Mascots and Team Names; Oorang Indians; Rockne, Knute Kenneth; Thorpe, James Francis.

Additional Reading:

Benjey, Tom. *Keep A-goin': The Life of Lone Star Dietz*. Carlisle PA: Tuxedo Press, 2006.

King, C. Richard, ed. *Native Americans in Sports*. 2 vols. Armonk NY: Sharpe Reference, 2004.

Oxendine, Joseph B. *American Indian Sports Heritage*. Lincoln: University of Nebraska Press, 1995.

Apparel

Tom Brady, looking a bit overweight, pulls out his wallet and slaps down a ten-dollar bill at the supermarket checkout counter to buy a bottle of Diet Coke. Looking much younger and thinner, he steps into the city bus, destination unknown. During an evening clash between the New England Patriots and Indianapolis Colts, several Tom Bradys, multiplied by some magical transaction, gather together in front of a big-screen television to watch the mighty struggle.

In another part of the country, Peyton Mannings are everywhere, taking their girlfriends to a movie (What does Peyton's wife think of that?), buying a cheeseburger at the local McDonald's, bringing an old Toyota into the shop for a lube job—and, in large numbers, watching that same football game.

It is Brett Favre, however, who is omnipresent in the home of cheese and milk cows. He fidgets in his pew during an unusually long homily. He shovels the latest snowfall, clearing his driveway, apparently unmindful of the cold. Another Brett Favre stops at the information desk at a hospital to locate the room where a buddy is recuperating.

There are even especially unusual-looking Tom Bradys, Peyton Mannings, and Brett Favres—with long hair and curves in places where they do not usually occur on the originals—inside football jerseys, which have popped up everywhere as a sign of solidarity with the local (or at least favorite) team. Yet, there are more than team jerseys strolling about

or relaxing at home: baseball-style caps, sweatshirts, T-shirts, jackets, sleepwear, cheerleading skirts for little girls, slippers, even underwear. No age is exempt, from the just-home-from-the-hospital baby to the great-grandfather or great-grandmother. It is easily noted as well that some teams, and on those teams, some players, are more likely than others to have their identities shared with the world, especially through the jerseys that proudly sport a player's name and number.

All of this is big business, especially for the National Football League. The NFL reportedly sells some three to four million jerseys annually. According to SportsScanInfo, the ten top-selling jerseys in 2008 were all from the NFL, with several featuring Dallas Cowboys players. Not surprisingly, Dallas has opted out of the league's merchandise revenue-sharing agreement, confident that it will continue to fare better on its own. According to Forbes, the Cowboys' brand logo is worth $200 million of the team's current $1.6 billion value. Whether a fan is wearing a Dallas, New England, or Green Bay jersey, or a clothing item from another team, the NFL is profiting from that choice of apparel.

Football clearly has established a new American fashion: the football look. Forget about Paris! Fashion for Americans emanates from the gridiron.

Additional Reading:
Joselit, Jenna Weissman. *A Perfect Fit: Clothes, Character, and the Promise of America*. New York: Metropolitan Books, 2001.

Arctic Football

Football has thrived in cold climates, even on days when players had to slip, slide, and stumble across snow-covered fields. Still, there is a limit to what football can endure, and the Arctic seemed beyond that limit—until recently.

A Florida woman named Cathy Parker saw a documentary about an attempt to create a football team at a high school in Barrow, Alaska, 340 miles into the Arctic Circle. School superintendent Trent Blankenship had decided that something needed to be done to address the 50 percent dropout rate at the Inupiat village of about 4,200. So he decided to start a football team to give students something more to connect them to the school and raise school spirit. A grant from the Alaska legislature and some willing amateur coaches helped bring the team to life in 2006. The venture did excite a lot of enthusiasm, and the Barrow Whalers even won a game while playing with makeshift facilities.

The field consisted of gravel and dirt. Telephone poles laid out on the sidelines provided seating, and buses served as locker rooms. Opponents were hard to come by since they were at least 500 miles away and had to be flown in. Yet the results were impressive. The graduation rate rose by 30 percent.

That is where Cathy Parker came in. She decided to start a fund-raising effort to provide a real football field for the Whalers. Project Alaska Turf's goal was to raise half a million dollars. ProGrass, a company from Pennsylvania that sells artificial turf, offered a discount. Cathy's husband, Carl, a former wide receiver with the Cincinnati Bengals and currently a high school football coach, offered moral support as well as an opportunity for the Whalers to go to Florida and train with his team.

A lot of dreams, no matter how well intentioned, die, but this one did not. Instead, it yielded a beautiful blue-and-gold football field ready for the 2007 season. Blue was decided on because the color holds the heat better than green. The Whalers, perhaps inspired by their improved surroundings, fought back from a 16–6 deficit (with the temperature in the low 40s) to win their first game of the new season 18–16. Afterward, the Barrow players celebrated by taking a dip in the Arctic Ocean. As of this writing, Cathy Parker was still raising money to continue upgrading the Barrow facilities. There is no telling what else may soon surround that gem of a football field nestled along the Arctic shore.

Additional Reading:

Demarban, Alex. "Florida Woman Strives to Help Alaska Football Team." *SitNews: Stories in the News*, February 20, 2007. http:www .sitnews.us/0207news/022007/022007_shns _akfootball.html.

"A Dream Realized in Barrow." *The Wizard of Odds: A College Football Site for Winners*, August 18, 2007. http://thewizardofodds .blogspot.com/2007/08/dream-realized-in -barrow.html.

Arena Football

"Don't throw that football inside the house!" is a command that a great many boys and girls have heard. It makes sense, of course, unless one likes to live with broken windows and shattered lamps. Playing football indoors, however, has its place in American society, just in buildings that are a lot bigger than most homes.

Arena football was the brainchild of Jim Foster, who knew quite a lot about football from his days as an executive of the short-lived United States Football League and the much longer-lived National Football League. He was attending an indoor soccer game in the early 1980s when the idea of indoor football came to him.

Foster set about formulating rules, trying them out in games, and garnering support for a new version of football. By 1987 he was ready for the Arena Football League to begin play.

Arena football is recognizably football, but there are some significant differences between it and the outdoor version. For instance, the field is only half as long (50 yards), and there are no sidelines. The player is out of bounds when he hits the wall surrounding the field of play. Teams play with eight players per side. The clock keeps running more consistently than in the NFL, with out-of-bounds plays and incomplete passes automatically stopping the clock only during the final minute of each half. Kicks and incomplete passes that bounce off an end zone net are considered in play. No punting is allowed, and there are some variations in scoring, a field goal by dropkick, for example, counting 4 points. Since punting is not allowed, a team must make 10 yards or score in four plays in order to avoid turning the ball over to the other side. Consequently, the game is more wide open than traditional American football.

High scoring is customary, and that is intended to increase excitement. Yet Foster included some regulations that are throwbacks to a distant past, such as returning the dropkick to the game and limiting substitutions to force the teams to use many players on both offense and defense. In 2007, however, unlimited substitution was finally allowed in an effort to improve the quality of play.

The Arena Football League consists of two conferences (National and American), each consisting of two divisions (Eastern and Southern in the National Conference, Central and Western in the American). As of 2007 each division included five teams, except the Eastern, which had four. An extensive playoff system includes twelve teams and began play on June 29 in 2007. The postseason concludes with the ArenaBowl. The 2007 championship game, played on July 29, pitted the favored San Jose SaberCats, which had won 13 of 16 games, against the upset-minded Columbus Destroyers, which despite a 7-9 regular-season record made it all the way to the final game. The top-seeded favorites, however, prevailed in ArenaBowl XXI, 55–33.

Arena football has gradually become part of American culture. Some of the games are available on ESPN and Sirius satellite radio. Jeff Foley, a journalist, spent two preseasons (1999 and 2000) with the Albany Firebirds, a team that no longer exists, played in preseason games, and chronicled his experiences in a book, *War on the Floor: An Average Guy Plays in the Arena Football League and Lives to Write About It*. An arena football game appeared in 2006 from the EA Tiburon, with a sequel the following year. The 2007 ArenaBowl festivities included a Saturday night concert in New Orleans featuring Styx as a prelude to the game the next day. ArenaBowl XXI became the first championship game to sell out at a neutral location, concluding a season during which attendance for the first time exceeded two million.

Despite continued success in attracting fans to games in 2008, the Arena owners decided in December to cancel the 2009 season with the hope that the league could resume play in 2010. The decision was based on concerns about the league's financial stability amid the national financial crisis that had developed during the year.

Additional Reading:

ArenaFootball.com: The Official Site of the Arena Football League. http://www.arenafootball.com.

Foley, Jeff. *War on the Floor: An Average Guy Plays in the Arena Football League and Lives to Write About It*. Bloomington IN: AuthorHouse, 2001.

AstroTurf

AstroTurf was the name given to the green knitted nylon carpet installed in the Houston Astrodome in the 1960s. The stadium, initially home to both football and baseball, included natural grass when it opened in 1965. Sunshine through windows in the roof, however, created glare that made it difficult for baseball players to catch fly balls. In response, the windows were darkened, but that caused the grass to die. The solution seemed to be artificial turf, named AstroTurf after the stadium in which it was first installed in 1966.

Thus was born the artificial turf craze, which promised a playing field with many wonderful qualities. It would be easy to maintain, not susceptible to bad weather, useful within enclosed stadiums, less likely to cause injuries, and guaranteed not to muddy players' uniforms.

As artificial turf spread, however, players quickly began to find problems with the new playing surface. Natural grass might be messy, but it was part of the long tradition of football. The vagaries of the natural environment could lead to difficult playing conditions, such as the 1967 "Ice Bowl" when, with a wind-chill factor of minus thirty-one degrees, the Green Bay Packers defeated the Dallas Cowboys for the right to play in Super Bowl II. Such games, however, also contribute to the legendary and heroic mystique of professional football.

Players also had immediate concerns about footing and injuries. Many felt that the artificial turf offered less sure footing than grass. AstroTurf (made by the Monsanto Company) was perceived as slippery when wet, while another version of artificial turf, Poly-Turf (from American Biltrite), was slippery when dry. The temperature on artificial turf also was a problem, tending to run much higher than the air temperature.

Of most significance were the injuries, which gave rise to new terms such as "turf toe" and "rug burn," and which included leg injuries caused by a shoe sticking to the surface on a quick turn.

Eventually AstroTurf's popularity faded, and by the 1980s stadiums began once again to feature natural grass. In 2004 Southwest Recreational Industries Sports in Texas, which had acquired the Astro-Turf brand in the 1990s, declared bankruptcy, helped along by a newer and better artificial surface product called Field-Turf (consisting of polyethylene fibers and rubber granules), made by FieldTurf Tarkett, Inc., of Canada.

GeneralSports Venue LLC acquired the North American rights to the AstroTurf name and is trying to revive the brand with a new and improved version called Gameday Grass (much like FieldTurf), which is made by Textile Management Associates of Dalton, Georgia. General-Sports hired former quarterback Archie Manning, better known in recent years as the father of two other NFL quarterbacks, as a spokesman for the new AstroTurf.

What will happen to the new AstroTurf product is uncertain, but its name will be forever linked to the tension between the natural and artificial in football. Artificial surfaces, though, have made a comeback, with over twenty NFL teams in 2007 using them rather than natural grass either in their stadiums or for their practice fields. In addition, large numbers of university football stadiums, and even high school fields, now sport artificial turf. There seems little chance that the natural is any more likely to shove aside the artificial in professional football than in this increasingly high-tech American society as a whole.

See also: Ice Bowl.

Additional Reading:
Doherty, Craig A., and Katherine M. Doherty. *The Houston Astrodome.* Woodbridge CT: Blackbirch Press, 1997.
Schmidt, R. C., et al., eds. *Natural and Artificial Playing Fields: Characteristics and Safety Features.* Philadelphia: ASTM, 1990.

Autry, Carlos Alan (b. 1952)

Alan Autry is best known as the police officer Bubba Skinner on the popular television series *In the Heat of the Night*, costarring Carroll O'Connor, which ran from 1988 to 1994. More recently, Autry has achieved distinction in the political arena as mayor of Fresno, California, a post to which he was elected in 2001 and reelected in 2005. However, he also was an outstanding football player at the University of the Pacific and later a backup quarterback with the Green Bay Packers.

Autry played football under the name Carlos Brown, using the surname of his mother's family. His parents were divorced shortly after his birth, and he and his mother went to live with the Browns. She later married a migrant farmer, and young Carlos followed his parents from field to field in California's San Joaquin Valley.

Autry earned a scholarship to the University of the Pacific and excelled as Pacific's starting quarterback as a sophomore in 1971. A serious knee injury wiped out most of his junior year, and a new coach installed an option system the next year, sending the strong-armed but not especially mobile Autry to the bench. He volunteered to switch to tight end in his final season, and despite his limited experience at quarterback, Green Bay drafted him in 1975.

Autry played sparingly his first year with the Packers but started three games in 1976 when starter Lynn Dickey was injured. He completed twenty-six of seventy-four passes for 333 yards and two touchdowns with six interceptions. The next year, Coach Bart Starr cut him from the squad, and the muscular young football player turned to acting.

After rediscovering his biological father in 1981, he resumed his original name but dropped "Carlos." One of his first acting roles (as Carlos Brown) was appropriately a part in the football film *North Dallas Forty* in 1979. It was his role as the tough and laconic but brave and good-hearted Sergeant Skinner (later promoted to captain) that earned him fame and fortune and laid the groundwork for his successful move into politics.

Additional Reading:
Moore, David Leon. "Actor-Turned-Fresno-Mayor Roots Against Old Pal Carroll." *USA Today*, November 18, 2005, section C.

Baugh, Samuel Adrian (Slingin' Sammy, the Texas Tornado) (1914–2008)

Slingin' Sammy Baugh transformed football, elevating the forward pass from an occasional change-of-pace play or desperation maneuver to a mainstream strategy, from something to be done judiciously, perhaps ten or so times per game, and never close to your own end zone, to a play appropriate anywhere and anytime. No wonder he was called Slingin' Sammy.

But there was more than the passer in Sammy Baugh, who was one of the most versatile of players. And not just football either, as Baugh, after earning All-America honors at Texas Christian in 1935 and 1936, signed as a third baseman with the St. Louis Cardinals. Deciding that his prospects were brighter in football, however, Baugh changed his mind and went with the Washington Redskins, who had just moved from Boston to the nation's capital. Impressed with his performance as a multitalented tailback who also could play great defense and punt farther than anyone, Washington had made him its first choice in the 1937 draft.

Baugh had the advantage of a redesigned, slimmed-down football in the second half of the 1930s, and with his big right hand he could really grip and throw it. But he also enjoyed passing and brought his passion to the pros, leading the NFL in passing six times and also topping the league in punting four years in a row (1940–43). In 1943 he won a triple crown, topping the NFL in passing, punting, and interceptions, the only player ever to lead the league in offensive, defensive, and special-teams categories in the same year.

Baugh played in some of the greatest games ever, usually against the Chicago Bears. As a rookie he led Washington over the Bears, 28–21, in the championship game, throwing for 354 yards and three touchdowns on a windy, icy day in Chicago's Wrigley Field as the temperature dropped to 15 degrees by the end of the game. The Bears turned the tables in the 1940 title game, demolishing Washington 73–0. Then Baugh and Company came back in the 1942 championship contest against an undefeated Chicago club, winning 14–6. The championship series between the two teams continued in 1943. Baugh, playing defense as usual, tackled Chicago's quarterback, Sid Luckman, and suffered a concussion. He returned in the second half to throw two touchdown passes, but Chicago won 41–21.

Baugh persuaded his coach, Dudley DeGroot, to switch to the T-formation in 1944, and the following year he completed 70.3 percent of his passes, a record that stood until Ken Anderson bettered it in 1982. Baugh also was a record-setting punter, averaging 45.1 yards per kick over his career. That average has since been exceeded, but Baugh's average of 51.4 yards per punt in 1940 remains the best single-season average ever almost seventy years later. Baugh's finest game came on Sammy Baugh Day in 1947. Facing the Chicago Cardinals, who would be NFL champions that year, he passed for 355 yards and six touchdowns to win, 45–21.

Enormously popular as a player, Baugh was hired by Republic Pictures to make a twelve-part movie serial called *King of the Texas Rangers* (1941). Baugh played Tom King Jr., who joins the Rangers after his Ranger father is murdered by Nazi saboteurs, although they are not explicitly identified as Nazis in the film. Like many B Westerns of the time, *King of the Texas Rangers* combined Old West elements (such as guns and cowboy clothing) with modern plot complications (the Nazis, whom the United States would soon be fighting).

Having played a pivotal role in changing the nature of football, Baugh retired after the 1952 season. After retirement he decided to enter coaching rather than return to films. He coached Hardin-Simmons University (1955–59), the New York Titans (later known as the Jets) of the American Football League (1960–61), and during the 1964 season the Houston Oilers (now Tennessee Titans). After that final coaching stint, Baugh stayed in his home state of Texas and ran a cattle ranch in Rotan.

See also: Forward Pass; Triple Crown.

Additional Reading:
Boswell, Thomas, et al. *Redskins: A History of Washington's Team.* Washington DC: Washington Post Books, 1997.
Loverro, Thom. *Washington Redskins: The Authorized History.* Dallas: Taylor, 1996.
Richman, Michael. *The Redskins Encyclopedia.* Philadelphia: Temple University Press, 2007.

Bednarik, Charles Philip (Concrete Charlie) (b. 1925)

A lot of people like to look back to the good old days when men were men, when people did their work with no nonsense and without complaining, and when there were no frills. Whether that viewpoint is accurate is another matter, but certainly the poster child (or more accurately poster man) for such a retro vision could well be Chuck Bednarik.

Bednarik is usually credited with being the last full-time two-way player. Even in recent years an occasional player has performed on both offense and defense, such as Troy Brown of the New England Patriots, a longtime receiver who doubled as a defensive back when injuries depleted the position on the Patriots. Bednarik, though, did it regularly, playing center on offense and linebacker on defense, a true sixty-minute player even after rules allowed for free substitution.

Bednarik came out of Bethlehem, Pennsylvania, itself a no-nonsense sort of place known for its steel production. After high school, this son of a steelworker entered World War II and ended up flying thirty missions over Germany as an aerial gunner on a B-24. After winning the Air Medal, Bednarik returned to the United States to get on with his life.

Bednarik stayed close to home, attending the University of Pennsylvania, where he played sixty minutes a game—at center and linebacker—for four years, earning All-America honors as a junior and senior. As a senior in 1948 he received the Maxwell Award as the finest player in the land, the first offensive lineman to win the award, although, of course, he also was a defensive standout. Still today, Bednarik is recognized, at least within the pages of the ESPN *College Football Encyclopedia*, as the university's all-time greatest football player.

Then he was drafted by the close-to-home Philadelphia Eagles as the team's bonus draft choice, which meant he was the first player chosen in the draft. He missed one game that first year but only two more in his rock-solid fourteen years with the Eagles. A ferocious blocker and tackler, he helped the Eagles win two NFL championships, in 1949 and 1960. His nickname, Concrete Charlie, came from his off-season job selling concrete, but it applied even more fittingly to his style of play.

The game that most epitomized the type of player Bednarik was occurred on December 26, 1960, in Philadelphia. The Eagles were facing the Green Bay Packers, just donning their mantle of greatness under Vince Lombardi, in the championship game. By this time Bednarik was in

his twelfth season, and the days of two-way players had ended. Injuries, however, had hit the Eagles hard earlier in the season, and Bednarik had returned to the offense along with playing his usual combative role at linebacker.

Philadelphia led 17–13 in a close, seesaw battle, but Green Bay had the ball late in the fourth quarter and was driving for the winning score. With eight seconds remaining, Bart Starr passed to powerful fullback Jim Taylor, who appeared headed for the goal line when Bednarik grabbed Taylor and wrestled him to the ground. Bednarik had not only saved the game but had played fifty-eight of the game's sixty minutes.

Bednarik also is remembered as the player who knocked Frank Gifford of the New York Giants out of football for a year and a half in the early 1960s with a powerful tackle. Bednarik, however, was not a dirty player, just a very tough one who never stopped playing as hard as he could.

It is not surprising that Bednarik, who retired after the 1962 season, grew increasingly intolerant of modern players with their part-time status, end zone high jinks, and stratospheric salaries. He also did not like it much that Eagles owner Jeffrey Lurie would not buy a copy of Bednarik's book for everyone on the team. After a period of estrangement that began in the mid-1990s, the Eagles reconciled in 2006 with one of their greatest players.

Each year the best college defensive player is given the Chuck Bednarik Award.

The name may not mean much to most modern players, but they would do well to find out about the man after whom the award is named. They could learn something about hard work, dedication to winning, service to one's country, and old-fashioned values that still evoke considerable nostalgia among those who prefer the quiet satisfaction of a job well done to a lot of posttouchdown posturing.

See also: Lombardi, Vincent Thomas; World War II.

Additional Reading:

Campbell, Donald P. *Sunday's Warriors: The History of the Philadelphia Eagles.* 2nd ed. Philadelphia: Quantum Leap Publisher, 1995.

Didinger, Ray, and Robert S. Lyons. *The Eagles Encyclopedia.* Philadelphia: Temple University Press, 2005.

McCallum, Jack. *Bednarik: Last of the Sixty-Minute Men.* With Chuck Bednarik. Englewood Cliffs NJ: Prentice-Hall, 1977.

Belichick, William Stephen (b. 1952)

As the New England Patriots established themselves as the dominant NFL team of the first decade of the twenty-first century, their head coach, Bill Belichick, became one of the most respected coaches in NFL history despite a personality that struck most people as decidedly underwhelming. Overcoming modest success at best in his first head-coaching job, with the Cleveland Browns, and a reputation for failing to communicate effectively, Belichick built a team that melded its parts into a machinelike whole, subjugating individual egos to a team-first attitude.

Belichick established himself as a top defensive coach while an assistant with the New York Giants under Ray Perkins and Bill Parcells from 1979 to 1990. A coach with the Super Bowl–winning Giants in games XXI and XXV following the 1986 and 1990 seasons, and highly praised for devising the defensive game plan that helped New York defeat the Buffalo Bills in the latter contest, Belichick earned a head-coaching position with the Browns in 1991.

In Cleveland Belichick came across as uncommunicative, did not relate well to the media, and incurred strong negative responses to cutting popular veteran players such as quarterback Bernie Kosar who in Belichick's opinion had outlived their usefulness. His best season was 1994, when he led the Browns to an 11-5 record and a playoff win.

Belichick's position with the Browns ended after the 1995 season, and he rejoined Bill Parcells, this time in New England. After the Patriots lost Super Bowl XXXI to the Green Bay Packers, Parcells left for the New York Jets and Belichick joined him there to serve as defensive coordinator from 1997 to 1999. When Parcells moved from head coach to vice president of football operations, Belichick briefly became his successor. At the news conference during which he was to meet the media as the Jets coach, however, he surprised the football world by announcing his resignation.

Belichick had accepted the position of coach of the New England Patriots instead, resulting in the Patriots having to give the Jets three draft choices, including a first-round pick, because Belichick broke his contract with New York. The Patriots went just 5-11 in 2000, but the next year they won the first of the three Super Bowls they would capture over a four-year period. Quarterback Tom Brady (installed as starter over veteran Drew Bledsoe in 2001) led a methodical and highly effective passing attack, and a strong defense along with a premiere kicker in Adam Vinatieri helped to pull out many close games during those championship years.

The Patriots had a down season by their standards in 2005, going 10-6. The next year they lost to the Indianapolis Colts and Peyton Manning, 38–34, in the AFC championship game. The Patriots led 21–3 in the second quarter but suffered an uncharacteristic defensive collapse.

The 2007 season saw the Patriots again become a powerful team, with an almost unstoppable passing attack that featured several new receivers, including a rejuvenated Randy Moss. A cheating incident, however, marred the early part of the season when it was discovered that the Patriots were apparently filming the New York Jets coaches' sideline signals. Commissioner Roger Goodell imposed a fine of $500,000 on Belichick, a fine of $250,000 on the Patriots, and a loss of one or two 2008 draft choices depending on whether the team made the playoffs. If the Patriots made the playoffs (as they subsequently did), they would forfeit a first-round choice; if not, they would lose second- and third-round picks.

The public also learned that Belichick had been the "other man" in a relationship that ended two marriages, including his own.

Nonetheless, Belichick, only slightly more outgoing and tolerant of the media than he had been in Cleveland and famously secretive about game plans and the status of injured players, retained the support of his team and of most New England fans—at least so long as his team continued winning. And continue winning it did, finishing the regular season as the only NFL team ever to win all of its games in a sixteen-game season, although its perfect season ended in the Super Bowl when the New York Giants defeated the Patriots 17–14. Belichick was rewarded personally by being voted Associated Press NFL Coach of the Year, the second time he had received that honor.

See also: Brady, Thomas Edward, Jr.; Cheating; Manning, Peyton Williams; Moss, Randy Gene; Parcells, Duane Charles; Perfection; Super Bowl.

Additional Reading:
Halberstam, David. *The Education of a Coach.* New York: Hyperion, 2005.
Holley, Michael. *Patriot Reign: Bill Belichick, the Coaches, and the Players Who Built a Champion.* New York: William Morrow, 2004.

Big Hit

A hit that reverberated throughout the National Football League, and certainly among fans of the New England Patriots, occurred during an exhibition game between New England and the Oakland Raiders on August 12, 1978. Darryl

Stingley, starting his sixth season with New England and seemingly on the verge of finally establishing himself as one of the league's premier receivers, went out for a pass. Oakland's Jack Tatum, known as the Assassin for his hard hits, went after him.

Tatum's hit left Stingley paralyzed—his neck broken and spinal cord injured—and a quadriplegic for the rest of his life. That life ended at age fifty-five in 2007, the result of bronchial pneumonia complicated by the permanent injuries inflicted by the hit. There was no penalty called for the blow that so changed Stingley's life. Two years after the hit, Tatum published an account of his career entitled *They Call Me Assassin.*

Tatum was doing what defensive players love to do and a great many fans love to watch—putting the big hit on a player. Tatum, of course, did not want to injure Stingley permanently; no players want to do that. The objective instead is to hurt the player enough so that he will be leery of future hits and perhaps take his eye off the ball or otherwise not play quite his best. The hit therefore has two dimensions: the physical and, of greater long-term value, the psychological.

Although some fans, sports journalists, and critics of football decry the extreme violence of the game, players continue trying for the big hit, all the bigger as players themselves become larger and faster. So popular is the big hit with fans that ESPN began offering a segment on its *Monday Night Countdown* in 2003 called "Jacked Up," hosted by former linebacker Tom Jackson. Jackson and his coanchors choose the five biggest hits from the weekend games to show. As the hit is replayed, the anchors shout, "He got jacked up!"

The only restrictions on the selection of hits are that they may not involve a serious injury or a penalty. The routine fogginess resulting from a big hit does not count under ESPN guidelines as a serious injury. Football players refer to the posthit state of mind as "blacking out," meaning not unconsciousness but wandering about in a daze and later not remembering what they were doing during their "black-out" plays, a condition usually indicative of a concussion.

So popular has the term *jacked up* become that, according to an article by Tim Layden in *Sports Illustrated*, Jackson has heard the expression in airports and grocery stores. If so, it surely has migrated to playgrounds as well.

The best-selling *Madden* NFL video game offers football fans and general devotees of violence the opportunity to get in on the action. The "hit stick" introduced with the *Madden* NFL 05 edition permits video gamers to accomplish devastating hits by defensive players. The following year a "truck stick" was added to permit offensive players to put the big hit on defensive players. Later, more violent hits were made possible, including the "helicopter spin."

One imagines that Darryl Stingley would not have enjoyed creating those hits, had he been able to use his arms sufficiently to play the game. Commissioner Roger Goodell also appears to be less than infatuated with the extreme violence in football. He has taken steps to reduce the incidence of head injuries through required testing of players and introduction of a whistle-blower system to guard against coaches and others pressuring players to perform when they are not well enough to do so.

The macho code operative in professional football requires players to play on despite the big hit and show neither fear nor pain. That is a dangerous pattern that can lead to long-term injuries. Goodell's system offers an out so players can be "real men" and still be safe. It likely will require a greater cultural awakening, however, to convince video gamers and the faithful fans of "Jacked Up" to understand the implications of their actions.

See also: Commissioners; Concussions; Disabilities; Suicide.

Additional Reading:

Gay, Timothy J. *Football Physics: The Science of the Game*. Emmaus PA: Rodale, 2004.

Layden, Tim. "The Big Hit." *Sports Illustrated*, July 30, 2007, 53–62.

Tatum, Jack. *They Call Me Assassin*. With Bill Kushner. New York: Avon, 1980.

Black College Football

Football flourished at black colleges (what now are often referred to as historically black colleges and universities) throughout much of the twentieth century. By the 1970s, however, universities that had long refused to admit African American students began to recruit black players in order to compete with northern schools in football. The civil rights movement of the 1960s had forced open the doors of academe in the South to African Americans, and southern coaches, some of whom (Bear Bryant of Alabama among them) had secretly longed for the great black athletes they had seen on northern squads, now were opening their programs to players of color.

That was good for society, for African American students, and for the universities, but not for black football. Integration of the baseball major leagues led to the demise of the Negro Leagues, and integration of college football would have only a slightly less drastic effect on football at historically black institutions. Football would survive at many of the schools, but the quality of football would decline, and far fewer graduates would find themselves drafted by the National Football League.

The first intercollegiate football game between teams from black colleges was played on December 27, 1892, in Salisbury, North Carolina. Livingstone College hosted Biddle University (renamed Johnson C. Smith University in 1923) and proved a hospitable host, losing 4–0. The contest occurred twenty-three years after what is usually considered the first intercollegiate game, the Rutgers victory over Princeton in 1869. To say that Livingstone did not have much money for this new extracurricular endeavor would be a great understatement. The players had to chip in to buy a regulation Spalding football. They applied cleats to their own everyday shoes but did not have to make their own uniforms. The young ladies of the Industrial Department sewed the uniforms using white ducking cloth.

Biddle scored first, taking a 4–0 lead at a time when a touchdown counted for 4 points. Later in the game, Livingstone's captain, J. W. Walker, grabbed a fumble and ran it across the goal line for an apparent tie. Unfortunately for the captain, snow had defaced some of the line markings, and Biddle's players argued that Walker had gone out of bounds. The complaint was accepted and the 4-point margin endured for the rest of the game. Livingstone would achieve vindication, though, fashioning an outstanding football program and winning several North Carolina Interscholastic Athletic Association championships and additional titles in other conferences, most recently the Central Intercollegiate Athletic Association championship in 1998. Throughout the years the rivalry between Livingstone and Biddle/Johnson C. Smith has endured. The football schedule for 2007 again pitted these two historic institutions against each other.

By the 1920s football had spread to many black colleges, but the greatest black football power of the decade was Tuskegee, with Cleve Abbott as coach. Abbott played football at Dakota State College where he was a star center and the team captain—the first African American to captain a predominately white team. At Tuskegee he set another first, becoming the first black coach to win two hundred games.

Also in the 1920s the *Pittsburgh Courier* in conjunction with black coaches began selecting Black College All-America teams. The first black college national champion was named in 1920, actually two that first year, with Howard University and Talladega College of Alabama sharing the title. Tuskegee did not win the honor in 1920 but won or shared the national title six times in the first eleven years that a national champion was named.

In later decades several black colleges became football powerhouses: Morgan State, Southern University, Florida A&M, among others, and most famously, Grambling State University under legendary coach Eddie Robinson.

Black colleges produced seventeen College Football Hall of Fame members and the same number for the Pro Hall of Fame as of 2005, as well as the first African American professional coach in modern times, Art Shell from Maryland Eastern Shore, hired to coach the Oakland Raiders in 1989.

The roster of players from black colleges who became star professionals is far too long to list, but a sampling includes Jerry Rice (Mississippi Valley State), Walter Payton (Jackson State), Steve McNair (Alcorn State), John Stallworth (Alabama A&M), L. C. Greenwood (Arkansas–Pine Bluff), Larry Little (Bethune-Cookman),

John Taylor (Delaware State), Willie Lanier (Morgan State), Ken Houston (Prairie View A&M), Harry Carson (South Carolina State), Aeneas Williams (Southern), and Michael Strahan (Texas Southern).

Before the 1970s were out, though, most of the top African American players, even from the South, were joining programs at large, primarily white universities, many of them in the South as well. In these big-time football programs, they could experience a higher level of competition, play in large stadiums, ensure greater media exposure, and improve their chances of being seen by NFL scouts. By 2004 only two players at black colleges were selected in the NFL draft: Lenny Williams from Southern and Isaac Hilton from Hampton. Yet if football at the historically black colleges and universities no longer is a common road to the pros, students at these institutions can still take pride in its tradition of excellence as well as enjoy the autumn contests between their own team and the school's rivals. That part of college football remains the same.

See also: African Americans (College); African Americans (Professional); Grambling State University; Rice, Jerry Lee; Robinson, Eddie Gay.

Additional Reading:
Chalk, Ocania. *Black College Sport.* New York: Dodd, Mead, 1976.
Hurd, Michael. *Black College Football, 1892–1992: One Hundred Years of History, Education, and Pride.* Virginia Beach VA: Donning, 1993.
———. "The Pride and the Passion: The Long, Hard Evolution of Black College Football," "Grambling," and "A Proud Legacy." In ESPN *College Football Encyclopedia: The Complete History of the Game.* Ed. Michael MacCambridge, 1102–21. New York: ESPN Books, 2005.
Roebuck, Julian B., and Komanduri S. Murty. *Historically Black Colleges and Universities: Their Place in American Higher Education.* Westport CT: Praeger, 1993.

Bowden, Robert Cleckler (Bobby) (b. 1929)

Bobby Bowden, inducted into the College Football Hall of Fame in 2006, continues to lead the Florida State Seminoles even as he closes in on the age of eighty. Something of a Southern philosopher and humorist as well as a coach, Bowden long ago secured his position as one of the best and most popular of college coaches.

After serving as an assistant coach at Florida State and West Virginia, Bowden became head coach at the latter in 1970. After a successful six-year run there, he returned to Florida State as head coach. Since 1976 he has guided that program, usually with remarkable results. He won national championships in 1993 and 1999 while finishing in the top five nationally for fourteen consecutive seasons (1987–2000). He also consistently proved his team's worth in bowl games, winning eleven in a row (1985–95).

By the end of the 2007 regular season, Bowden owned more victories (373) than any other Football Bowl Subdivision coach. He also had earned considerable renown for his religious faith and for establishing a coaching family. The Fellowship of Christian Athletes established the

National Bobby Bowden Award in 2004 to be given to a football player who demonstrates outstanding achievement athletically, academically, and in his community. Bowden also could take pride in the coaching accomplishments of three sons (Terry, Tommy, and Jeff) who followed him into the coaching profession. Among their successes is a selection as 1993 Coach of the Year (for Terry when he was head coach at Auburn) and an undefeated season by Tommy (at Tulane in 1998). Currently head coach at Clemson, Tommy has held his own against his father's team, beating the Seminoles four times against five losses.

As Bowden prepared to meet Kentucky in the Music City Bowl on New Year's Eve, 2007, he faced a serious cheating scandal on the part of some of his players. Reports from Florida State indicated that cheating on an online music history exam had cost the jobs of a full-time academic adviser and a student tutor and involved at least twenty-three athletes, not all of them in the football program.

Privacy rules prevented releasing most names, but Bowden found himself facing Kentucky without approximately thirty-six of his regular-season Seminoles. Some of the players missing from the bowl roster apparently were injured, academically ineligible, or in violation of other policies rather than implicated in the cheating. The list of missing players also may have included about ten walk-ons who would not have accompanied the team anyway. Nonetheless, a sizable contingent of Bowden's players was banned from the game because of involvement in the cheating incident. The Seminoles, not surprisingly, lost the game, 35–28. Florida State rebounded in 2008, however, with a 42–13 victory over the University of Wisconsin in the Champs Sports Bowl.

See also: Cheating; Religion.

Additional Reading:

Bowden, Bobby, told to Mike Bynum. *Bound for Glory: The Horatio Alger Story of FSU's Bobby Bowden*. College Station TX: We Believe Trust Fund at the Bank of A&M, 1980.

Bowden, Bobby, Terry Bowden, and the Bowden Family. *Winning's Only Part of the Game: Lessons of Life and Football*. With Ben Brown. New York: Warner Books, 1996.

Brown, Ben. *Saint Bobby and the Barbarians*. New York: Doubleday, 1992.

Bowl Games

Bowl games have been part of the way Americans have celebrated New Year's Day for over a century, and for much of that time they have also been part of late December festivities. It all started with the twentieth century in its cradle and the Tournament of Roses adding to its January 1 parade at Pasadena, California, a football game between a West Coast team and a club from the other side of the Mississippi River.

The January 1, 1902, game featured Fielding "Hurry Up" Yost's Michigan Wolverines and Stanford. It was no contest, as Michigan built a 49–0 lead behind running backs Willie Heston and Neil Snow before an exhausted and injury-depleted Stanford team suggested calling it a day.

Michigan complied, ending the contest some six minutes early.

The Tournament of Roses Association went back to other activities after that game, featuring polo matches, ostrich races, chariot races, and even a race between an elephant and a camel (won by the elephant) before returning to football on New Year's Day, 1916. That game featured Fritz Pollard of Brown, the first African American to play in a postseason game and later the first African American to coach in the National Football League. Pollard's team lost, however, 14–0, to Washington State.

The 1919 game, coming less than two months after the end of World War I, pitted two military teams against each other. The Great Lakes Navy team upset the Mare Island Marines 17–0 behind two future NFL Hall of Fame members. Paddy Driscoll, who later starred with Chicago's Cardinals and Bears, dropkicked a field goal and threw a 45-yard touchdown pass to future Bears owner and coach George Halas.

The 1920s witnessed additional postseason contests. Little Centre College of Kentucky overwhelmed Texas Christian 63–7 on New Year's Day, 1921, in the Fort Worth Classic. At the conclusion of the 1921 season, the San Diego East-West Christmas Classic on December 26 featured Centre College defeating Arizona 38–0. As new postseason games, all short-lived, were being inaugurated, the Tournament of Roses game, the "granddaddy of them all" as it would later be called,

moved into a new stadium in 1923. The stadium was bowl shaped, giving rise to the name "The Rose Bowl."

The Rose Bowl had the postseason to itself after the 1923 season, and tournament officials conferred responsibility for selecting teams on the Pacific Coast Conference, which would choose one of its own teams as the host. Twenty-three years later, in September 1946, the Big 10 entered into an agreement to send a representative to the Rose Bowl, an agreement that has endured, with the exception of those years when the Rose Bowl is home to the national championship game.

In the meantime, the Rose Bowl game of January 1, 1925, stirred hearts and elicited headlines throughout the country as Notre Dame under Knute Rockne and featuring the Four Horsemen defeated fullback Ernie Nevers and Stanford 27–10. Not until after the 1969 season would Notre Dame return to a bowl game.

As the Rose Bowl continued to prosper, other bowl games joined it: the Orange Bowl (in Miami) and the Sugar Bowl (in New Orleans) on January 1, 1935; the Sun Bowl (in El Paso) on January 1, 1936; and the Cotton Bowl (in Dallas) on January 1, 1937. These five bowl games held the field through 1945, although a number of military "bowls" were held during World War II in exotic locales and under exotic names, such as the Arab Bowl in Oran, North Africa; the Riviera Bowl at Marseille, France; the Potato Bowl in Belfast, Ireland; the Tea Bowl in London; the Lily Bowl at Hamilton, Bermuda; the

Coconut Bowl in New Guinea; and even the Atom Bowl at Nagasaki, Japan, the latter on January 1, 1946, not long after the dropping of the second atomic bomb, on Nagasaki, ended World War II.

By January 1, 1946, the list of official, NCAA-sanctioned bowl games started growing, with the addition of the Gator Bowl at Jacksonville, Florida; the Raisin Bowl at Fresno, California; and the Oil Bowl at Houston, Texas. The number of bowl games rose to eleven following the 1946 season, climbed to fourteen two years later (actually about fifty, although most were not officially recognized by the NCAA), and then dropped to nine sanctioned contests for the 1949 postseason.

Notre Dame returned to bowl competition against No. 1–ranked Texas in the Cotton Bowl on January 1, 1970, losing 21–17 despite the presence of three of the Four Horsemen in the stands. The Fighting Irish waged some of the most dramatic bowl battles over the ensuing years before falling into a lengthy bowl losing streak near the end of the century. Notre Dame returned to the Cotton Bowl the next year to play Texas, as in the previous year ranked first in the country. The result was different this time, however, as Notre Dame won 24–11. Playing Alabama for the national championship in the 1973 New Year's Eve Sugar Bowl, Notre Dame won a 24–23 nailbiter and the national title. The next year, Notre Dame cost Bear Bryant's Crimson Tide another opportunity for a national

championship by defeating Alabama 13–11 in the Orange Bowl. The Cotton Bowl on January 2, 1978, was the scene of another Irish victory and national title, the result of a resounding 38–10 upset of previously No. 1 Texas.

During the 1980s and 1990s the number of bowl games rose in response to the increased revenue available from participating, as well as the recruiting advantage from holiday television exposure. Contributing to the riches was the growing practice of selling bowl sponsorship, including bowl-naming rights. The 1992 postseason included eighteen bowl games, with the national championship decided in the Sugar Bowl when No. 2 Alabama defeated top-ranked Miami 34–13. The game brought the teams nearly a combined $8.5 million.

The 1992 postseason also marked the first effort to use bowls to decide a definitive national champion. The Bowl Coalition included four bowls (Cotton, Fiesta, Orange, and Sugar) that would take turns hosting the championship game. The Rose Bowl, for its part, refused to participate, remaining faithful to its Big 10–Pacific 10 agreement.

After just three years a new Bowl Alliance replaced the Coalition; this time both the Rose Bowl and the Cotton Bowl chose to remain outside. This attempt also endured just three years, its insufficiency demonstrated by the appearance of No. 1 Michigan in the Rose Bowl on January 1, 1998, where despite a victory Michigan dropped below Nebraska in the

USA *Today*/ESPN poll, although the Wolverines remained first in the Associated Press poll.

Then came the Bowl Championship Series (BCS) plan, implemented following the 1998 season. This time the Rose Bowl became involved, along with the Orange, Sugar, and Fiesta Bowls, which agreed to rotate as the site of the national championship game. Division I-A teams were selected for the title game based on a complex formula that factored in the AP and USA *Today*/ESPN polls, strength of schedule, and seven computer systems. Although the Rose Bowl came into the new system, it steadfastly refused to go along with the widespread corporate renaming of bowl games, declining to allow a sponsor to share equal billing with the traditional name of the event. However, it was agreed that the sponsor could be named as the "presenting sponsor," while the Rose Bowl remained the Rose Bowl. On January 3, 2002, the Rose Bowl hosted the championship game, with Miami defeating Nebraska 37–14, the first time in fifty-five years that the Pasadena contest did not feature Big 10 and Pacific 10 teams.

The NCAA continued to sponsor playoffs for Division I-AA, II, and III teams. The I-A and I-AA classifications would change in December 2006 to the awkward-sounding and virtually impossible to remember NCAA Football Bowl Subdivision (FBS) and NCAA Football Championship Subdivision (FCS). I-AAA, which referred to schools without football programs, became Division I.

Further refinement of the BCS poll system occurred during 2004. Polls conducted by human beings (as opposed to computer rankings) were given greater weight, with the AP and USA *Today*/ESPN polls counting one-third each. The other one-third depended on six computer rankings. In addition, a fifth BCS bowl game was added, raising the number of teams eligible for the prestigious BCS contests to ten. The fifth game, however, would not be at a different bowl site but rather the championship game held, as before, on a rotating basis at one of the four bowls already in the system.

By 2007 the number of bowl games stood at thirty-two. The championship game, held at the site of the Sugar Bowl in New Orleans on January 7, 2008, pitted Ohio State University against Louisiana State University. However, Ohio State had one loss and LSU two, while the sole major unbeaten team, Hawaii, was shut out of the championship game. In addition, an assortment of other teams with two losses, as well as Kansas, with just one loss and having earlier been ranked first, considered themselves equally deserving of selection for the championship contest. As a result, the BCS system again elicited considerable criticism, and many observers once more clamored for a playoff system. LSU's 38–24 victory over Ohio State, resulting in a national champion with two losses, only added to the discontent with the current system.

Regardless of whether the BCS system endures or some other postseason pattern develops, bowl games will remain part of the holiday season. By 2007 the bowl season had stretched out from December 20 to January 7, almost three weeks. Yet for American society, which has long started its holiday shopping and decorating right after Thanksgiving, if not earlier, that hardly seemed an unduly long bit of stretching.

See also: Bryant, Paul William; Four Horsemen of Notre Dame; Halas, George Stanley; Parseghian, Ara Raoul; Rockne, Knute Kenneth; World War II; Yost, Fielding Harris.

Additional Reading:

Hendrickson, Joe. *Tournament of Roses: The First 100 Years*. Los Angeles: Knapp, 1989.

Mulé, Marty. *Sugar Bowl: The First Fifty Years*. Birmingham: Oxmoor House, 1983.

Ours, Robert M. *Bowl Games: College Football's Greatest Tradition*. Yardley PA: Westholme, 2004.

Smith, Loran. *Fifty Years on the Fifty: The Orange Bowl Story*. Charlotte NC: East Woods Press and Orange Bowl Committee, 1983.

Bradshaw, Terry Paxton (b. 1948)

Terry Bradshaw serves as a cohost and analyst on *FOX NFL Sunday*, where he combines observations about football games with often self-deprecating humor. It is not difficult to see him as something of a clown and question his intelligence, as many have done, most famously former player Thomas "Hollywood" Henderson. Before Super Bowl XIII, one of four that the Pittsburgh Steelers would win with Bradshaw at quarterback (after the 1974, 1975, 1978, and 1979 seasons), the Cowboys linebacker said that Bradshaw could not spell *cat* "if you spotted him the *c* and the *t*."

Such a reading of Bradshaw is seriously flawed. In fact, along with his strong right arm, he demonstrated considerable leadership ability with the Steelers as well as enough intelligence for Coach Chuck Noll to let him call the plays himself. Bradshaw also has published five books (admittedly with some help), released several music albums, and acted in films. On any given Sunday, he also offers plenty of insights as a football analyst. Indeed, he seems to have learned how to spell *cat* quite some time ago.

Bradshaw starred in college at Louisiana Tech, where he developed into such an outstanding professional prospect that he became the first player chosen in the 1970 draft. Along with the four Super Bowl titles, Bradshaw led his team to eight Eastern Division championships and was named the NFL's Most Valuable Player in 1978. He retired after the 1983 season, having missed all but one game that year because of elbow surgery. He went out with a bang, however, throwing for a touchdown on his final pass. While throwing, he felt something pop in his elbow and left the game, never to return. His football exploits earned him induction into the Pro Football Hall of Fame in 1989 and the College Football Hall of Fame in 1996.

Bradshaw had begun making guest spots as a broadcaster on CBS while still a player and moved full-time into the role of a football analyst in 1984, working with play-by-play announcer Verne Lundquist. He later shifted to FOX. His albums of country, gospel, and seasonal music include *I'm So Lonesome I Could Cry* (1976) and *Terry Bradshaw Sings Christmas Songs for the Whole Family* (1996). Much of his film acting occurred with Burt Reynolds in such vehicles as *Hooper* (1978), *Smokey and the Bandit II* (1980), and *Cannonball Run* (1981).

Bradshaw's life has not been smooth sailing, though, as he has had to face a number of problems, all of which he has acknowledged over the years. He wrote in his early autobiography, *Terry Bradshaw: Man of Steel*, that he went through a period of feeling spiritually adrift and mired in a wild lifestyle alien to who he believed he really was until he came to feel a close relationship with God. He also suffered from depression and anxiety about being in crowds. The latter led to a period of alienation from his former team when he did not attend the funeral of longtime Steelers owner Art Rooney in 1988. In addition, his three marriages ended in divorce. Beneath the homespun, comic exterior, Terry Bradshaw is a man with many problems that he has had to face but also many talents and many accomplishments.

See also: Films; Immaculate Reception; Music; Super Bowl.

Additional Reading:
Bradshaw, Terry. *Terry Bradshaw: Man of Steel*. With David Diles. Grand Rapids MI: Zondervan Publishing House, 1979.
———. *It's Only a Game*. With David Fisher. New York: Pocket Books, 2001.
———. *Keep It Simple*. With David Fisher. New York: Atria Books, 2002.
———. *Looking Deep*. With Buddy Martin. Chicago: Contemporary Books, 1989.

Brady, Thomas Edward, Jr. (b. 1977)

Tom Brady, especially for New England fans, but also for the broader football community, is the embodiment of efficiency and unflappable leadership. Exemplifying the team-first approach of Bill Belichick and the New England Patriots, Brady consistently shifts attention from himself as much as he can, given his status as one of the NFL's genuine superstars.

Brady, however, did not reach the NFL with much of a star glow about him. Although a highly successful quarterback with the University of Michigan, whom he led to victories over Arkansas in the Citrus Bowl and Alabama in the Orange Bowl, he was not drafted until the sixth round in 2000. During his first season, he threw just three passes as an understudy to veteran Drew Bledsoe.

Brady began the 2001 season in the same role, but on September 23 in a game against the New York Jets, Bledsoe suffered a major injury. Brady was installed as starting quarterback and helped the Patriots not only make the playoffs but also win Super Bowl XXXVI against the heavily favored St. Louis Rams. With two minutes left in the game, Brady began a drive that resulted in the game-winning field goal by Adam Vinatieri. Two games earlier, Brady had been the principal participant in a historic play during the divisional playoff contest against the Oakland Raiders. With Oakland leading by three points near the end of the game,

Brady attempted a pass. Hit, he seemingly fumbled the ball, which was recovered by Oakland. However, the decision was overturned on replay when the referee ruled that Brady's arm had started forward, hence resulting in an incomplete pass rather than a fumble. The decision came under the so-called tuck rule. If the quarterback begins a passing motion, then decides to abort the pass and tuck the ball in against his body but drops the ball in the process of tucking it in, the play is ruled an incomplete pass rather than a fumble. The ruling permitted the Patriots to retain possession, tie the game, and win in overtime.

Brady continued to manage the Patriots' offense with accurate passing and intelligent decision making during the following years. He played a major role in his team's subsequent Super Bowl victories over the Carolina Panthers and Philadelphia Eagles after the 2003 and 2004 seasons.

Brady's personal life became uncharacteristically public in early 2007 when he acknowledged that former girlfriend Bridget Moynahan was expecting their child. John Edward Thomas Moynahan (the second and third names also Brady's names but reversed) was born on August 22, 2007, with Brady present and promising to fulfill his responsibilities as a father. Brady's acceptance of responsibility, his apparent cordial relationship with his son's mother, and his general "good guy" image all helped him avoid much negative publicity and retain his high level of popularity.

The 2007 season brought Brady more than fatherhood, however, as both he and the team scaled new heights. The Patriots became the first NFL team ever to conclude a sixteen-game regular season undefeated and untied. Brady meanwhile broke Peyton Manning's record for touchdown passes in a season by throwing for fifty scores along with setting a variety of other passing records, including most games with three or more touchdown passes in a season (twelve) and most scoring strikes in one month (twenty in October). For his remarkable play throughout the year, he was named the NFL's Most Valuable Player.

Unfortunately, Brady's 2008 season ended almost before it began. During the first quarter of the first regular-season game, he suffered a major knee injury that required multiple surgeries and sidelined him for the rest of the season.

See also: Belichick, William Stephen; Forward Pass; Perfection; Super Bowl.

Additional Reading:
Boston Globe Staff. *Greatness: The Rise of Tom Brady*. Chicago: Triumph Books, 2005.
Pierce, Charles P. *Moving the Chains: Tom Brady and the Pursuit of Everything*. New York: Farrar, Straus and Giroux, 2006.

Brown, James Nathaniel (b. 1936)

Jim Brown may have been the greatest runner in the history of professional football. The *Sporting News* thought so, naming him the greatest professional player ever in 2002. He also was a multisport star in high school and college, a film actor, and an individual dedicated to helping disadvantaged youngsters succeed.

Brown earned thirteen letters at Manhasset High School in New York State, excelling in football, lacrosse, baseball, basketball, and track. As a pitcher on the baseball team, he hurled two no-hitters. At Syracuse, he earned All-America honors in both football and lacrosse while also lettering in basketball and track. On a Saturday in May 1957, he won the high jump and javelin in a track meet, then helped his football team defeat Colgate, and ended his day with a win over Army in lacrosse.

The Cleveland Browns selected Brown in the first round of the 1957 draft, and Coach Paul Brown wasted no time installing him at starting fullback. As a rookie, he led the league in rushing with 942 yards, the first of eight rushing titles he would win in nine seasons. He gained a record-setting 1,863 yards in 1963, a total surpassed by O. J. Simpson ten years later.

Brown unexpectedly retired prior to the 1966 season although still at his peak, having gained 1,544 yards and scored twenty-one touchdowns in 1965. Despite playing just nine seasons, he set the all-time rushing record of 12,312 yards (broken by Walter Payton in 1984). He also established new highs for the most rushing touchdowns (106), most total touchdowns (126), and most all-purpose yards (15,549). The records that still stand are his career rushing average of 5.22 yards per carry (highest for a running back)

and his average of more than 100 yards per game for an entire career. In both 1958 and 1965 he received the NFL's Most Valuable Player award. Brown's football accomplishments led to induction into both the college and professional football halls of fame. He also is a member of the Lacrosse Hall of Fame.

Jim Brown embarked on an acting career while still playing football and went on to appear in many movies. His most famous role was as Robert Jefferson in the war film *The Dirty Dozen* (1967). Other films included the Western *Rio Conchos* (1964) and *Any Given Sunday* (1999), in which he plays a football coach. Spike Lee made a film about Brown's life and career, *Jim Brown: All-American* (2002).

Brown also devoted much of his post-football life to a variety of social causes. He organized Food First in 1972 to help feed residents of poverty-stricken Marshall County, Mississippi, and in 1988 he created Amer-I-Can, which helps youngsters exposed to urban gangs as well as individuals already in prison learn how to manage their lives in a productive way.

See also: Brown, Paul Eugene; Davis, Ernie; Films.

Additional Reading:
Brown, Jim. *Off My Chest*. Garden City NY: Doubleday, 1964.
———. *Out of Bounds*. With Steve Delsohn. New York: Kensington Publishing Corporation, 1989.
Freeman, Michael. *Jim Brown: The Fierce Life of an American Hero*. New York: William Morrow, 2006.
Isaacs, Stan. *Jim Brown: The Golden Year 1964*. Englewood Cliffs NJ: Prentice-Hall, 1970.

Brown, Johnny Mack
(the Dothan Antelope) (1904–1974)

Johnny Mack Brown starred in possibly the most important football game ever played by a southern team and later became the first football player to establish a new career as a top Western movie star. Brown was a great football player in high school and at the University of Alabama, deriving his nickname from his hometown of Dothan, Alabama, and his speed as an All-American halfback.

The game that secured Brown's lasting fame and induction into the National Football Foundation's College Football Hall of Fame in 1957 was the 1926 Rose Bowl. Southern football teams were generally scoffed at as inferior through the first half-century of college football. Only when a number of eastern schools turned down an opportunity to meet Washington in the 1926 Rose Bowl did Alabama receive an invitation, even though the Crimson Tide had gone undefeated during 1925 while allowing only seven points to be scored against them.

Coach Wallace Wade took his team to California on a laborious four-day train trip and, after arriving, put his players through rugged practices, partly to keep them away from the Hollywood press. Although most sportswriters expected an easy Washington win, the game generated a lot of interest and was the first Rose Bowl game to be broadcast locally on radio—by Pasadena station KPSN. The announcer was Charles Paddock, a former Olympic track star,

possibly the first athlete to enter a broadcast booth in a move that later would become commonplace.

Wade's careful preparations, however, did not seem to work as Washington built a 12–0 lead during the first half. At halftime Wade appealed to his players' pride in the South and the responsibility they were carrying on their shoulders as the region's representatives. It worked, as Alabama came out for the second half ready to fight.

"Pooley" Hubert ran for a touchdown and Brown scored twice on long pass plays of 61 and 38 yards, all in a space of twenty-two minutes. It helped that Washington's star back, George Wilson, was sidelined for part of the second half with an injury. When Wilson returned, he added a touchdown to bring Washington back within one point at 20–19, but Alabama held on for the victory.

On the train trip back home, the Alabama team was treated like conquering heroes. As the train stopped at stations along the way, local bands played and fans applauded. About a thousand Tulane students cheered the Tide in New Orleans, and most of Tuscaloosa turned out for a parade to accompany the team to campus.

Brown, a handsome as well as talented athlete, was portrayed on Wheaties cereal boxes and, in 1927, was invited for Hollywood screen tests. He quickly found himself in movies, playing the leading man in MGM silent films to such famous actresses as Joan Crawford, Greta Garbo, Mary

Pickford, and Norma Shearer. As the "talkies" came in, MGM apparently worried about Brown's slow southern drawl and replaced him with Clark Gable in a film titled *Laughing Sinners* (1931).

Brown, however, had no trouble getting roles with other film companies, and by the mid-1930s he was firmly established as a star of B Westerns and Western serials. Historically, his most important film was *Billy the Kid* for MGM (1930), directed by the great King Vidor. Along with Raoul Walsh's *The Big Trail*, starring John Wayne (1930), *Billy the Kid* used the new wide-screen as well as sound technology. The film, despite its unhistorical happy ending, was filmed in a gritty, realistic manner primarily on location in Johnson County, Wyoming, the actual site of the Johnson County Range War. Vidor produced outstanding panoramic shots and made effective use of natural lighting. The famous silent-film Western star William S. Hart advised Brown on the film and even lent him Billy the Kid's actual guns to use.

Mack starred in individual Western films and serials into the 1950s, with occasional guest appearances as late as 1966. From 1940 to 1950 he was consistently in the top ten popularity rankings for Western actors conducted by *Motion Picture Herald* and *Boxoffice*, generally behind such top-tier superstars as Gene Autry, Roy Rogers, and William Boyd (Hopalong Cassidy). Brown also starred in comic books. Dell's *Johnny Mack Brown* appeared from March 1950 to February 1959; in addition, Brown was featured in Dell's *Giant Series Western Roundup* along with Autry, Rogers, Wild Bill Elliott, and Rex Allen for twenty-one issues beginning in June 1952.

See also: Bowl Games; Films; Wheaties.

Additional Reading:

Copeland, Bobby J. *Johnny Mack Brown: Up Close and Personal*. Madison NC: Empire Publishing, 2005.

Everson, William K. *A Pictorial History of the Western Film*. New York: Citadel, 1969.

"Johnny Mack Brown." *The Old Corral: B-Westerns.com*. http://www.b-westerns.com/brown.htm.

Rutherford, John A. *From Pigskin to Saddle Leather: The Films of Johnny Mack Brown*. Waynesville NC: World of Yesterday, 1996.

Brown, Paul Eugene (1908–1991)

Paul Brown remains enshrined not only in the Pro Football Hall of Fame for his success on the gridiron but also in football and social history as a major contributor toward integrating professional football. His success in the short-lived All-America Football Conference paved the way for expansion of professional football throughout the country, and his innovations especially impacted offensive strategies and gave rise ultimately to the West Coast offense.

Brown learned his coaching trade across the football spectrum. At his own former high school, Massillon Washington High School in Massillon, Ohio, at the heart of the country that gave birth to the National Football League, Brown compiled a remarkable 80-8-2 record during the 1930s, including a thirty-five-game winning streak. Massillon was voted Ohio state champion six years in a row under him.

Brown then became head coach at Ohio State University, compiling an 18-8-1 record (1941–43) and winning a national championship in 1942. During his first season, his team's only loss was to Northwestern, starring Otto Graham, who later would become Brown's longtime quarterback with the Cleveland Browns. Most of the eight defeats he suffered at Ohio State came in his final season when he lost most of his players to military service during World War II.

Brown followed his players into service in 1944, serving as football coach at Great Lakes Naval Station. The Great Lakes team played against university teams as well as other military squads, winning fifteen games against five losses and two ties.

With World War II over, Brown moved into professional coaching with the Cleveland Browns of the new All-America Football Conference. The Browns were apparently named after boxing great Joe Louis, "the Brown Bomber" (with the team's name shortened from "Brown Bombers" to "Browns"), but the name quickly became associated in the public's mind with the team's coach.

In recruiting players, Brown looked especially to veterans of programs with which he was familiar—Massillon, Ohio State, Great Lakes Naval Station—or players he had competed against. Many of the players he signed became stars, including quarterback Otto Graham, fullback

Marion Motley, tackle and kicker Lou Groza, guard Bill Willis, and receivers Dante Lavelli and Mac Speedie. With Motley and Willis, Brown broke the color barrier in professional football that had been in force since the early 1930s and paved the way for the large number of African American players who have excelled in the NFL since the 1950s.

The Browns won the AAFC championship in each of its four years in existence (1946–49). When the league ended after the 1949 season, three of its teams (the Browns, the Baltimore Colts, and the San Francisco 49ers) entered the NFL, helping to spark expansion that over the following decades spread professional football throughout the country.

Brown continued his success in the NFL, much to the surprise of many football experts who thought that no AAFC team could compete with the top NFL clubs. Cleveland played in the title game each year from 1950 to 1955, winning the championship in its inaugural season in the NFL and in 1954 and 1955.

Brown proved himself a brilliant innovator, from his assessment of potential players to his game-day strategy. He used intelligence tests to determine whether players would be able to fit into his system and, perhaps influenced by his early high school coaching (he referred to himself as a "football teacher"), brought classroom pedagogy into his coaching. He would instruct his players from in front of a classroom while they sat at desks. Players were expected to take notes in three-ring binders, and Brown periodically collected the notebooks without warning as a type of "pop quiz." He was an early proponent of detailed film study and, borrowing yet another teaching strategy, graded his players on their performance on plays. Focus was especially important to Brown. He kept the team together in the same hotel the night before a game and even forbade his players from having sex with their wives after Tuesday so that the players would concentrate their attention and energy on the upcoming game.

During games, Brown called plays from the sidelines by using "messenger guards" who would shuffle in and out relaying plays. His exacting pass patterns laid the groundwork for what later would become the West Coast offense. Work did not end with the final game of the season. Brown hired more assistant coaches than other professional teams to enhance teaching effectiveness and paid them better than assistants were paid elsewhere so they would work year-round planning, analyzing, and assessing. Widely respected and imitated by his colleagues, by the late 1940s Brown had more than 2,000 coaches attending his coaching clinics.

The retirement of Otto Graham after the 1955 season ushered in a period of more modest success for the Cleveland team. The Browns fell to 5-7 in 1956 but rebounded to continue posting winning seasons but without any additional NFL championships. Brown drafted another Brown—Jim—in 1957, a fullback from Syracuse who became possibly the

greatest running back in NFL history. In 1962 Brown traded with Washington for the top choice in the draft in order to take Ernie Davis, the first African American Heisman winner, who like Jim Brown had been a great running back at Syracuse. However, during the summer Davis was diagnosed with leukemia. He improved temporarily but again worsened and died on May 18, 1963, without ever playing for Cleveland.

After the Browns recorded a 7-6-1 record in 1962, owner Art Modell, a New York advertising executive who bought the team in 1961, fired his coach. One of the issues dividing owner and coach was Brown's refusal to play Ernie Davis when his condition improved in the fall of 1962. Davis's doctors had told him that he could return to football, but other doctors informed Brown that they considered it too risky to let him play. Modell also recognized the tension that existed between the coach and his star running back and thought that Brown did not know how to deal with modern players.

Paul Brown, however, was not finished with football. He joined the American Football League as coach, general manager, and principal owner of the expansion Cincinnati Bengals in time for the 1968 season and returned to the NFL when the two leagues merged in 1970. Brown coached the Bengals through the 1975 season, making the playoffs three times. He then stepped down as coach but remained as team president until his death in 1991. Brown saw his Bengals make the Super

Bowl twice, following the 1981 and 1988 seasons, but lose to San Francisco by 5 and 4 points respectively.

Paul Brown died on August 5, 1991, almost half a century after the magical period during which his Cleveland Browns had played for a league championship for ten consecutive years, winning seven times. He had not been able to duplicate that success later with the Browns or with the Bengals, but he had continued to field strong teams and see his legacy endure in the profession he had helped so much to mold.

See also: African Americans (Professional); All-America Football Conference; American Football League (IV); Brown, James Nathaniel; Davis, Ernie; Graham, Otto Everett, Jr.; Radio Helmet.

Additional Reading:

Brown, Paul. *PB: The Paul Brown Story*. With Jack Clary. New York: Atheneum, 1979.

Cantor, George. *Paul Brown: The Man Who Invented Modern Football*. Chicago: Triumph Books, 2008.

Collett, Ritter. *Super Stripes: PB and the Super Bowl Bengals*. Dayton OH: Landfall Press, 1982.

Piascik, Andy. *The Best Show in Football: The 1946–1955 Cleveland Browns, Pro Football's Greatest Dynasty*. Lanham MD: Taylor Trade Publishing, 2007.

Bryant, Paul William (Bear) (1913–1983)

The tall, dignified figure in the houndstooth hat patrolling the sidelines during a University of Alabama football game is a picture etched in the minds of millions of football fans. One of the most successful college coaches ever, Paul "Bear" Bryant broke the record for most wins by a college coach (although his total has since been eclipsed). He also found himself in the middle of the movement to integrate football (and the broader society) in the South.

Bryant, who earned his lifelong nickname as a thirteen-year-old by wrestling a circus bear, played end for Alabama from 1933 to 1935, sharing in the glory of his team's national championship in 1934. Drafted by the Brooklyn Dodgers football team in 1936, he opted instead to enter coaching. He began at Union University in Jackson, Tennessee, in 1936 and later served as an assistant at his alma mater and at Vanderbilt before joining the United States Navy after the attack on Pearl Harbor, rising to the rank of lieutenant commander.

Bryant then coached the North Carolina Navy Pre-Flight football team before becoming head coach at the University of Maryland in 1945. He moved on to the University of Kentucky the following year. In both places he had considerable success, including a victory over No. 1–ranked Oklahoma in the Sugar Bowl on January 1, 1951. He is listed in the ESPN *College Football Encyclopedia* as Kentucky's all-time best football coach, a designation that he also holds for Alabama. In 1954 Bryant moved to Texas A&M University, taking over a football program that had gone into serious decline. That first year, he took his team to Junction, Texas, for a grueling training camp. Those who persevered became known as the "Junction Boys," a group to whom Bryant always felt especially close. The team won only one game that year but followed with three straight winning seasons, including an undefeated 1956 campaign. In 1957 running back John David Crow won the Heisman Trophy under Bryant's tutelage.

Then, in 1958, Bryant went home because, as he put it, "Mama called." The Crimson Tide had also been down when Bryant took over the football program, enduring four consecutive losing seasons, with just four wins over the previous three seasons.

Bryant had a winning record in his first year back at Alabama and never had a losing one. He won six national championships and thirteen Southeastern Conference titles, and he went to twenty-four straight bowl games. He coached Joe Namath and Kenny Stabler in the 1960s, helping prepare them to become great NFL quarterbacks. In the 1970s he switched to the wishbone offense, demonstrating his willingness to change in order to keep winning.

That acceptance of change also came in the area of race relations. Bryant won three national championships with all-white teams, but when his Crimson Tide were trounced by Southern California in 1970 by a score of 42–21, Bryant knew for sure that integration was necessary to remain competitive. Southern Cal featured several African American stars, including tailback Clarence Davis and fullback Sam Cunningham. After the game, just

seven years after Alabama Gov. George Wallace had stood in a doorway to block young black students from attending the University of Alabama, Bryant took Cunningham into Alabama's locker room and told his players to see what a football player looks like.

In fact, he already had signed an African American player, Wilbur Jackson, who was a freshman in 1970. Bryant won three more national championships with integrated teams. Although he had supported segregation when that was widely accepted in the South, he was ready to shift with the times. Much of that shift was dictated by practical concerns about winning, but he also seemed personally supportive of the new way. Eddie Robinson, the legendary Grambling coach and an African American, long held Bryant in high esteem.

Bryant retired after the 1982 season. His final victory, 21–15 over the University of Illinois, came on December 29, 1982, in the Liberty Bowl. It was win number 323. Less than a month later, on January 26, 1983, he was dead at the age of sixty-nine. It was almost as if Bear Bryant and football went so much together that it was impossible to separate Bryant from the sport without removing a crucial life principle from him. He was buried with the Junction Boys ring he had received during a reunion with his Texas A&M players.

The next month, Pres. Ronald Reagan bestowed the Presidential Medal of Freedom posthumously on Bryant, and in 1986 he was inducted into the College Football Hall of Fame. In 1996 the United States Postal Service honored him with a postage stamp bearing his image.

See also: African Americans (College); Namath, Joseph William; Parseghian, Ara Raoul; Robinson, Eddie Gay.

Additional Reading:

Barra, Allen. *The Last Coach: A Life of Paul "Bear" Bryant.* New York: W.W. Norton, 2005.

Bryant, Paul W., and John Underwood. *Bear: The Hard Life and Good Times of Alabama's Coach Bryant.* Boston: Little, Brown, 1975.

C

Camp, Walter Chauncey (the Father of American Football) (1859–1925)

Walter Camp is credited with being the Father of American Football, a title that he deserves as much as anyone, perhaps more than anyone. He took a game that was largely the same as rugby and quickly transformed it into a sport that observers today would recognize as the modern game of football.

Camp was an outstanding athlete, starring in baseball, track, soccer, and water sports at Hopkins Grammar School in New Haven, Connecticut. In 1876 he matriculated at Yale University. That was a momentous year in American history, as the nation celebrated the centennial of its birth and was shocked by the defeat of George Armstrong Custer and his Seventh Cavalry at Little Bighorn. It also was a watershed year for American sports, as Camp embarked on his long career in what would soon become American football.

The first efforts to codify rules for American rugby occurred in November 1876 at a gathering of representatives from several Ivy League schools in Springfield, Massachusetts. Essentially, however, the meeting resulted in a set of rules largely identical to those established by the Rugby Union Code of England for rugby.

Walter Camp meanwhile was establishing himself as an outstanding athlete at Yale, where he was pitcher and captain of the baseball team, a championship swimmer, an excellent hurdler, and a fine tennis player and rower. He also starred in rugby, where he especially excelled at the crucial skill of kicking, both punting and dropkicking. After graduation he continued to play for Yale while attending Yale Medical School for two more years (1880–81). He later coached at Yale and Stanford between 1888 and 1895, in 1892 actually coaching both teams as Stanford opened its season in December after the conclusion of Yale's competition. That year the two squads won a total of fifteen games with no losses and two ties.

It was in transforming rugby into American football, however, that Camp made his greatest contributions to the sport and to his country. Camp was a member of the second gathering of Ivy League representatives, which met in Springfield on October 9, 1878, and continued to exercise leadership at football's legislative sessions until his death in 1925.

A man of great vision as well as leadership skills, Camp argued diligently and effectively for a variety of rule changes that were adopted, beginning in 1880. They included reducing the number of players per side from fifteen to eleven, beginning play with the center kicking (later snapping) the ball rather than a scrum, establishing the position of quarterback, establishing a set number of plays to make a first down and maintain possession of the ball (initially five yards in three plays), using prearranged plays and signal calling, creating the T-formation, and moving to a point system of scoring. The points numbered four for a touchdown, two for a safety, two for a goal after a touchdown (today's extra point), and five for a goal from the field (field goal). Other alterations in the game affected the size of the field, the length of the game, and the organization of the officiating crew.

In 1888 Camp successfully lobbied for a change in tackling that permitted defenders to tackle the ball carrier below the waist. To some extent, this rule countered some of the previous changes in the game, which had increasingly opened up the contest. Fewer players, the requirement that a certain number of yards be made to keep the ball, planned plays, and calling of plays, for example, both permitted and required more assertiveness in moving the ball down the field. However, the new permissiveness in tackling shifted dominance to the defense as the offense found it much more difficult to gain yardage without being tackled. Consequently, the offense increasingly turned toward types of wedge formations, which involved the offense bunching up in order to escort the runner and keep him from being tackled. The wedge thus involved two groups of strong young men pushing and shoving each other mightily. Injuries multiplied, and even an occasional death resulted from the growing physicality of the game. Not until later rule changes, including legalization of the forward pass, would the game open up again.

Walter Camp also is credited with coselecting (along with sports journalist Caspar Whitney) the first All-America team in 1889, which was listed in Whitney's *The Week's Sport*. Camp also published several early books about football. And he did all of this while steadily moving up the career ladder at the New Haven Clock Company from assistant treasurer to treasurer, general manager, president, and chairman of the board. For his enormous contributions to football, he was inducted into the College Football Hall of Fame with the first class of inductees in 1951.

See also: Flying Wedge; Ivy League; Rugby.

Additional Reading:
Camp, Walter. *American Football; with Thirty-One Portraits*. New York: Harper & Brothers, 1891.
———. *The Book of Foot-Ball*. New York: Century Company, 1910.
———. *Walter Camp's Book of College Sports*. New York: Century Company, 1893.
Valenzi, Kathleen D., and Michael W. Hopps. *Champion of Sport: The Life of Walter Camp, 1859–1925*. Charlottesville VA: Howell, 1990.

Canadian Football League

Canadians have been playing football since the 1860s, the history of the sport north of the border paralleling the game within the United States as both descended from rugby and evolved over the years. Football in each country has also had to contend with another sport that adamantly refused to budge from its preeminent position: hockey in Canada and baseball in the United States. In the case of baseball, its designation as America's national pastime seems more rooted today in its long history and layered involvement with American society than in its current popularity.

Football in Canada is unlikely ever to leapfrog over hockey, but it retains considerable importance, and not just for Canadians. Many citizens of the United States have gone north to play, and players who established themselves in the Canadian Football League later transported their skills into the National Football League.

Doug Flutie was one of the most successful U.S. transplants, finding his scrambling ability especially suited to the more wide-open offensive brand of football practiced by the CFL. The former Boston College star, Heisman Trophy winner, and longtime NFL quarterback enjoyed his greatest football success in Canada. Flutie led the Calgary Stampeders in 1992 to their first Grey Cup in more than twenty years and was selected as the CFL's Most Outstanding Player, the second consecutive year he had won the award. He achieved the top player award four more times before returning to the United States.

Warren Moon starred at the University of Washington and was named Most Valuable Player of the 1978 Rose Bowl as he led his team to a 27–20 victory over Michigan. However, the NFL initially appeared uninterested, and he went to Canada. There Moon starred for six years and was later named to the Canadian Football Hall of Fame. He followed his CFL career with seventeen years in the NFL, earning induction into the U.S. Pro Football Hall of Fame as well.

Flutie and Moon are just two of the many U.S. players to star in the CFL, but there are other connections between the countries as well. During the 1990s the CFL expanded into the United States. One of the U.S. teams, the Baltimore Stallions, even won the Grey Cup, defeating Calgary 37–20 in 1995. The year before, Baltimore had lost in the Grey Cup to the British Columbia Lions, 26–23. Nonetheless, the expansion did not ultimately prove financially successful, and the CFL withdrew into Canada.

Football fans who wish to follow the Canadian Football League can do so through the medium of television. They will find that the game is quite recognizably football, although certain differences also are apparent. The league, in something like its present form and with its current name, has existed since 1958. Like the NFL, the CFL is divided into two units, divisions (the East and West) rather than conferences, with four teams in each division. The two divisional winners compete for the Grey Cup. The trophy has a long history, dating to 1909, when Earl Grey, the Canadian governor-general, donated a trophy for the Rugby Football Championship. Various Canadian rugby and football organizations have played for the Grey Cup since 1909, with the trophy awarded to the Canadian Football League champion since 1958.

The Canadian football field is longer and wider than the American field. Teams must move 110 yards for a touchdown and have only three downs to make a first down, factors that offer both a challenge and an opportunity for the offense. The offense must therefore try to make more yardage per play, which places a premium on the passing game. However, the larger field also offers more space for receivers to get open.

The most obvious difference between Canadian and U.S. football is that in the CFL each team has twelve players. Given the more offensively minded Canadian game, the extra player is essentially another receiver. A typical offensive formation features a five-man offensive line (a center plus two tackles and two guards) with four receivers lined up with the quarterback (two wide receivers and two slotbacks). Behind the quarterback and to his left is the running back; behind and to his right is the fullback.

A common defensive scheme is a 4-3-5 alignment. Two defensive ends and two tackles play on the line. Behind them are three linebackers and five defensive backs (a safety in the middle of the field, two defensive backs, and two cornerbacks).

Many other smaller rule changes pose

some initial difficulty for the fan and player alike, but given the apparent ease with which U.S. players have caught on to the game and been successful, the differences clearly do not affect the essence of the game. Like U.S. football, Canadian football is still about moving the ball by rushing or passing into the end zone, with the defense trying to prevent it.

Additional Reading:
Canadian Football Hall of Fame and Museum Web site. http://www.cfhof.ca.
Canadian Football League Web site. http://www.cfl.ca.
Cosentino, Frank. *A Passing Game: A History of the CFL*. Winnipeg: Bain and Cox, 1995.
Kelly, Graham. *The Grey Cup: A History*. Red Deer, Canada: Johnson Gorman, 1999.

Canton Bulldogs

The Canton Bulldogs of Canton, Ohio, along with the team's greatest star, Jim Thorpe, and the fact that the National Football League was created in Canton, help to explain why the Pro Football Hall of Fame is situated in Canton. The history of the Canton Bulldogs through the first quarter of the twentieth century was a proud history, and the Bulldogs deservedly continue a sort of eternal life through the Hall of Fame.

By the beginning of the twentieth century Canton was fielding outstanding amateur football teams. Its Stark County, Ohio, rival, Massillon, began in 1903 to hire top football players in order to establish superiority over Canton. Canton followed suit and, along with paying players, adopted the name "Bulldogs" in 1906.

Financial pressures, however, especially player salaries, drove the team out of business after that season, although the Canton Bulldogs would resurface to play a historically vital role in the rise of professional football.

A new Canton team was organized in 1912, with Jack Cusack initially serving as secretary-treasurer, but before the season began, he moved up to manager. The team took the name "Professionals" to avoid association with the original Bulldogs, who had been involved in a game-fixing scandal in 1906. Accusations had been made against Canton's coach, Blondy Wallace, alleging that he had attempted to fix a game between Canton and Massillon to ensure that both would have to play a third game in order to determine the better team, presumably to garner more money. Wallace was entirely innocent, despite erroneous reports that continued to be accepted for decades. However, bad publicity seriously hurt the Bulldogs financially and helped lead to the team's demise.

In 1915, however, when a new Massillon squad reactivated the old Massillon "Tigers" name, Canton brought back "Bulldogs." That year also saw Cusack sign Jim Thorpe, the great Olympic and Carlisle star, for the high sum of $250 per game. From then on, Canton ruled the Ohio League, tying for the championship with Massillon in 1915 and winning it outright in 1916, 1917, and 1919. During 1918, the manpower drain occasioned by World War I prevented Canton from fielding a team.

Canton boasted a long string of outstanding players. Three former Carlisle standouts—Thorpe (who was player-coach), Pete Calac, and Joe Guyon—starred for the Bulldogs. So many former All-Americans played for Canton that at times several were sitting on the bench.

Cusack took a job in Oklahoma working in the oil industry during the 1918 season and opted not to return after the war, turning the team over to Ralph Hay, a prominent Canton businessman who ran a Hupmobile dealership. Faced with problems of rising player salaries and teams raiding other teams' players, and in order to establish a more orderly professional game, Hay led the formation of the American Professional Football Conference in 1920. After its second season, the organization changed its name to the National Football League (NFL).

Hay's Canton Bulldogs thus were one of the original NFL teams, although at first it did not maintain the same level of excellence that the pre-NFL Bulldogs had enjoyed. Despite Thorpe's leadership, the team finished 7-4-2, well below the standard Canton fans had come to expect of their home team. Thorpe also served as president of the new league during 1920 but was replaced by Joe Carr for 1921.

The 1922 Bulldogs, now without Thorpe, finished 5-2-3. Then Hay brought in Guy Chamberlin to coach the team and play end. Future Hall of Fame tackles Wilbur "Fats" Henry and William Roy "Link" Lyman were among the Bulldogs' finest players. Under Chamberlin's leadership, the Bulldogs underwent a renaissance, winning the NFL title in both 1922 and 1923 as they went undefeated both years, winning twenty-one games with three ties. The Bulldogs earned the distinction of being the first NFL team to win back-to-back championships.

After the 1922 season Ralph Hay withdrew from running the team because its financial drain on his business was becoming too severe. He gathered many of the local businessmen, who agreed to support the team by levying on themselves a tax of one dollar per employee. Hay, although no longer owner, continued as manager. The local businessmen continued this support only through the 1923 season, after which the franchise was sold to Sam Deutsch, owner of the Cleveland Indians. Deutsch created a composite team out of the Indian and Bulldog players but kept his team in Cleveland while retaining the Bulldogs name.

After that one year without a professional team in Canton, several of the Cleveland players who had been with the Bulldogs, including Link Lyman, guard Rudy Comstock, and fullback Ben Jones, bought the Canton franchise from Deutsch, effectively splitting the composite team back into its original parts. Fats Henry and many of the previous Bulldogs players also returned to Canton.

The 1925 homecoming started well, with victories over Rochester and Dayton. Then a series of rain-hampered games undermined both the teams' play

and attendance. Canton finished with a disappointing 4-4 record. Attendance, which had been as high as 15,000, dwindled to 2,000 and 1,500 for later games. The 1926 season was even worse, as the team finished 1-9-3 for twentieth place. Even the return of Thorpe could not save the Bulldogs, and the franchise disbanded. Although there never again would be a Canton team in the NFL, the Bulldogs left behind a legacy intimately connected to the rise of professional football in the United States.

See also: Hay, Ralph E.; Hall of Fame (Professional); Ohio League; Professional Football Origins; Thorpe, James Francis.

Additional Reading:

Cusack, Jack. *Pioneer in Pro Football: Jack Cusack's Own Story of the Period from 1912 to 1917, inclusive, and the Year 1921.* Fort Worth TX: n.p., ca. 1963.

Maltby, Marc. *The Original Development of Professional Football, 1890–1920.* New York: Routledge, 1997.

Willis, Chris. *Old Leather: An Oral History of Early Pro Football in Ohio, 1920–1935.* Lanham MD: Scarecrow Press, 2005.

Carlisle Indian Industrial School

The Carlisle Indian Industrial School was the best known of the boarding schools for young American Indians established in the nineteenth century. The boarding schools were intended to educate young Indians and assimilate them into the dominant Euro-American culture when the youngsters were still young enough to discard their own cultural heritage. As idealistic as many administrators and teachers may have been, their effort was at best misguided for it in essence involved another way of trying to destroy the American Indian.

Lt. Richard Henry Pratt established the Carlisle school in Carlisle, Pennsylvania, in 1879. Pratt believed that sports were useful in contributing to the overall assimilation and acculturation that he desired. So in addition to learning English, dressing and cutting hair in imitation of Euro-Americans, embracing Christianity, and studying subjects that Pratt deemed relevant, Carlisle students were encouraged to play football as well as other sports. The philosophy behind football at Pratt and other boarding schools was essentially the same as that behind Gen. Douglas MacArthur's reintroduction of baseball into Japan at the conclusion of World War II: to inculcate what were seen as traditional American values. In Japan, however, MacArthur left the emperor in place and was satisfied with a synthesis of American democratic principles and traditional Japanese culture. In boarding schools throughout the United States, as at Carlisle, the effort was to eradicate traditional Indian culture.

Because good sometimes comes out of bad, there were some positives even to the boarding-school approach, especially in opening a new world of sports (and therefore also career opportunities) to male students. The sport most associated with Carlisle was football.

Pratt hired Glenn "Pop" Warner, a man who would come to be recognized as one of the nation's greatest football coaches, and Warner set about creating a new type of football style at Carlisle. Eschewing the massive and slow style of wedge-formation football, Warner opted for speed, strategy, and deception. His Carlisle players were typically smaller than the opposition, but speed and good coaching more than compensated for that deficiency, with pulling linemen and an assortment of alignments, including the single-wing and double-wing formations, confusing the opposition. Many great players starred for Carlisle, including Joe Guyon, Pete Calac, and, most famously, Jim Thorpe.

Carlisle football teams defeated many of the top college teams in the country, including Harvard, Cornell, Pennsylvania, and the University of Chicago. The most significant victory came against then powerhouse Army (captained by future president Dwight D. Eisenhower) in 1912, a year in which Carlisle may have been the greatest football team in the country. The great sportswriter Grantland Rice once said that he believed an all-star team from Carlisle could defeat an all-star team from any other football powerhouse, including Notre Dame and Michigan.

Ironically, the demise of Carlisle was partly related to football. Jim Thorpe, Carlisle's most famous athlete, had won the decathlon and pentathlon at the Olympics in 1912, but shortly afterward it was discovered that he had briefly played semipro baseball. Because he had thus forfeited his amateur status, he was ineligible for Olympic competition and had to yield his gold medals. Angered over Thorpe's treatment and believing that

Carlisle superintendent Moses Friedman and Coach Warner were aware that Thorpe had been playing baseball for money, students sent a letter to the secretary of the Interior demanding an investigation.

A congressional committee found no criminal wrongdoing but reacted negatively to the prominence given athletics at Carlisle. The fallout from the investigation led Friedman to resign in 1914. Warner left Carlisle the following February, the school's football fortunes quickly declined, and, with public policy regarding Indians turning against the boarding-school approach, Carlisle was closed in 1918, the institution converted into a military hospital.

See also: American Indians; Rice, Grantland; Thorpe, James Francis; Warner, Glen Scobey.

Additional Reading:

Adams, David Wallace. *Education for Extinction: American Indians and the Boarding School Experience, 1875–1928.* Lawrence: University Press of Kansas, 1995.

Anderson, Lars. *Carlisle vs. Army: Jim Thorpe, Dwight Eisenhower, Pop Warner, and the Forgotten Story of Football's Greatest Battle.* New York: Random House, 2007.

Bloom, John. *To Show What an Indian Can Do: Athletics in Native American Boarding Schools.* Minneapolis: University of Minnesota Press, 2000.

Jenkins, Sally. *The Real All Americans: The Team That Changed a Game, a People, a Nation.* New York: Doubleday, 2007.

Celebrations

Celebrating a great accomplishment is common. Joy needs an outlet, and a party or simply going out to dinner is a way to commemorate a happy occasion. It is no different in football, where making a great play often calls forth an emotional response by the player who made the tackle or scored the touchdown.

The danger of celebrating in football is that the celebration can easily evolve into an unsportsmanlike act that rubs the victim's face in the fact of his having been bested. Celebrations are seriously frowned on at the high school and college levels, where they are likely to incur a penalty against the celebrating team. Even some exuberant bouncing up and down after a score may well cost a college team field position on the ensuing kickoff.

At the professional level, however, celebrations are more widely tolerated, although within certain limits. The professional game is viewed as more of a public entertainment than high school or college football, and if a celebration is entertaining, it is apt to be accepted. In addition, much that would be considered unsportsmanlike at the other levels and draw a penalty is also tolerated. There is the sense that pros do not have to be as respectful toward each other. Trash-talking, for example, is widely practiced and almost never draws a penalty.

The broad limitations on celebrating in NFL games include prohibitions on taunting and group spectacles such as collective dances in the end zone after a touchdown. Essentially, if a player celebrates by himself and does not direct his actions toward the other team, he probably will not be flagged.

Credit (or blame, depending on one's point of view) for the rise of the most obvious type of celebration, the end zone dance after a touchdown, is usually given to wide receiver Elmo Wright, who performed what may have been the first end zone dance. Playing for the Kansas City Chiefs against the Houston Oilers on November 18, 1973, Wright caught a touchdown pass and did a short dance before spiking the ball. Wright actually had started celebrating touchdowns in college, somewhat spontaneously. While playing for the University of Houston in 1969, he caught a pass and started high-stepping in order to avoid the defensive back who dove at his feet. Wright then just continued his high-stepping into the end zone. Wright consequently has become the godfather of the end zone celebration.

Some professional players have earned considerable fame (or infamy) for their end zone dances, their performances earning distinctive names: Billy "White Shoes" Johnson's "Funky Chicken" and Ickey Woods's "The Ickey Shuffle," for example. Chad Johnson may have felt a tad less creative and went instead with a version of "Riverdance." Then there is "the Lambeau Leap," originated by safety Leroy Butler, who leaped into the stands at the Green Bay Packers' stadium after returning an interception for a touchdown. Receivers, of course, get more opportunities to score than do defensive backs, so it remained for Robert Brooks in the 1990s to establish the practice as a Lambeau tradition.

Some players have choreographed their celebrations ahead of time, even stashing props for later use. Terrell Owens once borrowed pom-poms from a cheerleader for a celebratory dance. Apparently deciding, however, not to rely on acquiring props on the spur of the moment, he prepared for another touchdown by stashing a pen inside one of his socks. After scoring, Owens pulled out his Sharpie, signed the football, and handed it to a person sitting in a box behind the end zone.

Joe Horn secreted a cell phone in the padding around the goalpost. He then feigned dialing and carrying on a conversation. Maybe he was calling home to tell his mother how well he did. Old-time football players likely would do their best to decapitate players performing such antics. And there is much of the juvenile "Hey, look how great I am" about such celebrations. Nonetheless, they are unlikely to end unless the NFL decides that sportsmanlike behavior belongs as much at the professional level as elsewhere.

Additional Reading:

Harvey, Walter. *Football's Most Wanted II: The Top 10 Books of More Bruising Backs, Savage Sacks, and Gridiron Oddities.* Washington DC: Potomac Books, 2006.

Wright, Elmo. "Father of End-Zone Dance Explains His Happy Feet." *New York Times Sports Sunday*, November 13, 2005.

Cheating

Cheating occurs in every area of human life, including sports. Not everyone, of course, is a cheater. Most people probably are essentially honest, although from time to time they may bend the rules a bit, usually in small ways. Even significant cheating in one particular area, say in sports, may be done by otherwise honest individuals.

In sports, cheating is often difficult to identify. Some practices that appear to be cheating actually are widely accepted, even expected. If a defensive lineman overhears a play being called and recognizes the play, he is expected to let his teammates know what is coming. If an official makes a mistake, perhaps spotting the ball a half yard ahead of where the play actually stopped, would anyone expect a member of the team benefiting from the placement, even if he recognizes the mistake, to correct the official? Certainly not; instead he will keep quiet and be grateful that his team caught a break.

If a quarterback or other player on the offense gives away plays through a subtle shift of the hand, nod of the head, or placement of a foot, would a defender do the honorable thing and point out the movement so that both teams are playing on an "even field"? Not likely.

So what defines the limit between acceptable, commendable actions that give one's team an edge and improper cheating? When is dishonesty actually dishonest?

The answer seems to be when a written rule is deliberately and clearly violated. Sometimes, of course, the violation is so intrinsically offensive even when there is no rule against it that a new rule is put in place to prohibit the act. That was the case with coaches instructing players to fake an injury to stop the clock and give the team a chance to score. When Notre Dame's Frank Leahy did that, not once, but twice, in a game against Iowa in 1953, the outrage led to the practice being banned. Plenty of other coaches had done the same thing, but usually not twice in the same game and not with such a demonstrable effect on the outcome. The two instances in the Notre Dame–Iowa game led each time to a Notre Dame touchdown and resulted in a 14–14 tie rather than a 14–0 Iowa victory. In that case, a particular type of cheating, reasonably acceptable before, had simply gone too far.

The use of steroids and certain other performance-enhancing substances that are both illegal and banned by the NCAA and the NFL comes under the heading of cheating along with being violations of society's law. Taking a substance that artificially makes the player stronger or faster gives the user an unfair advantage against his legal opponent.

Many other examples of cheating could be cited, including one early in the 2007 season that involved one of the most successful NFL teams and its highly respected coach, Bill Belichick. NFL rules prohibit the use of a video camera or any other recording device on the field, in the locker room, or in the coaches' box during a game. Videotaping may occur for later use by coaches, but from enclosed areas and conducted by designated and easily recognized individuals.

However, during the first quarter of the Patriots' season-opening 38–14 win over the New York Jets, Patriots video assistant Matt Estrella was discovered on the Jets' sideline videotaping the game and apparently taping the Jets' defensive signals. His camera was confiscated and the incident, which would come to be dubbed "Spygate," reported to the League office.

Within the week, Commissioner Roger Goodell, who had enacted strong penalties against Michael Vick and several other NFL players for inappropriate, in several cases illegal, activities, demonstrated that he was quite willing to be tough on teams and coaches as well. Goodell noted in a letter to the Patriots that the "episode represents a calculated and deliberate attempt to avoid long-standing rules designed to encourage fair play and promote honest competition on the playing field." In other words, the Patriots were caught cheating.

Goodell fined Belichick $500,000 and the team $250,000. He also decreed that the Patriots would lose a first-round draft choice in the 2008 draft if they made the 2007 playoffs, which, as expected, they did. If they did not make the playoffs, they would surrender second- and third-round picks.

Belichick apologized, although seemingly for the embarrassment and penalty rather than the act itself, and directed his apology to the Patriots family rather than

to the Jets. He also claimed that the videotaping had no impact on the game. Of course, the camera was confiscated early in the contest. Belichick also said in a statement released by the team that the Patriots "have never used sideline video to obtain a competitive advantage while the game was in progress," leaving unclear whether the team had used prohibited videotapes to prepare for a game. In fact, during a 35–0 victory over Green Bay the previous year, Estrella had been caught doing unauthorized videotaping and been ordered to stop.

Whether the cheating actually helped the Patriots may be difficult to determine. Certainly the Patriots would have been highly successful without it, but in a close game any small advantage may make the difference. And that, after all—whether the cheating involves stealing other teams' signals, using prohibited substances, faking injuries to get some undeserved time, or any of a myriad of other ways to bend the rules—is what cheating in sports is all about.

See also: Belichick, William Stephen; Bowden, Robert Clecker; Leahy, Francis William; Substance Abuse.

Additional Reading:

Bell, J. Bowyer. *Cheating: Deception in War & Magic, Games & Sports, Sex & Religion, Business & Con Games, Politics & Espionage, Art & Science.* New York: St. Martin's, 1982.

Feezell, Randolph M. *Sport, Play, and Ethical Reflection.* Urbana: University of Illinois Press, 2004.

Price, Christopher. *The Blueprint: How the New England Patriots Beat the System to Create the Last Great NFL Superpower.* New York: Thomas Dunne Books, 2007.

Cheerleaders

Cheerleaders had been inciting spectators to root for their favorite college football teams since the 1880s. Initially, all of the cheerleaders were males, cheering being a sufficiently manly activity to induce some of the most popular college students to volunteer their time and talents for the cause of victory over their pigskin rivals. Of course, in the late nineteenth century, most college students were male, and it would have been most unseemly for a proper woman to jump around in front of an audience anyway.

By the 1890s cheering had become more organized, with yelling captains brandishing megaphones and urging on the team's supporters. One of the most famous cheerleaders at the turn of the century was Franklin Delano Roosevelt of Harvard, leading cheers on behalf of the Crimson against Brown in 1903. Harvard won 29–0. The cheerleader would score some impressive victories of his own a few years later.

Those early cheers seem at best quaint today, but they evoked considerable emotion in the early days of the twentieth century. No Cornhuskers fans could have sat quietly while cheerleaders carefully enunciated the name of their school, building to a climactic crescendo: "U, U, U, N-I-Ver-er-Ver-Sit-Y Oh My!" And surely no Buckeyes quarreled with the seeming paucity of meaning in "Wahoo, Wahoo, Rip, Zip, Baz, Zoo, I yell, I yell, for O.S.U.!"

Initially, some university presidents opposed cheerleading as overly professionalizing the game, but by the 1920s it had spread far and wide in American colleges and universities; by then, high schools were imitating the higher institutions and incorporating cheering into their athletics programs as well. Evander Childs High School in New York, for example, had three female students cheering for the football team. Rather than merely calling out cheers, the cheerleaders by then were also engaging in gymnastics and tumbling. Some also began using large flashcards to help spectators follow the cheers.

One of the early female cheerleaders was Marion Draper, who cheered for Tulane against Northwestern in 1925. As a former member of the Ziegfeld Follies, a group of comely and talented women who starred in Florenz Ziegfeld's revues from 1907 to 1931, Draper would have been most fetching to the males in attendance. The idea of watching attractive young women jumping about proved quite appealing, and by World War II women comprised a majority of all cheerleaders.

Lawrence Herkimer, who had cheered while a student at Southern Methodist University, became an important figure in the history of cheering. He founded the National Cheerleaders Association in 1948 and invented the pom-pom, which soon became ubiquitous along sidelines. He also invented a jump named after him, the "Herkie Jump," during which the cheerleader leaps with one leg bent and the knee pointing toward the ground, with the other leg stretched out to the side as high as possible. Herkimer then proved to be a smart businessmen by starting the Cheerleader and Danz Team Company to supply uniforms and other items to the movement that he had helped make more popular, essentially helping to create a market and then developing a business to meet the needs of that market. Among the items his company manufactured and sold was the pom-pom.

By the beginning of the twenty-first century, cheerleading was firmly established as a major industry. Publications such as *American Cheerleader Magazine*, organizations such as Cheerleaders of America, summer camps, university-funded cheerleading scholarships, and televised cheerleading competitions contribute to the training and publicizing of cheerleaders. Films such as *Bring It On* (2000) and *Sugar and Spice* (2001) focus on high school cheerleaders. At the high school level, almost all cheerleaders are now girls, although the gender distribution at the college level is fairly balanced.

Apparel changed dramatically over the years, especially for female cheerleaders. Initially, women wore bulky sweaters and long skirts. By the 1950s college cheerleaders were increasingly coming to be viewed as sex objects. As Michael Oriard has pointed out in his *King Football*, cheerleaders embodied (in the media and in public perception) two ideals: the sweet and innocent beauty of the girl next door and a sexy voluptuousness. Costumes became more and more revealing: skirts shortened, tops grew tight and sometimes featured strategic sections cut away to show reasonably discreet portions of skin. College cheerleaders, of course, were eroticized considerably more than high school cheerleaders, although the latter today usually wear skirts short enough to have scandalized their pre–World War II predecessors.

Most professional football teams added cheerleaders in the 1960s; at first they usually were local high school girls dressed with suitable modesty. That changed in the early 1970s when the Dallas Cowboys jettisoned their high school CowBelles & Beaux in favor of dancers known as the Dallas Cowboys Cheerleaders. With short shorts, revealing tops, and go-go boots, they made the sidelines look more like Las Vegas than the local high school. Other teams have tried to compete, but none have been able to establish a cheerleading-dancing-entertaining corps with the panache and appeal of the DCC.

See also: Dallas Cowboys Cheerleaders; Purdue's Golden Girl; Sexuality.

Additional Reading:

Adams, Natalie Guice, and Pamela J. Bettis. *Cheerleader! Cheerleader!: An American Icon.* New York: Palgrave Macmillan, 2003.

"Dallas Cowboys Cheerleaders: America's Sweethearts." Dallas Cowboys Web site. http://www.dallascowboys.com/cheerleaders.

Falk, Gerhard. *Football and American Identity.* New York: Haworth, 2005.

Hanson, Mary Ellen. *Go! Fight! Win!: Cheerleading in American Culture.* Bowling Green OH: Bowling Green State University Popular Press, 1995.

Oriard, Michael. *King Football: Sport and*

Spectacle in the Golden Age of Radio and Newsreels, Movies and Magazines, the Weekly and the Daily Press. Chapel Hill: University of North Carolina Press, 2001.

Coin Toss

We tell our children not to throw their money around, meaning, of course, not to spend it unwisely, and certainly not to spend all of it. Yet in football, that is precisely what is done to get the game under way. Money, if only a small coin, is tossed to the ground.

The coin toss has a long history in football, predating modern American football. When the game still far more resembled its British antecedents soccer and rugby, a coin was used to determine which goal a team would defend at the start of the game. In October 1871 the Princeton Football Association was formed. Essentially a rules committee, the group established a number of regulations preserving the sport as strictly a kicking game in which players were prohibited from carrying or throwing the ball. The association included the stipulation that the winner of the coin toss would have the choice of goals. The Yale Football Association issued a set of slightly revised rules in 1872. Under this code the winner of the coin toss would benefit in two ways, by having first kickoff and the choice of goals.

The next alteration in the coin-toss procedures came from the most important early rule-setting meeting. On November 23, 1876, representatives from Princeton, Harvard, Yale, and Columbia met at the Massasoit House in Springfield, Massachusetts. Out of this meeting came a new organization, the Intercollegiate Football Association (although Yale did not formally join) and a set of sixty-two rules that set the game on its way to becoming the modern sport of American football. No longer was football to be merely a kicking game, as players were now permitted to carry the ball and to throw it backward. Regarding the coin toss, the respective captains conducted the toss with the winner having options. He could either pick the goal or choose whether to kick off.

A new body, the Intercollegiate Rules Committee, kept the procedures for the coin toss largely the same when revising football rules in 1894 but did stipulate that the same side would not kick off in both halves of the game. The team that won the toss and elected to receive in the first half would then kick to start the second half. That rule remains in effect today.

Still another rules body, the National Collegiate Athletic Association (NCAA) Rules Committee, which had become the governing body in 1916, removed the coin toss from the captains in 1921 and charged the referee with conducting it. The captains still had to call heads or tails and were prohibited from changing their initial call.

Other minor alterations in the coin-toss ceremony occurred later. The toss was set at three minutes before the game in 1952, teams were assigned a specific area to be in during the coin toss in 1979, and the number of captains permitted to be present for the ceremony was set at a maximum of four in 1990. Also in 1990 the location for the teams during the toss was revised again, with both teams to remain behind the 9-yard lines.

As with most aspects of the game, professional football followed college ball regarding the coin toss. Although minor differences have persisted between the two levels, they have played (and continue to play) essentially the same game. So it remains with the coin toss.

Additional Reading:

Davis, Parke H. *Football: The American Intercollegiate Game.* New York: Charles Scribner's Sons, 1911.

Nelson, David M. *The Anatomy of a Game: Football, the Rules, and the Men Who Made the Game.* Newark NJ: University of Delaware Press/Associated University Presses, 1994.

Commercials and Advertisements

Celebrities have been lending their names (in most cases for tidy sums of money) to products for about as long as advertising has been around. Football players are no exception, although college players are not permitted to participate in such mercenary activities, and current NFL rules prohibit its players from advertising certain products, principally alcohol, tobacco, gambling (or anything related to gambling, such as visiting Las Vegas), and outlawed supplements. That, however, was not always the case. Frank Gifford, for example, prominently pushed Lucky Strike cigarettes in the early 1960s. An advertisement in *Sports Illustrated* shows two pictures of the New York Giants star. On the left side of the page, the uniformed Gifford is featured in a rushing play; on the right, a smiling, contented Gifford is relaxing, attired in a sweater, reading a book, and holding a Lucky Strike in his right hand. A quotation by Gifford at the foot of the page extols the taste of Lucky Strikes.

Football players, of course, made their advertising mark in the pages of magazines and newspapers prior to moving into television commercials. The basic rule seemed to be that what mattered was the player, not necessarily that the joining of that particular player and a specific product had to make any rational sense. Hence, Otto Graham, a Hall of Fame quarterback with the Cleveland Browns, could advertise tea as a product that refreshes and keeps a person alert and going strong. A pro football player sipping tea? Or Vince Lombardi could offer a testimonial for National Car Rental in which he says nothing about National Car Rental but instead offers a lengthy epistle on "What it takes to be No. 1." Of course, the subliminal message is that National also is No. 1, without Lombardi actually having to lower himself to talk about the company. A reader of *Sports Illustrated* also might wonder why Ray Nitschke, the ferocious middle linebacker of Lombardi's Green Bay Packers in the 1960s, is kneeling on a football field holding a chainsaw. Presumably, Nitschke is not planning to take the chainsaw to a Chicago

Bears back coming through the line, but maybe running into Nitschke is as bad as running into a chainsaw.

Once football players gravitated to television commercials, they encountered a much wider audience. Out of this transformation came some of television's more memorable commercials. Joe Namath wearing Beautymist panty hose in 1974 comes immediately to mind. Namath surely took a lot of ribbing for showing off his newly shaved legs caressed by panty hose, but his paycheck apparently more than compensated for any embarrassment. In another commercial, Namath received $20,000 to shave off his moustache with a Schick razor, a moustache that, by NFL edict, had to come off anyway.

Today one can hardly imagine any company wanting O. J. Simpson to endorse its product, but in the 1970s Simpson was golden. *Advertising Age* in 1976 named him its Spokesman of the Year. In those days, Simpson, the record-setting running back for the Buffalo Bills, also was dashing through airports for Hertz, the car rental giant. The 1970s witnessed some of the best-known television commercials ever made by football players (with print versions also prevalent). Mean Joe Greene of the Pittsburgh Steelers makes his tired, aching, irritable way down a stadium tunnel when he is approached by a young boy who offers Greene his bottle of Coke. Greene inconsiderately chugalugs the Coke and continues without a thank-you. The boy, downcast, continues

on his way, but then Greene turns, calls after the boy, and tosses him his jersey as a trade. Hearts throughout the country go pitter-patter as Mean Joe turns nice. *TV Guide* rated this commercial one of the fifty best ever made. The spot won a Clio Award for creative advertising and was selected by *USA Today* in 2001 as the all-time best Super Bowl commercial.

A series of commercials for Miller Lite beer also sought to mold viewers' drinking habits in the 1970s. In one of the commercials, Bubba Smith, a defensive lineman for Baltimore, Oakland, and Houston in the 1960s and 1970s, proved willing to shed blood for Miller Lite. The commercials featured the debate over the beer's primary virtue: tastes great or less filling. Smith opts for both and still a third, the easy-opening can. He then rips off the top of the can with his bare hands. Viewers, however, did not get to see the lengthy, bloody gash he cut into his hand doing that stunt as the prop people somehow did not fix the can right. The former Oakland coach and longtime television announcer John Madden was another of the Miller Lite crowd. He endeared himself to viewers with his blustering, frenzied performance, capping his argument by smashing through the backdrop and demanding, "Hey, wait a minute!"

Many examples of football players advertising products lurk in the minds of viewers, perhaps still inducing certain buying choices, such as Dan Marino assuring us that he always buys Isotoner gloves for his linemen and receivers.

We may even pine for the long-defunct MCDLT sandwich from McDonald's, the kind that William "the Refrigerator" Perry, a bright but brief star with the Chicago Bears during the team's 1985 Super Bowl season, admired because of its packaging, which kept the hot parts hot and the cool parts cool. Advertising does not always work, even when it is entertaining, but player-made commercials will keep coming.

Still, there appear to be limits beyond those imposed by the NFL. Active players have not signed on to offer testimonials for erectile-dysfunction medicines. Former great tight end and Super Bowl coach Mike Ditka, however, was willing to stand up publicly for Levitra. It takes a really tough guy to admit certain things.

See also: Ditka, Michael Keller, Jr.; Gifford, Frank Newton; Graham, Otto Everett, Jr.; Greene, Charles Edward Joseph; Lombardi, Vincent Thomas; Madden, John Earl; Magazines; Marino, Daniel Constantine, Jr.; Namath, Joseph William; Newspapers; Perry, William Anthony; Simpson, Orenthal James.

Additional Reading:

Harvey, Walter. *Football's Most Wanted II: The Top 10 Book of More Bruising Backs, Savage Sacks, and Gridiron Oddities*. Washington DC: Potomac Books, 2006.

Reilly, Rick. "Introduction." In *The Football Book*. Ed. Rob Fleder, 12–17. New York: Sports Illustrated Books, 2005.

Commissioners

Every organization needs someone or some people in charge, and football is no exception. College conferences have commissioners, but there are a lot of college conferences in the United States, and the commissioners must share authority with the NCAA as well as with the individual educational institutions. In big-time professional football, however, there is only one league and one commissioner—the leader of the National Football League.

The NFL commissioner, of course, does not wield absolute authority, but his powers and influence are great. At the very dawning of the league in 1920, when it was still called the American Professional Football Association, league organizers realized the valuable role of a commissioner, then called the league president. At first, the owners opted for someone who would give the new league instant credibility and public name recognition. So they chose Jim Thorpe, possibly the best known football player in the country. Thorpe gave them recognition but little else, his mind and heart still focused primarily on playing.

After one year, the owners chose a new president, Joe Carr, a sportswriter and sports editor of the *Ohio State Journal* in Columbus and a machinist for the Pennsylvania Railroad. Carr served as league president until 1939. His leadership helped the league not only survive but also prosper and secure a lasting place for itself within American sports.

Carr's abilities were recognized across the sports spectrum, leading the American Basketball Association to tap him as its president for part of his football tenure (1925–28), and the National Association of Professional Baseball Leagues to put him in charge of its promotional department where he expanded the minor league system from 12 to 41 leagues.

Football, however, was where his star shone most brightly. He instituted official league standings in 1921 and supported a name change (to the National Football League) in 1922. Carr standardized players' contracts, mandated that a player's contract belonged to the team for which he played the previous year (thus sharply limiting free agency), and led creation of a new league constitution and bylaws.

Carr was a practical visionary who could clearly see what the league had to do to survive and keep growing over the long term. He understood, for example, that the league had to transform itself from an organization rooted in the towns and small cities of the Midwest to a league based in large cities, with large numbers of potential fans; in short, it had to become a national league as its name stipulated. That was not easy for Carr, whose whole existence had been focused on midwestern towns, where he had lived, worked, and even run a pre-NFL team, the Columbus Panhandles. To further this vision, he persuaded Tim Mara in 1925 to create a team in New York (the Giants) and Art Rooney a decade later to do the same in Pittsburgh (the Pirates, later the Steelers).

On Carr's watch the first College All-Star Game against the NFL champion was played in 1934. The first college draft was held in 1936 at the strong urging of Bert Bell, who later would hold the position

Carr filled so well. By the time Carr died in 1939, the NFL had quickly defeated competition by the first American Football League, survived its early years of rapid new-team creation and attrition, stabilized, and positioned itself for a bright future.

Carr's death led to selection of the veteran NFL secretary-treasurer Carl Storck. That proved a short-term answer, with Elmer Layden following Storck in 1941. Layden promised the kind of name recognition that Thorpe had once offered the league. A member of the famed Four Horsemen of Notre Dame, Layden became the league's first commissioner, the name change complementing the choice of Layden, both in line with the owners' desire to reach the level of public affection and acclaim accorded Major League Baseball.

Unfortunately, two events intervened to make Layden's years as commissioner (1941–46) difficult: World War II and the new All-America Football Conference. The war drained the league of manpower and led to a variety of temporary measures to keep the league functioning.

When Cleveland Rams owner Dan Reeves went into the navy, his team suspended play for the 1943 season. Also, the Pittsburgh Steelers and Philadelphia Eagles merged to form the Steagles, perhaps a necessary step but certainly an infelicitous name. The next year the Steagles dissolved, with the Eagles returning to action. The Steelers then merged with the Chicago Cardinals to form the Card-

Pitt team. In 1945 the Boston Yanks and Brooklyn Tigers (until 1944 named the Dodgers) merged, retaining the name Yanks and playing four games in Boston and four in New York. After the season, Dan Topping, owner of the Brooklyn team, deserted the NFL for the new league.

Arch Ward and other organizers of the fledgling All-America Football Conference sought a meeting with Layden but were rebuffed. Layden responded sarcastically to the request, suggesting that they get a football before talking. The league, of course, did just that, and soon the NFL had a new commissioner.

That new commissioner would be one of several outstanding leaders who occupied the position with impressive skill and acute judgment. Bert Bell was co-owner of the Steelers and before that owner and coach of the Eagles. Strong of purpose and prudent in his actions, he was able to unite owners and others associated with the NFL in a spirit of collegiality to work together to improve the league.

Bell had been largely responsible for the college draft, and now he turned to other matters, foremost among them a successful conclusion to the four-year experiment by the All-America Football Conference. A merger ended the competition and at the same time opened up new markets for the NFL, especially on the West Coast.

Bell also recognized the growing importance of television but, as he was accustomed to doing, moved prudently into televising games. CBS was permitted to televise some games in carefully chosen markets, but a blackout was enforced within seventy-five miles of the home stadium. Bell instituted the two-minute warning to assure CBS of at least one commercial break per half, a far cry from the many commercials that now permeate each football telecast. At the conclusion of the overtime championship game in 1958, when Johnny Unitas led the Baltimore Colts to victory over the New York Giants, Bell exulted triumphantly that this was football's greatest day. He well recognized what the dramatic contest would mean for the future popularity of the sport. Bell, however, would not live to see much of its future. The following season he died while watching a game between the Eagles and Steelers, the two teams he had once owned.

Bell had been highly popular with the owners who now had to find a successor. That proved difficult. It took twenty-three ballots to elect Pete Rozelle, then the thirty-three-year-old general manager of the Rams. Rozelle, however, exceeded almost everyone's most optimistic expectations.

Rozelle led the NFL through another period of competition by a new league, this challenge longer and even more difficult than the one posed by the All-America Football Conference. The American Football League (the fourth league by this name) enjoyed surprising success, lasting throughout the 1960s and finally merging with the NFL, all of its teams joining the

NFL, which was restructured into National Football and American Football Conferences. The competing league and the impending merger, announced in June 1966, led to the formation of the Super Bowl, which was first played on January 15, 1967, with the Green Bay Packers defeating the Kansas City Chiefs 35–10.

During Rozelle's almost thirty years at the helm of the NFL, *Monday Night Football* began (1970), Miami recorded the first and only undefeated season in the history of the NFL (1972), the NFL moved forcefully into television with large revenue rewards for the league, NFL Properties was formed to function as the NFL's marketing entity, and attendance rose by almost twenty thousand spectators per game.

Some of the greatest teams in league history performed during Rozelle's long tenure as commissioner. The Packers won five NFL championships (1961–62, 1965–67) and captured the first two Super Bowls. The mighty Dolphins of 1972 were followed by the Pittsburgh Steelers, who won four Super Bowls during the 1970s (after the 1974, 1975, 1978, and 1979 seasons). Teams also were added and moved. The Tampa Bay Buccaneers (1976) and Seattle Seahawks (1976) joined the league, the Cardinals moved from St. Louis to Phoenix (1988), and the Colts ignited considerable controversy by shifting from Baltimore to Indianapolis (1984).

Pete Rozelle, however, faced growing labor unrest. The increased strength of the National Football League Players Association posed challenges for league administrators and owners while, of course, benefiting players. A strike in 1982 limited the season to nine games, and another strike in 1987 eliminated one game entirely and left three other games to be played by replacement players. Among other gains for the players was limited free agency.

Al Davis became something of a Rozelle nemesis as the Oakland Raiders successfully sued the NFL in order to move his team to Los Angeles, a step he was able to take in 1982. The Raiders won the Super Bowl in January 1984. Nonetheless, Davis returned the Raiders to Oakland in 1995.

Rozelle stepped down in 1989 and was succeeded by Paul Tagliabue, who had been the NFL's legal counsel. Additional franchise shifts occurred during Tagliabue's reign: the Rams moved from Los Angeles to St. Louis (1995), and the Browns moved from Cleveland to Baltimore, where they became the Ravens (1996). The Jacksonville Jaguars and Carolina Panthers began play in 1995, and Cleveland received a new team, also called the Browns, in 1999.

The San Francisco 49ers continued to be successful in the 1990s, winning a fifth Super Bowl after the 1994 season. The Dallas Cowboys capped off their championship seasons of 1992, 1993, and 1995 with Super Bowl triumphs. The Green Bay Packers reclaimed their winning ways with a Super Bowl triumph after the 1996 season, then lost the following Super Bowl to the Denver Broncos. Denver made it two in a row in Super Bowl XXXIII. During Tagliabue's final years the New England Patriots became the most consistently powerful team in the NFL, winning three Super Bowls in four years (following the 2001, 2003, and 2004 seasons).

On the whole Tagliabue's tenure as commissioner was a time of labor peace and big television contracts. The league and union agreed on a free agency process and a salary cap in the 1992 contract, and in 1998, the NFL signed the largest television contract ever negotiated by any organization, one that would bring the teams $17.6 billion over eight years.

Shortly before retiring, Tagliabue saw new deals completed in both areas: television agreements with NBC and ESPN in 2005 (following agreements with CBS and FOX in 2004) and a new labor contract in March 2006.

If all looked serene for the new commissioner, Roger Goodell, he would quickly find that to be an illusion. Son of former New York Senator Charles Goodell, the new commissioner started his NFL career as a public relations intern in 1982. Since 2000 he had served as the NFL's chief operating officer.

Goodell had looked forward to addressing revenue sharing and stadium construction among other matters but was quickly faced with two difficult issues. One involved growing anger by former players and their families over what they perceived as insufficient concern for them by the Players Association. Although the anger was directed more toward the association and its executive director, Gene Upshaw, than toward league management, Goodell entered the discussion to try to find ways to care more effectively for retired players, especially those with serious medical problems.

The dominant issue facing Goodell, however, was criminal activity by current players. Off-field behavior was increasingly casting the NFL in an unfavorable light, and Goodell wasted no time in taking strong steps to correct the growing perception that improper behavior, including overt criminal actions, if not accepted, was at least tolerated for the sake of winning football games.

Brawls, drunken driving, even shootings came under scrutiny, and Goodell was ready with a new Personal Conduct Policy and heavy suspensions. Chicago Bears defensive tackle Tank Johnson was suspended for eight games of the 2007 season after violating probation on a gun charge. Adam "Pacman" Jones, a cornerback with the Tennessee Titans, received a year's suspension for behavior detrimental to the game after a series of five arrests. A sixth arrest followed the 2007-season suspension, and Goodell ruled out training camp as well for him. Cincinnati Bengals wide receiver Chris Henry received a two-game suspension in 2006 for violating the league's personal conduct and substance abuse policies, then drew a 2007 eight-game suspension for a series of violations, after which he would have to apply for reinstatement. Odell

Thurman, a Bengals linebacker, drew a four-game suspension to open the 2006 season after violating the substance abuse policy. A subsequent drunken driving incident extended that suspension to the rest of the season.

As serious as were these and other incidents (including nine Bengals arrested over a period of nine months), the football world was especially shocked when accusations arose regarding star Atlanta Falcons quarterback Michael Vick's alleged involvement with a dogfighting business on property he owned in Smithfield, Virginia. When Vick was indicted and pled not guilty to charges related to dogfighting, Goodell was left to sort out how to protect the NFL, respect the legal process and Vick's right to a presumption of innocence, and avoid a circus atmosphere around the Falcons as players began to prepare for the 2007 season. As a first step, he barred Vick from training camp while the NFL investigated. Vick subsequently admitted guilt and was sentenced to prison, as described elsewhere in this book.

See also: All-America Football Conference; American Football League (iv); Crime; Davis, Allen; Dogfighting; Four Horsemen of Notre Dame; Globalism; Greatest Game; Labor-Management Relations; Professional Football Origins; Super Bowl; Television Broadcasting; Thorpe, James Francis; Ward, Arch; World War ii.

Additional Reading:

Clary, Jack. "The History of the National Football League." In *Total Football ii: The Official Encyclopedia of the National Football League.* Ed. Bob Carroll et al., 14–33. New York: HarperCollins, 1999.

Davis, Jeff. *Rozelle: Czar of the NFL.* New York: McGraw-Hill, 2007.

MacCambridge, Michael. *America's Game: The Epic Story of How Pro Football Captured a Nation.* New York: Random House, 2004.

Concussions

Concussions are not unique to football, or to sports in general, but their prevalence in football is high because of the violent nature of the game. For most of the history of football, counting fingers accurately was sufficient evidence that the player was ready to return to the battle. In recent years, both medical and football personnel have come to realize how woefully inadequate that test really is.

A suicide brought the issue of concussions to the forefront of football consciousness again in 2006. Andre Waters, a defensive back for the Philadelphia Eagles and Arizona Cardinals from 1984 through 1995, committed suicide in the fall of 2006. A neuropathologist examined Waters's brain and determined that several concussions had resulted in his having the brain tissue of a man in his eighties. Soon after Waters's death, in early 2007, doctors concluded that Ted Johnson, only thirty-four years old, a recently retired New England Patriots linebacker, was exhibiting symptoms (depression and memory lapses) consistent with early Alzheimer's. Johnson had suffered two concussions in four days during the 2002 exhibition season.

Various studies, while not absolutely conclusive, demonstrate serious aspects of repeated concussions. According to a

2003 University of North Carolina study, 263 of 2,500 retired football players believed that concussions may have adversely affected their memory and their ability to think clearly.

A study published in the journal *Medicine & Science in Sports & Exercise* in June 2007 reported a connection between the number of concussions and clinical depression. According to the study, individuals who suffered three or more concussions were three times more likely than those who had no concussions to develop depression. Players with one or two concussions were one and a half times more likely to suffer depression. About 20 percent of those who said they had experienced three or more concussions were diagnosed with clinical depression. Concussions suffered in high school and college, although vitally significant to the person's health, were not included in the study. The survey relied on players' memories of concussions, raising the possibility that some may have suffered concussions and never realized it, or may have forgotten some of the concussions. Contributing to the need to take the study seriously was the response rate, as a remarkably large number of those who received the survey (2,552 of 3,683) responded.

Although NFL spokesman Greg Aiello denied that the study proved anything, he acknowledged the need to study the issue of concussions carefully. NFL Commissioner Roger Goodell convened a conference of medical personnel from every team in June 2007 to foster greater understanding of the danger of concussions. Further, Goodell initiated a whistle-blower system to start with the 2007 season. Under this system, anyone may anonymously report a doctor or coach who inappropriately clears a player to return to action or pressures anyone to play. New rules also will require each player to undergo neuropsychological testing and keep his chinstrap fastened while in action. Brochures were being prepared to help educate players and their families about concussions.

Contributing to the problem of concussions is the mind-set of football players who may worry that they will be looked down on if they complain about symptoms such as dizziness or headaches. That, of course, is one of the impediments to good health that the new educational program is intended to address.

Fear of losing one's job also has induced players to overlook concussions. Wayne Chrebet, a longtime receiver for the New York Jets, retired after the 2005 season—and after at least six concussions. Chrebet was honored by his former team at halftime of a 2007 game against the Miami Dolphins, but the ceremony could not restore his preconcussion state. He explained in an interview that the story of the New York Yankees' Wally Pipp sitting out a game and losing his job to Lou Gehrig was all too real to him, and he feared something similar happening if he took time off after an injury. An effective possession receiver, Chrebet lacked the great talent that might have given him more confidence about retaining his job. Now he has memory problems and cannot go on amusement-park rides with his children or do anything that might cause blood to flow suddenly to his head. The new rules also will impact a player like Chrebet, who will not be able to decide for himself whether to reenter a game. That might make him worry more about his job, but he could face the rest of his life with at least more certainty about his health.

See also: Big Hit; Suicide.

Additional Reading:

Guskiewicz, Kevin M., et al. "Recurrent Concussion and Risk of Depression in Retired Professional Football Players." *Medicine & Science in Sports & Exercise* 39 (2007): 903–9.

Rhoden, William C. "A Jet Who Led with His Head, and His Heart." *New York Times,* September 24, 2007.

Cosell, Howard William (1918–1995)

Howard Cosell, born Howard William Cohen, was perhaps the most recognized and controversial sports broadcaster of the 1960s and 1970s. Well-educated and highly intelligent, he enjoyed acquainting his audience with his erudition and vocabulary. His staccato-like, nasal speech pattern complemented perfectly his "telling it like it is" self-proclaimed mission. His voice was so distinctive as to be immediately recognized; it also was a voice people loved to imitate, including impressionist Rich Little.

Cosell came from a Jewish family and was the grandson of a rabbi but for much of his life did not actively practice his religion and anglicized his name from "Cohen" to "Cosell." The name change, however, actually was an effort to honor his father, whose surname, Kasell, had been changed to Cohen by immigration officials at Ellis Island. He earned a degree in English at New York University and a law degree from the New York University School of Law. He served during World War II in the U.S. Army Transportation Corps, where he rose to the rank of major. On returning from the war, he practiced law in Manhattan. Work with one of his clients, the Little League of New York, led to his first broadcasting job in 1953 on New York's WABC hosting a show on which Little Leaguers posed questions to major league players.

Cosell expanded his radio work and also began television reporting, including participating in ABC's Olympic telecasts and covering boxing matches. He excited considerable controversy with some of the positions he took in support of African American athletes, especially his support of Muhammad Ali's assumption of his Black Muslim name as a replacement for his "white" name, Cassius Clay, and Ali's refusal to accept induction into the military during the Vietnam War. Ali's refusal led to the New York State Boxing Commission's stripping him of his heavyweight championship, a move Cosell opposed. He also reported sympathetically on Tommie Smith's black-fisted black-power salute on the winner's stand at the 1968 Olympics in Mexico City.

Cosell's most famous Olympic reporting, however, came from Munich in 1972 during the murder of Israeli athletes by the Palestinian terror group Black September. Cosell's image and voice appear on Steven Spielberg's film about the attack, *Munich* (2005). The tragic incident reawakened in Cosell his Jewish heritage, and he became a member of the American Friends of the Hebrew University in Jerusalem, which named a physical education center after him and his wife, Mary Edith.

Cosell earned his greatest fame as a member of the broadcasting trio on *Monday Night Football* beginning in 1970. The program, part entertainment, part sports event, brought Cosell regularly into millions of homes. Viewers had something of a love-hate relationship with Cosell, caught up in his ability to sound the depths of football and its relationship to other aspects of American society and his witty repartee with fellow broadcasters Don Meredith and Frank Gifford, whom he nicknamed Dandy Don and the Giffer. At the same time, some viewed him as arrogant, pedantic, and pompous.

Cosell delighted in being iconoclastic and was not averse to putting football in its place to turn his attention to other, weightier matters, as when he announced to a shocked audience on December 8, 1980, that former Beatle John Lennon had been murdered.

Never reluctant to criticize either sports or his bosses, he strongly attacked the integrity of boxing after covering Larry Holmes's bloody battering of

Randall "Tex" Cobb in December 1982 and stopped covering boxing matches.

Despite, or perhaps because of, his ability to generate controversy, Cosell proved popular throughout the media world. He appeared in two episodes of the Jack Klugman–Tony Randall television comedy *The Odd Couple* (episodes 49 and 107, aired in 1972 and 1975) and in Woody Allen's film *Bananas* (1971). He hosted *Saturday Night Live* in 1985 and was an important part of the story in the film *Ali* (2001, with Jon Voight playing Cosell and earning an Academy Award nomination). The Monday football program he helped make successful resulted in both a book about it, *Monday Night Mayhem* (1988), and a television film of the same title on Turner Network Television, with John Turturro playing Cosell (2002).

Cosell suffered considerable criticism, probably unfairly, after he called an African American player, Alvin Garrett of the Washington Redskins, a "little monkey" during the *Monday Night Football* telecast of September 5, 1983. Cosell's extensive support of black athletes and the fact that he had used the same term in reference to white athletes—for example, Mike Adamle of the Kansas City Chiefs in a game against the New York Giants during the 1972 preseason—appear to contradict any notion that Cosell was a racist. The incident, however, led to his departure from *Monday Night Football* after that season.

Cosell believed that television broadcasting should be done by trained professionals and attacked the practice of bringing people into the broadcast booth just because they were successful and famous athletes. In his book *I Never Played the Game* (1985), he gave the practice a damning name—"jockocracy." Cosell's assault on the common hiring practice and his criticism of fellow ABC employees led to his removal from his television program, *Sportsbeat*.

Cosell continued, however, to work on ABC radio, with *Speaking of Sports* and *Speaking of Everything*, before retiring in early 1992 after surgery to remove a cancerous tumor. A series of strokes followed, and he died of a heart embolism at New York University Hospital on April 23, 1995.

His last great achievement came about two months earlier, when he received the Arthur Ashe Award for Courage during the ESPY ceremonies on ESPN. Cosell was not able to attend, but his friend, the comedian Bill Cosby, accepted on his behalf. Cosell may have felt some vindication for the earlier racial accusations, both in the award itself and in the prominent African American entertainer who stood in for him at the ceremony. Cosell was many things, including arrogant and self-righteous at times, but it is difficult to argue that he did not evince considerable courage in many ways as he argued and acted on behalf of what he believed.

See also: Gifford, Frank Newton; *Monday Night Football*; Television Broadcasting.

Additional Reading:

Cosell, Howard. *Like It Is*. Chicago: Playboy Press, 1974.
———. *I Never Played the Game*. With Peter Bonventre. New York: Morrow, 1985.
———. *What's Wrong with Sports*. With Shelby Whitfield. New York: Simon and Schuster, 1991.
Gunther, Marc, and Bill Carter. *Monday Night Mayhem: The Inside Story of ABC's Monday Night Football*. New York: Beech Tree Books, 1988.

Crime

Crime in connection with football was seldom mentioned during the first half of the twentieth century and remained largely hidden, if all too often a reality, for the second half. From time to time, a particular case would make the headlines, but many infractions were swept under the turf by officials and fans concerned with protecting their teams. That has changed dramatically in recent years, especially since the arrival of Roger Goodell as commissioner of the National Football League. Some of the most publicized criminal cases—the murder trial of O. J. Simpson, dogfighting-related charges against Michael Vick, and the gambling-related actions of Art Schlicter, for example—are discussed elsewhere in this book and therefore are not considered again here.

Crime affects individuals at every level of football, including high school athletes, as it does people across all areas of society. High school incidents, however, tend to be largely of interest locally and seldom come before the national public.

It is not that way at the college level, though, where crime is an increasing concern on campuses throughout the country. Most criminal acts at institutions of higher education have nothing explicitly to do with football programs. The mass murders at Virginia Tech University on April 16, 2007, and other serious crimes have raised concerns about accurate crime reporting by educational institutions and whether the schools are doing enough to make the campuses safe. Football-related criminal activity is a small although significant part of this issue. Cases that recently have come to public attention include a player found guilty of deliberately injuring his team's starting punter and criminal activity by former members of the Montana State University football team.

According to prosecutors, Mitch Cozad, a backup punter for Northern Colorado, stabbed starting punter Rafael Mendoza in his kicking leg during the night of September 11, 2006. In August 2007 Cozad was convicted of second-degree assault but acquitted of attempted first-degree murder. Witnesses testified that Cozad, a walk-on, was bitter over not being selected as his team's starting punter. Cozad subsequently received a prison sentence of seven years.

As reported in a *Sports Illustrated* article in August 2007, former Montana State receiver Rick Gatewood and his brother, Randy, were accused in May 2007, along with another, unnamed Montana State football player, of having operated a drug ring in Montana for almost two years. Randy later pleaded guilty to conspiring to distribute cocaine. Rick, as of this writing, had pleaded not guilty and was awaiting trial. The killing of Jason Wright, coach of an American Legion baseball team and allegedly a cocaine dealer, also reportedly involved former Montana State players. On an evening in June 2006, former defensive back John Lebrum and a former university basketball player named Branden Miller drove to a Perkins restaurant where they apparently thought Wright was dining. According to Miller, when Wright left the restaurant Lebrum charged Wright and knocked him down. Miller said that Lebrum, who had been dismissed from the university and later been convicted of felony criminal endangerment for beating up a man during a basketball game, loaded Wright into the victim's own car and drove away with him. Wright was found dead the next afternoon, the victim of several gunshot wounds and additional injuries apparently caused by being hit with a blunt instrument. Both Lebrum and Miller were arrested on June 29, 2006. Miller pleaded guilty in January 2008 to murder and tampering with evidence and was sentenced to 120 years in prison plus another 5 years for assault in another case. Lebrum pleaded guilty to helping Miller rob Wright. He received a sentence of 40 years for robbery plus 10 years for a probation violation.

Criminal behavior is a problem across the spectrum of college and university football programs, even within such a highly respected program as that at Penn State. According to a July 2008 report by ESPN, forty-six Penn State football players had been charged with 163 criminal offenses since 2002, and twenty-seven had been convicted of or pleaded guilty to 45 of the counts. These incidents included Chris Bell's pleading guilty to terrorist threats on July 22, 2008, after threatening a teammate with a knife in a dining hall. The same ESPN report notes that football players at the universities of Colorado, Georgia, and Iowa and Florida State University had been arrested on charges including sexual assault, robbery, and illegal drug activity since January 2008.

The NCAA is rightfully concerned about crime and sponsored a seminar on athletes and crime at its national convention in 2006. Those administrators who attended the seminar demonstrate the growing concern about crime on college campuses and in relation to sports programs as well, along with a serious commitment to ensure that young men and women who attend those institutions, many of whom also play sports, will be safe. More effective screening to detect past violent behavior by recruits also will help keep the surrounding communities freer of crime.

In professional football, crime has long been a problem, unfortunately a problem more tolerated than effectively addressed. A study conducted by Jeff Benedict and Don Yaeger for their book *Pros and Cons: The Criminals Who Play in the NFL* indicates that not only have many professional football players committed serious crimes but more often than not they have escaped punishment. Benedict and Yaeger based their research on the 1,590 men who played in the NFL during the 1996 season. They were able to research the criminal records of 509 of those players and found that of the 509, 21 percent had been arrested or indicted for a serious crime (including such acts as homicide, rape, kidnapping, assault, domestic violence, drug-related crimes, or illegal possession or use of a weapon). If their research is reasonably accurate, clearly a great many professional players have brought a high level of crime to their communities.

Benedict and Yaeger are less than enthusiastic about the way in which the NFL, individual teams, and local authorities responded to these crimes, although they single out certain individuals for having taken strong action. They note, for example, that former Colts and Dolphins coach Don Shula had a no-nonsense reputation for dealing with inappropriate conduct by his players, especially domestic violence. New England Patriots owner Robert Kraft is commended for immediately jettisoning fifth-round draft pick Christian Peter in 1996 once he became aware of the defensive lineman's college rap sheet, which included eight arrests and four convictions, including assaults against two women. Kraft was soon receiving congratulatory letters from college and high school coaches and others applauding his decisive action.

The future appears to promise that same sort of commitment to proper behavior and quick discipline under Commissioner Roger Goodell. Shortly after taking office in September 2006, he issued a Personal Conduct Policy that he obviously intends to enforce. Players are subject to serious penalties, including suspension or expulsion, for violating the policy even if they are not found guilty of illegal activities.

As Goodell began his five-year term, the Cincinnati Bengals were embarrassing the entire league through a string of arrests. When Johnathan Joseph, a Bengals cornerback, was charged with possession of marijuana in January 2007, he was the ninth Bengal to be arrested since the previous January. A few months later, the arrest of running back Quincy Wilson for disorderly conduct made it ten Bengals in fourteen months. One of the ten, linebacker Odell Thurman, began the 2006 season on suspension for the first four games for violating the league's substance abuse policy, and when he was arrested for drunken driving, Goodell suspended him for the rest of the year. Others who received significant suspensions from Goodell included Thurman's teammate, wide receiver Chris Henry (the first eight games of the 2007 season); Adam "Pacman" Jones, a Tennessee Titans cornerback since traded to the Dallas Cowboys (the entire 2007 season); and Chicago Bears defensive tackle Tank Johnson (the first half of 2007).

As the 2007 NFL season neared, Commissioner Goodell continued to deal with Michael Vick's situation while confronting issues posed by other players as well. Buffalo Bills defensive end Anthony Hargrove was arrested and faced three misdemeanor charges arising from a confrontation with police outside a nightclub in early August. Within a few days, he received a four-game suspension from the NFL for a substance-abuse violation. If the violations seemed to be coming in an unrelenting wave, at least they finally were being dealt with in a manner that may ultimately have a significant deterrent effect on players. Surely that will also have a trickle-down effect on college players, reinforcing the more proactive approach that at least some universities appear ready to take regarding athletes' misbehavior.

See also: Commissioners; Dogfighting; Gambling; Gangs and Street Violence; Gun Violence; Hnida, Katharine Anne; Sexuality; Simpson, Orenthal James; Substance Abuse.

Additional Reading:

Benedict, Jeff, and Don Yaeger. *Pros and Cons: The Criminals Who Play in the* NFL. New York: Warner Books, 1998.

Dohrmann, George. "Trouble in Paradise." *Sports Illustrated*, August 13, 2007, 60–64.

Lavigne, Paula. "Has Penn State's On-Field Progress Led to Off-Field Problems?" *Outside the Lines*. ESPN.com. Updated July 27, 2008. http://sports.espn.go.com/espn/otl/news/story?id=3504915.

Dallas Cowboys Cheerleaders

The Dallas Cheerleaders are the most famous group of cheerleaders in the world. The brainchild of Dallas Cowboys general manager Tex Schramm, the Dallas Cheerleaders were envisioned as not merely cheerleaders but professional dancers who could perform intricate routines on the sidelines. They were to be beautiful, sexy, talented, representative of women from many walks of life, outstanding representatives of the Cowboys organization, and beyond reproach in their personal lives. That was asking a lot, but Schramm enlisted talented professionals to help achieve his goals.

Texie Waterman, owner of a Dallas dance studio, judged the first auditions to help select the original seven Dallas Cowboys Cheerleaders and became their creative director. The new group, which began its cheering career in 1972, was quite a departure from the high school cheerleaders, who had generally cheered at professional games, and even from college cheerleaders. Dressed in white short shorts, revealing blue blouses, white vests, and white go-go boots, blue stars spangling their shorts and vests, they added to football games an erotic tinge not previously seen.

At the same time, they also exhibited a nice-girl-next-door persona. With Suzanne Mitchell, previously Schramm's secretary, as director to manage the many details involved with organizing the squad, arranging personal appearances, and other matters, the Dallas Cowboys Cheerleaders continued to grow in popularity.

Billed as "America's Sweethearts," they reached an even wider audience with their choreographed routines at Super Bowl x in January 1976. Within their first few years, the Dallas Cheerleaders appeared on television specials, were in a Faberge shampoo commercial, kicked off *Monday Night Football* in 1978 with a one-hour special called *The 36 Most Beautiful Girls in Texas*, and inspired two made-for-television movies. They have continued to appear at home and abroad ever since. Their television appearances have included additional specials, series, awards shows, and talk shows. They have appeared in Mexico, Japan, and U.S. military bases around the world. In addition, the Cheerleaders appear in an annual calendar that, to state the obvious, has proved enormously popular, and they have even appeared on three sets of trading cards.

The Dallas Cheerleaders also have become heavily involved with a wide range of good causes, appearing at events to benefit the Salvation Army, *Jerry Lewis Labor Day Telethon*, Special Olympics, Veterans Administration hospitals, March of Dimes, United Way, Make-A-Wish Foundation, and other charitable organizations.

Strict rules guide eligibility and personal conduct for the cheerleaders. To be considered for the group, aspirants must be at least eighteen years of age, have graduated from high school, be attending college or employed in at least a part-time job (or be a full-time mother and homemaker), and live in the Dallas–Fort Worth area during their time with the Dallas Cheerleaders. Selection is extremely competitive and includes rigorous training under current leaders Kelli McGonagill Finglass (director) and Judy Trammell (choreographer), both former Dallas Cowboys Cheerleaders. In addition, the staff aspires to choose cheerleaders who will represent a wide range of women. Over the years, cheerleaders have included teachers, secretaries, homemakers, dental hygienists, flight attendants, accountants, and women in many other careers.

Members of the Dallas Cheerleaders are not permitted to date anyone associated with the Cowboys organization, including players. They may not drink, smoke, or behave in any manner that would bring embarrassment to the Cowboys. During trips, they are always accompanied by at least one member of the administrative staff, and the cheerleaders always travel as a group.

With the Dallas Cowboys Cheerleaders now having passed their thirty-fifth year of existence and still counting, they are firmly established as an internationally renowned institution. The Cowboys organization has marketed the cheerleaders well, selling beauty, talent, sexiness, compassion, and, yes, even brains, while maintaining an invisible wall between the cheerleaders and the public. Onlookers may gaze, admire, fantasize, have their pictures taken with cheerleaders, buy their calendars, and enjoy their dance routines, but not touch. That is a formula that has worked effectively and promises to continue doing so.

See also: Cheerleaders; *Monday Night Football*; Sexuality.

Additional Reading:
"Dallas Cowboys Cheerleaders: America's Sweethearts." Dallas Cowboys Web site. http://www.dallascowboys.com/cheerleaders.
Evans, Mary Candace. *A Decade of Dreams: Dallas Cowboys Cheerleaders*. Dallas: Taylor, 1982.
St. John, Bob. TEX!: *The Man Who Built the Dallas Cowboys*. Englewood Cliffs NJ: Prentice Hall, 1988.

Davis, Allen (Al) (b. 1929)

Al Davis is one of the most influential and controversial figures in modern professional football history. His experiences have run the gamut from assistant coach to commissioner, but his fame and notoriety rest principally on his years as president and managing general partner of the Oakland Raiders.

Davis embarked on his career in football in 1950 after graduating from Syracuse University. He was an assistant coach at Adelphi College, head coach of the U.S. Army team at Fort Belvoir, Virginia, and assistant coach at the Citadel, the University of Southern California, and the Los Angeles/San Diego Chargers of the American Football League.

Davis began his decades-long run with the Oakland (sometimes Los Angeles) Raiders in 1963 as general manager and head coach, at thirty-three the youngest person to have held those positions in the modern history of professional football. In April 1966 he was named commissioner of the AFL as talks regarding a merger between the new league and the National Football League were heating up. Davis immediately set out to sign top players away from the older league, an effort that, depending on the interpretation, either hastened or threatened to undermine the merger talks.

A planned merger was announced in June of that year, to be completed by 1970, with interim steps such as a common college draft and a championship game (later dubbed the Super Bowl). Davis then returned to Oakland, although not as coach, and set out to acquiring firm control of the team from the other owners. Under Davis's highly personalized brand of leadership, the Raiders enjoyed great success, capturing thirteen division championships from 1967 to 1985 and winning Super Bowls XI, XV, and XVIII after the 1976, 1980, and 1983 seasons. The Raiders also won the AFL championship in 1967, losing Super Bowl II to the Green Bay Packers.

Davis favored an exciting, vertical passing game, coined the expression "Just win, baby," and personally chose the Raiders' striking silver-and-black uniforms. Beloved by many of his players, he was selected by nine Oakland Hall of Fame inductees to present them at their induction ceremonies.

Davis has spent much of his time also involved in confrontations with league management. With the proposed merger threatening to fall apart in 1970, Davis crafted a compromise proposal that included shifting three teams from the NFL to the AFL in order to create two thirteen-team conferences and paying $3 million to each of the three teams switching to the American Football Conference. Davis, however, then voted against his own proposal, demanding control over the divisional alignments. Oakland's majority owner, Wayne Valley, voted for the plan, thus overriding Davis's objections and permitting the merger to move ahead.

Davis tried to move the Raiders from Oakland to Los Angeles in 1980 and filed an antitrust lawsuit against the NFL when a court blocked the move. In 1982 a federal court removed the injunction, and Davis took his team to Los Angeles. By 1995 Davis was bringing his Raiders back to Oakland and again suing the NFL, this time charging the league with failing to adequately support construction of a new stadium in Los Angeles. The suit dragged on for over a decade before the California Supreme Court finally ruled against Davis in 2007.

If contrary at times, Davis also has been highly progressive socially and deeply committed to helping individuals in need, especially members of the Raiders family. Perhaps drawing on his own accomplishments as a very young man, Davis hired John Madden to coach the Raiders when he was just thirty-two years old. Davis was one of the first owners to scout historically black colleges. He hired the first African American coach (Art Shell) in the modern history of the NFL, was the first to draft an African American quarterback (Eldridge Dickey) in the first round, hired Tom Flores as the first Hispanic NFL coach, and made Amy Trask the first female NFL chief executive.

Davis gave many players a second (or later) chance, with such castoffs as quarterback Jim Plunkett and tight end Todd Christensen becoming top stars in Oakland. The Raiders became known as something of an outlaw team with a cast of players that in many cases had been found difficult to work with elsewhere. Davis, however, prized individuality in others as he had long practiced it himself. His compassion has consistently been triggered by illness befalling current or former Oakland associates or other friends, and that compassion has often been translated into financial support and personal visits.

The victories started coming less often after the Raiders made a losing appearance in Super Bowl XXXVII in January 2003, but nothing seems to keep Davis down or deter him from taking a chance. The 2007 season opened with a new Oakland coach, Lane Kiffin, at thirty-two just a hair younger than Davis was when he started his remarkable run with the Raiders. Unlike Davis, however, Kiffin did not remain long with the Raiders. He was fired early in the 2008 season.

See also: African Americans (Professional); American Football League (IV); Super Bowl.

Additional Reading:

Curtis, Bryan. "Just Live, Baby." *The New York Times Sports Magazine*, September 2007, 68–73, 86, 88.

Dickey, Glenn. *Just Win, Baby: Al Davis and His Raiders.* New York: Harcourt, Brace, Jovanovich, 1991.

Ribowsky, Mark. *Slick: The Silver and Black Life of Al Davis.* New York: Macmillan, 1991.

Simmons, Ira. *Black Knight: Al Davis and His Raiders.* Rocklin CA: Prima Publishing, 1990.

Davis, Ernie (the Elmira Express) (1939–1963)

Ernie Davis, one of college football's all-time great players and an important reflection of changes in racial attitudes in the United States, also is remembered as one of the most tragic figures in football history.

Davis's hero was Jim Brown, the outstanding running back for the University of Syracuse and the Cleveland Browns. A highly recruited high school star, Davis chose Syracuse because Brown had played there and also asked for Brown's jersey number, 44. He quickly established himself as an outstanding running back, helping Syracuse capture the national championship in 1959. Davis received the nickname the Elmira Express that year based on his rushing accomplishments and his hometown of Elmira, New York.

The 1959 season culminated in a Cotton Bowl victory over Texas for the Orangemen and a moment that reflected the racism still prevalent in much of the country, including Dallas, Texas, the site of the bowl. Davis was named Most Valuable Player of the game and was invited to receive his award at a postgame banquet. However, he was told that he would have to just pick up the award and leave. As an African American, he was not allowed to dine with the rest of the attendees. Two years later he became the first African American to win the Heisman Trophy. President John F. Kennedy, who was in New York attending a United Nations conference regarding the Berlin Wall on the weekend of the Heisman ceremony, asked to meet with Davis. The new Heisman winner was taken by limousine to the Waldorf-Astoria, where he and the president chatted and had their photograph taken.

Davis anticipated a successful professional career. When the Washington Redskins traded their No. 1 choice in the 1962 draft to the Cleveland Browns, and Cleveland used it to draft Davis, planning to unite him with Jim Brown, Davis surely felt on top of the world. Unfortunately, that future quickly disappeared. During the summer, Davis appeared listless in the College All-Star Game. Shortly afterward, when he went to a hospital to have swelling in his neck examined, he was diagnosed with acute monocytic leukemia. His condition improved somewhat by the fall, but his coach, Paul Brown, decided, on the advice of doctors, not to play him.

By March 1963 Davis was suffering from sudden nosebleeds and had been requiring regular blood transfusions. On May 16 of that year he entered Cleveland Lakeside Hospital, stopping off on the way to let Browns owner Art Modell know what he was doing. The next day he fell into a coma, and during the morning of May 18, 1963, he died, having never played in a professional game.

Rather than retiring No. 44 upon Davis's death, Syracuse made it a number of honor, given to the best of the university's running backs, including Floyd Little. After more than forty years Syracuse finally retired the number, on November 12, 2005. In 1979 Davis was inducted into the College Football Hall of Fame. A statue of Davis stands outside an Elmira middle school that bears his name. In October 2008 a film about Davis's life, *The Express*, starring Rob Brown as Davis and Dennis Quaid as his Syracuse football coach, Ben Schwartzwalder, opened in theaters around the country.

See also: African Americans (College); African Americans (Professional); Brown, James Nathaniel; Brown, Paul Eugene; Heisman Trophy.

Additional Reading:
Gallagher, Robert C. *Ernie Davis, the Elmira Express: The Story of a Heisman Trophy Winner.* Silver Spring MD: Bartleby, 1983.

Pennington, Bill. *The Heisman: Great American Stories of the Men Who Won*. New York: ReganBooks, 2004.

Disabilities

Football is such a physically demanding game that physical disabilities have long seemed to disqualify individuals from participation. That principle may need to undergo renewed scrutiny given the work of Brian Kajiyama, a graduate assistant with the University of Hawaii football team.

Kajiyama lives with cerebral palsy—that is to say, he actively lives, engaging life on many fronts. An excellent student, he graduated from Hawaii with honors in 2003 and then earned a master of education in guidance and counseling. His thesis was on using technology to improve an individual's quality of life, a subject about which he had considerable personal experience. Next on his academic agenda, according to his blog, is a doctorate in exceptionalities from the Special Education Department at Hawaii.

The doctorate, however, is only one area of endeavor for Kajiyama. A lifelong fan of Hawaii's football program, he became a volunteer assistant in 2006, helping to edit game film of Hawaii's opponents. In 2007 he was named a graduate assistant under head coach June Jones. He quickly demonstrated a genuine facility for breaking down a team's offense and preparing scouting reports for his own team's defensive unit to use.

All of this would have been a considerable accomplishment under any conditions, but for Brian Kajiyama it was historic. Kajiyama moves about in a motorized wheelchair and communicates by typing his comments into a computer that then speaks through a robotic voice. Assistant coach Jeff Reinebold has said, probably correctly, that Kajiyama is the first-ever wheelchair-bound, nonspeaking college football coach.

The University of Hawaii enjoyed a memorable 2007, going through its regular season undefeated and untied. Many people contributed to the team's success, including its highly respected head coach and Colt Brennan, possibly the best quarterback in the country. However, a graduate assistant in a wheelchair speaking through a computer had a fair amount to do with that success too.

See also: Concussions; Retirement.

Additional Reading:
DePauw, Karen P., and Susan J. Gavron. *Disability and Sport*. Champaign IL: Human Kinetics, 1995.
———. *Disability Sport*. Champaign IL, Human Kinetics, 2005.
Kajiyama, Brian. Personal blog. http://bkajiyama.blogspot.com.

Ditka, Michael Keller, Jr.
(Iron Mike, Da Coach) (b. 1939)

Mike Ditka in recent years has been seen regularly on television analyzing and selling—and even considering a run for the United States Senate. A commentator on ESPN's *Sunday NFL Countdown*, Ditka, referred to as "Coach," offers forceful, frank, and insightful comments on the weekend's games. Previously, he had worked on *The NFL Today* for CBS Sports.

Television viewers are just as likely to see Iron Mike—so named for his no-nonsense personality and rugged dependability as a player, and also reflecting his origins in the coal-mining and steel-manufacturing area of western Pennsylvania—pushing a variety of commercial products. Companies like to have a product endorsed by someone whose qualities coincide with the item or whose appearance with the product appears so startling that it jolts viewers into paying closer attention. Ditka generally has fit the latter advertising model.

Mike Ditka on YouTube? Seems far-fetched, but that is where viewers have been able to see him urging those youngsters to enjoy a good bowl of Campbell's Chunky soup. There as well as on network television, Ditka also has participated in the series of commercials for Coors Light designed to simulate a coach's press conference regarding an upcoming game. Ditka's "The Past Is for Cowards" spot includes a youthful questioner mentioning that he is going to a '70s-style party. Ditka's response, deviating only slightly from the typical quasi–non sequitur responses common to the series of commercials, is to assert that "the past is for cowards." In other words, let's get on with the game— or something like that.

But most memorable of all is Ditka's association with Levitra, a performance-enhancing drug permitted by the NFL. Iron Mike admitting to erectile dysfunction? The ultimate man's man acknowledging problems performing in bed?

Well, if Mike needs a little help along that line, then what man should feel bad about sharing the same problem? "Take the Levitra challenge!" Iron Mike commands the viewer. And if you don't, he seems to imply, he may just smash you over the head.

Want a good meal when you're in Chicago? Ditka can solve that problem as well. He operates a restaurant with the basic name, befitting the son of a Ukrainian family from western Pennsylvania, Mike Ditka's Restaurant. As one might expect, the restaurant specializes in chops and steaks, offers what it calls the "Best Burger in Chicago," and has a special entree named after the owner—"Da Pork Chop." The "Da," as in "Da Coach," reflects Ditka's slight residue of an East European accent while also mimicking the Chicago south side accent. Yet, the restaurant also contrasts with Ditka's public persona. It is, after all, what a young Ditka surely would have considered a "fancy restaurant" with its valet parking, business-casual dress code, self-described "casual elegant" style, and entrees that run to $50 each.

Then there was Ditka's flirtation with elective politics, and what could be more incongruous than no-nonsense Iron Mike engaging in the life of a politician, urging people to vote for him, kissing babies, making nice with wealthy would-be donors? Yet he considered challenging Barack Obama for the U.S. Senate from Illinois in 2004. The Republicans, finding themselves short of traditional sorts of candidates, wooed Da Coach hard. Finally, though, he declined, no doubt himself seeing the incongruity in this match.

Younger television (and YouTube) viewers, football fans, and diners may not remember what originally made Ditka famous or realize what a great football player and successful coach he really was. Ditka was one of the great tight ends of all time. An All-American at the University of Pittsburgh where he played both offensive and defensive end, Ditka was inducted into the College Football Hall of Fame in 1986.

Ditka was the first choice of the Chicago Bears in the 1961 draft and became one of the first professional tight ends to catch a lot of passes as well as block. He had a tremendous rookie season, catching fifty-six passes for 1,076 yards and twelve touchdowns. His receptions kept rising during his first four seasons to peak at seventy-five in 1964. He played six years with the Bears, then two somewhat disappointing seasons with the Philadelphia Eagles before concluding his playing career with four seasons for the Dallas Cowboys. In Dallas he was a member of the 1971 championship Cowboys, catching a touchdown pass in Super Bowl VI. When Ditka retired after the 1972 season, he had the second highest total of career receptions ever by a tight end. Not surprising, he was inducted into the Pro Football Hall of Fame, entering with the class of 1988 as the first full-time tight end to make the Hall.

Then Ditka turned to coaching. He spent nine seasons as an assistant with Dallas (with a win in Super Bowl XII) before returning to the Bears as head coach. In his eleven years (1982–92) as coach of the Bears, they won six divisional titles and Super Bowl XX after the 1985 season. That year Chicago—featuring running back Walter Payton, defensive lineman and sometime goal-line runner William "the Refrigerator" Perry, and an overpowering defense coached by Buddy Ryan—went 15-1 in the regular season and demolished the New England Patriots 46–10 in the Super Bowl. Ditka earned Coach of the Year honors both that year and in 1988.

Ditka's later term as coach of the New Orleans Saints (1997–99) was less successful. The Saints suffered losing records each season, and Ditka came under considerable criticism for giving the Washington Redskins all of the team's 1999 draft picks plus its first-round 2000 pick so the Bears could move up in the draft and take running back Ricky Williams of Texas. The transaction yielded an infamous ESPN *The Magazine* cover featuring Ditka and Williams together as man and wife with Williams bedecked in a white wedding dress. Williams had a so-so rookie season, gaining 884 yards but averaging just 3.5 yards per carry; the Saints, their future mortgaged, went a disastrous 3-13; and Ditka was gone.

Gone but hardly forgotten, as television viewers can easily substantiate. In addition, Ditka has recently been making headlines and appearances, including be-fore Congress, lobbying the NFL and the NFL Players Association for better treat-ment of retired players, especially those who are indigent or ill. Iron Mike may be made of stern stuff, but clearly, where old players are concerned, his heart is plen-ty soft enough.

> See also: Commercials and Advertisements; Payton, Walter Jerry; Perry, William Anthony; Politicians; Retirement; Super Bowl; Television Broadcasting.
>
> Additional Reading:
> Ditka, Mike. *Ditka: An Autobiography*. 2nd ed. With Don Pierson. Chicago: Bonus Books, 1987.
> Keteyian, Armen. *Ditka: Monster of the Midway*. New York: Pocket Books, 1992.

Dogfighting

Dogfighting is the most heinous of all pseudosports involving animals. It puts dogs, so cherished as pets, in a fight to the death as human beings, the suppos-edly civilized and rational animals, watch and cheer while often placing heavy bets on the outcome.

There was a time when dogfighting was viewed as primarily a rural, lower-class pastime, but no more. The brutal spectacle has crossed economic, social, and racial lines and may now be more common in urban areas than in rural, with urban gangs joining the dogfight-ing crowd. Pit bulls trained to kill are the most common dog used, often turned into killers through practicing on "bait" dogs, harmless creatures used to whet the fighter's appetite for violence.

The American public was shocked in 2007 when one of the National Football League's greatest stars, quarterback Mi-chael Vick of the Atlanta Falcons, was charged with involvement in a dogfight-ing ring allegedly operated out of a home he owned in Smithfield, Virginia. There already were indications, however, that athletes, including football players, per-haps in large numbers, were participants in this shameful activity.

Former NFL running back LeShon Johnson pleaded guilty to dogfighting in 2005 in a case brought to light by an undercover member of the Oklahoma Bu-reau of Narcotics and Dangerous Drugs who infiltrated the dogfighting ring that included the former player. Johnson, who played five years in the NFL with Green Bay, Arizona, and the New York Giants (1994–97, 1999), ran the Krazyside Ken-nels and regularly branded his dogs with a "5." He was arrested in his Tulsa apart-ment in 2004, and a calendar discovered at the time indicated that he may have been involved in dogfighting while still playing football. Johnson received a five-year deferred sentence.

Nate Newton, an offensive lineman with the Dallas Cowboys (1986–98), was arrested for participating in a fight at a dogfighting match in Texas in 1991. The authorities later dropped the charges against him. Tyrone Wheatley, a run-ning back with the New York Giants and Oakland Raiders (1995–2004), publicly praised fighting dogs for their spirit in a *Sports Illustrated* issue in 2001. So Vick was certainly not the first NFL player to be associated with the activity.

Vick, however, brought dogfighting to the front pages and the evening news. Seldom had a player of his stature been so caught up in an event people found so revolting, along, of course, with its being illegal. Dogfighting is a crime in all fifty states, a felony in all but two (Idaho and Wyoming, where it is a misdemeanor). Vick had led the Falcons to within a game of the Super Bowl in 2004 and in 2006 became the first quarterback to run for a thousand yards in a season. He had signed a ten-year contract in 2004 worth about $130 million. Contributing to the surprise was that Vick generally was well liked and viewed as a quiet, hardworking player.

Two other cases directed attention toward Vick and ultimately led to his being indicted along with three other men for conspiring to engage in interstate commerce in support of an illegal activity and for sponsoring a dog in a dogfighting action.

One case, a house invasion and murder of Thomas Weigner in Texas during August 2006, a man reputed to be heavily involved in dogfighting, had nothing directly to do with Vick but caused the player's name to surface in connection with dogfighting. The other case concerned Vick's cousin Davon Boddie, who was arrested for alleged drug possession. Boddie gave Vick's house as his address, which led authorities in April 2007 to search the premises in connection with Boddie's possible drug use.

What they found was shocking. There were approximately sixty dogs, mainly pit bull terriers, some with wounds indicating that they had been fighting. Also discovered were a "rape stand" used to hold a female dog during breeding, an electric treadmill for dogs, a sixteen-foot-square room apparently used as "the pit" for the actual fights, a bloody carpet that could have been placed in the pit so that the dogs would have good footing and not slip while fighting, and "break sticks" used to pry dogs' jaws open.

Authorities claimed that the Bad Newz Kennels was operated on the Vick property and had been the sponsoring organization for dogfights since 2002. Since transporting dogs across state lines for the purpose of fighting is a federal offense, federal as well as Surry County officials were involved in the searches and investigation.

Vick was indicted in July 2007, the document also alleging that dogs had been executed by drowning, hanging, electrocution, or other means for not fighting well enough. Such specific and vivid details contributed to public disgust. Later that month one of his codefendants, Tony Taylor, pleaded guilty and told officials that Vick had been the primary financial supporter of the dogfighting and that he had been present for several dogfights. Taylor's sentencing was delayed until after the scheduled trial of Vick and the other defendants, seemingly to pressure

Taylor into cooperating with the investigation. In August two other codefendants, Quanis Phillips and Purnell Peace, entered into a plea agreement. Along with pleading guilty to sponsoring dogfighting, they implicated Vick in gambling, primarily funding the gambling that occurred, and helping to kill dogs (methods that included hanging and drowning) that did not perform well enough in the fights. Phillips was sentenced to twenty-one months in prison and Peace to eighteen months on the federal charges.

Meanwhile, NFL Commissioner Roger Goodell ordered Vick to stay away from training camp while the league investigated. To head up the investigation, Goodell employed Eric Holder, later attorney general under President Obama.

Along with facing criminal charges, Vick immediately began suffering the consequences of his behavior. Organizations such as People for the Ethical Treatment of Animals (PETA) and the Humane Society of the United States protested and demanded speedy action against Vick. Goodell met with a similar organization, the American Society for the Prevention of Cruelty to Animals, to prepare a program to educate NFL players about appropriate treatment of animals, an indication that the commissioner saw a problem greater than one isolated case involving Vick.

Vick also began to take a heavy financial hit apart from what might transpire regarding his NFL contract. Nike, which had worked with Vick to design a line of athletic shoes and had used Vick in commercials, ended its relationship with him. Reebok stopped sales of Vick's No. 7 jersey; AirTran Airways, which had employed Vick to do radio and billboard advertisements, severed its involvement with him; and Rawlings, the famous sporting goods company, ended its use of Vick's image in store displays. In addition, Upper Deck removed from its online store all Vick items (including autographed helmets, jerseys, and footballs) and announced that it, like another producer of football cards, Donruss, would remove Vick's trading card from its NFL sets.

Vick and his attorney had consistently maintained his innocence, but that changed after the codefendants worked out their own plea deals. As Vick faced almost certain conviction and prison time, he decided to plead guilty to federal charges of conspiracy to travel in interstate commerce for illegal purposes and conspiracy to sponsor dogfighting. Vick entered his plea on August 27, 2007, and sentencing was set for December 10. By that time it was clear that Vick's venture into dogfighting would cost him dearly, legally, financially, and in loss of public esteem. Beyond the federal charges, Vick remained subject to possible state charges and punishment by the league. Under the new Personal Conduct Code, Goodell could impose penalties, including suspensions, even if Vick had not committed crimes. After Vick announced on August

24 his intention to plead guilty, Goodell suspended him indefinitely. Michael Vick, the ultimate running quarterback, found himself unable to run from his new image as the poster boy for dogfighting.

Vick publicly apologized for not being "honest and forthright" with Commissioner Goodell, Falcons owner Arthur Blank, Coach Bobby Petrino, and his teammates. He acknowledged complicity in killing dogs and vowed to redeem himself. For his part, Blank said that the Falcons would not immediately cut Vick from the team (a decision made for legal and financial reasons) but would seek to recover the $22 million signing bonus paid to him. An arbitrator later ruled that Atlanta was entitled to receive approximately $20 million back, a judgment overturned by a federal judge in February 2008. According to U.S. District Judge David Doty of Minneapolis, Vick was entitled to retain all but $3.75 million of the $22 million under the NFL collective bargaining agreement. However, Vick stood to lose the remainder of the $130 million not yet paid to him under his current contract.

On December 10 Vick received his sentence: twenty-three months in prison. He had voluntarily started serving his sentence on November 19, a decision, according to his lawyer, designed to demonstrate his acceptance of responsibility for his actions. With time off for good behavior, Vick could be out of prison sometime in the summer of 2009. A state trial date was set for June 27, 2008, but Virginia authorities decided in June to postpone Vick's state trial and that of three codefendants until they are released from federal prison. Vick was released from prison on May 20, 2009, and ordered to spend the final two months of his sentence at a halfway house and work construction for $10 an hour.

At the very least Vick would miss two full seasons of football (2007 and 2008), but most likely he would not be ready to play in 2009 even if he received early release and clearance from the league. It also is possible that Commissioner Goodell might continue Vick's suspension, or even that Vick might face conviction and further prison time from state charges on top of the federal charges to which he pleaded guilty. Still, freed at the age of twenty-nine, Vick has the majority of his years still ahead of him—and with the chance to reclaim his life even if he cannot reclaim his football career.

See also: Commissioners; Crime.

Additional Reading:

"Dogfighting Fact Sheet." *Humane Society of the United States.* July 31, 2007. http://www.hsus.org/hsus_field/animal_fighting_the_final_round/dogfighting_fact_sheet.

Dohrmann, George. "The House on Moonlight Road." *Sports Illustrated,* June 4, 2007, 45–49.

Sinclair, Leslie, Melinda Merck, and Randall Lockwood. *Forensic Investigation of Animal Cruelty: A Guide for Veterinary and Law Enforcement Professionals.* Washington DC: Humane Society Press, 2006.

Downtown Athletic Club

The 1920s was a golden age of sports in America. Fans eagerly followed the exploits of Red Grange, Babe Ruth, Bobby Jones, Jack Dempsey, the Four Horsemen of Notre Dame, and a slew of other sports heroes. At the same time, spectators also were increasingly becoming participants, turning to sports and exercise as a way to have fun and improve their health. Athletic clubs sprouted up throughout the country, and in New York City, James Kennard and Philip Slinguff, who had been prominently involved in developing a form of social exclusivity known as the gentlemen's social club, joined the athletic craze. Their plan: to build an exclusive club that would combine social status and comfort with physical exercise and relaxation.

Kennard and Slinguff decided on a site within a five minutes' walk of both Wall Street and Broadway in order to appeal to the successful and cultured businessman who also had a keen interest in athletic activity. Groundbreaking at 19 West Street occurred on March 12, 1929. A few months later at the New York Stock Exchange, hardly a stone's throw from the ongoing construction, "Black Thursday" (October 24, 1929) hit. The stock market collapsed, and the Great Depression struck with a thunderous crash.

Yet, aided by loans, construction of the Downtown Athletic Club continued, and the building opened in 1930 bedecked in all its glamour and grandeur. The Art Deco skyscraper soared aloft for thirty-five floors. Facilities included 137 hotel rooms, seven banquet rooms, a formal dining room, a fitness center, a gymnasium, and squash, handball, and racquetball courts. On the twelfth floor the club featured a swimming pool, at the time the highest indoor pool in the world.

Membership grew to approximately 4,500 in the 1960s but declined over the following decades. Faced with bankruptcy, the Downtown Athletic Club sold the building to an investment firm in 1999 and then repurchased the first thirteen floors, including the Heisman room. The DAC planned renovations and began negotiating with a management company to run the building. Then came September 11, 2001.

With renovations in process, the windows above the fourteenth floor were open to improve ventilation. When the two hijacked planes smashed into the Twin Towers of the World Trade Center two blocks away, dust and debris poured through the open windows clogging the building's air ducts. Many injured in the terrorist attack were brought into the lobby, where DAC staff set up a sort of emergency room, using dining tables as stretchers, pulling down drapes for blankets, and tearing up tablecloths and napkins to apply as bandages.

The DAC building itself suffered no structural damage, but additional renovations were estimated to cost between $20 million and $30 million. Of greatest consequence, of course, were those who died, including eleven club members.

The club considered a variety of financial options but, given the much larger issues facing New York, found limited interest on the part of club members. The decision was made to relinquish the lease to the mortgage holders, a step finally taken in July 2003.

The club donated much of its exercise equipment to the Boys Club of New York and the New York Fire Department and over the next few years used various venues for its Heisman Trophy presentation. In 2008 the Heisman Trophy program received a new home in the Sports Museum of America a few blocks from the Statue of Liberty in the building that once housed the Cunard Passenger Ship Line. Many will surely miss the Downtown Athletic Club building. However, an award housed in a museum that celebrates all sports rather than football alone, almost within the shadow of the statue that welcomed the ancestors of many Heisman recipients, may be even more meaningful than it was in its original, grand setting.

See also: Heisman, John William; Heisman Trophy.

Additional Reading:
Pennington, Bill. *The Heisman: Great American Stories of the Men Who Won.* New York: ReganBooks, 2004.

Draft

Most people at least partly choose where they will work. That is not the case initially with professional football players. There was a golden age when players were able to sell their services to the highest bidder or pick an employer for any other reason that seemed important, but that ended in 1936 with the first college draft. The person behind the draft was Bert Bell, then owner of the Philadelphia Eagles and a future commissioner of the National Football League. His objective was to inhibit a bidding war for players, keep salaries down, and establish a competitive balance among teams.

To a great extent, professional sports have deviated sharply from most American businesses, where employees' freedom of movement is much greater, unencumbered by management policies and employee contracts that, until the advent of free agency, made players lifelong employees of their original organizations until they were traded, sold, or released. To put it another way, most people in the United States have traditionally been able to become free agents after a limited-term contract (often one year), subject to market conditions.

To enhance competitiveness, which Bell understood to be good for business (fans would tire of paying to see teams that had no real chance to win), Bell and the other owners agreed to have teams select players one at a time according to their records of the previous year. The team with the worst record would draft first, the champion, last, and everybody else in between. Over the years, rules regarding players with remaining college eligibility have changed, and the number of drafting rounds has decreased. The draft has moved among winter, fall, and spring dates, and the process has faced competing drafts by leagues that arose to challenge NFL supremacy. The term *draft* was dropped during World War II to avoid confusion with the military draft, replaced by the awkward term *preferred negotiations list*. Yet through it all, the basic process envisioned by Bert Bell has endured down to the present.

The draft, of course, is as much art as science, even today with so much effort and expertise going into scouting the best choices. From the start, there were wasted picks. The first player chosen in the first draft was Jay Berwanger, a University of Chicago halfback who also was the first Heisman Trophy winner. Berwanger, however, chose not to join the Eagles. Nor would he play with the Chicago Bears, who traded for him, or for anyone else. Plenty of No. 1 choices over the following drafts never achieved the level of success expected of them. Yet twelve first selections are in the Pro Football Hall of Fame, from halfback Bill Dudley, taken by the Pittsburgh Steelers in 1942, to quarterback Troy Aikman, drafted in 1989 by the Dallas Cowboys.

Drafts today excite great interest with many sports publications, including separate magazines, offering predraft predictions and postdraft analyses. The draft is a popular, if rather long, television production, followed closely by football fans, especially through the early rounds. It is certainly a matter of great import to the players, whose future earnings hinge on how early they are drafted. Underclassmen

may enter the draft but have to decide whether entering the draft, with the outcome always somewhat uncertain, is a better choice than staying in college and playing another year, risking injury but also perhaps improving their draft position with another good season.

Sometimes the draft offers individual minidramas, such as the story of Notre Dame quarterback Brady Quinn and the 2007 draft. Highly successful under the tutelage of Notre Dame coach Charlie Weis, who while with the New England Patriots had helped Tom Brady become an All-Pro quarterback, Quinn was expected to go high in the draft. Yet team after team passed him by while Quinn sat with his girlfriend on very public view at the draft site trying to answer questions and put the best face possible on the disappointing, if not devastating, development. Finally, Quinn was ushered into another room away from television cameras to await his fate. Then, with the twenty-second pick, the Cleveland Browns, who had already made their first-round choice, engineered a trade to draft Quinn. That the Browns offered him an opportunity to become the starting quarterback early in his career, thus perhaps making the long fall throughout round one a positive over the long haul, did not detract from the immediate disappointment, short-term financial loss, and personal embarrassment Quinn endured. On the other hand, even Notre Dame haters seemed to sympathize with him.

Today an NFL player is not tied for the

duration of his career to the team that drafted him, as limited free agency gives him the opportunity later in his career to sign with another team. Still, he has less freedom of choice than most American workers. However, he also is likely to make more money than most people. That may be sufficient compensation for some loss of personal freedom. It may even compensate for some public embarrassment on draft day.

See also: Commissioners; Magazines; Television Broadcasting.

Additional Reading:

Carroll, Bob, et al., eds. *Total Football II: The Official Encyclopedia of the National Football League.* New York: HarperCollins, 1999.

"Pro Football Draft History." The Pro Football Hall of Fame Web site. http://www.profootballhof.com/history/general/draft.

Whittingham, Richard. *The Meat Market: The Inside Story of the NFL Draft.* New York: Macmillan, 1992.

Williams, Pete. *The Draft: A Year Inside the NFL's Search for Talent.* New York: St. Martin's, 2006.

Drive, The

Perhaps nothing is so heroic in a football game or so captures the imagination of spectators as the winning drive in the final minutes of the game. Although a successful drive to pull victory out of the snarling mouth of defeat requires everyone to play well—the blockers to block, receivers to get open, the quarterback to throw accurately—the quarterback is the person who engineers the drive. Ultimately, he, more than any other player, receives the credit or blame for the outcome.

Many outstanding quarterbacks built a reputation for being able to bring their teams downfield in the closing minutes and get the ball into the end zone for the winning score: Johnny Unitas, Roger Staubach, Brett Favre, John Elway, Peyton Manning, Tom Brady, and, both at Notre Dame and with the San Francisco 49ers, Joe Montana, to name just a few.

Many football observers consider the Elway-led drive in the 1986 AFC championship game the best drive ever. The Denver Broncos, trailing the Cleveland Browns 20–13 with 5:32 remaining in the game, had the ball on its own 2-yard line. Elway methodically led his team downfield in fifteen plays, culminating in a 5-yard scoring pass to Mark Jackson. The extra point tied the game with 31 seconds left. In overtime, Denver scored a field goal on its first possession to complete its come-from-behind victory.

Fans of other great quarterbacks will likely prefer their drives to Elway's. Roger Staubach, after all, led Dallas to twenty-three fourth-quarter wins, and all of the quarterbacks mentioned above were adept at pulling their teams through. Regardless of who engineered a particular last-minute victory, winning drives reflect how people like to see themselves: tough in the clutch and at their best when the game (whatever the game may be) is on the line. In short, the kind of person who can be counted on to overcome all obstacles and come through when he or she is most needed.

See also: Brady, Thomas Edward, Jr.; Elway, John

Albert; Favre, Brett Lorenzo; Greatest Game; Manning, Peyton Williams; Montana, Joseph Clifford; Unitas, John Constantine.

Additional Reading:

Latimer, Clay. *John Elway: Armed and Dangerous*. Rev. ed. Lenexa KS: Addax, 2002.

Dropkick

The dropkick, more than any other play, conjures images of old leather helmets and primitive films of players dashing jerkily at unnatural speeds down the field. In truth, the dropkick, as a practiced phenomenon, is as dead as the dinosaurs. Yet it lives in fans' imaginations as surely as covered wagons and one-room schoolhouses. And, in a bow to its past, the National Football League continues to keep the dropkick on the books as a legal maneuver.

In fact, Doug Flutie, the diminutive quarterback who starred in the Canadian Football League and acquitted himself all right in the NFL as well, himself something of a throwback to past quarterbacks in size, determination, and grit, resurrected the dropkick. Playing for the New England Patriots in the final game of the 2005 season, Flutie dropkicked an extra point, and he made it.

The dropkick is defined by the NFL as "a kick by a kicker who drops the ball and kicks it as, or immediately after, it touches the ground." As such it differs from the placekick, which is kicked off a tee or off the ground with someone holding the ball. The punt is like the dropkick except that the kicker kicks the ball before it touches the ground. Both punts and placekicks seem to promise a lot more accuracy than risking the ball heading off in a strange direction as it touches the ground, yet kicker after kicker proved proficient with the dropkick in the early years of football. Jim Thorpe was a master of the dropkick, but he was just one of many. The best may have been Paddy Driscoll, who kicked his way into the hearts of Chicago fans (for the Cardinals and Bears) throughout the 1920s. Driscoll shares the record for most dropkick field goals in one game (four) and accomplished the longest dropkick field goal (50 yards, which he did twice).

There is logic to the abandonment of the dropkick, though, and that logic lies in the changing shape of the football. During the heyday of the dropkick in the 1920s and 1930s, the ball was a bit more round than it is today. The ball reached approximately its current shape, technically known as a "prolate spheroid," by 1934. The new shape made passing a lot easier but dropkicking chancier as the less rounded ball could not be counted on to bounce quite as regularly as its predecessor.

So when Flutie dropkicked that extra point, he was hearkening back to something that had not been done successfully for over six decades, not since Ray McLean of the Chicago Bears dropkicked an extra point against the New York Giants in the 1941 championship game. The last dropkicked field goal was by Earl "Dutch" Clark of the Detroit Lions against the Chicago Cardinals in

1937. Dropkicks are not apt to return on
a regular basis, but they are likely to hang
around in old newsreels, reminding fans
of what used to be.

See also: Canadian Football League; Equipment;
"Hail Mary" Pass.

Additional Reading:

Cope, Myron. *The Game That Was: The Early
    Days of Pro Football.* New York: World Pub-
    lishing Company, 1970.

Education

Getting a good education is a goal for most Americans as an avenue toward a better life. Getting a good job, buying a house, having a richer cultural experience, and many other benefits accrue to studying hard, completing one's homework, developing reading and writing skills, and doing well on tests. Although some high school and college football players may like what they do on the gridiron more than what transpires in the classroom (as difficult as that is to believe), most of them will not make a career in football. For them a sound education is all the more important. Yet even for that tiny minority of athletes who do achieve success in professional football, their playing careers will constitute a relatively short period in their lives, but a good education will help them prepare for their next and, presumably, much longer career.

Consequently, schools and the world of football itself regularly urge athletes toward academic success and degree completion. An especially supportive organization is the American Football Coaches Association, which annually issues its report card on how well academic institutions do regarding graduation rates. The AFCA's 2007 Academic Achievement Award, presented by the Touchdown Club of Memphis, honored Northwestern University and the University of Notre Dame for achieving a graduation rate of 95 percent of its 2001–02 freshman football class.

Northwestern and Notre Dame led all 107 Football Bowl Subdivision schools that completed the AFCA's Graduation Rate Survey. Graduating their football players, however, is nothing new for these two institutions, as 2007 marked the seventh time that Notre Dame has finished first and the fifth time for Northwestern since the award was inaugurated in 1981 (it was sponsored by the now defunct College Football Association through 1997). Both programs, however, trail Duke University, which has won the award twelve times, and which once again, along with Vanderbilt, graduated more than 90 percent of its football players.

The AFCA found that 34 of the 107 institutions graduated 70 percent or more of their football players, and that the average graduation rate was 60 percent, up from the 58 percent mark of the previous two years. Among the conferences, the Big 10, Atlantic Coast, and Mid-American Conferences tied for most teams making the 70 percent or better rate, each with five teams.

The National Collegiate Athletic Association, of course, is the dominant organization regarding standards for college and university sports programs. Criticized in the past for not giving enough attention to academic excellence, the NCAA has moved forcefully in recent years to support classroom as well as athletic accomplishments.

The NCAA argues that athletics should be seen as part of an institution's academic mission rather than as a separate area of college life. Consequently, the organization has been striving to ensure that athletes come to college adequately prepared and that they make steady academic progress toward graduation.

The NCAA established its current high school criteria for college eligibility in 2002. The freshman athlete must have taken at least fourteen core courses in English, history, mathematics, and sciences with a minimum grade point average (GPA) of 2.0. Most Division I schools now require core courses in excess of fourteen, typically fifteen to eighteen, and in some cases even more.

Faced with bogus high schools selling high school course credit while requiring virtually no academic effort on the part of the student, the NCAA has limited the amount of course work that a student may complete after high school. Students who have not met the minimum core and GPA requirements for college eligibility increasingly must turn to two-year colleges to establish their eligibility. A complaint regarding a possible downside of this policy is that legitimate post–high school prep schools may suffer unfairly and even be forced to close despite the good work that they have done in the past in helping students prepare for college.

Only part of the equation, however, is initial eligibility. The NCAA is also committed to fostering steady academic progress during the college years, with the first-year student having to complete at least twenty-four credits of course work with a minimum GPA of 1.8. Acceptable progress after the first year means satisfactory completion of 40, 60, and 80 percent of degree requirements by the end of the second, third, and fourth years, with the GPA also rising.

Beginning in August 2007 the NCAA began mandating that eligibility for all athletes be determined at the conclusion of the fall semester rather than at the beginning of the spring semester. Previously, only seniors were assessed at the end of the first semester. The change means that football players who do badly academically in the fall may now be ineligible for bowl games that in most cases are played during the break between the two semesters.

Recognizing the heavy time commitment involved in some sports, including football, the NCAA views six years as an acceptable time frame to complete all degree requirements and computes its Graduation Success Rate (GSR) accordingly.

The GSR differs from the graduation rate computed by the U.S. Department of Education in that it takes into account students who transfer to another school but are in good academic standing when they do so. The NCAA believes that students transfer for a variety of legitimate reasons, and that the school should not be penalized if the student has been making good academic progress.

Another NCAA program, developed in 2004, is the Academic Progress Rate (APR), which rates institutions on the academic standing and progress of their students on a semester-by-semester basis, that is, on a "real-time" continuum. The NCAA awards one point for each athlete who meets academic-eligibility standards in a given semester and a second point if that student remains at the same institution. The team's total points are divided by the total points possible for the team, and the quotient is multiplied by 1000. The result is that team's APR. The NCAA views an APR of 925 as acceptable, which corresponds roughly to a graduation rate of 50–60 percent.

Teams that fail to reach the 925 mark may face "contemporaneous" (that is, immediate) penalties of loss of scholarships in that sport. Teams that consistently fall below a 900 APR face "historical" penalties. These historical penalties are graduated: a warning, practice and financial restrictions, a ban on postseason play, and restricted membership status in the NCAA.

Since the NCAA is concerned not just with punishing offenders but also with facilitating a stronger commitment to academics, it makes available financial resources to low-resource colleges that need assistance in developing academic support systems. It is now common for colleges and universities to offer academic support programs for their athletes. These programs typically include tutors and a monitoring system to check on the athletes' progress within courses and within their overall programs of study.

Increasingly, the divide that once existed at some institutions between the athletics department and the faculty is being replaced with regular interaction. Both parties find it in their mutual interest to work together to establish a seamless higher education experience for athletes. Coaches and faculty both invest much time and effort in the students, and the university has a financial stake in students' success, so helping the football player (or other athlete) succeed academically, athletically, and socially is widely perceived to be in everyone's interest.

With this growing partnership, the term *student-athlete* appears to be an increasingly accurate description of the football player at Notre Dame, Northwestern, and many other colleges and universities throughout the country.

See also: Eliot, Charles William; Pop Warner Little Scholars.

Additional Reading:
American Football Coaches Association Web site. http://www.afca.com.
National Collegiate Athletic Association Web site. http://www.ncaa.org.
Thamel, Pete, and Duff Wilson. "Poor Grades Aside, Top Athletes Get to College on $399 Diploma." *New York Times Sports Sunday*, November 27, 2005.

Eliot, Charles William (1834–1926)

Critics of football have had no more learned or forceful ally than Charles W. Eliot, president of Harvard University from 1869 to 1909. Eliot was one of the greatest of Harvard's presidents, taking the institution into the twentieth century and building it into the great university that it has remained ever since.

Eliot was an innovative educator who penned "The New Education," a two-part article for *The Atlantic Monthly* in 1869. The article helped him gain the Harvard presidency. There he strengthened the elective system, greatly expanding the curriculum, especially with a deeper commitment to science, mathematics, history, and modern languages. He increased the faculty, strengthened entrance examinations, and encouraged pedagogy that engaged students in the classroom rather than just relying on the old methods of formal lectures and recitations. He also emphasized serious assessment of student performance. Committed to a useful education, he reformed the professional schools while also improving research facilities. Not least among Eliot's interests at Harvard was his effort to promote racial equality. One of his Harvard students was W. E. B. DuBois, and he awarded Booker T. Washington an honorary degree.

Football, however, was a grave concern to Eliot. He was not opposed to football per se, but to the violence and commercialism that he saw spreading throughout the sport. He was the first president of a major university to combat football as it developed. The faults that he found in the sport included a win-at-all-costs mentality and deception in playing the game. Possessor of a finely honed sense of honor, Eliot believed that any trickery was wrong, even the curve ball in baseball.

Eliot proposed such changes to the game as prohibiting freshmen and graduates from playing, altering rules to reduce dramatically the game's violence, playing all games on school grounds, and limiting athletes to one sport.

He supported sports and physical exercise as conducive to health if done properly, but he believed they should be kept subsidiary to academics. The enormous excitement generated by football, especially the Harvard-Yale rivalry, deeply bothered him.

Opposition to violence was a fundamental tenet for Eliot, who believed that nations should use arbitration rather than war to settle their international conflicts. Football for Eliot was war writ small. Unlike other sports, football, in his view, employed violence as a planned strategy, whereas in other sports violence was the result of an occasional accident. He believed football to be more brutal than even boxing, for the latter followed clear, enforceable rules.

Much of what Eliot saw in the game was only part of the story. However, his concerns with violence and commercialism, and his worries that athletics were superseding academics for many students, remain still today serious and relevant issues.

See also: Education; Ivy League.
Additional Reading:
Eliot, Charles W. *Charles W. Eliot: The Man and His Beliefs.* 2 vols. Ed. William Allan Neilson. New York: Harper and Brothers, 1926.
James, Henry. *Charles W. Eliot: President of Harvard University, 1869–1909.* 3 vols. Boston: Houghton Mifflin, 1930.
Watterson, John Sayle. *College Football: History, Spectacle, Controversy.* Baltimore: Johns Hopkins University Press, 2000.

Elway, John Albert (b. 1960)

People like to think that they always have a chance, that it is never too late. John Elway became a football legend by demonstrating that if someone named John Elway is in your corner, you probably always do have a chance. A record-setting forty-seven times, Elway led his Denver Broncos back to tie or win a game in the fourth quarter. The comeback that cemented his reputation for pulling games out at the last minute occurred in the American Football Conference title game in 1986. The Broncos trailed the Cleveland Browns by 7 points with less than six minutes to play. The Browns pinned the Broncos on their own 2-yard line with a punt.

Then Elway got down to business, leading a 98-yard drive to tie the game. He threw a touchdown pass to Mark Jackson with under a minute remaining. The extra point tied the contest, sending it into overtime. Then Elway led another drive, this one culminating in a game-winning field goal by Rich Karlis. The tying drive became known as simply "The Drive" and has continued to be called that ever since.

John Elway, son of a college football coach, Jack Elway, already was one of the most highly touted athletes in the country as a high school player. Starring at Granada Hills High School in Granada Hills, California, near Los Angeles, he made the *Parade Magazine* All-America team. He also excelled in baseball and was drafted by the Kansas City Royals.

Elway chose Stanford over professional baseball and became an outstanding quarterback as well as a fine baseball player at the college level. As a senior he was selected as an All-American at quarterback while batting .361 and also pitching for the baseball team. Elway's final football game, against California, included what has become known as "The Play": a game-winning kick return with five laterals by California as time expired. The Stanford band thought that the game was over, as Stanford had taken a 3-point lead just before the kickoff. The band therefore found itself on the field of play as the California players concluded their remarkable return, and some band members were understandably run over by anxious players trying to win the game.

Once again professional baseball sought Elway, this time the New York Yankees. He went on to play two summers in their minor league system. In the 1983 NFL draft the Baltimore Colts made Elway the first overall pick, but he refused to play for Baltimore, forcing a trade. The Denver Broncos acquired him, and the stage was set for his Hall of Fame career that included not only the forty-seven comebacks but also selection as NFL Most Valuable Player in 1987, five Super Bowl appearances, and two Super Bowl wins.

In his final professional game, Super Bowl XXXIII, on January 31, 1999, Elway passed for 336 yards to lead his team to victory, the performance earning him recognition as the game's Most Valuable Player. Coupled with a Super Bowl upset of the favored Green Bay Packers the previous year, Elway could really go out a winner.

Elway retired as one of the greatest quarterbacks ever to play in the NFL. He then proved himself an able businessman, owning car dealerships and restaurants and serving as co-owner of the Arena Football Colorado Crush. Nor has his name been absent from television, with characters on *South Park*, a series on Comedy Central, several times referring to him as a football hero. In 2007 he appeared in the ABC reality series *Fast Cars and Superstars: The Gillette Young Guns Celebrity Race*. After a series of stock car races, Elway won the final competition on June 24.

Also in 2007 Elway signed on as quarterbacks coach at Cherry Creek High School in Englewood, California, to tutor his son, Jack, the team's starting quarterback, as well as the other quarterbacks on the team. His Elway Foundation is engaged in attempting to prevent and treat child abuse. The foundation hosts an annual golf tournament, the John Elway Golf Classic, with the profits split among charities that combat child abuse.

In 2000 Elway was inducted into the College Football Hall of Fame. Four years later he became a member of the Pro Football Hall of Fame.

See also: Drive, The; Super Bowl.

Additional Reading:

Christopher, Matt. *In the Huddle with . . . John Elway*. Boston: Little, Brown, 1999.

Fox, Larry. *Sports Great John Elway*. Hillside NJ: Enslow, 1990.

Green, Jerry. *Mile High Miracle: Elway and the Broncos, Super Bowl Champions at Last.* Indianapolis: Masters, 1998.

Equipment

Football, like most activities, has its equipment, its tools of the trade. These have changed greatly since the earliest days of football, primarily by addition and improved manufacturing. A lot of the equipment has been created to make football less dangerous to the health of the participants.

The most essential piece of equipment, the only item absolutely necessary to the sport, is the football itself. Many people play football with no other items at all, and in so doing come close to replicating the way football was played at the very beginning of its history.

The football is regularly referred to as the pigskin, but it really should be called the steerskin because it usually is made from a steer's hide. At first, when the sport was still completely a kicking game, the football was round. As the game began its evolution in the 1870s away from soccer and rugby and toward what is played today, the shape of the ball began to change.

Once running was permitted, the ball became more elongated and therefore easier to carry in the crook of one's elbow. Legalizing the forward pass in 1906 gave further impetus to alterations in the ball, and it became yet more elongated, assuming the shape officially referred to as a "prolate spheroid." The short axis of the ball (the distance around the fat part) was decreased in several stages: to 22 1/2–23 inches in 1912, 22–22 1/2 inches in 1929, 21 1/4–21 1/2 inches in 1934. These reductions made it easier for a quarterback to grip the ball and pass it effectively.

The official football for the National Football League has long been manufactured by Wilson Sporting Goods and is strictly regulated regarding weight, size, and amount of inflation.

Maintaining the integrity of game balls has been a constant concern for officials, so in 1999 the NFL initiated a new procedure for ensuring that footballs used in kicking have not been altered. Suspicions had long circulated regarding efforts to make the ball carry a greater distance. It was believed that on occasion balls had been overinflated, seams spread, or the leather dried out in dryers or microwave ovens to make a punt, kickoff, or field-goal attempt carry farther.

Starting in 1999 twelve footballs to be used by the special teams (that is, for kicking) were carefully guarded and not distributed to the teams until shortly before kickoff. These balls are referred to as K-balls. Kickers and holders have regularly complained that the balls are slick because they have not been rubbed sufficiently, although a representative from each team is permitted to rub and brush the balls two hours before the game starts.

At the dawn of American football, uniforms, helmets, pads, and special shoes simply did not exist. In the 1870s, however, team members started dressing alike in order to establish their team identities and make it easier for a player to recognize teammates in the heat of battle. At first, the uniform was quite simple, such as trousers and jerseys of the same colors and patterns, the same type of sweater (with turtleneck sweaters popular in the 1880s and 1890s), or even a handkerchief around the head. Princeton players were wearing a "P" on their sweaters by the 1870s, and numbers were added to uniforms around 1905. Names appeared with the American Football League in 1960.

Initially, the uniform was strictly a matter of clothes. Players wore no pads and certainly no helmets. Once tackling below the waist was permitted in 1888, the game became more dangerous, and players soon realized that they needed some protection. Pads were introduced to protect the player's knees, hips, thighs, ribs, shoulders, kidneys, and other portions of the anatomy. At first pads were strapped on or sewn into the pants, but in 1915 A. G. Spalding and Company Sporting Goods developed a harness of pads to be worn under the uniform. Later, pants included pockets on the inside into which pads could be inserted, and a type of girdle was manufactured to include hip and tail pads.

The pad most associated with football is the shoulder pad, which helps give the player the wide-shouldered look. The first shoulder pads were not much like the modern ones, with strips of leather stretched over the shoulders. By the 1930s significant improvements were being made in the shoulder pads to absorb shock much better. At first, shoulder pads mainly came in one size, but that changed to reflect the variations in player sizes and to ensure that the pads offered good protection. The shoulder pads also became lighter in the 1970s while supplying even more protection, certainly a great boon to the players who had to run up and down the field wearing considerable equipment. Other pads were added to protect ribs, neck, and biceps, especially for players who were susceptible to injuries in those areas.

Gloves started appearing on players in the 1980s, especially on receivers, who thought they could catch the ball better in cold weather wearing gloves. Some players did not view gloves as sufficiently manly, but that attitude has largely dissipated.

Shoes underwent considerable change over the years, especially regarding the cleats. Some of the stages of cleat development included cleats that could be screwed onto and off metal posts on the shoe, outlawing of permanently attached metal posts as a health hazard, and shorter and harder cleats that were more suitable to artificial turf. In addition, high-topped shoes began yielding to low-cut shoes as early as 1940, when George Halas, who had worked with sports equipment manufacturer John T. Riddell of Chicago to design the low-cuts, had his Bears wear them.

Of all items worn by the football player, none is more visible and emblematic of the sport than the helmet. However, it took a long time for the helmet to become both an effective protection and a requirement. Helmets remained optional in college football until 1939 and in the NFL until 1943. By those dates, most players were wearing helmets, although a few holdouts remained. Dick Plasman of the Chicago Bears is generally believed to be the last player to perform bareheaded (in 1940 or 1941).

Before the helmet, some efforts were made to protect the head and face. Edgar Allan Poe of Princeton, grandnephew of the famous writer, used a nose protector in 1890, but the attachment was difficult to keep on and interfered with vision and breathing. In 1896 George Barclay of Lafayette College tried a head harness, a set of three leather straps constructed by a harness maker.

The head harness soon included pads and then evolved into a leather cap. Flaps were added to protect the ears, and early in the twentieth century the helmet was born. The early helmets unfortunately rested directly on the head and therefore did little to cushion the skull when the player took a hard hit. In 1917 a suspension system of straps was created to keep the leather shell off the head, thus better cushioning the head and also improving ventilation.

Plastic helmets were introduced in 1938, briefly banned in the late 1940s, and then brought back. In 1940 a chinstrap replaced the strap that went around the Adam's apple, a great benefit to everyone who wanted to avoid being choked. In the same year, a plastic facemask was added to the helmet, replacing the earlier rubber-covered wire mask. During the following decades great improvements were made to both the helmet and the facemask. Ultimately, most players accepted the greater protection afforded by the facemask even if some continued to complain about its impact on their vision. Bobby Layne, an outstanding Detroit Lions quarterback renowned for both his talent and his toughness, however, eschewed the facemask throughout his career until he retired in 1962. Billy Kilmer, who played quarterback for the San Francisco 49ers, New Orleans Saints, and Washington Redskins in the 1960s and 1970s, yielded only enough to use a single-bar facemask.

The mouthpiece was common in high schools and colleges by the 1950s, and players who had become accustomed to the mouthpiece continued using it at the professional level. The protection may have deprived dentists of considerable income but did much for players' appearance when they went home after the game.

Football is a violent game, but it would be even more dangerous without the considerable technological advances in safety equipment over the years. Injuries still abound, of course, but having three-hundred-pound behemoths smashing into each other without helmets, facemasks, and pads would result in enough carnage to make the gridiron look like a miniature battle scene.

See also: Dropkick; Forward Pass; Halas, George Stanley; Poe, Edgar Allan; Professional Football Origins.

Additional Reading:

Nelson, David M. *The Anatomy of a Game: Football, the Rules, and the Men Who Made the Game.* Newark NJ: University of Delaware Press/Associated University Presses, 1994.

Riffenburgh, Beau. "Tools of the Trade." In *Total Football II: The Official Encyclopedia of the National Football League.* Ed. Bob Carroll et al., 34–38. New York: HarperCollins, 1999.

Extreme Football

The first, and so far only, serious excursion into extreme football occurred at the beginning of the twenty-first century with the league known as the XFL. It failed after a single season (2001), the victim of false assumptions, bad decisions by people who did not adequately understand the appeal of mainstream football, and perhaps bad timing.

The XFL was the creation of Vince McMahon of the World Wrestling Federation (later renamed World Wrestling Entertainment). The assumption apparently was that a more violent version of football would be exciting and draw wrestling fans while retaining football fans. The league was conceived as the "Xtreme Football League," but that name was already in use by a league that did not materialize.

To avoid legal problems, the "X" in XFL then was explained as signifying nothing, although the connotation obviously continued to smack of the "extreme" concept.

The new league resembled traditional football in a multitude of ways but also incorporated a number of different rules as well as violent-sounding names: the Orlando Rage, Chicago Enforcers, New York/New Jersey Hitmen, Birmingham Thunderbolts, Los Angeles Xtreme, San Francisco Demons, Memphis Maniax, and Las Vegas Outlaws.

McMahon's creation was truly his, as teams were not individually owned. Rule changes designed to enhance the level of action included legalizing the bump and run by defensive backs against receivers, abandoning the in-the-grasp rule for quarterbacks, permitting a back to be in motion toward the line of scrimmage, dropping the fair catch on kickoffs and punts while allowing a 5-yard "halo" around the returner as he caught the ball, and making punts live and therefore subject to recovery by the kicking team after the ball traveled 25 yards. In addition, roughness calls were more limited. The receiving team was determined not by a coin toss but by having a player from each team line up at the 35-yard line and race to the 50 where a ball was placed. The two battled for the ball, and the one who got it chose whether to receive or kick.

Since extra points were viewed as largely automatic and therefore not exciting, extra-point kicks were discarded in favor of conversions by running or passing, the team having the choice of going for one, two, or three points by starting at various distances from the end zone. Ties were not allowed, with the league using an overtime approach similar to what is now employed in college ball. A team had four plays from the 20 to score, with a field-goal attempt not permitted until fourth down. If a team scored in fewer than four plays, the other team had only the same number of plays the first team used.

Along with transporting more of the violence of wrestling into football, the XFL also featured provocatively dressed cheerleaders and trash-talking public-address announcers. Viewers were invited to see much more than was made available at NFL games, with cameras on the sidelines, in the huddle, and in the locker room before and after games. Coaches were wired for sound, so the audience could share in coach-quarterback communications as well as hear any off-the-cuff comments the coach might make in the heat of the game.

The XFL had the advantage of no college or NFL competition because it began play in early February. It also had strong television coverage. NBC aired a game on Saturday at 8:00 p.m. and taped a second game for broadcast in the primary game's home-team market; the alternate game also could be substituted if the first game was not competitive. On Sunday, TNN (The Nashville Network, since transformed into Spike TV) broadcast a game at 7:00 p.m., followed by a game on UPN (United Paramount Network, which ceased broadcasting in 2006).

There was great initial interest. The first game, on February 3, 2001, an NBC broadcast of the Las Vegas Outlaws defeating the New York/New Jersey Hitmen 19–0, drew a 9.5 rating. After that, viewers quickly disappeared. The rating for the second broadcast was sliced in half, at 4.6, and some games failed even to reach a 1.0 rating.

Despite the hoopla, the games tended to be boring with little scoring because of rules that in adding violence also tilted the advantage to the defense. Few players had much name recognition. Quarterback Tommy Maddox was the league's brightest star and the player who enjoyed the most success in the NFL after the XFL's demise. The mainstream never took the league seriously or viewed XFL football as real football. Some viewers questioned whether the games were honestly played or contrived, as are wrestling matches, although surely no one would have contrived to make the games as tedious as they were.

NBC rejected a second season of XFL, and UPN was willing to continue only if McMahon shortened his WWF Smack-Down! broadcasts to accommodate the network's schedule. He refused and ended his short-lived football experiment.

Perhaps with a clearer understanding of what football audiences want (including a reasonable amount of scoring and confidence in the integrity of the game), and more fortuitous timing, the league might have had a chance. Since XFL, extreme sports have grown in visibility and popularity, although they still have not become part of mainstream American sports. With their growing stature, however, the XFL, if it had come along a few years later, might have fared better.

See also: Television Broadcasting.

Additional Reading:
Remember the XFL Web site. http://www.rememberthexfl.8m.com.
Forrest, Brett. *Long Bomb: How the XFL Became TV's Biggest Fiasco.* New York: Crown, 2002.

Eyeglasses

Eyeglasses to most people would likely seem thoroughly incompatible with the physical violence of a football game. Contact lenses are less burdensome, less likely to be rammed back into one's face with a strong block or tackle. Further, eyeglasses for many people symbolize an intellectual dimension that, rightly or wrongly, appears contradictory to the image of three-hundred-pounders doing their best to pulverize each other.

Nonetheless, eyeglasses have found their way into the game, most famously on the face of Bob Griese, Hall of Fame quarterback with the Miami Dolphins. In fact, a pair of Griese's glasses is on display at the Pro Football Hall of Fame in Canton, Ohio.

Bob Griese was the first quarterback to wear glasses successfully in a National Football League game (meaning they let him see better and were neither destroyed nor routinely knocked off). The particular pair on display at Canton is the one Griese used in the 1978 Hall of Fame game played at Fawcett Stadium next to the Hall.

Bob Griese may have been the ideal player to show that eyeglasses could work in a game. Known as "the thinking man's quarterback," Griese has always had a professorial air about him, so on him eyeglasses looked almost natural, even in a professional football game.

Additional Reading:

Griese, Bob, and Gale Sayers. *Offensive Football.* Ed. Bill Bondurant. New York: Atheneum, 1972.

Griese, Bob, and Brian Griese. *Undefeated: How Father and Son Triumphed over Unbelievable Odds Both on and off the Field.* With Jim Denney. Nashville: T. Nelson, 2000.

F

Falwell, Jerry Lamon (1933–2007)

Jerry Falwell is best known as one of the twentieth century's most prominent televangelists and religious leaders of the Christian right. He came to prominence with his *Old-Time Gospel Hour* in the 1950s, which helped him acquire the following necessary to make a success of the Thomas Road Baptist Church, which he had begun in his hometown of Lynchburg, Virginia. He established Liberty University in 1971 and continued to lead it until his death in 2007. In 1979 he founded the Moral Majority movement, which became a highly influential effort to unite conservatives of various faiths in support of issues and political candidates consistent with his positions on such matters as abortion, gay rights, and what he considered traditional family values.

What Falwell is less well known for, however, is his strong commitment to football. He was captain of his football team in high school and continued to be a lifelong football fan. At Liberty University, he hoped to create a football program that would rival those at such other religious-affiliated universities as Notre Dame and Brigham Young. He wanted to make his Division I-AA program strong enough to justify moving up to Division I-A.

Falwell's desire to promote football was more than a manifestation of his personal love for the game or a strategy to bolster admissions. He believed that football was another avenue for disseminating moral and cultural principles. If he could place graduates of Liberty University, professing the values that the institution seeks to inculcate in its students, within the National Football League, he would have still another prominent stage from which to spread his message.

Toward that end he hired a new athletics director and new head football coach after a disastrous 2005 season in which Liberty won only one game. Danny Rocco, formerly associate head football coach at the University of Virginia, signed on to build the football program, and Jeff Barber, senior associate athletics director at the University of South Carolina, became director of athletics. The improvement was quick and dramatic, with Liberty winning six games while losing five in 2006, and Rocco being named Big South Conference Coach of the Year.

Liberty University upgraded its football stadium for 2007 by adding luxury suites, each complete with a climate-controlled environment, an open-air observation deck, a private restroom, and a catering service. The university also opened a new football operations and training facility that cost $10 million, funded by a wealthy supporter of Liberty University, Arthur L. Williams. Williams also pledged to finance a new football stadium with a seating capacity of 36,000 once the program started regularly selling out its current 15,000-seat stadium. Although Jerry Falwell did not live to see the new stadium built or the team complete its rise to excellence, the football program appears to be on track to achieve the goals that he set for it.

See also: Religion.

Additional Reading:

Falwell, Jerry. *Falwell: An Autobiography.* Lynchburg VA: Liberty House, 1997.

Woo, Stu. "Falwell's Football Dream." *The Chronicle of Higher Education,* June 1, 2007, A31–32.

Fantasy Football

Fantasy football offers people, even if they are not athletic enough to play the game for real or wealthy enough to own a team, the ability to manage every aspect of a team, from choosing the players to making trades and even, potentially, competing for a league championship. Everyone can be a Walter Mitty, or in this case, a combination coach, general manager, and owner.

Of course, fantasy has always been involved in football. The young boy imagining himself scoring the winning touchdown as time expires or the girl kicking field goals over a clothesline in her backyard is engaged in fantasy football. The youngster collecting football cards is also surely engaged in fantasy, either on an athletic or financial level.

Today, however, the term is most commonly applied to an often complicated, and sometimes expensive, type of competition in which the player has his or her own team and competes against other individuals who have joined the league.

Rules vary widely, but participation begins with an individual joining a league, which may involve a significant membership fee. The individual owner participates in a draft in order to stock his or her team. The draft usually is what is called a serpentine draft, with participants during each round reversing their order of drafting to give each owner an equal opportunity to pick good players. Another type of player selection is the auction draft, with each owner having a set amount of money to spend for the whole team. Most leagues require owners to start over the next year, but dynasty leagues permit teams to retain their players unless they are released or traded, which gives participants a more real-life experience as team owners. Keeper leagues allow teams to retain a certain number of players from one season to the next.

The owner and general manager, of course, must also be the coach and establish the starting lineup that offers the best chance for victory. Players for one team earn points depending on what their real-life counterparts do in that week's games. Certain numbers of points are allotted for touchdowns, yardage, field goals, and so forth. If the real players collectively have a bad day, the fantasy team will likely lose.

At all of these stages, fantasy owners have a multitude of aids—Internet sites, magazines, supplements in sports publications—to help them make decisions, from which players to draft to which players to play during a particular week. These aids offer rankings of players, suggest good buys, identify sleepers and snoozers (players who are likely to surprise or disappoint), and provide many tips for effective playing.

There are other types of fantasy football games as well. Board games such as Blood Bowl, Deathball, and Elfball are popular. Blood Bowl, for example, is played by two people fittingly called the coaches. They move miniature figures representing players across a grid of squares. The objective, as in real football, is to reach the other team's end zone, and scoring is accomplished by use of dice, cards, and counters. The blood figures into the game because players may try to injure their opponents. The figures are fantasy creatures with football-related skills. For example, elves are reputed to be fast runners. All of the figures are ranked statistically according to certain abilities, such as speed, fighting potential, or resistance to injury. The game proved so popular that by August 2006 it had appeared in its fifth edition.

One of the great aspects of fantasy is that it offers something very personal for everyone. So is it in football. Fantasy leagues that simulate ownership and management of a professional team, card collecting, board games, watching a game from the stands or on television, or playing in a backyard can all trigger that uniquely human attribute known as fantasy. And through fantasy, everyone can be a great player, coach, general manager, or owner.

See also: Trading Cards.

Additional Reading:
Dorey, David. *Fantasy Football: The Next Level: How to Build a Championship Team Every Season.* New York: Warner Books, 2007.
"Fantasy Football." About.com: Football. http://football.about.com/od/fantasyfootball/Fantasy_Football.htm.
Harmon, Michael. *The Savvy Guide to Fantasy Football.* Indianapolis: Indy-Tech Publishing, 2006.

Favre, Brett Lorenzo (b. 1969)

Brett Favre, the longtime star of the Green Bay Packers, rewrote the record book for quarterbacks during the 2007 season while continuing to set the standard for quarterback durability and playing old-fashioned, hard-nosed football. The graybeard on a relatively young team, Favre also assumed the role of elder statesman while playing, as he always had done, with the enthusiasm of a rookie.

Favre enjoyed great success from his first joining Green Bay in 1992 after being acquired in a trade with the Atlanta Falcons, who drafted him out of the University of Southern Mississippi in 1991. By 1993 the Packers were in the playoffs for the first time since 1982, and in 1996 Green Bay reclaimed the top spot it had held under Vince Lombardi. After going 13-3 in the regular season, the Packers marched through the playoffs, winning Super Bowl XXXI 35–21 over the New England Patriots. The next year, the Packers returned to the Super Bowl but were defeated by the Denver Broncos.

Favre became the first player in NFL history to win three consecutive Most Valuable Player awards (1995–97, sharing the honor with Detroit's Barry Sanders in 1997). Noted as something of a gunslinger, Favre was not afraid to take risks with his passes. Nor was he afraid to butt heads with defensive players. His determined play excited respect in his opponents as well as in his fans and teammates, leading Favre to become one of the game's most consistently admired players.

Contributing to the widespread respect accorded Favre was the considerable adversity he overcame. After incurring an ankle injury in the mid-1990s, Favre became addicted to Vicodin, a narcotic painkiller. Coupled with excessive drinking, Favre's use of Vicodin (by his own admission he was taking fifteen at a time followed by heavy drinking) led to a seizure in February 1996 that might well have proved fatal. He set out to reshape his life by abandoning both drugs and alcohol. Favre's commitment to a changed lifestyle was as successful as his commitment to excellence on the football field, and he began to speak publicly about his previous addictions. By 2007 he could report that he had not had a drink in approximately eight years.

Favre faced other personal crises as well. On Sunday, December 21, 2003, his father, Irvin Favre, with whom he was very close, suffered a fatal heart attack during an automobile accident. Despite his father's death, Favre played football the next evening and passed for 399 yards and four touchdowns as the Packers defeated the Oakland Raiders 41–7.

The following October, Favre's brother-in-law, Casey Tynes, died in an automobile accident on Favre's own Hattiesburg, Mississippi, property. Shortly afterward, Favre's wife, Deanna, learned that she had breast cancer. Fortunately, she recovered, and she and her husband created The Deanna Favre Hope Foundation to support breast cancer education and diagnosis. Then, in August 2005, Hurricane Katrina struck, destroying the Favre family home and damaging Brett and Deanna's home property in Hattiesburg.

Despite these difficulties and a decline in the team's fortunes during the middle of the new century's first decade, Favre kept playing. In 2007 the team rebounded, and Favre added to his illustrious career by breaking some of the NFL's most impressive quarterback records. On September 16 Green Bay defeated the New York Giants, providing Favre with career win number 149, the most ever by an NFL quarterback, as he surpassed John Elway, Favre's opposing quarterback in Super Bowl XXXII.

Against the Minnesota Vikings on September 30, 2007, Favre came to the line of scrimmage, surveyed the defense, changed the play, and hit receiver Greg Jennings on his jersey numbers for a touchdown. It was Favre's 421st touchdown pass, one more than Dan Marino had thrown in his great career with the Miami Dolphins. At the same time, he continued adding to his record of consecutive starts at quarterback in regular-season play, a total that had reached 253 by the end of the 2007 season.

Later in the season Favre broke Marino's career record for total yards gained passing. *Sports Illustrated* named him Sportsman of the Year. Most importantly of all for Favre, he helped his youthful Packers finish the regular season 13-3 and return to the playoffs. Although Green Bay lost in the NFC championship game to the eventual Super Bowl–winning New York Giants, the Pack was back again, and fans realized that the real Favre had never actually left. Unlike the proverbial old soldier, Favre did not seem inclined to fade away, instead continuing to play—and win.

Then came Favre's surprise announcement that he was retiring. By the time practice resumed for the 2008 season, however, Favre had experienced a change of heart and announced his intention to return to playing. By then Green Bay had moved on, naming Aaron Rodgers as starting quarterback, but after considerable back and forth between the Packers on the one hand and Favre and his agent on the other, Favre was reinstated and returned to the Packers, who subsequently traded him to the New York Jets.

See also: Drive, The; Elway, John Albert; Katrina (Hurricane); Magazines; Marino, Daniel Constantine, Jr.; Substance Abuse; Super Bowl.

Additional Reading:
Favre, Brett. *Favre: For the Record*. With Chris Havel. New York: Doubleday, 1997.
———, and Bonita Favre. *Favre*. With Chris Havel. New York: Rugged Land, 2004.
Gutman, Bill. *Brett Favre: A Biography*. New York: Pocket Books, 1998.

Films

Football films initially focused on the college rather than the professional game. In fact, college football and the film industry, as Ed Krzemienski points out in the ESPN *College Football Encyclopedia*, grew up together, moving from their infancy in the late nineteenth century through various stages of adulthood.

By the 1920s college football was enormously popular, a vital part of the golden age of sports. Professional football, however, was confined to the Northeast and Midwest, yet to take its place with college football, baseball, boxing, and horse racing as a top-tier sport.

The Halfback (1917), a short film by Conquest Film Company, reflected the juvenile nature of some of the early excursions into football films. Based on a popular prep-school novel by Ralph Henry Barbour, *The Halfback* depicts the efforts of Joel March (played by Yale Boss, a well-known juvenile actor of the time), to make a success of himself first in baseball and then in football.

Before long, however, films about college football were beginning to reflect the considerable public discourse already occurring about the game, including accusations that it was departing from its amateur ideal by becoming too commercialized and professional, a discussion that followed the Jazz Age into the Depression and beyond. Hollywood joined this public reexamination with such releases as *The Freshman* (1925), *Horse Feathers* (1932), and *Saturday's Heroes* (1937).

The Freshman and *Horse Feathers*, comedies starring, respectively, Harold Lloyd and the Marx Brothers, engage in considerable social criticism without diminishing their humor. Lloyd produced and starred in *The Freshman* (a silent film) as Harold "Speedy" Lamb, a naïve college student who longs for fame and knows that becoming a gridiron hero is a surefire avenue to popularity. The film satirizes the "big man on campus" theme, which was already raising questions on and beyond campuses about the proper place of football in academic institutions. Speedy eventually gets into a game and scores the winning touchdown. He comes to realize, however, that being the big man on campus is not what matters most after all but rather it is the love of Peggy, a boardinghouse desk clerk played by Jobyna Ralston, that really matters.

Horse Feathers is a more rollicking comedy than *The Freshman* and remains one of the most popular Marx Brothers films. Groucho, who plays Quincy Adams Wagstaff, president of Huxley College, laments that his son, played by Zeppo, is "neglecting football for education,"

and he hires professional players to ensure a victory over archrival Darwin College. Beneath the humor, at least for the more perceptive viewers, is a depiction of college football a bit too near the truth to be comforting.

Saturday's Heroes continued to highlight problems with college football but without the comedy. Van Heflin stars as Val Webster, a player dropped from the team for scalping tickets. He then signs on with the rival team as an assistant coach to help defeat his former squad. The film raises the subject of financially supporting college players, a topic that long remained relevant along with the issues raised by the earlier films. By the 1950s illegal recruiting practices involving payments to players would lead to serious penalties against several college teams, including banishment from television broadcasts.

A common figure in early football pictures was the then little-known actor who began his career as Marion Michael Morrison before changing his name to John Wayne. The great director John Ford put Wayne in *Salute* (1929), about the Army-Navy football rivalry. In his role, for which he did not receive a screen credit, Wayne plays one of three midshipmen who engage in some hazing (mild by later standards) of younger players. The film began Wayne's long acting association with Ward Bond. Wayne's early football films also included *The Forward Pass* (1929) and *Maker of Men* (1931). In the former, Wayne again appears as an uncredited extra, but

Maker of Men presents Wayne in a credited, supporting role as Dusty Rhodes, a football player not to be confused with the later pinch-hitting star of the 1954 New York Giants baseball team.

Wayne was an appropriate casting choice for football games. Along with possessing the physique and good looks appropriate to a cinematic football player, he actually was a football player, albeit briefly, at Southern California under the legendary coach Homer Jones. An outstanding guard in high school, Wayne lost his athletic scholarship at USC after his freshman year as a result of a serious shoulder injury suffered while surfing.

In a 1953 football film, *Trouble Along the Way*, Wayne is the lead, playing a college coach named Steve Williams. An alcoholic with a broken marriage, Williams is coaching at a small Catholic college in New York named St. Anthony's that is undergoing a financial crisis. His task is to resurrect the football program in order to save the college from having to close. He also is trying to take care of his daughter, Carol. Williams willingly breaks a variety of rules to build up the team, for example, luring a professional quarterback from Canada, hiring other players, and conducting workouts all summer despite collegiate limitations on practice schedules. He enters into unethical arrangements with a sporting goods store to acquire equipment and coerces the Polo Grounds in New York into booking his team by threatening a religious demonstration against the Polo Grounds officials.

While watching St. Anthony's take a 13–0 lead, Carol quotes her father with the line later attributed to Vince Lombardi, "Winning isn't everything, it's the only thing." Ultimately, however, the denouement is happy. Father Burke, the rector (played by Charles Coburn), discovers his coach's tactics but acknowledges that the blame is not solely his. Williams reforms, changes his philosophy of life, establishes a better relationship with his daughter, and, as the film concludes, attends church services with Carol and Miss Singleton (Donna Reed), a social worker who had befriended Carol and ultimately fallen in love with Williams. The film did not prove successful at the box office, largely because viewers much preferred John Wayne fighting Indians or Nazis to coaching football, but it did highlight a range of practices not far off the mark for some football programs.

Analyses of college football continued beyond film's early decades, although a growing genre of heroic and tragic biographies tended to mute criticism of the sport in the years shortly before and after World War II. *Knute Rockne, All American* (1940) had a large impact on this new direction. The film, which takes considerable liberty with the facts, is strongly hagiographic in its depiction of Rockne (Pat O'Brien) while making George Gipp, played by Ronald Reagan, a tragic hero: the youthful football star who dies young. The film includes a deathbed scene with

Gipp urging his coach, "Sometime when the team is up against it and the breaks are beating the boys, tell them to go out there with all they've got and win just one for the Gipper." The highly sentimental tone of the film was criticized at the time. However, the film earned lasting fame and provided a future president of the United States (Ronald Reagan) with an enduring nickname (the Gipper). It later was declared "culturally, historically, or aesthetically significant" by the United States Library of Congress and chosen for preservation in the Library's National Film Registry, a designation also accorded *The Freshman*.

One could easily fashion a whole film festival out of movies about Notre Dame's football team. Two of the most interesting are *John Goldfarb, Please Come Home* (1965) and *Rudy* (1993). *John Goldfarb*, based on a novel written by William Peter Blatty, was inspired by the shooting down of U2 pilot Gary Powers by the Soviet Union in 1960. John "Wrong Way" Goldfarb (Richard Crenna) had once been a college star who ran 95 yards the wrong way in a game. In the film, his spy plane develops mechanical problems and he is forced to land in Fawzia, a fictitious Arab nation. King Fawz (Peter Ustinov) threatens to turn Goldfarb over to the Russians unless he coaches the Fawz University football team. The U.S. State Department agrees to arrange a game between Notre Dame and the king's team, both to avoid a diplomatic crisis with the Russians and to maintain an American military base in Fawzia. To support its nation's interests, the Notre Dame team agrees to play and deliberately lose the game. Notre Dame took exception to a number of elements in the film—including depictions of Notre Dame players in a harem scene and the supposed overall harm the film would do to the prestige of the university—and sued 20th Century-Fox (unsuccessfully) to prevent distribution of the film.

A much more successful Notre Dame film, and one that the university much preferred, was *Rudy*. The film is about a young man who longs to play football for Notre Dame but lacks the grades and athletic ability to earn a football scholarship or even admission to the school. Sean Astin plays the real-life Daniel "Rudy" Ruettiger effectively, and the film generally adheres, with some small alterations, to the facts. Rudy eventually makes it to Notre Dame, joins the team as a walk-on, becomes a member of the practice squad, and is told by Coach Ara Parseghian (Jason Miller) that he will get to play in a game his senior year. However, Parseghian retires, and his successor, Dan Devine (Chelcie Ross), seems reluctant to carry out Parseghian's commitment but changes his mind when several starters urge him to play Rudy. In a dramatic scene, they walk into the coach's office and drop their game jerseys on his desk. Devine agrees and inserts Rudy at the end of the final home game. Rudy enters, sacks the opposing quarterback, and is carried off the field on his teammates' shoulders. Notre Dame abandoned its longtime arm's-length approach to films about its football team to support the making of this feel-good movie, even permitting filming during halftime of a Notre Dame game.

One of the best recent films about college football is *We Are Marshall* (2006), which tells the story of the 1970 plane crash that decimated the football program at Marshall University in Huntington, West Virginia. The crash took seventy-five lives, including those of the head football coach, most of his staff, the athletics director, most members of the team, twenty-two other supporters of Marshall University, and five crew members of the plane.

Most of the film deals with attempts to come back from the tragedy. Matthew McConaughey plays Jack Lengyel, the coach who has the challenging task of rebuilding the program. Red Dawson (Matthew Fox), an assistant coach who was not on the plane, struggles with survivor's guilt as he tries to assist the new coach. Also contributing to the effectiveness of the film is a strong performance by David Strathairn as Marshall's president. The title comes from a Marshall cheer performed by students and players. Among those offering help to the new coach is Bobby Bowden (Mike Pniewski), later Florida State's coach who at the time was coaching at West Virginia University. Bowden gives Lengyel access to game film and playbooks so the Marshall coach can learn the veer offense. Bowden reportedly had been a candidate for the head coaching position at Marshall that went instead to Rick Tolley, who died in the plane crash.

As professional football rose in popularity, Hollywood increasingly turned to it as well. By 1946 the National Football League and the new All-America Football Conference had moved west, with the NFL Rams in Los Angeles and the AAFC 49ers in San Francisco. It is not surprising that one of the first successful films about professional football was *Crazylegs* (1953), featuring Elroy "Crazylegs" Hirsch, star receiver for the Los Angeles Rams, playing himself in the film.

By 1966 Jim Brown, the great running back for the Cleveland Browns, abandoned football for a full-time acting career, appearing in such movies as *The Dirty Dozen* (1967), *Ice Station Zebra* (1968), and *The Towering Inferno* (1974). Many other pro football players also migrated into films, including Joe Namath, O. J. Simpson, Merlin Olsen, Alex Karras, and Howie Long. The popularity of professional football, especially from the 1960s on, meant that star players had instant name and face recognition as well as the athletic ability (if not always comparable acting ability) to play energetic film roles.

One of the most successful former football-playing actors was Woody Strode, an African American who helped reintegrate professional football as an end with the Los Angeles Rams in 1946. Strode's football career was brief—one season, four receptions, and one kick return—but he went on to a long acting career. Some of his most memorable performances came in the John Ford Westerns *Sergeant Rutledge* (1960) and *The Man Who Shot Liberty Valance* (1962). Strode was not alone among former football players who became acclaimed actors, although they tended to be former college players such as Burt Reynolds (a running back at Florida State) and the aforementioned John Wayne.

Some of the pro football films are iconoclastic, laying bare less than savory aspects of pigskin life. *North Dallas Forty* (1979), based on the novel of the same title by former Dallas Cowboys receiver Peter Gent, exposes players' involvement with alcohol, sex, and drugs. The novel and film base a number of characters partly on real-life individuals, for example, quarterback Seth Maxwell on Don Meredith, coach B. A. Strothers on Tom Landry, and protagonist Phillip Elliott on Gent. Mac Davis, G. D. Spradlin, and Nick Nolte, respectively, play the roles.

Still, there is considerable variety in the pro football films. *Semi-tough* (1977), adapted from Dan Jenkins's novel, stars Burt Reynolds and Kris Kristofferson as pro football players who compete for the same girl (Jill Clayburgh). That competition leads into an extensive parody of Werner Erhard's E.S.T. (Erhard Seminars Training) self-awareness program. *Black Sunday* (1977) is a thriller inspired by the attacks on Israeli athletes at the 1972 Olympics and involves a terrorist plot to detonate a bomb over the Super Bowl game from a blimp.

Everybody's All-American (1988) is a film version of Frank Deford's novel. The film follows the life of Gavin Grey, the Grey Ghost (Dennis Quaid), from his All-American career in college to his professional stardom and decline into alcoholic, financial, marital, and legal problems. Possible models for the protagonist have been identified as Charley "Choo Choo" Justice (of North Carolina and the Washington Redskins) or Billy Cannon (a Heisman Trophy winner at lsu and a professional with Houston, Oakland, and Kansas City), although Deford, a longtime contributor to *Sports Illustrated*, denies those connections.

One of the most moving football films, certainly the one that made more men cry than any other, is *Brian's Song* (a made-for-television movie from 1971). The film stars James Caan as the dying Brian Piccolo, a Chicago Bears running back, and Billy Dee Williams as his teammate and close friend, Gale Sayers. Generally based on the true story, the film is more about male friendship than football. The theme song, "The Hands of Time," also enjoyed considerable popularity.

Although college and professional football have dominated the football film genre, high school football has not been totally absent. Among those that achieved considerable attention are *All the Right Moves* (1983) and *Remember the Titans* (2000). The former is about a number of people, including Coach Nickerson (Craig

Nelson) and Stef Djordjevic (Tom Cruise as a player just on the verge of superstardom), trying to make the right moves to advance their own causes. *Remember the Titans* chronicles true events (with some embellishments) in 1971 at T.C. Williams High School in Alexandria, Virginia, which not only was integrated that year but became the only senior high school in the city. An African American, Herman Boone, played by Denzel Washington, is hired as the new football coach although Bill Yoast (Will Patton), a successful veteran white coach, also was a candidate for the position. Boone persuades Yoast to serve as his assistant, takes the team away to a team-building camp, and overcomes considerable racial conflict on the team to coach the Titans to an undefeated, championship season. A song from the soundtrack, "Titan's Spirit," composed by Tevor Rabin, has since been used extensively on sports telecasts.

The most Academy Award nominations for any football film went to *Heaven Can Wait* (1978), which previously had existed as a stage play written by Harry Segall, and before that as a film, *Here Comes Mr. Jordan* (1941), about a boxer. Warren Beatty stars as Joe Pendleton, a backup quarterback for the Los Angeles Rams, who is involved in an automobile collision. An angel pulls him out of his truck and wings him off to heaven without realizing that Joe is not supposed to die yet. Among many plot complexities, Joe returns and sets out to become both a team owner and the team's quarterback.

The film was nominated for ten Academy Awards, including Best Actor in a Leading Role (Beatty) and Best Picture, and won for Best Art Direction. The theme of reincarnation nicely fits the whole genre of football films, as the sport, in both its college and professional manifestations, keeps showing up again and again in films. Undoubtedly it will continue to do so.

See also: Bowden, Robert Clecker; Bradshaw, Terry Paxton; Brown, James Nathaniel; Brown, Johnny Mack; *Friday Night Lights*; Gipp, George; Greene, Charles Edward Joseph; Hirsch, Elroy Leon; Landry, Thomas Wade; Literature; Marshall University Air Tragedy; Mr. Inside and Mr. Outside; Namath, Joseph William; Olsen, Merlin Jay; Parseghian, Ara Raoul; Robeson, Paul Leroy Bustill; Rockne, Knute Kenneth; Sayers, Gale Eugene; Simpson, Orenthal James; Taylor, Lawrence Julius.

Additional Reading:

Carroll, Bob, and Michael Gershman. "Three Reels and a Cloud of Dust." In *Total Football II: The Official Encyclopedia of the National Football League.* Ed. Bob Carroll et al., 517–20. New York: HarperCollins, 1999.

Harvey, Walter. *Football's Most Wanted II: The Top 10 Book of More Bruising Backs, Savage Sacks, and Gridiron Oddities.* Washington DC Potomac Books, 2006.

Krzemienski, Ed. "College Football and the Movies." In ESPN *College Football Encyclopedia.* Ed. Michael MacCambridge, 52–57. New York: ESPN Books, 2005.

Fitzgerald, F. (Francis) Scott Key (1896–1940)

No American writer equal to F. Scott Fitzgerald has so glorified the football hero as Fitzgerald did. As a young boy, Fitzgerald, who later would write one of the twentieth century's greatest novels, *The Great Gatsby* (1925), and some of its finest short stories, fantasized about becoming a great football hero. That fantasy took dual paths: playing the game and writing about it. He would become far more accomplished doing the latter.

During his years at St. Paul Academy in St. Paul, Minnesota, from 1908 to 1911, Fitzgerald played end on the St. Paul football team, although he never rose above second-team status. The broken rib he suffered on the gridiron he cherished as a badge of honor. During those years, Ted Coy, a Yale football star, was a special hero to young Scott, who also started writing for the *St. Paul Academy Now and Then*, publishing within its pages the story "Reade, Substitute Right Half." In the story, Reade, like Fitzgerald smaller than most of the boys and only a substitute, is summoned by his coach with the game on the line and delivers the winning touchdown on an interception that he returns for a score.

The dream of football heroics stayed with Fitzgerald, with the exploits of the fictional Reade reappearing in the daydreaming of Basil Duke Lee, protagonist of "The Freshest Boy" (1928). Fitzgerald also tried football at Newman Academy and later as a freshman at Princeton University. He achieved some success on the Newman team and was praised in the *Newman News* for a run against Kingsley School that set up the winning touchdown; at Princeton, however, his enthusiasm did not translate into

success. Accounts vary regarding Fitzgerald's short-lived Princeton football career, which may have lasted no longer than one practice, the aspiring footballer succumbing either to a wrenched knee or simply lack of talent.

Nonetheless, Fitzgerald continued to follow Princeton football throughout his life. Hobey Baker, still revered as a great football and hockey player, was a Princeton senior when Fitzgerald was a freshman and became the model for Allenby, the football captain in *This Side of Paradise* (1920), and Ted Fay in "The Freshest Boy." Years later, in an essay on insomnia called "Sleeping and Waking" (1934), Fitzgerald recalled a dream that he had courted for twenty years to induce sleep: Princeton's football team needing a quarterback, the coach noticing Fitzgerald kicking and passing a football around on the sidelines, the coach wanting to know the identity of the young athlete, Fitzgerald being inserted into the third quarter of the big game against Yale. Of course, it was only a fantasy, but one that the famous author had entertained well into adulthood.

Princeton games continued to attract Fitzgerald, and he attended them with individuals as diverse as Ernest Hemingway and a youthful Andrew Turnbull, who later would write the first major biography of the author. On December 21, 1940, Fitzgerald was sitting in his easy chair beside the fireplace reading a recent issue of *The Princeton Alumni* and making notes on Princeton's 1941 football season.

Suddenly, he arose from his chair, reached for the mantel, and fell to the floor. His final act involved his favorite sport and his favorite team—and surely that long-held desire that in "Sleeping and Waking" he had referred to as "that dream of a defeated dream."

See also: Ivy League; Literature; World War I

Additional Reading:
Bruccoli, Matthew J. *Some Sort of Epic Grandeur: The Life of F. Scott Fitzgerald.* 2nd rev. ed. Columbia: University of South Carolina Press, 2002.
Fitzgerald, F. Scott. "Sleeping and Waking." In *The Crack-Up.* Ed. Edmund Wilson, 63–68. New York: New Directions, 1945.
Rielly, Edward J. *F. Scott Fitzgerald: A Biography.* Westport CT: Greenwood Press, 2005.

Flag Football

Flag football is a version of American football that requires defensive players to remove a flag (often attached to a belt) from the ball carrier rather than tackle the individual. This version of football therefore offers safer competition than tackle football and removes the need for helmets and pads. It also lends itself to mixed competition between girls and boys (or women and men) regardless of their size.

Rules vary widely and can be modified to fit the playing field, which in many cases will lack such fixtures as goal posts and yard markings. The game can be played, for example, in a park, on a beach, or in a backyard.

Variations include size of the individual team, which most commonly ranges

from four to nine members but in reality may include any number desired by the participants. In some versions of flag football, limited blocking is allowed, but only to the chest. Kicking and punting may be allowed or not, and linemen may be eligible or ineligible to catch passes.

National and international competitions include a World Cup of Flag Football that has included teams from the United States, Mexico, and other countries. In addition, the National Football League has attempted to both encourage and regulate flag football. Begun in 1996, the NFL Flag League offers football for boys and girls ages five to seventeen. Rules include ten-person teams with five from each team on the field at one time, limitations on rushing the passer, prohibitions against tackling and trash-talking, and no punting or kicking.

See also: Touch Football.

Additional Reading:
NFL Youth Football Network Web site. http:www.nflyouthfootball.com.

Flying Wedge

The flying wedge symbolizes early football, a game in which power dominated, tactics were primitive, and many calls for abolishing the game because of its level of violence echoed across the land. The play itself was strictly a power play mobilizing force in imitation of war.

Lorin Deland, a student of Napoleonic warfare, did not play college football himself but developed a real interest in the game and volunteered to assist the Harvard football team in 1892. At the time, one of the ways to begin a game or resume play after a score was to engage in a sort of symbolic kickoff by tapping the ball on the ground. Then a player could pick up the ball and hand it off to a teammate who would attempt to advance the ball. The runner, of course, was usually quite exposed to the opposing players.

Deland came up with the idea of having the teammates form a wedge and rush ahead of the ball carrier, protecting him from the advancing defenders. Deland had the nine players not tapping or running with the ball form two groups of five and four players respectively. The two groups began to run toward the captain of the team, who tapped the ball on the ground. As the groups converged in front of the captain, forming a wedge, the captain handed off to the carrier, who followed the wedge downfield.

The military strategy behind the play involved the principle of attacking a single point with maximum force to permit a breakthrough. The flying wedge would meet individual players and cast them aside, allowing the runner to continue uninterrupted toward the awaiting goal.

The flying wedge quickly began to generate excitement and considerable criticism. The wedge, according to its critics, seriously endangered the individual player who was being hammered by the collective might of the other team.

Teams, of course, saw the play's utility, and Yale created a version suitable for plays from scrimmage. Called a power V-wedge, the play originated at the line of scrimmage with most of the linemen starting in the backfield. The center snapped the ball once the wedge of players was in place and ready to strike with the ball carrier following.

The flying wedge, however, did not last long. In 1894 the play was banished from the gridiron. The rule change permitted only two players to be in motion prior to the start of the play, and two players could not an effective wedge make.

See also: Camp, Walter Chauncey; Forward Pass; Ivy League.

Additional Reading:
Camp, Walter, and Lorin F. Deland. *Football.* Boston: Houghton, Mifflin, 1896.
Nelson, David M. *The Anatomy of a Game: Football, the Rules, and the Men Who Made the Game.* Newark: University of Delaware Press, 1994.
Watterson, John Sayle. *College Football: History, Spectacle, Controversy.* Baltimore: Johns Hopkins University Press, 2000.

Forward Pass

As the flying wedge symbolized the early days of football, the forward pass represented the sport's movement into the modern age. The pass was to football what the jet plane was to transportation, ushering in a new era of speed and excitement, allowing participants to cover much territory in a relatively short space of time.

The forward pass was not an easy play in the game's infancy, as the ball was far more rounded than it is now, making it easy enough to carry but difficult to throw far with much accuracy. Early football was a ground game utilizing power, a game involving a lot of pushing and shoving but not a lot of open-field action or scoring. The transformation in the game would come from discontent with the way things were, which in turn resulted in changes in both the rules of the game and the shape of the football.

That transformation began in 1906 with legalization of the forward pass. The pass, however, was not envisioned so much as a way to increase scoring as a means for opening up play. The rules committee overseeing college football was hesitant to move too quickly, so it imposed strict limitations on the forward pass.

The ball had to cross the line of scrimmage at least 5 yards to the left or right of where the snap was received from the center. Only players at the end of the line were eligible receivers. Throwing the ball over the center of the line would lead to a turnover with the opposing team taking possession of the ball. In addition, incomplete passes resulted in loss of possession, as did a touch by an ineligible receiver or a pass that hit the ground before being touched by the receiver. A pass out of bounds was considered a fumble, and no pass could be thrown across the goal line.

Despite these limitations, the forward pass caught on and became a valuable offensive weapon. Coach Eddie Cochems of St. Louis University, for example, quickly incorporated the pass into his arsenal and beat some of the best midwestern teams with it as halfback Bradbury

Robinson demonstrated great facility with the rounded ball. St. Louis, using the pass, whipped Iowa 39–0 after losing to the same team 31–10 the previous year, and throughout the season consistently completed long passes of 30, 40, or even more yards.

Traditionalists, however, disliked the pass and sought to curtail it. Proposals in 1910 included limiting the pass to behind the line of scrimmage, a sort of forward lateral. Fortunately, those efforts did not carry the day, and instead rules limiting the forward pass were relaxed. The pass would be permitted to cross the line of scrimmage anywhere so long as the passer remained at least 5 yards behind the line and the receiver was at least 20 yards beyond the line of scrimmage. The ends and backs were now eligible to catch passes. An incomplete pass on first or second down was brought back to where the pass was thrown. An incomplete pass on third down resulted in loss of possession because at that time a team had only three chances to make a first down. The 1910 rule changes included increasing the first-down yardage from 8 to 10 yards, a change that also encouraged more passing.

In 1912 the 20-yard rule was dropped, and in order to increase scoring the field was reduced from 120 to 100 yards while teams were given a fourth down to make the requisite 10 yards. The touchdown was increased from 5 to 6 points, and with the extra point at 1 point, the game was coming to resemble much more closely the version played today.

The greatest change in 1912, however, affected the shape of the ball. The ball became more elongated, its long axis (around its ends) measuring 28 to 28 1/2 inches in circumference, its short axis (around the middle) 22 1/2 to 23 inches. Over the years the ball would become slightly more elongated. The new shape was much easier to grip and throw for longer distances and with greater accuracy than its more rounded predecessor allowed.

Any remaining doubt about the value of passing was erased on November 1, 1913 (All Saints' Day), when something of a football upstart, a little midwestern college named Notre Dame, went East to play Army. Coach Jesse Harper had found the forward pass an effective way for his lighter players to overcome the physical advantages larger opponents enjoyed. On that autumn day, quarterback Gus Dorais and a receiver named Knute Rockne, who later would make something of a name for himself as a coach, teamed up to lead the Irish to a 35–13 win. Dorais completed thirteen of seventeen passes for 243 yards, Rockne scored a touchdown, and Notre Dame went on to complete the season undefeated and untied.

The New York Times blazed forth the headline, "Notre Dame's Open Play Amazes Army." Princeton coach Bill Roper noted that he had never seen the pass play used so effectively. The forward pass was here to stay, and future generations of quarterbacks and receivers would rewrite the passing record book many times as they filled the air with footballs.

See also: Elway, John Albert; Equipment; Favre, Brett Lorenzo; Flying Wedge; Marino, Daniel Constantine, Jr.; Rockne, Knute Kenneth; Unitas, John Constantine.

Additional Reading:

Maggio, Frank P. *Notre Dame and the Game That Changed Football: How Jesse Harper Made the Forward Pass a Weapon and Knute Rockne a Legend.* New York: Carroll and Graf, 2007.

Nelson, David M. *The Anatomy of a Game: Football, the Rules, and the Men Who Made the Game.* Newark: University of Delaware Press, 1994.

Watterson, John Sayle. *College Football: History, Spectacle, Controversy.* Baltimore: Johns Hopkins University Press, 2000.

Four Horsemen of Notre Dame

The quotation still lingers in the public consciousness: "Outlined against a blue-gray October sky the Four Horsemen rode again. In dramatic lore they are known as Famine, Pestilence, Destruction and Death. These are only aliases. Their real names are Stuhldreher, Miller, Crowley and Layden." Grantland Rice drew this dramatic, biblical image in the pages of the New York *Herald Tribune* on October 19, 1924, following the previous day's victory by Knute Rockne's Fighting Irish over Army, 13–7.

In truth, the backfield that Rice noted by their destructive aliases—the Four Horsemen of the Apocalypse—formed one of the greatest backfields in college football history. Yet for all the players' accomplishments, they might have been no more than a forgotten footnote in football history were it not for a happy conjunction of one of the nation's most revered sportswriters and an imaginative and enterprising Notre Dame student publicity aide, George Strickler. Strickler mounted the four players, in uniform, each holding a football, on four horses, and created a photograph that remains one of the most recognized football pictures.

All four of the players, however, deserved remembering. They led their team to an unbeaten season and the national championship in 1924, culminating in a 27–10 victory over Stanford in the Rose Bowl on January 1, 1925. Harry Stuhldreher (1901–65), the quarterback, was the leader as well as a skilled runner and passer and the team's best punt returner. He later coached at Villanova and the University of Wisconsin, became a successful businessman, and authored two football books, one of them about his former coach, Knute Rockne.

Jim Crowley (1902–86), the left halfback, also became a head coach, at Michigan State and Fordham. He later served in the navy in World War II, became the first commissioner of the All-America Football Conference in 1944, and worked as a broadcaster. His career included relationships with two of football's most important figures: Curly Lambeau, the founder and longtime coach of the Green Bay Packers, who recommended Crowley to Rockne; and Vince Lombardi, another legendary Packers coach, who played under Crowley at Fordham, where Lombardi was one of the "Seven Blocks of Granite," the name given to the powerful Fordham line.

Don Miller (1902–79), the right halfback, was called by Rockne the greatest open-field runner he ever coached. Along with his rushing, he led the Irish in receiving three years in a row. Despite leading his team in rushing in 1924 with a career-high 763 yards, he was the only member of the backfield not to make All-American, an honor, however, that he had earned the previous year. Miller earned a law degree, was an assistant coach at Georgia Tech and Ohio State, and practiced law with a Cleveland law firm. In 1941 Pres. Franklin Roosevelt appointed him U.S. District Attorney for northern Ohio.

The fourth member of the group, Elmer Layden (1903–73), was the fullback. He was perhaps the team's best defensive player and also handled the punting. In the Rose Bowl game against Stanford, Layden scored three times: on a 3-yard run and on interception returns of 78 and 60 yards. Like Miller, he became a lawyer, and after graduation from Notre Dame returned to his home state of Iowa to practice law and coach football at Columbia (later Loras) College. He also coached the football team at Duquesne University and, in 1933, became Notre Dame's coach, producing an 11-0 team in 1938 that was named national champion by several organizations. He became commissioner of the National Football League in 1940, where, after creation of the All-America Football Conference headed by Jim Crowley, he found himself in competition against his former backfield partner.

All four men were named to the College Football Hall of Fame, an honor that cemented their joint position as a legendary backfield. It seems only fitting that the Four Horsemen continue to ride together so close to the campus where they achieved stardom.

See also: Commissioners; Nicknames; Lombardi, Vincent Thomas; Rice, Grantland; Rockne, Knute Kenneth.

Additional Reading:

Heisler, John, ed. *Echoes of Notre Dame Football: The Greatest Stories Ever Told.* Chicago: Triumph Books, 2005.

Peterson, James. *The Four Horsemen of Notre Dame.* Chicago: Hinckley and Schmitt, 1959.

Friday Night Lights

Friday Night Lights, which debuted on NBC in the fall of 2006, is not the first television series dealing with football. *Against the Grain*, for example, ran briefly on NBC in 1993. That series, however, was canceled after just eight episodes, forcing high school quarterback Ben Affleck and the rest of the gridiron cast to turn in their cleats. *Friday Night Lights* does qualify, though, as the first successful football series, especially with the critics. As of 2009, with the series airing on DirectTV and NBC, it was still waging a battle to attract viewers.

The show is a fictional iteration of the nonfiction book *Friday Night Lights: A Town, a Team, and a Dream* (1990). H. B. Bissinger, a Pulitzer Prize–winning journalist, followed the fortunes of the Permian High School Panthers of Odessa, Texas, during the 1988 season, while closely examining the town as well. The book focuses on several individuals associated with the team, including the head coach, laying bare interpersonal relationships and the town's passion for its team.

Along the way, Bissinger exposes such unsavory aspects of football worship in Odessa as racism and misplaced priorities regarding academics. Although the book was highly regarded as an outstanding piece of journalism almost everywhere else, many residents of Odessa saw it as a putdown of their town. Bissinger even received threats after the book's publication, which prevented his returning to Odessa where he was scheduled to appear as part of his book tour.

The book led to a film (2004) that generally follows the book and keeps the real names of the people. It does differ in a number of specific details, including Permian's final game of the season, which was a defeat in the semifinals, not in the state championship game as depicted in the film. The film stars Billy Bob Thornton as Coach Gary Gaines, with Detroit Lions receiver Roy Williams, a Permian alumnus, in a cameo role as an assistant coach for a rival team. Country music star Tim McGraw plays the father of Don Billingsley, one of the Permian players.

The film's director, Peter Berg, and producer, Brian Grazer, along with David Nevins, adapted the television series from the book. Names are changed, including Odessa to Dillon, and fictional characters, some of whom bear a general resemblance to real-life figures, are created. Jason Street, for example, sees his football career ended by a spinal injury. In the book, Boobie Miles suffers a leg injury when he catches his foot on the AstroTurf.

The series mixes in a lot of soap opera material with its social criticism and football drama. It strives for a documentary style by using three cameras that follow the characters without rehearsals or much blocking of scenes. The effect for the audience is one of following the characters as they move around naturally rather than having them perform for a camera.

Initial marketing of the show was aimed at a largely young and male audience. That proved to be a mistake that limited the audience, so NBC changed its tactics in order to appeal to female viewers and, more broadly, the entire family by emphasizing family and other relationships. In addition to football, the series explores a wide range of issues and conflicts, such as parental disapproval of a daughter's boyfriend, the former starting quarterback suffering paralysis, the killing of a would-be rapist, a member of a Christian speed-metal band joining the team to please his father, and problems of drug and alcohol use.

The series quickly started winning prestigious awards. The Writers Guild of America named *Friday Night Lights* the best new series of 2006–07, and Peter Berg earned an Emmy as Outstanding Director for a Drama Series for the "Pilot" episode.

See also: Films.

Additional Reading:
Bissiner, H. G. *Friday Night Lights: A Town, a Team, and a Dream.* 1990. Cambridge MA: Da Capo, 2000.
MySpace.com—NBC Friday Night Lights TV Series. http://www.myspace.com/nbcfnl.
Friday Night Lights (television series) Web site. http://www.nbc.com/Friday_Night_Lights.

Gambling

Gambling is one of those aspects of football seldom talked about openly. Take, for example, the section of sports pages usually headed something like "Latest Line." It states by how many points teams are favored. Although fans may like knowing whether their favorite teams are likely to win the next game, there is no practical use of these "lines" except in gambling. Yet sports gambling is legal only in Nevada casinos. The legal issues related to Internet betting are not clear because most online bookmakers operate outside the United States.

Betting usually takes one of two forms. Moneyline wagering involves betting on a team to win without concern for the final score or margin of victory. Betting the point spread is more popular for football. In this form of wagering, individuals betting on the favored team win only if the team wins by the projected margin of victory or more. This is referred to as "covering the spread." A bettor can win even when his or her team loses so long as the team loses by fewer points than the spread.

A lot of betting involves a betting pool, sometimes called an office pool when the betting occurs among a group of co-workers. Here odds are not considered, and those who win split the money that was bet. In a small, friendly pool, usually all of the money is distributed with no "house take," what technically is called a vig.

Not surprisingly, the NCAA and the NFL both outlaw betting on football by players and others associated with football teams. The fear is that betting can lead to associations with unsavory types, including mobsters, who can put pressure on players or coaches to throw games or shave points in order to keep a team from covering the spread. Even if football personnel who bet try their best to win their games, gambling can call into question their integrity and that of the sport itself.

One of the most famous gambling episodes in football occurred in the spring of 1963 when Commissioner Pete Rozelle suspended Green Bay Packers halfback Paul Hornung and Detroit Lions defensive tackle Alex Karras, two of the NFL's top stars, for betting on football games. There was no indication that either player had ever bet against his own team, much less attempted to throw a game or shave points. Just betting on games, however, put the players in violation of their contract and permitted the commissioner to suspend them indefinitely. Both ended up serving a one-year suspension.

Owners also have engaged in gambling

on football games. For example, Carroll Rosenbloom, owner of the then Baltimore Colts, had bet on his team to defeat the New York Giants in the 1958 championship game, often called the greatest game ever played, by at least 4 points. The game went into overtime with the two teams tied, and Rosenbloom reportedly told his coach, Weeb Ewbank, to go for a touchdown in order to cover the spread. He did, and fullback Alan Ameche obliged with a touchdown, winning the game for the Colts and the bet for Rosenbloom. Rozelle had been investigating the owner's gambling at the same time he was looking into the actions of Hornung and Karras. He handled Rosenbloom's actions much more privately, however, accepting a written promise from Rosenbloom that he would not bet again on football, a promise that, according to some observers, he failed to keep.

Perhaps the most publicized and costly addiction to gambling by any football player in modern times was suffered by quarterback Art Schlicter. He was selected by the Baltimore Colts in the first round of the 1982 draft out of Ohio State. He then gambled away his $300,000 signing bonus, was suspended by the NFL in 1983 for gambling, and after being reinstated found himself arrested in 1987 for bank fraud and illegal gambling. He later served four years in prison, made a comeback as a minor league football player and sports show host, was convicted of grand theft, and returned to prison. Released, he again got into trouble,

apparently because of his addiction; he was convicted in 2000 of money laundering and fraud and imprisoned again, this time sentenced to sixteen years, six of them suspended. Schlicter was released from prison again in 2006 and started a nonprofit organization, Gambling Prevention Awareness, to help others learn about the dangers of gambling.

College players as well as professionals are susceptible to becoming involved in gambling. Adrian McPherson, a quarterback at Florida State, was dropped from the team in 2002. Shortly afterward, he was arrested for gambling and theft, having allegedly bet on Florida State games and stolen a $3,500 check from a truck and auto accessories business. McPherson pleaded no contest and was sent to prison for two and a half years.

During the 1990s three Northwestern players placed bets through a bookie who was also a former player. One of the players, Dennis Lundy, was charged with lying to a grand jury when he denied deliberately fumbling in a 1994 game against Iowa. He later admitted fumbling in order to keep his team from covering the point spread so that he would win a bet. Lundy was sentenced to one month in prison and two years of probation. During the 1996 football season, a betting scandal involving Boston College football players came to light. Eventually thirteen players were suspended for the rest of the season and six were banned permanently. The betting was on college and professional football games and major league baseball contests, with some of the players reportedly betting against their own team.

The extent to which gambling has led players to become involved in organized crime is uncertain. Serious charges concerning football-mob ties and even fixing of games have been leveled by various individuals, including former players Bernie Parrish and Reggie Rivers.

So long as newspapers consistently print betting lines and individuals routinely place "friendly" bets on football games, a culture of gambling will be difficult to combat. What many people associated with football fear and attempt to prevent is the undermining of the integrity of the game that can easily occur if incidents such as those mentioned here proliferate—and especially if organized crime is able to exercise control over what happens on the field of play.

See also: Commissioners; Crime; Dogfighting; Greatest Game; Hornung, Paul Vernon.

Additional Reading:

MacCambridge, Michael. *America's Game: The Epic Story of How Pro Football Captured a Nation.* New York: Random House, 2004.

Orkin, Michael. *Can You Win? The Real Odds for Casino Gambling, Sports Betting, and Lotteries.* New York: W.H. Freeman, 1991.

Parrish, Bernie. *They Call It a Game.* New York: Dial, 1971.

Rivers, Reggie. *4th and Fixed: When the Mob Tackles Football, It's No Longer Just a Game.* Naperville IL: Sourcebooks, 2004.

Gangs and Street Violence

Gangs of young, violent individuals are a serious problem throughout the United States, especially in economically depressed inner-city areas. According to an attorney general's report of April 2008, there are approximately twenty thousand street gangs in the country. Members may deal drugs, rob, commit assault, and murder while attempting to extend absolute control over their neighborhood. Many members are not yet even in their teens, with some gangs establishing junior-gang organizations to direct neighborhood children into full-fledged membership when they are older. Although some members escape from that lifestyle, by the time they have reached their teens they are usually firmly entrenched in the gang culture with little facing them except crime, violence, and, if they live long enough, prison.

Efforts to reach out and save youngsters from this gang life come from many quarters, including concerned parents, schools, and churches. Traditionally, sports also have offered a path to a better, more responsible, and fulfilling life, typically in concert with efforts to encourage academic success.

Yet as an article in *Sports Illustrated* points out, the effectiveness of sports as a path away from gang life is declining amid increasingly indiscriminate violence. As the article notes, gangs in the past generally left athletes alone; now, though, the athlete is likely to be as much a target for gang violence as anyone else. In fact, many gang members will be especially angry at anyone, including an outstanding student or a talented athlete, who works toward a new life, seeing that effort as an insult against those who remain in the neighborhood.

An especially tragic example of a gifted athlete with the world seemingly open before him but whose future was snuffed out by street violence is Terrance Kelly. Kelly lived in Richmond, California, north of Oakland. His father was a former drug dealer who broke with his criminal past, reformed his life, and even became his son's football and baseball coach. Kelly's grandmother, Bevlyn Kelly, took special care of her grandson and made sure that he went to a Catholic elementary school and later De La Salle High School in Concord in order to have the best chance possible to escape the gang culture and enjoy a bright future. At De La Salle, a football power, young Kelly starred as a linebacker, earning Super Prep All-American honors and winning an athletic scholarship to play football at the University of Oregon. He seemed on his way out and up.

On August 12, 2004, two days before he was scheduled to return to Oregon where he had spent most of the summer with his new teammates, he drove to an especially dangerous area of Richmond to pick up the son of his father's girlfriend. There fifteen-year-old Darren Pratcher, who apparently knew and resented Kelly, approached within about three feet of where Kelly sat waiting in a car. Pratcher shot his victim four times, including one bullet to the head. When Kelly's grandmother arrived at the scene, she was so overcome with grief that she suffered a heart attack and died two months later.

Darren Pratcher was convicted of first-degree murder and sentenced to a prison term of fifty years to life. No number of years behind bars for Pratcher, however, could erase the tragedy of young Terrance Kelly. Nor could any sentence remove the hopelessness that envelops so many young men and women who long to find a better life but see in Kelly's story a powerful message that no matter how hard they try they will not be able to break free.

It is the task of American society to find ways to reduce the influence of street gangs and the prevalence of street violence and offer young men and women who otherwise would be susceptible to joining gangs a vision of a better life and the means to achieve that life. There are no easy solutions to the issues of poverty, distorted values, cynicism regarding mainstream goals, and peer pressure that lead young people into gangs. Certainly football and other sports have a role to play in helping at-risk youth to accept responsibility and develop a sense of self-worth. The fate of Terrance Kelly can breed greater despair, or it can motivate people to try harder and more wisely to change the street culture that cut short his dreams and his life.

See also: Crime; Gun Violence.

Additional Reading:
Dohrmann, George. "How Dreams Die." *Sports Illustrated*, June 30, 2008, 54–60.
Huff, C. Ronald, ed. *Gangs in America III*. Thousand Oaks CA: Sage Publications, 2002.
Petersen, Rebecca D., ed. *Understanding Contemporary Gangs in America: An Interdisciplinary*

Approach. Upper Saddle River NJ: Prentice Hall, 2004.

Gibbs, Joe Jackson (b. 1940)

Joe Gibbs was a highly successful coach with the Washington Redskins from 1981 to 1992, winning Super Bowls XVII, XXII, and XXVI after the 1982, 1987, and 1991 seasons. After retiring, he found a new vocation as a NASCAR team owner. Then, after being repeatedly wooed by NFL owners, he returned to Washington as head coach in 2004.

Winning three Super Bowls was an extraordinary achievement in itself, but the variety involved in winning them added to the accomplishment. Gibbs won with three different starting quarterbacks: Joe Theismann, Doug Williams, and Mark Rypien. Gibbs emphasized a strong running game with Washington, which showed up clearly in his first Super Bowl as John Riggins carried the ball thirty-eight times for 166 yards, running in front of an outstanding offensive line dubbed "the Hogs."

Yet Gibbs also liked the deep passing game, and in Super Bowl XXII he meshed rushing and passing to produce an overwhelming offensive performance of 602 yards. Timmy Smith gained 204 yards on twenty-two carries, including a 58-yard touchdown run. Quarterback Doug Williams passed for 340 yards and four touchdowns in possibly his finest game as a pro quarterback. In Gibbs's final Super Bowl appearance, Washington relied primarily on the pass, netting 292 yards by air and just 125 on the ground. Gibbs coached one more year and retired in early 1993; approximately three years later he was inducted into the Pro Football Hall of Fame.

Gibbs already had his second career up and running by the time he left Washington. He created Joe Gibbs Racing in 1991, with Dale Jarrett driving for him. He had three cars in National Hot Rod Association competition by 1995, and he won NHRA championships in 1996 and 1997 with Jim Yates driving. He also won three NASCAR championships, in 2000, 2002, and 2005, with Bobby Labonte driving the first championship car and Tony Stewart the next two. Denny Hamlin won the Pocono 500 and the Pennsylvania 500 for Joe Gibbs Racing in 2006.

Despite his success in racing, Gibbs finally agreed to return to coaching in 2004, signing a five-year contract with Washington Redskins owner Daniel Snyder and leaving his son, J. D. Gibbs, in charge of his NASCAR team. The return, however, proved challenging, and as of 2007 Gibbs's earlier level of success continued to elude him. His record was 6-10 in his return season. The following year, 2005, Washington improved to 10-6 and made the playoffs for the first time since 1999. After defeating Tampa Bay in the first round of the playoffs, Washington lost to Seattle. The team dipped to 5-11 in 2006 and continued to struggle in 2007, suffering a 52–7 defeat at the hands of the New England Patriots. Although Gibbs stood alone as the only Hall of Fame coach actively coaching in the NFL, increasing numbers of observers were wondering if perhaps the game had passed him by, or perhaps he had simply been away from it too long.

Then, as the 2007 season progressed, the team learned of the shooting death of safety Sean Taylor, a young man much liked by his teammates. Coach Gibbs helped to hold the team together, and the team, determined to do their best at least partly in honor of Taylor, made a late-season run to reach the playoffs. Although Washington was defeated in the first round of the playoffs, the comeback was a notable achievement. Within a week of the loss, however, Gibbs announced that he was retiring as coach to be closer to his family. Undoubtedly, Taylor's death and the aftermath of that loss took a huge emotional toll on Gibbs. In addition, a three-year-old grandson of the coach was undergoing regular chemotherapy treatments for leukemia. Although Gibbs's return to coaching had not produced the championships that Washington fans had hoped for, certainly his final season was remarkable for his overcoming perhaps the greatest challenges he had ever faced as a head coach.

See also: Super Bowl.

Additional Reading:
Gibbs, Joe. *Racing to Win*. With Ken Abraham. Sisters OR: Multnomah, 2002.
———. *Joe Gibbs: Fourth and One*. With Jerry Jenkins. Nashville: T. Nelson, 1991.

Gifford, Frank Newton
(the Giffer) (b. 1930)

Frank Gifford was an outstanding halfback and receiver for the New York Giants from 1952 to 1964, overcoming a devastating injury in 1960 to resume his career. Later he became a friendly and informative presence for new generations of football fans through his work in the broadcast booth.

Strikingly handsome, Gifford was a multitalented All-American at the University of Southern California in 1951, contributing at halfback, fullback, and quarterback, and as a punter and placekicker. The Giants made him their No. 1 draft pick in 1952. Skilled on defense as well as offense, Gifford initially was a two-way player for New York. By 1956 he was firmly established as a superstar, rushing for 819 yards, catching fifty-one passes for another 603 yards, earning Most Valuable Player recognition, and leading the Giants to the NFL championship. In 1958 Gifford caught a touchdown pass in New York's famous overtime loss to Baltimore in the title game. He also played in the losing championship game against the Colts the next year.

Gifford's career almost came to an end during the 1960 season when Philadelphia Eagles linebacker Chuck Bednarik hit him so hard that he suffered a serious head injury. Gifford missed all of 1961 but returned the following year to play three more seasons, principally as a flanker. The Giants were Eastern Conference champions in 1962 and 1963, losing to the Green Bay Packers and the Chicago Bears, respectively, in the championship games, with Gifford accounting for the only touchdown in the latter contest.

After retiring as a player, Gifford turned to broadcasting. He worked NFL games for CBS and was a member of the *Monday Night Football* broadcasting team on ABC from 1971 through the 1997 season, continuing an additional year as part of the pregame show. His honors included induction into both the college and pro football halls of fame and the Pete Rozelle Award for his television broadcasting.

Gifford's departure from *Monday Night Football* occurred as his affair with former airline flight attendant Suzen Johnson was being widely publicized. Johnson allegedly spent a week with Gifford in a Manhattan hotel during the spring of 1997, a liaison taped by a tabloid paper, *The Globe*. The paper published the story in May, and Johnson appeared on the cover of *Playboy*, as well as in a nude pictorial inside, in November.

Gifford's 1986 marriage to television talk-show host, singer, and actress Kathie Lee Gifford survived the affair. Kathie Lee at the time was still cohosting with Regis Philbin the television talk show *Live with Regis and Kathie Lee*, which she left in 2000 after fifteen years on the program.

See also: Bednarik, Charles Philip; Literature; Cosell, Howard William; *Monday Night Football*.

Additional Reading:
Gifford, Frank, and Harry Waters Jr. *The Whole Ten Yards*. New York: Random House, 1993.
Smith, Don. *The Frank Gifford Story*. New York: Putnam, 1960.
Wallace, William N. *Frank Gifford*. Englewood Cliffs NJ: Prentice-Hall, 1969.

Gil Thorp

The comic strip *Gil Thorp* has found itself confronting adversaries that are even stronger than the teams facing Coach Thorp's high school squads. Political and religious positions taken by the author of the strip in recent years have seemingly been behind some newspapers, including the *Chicago Tribune*, pulling the strip from their pages.

Gil Thorp was the creation of Jack Berrill in 1958, who continued to write it until his death in 1996. It features a former athlete who serves as athletics director and football, baseball, and basketball coach at Milford High School. Berrill named his character after baseball great Gil Hodges and the Olympic and football star Jim Thorpe. The strip continues to be distributed by Tribune Media Services, and a Tribune Company subsidiary, Chicago Sports.com, maintains the strip's official Web site despite the newspaper's dropping of the strip.

After Berrill's death, the Tribune syndicate tabbed Jerry Jenkins to continue writing the strip. Jenkins, the author of the *Left Behind* religious novels, received occasional help from his son, Chad, currently a baseball coach at MidAmerica Nazarene University in Olathe, Kansas. Several cartoonists have drawn the strip since Berrill's last few years, when his vision declined.

Given the placement of the strip in a high school, it has necessarily dealt with teen-related issues, and in recent decades it has included such serious matters as steroid use and teen pregnancy. Jenkins, after taking over, introduced more overtly religious themes into his stories. One story line dealt with an Orthodox Jewish football player. Another not only presented a fifteen-year-old girl becoming pregnant but also had Thorp talk her out of having an abortion. He then took her into his home (over the years he had married the high school girls' physical education teacher and had two children with her) in order to support the girl through her pregnancy. The strong antiabortion stance evoked criticism, although the *Chicago Tribune* denied that it dropped the comic strip because of the abortion theme.

Neal Rubin followed Jenkins as author in 2004. The current artist is Rod Whigham. As of 2007, sixty-five newspapers continued to carry the strip.

See also: Peanuts; Tank McNamara.

Additional Reading:

Berrill, Jack. *Best of Gil Thorp: Volume 3.* Arlington Heights IL: Take Five Publishers, 1989.

The Official Gil Thorp Web Site. http://www.gilthorp.com.

Snyder, Eldon E. "Teaching the Sociology of Sport: Using a Comic Strip in the Classroom." *Teaching Sociology* 25, 3 (1997): 239–43.

Gipp, George (the Gipper) (1895–1920)

George Gipp is associated with football greatness, the early death of a popular sports hero, a deathbed request, a dramatic honoring of that request, and one president of the United States. How much some of these associations are completely rooted in fact remains uncertain, but they, and George Gipp, are forever enshrined in the story of college football and in America's consciousness.

George Gipp's story was reborn for the general public during the presidency of Ronald Reagan, who played Gipp in a sentimental film called *Knute Rockne: All American* (1940), with Pat O'Brien as Rockne. In the death scene, Gipp, who had suffered a streptococcus infection and pneumonia, and, although he had overcome the pneumonia, was dying of the infection, offers his final request. Someday, he implores Rockne, when the team is having a tough time and the breaks are going against the team, tell the players "to go out there with all they've got and win just one for the Gipper." He does not know where he will be, he says, but "I'll know about it, and I'll be happy."

It is uncertain whether George Gipp, dying of pneumonia in St. Joseph's Hospital in South Bend, Indiana, in December 1920, actually said anything like that. It was not beyond Rockne to make up a good story if he thought it would contribute to victory. If Rockne did promise Gipp to ask the team to win one for him, he waited eight years to fulfill that promise—until the Fighting Irish were locked in a tough contest with powerful Army on November 10, 1928. At halftime, with the game still scoreless, Rockne told his players about George Gipp and asked his team to remember the dying man's plea. They did, winning the game 12–6; afterward, halfback Jack Chevigny, as the story goes, shouted, "That's one for the Gipper."

As both California governor and president, Reagan liked to use the line about winning one for the Gipper as something of a political slogan, until in the public mind the actor turned politician merged with the football player, "the Gipper" becoming Reagan's nickname, usually employed affectionately.

What is certain about George Gipp is that he was an extraordinarily talented football player whose entrance into Notre Dame history in 1917 was itself suitable for the movies. He did not go out for the football team, but when Rockne, then an assistant coach, saw him dropkicking the ball on the sidelines, he recruited him for the team. The following year Rockne became head coach, and Gipp became one of his stars, excelling on both offense and defense. For three consecutive years (1918–20) he led the team in both rushing and passing. He also starred on defense, punted, and kicked field goals and extra points. In 1920 he was a consensus All-American, but that season almost did not happen for Gipp. He was elected captain of the football team, but before the season could get under way, he found himself faced with expulsion over class absences. He pleaded with a disappointed and angry Rockne to help arrange an oral makeup exam to show that he knew the material from those class meetings he had missed. Rockne in turn pled Gipp's case with Father James Burns, the Notre Dame president, who finally agreed to give Gipp the requested chance. Gipp passed the test, remained a Notre Dame student, and was reinstated to the team, although not as captain.

George Gipp's gridiron feats made him a hero to his fellow students. After the on-campus funeral service at the Church of the Sacred Heart, a grieving student body turned out en masse in a blinding snowstorm to accompany the body to the South Bend train station for George Gipp's final trip home to Laurium, Michigan. The starting eleven marched together, the left halfback position empty.

The story of George Gipp, though, which consistently hovers between fact and legend, took a strange twist in the autumn of 2007. His body was exhumed for DNA testing at the request of family members. According to the medical examiner of Houghton County, Michigan, Dr. Dawn Nulf, his remains were removed on October 4 and returned to his burial site later that same day. No explanation for the testing was given. The resolution of that chapter of the Gipp story certainly invites devotees of Notre Dame football lore to keep tuned in.

See also: Films; Presidents of the United States; Rockne, Knute Kenneth.

Additional Reading/Viewing:

Chelland, Patrick. One for the Gipper: George Gipp, Knute Rockne, and Notre Dame. Chicago: H. Regnery, 1973.

Knute Rockne: All American. Dir. Lloyd Bacon. Warner Brothers, 1940.

Vaughn, Stephen. Ronald Reagan in Hollywood: Movies and Politics. New York: Cambridge University Press, 1994.

Globalism

Throughout much of the world, *football* means "soccer." In recent decades, however, American football has been spreading, largely through marketing efforts by the National Football League.

The NFL has been playing exhibition games abroad since 1950, when the New York Giants defeated the Ottawa Rough Riders 27–6 in Ottawa. Another Ottawa game followed in 1951, but not until 1959 did an NFL team venture abroad again as the Chicago Cardinals bested the Toronto Argonauts 55–26. From 1969 on, exhibition games in other countries were between two NFL teams. The first NFL game played beyond the Americas was in Tokyo in 1976; two years later the NFL moved south of the border for the first time, to Mexico City.

The NFL inaugurated the American Bowl Games in 1986 in London and continued with the series in games abroad through 2005. The locales included Berlin, Barcelona, Monterrey, Dublin, Vancouver, Sydney, and Osaka, along with cities previously visited.

A new step was taken on October 2, 2005, when the NFL staged its first regular-season game abroad. Arizona defeated San Francisco 31–14 in Mexico City, site of six previous exhibition games. Mexico City was chosen because NFL games had consistently drawn well there, with attendance surpassing 112,000 for a Houston Oilers–Dallas Cowboys game in 1994. Mexicans did not disappoint for the Arizona–San Francisco contest, as attendance exceeded 103,000. The attendance figures were no anomalies. Football is popular throughout much of Mexico, which has about fifty university football teams and a great many Mexican youths playing Pop Warner Football.

The NFL followed the successful excursion to Mexico City by scheduling a regular-season game for London in October 2007 between the Miami Dolphins and the New York Giants. The game in London's mud-soaked Wembley Stadium, the first NFL regular-season game outside the United States, was hardly a pretty contest as the Giants slogged to a 13–10 win over the Dolphins. Nonetheless, another game was scheduled for October 26, 2008, in Wembley Stadium, this one between the New Orleans Saints and San Diego Chargers. In a significant broadcasting upgrade over the previous airing by the satellite subscription channel Sky Sports, the BBC planned to televise the game on two of its channels, beginning the broadcast on BBC Two and after two hours switching to BBC Three.

The NFL staged its first regular-season game in Canada in December 2008. In a contest dominated by field goals and played before a disappointingly small crowd at Rogers Centre in Toronto, the Miami Dolphins defeated the Buffalo Bills 16–3. There was considerable negative reaction in Canada to the game because of suspicion that it was a prelude to NFL efforts ultimately to supplant the Canadian Football League.

There are, of course, many other ways

in which American football has traveled abroad. About the same time that Gen. Douglas MacArthur was helping to reintroduce baseball into Japan, the U.S. Marines were preparing to play football on a field in Nagasaki. The game occurred on New Year's Day, 1946, less than five months after an atomic bomb dropped on that city had ended Japan's involvement in World War II.

The Nagasaki Bears starred former Notre Dame quarterback Angelo Bertelli, the 1943 Heisman Trophy winner. Leading the Isahaya Tigers was Chicago Bears fullback Bullet Bill Osmanski. The playing field, known as Atomic Field No. 2, had been cleared of most debris but still contained tiny shards of glass. Consequently, the Marines decided to play two-handed touch rather than tackle football. Organizers of the contest agreed that the game should end in a tie, which made sense for morale but ran up against the competitive fire of Osmanski. The Nagasaki Bears built a 13–0 lead on two Bertelli touchdown passes, but the Tigers roared back with two touchdowns. Needing an extra point to win 14–13, the Bears converted rather than settle for the agreed-on tie.

By 1989 the NFL was ready to support a truly international league. It created the World League of American Football, which began play in the spring of 1991. During those first two years, ten teams competed within three divisions: the European, North American East (including a Montreal team), and North American West. The European Division included the London Monarchs, Barcelona Dragons, and Frankfurt Galaxy. Each team played ten games, with London winning the first World Bowl. The three European clubs all finished in the top five in attendance.

The success of the European teams led the NFL to make a radical change in the league. It suspended play for two years while restructuring into a six-team, all-European league for 1995. NFL teams contributed thirty-seven players to the league that year.

The NFL changed the league's name to NFL Europe in 1998 and later to NFL Europa, steadily increasing its allotment of players under contract to NFL teams. NFL Europa became a developmental league for the NFL while establishing a European fan base. Quite a few NFL players gained important game experience in the league, in some cases returning to star in the United States. Among the NFL Europa graduates were quarterbacks Jon Kitna, Kurt Warner, and Jake Delhomme, as well as kicker Adam Vinatieri.

By 2007, however, the league had lost much of its geographic diversity, consisting of one team in Amsterdam, Netherlands, and five in Germany. In addition, the league was losing about $30 million annually. Commissioner Roger Goodell announced that NFL Europa would cease operation after the 2007 championship game, which the Hamburg Sea Devils won, defeating the Frankfurt Galaxy 37–28. According to Goodell, the NFL would focus instead on regular-season games abroad and other international initiatives.

One of those initiatives, through NFL International, was an agreement between the NFL and Titan Media, which became the league's media partner in China. Titan publishes *Titan Sports*, a widely read newspaper in China that appears three times per week, and a monthly magazine, *All Sports*. Titan agreed that both publications would give increased coverage to the NFL and American football.

Building on this agreement and the 2008 Summer Olympics held in China, the NFL has considered playing a football game in China. Already, thousands of Chinese youth play NFL-sponsored Flag Football. Commissioner Goodell also announced that he plans to look into the possibility of locating a future Super Bowl game in London.

With the NFL moving ambitiously toward greater involvement with the rest of the world, the league has firmly embraced globalism, as have many other American businesses. It may be American football being played in NFL games, but the league would like to export it throughout the world. That makes good business sense, and China offers a huge potential market. It is a long way from Canton, Ohio, to Beijing, a journey the founders of the National Football League could never have envisioned from the Canton car dealership where they created the new league. Yet, that journey, along with many others across international borders, is now part of the world of the NFL.

See also: Commissioners; World War II.

Additional Reading:

Anderson, Lars. *The Proving Ground: A Season on the Fringe in NFL Europe.* New York: St. Martin's, 2001.

Lukacs, John D. "Nagasaki, 1946: Football Amid the Ruins." *New York Times,* December 25, 2005, section 8.

Weir, Tom. "*Futbol*-Mad Mexico Ready for Football." *USA Today,* September 30, 2005, section C.

Golden Dome

The Golden Dome, like the mural routinely referred to as Touchdown Jesus, is an image with far broader reference than football, yet it also has come to be a nationally recognizable symbol of University of Notre Dame football. The original golden dome sits atop the Administration Building, once virtually the entire university, but now just one, albeit the most famous, of the university buildings.

Destroyed by fire in 1879, the building was rebuilt within months, this time with the addition of a golden dome. Since then the dome has been regilded ten times, most recently in 2005. It is this brilliant expanse of gold, whether for a traveler approaching South Bend, Indiana, or someone coming upon the image in a photograph, that instantly identifies the institution as Notre Dame.

Notre Dame students and alumni are referred to as "Domers," and the golden dome is replicated every Saturday in the helmets worn by the football players. Each week before a home game, student-managers repaint the helmets so that the golden paint, which includes some real gold dust, shines as radiantly as the larger dome. Each player who takes the field is thus representing the university and what it stands for—academic and spiritual excellence, of course, but also victory on the field.

The golden helmet is a long-running Notre Dame tradition, yielding only twice: when a green shamrock was included on the helmet from 1959 to 1962, and, in 1963, when a white number was added to the gold. Ara Parseghian returned the helmet to a solid gold color when he became head coach in 1964. His explanation was that he wanted the uniform to be simple, without ornamentation, and that the team's intensity would be what gave the team its identity. He probably also saw the symbolism in the solid gold minidome, and he could hardly have missed the dismal team record (nineteen wins, thirty losses) during those years when the pure-gold tradition was violated.

See also: Parseghian, Ara Raoul; Tailgating; Touchdown Jesus.

Additional Reading:

Schlereth, Thomas J. *The University of Notre Dame: A Portrait of Its History and Campus.* Notre Dame IN: University of Notre Dame Press, 1976.

Graham, Otto Everett, Jr.
(Automatic Otto) (1921–2003)

Otto Graham was a man for all seasons and a winner year-round. At Northwestern University, he was an All-American in football and basketball and also lettered in baseball. He played in the school band and proved as versatile there as in athletics, playing the violin, cornet, and French horn. Football, of course, was the area in which he would achieve his greatest fame. As a halfback in the single-wing offense, he ran, passed, and handled the punting and place-kicking.

Graham was drafted by the Detroit Lions but was committed to the United States Navy, where he also played football under Paul "Bear" Bryant. While still in the military, Graham signed with Paul Brown, who was organizing the Cleveland Browns in the new All-America Football Conference. As coach at Ohio State, Brown had acquired firsthand knowledge of Graham's talents and made the former Northwestern star the first player he signed for his new team.

Graham switched to T-formation quarterback in the pros and led the Browns to four consecutive AAFC titles before the league ended following the 1949 season. He was named MVP of the league in both 1947 and 1948, sharing the honor the second year with San Francisco 49ers quarterback Frankie Albert. For a time, Graham also looked to a career in basketball. He played for the Rochester Royals (now the Sacramento Kings) during the 1945–46 season and, prefiguring his future winning ways on the gridiron, helped his team to the NBA title. His teammates on the Royals that year included future Hall of Fame New York Knicks coach Red Holzman and Chuck Connors, who would achieve fame on television in *The Rifleman* series.

Many observers thought that the

Browns (one of three AAFC teams incorporated into the National Football League in 1950) would find themselves overmatched in the older league. Instead, Graham and his teammates showed they were very much for real, playing in the title game every year but one from 1950 through Graham's final season in 1955. In their first year, they stunned the Los Angeles Rams, 30–28, in the championship game as Graham threw four touchdown passes and then led an end-of-game drive to set up the winning field goal by Lou Groza with twenty-eight seconds left. The Browns repeated as NFL champions in 1954 and 1955. In Graham's final game, he ran for two touchdowns and passed for two more in the Browns' 38–14 romp over the Rams.

All together, Graham was his league's first-team All-Pro quarterback nine times in his ten professional seasons. Five times he was named his league's Most Valuable Player, adding to his selections with the AAFC by winning the honor in the NFL in 1951, 1953, and 1955. In his final season he also was awarded the Hickok Belt as the year's top professional athlete. His induction into the various halls of fame was virtually automatic: the College Hall of Fame in 1956 and the Pro Football Hall of Fame in 1965.

Graham's postplaying days were filled with activity. He coached the College All-Stars to a win over the NFL champion Detroit Lions in 1958, served as football coach of the Coast Guard Academy (1959–65, with an undefeated season in 1963) and the Washington Redskins (1966–68), and was athletics director at the Coast Guard Academy (1970–84). Having survived colorectal cancer, Graham became a lecturer on cancer detection. He became an accomplished expert on that as well, as he had on almost everything he experienced over the years, from the violin to the pigskin.

See also: All-America Football Conference; Brown, Paul Eugene; Bryant, Paul William; World War II.

Additional Reading:
Graham, Duey. *Ottomatic: The Remarkable Story of Otto Graham*. Wayne MI: Immortal Investments, 2004.
Graham, Otto. *Otto Graham: "T" Quarterback*. New York: Prentice-Hall, 1953.

Grambling State University

Grambling State University is home to one of the most famous football programs in college football. Known as the Cradle of the Pros for the many players that Grambling sent to professional football during Coach Eddie Robinson's long tenure as head football coach (1941–97), the university had a powerhouse football program for decades.

Grambling began in 1901 as the Colored Industrial and Agricultural School. The school moved a few miles to its present location, Grambling, Louisiana, in 1905 and was renamed the North Louisiana Agricultural and Industrial School. It later was called the Louisiana Negro Normal and Industrial Institute, Grambling College, and, in 1974, Grambling State University. The school was initially formed to educate rural African Americans. In 1936 it developed a primary focus on teacher education, and over the years it steadily increased its programs and degree offerings.

Prior to Eddie Robinson's arrival, the football program was not particularly distinguished. Robinson quickly turned the program around and by his second year he had an undefeated, untied, and unscored-on team. The excitement that he generated for football at Grambling was evidenced by thirty-three of the school's sixty-seven male students going out for football in that 1942 season. Over the years Robinson had seven first-round draft picks among the more than two hundred players he sent on to professional football. Under Robinson, the Tigers were named Black College National Champion (or co-champion) nine times. His successor, former Grambling quarterback Doug Williams, the first African American quarterback to win a Super Bowl (Super Bowl xxII on January 31, 1988), won national championships in 2001 and 2002. Coach Melvin Spears took the Tigers to still another national championship in 2005.

The Grambling players, with their black, red, and bright gold uniforms, looked as striking as their performance on the field. So many star athletes wore those uniforms that the All-Time Black College Football Team chosen by the Sheridan Broadcasting Network in 1993 included five former Tigers: quarterback Doug Williams, running back Tank Younger, wide receiver Charlie Joiner, defensive lineman Willie Davis, and defensive back Everson Walls.

Grambling's football success also owed much to Collie Nicholson, who as sports information director complemented Robinson's on-field genius with his own off-field creativity. Nicholson did much to publicize Grambling, thus contributing to recruiting success as well as financial support for the institution. He came up with the idea of an annual Bayou Classic between Grambling and rival Southern University to be played in the New Orleans Superdome, which became the only black college game broadcast regularly on network television. Since recovery efforts following Hurricane Katrina repaired the Superdome, the game returned to New Orleans after being moved to Houston for the 2005 meeting of the rivals.

Nicholson would go to great lengths to bring Grambling to new audiences. For example, he learned the Japanese language at least passably well in order to negotiate scheduling a game between Grambling and Morgan State in Tokyo in 1976. Grambling drew crowds so well, partly because of Nicholson's successful publicity campaigns, that other teams clamored to host the Tigers at their stadiums. As a result, Grambling often played the majority of its games on the road and was still good enough to continue its winning ways.

Today Grambling State University maintains its tradition of excellence in academics and athletics. Objectively speaking, the quality of the football it plays may have dropped, as it has across the world of black football since previously all-white universities began to recruit African American players in the 1970s; however, Grambling continues, more often than not, to field one of the best black college football teams in the country.

See also: African Americans (College); Black College Football; Katrina (Hurricane); Robinson, Eddie Gay.

Additional Reading:

Davis, O. K. *Grambling's Gridiron Glory: Eddie Robinson and the Tigers' Success Story: Complete with Photographs from the Author's Collection.* Ruston LA: O. K. Davis, 1983.

Grambling State University Web site. http://www.gram.edu.

Hurd, Michael. *"Collie J": Grambling's Man with the Golden Pen.* Haworth NJ: St. Johann, 2007.

Grandfathers

Plenty of grandfathers are associated with football, but not as professional or college players—except for one grandfather in southwest Texas at Sul Ross State University in Alpine. The university, referred to by longtime CBS news anchor Dan Rather, according to the university's Web site, as "possibly the most underrated little university west of the Mississippi," is named after Sullivan "Sul" Ross. Ross fought against the Comanches, served with the Texas Rangers, and was a Confederate officer in the Civil War. Later he served as a sheriff, a state senator, governor of Texas, and president of the institution now known as Texas A&M.

So it may be appropriate that Sul Ross State University, given the adventurous nature of its namesake, is home to the grandfather who defied age to return to the gridiron. Mike Flynt had played football for Odessa Permian High School and then for two years at Sul Ross State. However, he was not able to compete during his senior year because he was kicked off the team for fighting prior to the season.

So having played his last collegiate game in 1970, but with one year of football eligibility remaining, and wanting to dispel that feeling that he had let his former teammates down, Flynt set out to make the 2007 football team. With the support of head coach Steve Wright, eight years Flynt's junior, he did just that. And it was not as if the university were a Johnny-come-lately in the world of football looking for any warm body to fill a pair of shoulder pads. In fact, the Sul Ross football team had won five conference titles in the previous twenty years.

For Mike Flynt, being a grandfather means a lot more than sitting in a rocking chair and telling stories of the good old days. It also means donning a helmet and heading out to butt heads with players young enough to be his children, almost young enough to be his own grandchildren. Now he has another story to tell those grandchildren of his own when he finally does decide to settle down into a rocking chair: how a fifty-nine-year-old, the oldest individual ever to play in a college game, was on the field blocking like crazy while a teammate booted the game-winning field goal in triple over-time against Texas Lutheran. Not bad for an old man!

See also: Middle Age.

Additional Reading:
"Mike Flynt and Lobo Football." Sul Ross State University Website. http://www.sulross.edu/pages/6271.asp?nid=1613.

Grange, Harold Edward (Red, the Galloping Ghost) (1903–1991)

Red Grange, the Galloping Ghost from Illinois, was one of the greatest college football players ever. Then he helped to establish professional football as a legitimate sport. In a golden age of sports during the Jazz Age, few if any athletes achieved greater fame than this extraordinary running back. According to National Football League cofounder and long-time Chicago Bears owner and coach George Halas, Grange was the best runner he ever saw.

Grange was so fast and shifty that he seemed almost to disappear, here one moment, there the next. The legendary football writer Grantland Rice referred to him as a "gray ghost," and Damon Runyon called him "three or four men and a horse rolled into one." But it was sportswriter Warren Brown who dubbed him "the Galloping Ghost."

At every level—in high school at Wheaton, Illinois, at the University of Illinois, and as a professional—Grange excelled in breaking long runs. His biographical sketch on the College Football Hall of Fame Web site notes that he carried the ball 4,103 times at those three levels combined and gained 33,920 yards, an average of 8.4 yards per carry. The Hall's math, however, is incorrect; the average actually is a mere 8.267 yards per try.

Grange was a national superstar (or phantom) from his first game with the University of Illinois in 1923, when he scored three touchdowns against Nebraska. The next fall, he scored four touchdowns in the first twelve minutes of the game against Michigan, returning a kickoff 95 yards and rushing 67, 56, and 44 yards from scrimmage. He added a fifth touchdown in the second half and also threw a touchdown pass, totaling 402 yards. Michigan had won twenty-two consecutive games before the Galloping Ghost confounded them, leading the Illini to a 39–14 victory. Later that autumn he ran for 300 yards and passed for 177 against the University of Chicago. In 1925 he carried the ball thirty-six times for 363 yards and three touchdowns against Pennsylvania. In just twenty college games, he scored thirty-one touchdowns.

As soon as Grange completed his collegiate play in 1925, George Halas signed him, knowing that the most famous football player in the land could add instant credibility to the NFL, born at the beginning of the decade and hardly out of its swaddling clothes. Grange played his first professional game on Thanksgiving Day, and thirty-six thousand came out to Wrigley Field to watch. The official program featured Grange on the cover, proving that the game's organizers knew full well what was attracting the spectators. By Grange's standards, it was not a particularly good performance. He gained 92 yards from scrimmage, picked up 56 yards on punt returns, threw a few passes, and intercepted a pass but scored no touchdowns. The game ended in a scoreless tie, for which the Galloping Ghost received the extraordinary sum of $12,000.

Both the Bears and Grange's agent (as unusual then as his salary) knew, though, that Grange more than earned his pay by pulling in paying crowds. The agent, C. C. "Cash and Carry" Pyle, arranged with Halas for a whirlwind schedule of exhibition games across the country. Grange, who had already played nine games with Illinois that year, played eight more with the Bears. After a holiday week off, he joined the Bears for another nine games, a total of twenty-six that he played that fall and winter. Huge crowds continued to show up for Grange's games, including some 70,000 in New York and about 73,000 in Los Angeles.

After the tour ended, Pyle and Grange asked for a five-figure salary and part ownership of the Bears. When Halas refused, Pyle sought a team of his own to feature Grange. That request also was denied, so Pyle and Grange started their own league, the first of several to be known as the American Football League. Pyle's New York franchise, featuring Grange, did well, but most of the league did not, and the AFL lasted just one year. The NFL,

however, desperately wanting Red Grange for its own games, offered to bring Pyle's New York Yankees into the NFL.

The 1927 season was a bad one for the great running back, as he suffered a knee injury early in the year, ironically against the Bears, and missed the rest of the season and all of 1928. With Grange on the sidelines, the Yankees suffered financially and folded.

Grange then returned to Halas and the Chicago Bears, somewhat slowed by his injury but still very good, and played through 1934. He himself thought that he was a better defensive back than a runner in those years, and one of his most memorable plays was a tackle in the 1933 championship game against the New York Giants to preserve his team's 23–21 victory.

Acclaim for the Galloping Ghost came steadily. He was a charter member of both the college and professional football halls of fame. The Football Writers Association of America chose an all-time All-America team in 1969 on the 100th anniversary of college football. Only one player was a unanimous choice: Red Grange.

See also: American Football Leagues (I, II, III); Halas, George Stanley; Professional Football Origins; Rice, Grantland.

Additional Reading:

Carroll, John M. *Red Grange and the Rise of Modern Football.* Chicago: University of Illinois Press, 1999.

Grange, Red [told to Ira Morton]. *The Red Grange Story: The Autobiography of Red Grange.* New York: Putnam, 1953.

Schoor, Gene. *Red Grange: Football's Greatest*

Halfback. With Henry Gilfond. New York: J. Messner, 1952.

Greatest Game

The truth is that no single football game can definitively be called the greatest ever. Too many variables come into play for that to happen. A particular individual will prefer a game based on level (high school, college, or professional), allegiance to a particular team, what the person likes to see in a game (high scoring, rugged defense, etc.), and a myriad of other factors. Nor is it possible to determine which game has had the greatest impact on American society. Was it the first officially recognized college game, between Rutgers and Princeton on November 6, 1869? The epic 10–10 tie between unbeaten powerhouses Notre Dame and Michigan State on November 19, 1966? The first Super Bowl, when the Green Bay Packers defeated the Kansas City Chiefs on January 15, 1967? All of these games would have their advocates, as would any number of other contests.

Yet many people, including the Pro Football Hall of Fame, consider the greatest game ever to have been the National Football League championship contest of December 28, 1958, between the New York Giants and Baltimore Colts. Certainly, this game qualifies as well as any, especially if the focus is on not the quality of play but the impact on society.

David Halberstam, the highly acclaimed journalist whose books traversed such topics as the Vietnam War, terrorism, the Kennedys, the civil rights movement, and a variety of sports topics (the 1964 World Series, Bill Belichick, Michael Jordan, and the Red Sox), was working on a book about the 1958 Colts-Giants game when he was killed in an automobile accident on April 23, 2007. At the time of the accident, he was being driven to a meeting with former Giants quarterback Y. A. Tittle, whom he wanted to interview in order to gain a better understanding of Johnny Unitas's performance in the game.

In fact, the quality of play overall in that championship encounter was not exceptional, even with Johnny Unitas passing for 361 yards. The Giants fumbled the ball away four times, the Colts once. Unitas was the fumbler, losing the ball in the first quarter. He also threw a first-quarter interception. In addition, Baltimore missed two field-goal attempts, one by Steve Myhra, the other by the team's long kicker, Bert Rechichar.

What set this game apart, however, were several factors: that it was a championship game, that it was the first NFL championship decided in sudden-death overtime, that the contest occurred in New York (the nation's media center), and that the television audience was expanding in the country so a lot of people were able to watch the game unfold. Ironically, most New Yorkers suffered disadvantages that others did not have. A delivery workers' strike in the city made delivery of newspapers impossible, and a seventy-five-mile television blackout (on orders of Commissioner Bert Bell) because the game was not sold out kept them from watching it.

As Tom Callahan, a sports columnist for the *Washington Post* and biographer of Johnny Unitas, has pointed out, most sports columnists of the time cared principally about four sports: baseball, boxing, horse racing, and college football. Professional football had not yet secured an equal place for itself at the table of major American sports—for columnists and the general public—but that would soon change. Throughout the country, television watching was on the rise, and about forty-five million people (the largest television audience ever to see an NFL game) tuned in.

The Giants struck first, on a Don Chandler field goal in the first quarter. The second quarter, however, belonged to the Colts, as Alan "the Horse" Ameche, their fullback, scored from the 2-yard line; and Unitas passed to end Raymond Berry, his favorite receiver, for another score. Myhra added both extra points. It looked at halftime as if the Colts, leading 14–3, were on their way to victory over the hometown team.

In the third quarter, the game swung the other way. Mel Triplett ran for a touchdown, and, early in the final quarter, Charlie Conerly passed to Frank Gifford for another. Pat Summerall kicked both extra points, and the Giants led 17–14. Rechichar missed a 46-yard field-goal attempt, following Myhra's first-quarter miss.

With about two and a half minutes remaining, Gifford took a handoff and ran for what he always believed was a first down. If he had made it, the Giants could have run out the clock. However, Baltimore's great defensive end Gino Marchetti suffered a broken leg on the play. In the confusion surrounding Marchetti's injury, Gifford insisted the referees spotted the ball short of where he had been tackled, depriving the Giants of a first down.

New York punted, and Baltimore took over at its own 14-yard line with 2:20 to go. Then, in one of the many late-game drives he engineered in his Hall of Fame career, Unitas moved his team down the field, three times connecting with Berry, to set up a Myhra 20-yard field goal. The game was tied with seven seconds left.

In overtime, the Giants received the kickoff but could not make a first down. The Colts received the punt and started from their own 20. Mixing runs and passes, Unitas again directed his team downfield. With the ball on the Giants' 1-yard line, Unitas gave the ball to Ameche, who drove across the goal line for the winning score and the championship. The final score: 23–17.

The championship contest involved seventeen future members of the Hall of Fame, including Tim Mara, owner of the Giants; the team's vice president, Wellington Mara; and two New York assistant coaches, Vince Lombardi (the offensive coach) and Tom Landry (the defensive coach).

The drama of the game, the cult status that Johnny Unitas immediately assumed, and the growing television audience, which increasingly found football, with its excitement and violence, especially suited to television broadcasts, began to change America's view of professional football. It really was worth watching, Americans were deciding. The close alliance of football and television was moving forward, and together they would help alter forever the viewing habits of America's sports audience.

See also: Drive, The; Gambling; Gifford, Frank Newton; Landry, Thomas Wade; Lombardi, Vincent Thomas; Television Broadcasting; Tittle, Yelberton Abraham; Unitas, John Constantine.

Additional Reading:
Callahan, Tom. *Johnny U: The Life and Times of John Unitas*. New York: Crown Publishers, 2006.
Gifford, Frank, and Harry Waters Jr. *The Whole Ten Yards*. New York: Random House, 1993.

Greene, Charles Edward Joseph (Mean Joe) (b. 1946)

Mean Joe Greene slowly limps down the tunnel leading to the Pittsburgh Steelers' locker room, his jersey bearing his No. 75 draped over a shoulder. A boy stands behind him at the entrance to the tunnel holding a bottle of Coke. The boy tells Greene he thinks he is the best ever and offers him the soft drink. Greene takes the bottle, hoists it, and consumes the drink. The boy then turns and starts to trudge off until Greene calls to him. The boy turns, and Mean Joe, not so mean

now, tosses the prized jersey to the boy. It is a touching moment ranked by *TV Guide* as one of the top ten commercials of all time and named by *USA Today* as the best Super Bowl ad ever. The commercial also won a Clio.

The Mean Joe Greene Coke commercial is from 1979, and other memorable commercials and players have arrived since then. It remains, however, immortalized in commercial history, as Greene stands enshrined in both the college and pro football halls of fame.

Greene was an All-American defensive tackle at North Texas State University before being selected by the Pittsburgh Steelers in the first round of the 1969 draft. Pittsburgh was a terrible team in those days, going just 1-13 in Greene's rookie season. Under Coach Chuck Noll, however, Pittsburgh's fortunes would turn around quickly, and Greene had much to do with that reversal.

Greene played for the Steelers through the 1981 season, helping his team win four Super Bowls in the 1970s. He was Defensive Rookie of the Year in 1969, made the Pro Bowl ten times, was All-NFL five times, and was named NFL Defensive Player of the Year in 1972 and 1974. He teamed with defensive ends L. C. Greenwood and Dwight White and tackle Ernie Holmes to form the outstanding front four known as the Steel Curtain, a play on the geopolitical Iron Curtain, the line's great defense, and the team's name. The nickname later was expanded to refer to the entire defensive unit.

Fast, quick, and strong, Greene also

was a highly intelligent and unselfish player. He devised a clever tactic, lining up at an angle between the center and guard to disrupt the offensive linemen's blocking assignments. It usually required two linemen to block Greene, so he tied up blockers, thus cutting down on the sacks he was able to register but freeing up other defensive players to get after the quarterback. While opposing players trying to block Greene or run through him certainly felt that he was plenty mean, he inherited the nickname "Mean Joe Greene" from North Texas State, known as the Mean Green.

After retiring as a player, Greene acted in several films, including a television movie based on the famous Coke commercial called *The Steeler and the Pittsburgh Kid* (1981), with Henry Thomas, who later starred as Elliot in *E.T. The Extra-Terrestrial* (1982). Greene also served as an assistant coach with Pittsburgh, Miami, and Arizona in the NFL, returning to Pittsburgh in 2004 as special assistant for player personnel.

See also: Bradshaw, Terry Paxton; Commercials and Advertisements; Films; Nicknames; Super Bowl.

Additional Reading:
Fox, Larry. *Mean Joe Greene and the Steelers' Front Four.* New York: Dodd, Mead, 1975.
Zittrain, Jonathan L., and Jennifer K. Harrison. *The Torts Game: Defending Mean Joe Greene.* New York: Aspen, 2004.

Gridiron

Everyone conversant with football understands that the gridiron is another name for the football field. What many people do not know, however, is why that term has been applied to football.

The quick and easy answer is that the football field with its lines designating yardage at 10-yard intervals looks somewhat like a gridiron. A gridiron is a flat framework consisting of parallel metal bars on which food, usually meat, is placed for cooking. The gridiron is then placed over a fire. According to *The Oxford English Dictionary*, the term *gridiron* has been used at least since the thirteenth century. Anyone cooking hamburgers or steaks in a backyard is likely experienced with a gridiron.

There are other definitions for a gridiron, however; for example, the structure above the stage of a theater from which scenery and lights are hung by cables or ropes. Most of these definitions have no relevance to football, except for one. The gridiron was also a medieval instrument of torture. The person being tortured was placed on the gridiron and subjected to the horrible pain of being burned to death.

The fusion of these two medieval uses of the word *gridiron* within the context of football occurred in a book by the prolific author of juvenile stories, H. (Harrie) Irving Hancock (1868–1922). Among Hancock's many books for youths is the High School Boys series, consisting of four books, among them *The High School Left End* (1910), also known as *Dick & Co. Grilling on the Football Gridiron*, as the books in the series had alternate titles. The series features Dick Prescott and his friends (the "Company" referred to in the title).

As with so many books by Hancock and others from the early twentieth century, this series about Dick and his pals is designed to provide uplifting reading for adolescents, imparting both entertainment and traditional values, including the development of a spirit of teamwork. The chapter titles indicate the moral growth that Dick and friends undergo. At the beginning they are "Sulking in the Football Camp." Later chapter headings include "Does Football Teach Real Nerve," "Facing the 'School,'" "The Price of Bravery," and after "The Thanksgiving Day Game," "Sulker and Real Man."

There is no actual torture, of course, despite the reference to the "grilling," but a metaphoric allusion to testing by the fire of competition. Dick is not burned to death but comes out a "real man": stronger, responsible, more morally mature, and ready for the next challenge. For those not able to locate a hard copy of *The High School Left End*, a copy is available online through Project Gutenberg.

See also: Language; Literature.

Additional Reading:

Hancock, H. Irving. *The High School Left End (or Dick & Co. Grilling on the Football Gridiron).* Philadelphia: Henry Altemus, 1910.

———. *The High School Left End (or Dick & Co. Grilling on the Football Gridiron).* Project Gutenberg. http://infomotions.com/etexts/gutenberg/dirs/1/2/6/9/12691/12691.htm.

Gun Violence

Gun violence has been a problem in the United States since the country was formed, and it continues to be so. The majority of homicides in the United States are committed with guns, and the same is true of suicides. Approximately one-fourth of robberies involve gun use, and robberies when the perpetrator is armed with a gun are three times as likely to result in a death than when other weapons are used. The latter statistic was confirmed in the recent death of Sean Taylor.

Football was thrust into this gun-violence arena on November 26, 2007, when Taylor, a twenty-four-year-old Washington Redskins safety and former University of Miami All-American, was shot during a burglary of his home. The following day, he died.

Four young men ages seventeen to twenty were arrested for the crime. They entered Taylor's Miami, Florida, home early in the morning of Monday, November 26, expecting Taylor to be with his Washington team. However, Taylor had suffered a leg injury that had caused him to miss the two previous games. As a result, he was home with his girlfriend, Jackie Garcia, and their eighteen-month-old daughter when the intrusion occurred. Taylor heard noises and grabbed a machete that he kept in his bedroom. Then the bedroom door burst open, and one of the burglars shot him in the upper leg. The bullet hit the femoral artery, causing sudden and extensive blood loss.

Despite some optimism that Taylor might survive, he died the next day, cutting short a season in which despite his injury he was leading the league in interceptions. More importantly, it cut short a valued life, devastating his family, friends, and teammates.

This was not the first time, however, that gun violence had intervened in football. In November 2006, another University of Miami player, defensive lineman Bryan Pata, was shot to death just a few miles from Taylor's Miami home. After practicing with his Hurricanes team, Pata returned to his apartment, where he was shot. At the time of Taylor's death, Pata's murder remained unsolved.

On January 1, 2007, Darrent Williams, a cornerback with the Denver Broncos, was murdered in a drive-by shooting in downtown Denver. He had attended a birthday party for a Denver Nuggets player and was riding in a limousine. Shot in the neck, he fell over onto teammate Javon Walker and died instantly. Also in this case, no one had been charged with the murder at the time of Taylor's death, although police had identified a number of possible leads.

Richard Collier, a tackle for the Jacksonville Jaguars, was ambushed outside an apartment complex in Jacksonville during the early morning of September 2, 2008. While sitting in a car, Collier was shot fourteen times, with one bullet striking his spinal cord. Weeks later, he awoke to find himself paralyzed below the waist and with his left leg amputated above the knee. The assailant, later arrested, apparently was angered by a reputed altercation with Collier at a nightclub.

Regrettably, these young men were neither the first, nor are they likely to be the last, football players to fall victim to gun violence.

See also: Crime; Gangs and Street Violence; Kennedy, John F., Assassination of.

Additional Reading:

Cook, Philip, and Jens Ludwig. *Gun Violence: The Real Costs*. New York: Oxford University Press, 2000.

Haerens, Margaret, ed. *Gun Violence*. Detroit: Greenhaven, 2006.

Wellford, Charles F., John V. Pepper, and Carol V. Petrie, eds. (the National Research Council [U.S.], Committee to Improve Research Information and Date on Firearms). *Firearms and Violence: A Critical Review*. Washington DC: National Academies Press, 2004.

H

"Hail Mary" Pass

The "Hail Mary" may be the only prayer after which a play in any sport has been named. The play is a long pass thrown in desperation with time running out at the end of the first half or at the conclusion of the game. In football, the quarterback throws the ball deep and hopes for a miracle catch. The play is like a prayer said when all other hope has vanished.

People usually pray with the expectation, or at least the hope, that their prayers will be answered. Unfortunately, the "Hail Mary" pass seldom succeeds because everyone, most significantly the defense, knows precisely what is coming. Yet, on rare occasions, the play works.

The most memorable "Hail Mary" pass occurred on Friday, November 23, 1984, in a high-scoring seesaw contest between Boston College and the University of Miami, the defending national champion, in the Orange Bowl. Miami took the lead, 45–41, with approximately twenty-eight seconds left.

After the ensuing kickoff, Boston College quarterback Doug Flutie, who would win the Heisman Trophy that year, led his team to their own 48-yard line with six seconds remaining. Eluding Miami rushers, Flutie bought enough time for his receivers to reach the end zone but was forced back to about his own 36-yard line to throw. Three defenders leaped for the ball but struck each other, as the ball settled against the stomach of Gerard Phelan, who clutched the football and fell to the turf in the end zone: the final score 47–45. The miracle finish continues to be replayed on television often enough so that new generations of football fans are sure to see it and learn that sometimes a prayer can make all the difference, especially when thrown with a strong arm.

See also: Dropkick; Holy Roller; Immaculate Reception; Religion.

Additional Reading:

Flutie, Doug. *Flutie*. Rev. ed. With Perry Lefko. Champaign IL: Sports Publishing, 1999.

Krantz, Les, ed. *Not Till the Fat Lady Sings: The Most Dramatic Sports Finishes of All Time*. Chicago: Triumph Books, 2003.

Mandell, Ted. *Heart Stoppers and Hail Marys: The Greatest College Football Finishes (Since 1970)*. South Bend IN: Hardwood, 2006.

Halas, George Stanley (Papa Bear) (1895–1983)

The nickname *Papa* is a sign of respect and endearment, the mark of a child loving and honoring his or her father. The great writer Ernest Hemingway encouraged his associates, admirers, and hangers-on to refer to him that way, the request helping to fulfill his need to be venerated. The term came naturally where George Halas was concerned. Not that the legendary owner, general manager, and coach of the Bears who also was a pioneer in the formation of the National Football League was always lovable. In fact, he often was hard and demanding, pushing his players to do their best. Of course, most parents want their children to excel, so even there the nickname seemed to work.

George Halas was in on the ground floor of the National Football League. When a group of representatives from professional teams met in Ralph Hay's Hupmobile auto agency in Canton, Ohio, on September 17, 1920, Halas, the player-coach of the Decatur Staleys, was present. Out of this meeting came the American Professional Football Association, renamed the National Football League (NFL) after the 1921 season.

The Staleys under Halas were thus one of the original NFL teams, although its name also changed. A. E. Staley, who owned both the team and the A. E. Staley Manufacturing Company of Decatur, Illinois, which made starch, turned the team over to Halas in 1921. In 1922 the team, now based in Chicago, became the Bears. In the early 1930s Halas bought out Ed Sternaman, whom Halas, after taking over the team, had brought on as a partner. Halas continued to be not only the owner but the face, even the very embodiment of the Bears, until his death in 1983.

Halas was responsible for many innovations in professional football. He was the first coach to hold daily practices, to cover the field with a tarpaulin, to use films of his opponent, to take his team barnstorming, and to have his games broadcast on radio. He pioneered use of a public-address system to help fans follow what was happening on the field. His 1925 signing of Red Grange, one of the most popular sports figures in the nation, gave the youthful NFL increased public awareness as Halas immediately began a seventeen-game barnstorming tour.

Halas also was innovative in on-field strategy. His refinement of the T-formation with a man in motion helped the 1940 Bears register one of the most extraordinary victories in NFL history. In the championship game, the Bears used the formation with overwhelming efficiency to demolish the Sammy Baugh–led Washington Redskins 73–0. Such assistant coaches as Clark Shaughnessy (and his 1930–32 replacement, Ralph Jones) had much to do with Halas's success, but even here he was a pioneer, early on recognizing the importance of good assistants. Halas helped popularize the practice of having a coach observe the game from the press box and relay his observations from there.

Occasionally over the years Halas stepped away from coaching (in 1930–32, 1942–45, and 1956–57). The second of these periods permitted Halas to join the war effort during World War II. In forty seasons as coach before leaving the sidelines for good after the 1967 season, Halas won five NFL titles, with the Bears winning two more during his coaching absences.

His coaching totals of 318 regular-season victories and 324 overall wins were records when he retired as coach.

See also: Baugh, Samuel Adrian; Grange, Harold Edward; Hay, Ralph E.; Professional Football Origins; Sayers, Gale Eugene.

Additional Reading:
Davis, Jeff. *Papa Bear: The Life and Legacy of George Halas*. New York: McGraw-Hill, 2005.
Halas, George. *Halas by Halas: The Autobiography of George Halas*. With Gwen Morgan and Arthur Veysey. New York: McGraw-Hill, 1979.
Vass, George. *George Halas and the Chicago Bears*. Chicago: Regnery, 1971.

Hall of Fame (College)

The desire for immortality appears endemic in human nature. It is no less prevalent in football players, although their vision of immortality is a bit different, consisting of a plaque, certain mementos placed on display (not unlike relics), and an association forever with what one might call the saints of the sport. The word *forever* is a vital element in reference to membership in the College Football Hall of Fame, or to its professional counterpart, or for that matter, to the National Baseball Hall of Fame at Cooperstown, New York. There are moral reasons for excluding one from membership, but there is no provision for removing anyone from it regardless of what the individual has done. Even murder, the act widely believed to have been committed by O. J. Simpson, has not led to his removal from either the college or professional hall.

The College Football Hall of Fame is operated by the National Football Foundation, which was founded in 1947 to promote amateur football and to encourage certain virtues, including leadership and academic excellence. Selection to the College Hall of Fame requires, according to its eligibility rules, good citizenship after the candidate's football career has ended. The individual also must have been a first-team selection to a major All-America squad, be at least ten years beyond his college football career, and be retired from the professional game. A coach must have been a head coach for at least ten years, coached at least one hundred games, and won at least 60 percent of his games. A coach is to be three years beyond retirement; however, he can be immediately eligible if he retires after seventy years of age, or he can be selected while still active if he is seventy-five or older. This latter exception explains the eligibility of Joe Paterno, who was elected to the Hall of Fame in 2006 while still coaching Penn State. There also is a fifty-year rule, which states that players must have performed within the past fifty years. However, review committees may waive the requirement for particularly deserving individuals from the early days of college football.

The first class of inductees—including such football legends as Jim Thorpe, Red Grange, Amos Alonzo Stagg, and Knute Rockne—entered the College Football Hall of Fame in 1951. At the time, however, there was no physical hall. A permanent site for the Hall of Fame was to have been built on the campus of Rutgers University, but those plans never materialized. The first College Football Hall of Fame building opened in 1978. The setting, Kings Island Amusement Park near Cincinnati, evoked no great association with college football, and perhaps not surprisingly the Hall of Fame never seemed to catch on particularly well with the public. The Hall of Fame closed its doors, but not its selection process, in 1994.

Since 1995 the College Football Hall of Fame has been located in a far more appropriate place, South Bend, Indiana, not far from the University of Notre Dame, home to possibly the best-known college football team in the country. There the Hall of Fame seems to have found not only a permanent home but also an entirely fitting location.

Today, more than nine hundred important figures from college football, covering a wide range of competitive levels—NCAA FBS, FCS, Divisions II, III; and NAIA—are enshrined. Any dues-paying member of the National Football Foundation may nominate a candidate. Coaches and athletics directors also may make nominations. After an initial screening by NFF staff to ensure that candidates meet the minimum requirements, district screening committees examine the nominees. Nominees with the most votes are put on the ballot, and the Honors Court rules on which past nominees will be kept on the ballot. All dues-paying foundation members vote, with the results sent to the Honors Court, which selects the class of inductees.

See also: Grange, Harold Edward;; Hall of Fame (Professional); Paterno, Joseph Vincent; Rockne, Knute Kenneth; Stagg, Amos Alonzo; Thorpe, James Francis.

Additional Reading:
College Football Hall of Fame Web site. http://collegefootball.org.
National Football Foundation Web site. http://www.footballfoundation.com.

Hall of Fame (Professional)

The Pro Football Hall of Fame is located in Canton, Ohio, the town where seven men, including Jim Thorpe, gathered in a Hupmobile auto agency in August 1920 to search for solutions to problems facing professional football. A second Canton meeting, in September, included George Halas. Out of these meetings came the American Professional Football Association, which began play that same year. The next year the league's name changed to the National Football League, the name that it retains today.

Many decades passed, though, before a hall of fame for the league was established. In fact, the idea for a hall did not come from the league itself but from an enterprising local newspaper and several Canton businessmen who were anxious to promote their town, today still a modestly sized city with a population of just over eighty thousand. Somewhat isolated from large metropolitan centers, Canton is located fifty miles south of Cleveland and a two to four hours' drive from such

NFL cities as Pittsburgh, Buffalo, Cincinnati, and Detroit.

The *Canton Repository* began pushing for a football hall of fame in 1959, and civic groups took up the fight. William E. Umstattd of the Timken Company (a manufacturer of friction management and power transmission products) represented Canton in making a formal proposal to the NFL in January 1961. After that, the project moved rapidly through acceptance, groundbreaking on August 11, 1962, and the official opening on September 7, 1963. Additions have been made to the original two-building complex three times (1970–71, 1977–78, 1994–95), with a major renovation in 2003 to add the Hall of Fame Gallery, resulting in the current five-building Pro Football Hall of Fame.

Visitors today enter near a seven-foot statue of Jim Thorpe and proceed to a variety of rooms and exhibits, including the Pro Football Today Exhibition Area, the Hall of Fame Gallery with busts of the inductees, the Pro Football Adventure Room featuring information about other professional football leagues, the Enshrinee Mementos Room, and the Super Bowl Room. The Game Day Stadium includes a turntable theater with a large Cinemascope screen. An interactive area offers visitors an opportunity to call plays, throw passes, and play a football trivia game, among other activities. Researchers and others may visit the Hall's Archives and Information Center, which houses an extensive collection of materials relating to professional football.

Attendance stayed below 100,000 through the 1960s but increased dramatically in the 1970s, reaching its peak after the first expansion. In 1973, 330,029 visitors passed through the Hall's doors according to the Hall's attendance figures. Attendance has not approached that figure again. It dipped to a level between 160,000 and 170,000 in 1984 and 1985, then rebounded to surpass 200,000 from 1988 to 1991. After another dip at the beginning of the new century, attendance climbed modestly, reaching 194,508 in 2006, the highest level since 1999.

The Pro Football Hall of Fame reaches out to the public in a variety of ways, including through an informative Web site, traveling exhibits, and youth educational programs.

The annual induction of new members is an extensive celebration lasting ten days. Events include, in addition to the induction ceremony, concerts, fireworks, hot-air balloon flights, and parades. There also is a preseason football game. The 2007 contest pitted the Pittsburgh Steelers against the New Orleans Saints.

The heart of the festival, however, is the enshrinement of the new members, a group that in 2007 featured Gene Hickerson, Michael Irvin, Bruce Matthews, Charlie Sanders, Thurman Thomas, and Roger Wehrli, bringing the total number of players, coaches, and other contributors to professional football (e.g., owners, executives, officials) who have been inducted to 241. Writers and broadcasters are not eligible for induction into the Hall, but they are eligible for the Dick Mc-Cann Award for writers and the Pete Rozelle Award for broadcasters, named after the first Hall of Fame director and a former NFL commissioner, respectively. The first class of inductees was chosen in 1963, a group of seventeen that included Sammy Baugh, Red Grange, George Halas, Don Hutson, Bronko Nagurski, and Jim Thorpe.

A forty-member Board of Selectors chooses the new members. This board comprises one member from each of the thirty-two NFL cities (with two from New York because the city includes two teams), a representative from the Pro Football Writers of America, and seven at-large members. The PFWA member is appointed for a two-year term, but the other members serve until they retire or resign from the board. Three to six inductees are chosen annually. Nominations may come from anyone, including fans, but a player must have been retired at least five years. A coach also must be retired, but other contributors may still be active. To be chosen, a candidate must first survive initial screening by the Board of Selectors. Seventeen finalists are chosen, including two senior nominees (from before 1982) chosen by the Seniors Committee, which consists of nine veteran members of the Selection Committee. Once on the ballot, the individual must be approved by 80 percent of the selectors.

As with the College Football Hall of Fame, membership is permanent, with no provisions for removing someone already selected. Once in, always in, and that permanent enshrinement among professional football's immortals is a powerful attraction for those who have been part of the professional football world. The Hall, it should be noted, does not select from every facet of professional football, but largely from the National Football League with, one might say, some credit given to those who were members of organizations later incorporated into the NFL, such as the American Football League and some teams from the All-America Football Conference.

See also: Baugh, Samuel Adrian; Canton Bulldogs; Eyeglasses; Grange, Harold Edward; Halas, George Stanley; Hall of Fame (College); Hay, Ralph E.; Professional Football Origins; Nagurski, Bronislaw; Thorpe, James Francis.

Additional Reading:

Brantingham, Barney. *Pro Football Hall of Fame: The Story Behind the Dream.* Canton OH: Sequoia Communications (for the Pro Football Hall of Fame), 1988.

The Pro Football Hall of Fame Web site. http://www.profootballhof.com.

Pro Football Hall of Fame Festival Web site. http://www.profootballhoffestival.com.

Smith, Ron. *Sporting News Books Presents Pro Football's Heroes of the Hall.* St. Louis: Sporting News, 2003.

Hay, Ralph E. (1891–1944)

Most people at some point have great dreams. Many discard those dreams in the face of daily doses of reality. Others do not. Ralph Hay not only held on to his dream but did something about it.

Hay's dream, according to his brother-in-law Lester Higgins, was that professional football someday would be as large as major league baseball. Hay, who owned the Canton Bulldogs as well as a Hupmobile dealership in Canton, Ohio, set out to follow his dream as well as to establish reasonable controls over salaries and player movement from team to team—and he succeeded in a measure surely beyond his imagining.

The date was August 20, 1920, when Hay welcomed six other individuals involved with professional football teams into his auto agency for a discussion. The subject was a new league, to be called the American Professional Football Conference. All six were deeply interested, as were owners of other teams not represented in person that day.

Consequently, Hay hosted a second meeting, this one on September 17. Ten teams sent representatives, too many to fit into Hay's small office, so they met in the showroom, taking seats on running boards and fenders. The day was warm, so the men refreshed themselves by drinking beer from pails, a pail being the usual way to carry beer home from a saloon.

Jim Thorpe and George Halas were among the participants. Agreement was quickly reached. The group asked Hay to become president of the new league, but he demurred in favor of Jim Thorpe, explaining that Thorpe would bring credibility and public acclaim to the position. In all, fourteen teams signed up, extending beyond Ohio to include teams from Illinois, New York, Michigan, and Indiana.

In little more than two weeks, the season was under way, the Dayton Triangles defeating the Columbus Panhandles 14–0 on October 3. After the 1921 season the league changed its name to the National Football League. Fans today who follow their favorite NFL teams and revel in the national extravaganza known as the Super Bowl should remember that it all started with one man's dream. Many might see the essence of America in that fact, and in the proof echoing down almost a century later that one person can indeed make all the difference in the world.

See also: Canton Bulldogs; Halas, George Stanley; Hall of Fame (Professional); Ohio League; Professional Football Origins; Thorpe, James Francis.

Additional Reading:
Willis, Chris. *Old Leather: An Oral History of Early Pro Football in Ohio, 1920–1935.* Lanham MD: Scarecrow Press, 2005.

Hayes, Wayne Woodrow (Woody) (1913–1987)

Woody Hayes was a lieutenant commander in the U.S. Navy commanding ships in the Atlantic and Pacific theaters during World War II, an amateur historian, and a football coach who saw football as a lot like war. That combative approach to the game stood him in good stead for many years but ultimately brought an untimely end to his coaching career.

Hayes learned the coaching business in high school football and at Denison University and Miami University in Ohio before becoming coach at Ohio State University in 1951. He stayed there for twenty-eight years, compiling a record of 205-61-10 with the Buckeyes, won thirteen Big 10 titles and three national championships, and saw his players earn fifty-one first-team All-America selections and three Heisman Trophies. Archie Griffin, a running back under Hayes, was the first and so far only player to win two Heisman awards (1974–75).

Hayes favored a ground attack, the football equivalent of the infantry. His approach was often referred to as "three yards and a cloud of dust." Leery of relying too much on a passing game, he reminded people that "there are three things that can happen when you throw a pass, and two of them are bad" (referring to a completion, an incomplete pass, and an interception).

Hayes also was a strong advocate of academic excellence. An English major during his student days at Denison, he received an academic appointment at Ohio State in physical education and taught basic English and vocabulary classes for his freshmen. He maintained high academic expectations for his players and interacted regularly with university faculty, often dining with them at Ohio State's university club.

Hayes was also passionate about football, and that passion at times translated into outbursts of anger. A number of angry incidents marred his coaching career at Ohio State, including an attack on a television cameraman in 1956, an angry exchange with a referee in 1971 during which Hayes ripped up sideline markers, and a confrontation prior to the 1973 Rose Bowl game during which he shoved a camera into a photographer's face.

The final straw that broke the back of Woody Hayes's coaching career came on December 29, 1978, against Clemson in the Gator Bowl. With Ohio State trailing 17–15 and desperately trying to score near the end of the game, Charlie Bauman of Clemson intercepted a Buckeyes pass. As he ran out of bounds on the Buckeyes side of the field, Hayes erupted, punching Bauman in the throat. Upon Hayes's return to Ohio, he was fired.

The ignominious end to Hayes's tenure at Ohio State, however, did not completely sever the bond between him and the university. Upon his death in 1987, his family requested that donations be made to the university to further its academic work. In addition, a Wayne Woodrow Hayes Chair in National Security Studies was established in the International Security Studies program to commemorate the coach's longtime commitment to academics and his special interest in history. The College Football Hall of Fame had already honored him for his football accomplishments by inducting him into the Hall in 1983.

See also: Education; Heisman Trophy; World War II.

Additional Reading:
Brondfield, Jerry. *Woody Hayes and the 100-Yard War*. New York: Random House, 1974.
Hayes, Woody. *Hot Line to Victory*. Columbus: Ohio State University, 1969.

Vare, Robert. *Buckeye: A Study of Coach Woody Hayes and the Ohio State Football Machine.* New York: Harper's Magazine Press, 1974.

Heffelfinger, William W. (Pudge) (1867–1954)

Pudge Heffelfinger was the finest lineman of his day, but his place in history owes more to his having been the first football player absolutely known to have been paid for his services—not in an inflated expense account or expensive gifts, but in hard cash. Heffelfinger received $500 from the Allegheny Athletic Association (AAA) to play against its chief rival, the Pittsburgh Athletic Club (PAC), on November 12, 1892. The payment was well worth it, as Heffelfinger jarred the ball loose from the PAC runner during the first half and ran it back for a touchdown, giving the AAA a 4–0 victory at a time when a touchdown counted for 4 points. Documentation proving the payment came to light in the 1960s when Dick Mc-Cann of the Pro Football Hall of Fame discovered an entry in the AAA's account ledger for 1892. Unless proof of an earlier payment to another player surfaces, Heffelfinger will continue to enjoy his place in history.

Heffelfinger, however, accomplished much more in his life than earning a one-time payment from the AAA. He was a three-time All-American at Yale (1889–91), where he starred at guard. At six feet three inches and almost two hundred pounds, he was among the biggest players of his time, and he also was one of the fastest. He was especially adept at leaping over blockers to break up a flying wedge and tackle the runner.

After Yale Heffelfinger went to work for a railroad in Omaha, Nebraska, but also played for independent football teams. In 1892 he went East with the Chicago Athletic Association team to play six games, a trip that alerted the AAA to his possible availability for their own purposes. His athletic skills remained with him throughout much of his life, and he continued to play football occasionally even into middle age. At the age of fifty-three in 1920 he played most of the game for the East All-Stars against the Ohio State All-Stars at Columbus. At sixty-three he suited up a final time, appearing in a game in Minneapolis. Heffelfinger also coached the University of California team in 1893, going 5-1-1.

Heffelfinger enjoyed plenty of success off the football field as well. As with his pioneering professional status as a player, he was somewhat ahead of his time in using the media effectively. Along with publishing an annual *Heffelfinger's Football Facts*, he produced the first radio sports show and first spy show (*Secret Agent K-7*). In 1951 he was inducted as a charter member of the College Football Hall of Fame.

See also: Ivy League; Professional Football Origins; Radio.

Additional Reading:
Heffelfinger, W. W. *This Was Football, by W. W. "Pudge" Heffelfinger, as told to John McCallum.* New York: Barnes, 1954.

Heisman, John William (1869–1936)

John Heisman, whose name endures with the trophy given annually to college football's best player, was a pioneering and highly successful college coach whose innovations helped make football the game it is today. Heisman was born in Cleveland in 1869 but grew up in northwestern Pennsylvania, where he developed his physical strength helping his cooper father make wooden barrels.

Heisman was a star lineman for Brown University (1887–89) and earned a law degree at the University of Pennsylvania in 1892. He chose, however, to pursue a football rather than legal career and accepted the position of football coach at Oberlin College in Ohio the same year that he became a lawyer. He later coached at Akron, Oberlin again, Auburn, Clemson, Georgia Tech, Pennsylvania, Washington and Jefferson, and Rice, concluding his career in 1927 with a record of 185 wins, seventy losses, and seventeen ties. At Georgia Tech, he had three consecutive undefeated teams (1915–17) and won the national championship in 1917.

Even more significant than his impressive record of wins and losses was the level of innovation that he introduced into college football. Heisman hardly looked the part of a football player or coach. Short and bespectacled, he appeared more professorial than athletic. Highly intelligent and imaginative, he was an outstanding student and later an accomplished Shakespearean actor who spent his off-seasons on the stage. He often brought that sense of drama into the locker room and became noted for the "stage English" he employed in pep talks.

Heisman wanted to make football more intellectual and less brutish. In that he succeeded well. He was a strong advocate of the forward pass and lobbied hard, and successfully, to have it legalized. He knew that passing would force some of the defenders back away from the line and open up the running game, making plays dependent more on tactics and execution and less on two piles of bodies smashing into each other.

Other Heisman innovations included the center snap, a vocal hike signal from the quarterback, posting the down and yardage on the scoreboard, playing the quarterback at safety on defense (at a time when the same individuals played both offense and defense), and the hidden-ball play. During this trick play, the backs would perform several fakes, one of them ending up with the ball tucked under his jersey. The play was almost impossible to defend and, not surprisingly, was eventually outlawed.

Ironically, it was in retirement that Heisman played the role for which he is best remembered. In 1930 he accepted the position of athletics director at the new Downtown Athletic Club in New York City. Willard Prince, a club executive, pushed to have the Athletic Club present an annual award to college's finest football player, which Heisman, believing that teamwork rather than individual accomplishments should be honored, initially opposed. Nonetheless, the award was instituted in 1935 (in that first year actually honoring the best player east of the Mississippi River).

Prince had wanted to name the award after Heisman, but the athletics director adamantly refused. However, after Heisman died of bronchial pneumonia on October 3, 1936, the club renamed the award The Heisman Memorial Trophy Award. Ever since, the Heisman Trophy has been the most coveted college football individual award. Many of its recipients may know nothing about the man after whom it was named, but the game as it is today owes much to John Heisman, Shakespearean actor and coach extraordinaire.

See also: Downtown Athletic Club; Forward Pass; Heisman Trophy.

Additional Reading:

Heisman, John W. *Principles of Football.* 1922. Athens GA: Hill Street Press, 2000.

Umphlett, Wiley Lee. *Creating the Big Game: John W. Heisman and the Invention of American Football.* Westport CT: Greenwood Press, 1992.

Heisman Trophy

The Heisman Trophy is given annually to the individual chosen as the nation's best college football player. The award, named after legendary coach John Heisman, was the brainchild of Willard B. Prince, an executive with the Downtown Athletic Club of New York City, the organization that originated the Heisman in 1935 and continued to award it through the Heisman Trophy Trust.

The trophy was designed by Frank Eliscu, who had a friend of his, Ed Smith, a running back for the New York University football team, pose while Eliscu created a clay model. Eliscu later modified his statue based on conversations with Jim Crowley, a former member of Notre Dame's Four Horsemen and at the time coach at Fordham University, and some of Crowley's players who said they had difficulty assuming the pose that Eliscu had initially sculpted.

The final trophy, in bronze, depicts a halfback in motion holding the football with his left arm and stretching out his right to stiff-arm an invisible would-be tackler. The halfback appears to be cutting sharply, his right leg forward, left leg stretched backward. The sculpture is one of the most famous sports trophies. Heisman aspirants are well aware of its details, as evidenced by the public posturing of Desmond Howard, a former wide receiver for the University of Michigan. Howard earned considerable attention, undoubtedly his objective, when he struck a Heisman pose (although with reverse use of his arms) after scoring a touchdown against Ohio State during the 1991 season. Howard proved prophetic when he subsequently was awarded the Heisman.

Jay Berwanger, a halfback at the University of Chicago, was the first recipient, in 1935. That first year the award was given to the best player east of the Mississippi River, but the next year the selection process was extended to the whole nation, with the Heisman going to Yale end Larry Kelley. As of 2007 the only two-time winner of the Heisman remains Ohio State running back Archie Griffin (1974–75). However, Florida quarterback Tim Tebow in 2007 became the first sophomore to win the award, giving him a good chance to join Griffin in that elite class.

The most memorable acceptance speech probably was given by Penn State tailback John Cappelletti in 1973. In the audience was Cappelletti's younger brother, Joseph, terminally ill with leukemia. Tears rolling down his face, the Heisman recipient dedicated the trophy to his brother, noting that Joseph had to fight his battle every day, not just on Saturdays in the fall, and that his younger brother had been a great inspiration to him. Bishop Fulton J. Sheen was scheduled to give a benediction after Cappelletti's speech but instead rose to announce that a blessing was unnecessary, that God had already blessed everyone in attendance through John Cappelletti. Approximately two and a half years later, Joseph Cappelletti died.

One of the more entertaining presentation speeches was Attorney General Robert F. Kennedy's in 1962. A football player at Harvard in 1947, Kennedy joked that when he received his letter from the Heisman Award Committee he first thought that the letter had been delayed in the mail for fifteen years. He added that a Yale player whose name started with "K," Larry Kelley, had once won, and that a "K" from Princeton, Dick Kazmaier,

had been selected, but that the Harvard contingent was still waiting for its own "K"—with a Kennedy obviously willing to fill the gap. Kennedy finally got around to presenting the award to Oregon State's Terry Baker, whose name included but did not start with a "K."

The Heisman Trophy Trust selects the recipient through a national election. Six Sectional Representatives appoint State Representatives, who select voters within in their state, the number of state voters depending on the size of the state and the number of its media outlets. Each of the six sections of the country has 145 media votes. In addition, each former Heisman Trophy recipient is eligible to vote. There also is a provision for the public to express its preference, although the public has just one collective vote out of, for example, the 923 votes provided for in the 2005 balloting. Voters indicate first, second, and third choices on their ballot, a point system having been developed to lessen the possibility of a particular section dominating the vote.

Although the Downtown Athletic Club did not reopen its building after it was damaged by the terrorist attacks of September 11, 2001, the organization continued to give the award through the Heisman Trophy Trust. The new physical home for the Heisman, the Sports Museum of America, opened in 2008 a few blocks from the Statue of Liberty. College football once had its own statue of liberty play, but the greater relevance may be that college football continues to be played by descendants of people who arrived at Ellis Island from a variety of distant locations, carrying with them their own dreams. Whatever the origin of a player's family, however, it is good for Heisman Trophy winners, as for everyone, to keep in mind the freedom and the responsibility symbolized by the tall lady holding aloft her lamp.

See also: Downtown Athletic Club; Four Horsemen of Notre Dame; Hayes, Wayne Woodrow; Heisman, John William.

Additional Reading:
Heisman Trophy Web site. http://www.heisman.com.
Pennington, Bill. *The Heisman: Great American Stories of the Men Who Won.* New York: ReganBooks, 2004.
Whittingham, Richard. *Rites of Autumn: The Story of College Football.* New York: The Free Press, 2001.

Hirsch, Elroy Leon (Crazylegs) (1923–2004)

Great halfback, outstanding receiver, movie actor, athletics director at a leading university: all by a person named Crazylegs. It is unlikely that anyone would take seriously today a person named Crazylegs, but everyone, especially opposing defenses, took Elroy Hirsch very seriously indeed.

Elroy Hirsch got his nickname from his unusual style of running, with his left foot seeming to point to the side. The gait gave him a sense of wobbling while he ran, but it did not hurt his speed or cutting ability. Hirsch came to prominence as a running back at the University of Wisconsin. After he broke off a 62-yard touchdown run against the Great Lakes Naval Training Center team in 1942, Chicago *Daily News* sportswriter Francis Powers bestowed on him the name that he would carry for the rest of his life.

With his country engaged in World War II, Hirsch signed up with the United States Navy v-12 program. That required his transfer to the University of Michigan, where the navy program was located. At Michigan in 1943 he lettered in football, baseball, basketball, and track, the first Wolverine ever to earn letters in four sports. While fulfilling his military obligation, he also played with the El Toro Marine team in 1945.

The war over, Hirsch scored two touchdowns in the 1946 College All-Star Game as the collegians defeated the Washington Redskins 16–0. He then joined the Chicago Rockets of the All-America Football Conference and spent three unhappy, injury-plagued seasons with the new league. After completing his Rockets contract, he joined the Los Angeles Rams of the National Football League as a halfback in 1949. Los Angeles coach Clark Shaughnessy recognized Hirsch's explosiveness as a pass catcher and flanked him out to the side, making him the first full-time flanker. The decision turned Hirsch's career around and enabled him to become the most exciting receiver of his time.

Hirsch's greatest season was 1951, and his signature game was the contest against the Chicago Bears that year. The coach was Joe Stydahar, who had replaced Shaughnessy in 1950. Down 14–0, the Rams had the ball on their own 9-yard line. Quarterback Bob Waterfield threw a deep pass. Hirsch caught it and went the rest of the way for a tide-turning 91-yard touchdown. The Rams went on to demolish the Bears 42–17. The Rams won the NFL title that year, defeating the mighty Cleveland Browns 24–17. Crazylegs caught sixty-six passes for 1,495 yards, an average of 22.7 yards per reception, and scored seventeen touchdowns, six on plays of 70 yards or more. He teamed with another Hall of Famer, the great possession receiver Tom Fears, to give the Rams one of the best pairs of receivers ever. He remained an effective receiver until the very end of his career, which came after the 1957 season. Hirsch was inducted into the Pro Football Hall of Fame in 1968 and the College Football Hall of Fame in 1974.

Hirsch's good looks and gridiron-generated fame led him into the movie business while he was still playing for the Rams. So popular was he throughout the nation, and especially in Los Angeles (Hollywood country), that Republic Pictures made a film, *Crazylegs* (1953), about his life. And who better to play the lead than Crazylegs himself? The film included actual footage from some of his college and professional games and stressed the theme of an athlete battling to overcome injuries and ultimately achieving stardom.

Other films followed. Hirsch played the lead in *Unchained* (1955), based on a book by real-life prison supervisor Kenyon Scudder. The football star appears as inmate Steve Davitt, who must decide whether to attempt an escape or put his family first and complete his sentence. Most of the scenes were shot at Chino Prison. Today the most recognizable performer probably would be Barbara Hale, who played secretary Della Street on the *Perry Mason* television series. The film also is memorable for having given the world the song "Unchained Melody," composed by Alex North.

Hirsch continued his acting in the film *Zero Hour* (1957), playing an airline pilot along with an all-star cast of Hollywood favorites, including Dana Andrews, Linda Darnell, and Sterling Hayden. The film later inspired *Airplane!* (1980), a parody of airplane disaster films that closely follows *Zero Hour*.

Hirsch's long-term career, however, did not lie in acting but in sports administration. He became athletics director at the University of Wisconsin in 1969 and held the post until retiring in 1987. The position brought him back full circle to the state where he was born and the university where he first achieved football fame. Annually, new generations of athletes are able to try out their own "Crazylegs" in an eight-kilometer race through downtown Madison named after the football great: the Crazylegs Classic.

See also: Films; World War II.

Additional Reading/Viewing:

Crazylegs. Dir. Francis D. Lyon. Republic, 1953.

Hession, Joseph. *Rams: Five Decades of Football.* San Francisco: Foghorn Press, 1987.

Hnida, Katharine Anne (Katie) (b. 1981)

Katie Hnida was an outstanding kicker at Chatfield High School in Littleton, Colorado, making honorable mention All–Jefferson County as a senior in 1999. She also was a letter winner in track and homecoming queen, in the latter role participating in halftime ceremonies wearing her football uniform. Hnida was named Colorado Sportswoman of the Year during her senior year and selected by the magazine *Teen People* as one of the twenty most influential teenagers in the country. Her final high school year was marked by the tragic shootings at nearby Columbine High, with the Columbine students completing their academic year at Chatfield.

Hnida was invited by Coach Rick Neuheisel to walk on at the University of Colorado, but shortly thereafter Neuheisel left for the University of Washington and was replaced by Gary Barnett. Hnida therefore began her football career playing for a coach who had not been involved in inviting her to join the Colorado football team. Hnida would go on to achieve several important firsts in college football but pay a heavy price to do so. During her freshman year, she became the second female to dress for a Division I game (against Kansas on September 18, 1999) and the first to dress for a bowl game (against Boston College in the Insight .com Bowl on December 31, 1999). Hnida played only one season before Barnett cut her from the team at the end of summer when, ill and facing surgery to have her

tonsils removed, she was unable to compete in a tryout against other kickers he had recruited. After her sophomore year, she withdrew from Colorado and transferred to Santa Barbara City College but did not play football there.

Hnida's love for football, however, had not disappeared. She sent out tapes to eighty Division I programs and accepted an invitation from head football coach Rocky Long of the University of New Mexico to participate in tryouts as a walk-on. She spent three seasons as a member of the Lobos, achieving her second and third firsts for women players. On December 25, 2002, she became the first woman to play in a Division I game when she attempted an extra point in the Las Vegas Bowl against UCLA. The kick unfortunately was blocked. After her history-making appearance, she was interviewed on NBC's *Today*, ABC's *Good Morning America*, CBS's *The Morning Show*, Fox News, ESPN, and CNN. The following year, she became the first woman to score in a Division I game when she converted two extra-point attempts against Texas State on August 30, 2003.

During Hnida's years at New Mexico, she finally spoke about what she had endured at Colorado. According to Hnida, Colorado players had physically, verbally, and sexually harassed her. Teammates, she said, had groped her and called her sexually explicit, obscene names. Even worse, she charged that a teammate, an individual she had previously trusted, had raped her. These accusations came amid a variety of charges and lawsuits against the Colorado football team under Coach Barnett, which included accusations of other rapes and accounts of strippers being hired to entertain football recruits.

A University of Colorado Board of Regents inquiry found that recruits had been enticed with alcohol, drugs, and sex, but stated that officials had not sanctioned these actions. The sex scandal led to the university president and athletics director resigning and institution of major changes in recruiting policies and oversight of the athletics programs. After Barnett lost the last two games of the 2005 season by a combined 100–6 score, his contract was bought out. Ironically, his replacement, Dan Hawkins, had been coach at Willamette University when Liz Heaston kicked two extra points, becoming the first woman to play in a college football game.

Hnida today is no longer directly involved with football. However, she has written a book about her experiences, and her pioneering role in college football is honored by the College Football Hall of Fame, which includes, among its many historic artifacts, Hnida's football uniform and cleats.

A lawsuit against the University of Colorado by two women alleging they were gang-raped at a Colorado football recruiting party continued into 2007. The 10th U.S. Circuit Court of Appeals reinstated their lawsuit on September 6, 2007, saying that the university demonstrated "deliberate indifference" to sexual harassment, and referred the case back to the trial court. In December, the university agreed to settle the suit by paying the two women $2.85 million.

See also: Crime; Sexuality; Women Players.

Additional Reading:
Hnida, Katie. *Still Kicking: My Journey as the First Woman to Play Division 1 College Football*. New York: Scribner, 2006.

Holy Roller

Religious terminology is never far beneath the surface when unusual plays occur in football, especially when they develop near the end of a game and decide the outcome. So when an especially strange play occurred in a San Diego Chargers–Oakland Raiders contest on September 10, 1978, football observers pulled out their religious vocabulary once again.

Oakland had the ball with ten seconds left and trailing 20–14. Quarterback Kenny Stabler attempted to pass but was hit by defensive end Fred Dean. The ball, as it later turned out, was tossed to the ground by Stabler, who knew that being tackled would permit time to run out.

As the ball rolled toward the end zone, Stabler's teammates conspired to keep it moving in the right direction. Running back Pete Banaszak hit the ball forward. Tight end Dave Casper gave it a little kick, propelling the football into the end zone. Then Casper fell on the ball for a tying touchdown as time expired. All that remained to give Oakland the victory was a sure-footed extra point, and Errol Mann delivered, making the final score Oakland 21, San Diego 20. The feigned fumble that kept advancing was dubbed the Holy Roller, although the agents of motion clearly were mere Oakland mortals.

Stabler admitted after the game that he had deliberately fumbled the ball forward. The Oakland machinations would seem to cry out for a foul ruling by the officials, but the sequence of actions violated no rules in place at the time. Still, league officials recognized the schoolyard antics that concluded the game and moved swiftly to guard against any repetition of that sort of "team" effort. The new rule, enacted during the off-season, stipulated that in the final two minutes of a game a fumbled football may be advanced by only the player who fumbled it.

See also: "Hail Mary" Pass; Immaculate Reception; Religion.

Additional Reading:
Stabler, Ken. *Snake*. Garden City NY: Doubleday, 1986.

Hornung, Paul Vernon
(the Golden Boy) (b. 1935)

Paul Hornung, with his many football talents and golden hair, became the darling of football fans at Notre Dame and Green Bay as well as an attractive figure to women throughout the country, a good many of whom he dated. Three seasons after he set the National Football League record for most points scored in a single season, he was suspended for a year for betting on football games but returned to help the Packers to their first Super Bowl and ultimately earn induction into both the college and professional football halls of fame.

Hornung won the Heisman Trophy at Notre Dame after the 1956 season despite one of the worst seasons in Irish football history—just two wins and eight losses. Hornung, however, became the first and still the only player to win the Heisman on a losing team, the result of his finishing second in the country in total offense, second in kickoff returns, fifteenth in passing, and sixteenth in scoring.

The Green Bay Packers selected Hornung as a bonus pick in the 1957 draft. After struggling to find his best position during his first two years (moving among quarterback, fullback, halfback, and tight end), he settled in at halfback once Vince Lombardi joined the Packers in 1959. Under Lombardi, Hornung did just about everything. He ran effectively, complementing fullback Jim Taylor and proving himself almost unstoppable near the goal line. He also caught passes, blocked well, kicked extra points and field goals, and threw the option pass.

Hornung led the National Football League in scoring in 1959, 1960, and 1961, setting the one-season record of 176 points in 1960—a mark not broken until LaDainian Tomlinson scored 186 points for San Diego in 2006. Hornung, who was in the Army Reserves, was called to active duty during the 1961 season but received weekend passes to play on Sundays. It took a phone call from Lombardi to Pres. John Kennedy and the president's personal intervention, however, to free up Hornung to play in the championship game. Despite Hornung's multiple responsibilities that year, he was named the National Football League's Most Valuable Player. During Hornung's years with the Packers (1957–66), they won the NFL championship four times (1961–62 and 1965–66), along with the first Super Bowl, played on January 15, 1967.

Hornung's career, however, was not without its difficulties. An inveterate partygoer, he suffered occasional fines for being out past curfew. More importantly, he was suspended along with Detroit Lions defensive star Alex Karras for the entire 1963 season for betting on football games. He returned in 1964, but injuries curtailed him during his final two seasons with the Packers and prevented his playing in Super Bowl I. After the 1967 season Hornung, much to Coach Lombardi's dismay, was selected by the New Orleans Saints in the expansion draft. A partial dislocation of two vertebrae, however, forced him to retire before playing for the Saints.

After retiring as a player, Hornung went into broadcasting and for many years broadcast Notre Dame games. During a radio interview in March 2004, he said that Notre Dame would have to lower its academic standards and recruit more top African American players if the university wanted to compete successfully in football. Although Hornung had a long history of supporting racial justice, detailed in his book *Golden Boy*, his comments were strongly criticized by Notre Dame and he lost his position broadcasting Irish football games. Hornung's accomplishments, however, remained undimmed, as did his support of Notre Dame, which includes an annual scholarship to Notre Dame for a student from the Louisville area.

See also: Gambling; Heisman Trophy; Lombardi, Vincent Thomas; Sexuality; Super Bowl; Tomlinson, LaDainian.

Additional Reading:
Hornung, Paul. *Football and the Single Man.* As told to Al Silverman. Garden City NY: Doubleday, 1965.
———. *Golden Boy.* As told to William F. Reed. New York: Simon and Schuster, 2004.
———. *Lombardi and Me: Players, Coaches, and Colleagues Talk about the Man and the Myth.* With Billy Reed. Chicago: Triumph Books, 2006.

Hudson, Donald Edward (b. 1929)

Sometimes what people think is history really is not, but it is never too late to get the facts straight. That proved true again in 2007 when it came to light through the efforts of Donald Hudson's son-in-law, Eric Parris, and Macalester College that the first African American football coach at a predominately white college in the modern era was neither Ron Stratten at Portland State in March 1972 nor Cass Jackson at Oberlin College in 1973 but Don Hudson. Hudson became head football coach at Macalester College in St. Paul, Minnesota, during December 1971.

The first black football coach ever at a primarily white college apparently was Matthew Washington Bullock, who coached at Massachusetts Agricultural College in 1904. The Agricultural College now is known as the University of Massachusetts.

Hudson served his apprenticeship at Lincoln University in Missouri, at Central High School in Minneapolis, and as an assistant at Macalester. At Central High and after being named head coach at Macalester, Hudson faced the same problem, losing most of his assistant coaches. Some quit after being passed over for the head coaching positions, but Hudson thought others likely quit at least partly for racial reasons.

Macalester posed challenges apart from racial issues. The college was (and remains) proud of its academic commitment and considered football useful but clearly subsidiary to academics. Hudson learned to accept his players missing practices in favor of classes. He regularly had to make do with a modest roster size of about thirty players. The team consisted of true scholar-athletes, but wins on the football field were elusive.

Macalester won only three games against thirty-six losses during Hudson's four seasons heading the football program (1972–75). He then returned to his alma mater, Lincoln University, as football coach. Eventually he moved to Colorado and served as the athletics director of a school system there.

Throughout the years, Hudson's former Macalester players remembered their coach with respect and affection even if history overlooked him. Finally,

Hudson got his due recognition. Part of that recognition came during halftime of a Macalester football game in 2007 when he was honored for writing that long-neglected chapter in the history of college football.

See also: African Americans (College).

Additional Reading:
"Macalester Honors First African American Football Coach at a Predominately White College." Macalester College Web site. http://www.macalester.edu/athletics/athletic _news/07_1001_don_hudson_day.html.
Weiner, Jay. "A Sports Writer Corrects a Mistake." *Chronicle of Higher Education*, November 23, 2007, B5.

Hypertrophic Cardiomyopathy

Hypertrophic cardiomyopathy (HCM) is a secret and silent killer, especially of young athletes. HCM is a genetic disorder in which the walls of the left ventricle of the heart become enlarged, although the chamber itself does not increase in size. The ventricle therefore does not properly relax, resulting in a decreased blood flow into the heart. In addition to the thickening of the ventricle wall, the cells in the ventricle walls do not arrange uniformly, so an electrical signal can take an erratic path, causing a fatal disruption in the heart's normal flexing and contracting.

Each year, approximately six thousand people, most of them in their teens or twenties, die of HCM. The disease is the most common cause of sudden death in young athletes. Every two weeks on the average, a young athlete dies of HCM immediately after or during strenuous exercise. The exercise imposes sufficient stress on the heart with its enlarged ventricle walls to cause fatal arrhythmia. Often the athlete has experienced no prior symptoms and is unaware of family members who may have suffered from the same heart defect.

Thomas Herrion, an offensive lineman with the San Francisco 49ers, collapsed and died in the locker room shortly after a preseason game in Denver on August 20, 2005. Herrion had been popular with teammates and coaches at both the University of Utah and San Francisco, who praised him for being consistently positive. Friends and family members noted that Herrion did not smoke, drink, or use drugs, and he apparently had passed five physicals within two years of his death.

Most athletes who die of HCM are not as well known as Herrion and do not receive the same level of press coverage. In fact, few come to the attention of the nation at all. Most are like a high school graduate named DeCarlo Polk, who collapsed and died while playing a pickup game of basketball on June 27, 2007, and, were it not for an article in *Sports Illustrated*, would have been mourned only by those family and friends who knew him personally.

Polk was a seventeen-year-old, 237-pound football player at Hillside High School in Durham, North Carolina, where he had been an honor student as well as an outstanding defensive lineman. He had looked forward to attending St. Augustine's College, which had given him a football scholarship.

Had Polk's and Herrion's condition been diagnosed, football might have been gone but they probably could have lived long and happy lives, perhaps with an implanted cardioverter-defibrillator. Diagnosis, however, is difficult. If there are symptoms, such as shortness of breath or fatigue, they can easily be incorrectly associated with asthma, and using an asthma inhaler with HCM can cause fatal irregular heartbeats. One invaluable approach is to study family history for signs of the disease in a relative. That simple step can lead to the sort of testing that can correctly diagnose HCM and save lives.

Additional Reading:

Corbett, Jim. "49ers Reel from Untimely Death." USA *Today Sports Weekly*, August 24–30, 2005, 66.

Epstein, David. "Following the Trail of Broken Hearts." *Sports Illustrated*, December 10, 2007, 90–98.

Hypertrophic Cardiomyopathy Association Web site. http://www.4hcm.org/WCMS/index.php.

Maron, Barry J., and Lisa Salberg. *Hypertrophic Cardiomyopathy: For Patients, Their Families, and Interested Physicians*. 2nd ed. Malden MA: Blackwell, 2006.

Ice Bowl

The Ice Bowl is one of the most memorable National Football League games and certainly one of the most aptly named. The more official designation is the NFL Championship Game between the Green Bay Packers and Dallas Cowboys. The two teams met in Green Bay on December 31, 1967, to determine which team would represent the NFL in Super Bowl II.

At the kickoff, the temperature was minus thirteen degrees with a wind chill of minus forty-six. The general assumption was that the extreme weather would hurt the warm-weather Dallas Cowboys a lot more than the Packers. For a time, that seemed to be holding true.

Green Bay scored a touchdown on its first possession with quarterback Bart Starr leading a drive of 80 yards and throwing to Boyd Dowler for the score. Again in the second quarter, Starr hit Dowler for a touchdown, and the score stood at 14–0.

With four minutes remaining in the first half, however, the tide turned. Starr dropped back to pass, was rushed, retreated farther, was hit, and fumbled. Dallas's George Andrie picked up the ball and carried it into the end zone for a touchdown, cutting the Green Bay lead in half. With two minutes remaining, Willie Wood fumbled a punt, only the second punt he had fumbled in eight seasons. The Dallas recovery led to a field goal, making the score 14–10 at halftime.

Throughout the third quarter and most of the fourth, Dallas dominated, looking far more than Green Bay like a team accustomed to frigid weather. With the temperature dropping even farther, line judge Bill Schliebaum had his whistle freeze to his lips and lost some skin pulling it loose. Jim Huxford, who helped move the chains, had his ski mask freeze to his mouth. Huxford, recovering from a heart attack and increasingly feeling the tension of the game as well as the cold, later required medical assistance from the Packers' team physician, Dr. Eugene Brusky, who administered a nitroglycerin pill.

Reporters found their typewriters freezing to the wooden ledge in the press box. Ray Scott, broadcasting the game for CBS, insisted on having a window open so that he could get a real feel for the game. One of his broadcasting partners, Frank Gifford, got off one of the great cold-weather lines of all time when he remarked, "I think I'll take another bite of my coffee."

Meanwhile, Dallas was threatening to score but falling short. On the first play of the fourth quarter, however, the Cowboys broke through on an option pass from Dan Reeves to Lance Rentzel for the go-ahead touchdown. The Cowboys led 17–14.

Twice in the final quarter, Green Bay had the ball but could not score. Then, with just under five minutes to go, the Packers had what probably would be their final chance. Willie Wood cradled a punt, determined not to muff this one, and returned it to the 32-yard line. The Packers huddled, and Starr said, simply, "This is it. We're going in." His teammates later said that his calm confidence convinced them that this time they were going to score. And they did, Starr leading his troops downfield, dumping off short passes to halfback Donnie Anderson, handing off to fullback Chuck Mercein. A great catch by Mercein took the ball to the Dallas 11. Mercein ran for 8 more yards, stumbling on the icy turf into one of his own linemen, Forrest Gregg, and going down at the 3. Two more running plays put the ball just 1 yard away from a touchdown.

It was now third down with sixteen seconds remaining and no more Green Bay timeouts. A pass play seemed the safest call because an incompletion would at least stop the clock. A field goal would tie the game, but even at such a short distance a kick was chancy. The holder could drop the ball, or the kicker might slip on the frozen field. Starr went to the sideline to confer with Vince Lombardi, who was coaching his final season at Green Bay. Starr thought that a wedge play with the fullback going in behind guard Jerry Kramer and center Ken Bowman would

work. If it did not, however, time probably would run out before the field-goal unit could get onto the field. Lombardi agreed with his quarterback. He had been preaching "Run to win," a quote from St. Paul, to his team, and now was the time to do it.

Starr called the play in the huddle: "Brown right, 31 wedge." At the snap, Mercein moved forward to take the handoff, but Starr was not there. Starr had second thoughts at the line of scrimmage. He worried that Mercein might slip and never make it to the goal line, and he remembered successfully improvising a quarterback sneak the year before. A quarterback sneak was so rare for the Packers that they did not even have it in their playbook. Yet, Starr made his decision. With the rest of the team expecting a handoff, Starr kept the ball and followed Kramer and Bowman. The touchdown and extra kick gave Green Bay the victory, 21–17, and sent them on to a second consecutive Super Bowl victory. Vince Lombardi had one more championship to close out his legendary run as Green Bay's coach.

Few plays have been rerun more often over the years than Bart Starr's sneak into the end zone. The game was important regardless of the weather because it decided the NFL championship. However, it was the weather even more than the championship drama that immortalized the contest.

See also: Gifford, Frank Newton; Hornung, Paul Vernon; Landry, Thomas Wade; Lombardi, Vincent Thomas.

Additional Reading:

Kramer, Jerry. *Instant Replay: The Green Bay Diary of Jerry Kramer.* Ed. Dick Schaap. New York: World Publishing Company, 1968.

Maraniss, David. *When Pride Still Mattered: A Life of Vince Lombardi.* New York: Simon and Schuster, 1999.

Immaculate Reception

In the realm of football, any occurrence that transcends the norm is susceptible to being interpreted as if it were a matter of divine intervention. Most football announcers, players, and fans probably do not actually believe that deities intervene to ensure a completed pass, successful block, or sure tackle, but they often talk that way.

The pass completion routinely referred to as the Immaculate Reception is a case in point. The name borders on bad taste if not disrespect, although most who use the term probably do not understand precisely what religious concept it verbally parodies. The Immaculate Conception refers to the belief that Mary, mother of Jesus, was born without original sin, hence that she was conceived immaculately, or, in terms of sin, spotlessly.

The analogy is that this particular pass was caught without being touched by an inappropriate hand, or something like that. The reality is that the sound of the phrase "the immaculate reception," along with some vague understanding that the term refers to something religious, is probably what led to its use rather than any clearly intended theological parallels.

The incident occurred in the December 23, 1972, playoff game between the Pittsburgh Steelers and Oakland Raiders. Pittsburgh trailed 7–6 and had the ball fourth-and-ten on its own 40-yard line with twenty-two seconds left in the game. The situation was desperate, and Terry Bradshaw dropped back to pass. Under a heavy pass rush, he moved right, saw John Fuqua, and threw in his direction. The intended receiver and Oakland defender Jack Tatum converged, and somehow the ball popped up out of the collision. Rookie running back Franco Harris, following the play, grabbed the ball out of the air and headed for the Oakland end zone.

The touchdown gave Pittsburgh the lead, but was it a touchdown? That depended on whether Fuqua had touched the ball. Rules in effect at the time required a defensive player to touch the ball between touches by offensive players in order for the touchdown to count. Officials, apparently not able to tell for sure whether Fuqua had made contact, ruled a touchdown. The ensuing extra point put the Steelers up 13–7 with five seconds left.

The playoff victory was the first ever for Pittsburgh. Although the team did not advance farther in 1972, Super Bowl victories would come after the 1974, 1975, 1978, and 1979 seasons as Bradshaw, Harris, and teammates established one of the greatest NFL teams in history. And it all started with that Immaculate Reception, which really did not have anything to do with deities real or imagined, but had a lot to do with a quick-thinking running back.

See also: Bradshaw, Terry Paxton; "Hail Mary" Pass; Holy Roller; Religion; Super Bowl.

Additional Reading:

Fitzgerald, Francis J., ed. *Greatest Moments in Pittsburgh Steelers History*. Louisville: Adcraft, 1996.

Mendelson, Abby. *The Pittsburgh Steelers: The Official Team History*. 3rd ed. Lanham MD: Taylor Trade Publishing, 2006.

Instant Replay

Did we make the right decision, or was it a terrible mistake? What could we have done differently? What exactly did happen, and how did it occur? Can we rectify that error and get it right next time? How nice it would be if we could answer these questions definitively and make things right.

One of the nation's most beloved films, *It's a Wonderful Life* (1946), raises some of these questions as George Bailey, played by Jimmy Stewart, laments his supposed failures and thinks that it might have been better if he had never been born. An angel hears and arrives to cure George's anguish by showing him an instant replay of what would have happened had he never existed.

It is a wonderful fantasy, but in sports we can really do something along these lines, thanks to instant replay. Before sports officials and fans had access to instant replay, Jerry Kramer, the great Green Bay Packers guard, entitled his diary of the 1967 season *Instant Replay*, after the practice of television networks showing the same play again in newscasts. Now football offers instant replay on a regular basis during games.

The process of checking officials' initial rulings was controversial, as football officials worried about undermining referees and slowing down games. The National Football League experimented with instant replay on a limited basis from 1986 through the 1991 season and again during 1996 and 1998 preseason play. It was approved for the 1999 season, extended for 2000, continued through 2003, approved for an additional five years in 2004, and then made permanent in March 2007.

Many, but not all, plays are reviewable under the NFL system. Essentially, anything that involves the sidelines, goal line, end zone, or end line may be reviewed. Passing plays and a variety of other situations, such as whether a runner is down by defensive contact and determination of forward progress, also are subject to review. Most penalties are not included in the system.

The head coach may challenge two calls during the game so long as he has a timeout left. If he challenges, and the call remains unchanged, his team loses a timeout. If both challenges result in plays being overturned, he is permitted to make a third challenge. During the final two minutes of each half and in overtime, however, only a replay assistant may issue a challenge. The replay assistant monitors each play and informs the referee if a play should be reviewed. Regardless of the source of the challenge, the referee reviews the play by watching it replayed on a field-level monitor. The NFL requires "indisputable visual evidence" for the play to be overturned.

The NFL improved its instant-replay capabilities for the 2007 season, substituting high-definition technology for its previous standard-definition system. The high-definition images are considered about five times sharper than the previous technology, enabling the referee to review plays more accurately and quickly.

Since 1999, the number of challenges has gradually increased from 195 reviewed plays in the first year to 311 in 2006. Similarly, the reversals have increased, from 57 to 107. The effect of this increase in reversed calls is to increase the likelihood that the team that deserves to win the game actually does win it. The desire to "get it right" has largely overcome initial concerns about the process.

Colleges were slower to move into instant replay, beginning their experimentation during the 2004 season in Big 10 games. All conferences were permitted to use instant replay for the 2005 season, and most did so. It was also used that year for all bowl games and championship playoff games in Divisions I-AA, II, and III.

The college system is similar to the NFL's in types of plays that may be reviewed. However, rather than challenges from a coach, a replay official monitors every play and determines which ones should be reviewed. The head coach may call a timeout and challenge one ruling per game, losing the timeout if the previous call is not reversed.

The Canadian Football League follows a system similar to that used by the NFL, although differences in game rules require some adjustments. CFL teams have only one timeout per half, so the first challenge, even if unsuccessful, does not cost the team a timeout. A replay official replaces the coach as the person initiating a review during the final three minutes of each half because the CFL issues a three-minute warning.

So football has caught up with George Bailey, and, if the game cannot be viewed as exactly a wonderful life, at least the outcome will be less likely to hinge on a missed call.

See also: Canadian Football League; Television Broadcasting.

Additional Reading:

Kramer, Jerry. Instant Replay: The Green Bay Diary of Jerry Kramer. Ed. Dick Schaap. New York: World Publishing Company, 1968.
NFL Communications Department and Seymour Siwoff (Elias Sports Bureau), eds. Official 2007 National Football League Record & Fact Book. New York: National Football League/Time Inc. Home Entertainment, 2007.

Internet

Football has moved firmly into the Internet world with a multitude of useful sites available for casual fan and serious scholar alike. It is now common for high schools to have their own Web sites, which typically feature a link to the school's athletics program. In some cases the football fan will find little more than the schedule of games; on many other sites, however, there will be in-depth information about the team's past records, top players, and other matters.

The National Football League sponsors its own site dedicated to high school football, www.nflhs.com, which includes news from high school programs throughout the country. Included is information related to academics, fitness, and ways to improve one's play. The Web site also offers stories about current professional players' high school experiences; for example, a video posted for downloading in August 2007 featured Brett Favre.

Every college and university in the United States must have its own Web site by now as an important part of its recruiting efforts. The areas of college life highlighted always include athletics. If the school has a football program, information will be available regarding the current season, and in many cases archived articles and press releases from past seasons can be accessed. Fans are able to follow their favorite team's fortunes online and often are able to read weekly comments by the coach, updates on individual players, and previews of future games.

The National Football Foundation's College Football Hall of Fame site (www.collegefootball.org) is a must for fans of college football. There is practical information for anyone planning a trip to the Hall of Fame, located in South Bend, Indiana, but also biographical and statistical information on every person who has been inducted into the Hall. News about Hall-related activities is posted, and archived articles are available.

For professional football, the NFL and the Pro Football Hall of Fame offer two outstanding Web sites. First, www.nfl.com provides extensive history of the NFL along with information relating to fantasy football, the media, current player situations, and other matters. The history-minded reader may explore NFL legends, team histories, records, past drafts, and Super Bowls, among other topics. Current scores, of course, are included, as are analyses by sports journalists. Links abound, including one to the Pro Football Hall of Fame.

The Pro Football Hall of Fame site (www.profootballhof.com) is of tremendous value to anyone interested in pro football history and information about the inductees. The site includes biographical information on each member of the Hall, and the History Index offers stories on many matters great and small. Anyone planning a trip to Canton, Ohio, can find the obvious information about hours and ticket prices but also will get more out of the visit by surfing the site beforehand to become familiar with some of the items that are available for viewing.

Other sites also are of considerable use to the serious student of football. For example, the Professional Football Researchers Association sponsors a particularly helpful site (www.footballresearch.com/index.cfm). Its most valuable dimension may be the archive of articles, many of which explore aspects of football history not examined in-depth anywhere else.

Each NFL team has a Web site, and these also are rich in information. The site of the Green Bay Packers, www.packers.com, to cite just one example, includes a detailed history of the franchise as well as a briefer chronological listing of significant events in Packers history. There is information about Lambeau Field, a pro shop where people may order Packers-related items, and up-to-the-minute news on the Packers, especially from the pre-season through the final game of the year. Other NFL sites are similar in content.

Team sites, as would be expected, tend to be as upbeat as possible about their teams. Anyone wishing for a more objective analysis of a team is more likely to get that in sites run by organizations independent of the NFL. Sports publications such as *Sporting News* and *Sports Illustrated* offer Web supplements (www.sportingnews.com/index.html; sports illustrated.cnn.com) that usually include information about professional, college, and, to some extent, high school football not in the print publication. Newspapers and television networks also offer online versions that usually include stories unique to the Web sites.

The sites mentioned here comprise a mere sampling of what is available to anyone interested in football. With increasing numbers of people turning to online sources for most of their news, such sites will continue to grow in importance.

See also: Hall of Fame (College); Hall of Fame (Professional); Magazines.

Additional Reading:
See the sites mentioned above as well as other Internet sites referenced throughout this book.

Ivy League

Is it just a fantasy? Football players who excel academically while choosing challenging majors and taking the same courses that other students take, truly justifying the "scholar-athlete" designation. Players who play for the love of the game, not because they are receiving athletic scholarships to play and not because they will receive postseason television exposure—because they will not. Yet playing well enough so although usually shut out of serious All-American and Heisman consideration, they still have a shot at the National Football League.

Maybe it is a fantasy, but there is another option. We could be talking about the Ivy League. The Ivy League consists of eight outstanding academic institutions: Brown, Columbia, Cornell, Dartmouth, Harvard, Pennsylvania, Princeton, and Yale. They also encourage athletics because a healthy body is part of a complete person and school sports can improve school spirit.

However, it was not always thus. Once upon a time, before there was an Ivy League, some of these institutions were not only important in the early development of football but also football powerhouses. What is usually considered the first American football game featured one of these schools, Princeton, defeating Rutgers 6–4 on November 6, 1869. Perhaps no school was more instrumental in the evolution of nineteenth-century football than Yale, thanks especially to Walter Camp, who played and coached for Yale, served on the Rules Committee from 1879 until 1925, helped bring about enormous change in the game, and is considered the father of American football.

Some of the most magical names in football history come from the institutions that later comprised the Ivy League, including Walter Camp, Amos Alonzo Stagg, Pop Warner, and John Heisman. Fritz Pollard starred at Brown in the second decade of the twentieth century, becoming the first African American to play in the Rose Bowl and later the first African American NFL coach.

By the end of the Roaring Twenties, Yale had won eighteen national championships in football and Princeton fifteen, while Harvard had registered forty-two consecutive winning seasons from 1881 to 1923. Yale compiled one of the most unbelievable seasons in football history in 1888 when it not only won all of its thirteen games but also outscored its opponents 698–0, one of eleven seasons in which Yale did not allow a single point. In the 1930s, Princeton put together a remarkable three-year 25-1 run with two more national championships.

Yet it is only proper to point out that during much of this early football, these Eastern powerhouses were no more pure and honorable than many other football programs across the country. However, unlike many other football institutions, these schools came to recognize that academic excellence and national football achievement often clash. They also determined that football should be part of the whole but integrated into the whole and consistent with a principle once dear to most university hearts, that of the football player as a true amateur.

In 1945 the eight universities entered into the Ivy League Agreement, which included a provision that would establish a fundamental difference between their approach to football and that of the remaining major football powers: no athletic scholarships. The eight instituted a ban on postseason play in 1952, perhaps concluding that students should be focusing more on final exams than preparing for another football game. The renewal of the Ivy League Agreement in 1954 with the stipulation that the eight teams would play each other annually (plus the extension of a similar philosophy to all of their sports programs) formalized the Ivy League.

It took a while for the difference to sink in. When Yale went undefeated in 1960, it was ranked fourteenth in the final Associated Press poll. Ten years later, Dartmouth won all of its games, finished fourteenth nationally, and beat out Penn State for the Lambert Trophy, given annually to the best football team in the East.

Yet as the rest of the football world began to discount Ivy League football, the schools continued playing good football and producing good football players. As Bruce Wood points out in his essay "The Roots of the Game," all Ivy League schools were represented on NFL rosters in 2003. Among players who have moved in recent years from the Ivy League to the NFL is Jay Fiedler, who came out of Dartmouth to become the Miami Dolphins' starting quarterback from 2000 to 2004. Reggie Williams—a Dartmouth graduate and in the 1970s the last Ivy League player to be named All-American, as well as a four-teen-year linebacker with the Cincinnati Bengals—was inducted into the College Football Hall of Fame in 2007. The big man on campus at Princeton or Yale may no longer be the star football player, but he may well be a well-rounded individual who also plays football.

See also: Camp, Walter Chauncey; Education; Heisman, John William; Pollard, Frederick Douglass; Stagg, Amos Alonzo; Warner, Glen Scobey; World War I.

Additional Reading:

Bernstein, Mark F. *Football: The Ivy League Origins of an American Obsession.* Philadelphia: University of Pennsylvania Press, 2001.

Lincoln, Chris. *Playing the Game: Inside Athletic Recruiting in the Ivy League.* White River Junction VT: Nomad, 2004.

McCallum, John Dennis. *Ivy League Football Since 1872.* New York: Stein and Day, 1977.

Wood, Bruce. "The Roots of the Game: The Resilient Glory of Ivy League Football." In ESPN *College Football Encyclopedia: The Complete History of the Game.* Ed. Michael MacCambridge, 1032–35. New York: ESPN Books, 2005.

Jackson, Vincent Edward (Bo) (b. 1962)
"Bo Knows" was a popular advertising campaign for a Nike athletic shoe in 1989 and 1990. The slogan played off Bo Jackson's genuine expertise in a number of sports by exaggerating the already extensive number of sports in which he excelled.

Jackson starred at Auburn in any sport he attempted, and he attempted several. He was a standout baseball player, hitting as high as .401. On the track team, he ran the 100 meters in 10.4 seconds. In football, he became arguably the best player in the land, winning the Heisman Trophy as a senior and also being named the country's best football player by the Walter Camp Foundation, the *Sporting News*, and United Press International. He was big, strong, and lightning fast, qualities that helped earn him the childhood nickname "the wild boar," later shortened to "Bo."

The New York Yankees drafted Jackson in the second round of the baseball draft in 1982, but he declined in favor of a football scholarship to Auburn. There, he recorded a remarkable rushing average of 7.7 yards per carry as a sophomore in 1983. In his senior year, 1985, he rushed for 1,786 yards.

Both major league baseball and the National Football League wanted Jackson.

The Tampa Bay Buccaneers made him the first pick in the 1986 NFL draft, but he chose baseball and the Kansas City Royals. He reached the majors that year and made the All-Star team in 1989 when he hit thirty-two home runs and recorded 105 runs batted in. He also stole twenty-six bases and demonstrated great speed and a powerful throwing arm in the outfield.

Although baseball seemed to be Jackson's primary love, he also wanted to play football, and when Al Davis, owner of the Oakland Raiders, offered him the opportunity to do both, Jackson signed on. In 1987 he rushed for 554 yards in just seven games for Oakland, averaging 6.8 yards per carry. Splitting time between baseball and the NFL limited his football statistics, but he still managed to gain as many as 950 yards rushing in a season (1989) and average 5.4 yards per carry through his abbreviated four-year career. That career included All-Pro selections in 1989 and 1990, making him the only athlete to be an All-Star in two major sports.

During a postseason game against the Cincinnati Bengals in 1990, Bo Jackson's football career came to an end and his baseball career was sharply curtailed by an injury. Jackson's hip was injured when he was tackled. Surgery was required, and afterward doctors discovered that he had avascular necrosis, a deterioration of the hip occasioned by insufficient blood supply. He never played football again and missed most of the 1991 baseball season and all of 1992. He returned in 1993 to play two final seasons with the Chicago White Sox and California Angels. Jackson could still hit, but his speed was gone.

The day after his 1993 return, the first of the "Bo Knows" ads ran in USA *Today*. The series of ads featured Jackson taking up one sport after another, including tennis, golf, hockey, auto racing, and even luge and the guitar. A staple of the ads was someone actually expert in the field responding to Jackson's attempt.

A digital counterpart of Jackson, Tecmo Bo, starred in the Nintendo game *Tecmo Super Bowl*, and Jackson also had his own video game, *Bo Jackson's Hit and Run*, which drew upon both baseball and football. Jackson has acted in a number of television shows and, honoring a promise to his deceased mother, returned to Auburn to complete his college degree. He currently is CEO and part owner of a large multisports facility in Lockport, Illinois, the Bo Jackson Elite Sports Complex.

Bo Jackson remains one of sports most prominent what-ifs. Had he remained healthy and chosen to concentrate on football, he likely would have made the Pro Football Hall of Fame. His talents in baseball were not quite that great, but he might well have made additional All-Star teams. As it was, he may have been the best two-sport professional athlete in the history of American sports.

See also: Commercials and Advertisements; Heisman Trophy.

Additional Reading:
Gutman, Bill. *Bo Jackson: A Biography*. New York: Pocket Books, 1991.
Jackson, Bo, and Dick Schaap. *Bo Knows Bo: The Autobiography of a Ballplayer*. New York: Doubleday, 1990.

Jewelry (Bling)

Football players, as with men generally, wear more jewelry (or at least different types of jewelry) than men wore several decades ago. In the general male population, cufflinks, tie clasps, and studs have largely given way to chains, earrings, and rather sizable rings.

Football players, of course, are not likely to play in a game with anything as potentially dangerous as a chain or a dangling earring inviting a severe choking or torn earlobe. Jewelry is primarily for after the game, when the player exchanges his gladiatorial accouterments for sartorial splendor.

Despite what the football player may wear away from work, the type of jewelry that continues to speak most loudly of football accomplishments is the ring. And not just any ring, but the large, expensive, ornate, even beautiful ring that goes to those players, coaches, and other personnel who participated in a Super Bowl triumph. The Super Bowl ring is the symbol of the ultimate victory at the highest level of football competition.

There was a time when other items denoted a championship title. Members of the 1922 Canton Bulldogs, for example, received a football-shaped charm, the lettering proclaiming them "WORLD'S PROFESSIONAL CHAMPIONS." A diamond-studded tie clip did the same for the 1948 Cleveland Browns, even if the Browns were champions only of the All-America Football Conference portion of the world. By the time the Browns were champions of the National Football League, the designation was more accurate, and they may have appreciated the gold watch they received in 1954 even more than the tie clip.

The Super Bowl ring has been around as long as the Super Bowl itself, with the Green Bay Packers winning the first game—and earning the first Super Bowl ring—following the 1966 season. The Packers, after the first two Super Bowls, and most victors since, have received their rings from the skilled jewelers at Jostens in Denton, Texas. The winning team, however, may choose the manufacturer, and from time to time another company has received the contract. The Indianapolis Colts, for example, winners of Super Bowl XLI, opted for a local company, Herff Jones of Indianapolis.

Whatever the year or manufacturer, the Super Bowl ring usually has certain features. It is large and made of gold. The ring also includes a diamond design that represents the number of Super Bowls the team has won throughout its history. The ring also typically includes the name of the team and its logo.

The NFL makes available $5,000 for each ring, the number of rings running as high as 150. If the cost of the ring exceeds $5,000, the team makes up the difference. The NFL does not announce the value of the Super Bowl rings, perhaps in an attempt not to encourage potential thieves.

As not only a piece of jewelry but also a symbol of the ultimate football accomplishment, the Super Bowl ring is something that recipients usually treasure for the rest of their lives. Some talented (and lucky) individuals have received more than one, although wearing several at once might prove a bit cumbersome if not overly ostentatious.

As of 2007 the record for most Super Bowl rings won is seven, the number that may grace the fingers of Neal Dahlen, who earned them as a staff member of the San Francisco 49ers and Denver Broncos. The most won by a player is five, earned by linebacker Charles Haley with San Francisco and the Dallas Cowboys.

The Super Bowl ring can serve practical purposes. Charlie Weiss, for example, won four Super Bowl rings as an assistant coach with the New York Giants and New England Patriots. After becoming head coach at the University of Notre Dame, he commented on the advantage of wearing his rings (although perhaps not all four at once) when meeting with recruits.

Without a doubt, the most finely crafted chain or earring pales in comparison to a Super Bowl ring. Fashion experts have long asserted that there are some items that go with just about anything.

Certainly the Super Bowl ring is right at the top of that list.

See also: Super Bowl.

Additional Reading:
Fleder, Rob, ed. *The Football Book*. New York: Sports Illustrated Books, 2005.

Ossé, Reggie. *Bling: The Hip-Hop Jewelry Book*. New York: Bloomsbury, 2006.

"Sports Collections." Jostens Web site. http://www.jostens.com/sports.

Katrina (Hurricane)

Hurricane Katrina, which struck Louisiana and Mississippi on August 29, 2005, was one of the worst natural disasters in United States history. The impact of the 145-mile-per-hour winds and heavy flooding wreaked devastation on New Orleans and other large segments of both Louisiana and Mississippi. The hurricane caused close to two thousand deaths, destroyed people's homes and businesses, and left much of New Orleans looking as if it had suffered a nuclear attack. The effect of Katrina, of course, far transcended its impact on sports, yet the hurricane also affected sports, including football, in a variety of ways, leading to its second-place finish in balloting by members of the Associated Press for 2005 sports story of the year. Only the World Series triumph by the Chicago White Sox received more votes.

Along with homes and businesses, Hurricane Katrina destroyed schools throughout its ruinous path. Although paling in comparison to the damage done to students' academic pursuits, the loss of schools, especially high schools, also wiped out athletic seasons for many students, including the football season that was soon to start.

With many schools completely, in some cases permanently, destroyed, students were faced with relocating for the beginning of the 2005–06 school year. Along with this relocation occurred the dispersal of student-athletes to other institutions in their home states and throughout the country.

The stories of disruptions in people's lives and of their attempts to cope are so many that only a few examples can be offered here. South Plaquemines High School, for instance, opened in Port Sulphur, Louisiana, in August 2006 for students from the hard-hit communities of Buras, Bothville-Venice, and Port Sulphur. On the football team, players who had once competed against each other now found themselves teammates and adopted the nickname "The Hurricanes" to remind themselves what had brought them together to build a new community.

One of the most publicized stories involving high school football in the aftermath of Katrina involved Bastrop High School in Louisiana. Five former Port Sulphur High School players transferred to Bastrop three hundred miles northwest of New Orleans. The five included an unusually talented sophomore quarterback named Randall Mackey. Given the extraordinary circumstances, the Louisiana High School Athletic Association permitted students to play on their new teams immediately, but the organization retained sharp limits on recruiting players.

When one Bastrop quarterback hurt his knee and another left school, the recently arrived Mackey became the starter. He played brilliantly, making all-state and helping his new team win the 2005 Class 4A State Championship. However, accusations arose regarding recruiting improprieties, and eventually Bastrop was stripped of the title. In addition, Mackey and another player from Port Sulphur were given season-long suspensions.

The Louisiana High School Athletic Association then reconsidered and reduced the suspensions to two games. Mackey led his team to yet another state championship in 2006, this one officially recognized, perhaps finally putting behind him at least some of the horrors and disappointments caused by Hurricane Katrina.

College football also was disrupted, although less seriously than at the high school level. The Tulane University football team was evacuated to Jackson, Mississippi, later moving to Dallas and finally to Louisiana Tech University in Ruston, Louisiana, where it had its home base for the 2005 season. Instead of playing its home games in the Louisiana Superdome, Tulane struggled through a difficult season, playing in ten different stadiums and going 2-9 for the year. In recognition of its perseverance in overcoming a myriad of physical and emotional difficulties, Tulane's football team was presented with the 2005 Courage Award by the Football Writers Association of America and the FedEx Bowl.

Perhaps the greatest college football loss because of the hurricane was the Sugar Bowl. The bowl game had been played in New Orleans since its inaugural contest in 1935; since 1975 its home had been the Superdome. With the Superdome severely damaged, the 2006 Sugar Bowl was held at the Atlanta Georgia Dome, depriving New Orleans of its annual revenue from the game, which usually runs between $150 million and $200 million.

At the professional level, Hurricane Katrina most affected the New Orleans Saints, who lost their home stadium, the Superdome. As the hurricane approached, city officials decided to use the Superdome to house evacuees. Eventually, thirty thousand people huddled in the stadium while floodwaters rose, the wind tore off much of the roof, and lack of sanitation, food, water, and security turned the Superdome into a ring of Dante's hell.

In the aftermath of Katrina, uncertainty abounded regarding the future of the building, including whether it even had a future. Uncertainty also surrounded the future of the New Orleans Saints. The immediate problem for the team was finding places to practice and play their home games. As the Saints prepared for their first game of the season, against the Carolina Panthers on September 11, they were forced to improvise. Still without much of their equipment, the Saints held team meetings at the convention center in San Antonio, practiced at an area high school, used a Gold's Gym for weightlifting and other exercising, and dressed at the Alamodome.

The Saints' scheduled home opener, the second game of the season, was moved from September 18 to Monday, the 19th, and played at the home stadium of their opponents, the New York Giants. Their remaining home games were scheduled in either Louisiana State University's Tiger Stadium at Baton Rouge or the Alamodome in San Antonio.

As the Saints played out their season, winning just three games while losing thirteen, New Orleans fans wondered whether they would ever get their team back. Owner Tom Benson did not commit to returning to New Orleans and seemed to be considering moving the team to another city. The response to this indecision was considerable anger from Mayor Ray Nagin and the citizens of New Orleans. Although contractually tied to New Orleans until 2010, the Saints had certain avenues by which they could break the contract. Benson could opt out by paying Louisiana $81 million after the 2006 season. In addition, a clause in the team's contract permitted the Saints to leave if the Superdome were unusable.

The decision to stay or leave, however, was not solely up to Saints ownership. Twenty-four of the thirty-two National Football League teams would have to approve a move. Commissioner Paul Tagliabue established a New Orleans Advisory Committee, consisting of eight owners, to consider the Saints' future.

With the strong support of Commissioner Tagliabue, two major, complementary decisions were made: to repair the Superdome and to keep the Saints in New Orleans. The 2006 season marked the return of both. After extensive work in a relatively short space of time, the Superdome reopened, and the Saints played the Atlanta Falcons there on Monday, September 25. The game was treated like a Super Bowl contest, with a variety of musical performers, former Pres. George H. W. Bush presiding over the coin toss, 150 Katrina first responders accompanying the former president, and other dignitaries in attendance, including Louisiana Gov. Kathleen Blanco, New Orleans Mayor Ray Nagin, NFL Commissioner Roger Goodell, and former Commissioner Paul Tagliabue.

The Superdome itself was better than ever. Much of the roof had been replaced, 137 box suites had been remodeled, club-level seats were now leatherette, new scoreboards had been erected, new turf had been installed, and four club lounges and remodeled concession stands awaited the fans. The renovation had cost approximately $184 million, $115 million of it coming from the Federal Emergency Management Agency and $15 million from the NFL. The state and a bond refinanced by the Louisiana Stadium and Expedition District provided the rest.

In their new home, the Saints, with the nation rooting for them, won 23–3. The victory gave the Saints three wins in a row to open the season. They finished with a regular-season record of ten wins and six losses, a huge turnaround from the previous season. With a new quarterback, Drew Brees, and the exciting rookie running back Reggie Bush leading the way, the Saints made the post-season. There they defeated Philadelphia 27–24 before losing in the conference title game to Chicago, 39–14.

Members of the Saints and many others involved with the NFL contributed time, talent, and money to help those displaced by Hurricane Katrina. Saints owner Tom Benson and his family established the New Orleans Saints Hurricane Katrina Relief Fund and made it possible for individuals and organizations to contribute online at the Saints' Web site. The Saints also contributed $100,000 to rebuild the NFL's youth education center in New Orleans and made plans to help rebuild forty football fields in Louisiana and Mississippi. The NFL-organized telethon three weeks after Katrina raised $5 million.

Louisiana native Warrick Dunn of the Atlanta Falcons initiated a players' fund to help Habitat for Humanity rebuild homes in Baton Rouge. Reggie Bush made two large donations totaling $100,000 to Holy Rosary High School in New Orleans, which specializes in helping learning-challenged students. A number of Saints players—including Joe Horn, Deuce McAllister, Ernie Conwell, and T. J. Slaughter, among others—visited evacuees at USA Kelly in San Antonio, a former air force base, bringing them

clothes, food, and other items. Many others associated with the NFL contributed in a multitude of ways to help Katrina victims. Indianapolis quarterback Peyton Manning received the NFL's Walter Payton Man of the Year Award for 2005 for his work to help residents of the Gulf Coast, including his hometown of New Orleans. Among other projects, Peyton, with his brother, Eli, a New York Giants quarterback, delivered relief supplies to storm evacuees in Baton Rouge shelters.

Drew Brees has become known as "the patron Saint" of New Orleans because of the extensive efforts that he and his wife, Brittany, have made to help the city rebuild. The Breeses established a $2.5 million Brees Dream Foundation to help breathe new life into eight sites that will feature schools and athletic fields. The foundation also is initiating after-school mentoring programs.

As part of the Brees Dream program, children are invited to sign an "Expect More" pledge as an expression of their willingness to demand more of others and of themselves. Along with the child, Drew Brees signs each pledge sheet. The final statement of expectation reads as follows: "I have a responsibility to make a positive difference in my community." In addition, Brees, a former Purdue student-athlete, secured the help of more than eighty of his Purdue Sigma Chi fraternity brothers to help Habitat for Humanity rebuild homes in New Orleans' Upper Ninth Ward.

In some ways, what happened to football during and after Hurricane Katrina was a microcosm of the storm's impact on the broader society: much destruction and suffering, displacement and even despair, but also a commitment to go forward, to rebuild, and to help one another.

See also: Commissioners; Favre, Brett Lorenzo; Manning, Peyton Williams.

Additional Reading:
Brinkley, Douglas. *The Great Deluge: Hurricane Katrina, New Orleans, and the Mississippi Gulf Coast.* New York: Morrow, 2006.
Corbett, Jim. "New Orleans' Patron Saint." USA *Today Sports Weekly* July 4–11, 2007, 38–41.
Reed, Betsy, ed. *Unnatural Disaster: The Nation on Hurricane Katrina.* New York: Nation Books, 2006.
Time Editors. *Hurricane Katrina: The Storm That Changed America.* New York: Time Books, 2005.

Kennedy, John F., Assassination of

Most people who were old enough to understand what was happening still remember the precise date that Pres. John F. Kennedy was assassinated in Dallas, Texas: November 22, 1963. In fact, many who were not yet born on that terrible Friday can recite the date, while their parents and grandparents, probably with few exceptions, can recall where they were when they heard what had happened.

The assassination of President Kennedy affected the entire nation in a myriad of ways. Football was no exception. At every level, games were canceled, student-athletes were called together in prayer, and businesses found more people watching

television in their stores or grieving together than buying.

Roger Staubach was the Navy quarterback and Heisman Trophy winner in 1963. He had become friendly with the president, himself an old Navy man and war hero, when President Kennedy would stop by to watch the Navy football team practice at the Quonset Point Naval Air Station in Rhode Island.

Staubach heard of the shooting in Dallas in his dormitory room as he was about to leave for a thermodynamics class. Classes were canceled, and Staubach went to the athletics complex and just sat by his locker. The football coach, Wayne Hardin, prayed with the team. The big game against Army was rescheduled for two weeks later.

Just four days after the assassination, November 26, Staubach learned that he would receive the Heisman Trophy. There was no celebratory party. Nor were there the usual bonfires and pep rallies when Navy finally played Army on December 7, ironically the anniversary of another terrible day in American history. Navy hung on to win, 21–15. Staubach later would have a Hall of Fame professional career with the Dallas Cowboys, helping Dallas to remove at least some of the stigma of being the city where the president was murdered.

On November 22, in South Bend, Indiana, home of one of Navy's traditional rivals, the University of Notre Dame, the news of President Kennedy's assassination hit especially hard. The Irish

Catholic president was a great favorite at the Catholic university known as the Fighting Irish.

The team was practicing at Notre Dame when word came that the president had been shot. Coach Hugh Devore, whose team was suffering through a horrible 2-7 season that would cost him his job after just one year as coach, canceled the practice and led the team in prayer. Uncertain what the next day would bring, the team flew to Iowa City for the game against the University of Iowa. The game, however, was canceled. Back on campus, players read the newspapers, attended church services, and watched the events of the funeral on television.

Throughout the nation, football games were postponed or canceled, including all games by the American Football League. The National Football League, though, was another matter. When he heard of the assassination, NFL Commissioner Pete Rozelle called President Kennedy's press secretary, Pierre Salinger, who was aboard a plane bound for a summit in Asia. Rozelle and Salinger were friends and fellow alumni of the University of San Francisco.

Rozelle wanted to get Salinger's advice regarding whether to cancel Sunday's games. Salinger and Rozelle both thought that President Kennedy, who loved football, would want the games to be played. The fact that no games were scheduled for Dallas or Washington DC made the decision to play easier.

Before long, however, Rozelle saw that he had made a terrible mistake. He was roundly criticized for supposedly choosing business as usual over paying respect to the nation's fallen leader.

The games went on but with little fanfare. Halftime events were canceled, the national anthem typically was the only music heard, and the crowds were subdued. Yet Rozelle's decision looked even worse when Jack Ruby shot and killed Kennedy assassin Lee Harvey Oswald on Sunday, at approximately 11:20 a.m., a shooting watched by millions on television.

The Dallas Cowboys, playing in Cleveland, heard the announcers consistently refer to them, on orders of Browns owner Art Modell, as the Cowboys, never the Dallas Cowboys. Aware of the animosity felt toward Dallas, the players feared for their safety and kept their helmets on as some protection even when not playing. Some players wondered if there might be snipers in the stadium.

Rozelle later admitted that deciding to play the games that Sunday was his greatest regret as commissioner. He had acted in good faith, however, not out of disrespect or a crass desire for money. In fact, the NFL lost money because CBS did not televise the games, costing the league one-fourteenth of its television revenue for the season. If the league had played that game later in the year, it would have been better off financially.

The nation, including its football players, suffered a great loss that Friday in November. It was stunning to believe that a president in modern times could be killed so easily, all the more shocking when the president was such a young, vibrant leader. Camelot came to an end, and those who wore football helmets and shoulder pads mourned the loss as much as anyone else. Roger Staubach felt that he had lost a friend in addition to a president. Much of the nation felt the same.

See also: Presidents of the United States; Television Broadcasting.

Additional Reading:
Associated Press. *The Torch Is Passed: The Associated Press Story of the Death of a President.* Cleveland: The Plain Dealer, 1963.
Delsohn, Steve. *Talking Irish: The Oral History of Notre Dame Football.* New York: Avon Books, 1998.
MacCambridge, Michael. *America's Game: The Epic Story of How Pro Football Captured a Nation.* New York: Random House, 2004.

Kerouac, Jack (Jean Louis Lebris de Kerouac) (1922–1969)

Jack Kerouac is best remembered for his novel *On the Road* (1957), long viewed as perhaps the most important literary reflection of the Beat Generation of the 1950s. Before becoming a writer, however, young Jack Kerouac was an outstanding football player, possibly the finest football player ever to trade the pigskin for a pen.

Kerouac grew up in Lowell, Massachusetts, where he became a star player for Lowell High School. A speedy runner, Kerouac had perhaps his finest game as a senior against Lawrence High School on Thanksgiving Day, 1938. The game was especially important because the two mill towns were keen rivals in football. In the second half, Kerouac secured the win in front of college scouts who already had become enamored of the young speedster. Lowell led just 2–0, as precarious a lead as possible against the dangerous Lawrence offense. With only a few minutes remaining in the game, Lowell quarterback Art Coughlin lobbed a wobbly pass in Kerouac's direction, but a Lawrence defensive end touched the ball, sending it off course. Kerouac, however, did not give up. He raced downfield, stretched back, and hauled the pass in inches from the ground. Keeping his balance, he raced for the end zone, met two defenders at the 5-yard line, and smashed through them, ending up inches beyond the goal line.

Young Jacky had grown up following the football exploits of such gridiron greats as Red Grange. He early on imagined football as an avenue out of a Lowell future that promised little for him beyond a job in one of the textile mills. Although slow to establish himself with his high school coach, by his senior year he was a star, and not just against Lawrence. He scored three touchdowns against Worcester Classical and two against Keith Academy. The Boston *Herald* immortalized his name in a sports headline.

Both Columbia University, coached by Lou Little, and Boston College, with a new coach, Frank Leahy, who would later achieve legendary status at Notre Dame, wanted Kerouac. He chose the more distant Columbia in New York City. Little already was a legend there, having led his team to a Rose Bowl victory over Stanford on January 1, 1934. Little had lost only one game per year from 1931 through 1934, but then victories had started proving more elusive, although Little would remain Columbia's football coach through 1956, a year before *On the Road* was published.

Before Columbia, though, Kerouac needed a year at Horace Mann Prep School in the Bronx to get himself physically and academically ready for college. There he quickly established himself as a presence on the Horace Mann football team. He scored a touchdown in the second game of the season, against the Columbia freshman team, to help his squad prevail 20–0. In attendance was Coach Little. In the season-ending game against Tome, he returned a punt 72 yards to give Horace Mann a 6–0 win and the unofficial prep school football championship of New York City.

Life at Columbia, unfortunately, did not go as Kerouac had anticipated. Jack was a freshman in the fall of 1940 with Europe engulfed in the flames of war and many Americans expecting their own country's imminent involvement. He played on the freshman team as freshmen were not then permitted on the varsity squad. In his second game, against St. Benedict's Prep School, he ran the opening kickoff back for 90 yards and was stopped just short of the goal line. Three plays later, he suffered a broken leg. The freshman coach, Ralph Furey, did not believe the injury to be severe and urged

him to keep running. Ten days later, an X-ray showed the break.

Kerouac returned to practice the next year hoping to make the varsity. Although the United States was still not officially in the war, many Americans were going abroad to help the lands of their ancestors, and Jack had trouble taking football as seriously as he had earlier viewed it. He packed his suitcase and went home by way of Washington DC. Pearl Harbor was attacked in December, and in July Kerouac sailed out of Boston Harbor as a merchant seaman aboard the S.S. *Dorchester*.

By fall of 1942 he was back in Lowell and reading an invitation by Coach Little to return to Columbia. He decided to do that, but Little refused to put him into his first game, against the West Point team. A week later Kerouac departed Columbia. He joined the navy in February 1943 and, after returning, decided to be a writer.

Kerouac's first novel, *The Town and the City* (1950), replays some of his own football exploits, but by then the football player had yielded firmly to the author. By the time he died in 1969, he had published sixteen books and attained lasting fame as the voice of a generation.

See also: Leahy, Francis William; Literature; World War II.

Additional Reading:

Charters, Ann. *Kerouac: A Biography*. San Francisco: Straight Arrow Books, 1973.

Kerouac, Jack. *On the Road*. New York: Viking, 1957.

———. *The Town and the City*. New York: Harcourt, Brace, Jovanovich, 1950.

Maher, Paul, Jr. *Kerouac: The Definitive Biography*. Lanham MD: Taylor Trade Publishing; distributed by National Book Network, 2004.

McNally, Dennis. *Desolate Angel: A Biography of Jack Kerouac, the Beat Generation, and America*. New York: Random House, 1979.

Kickoffs

The opening kickoff is one of the most exciting plays in a football game. As the toe prepares to meet the ball, fans stand, their cheers building to a crescendo and exploding as the ball rises. Anticipation gives way to action, and the spectators await the long runback or the bone-jarring tackle. Often, of course, neither happens as the ball sails far into the end zone.

That is likely to change, at least at the college level, through a new rule effective with the 2007 season. The new rule moves the ball back from the 35-yard line to the 30-yard line for all kickoffs. The extra 5 yards will mean fewer touchbacks, more returns, better starting position much of the time, more excitement, and probably more scoring.

The new rule change also is likely to mean more injuries in a game that officials have been trying to make safer. The kickoff already is a highly dangerous play, possibly the most dangerous play of the game. A five-year study that concluded in 1998 showed that special-teams plays result in almost one-third (31.7 percent) of anterior cruciate ligament injuries. That despite the fact that special-teams plays account for a small percentage of total plays in a game.

The high rate of injuries is easy to understand. Members of the kicking team race as fast as they can down the field and have a lot of the field to reach maximum speed and therefore maximum force as they smash into the ball carrier. The confrontations between blocker and would-be tackler also are at maximum force, and many times the player being blocked is struck from the side or without seeing the blocker.

Plenty of people associated with football worry about an increase in injuries as a result of the change, and not just to legs. Harold King, a longtime trainer for the Atlanta Falcons who now supervises high school athletic trainers in Atlanta, expressed even more concern about a rise in concussions.

Another certain change is that given the increased number of kicks being returned, more starting defensive players will be on special teams to try to prevent long runbacks. That may well increase the number of starters being injured as well.

So why the change? The rationale given by the NCAA was to speed up the game by eliminating the down time as touchbacks are marked off. Time versus safety is a balancing act that people confront every day in their lives—when they are driving, crossing a street, applying a chainsaw to a tree branch, unclogging a grass-filled lawnmower, and performing a myriad of other common actions. What will the result be of shifting the balance in college games? Time will tell, perhaps in both the saving of it and the losing of more than just a few minutes.

See also: Big Hit; Coin Toss; Concussions; Dropkick.

Additional Reading:

Glier, Ray. "End Zone to Danger Zone." *New York Times Sports Sunday*, August 26, 2007.

Nelson, David M. *Anatomy of a Game: Football, the Rules, and the Men Who Made the Game*. Newark: University of Delaware Press, 1994.

Watterson, John Sayle. *College Football: History, Spectacle, Controversy*. Baltimore: Johns Hopkins University Press, 2000.

Korean War

The Korean War (1950–53) followed a successful post–World War II half decade for the National Football League that saw the NFL survive a serious challenge by the All-America Football Conference and effect a merger that ended the competition. The new teams created by the merger—the Cleveland Browns, San Francisco 49ers, and Baltimore Colts—would provide some of the NFL's greatest moments in future years. The challenge from the competing league also precipitated the reintegration of the NFL, which was a significant victory for racial justice and also boosted the quality of play by opening the NFL doors to talented African Americans.

The Korean War, however, threatened to sidetrack the NFL—not, of course, a threat that came anywhere close to equaling the larger danger to the world as China's engagement in military action against the United States on the Korean peninsula raised the possibility of another world war. The Korean War also heightened America's concern with Communist aggression abroad and Communist infiltration into the United States.

As the United States faced yet another war, football players, as they had done less than a decade earlier, joined the battle. More than 225 current and future NFL personnel served during the Korean War, many with great distinction. Fourteen players found themselves in their second war.

Cloyce Box spent four years with the U.S. Marines during World War II. In 1949, then twenty-six years old, he finally received his professional opportunity, joining the Detroit Lions as a halfback and end. The Lions quickly found that his greatest skill was as a receiver, and in his second season he caught fifty passes for 1,009 yards, a 20.2-yard average per reception, and eleven touchdowns. Then came the Korean War, and Box was recalled to active duty. In 1952 he returned to the Lions and caught forty-two passes for 924 yards, a 22-yard average, and a league-leading fifteen touchdowns. By this time, though, he was approaching thirty years old and played just two more years, his war service preventing a probable Hall of Fame career.

Bob Forte served as a tank officer with the army during World War II before joining the Green Bay Packers. He played as a halfback, defensive back, linebacker, kick returner, and punt returner with Green Bay from 1946 through 1950, and he even threw an occasional pass. Although he did not see a lot of action carrying the ball, he excelled defensively as a ballhawk, intercepting nine passes, which he returned for a total of 140 yards and a touchdown, in 1947. He also recovered a fumble that year and scored twice on receptions. Forte then returned to military duty in Korea in 1951. He rejoined the Packers in 1952 to play two more years, finishing his career with twenty-three interceptions.

Ralph Heywood did Box and Forte one better, serving in three wars: World War II, the Korean War, and the Vietnam War. He is the only NFL player to participate in all three conflicts. Heywood, an offensive and defensive end as well as a punter, was selected by the Detroit Lions in the third round of the football draft in 1944 but had his football career delayed by World War II. He returned stateside in 1946 to play with the Chicago Rockets of the All-America Football Conference and the Lions, Boston Yanks, and New York Bulldogs of the NFL. His final season was 1949. Three years later, still in the Reserves, he returned to active duty during the Korean War and later served with the marines in Vietnam.

Box, Forte, and Heywood, along with the eleven other NFL players who served in both World War II and the Korean War, deserve special appreciation for their sacrifice. However, the NFL Korean War veteran who may have most distinguished himself in combat was Eddie LeBaron.

LeBaron stood only five feet seven inches tall and weighed just 166 pounds, but he played much larger than that in both college and professional ball. At the College of the Pacific (now University of the Pacific), he was an All-American quarterback his senior year (1949) as he led his team through an undefeated season. He also starred at safety on defense and as a punter, and he quarterbacked the College All-Stars to a 17–7 win over the NFL champion Philadelphia Eagles. His college accomplishments earned him induction into the College Football Hall of Fame in 1980.

After graduation, LeBaron served in the Korean War with the marines. He spent nine months in Korea, seven of them on the front lines, where he was wounded twice. He received the Bronze Star for his actions at Heartbreak Ridge where, under heavy fire, he risked his life to contact a mortar platoon's forward observation post and then assumed command of a rifle platoon that had lost its commander and led it back into battle. In addition to the Bronze Star, LeBaron was awarded a Purple Heart and a Letter of Commendation. He earned his nickname "the Littlest General" not only for his size but also for his leadership abilities, which he displayed on both the field of battle and the football field.

After Korea, LeBaron played professional football for eleven years in the NFL (1952–53, 1955–63) with the Washington Redskins and Dallas Cowboys and one year (1954) in the Canadian Football League for his college coach, Larry Siemering, who was coaching the Calgary Stampeders. LeBaron was Rookie of the Year in 1952, made the Pro Bowl four times, and led the league in passing in 1958. He later was a football announcer with CBS Sports and served as general manager of the Atlanta Falcons (1977–82) and as the team's executive vice president (1982–85). While playing professional football, LeBaron earned a law degree, which he put to use practicing law in Nevada after retiring as a player and before becoming the Falcons' general manager. After leaving Atlanta, he returned to his law practice.

By 1953 the shooting war in Korea had ended, an uneasy partition of the peninsula continued to separate the two Koreas, and the United States had returned to its cold war standoff with the Soviet Union and China. Many of the football players who had gone to war resumed their careers. They, like virtually all Americans, hoped for a lasting peace. The peace, however, would not last nearly as long as they wished. By the next decade, the United States would find itself once again involved in a war in Asia.

See also: World War II.

Additional Reading:

Edwards, Paul M. *Korean War Almanac.* New York: Facts on File, 2006.

"Football and America: The Korean War." The Pro Football Hall of Fame Web site. http://www.profootballhof.com/history/general/war/korean.

Labor-Management Relations

The relationship between labor and management during most of professional football's history was thoroughly one-sided with management holding the power. Players for the most part had little recourse if they did not like their team or their salary. They could make the best of it or find another line of work. The absolute power of a team to keep its players from playing for another team removed most pressure from management to accommodate players' wishes. Except when another league attempted to compete with the NFL, there was no meaningful competition.

As in other sports and in industries throughout the United States, NFL employees (in this case the players) sought to form a union that would help them earn more money, have some security if they were injured, and have a pension plan for the postfootball years. Some dreamed of free agency, but that would be long in coming and prove to be the issue over which some of the strongest battles would be fought.

The National Football League Players Association (NFLPA) was born in 1956 when a group of Cleveland Browns players sought help in setting up an association from former Browns general manager Creighton Miller, a Notre Dame defensive end in the 1940s whose father and two uncles (including Don, one of the Four Horsemen) had also played at Notre Dame. Miller began approaching players from other teams, including Frank Gifford of the Giants and Don Shula of the Colts. By November 1956 the new association was approved by a majority of the players.

The original player proposals, presented to Commissioner Bert Bell in 1957, seem embarrassingly mild today: a minimum $5,000 salary, continued payment if a player were injured, and payment for players' equipment by the clubs. The effort, however, met with no success.

The players then threatened an antitrust lawsuit against the owners. The timing of that threat was fortuitous, as a previous antitrust suit filed some dozen years earlier by Bill Radovich of Detroit was finally reaching the Supreme Court, which ruled that the NFL was indeed subject to antitrust legislation. To quiet player opposition, owners agreed to several player demands, although it would take additional threats of antitrust suits to get the NFL to move forward on hospitalization, medical and life insurance, and retirement benefits.

Relations between the league and the NFLPA remained difficult, with brief strikes occurring in 1968 and 1970. Each work stoppage led to a Collective Bargaining Agreement, although player gains remained small. However, the NFL in 1970 did accept the right of players to be represented by agents and to have an impartial arbitration of injury-related grievances. Even these small accommodations by the league, however, were followed by apparently retaliatory actions as player representatives were cut and NFLPA president John Mackey, the Colts Hall of Fame tight end, was traded to San Diego.

The NFLPA took an important step in 1971 when it hired its first executive director, attorney Ed Garvey. Players began to work toward a new agreement in 1974, with the NFLPA pushing for free agency, elimination of the draft, and arbitration of all grievances, among other proposals. The owners refused to negotiate, and the players went on strike. In August they called off the strike and fought the battle through the courts, winning a decision in 1976 that found the owners guilty of violating federal antitrust laws. A new agreement was signed in 1977, with the NFLPA winning arbitration for noninjury grievances, improved benefits, and limited free agency.

The new process for free agency, however, proved to be largely an illusion. The new system aligned salary offers made to free agents with draft-choice compensation, making the price of signing free agents too high to be worth it. With negotiations toward a new agreement again stalled, the players went on strike in 1982—at the time the most significant strike that the NFLPA had called. The strike began after the first game of the season but was called off when the owners, already having received television revenue for the season, appeared ready to cancel the remaining games. The new Collective Bargaining Agreement did not materially change free agency but did involve several important features for the players. The owners agreed that the salary/benefits package would be worth at least $128 billion over five seasons, which translated into over one-half of projected team revenues. Players also received a variety of medical benefits, including the right to receive a second medical opinion, inspect their team medical records, and approve surgeons for team-related injuries.

In 1983 Ed Garvey resigned as executive director and was replaced by Gene Upshaw, who surveyed players and found that the issue most important to them was free agency. Players had improved their financial lot and had secured a variety of improved benefits, but they still had no real control over their choice of an employer, a basic right that most Americans enjoyed.

A major turning point developed in 1987 when the players decided to strike. This time, the television revenue had not been paid up-front, so the owners were not about to cancel the season. They prepared for the strike by employing Eddie LeBaron, a former quarterback and war hero who until recently had been general manager of the Atlanta Falcons, to prepare a roster of replacement players. When the players went out on strike in mid-September, the owners were ready. They played three games with replacement players—from the regular players' perspective, "scab players." In addition, approximately 15 percent of the regular players crossed picket lines to play. The NFLPA ended the strike after two games were conducted with replacement players, but the league did not permit the original players back until after a third game. The association filed an antitrust lawsuit against the NFL over the free agency issue and also filed unfair labor charges with the National Labor Relations Board (NLRB) over the league's refusal to permit the striking players back immediately.

The owners agreed to a new free agency plan, their "Plan B," which freed some of the players. Each team could restrict thirty-seven players, which, of course, meant that most of the top players, those who would likely draw the highest salary offers in a genuinely open free-agent system, would be ineligible. The NFLPA, knowing that it would be extremely expensive to continue the legal fight, increased its group licensing program, with most players signing an exclusive licensing contract with the NFLPA to allow the association to market their names and images.

Over the next few years the NFLPA conducted a complex series of legal maneuvers, including decertification of the association as a union and then reinstitution of the collective bargaining unit. Along the way, increasing numbers of players defected from the NFLPA licensing program to sign with NFL Properties, which offered at least $10,000 to each player who signed with the league's marketing arm.

Slowly but steadily, the NFLPA won some battles in the federal courts and before the NLRB in the early 1990s, leading the league to enter negotiations. Lengthy discussions led to the signing of a Collective Bargaining Agreement in January 1993. A genuine compromise, which meant that it completely satisfied no one but offered each side something of what it wanted, the new contract included a true free-agency process while including the salary cap that the owners demanded. The players also received a guaranteed 58 percent of gross league revenues.

The 1993 Collective Bargaining Agreement was extended in 1998, 2002, and 2006. The 2006 agreement proved especially difficult because the issue of revenue sharing for the owners became tied up with renewal of the agreement. The owners thus had to agree among themselves before they could come to an agreement with the players. In fact, the owners voted 32–0 in early March 2006 to reject the final NFLPA offer. Then the owners requested a seventy-two-hour extension of the deadline for coming to an agreement, a request to which the players acceded. Robert Kraft, owner of the New England Patriots, crafted a compromise revenue-sharing plan and along with Jets owner Woody Johnson persuaded the other owners to buy into it.

Under the revenue-sharing plan, the top fifteen revenue-producing teams would contribute $900 million over six years, with low-revenue teams having to qualify to receive money from the fund. The owners then passed Kraft's plan 30–2, as they did an extension of the Collective Bargaining Agreement for six years, although either side would be free to opt out of the agreement after four years.

Ultimately, the owners seemed to understand that there is simply too much money coming in (at least for most teams), including huge television contracts, to run the risk of a work stoppage that would disrupt revenue streams even temporarily. The public's negative reaction to the most recent Major League Baseball players' strike (1994–95) essentially involved a "pox on both your houses" attitude, and owners likely feared a similar rejection of both parties if they could not come to an agreement. Such a rejection, they understood, could have long-term financial implications by essentially cooking the goose that has been laying the golden egg of NFL prosperity.

For the players, the system, while not perfect, continues to guarantee them high salaries, excellent benefits, and, with some limitations, free agency, which itself is a key to maximizing career earnings. Under the current system, a player may become an unrestricted free agent after four years unless he is designated a franchise player or transition player. Either of these designations impacts a very small percentage of players, as each team may use just one of those categories per year and must still pay the designated player at a level high enough to make him one of the best-paid players at his position in the league.

The relationship between labor and management has evolved mightily over the decades. Although tension still exists, there is enough cash coming in to please almost everyone and grease the wheels of reconciliation quite nicely. Given the NFL's popularity and prosperity, it appears unlikely that relations will deteriorate markedly anytime soon.

See also: Commissioners; Substance Abuse; Television Broadcasting; Upshaw, Eugene Thurman, Jr.

Additional Reading:
Borges, Ron. "Driving Force Behind NFL's Deal." *Boston Sunday Globe*, March 12, 2006.
MacCambridge, Michael. *America's Game: The Epic Story of How Pro Football Captured a Nation.* New York: Random House, 2004.
NFL Players Association Web Site. http://www.nflpa.org.

Landry, Thomas Wade (1924–2000)

Tom Landry, first coach of the expansion Dallas franchise in the National Football League, established the Cowboys as "America's Team." He led the Cowboys for their first twenty-nine years and won thirteen divisional championships, five National Football Conference titles, and two Super Bowls. Along the way, the reserved and deeply religious coach was branded a "plastic man," became the model for the coach in one of the most famous football novels, and ended up being fired despite his accomplishments. He also made the Pro Football Hall of Fame in 1990, just two years after the end of his long tenure as the Cowboys' coach.

Landry came to his head coaching job with considerable experience. An excellent fullback and defensive back at the University of Texas and an All-Pro defensive back with the New York Giants, Landry also proved his mettle during World War II when as a copilot on a B-17 Flying Fortress bomber he flew thirty combat missions over Europe and walked away from a crash landing in Belgium.

Landry's academic background in industrial engineering likely helped him structure new defensive strategies with the New York Giants in the 1950s in his role as what later would be called a defensive coordinator. Another future coaching immortal, Vince Lombardi, handled the offense. Landry devised the 4-3 defense, replacing the nose tackle with a middle linebacker in order to have four men on the line backed up by three linebackers. The Hall of Fame middle linebacker Sam Huff helped to ensure that the new position would catch on in the NFL.

A thinking man's coach and clever innovator, Landry brought his ability to devise new schemes to Dallas in 1960. He created the flex defense by incorporating additional flexibility into the 4-3 scheme. Landry moved two of his linemen back about a yard, choosing the players to move based on the play he anticipated the offense to be running. On offense he added a man in motion and the shotgun (a formation in which the quarterback stands about 7 yards behind the center to have a wider view of the playing field). Neither was his personal creation; in fact, putting players in motion had a long history. However, Landry used both to great effect. An innovative aspect of the shift was having the offensive linemen squat, then stand up before going down again, this time into their final stance. The point was to hinder the defensive players from seeing the movement of the backs.

By 1966 the Cowboys were playing (and losing to) the Green Bay Packers for the NFL championship, the first of twenty consecutive winning seasons for Dallas. Dallas lost again to Green Bay in the championship game in 1967 in what became known as the Ice Bowl. The next step for Dallas was the National Football Conference championship, which it won in 1970, only to lose Super Bowl V to the Baltimore Colts. The following year, however, Dallas won the Super Bowl, defeating the Miami Dolphins. The Cowboys had moved from nonexistence to the pinnacle of the NFL, and more was to come. Landry's Cowboys returned to Super Bowls X, XII, and XIII, winning number XII.

After the 1978 season, however, Dallas never again made the Super Bowl during the Landry years. Landry's final winning season was 1985, followed by three consecutive losing seasons.

Landry was respected by most of his players and revered by many. However, there were some dissenting opinions, especially in the early years when

Landry was impatiently pushing his new team to start winning. Some players referred to him as "Pope Landry I" in reference to his obvious religious devotion. In fact, Landry was quite willing to acknowledge his religious beliefs, felt that coaching was part of God's plan for him, and was a strong supporter of the Fellowship of Christian Athletes. In 1971 Duane Thomas, a gifted but controversial running back, called Landry "a plastic man, no man at all," referring to his seemingly dispassionate, aloof demeanor. Peter Gent, a wide receiver for the Cowboys from 1964 to 1968, modeled the coach in his novel *North Dallas Forty* after Landry, a less than flattering depiction of his former boss.

As the Cowboys' fortunes declined, Landry was subject to increasing criticism, including a death threat in 1986 that led him to coach wearing a protective vest. H. R. "Bum" Bright, who bought the Cowboys in 1984 from original owner Clint Murchison, criticized the play selection but gave Landry a new three-year contract in 1987. During a game in 1988, as Dallas was suffering through a thirteen-loss season, the coach lost track of where the football was and called a play that contributed to another loss. Yet after the season, Landry announced that he planned to continue coaching and return the Cowboys to their winning tradition. That was not to be, as new owner Jerry Jones and Landry's partner of twenty-nine years, general manager Tex Schramm, informed him on February 25, 1989, that he was being fired and replaced by Jimmy Johnson.

Commissioner Pete Rozelle likened the departure of Landry to Vince Lombardi's death. Landry's Hall of Fame quarterback, Roger Staubach, called him the best professional coach ever. Saying his farewells to his players shortly after his dismissal, the supposedly unemotional Landry could not contain his tears, and his players responded with a standing ovation.

See also: Literature; Lombardi, Vincent Thomas; Religion; Super Bowl; World War II.

Additional Reading:

Freeman, Denne H., and Jaime Aron. *I Remember Landry*. Champaign IL: Sports Publishing, 2001.

Gent, Peter. *North Dallas Forty*. 1973. Toronto: Sport Classic Books, 2003.

Landry, Tom. *Tom Landry: An Autobiography*. With Gregg Lewis. Grand Rapids MI: Zondervan Books, 1990.

St. John, Bob. *Landry: The Legend and the Legacy*. Nashville: Word Publishing, 2000.

Language

Football has a living language. Like other languages that remain functional, football's language has borrowed its lexicon from various sources, continues to evolve, and influences communication in other areas of life. Although some concepts may bewilder those unfamiliar with the sport, speakers of English on the whole can understand most of football language, with the result that it could almost be considered a dialect of English.

One of the first aficionados of language to analyze football's unique language status was the humorist and social satirist George Carlin. Applying basic comparative linguistics, with a strong social slant and considerable humor, to contrasting football and baseball language, Carlin noted in his "Baseball-Football" routine, which he continued to revise over the years, that football language borrows heavily from military terminology. Football and war are both violent, although the difference in degree clearly is massive. Thus warlike terms fit the physicality of football: driving against the enemy, combining an aerial and a ground attack, employing bombs and bullet passes on offense, having the quarterback operate out of the shotgun, blitzing on defense, even spearing. The game includes unnecessary roughness and penalties, and sometimes results in sudden death. These parallels are amusing, but they also convey considerable truth. Football is a rough game, and its basic principles, minus killing and deliberate bloodshed, are similar to the principles of warfare. It is not a coincidence that Woody Hayes, the former great football coach who won three national championships at Ohio State University, was a devoted student of military history and an avid student of Gen. George Patton.

Carlin ignored a few other terms that involve violence and death, such as spiking and the coffin corner, but despite the many military terms, football language is more than just military talk. Football language has made its way into many realms of American society, where it is used by people who often have no idea they are employing football terms.

So an office staff may huddle to come up with a good solution to a business problem. People express their inability to solve problems by admitting that they had to punt. If their failure included a mistake, they fumbled the ball. Yet almost everyone knows that it is easy to criticize others after the fact, hence the aversion people feel for Monday-morning quarterbacking. The workers who deal directly with customers, such as bank tellers, are said to be in the trenches, a term whose evolutionary etymology can be traced back through football (line play) to that great source of football language, warfare, as in trench warfare during World War I. A subordinate who fails to follow the chain of command (itself a military concept) is attempting an end run, and is certainly out of bounds.

As football language borrowed heavily from military language, so it now especially influences business, which itself can be viewed as something of a war among competitors. The concept behind a hostile takeover is not much different from driving through enemy territory to score a touchdown. A business plan is just a game plan transferred for another type of enterprise. Blue-chip football prospects are considered as promising an investment as blue-chip stocks, although both football and business are ultimately indebted to poker for the term.

Football language thus keeps evolving, and with the sport growing in popularity, increasing numbers of people will be able to include, when asked what languages they speak: football English.

See also: Hayes, Wayne Woodrow; Literature; Mascots and Team Names; Nicknames.

Additional Reading/Listening:

Brock, Ted. "Blitzing the English Language." In *Total Football II: The Official Encyclopedia of the National Football League*. Ed. Bob Carroll et al., 509–10. New York: HarperCollins, 1999.

Carlin, George. "Baseball-Football." *An Evening with Wally Londo Featuring Bill Slaszo*. 1975. Atlantic, 2000.

———. *Brain Droppings*. New York: Hyperion, 1997.

Shefski, Bill. *American Football Language: The Jargon Explained*. New York: Random House, 1987.

Leahy, Francis William (Frank) (1908–1973)

Frank Leahy, football coach at the University of Notre Dame, was perhaps the most famous college coach of the post–World War II era despite his unenviable task of trying to live up to the standard set by Knute Rockne. Despite his considerable accomplishments, Leahy also was a controversial coach who was not averse to pushing the legal limits in order to win.

Leahy played tackle for Rockne's national champion Irish team in 1929 but tore cartilage in a knee before the 1930 season, which ended his playing career. A favorite of Rockne's, Leahy spent the 1930 season beside his coach on the sideline and later accompanied Rockne to the Mayo Clinic in Rochester, Minnesota.

Rockne sought treatment for phlebitis and Leahy, at Rockne's invitation, went along to have his knee examined by the Mayo specialists. While there, the two men shared a hotel room for a week. The closeness that developed over the year convinced Leahy to follow Rockne into coaching.

Leahy began his coaching career as line coach at Georgetown in 1931 and joined Jim Crowley, one of Notre Dame's Four Horsemen, at Michigan State the following year. Leahy followed Crowley to Fordham in 1933, where he remained through the 1938 season. As Fordham's line coach, he was responsible for instructing the team's famous Seven Blocks of Granite line, which included future coaching great Vince Lombardi.

Leahy became the head coach at Boston College in 1939 and compiled a 20-2 record in two years, finishing with an undefeated season and a 19–13 Sugar Bowl victory over previously undefeated Tennessee. One of the few times Leahy came up short at Boston College was his attempt to recruit future Beat novelist Jack Kerouac. Leahy's success at Boston College earned him the position at Notre Dame that Rockne had held until his death in the spring of 1931.

Notre Dame held special meaning for Leahy, not only because it was his alma mater but also because the devoutly Catholic coach felt at home there. In fact, most of his coaching had been at Catholic institutions, and in 1951 Pope

Pius XII honored Leahy by making him a Knight of Malta.

Leahy surprised many followers of Notre Dame football by abandoning Rockne's box formation (which included considerable motion by the backfield) in favor of the T-formation. He also introduced to college football audible calls by the quarterback and the pro-type zone defense. Leahy consistently downplayed his team's chances while referring affectionately to his players as his "lads." Although very different in personality from his mentor (Leahy was far less emotional and outgoing than Rockne), he enjoyed a level of success that came close to Rockne's.

Leahy coached Notre Dame for eleven seasons (1941–43 and 1946–53) with the intervening years spent in the navy during the war. His Irish teams went 87-11-9 and were national champions in 1943, 1946, 1947, and 1949. In the late 1940s his teams went thirty-nine games without a loss, including four undefeated seasons in a row (1946–49). Four of his players—Angelo Bertelli, Johnny Lujack, Leon Hart, and John Lattner—won the Heisman Trophy. A fifth, Paul Hornung, whom he had recruited, won the award under Leahy's successor, Terry Brennan. After slipping to 4-4-1 in 1950, Notre Dame rebounded, losing just four games in the next three years and going undefeated in 1953.

That 1953 season would be Leahy's last at Notre Dame. He was beginning to suffer from health problems and collapsed with a pancreatic attack at halftime of the Georgia Tech game. The Iowa contest proved especially stressful for Leahy as his team fell behind 7–0. With time running out in the first half and no timeouts remaining, Leahy had a player feign an injury to stop the clock. Notre Dame scored a touchdown with the extra seconds. Then in the second half, with Notre Dame again behind, this time 14–7, the clock again winding down, and no timeouts left, Leahy pulled the same trick. Again the extra time allowed the Irish to score, pulling even at 14–14. The game ended in that score, preserving the undefeated season but probably costing Leahy a fifth national championship, although Notre Dame was ranked first in some polls.

Leahy was far from the only coach to pull the fake-injury ploy, but other teams did not have Notre Dame's high profile. Leahy came in for considerable criticism, the team incurred the unpleasant nickname "the Fainting Irish," and the NCAA Football Rules Committee outlawed the trick. Without much opposition from the Notre Dame administration, Leahy resigned as coach on January 31, 1954. The reason given to the press was Leahy's health, but Leahy apparently had come to feel that he was not especially wanted at Notre Dame anymore. The resignation started Notre Dame's football program on a downward slide that would not be reversed until the arrival of Ara Parseghian as coach in 1964.

Leahy remained sufficiently popular to be tabbed to give a seconding speech at the Republican National Convention in

1956 on behalf of Gen. Dwight Eisenhower. He served briefly as general manager of the American Football League Chargers in 1960 but did not return to coaching. Leahy died of leukemia in 1973, three years after being inducted into the College Football Hall of Fame.

See also: Cheating; Four Horsemen of Notre Dame; Heisman Trophy; Kerouac, Jack; Lombardi, Vincent Thomas; Rockne, Knute Kenneth.

Additional Reading:

Bynum, Mike, ed. *Many Autumns Ago: The Frank Leahy Era at Boston College and Notre Dame*. N.p.: October Football Corporation, 1988.

Leahy, Frank. *Notre Dame Football: The T Formation*. New York: Prentice-Hall, 1949.

Twombly, Wells. *Shake Down the Thunder: The Official Biography of Notre Dame's Frank Leahy*. Radnor PA: Chilton, 1974.

Ward, Arch. *Frank Leahy and the Fighting Irish: The Story of Notre Dame Football*. New York: G. P. Putnam's Sons, 1944.

Literature

Football has never equaled baseball as an inspirer of great literature. The latter remains the sport of poets, and no football play has come upon the stage to rival August Wilson's *Fences*. That is not to say that readers cannot locate a good poem about football from time to time. A useful source for such poetic nuggets, as well as an occasionally exciting short story, is *Aethlon: The Journal of Sport Literature*, the publication of the Sport Literature Association.

Leading poets, it is true, do mention football on occasion. Yet even when that occurs, as in Howard Nemerov's "Poetics,"

Billy Collins's "Invention," or Delmore Schwartz's "The Heavy Bear Who Goes with Me," the sport tends to be a minor element in the poem.

In the novel, however, if football has not seriously rivaled baseball, it has at least become competitive. A number of good football novels have appeared over the past few decades offering entertainment as well as insights into the sport. Often, especially when professional football is depicted, the seamier side of football appears: its violence, its traditional propensity for drug and alcohol abuse, its supposed hypocrisy and corruption. Football, of course, has plenty of positives as well, and a great many members of the football fraternity have demonstrated admirable virtue, but that perspective is less prevalent in football fiction than in its baseball counterpart.

F. Scott Fitzgerald, however, one of the true giants of American literature, did see in football a game of honor, courage, and even heroics. Fitzgerald longed to be a football star (a goal he never attained) and reflects his love for the game and admiration for the football hero in such works as the short story "The Freshest Boy" (1928), the novel *This Side of Paradise* (1920), and the essay "Sleeping and Waking" (1934). In both the short story and the novel, Fitzgerald's early idol, the great Princeton football and hockey star Hobey Baker, is a model for fictional star athletes; and in the essay, Fitzgerald recalls his lifelong fantasy of playing quarterback for Princeton.

Recent football novels that deserve reading include Frederick Exley's *A Fan's Notes* (1968), Don DeLillo's *End Zone* (1972), Dan Jenkins's *Semi-tough* (1972), Peter Gent's *North Dallas Forty* (1973), Frank Deford's *Everybody's All-American* (1981), and Tim Green's series of football thrillers featuring attorney Madison McCall.

Exley's *A Fan's Notes* was his first novel. It is a heavily autobiographical piece of writing, subtitled *A Fictional Memoir*, with enough alterations to help it cross over into at least semifiction. The first volume in a three-part trilogy (the other volumes are *Pages from a Cold Island*, 1975, and *Last Notes from Home*, 1988), *A Fan's Notes* draws upon Exley's early introduction to sports through his basketball-coach father and the author's growing obsession with sports. The novel also portrays Exley's experiences as a student at Southern California when Frank Gifford was starring in football there, his struggles with alcoholism and mental illness, and his continuing obsession with Gifford as the former USC star played out his Hall of Fame career with the New York Giants.

A Fan's Notes excited considerable critical acclaim, earning for Exley the William Faulkner Award for best first novel of the year as well as a nomination for the National Book Award. The book was made into a film, released in 1972, starring Jerry Orbach.

Don DeLillo is recognized as one of America's leading novelists, especially since the publication in 1985 of his *White Noise*, which won the National Book Award. A later novel, *Underworld* (1997), finished second in a 2006 survey by *The New York Times* of the best American fiction of the past quarter century.

DeLillo's second novel, *End Zone*, took the author into the world of football while introducing some of the concerns that would reappear in his later works, including nuanced explorations of family disintegration and the effects of violence. The book's protagonist, Gary Harkness, has failed as a football player and student at several leading universities before ending up at Logos College in Texas. At Logos, he interacts with the first African American student (an outstanding running back) ever enrolled there, establishes a romantic relationship with a very large young woman wearing an orange dress with a mushroom cloud on its front, and plays for a once-famous football coach increasingly hiding within his own spiritualism. He also audits an ROTC course that leads him into a fascination with nuclear war. Among football novels, the book stands out as one of the most unusual and interesting.

Dan Jenkins's *Semi-tough* is markedly different from DeLillo's novel. It narrates the adventures of Billy Clyde Puckett, a star halfback playing for the New York Giants. Puckett finds himself in Los Angeles facing the Jets in the Super Bowl. The story includes much free-flowing whiskey and equally free women with considerable humor, all leavened with Puckett's agreement to keep a journal account of the game as well as events preceding and following it for a book publisher. The film based on the novel (1977) stars Burt Reynolds as Puckett and Kris Kristofferson as Marvin "Shake" Tiller, Puckett's buddy and rival for the affections of Barbara Jane Bookman, played by Jill Clayburgh. The film introduces an extensive spoof of self-improvement programs, specifically Werner Erhard's E.S.T. (Erhard Seminars Training) program.

One of the most praised football novels is Gent's *North Dallas Forty*. Gent is a former receiver with the Dallas Cowboys who models his main characters (the receiver-protagonist, Phil Elliott; the quarterback, Seth Maxwell; and the coach, B. A. Quinlan) partly after himself, Don Meredith, and Tom Landry respectively. Overall, the Dallas team in the novel is based on Gent's former club. The novel is filled with drinking, drug use, and sexual escapades. It also presents coaches and owners as hypocritical and corrupt. The film version, released in 1979, stars Nick Nolte as Elliott, Mac Davis as Maxwell, and G. D. Spradlin as Coach Quinlan.

Gent published a sequel, *North Dallas After 40* (1989), that reprises many of the characters from the first novel but in a plot that expands into drug smuggling, money laundering, and other criminal activities. Both it and Gent's *The Franchise* (1983) continue to depict the seamier side of football, including the corrupting influence of big money on the sport.

Frank Deford, a longtime writer for *Sports Illustrated*, is one of the nation's most respected sports journalists and also has written highly regarded fiction. The protagonist of Deford's *Everybody's All-American* is Gavin Grey, "the Grey Ghost," who stars as a running back at the University of North Carolina. He wins the Heisman Trophy and embarks upon a professional career, only to run into trouble with alcoholism and his businesses, as well as in his marriage. Charlie "Choo Choo" Justice, an All-American at North Carolina in the late 1940s, and Billy Cannon of Louisiana State University, who won the Heisman in 1959, have been proposed as possible models for Grey, although Deford has denied basing his depiction on either player.

The film of *Everybody's All-American* (1988) stars Dennis Quaid as Gavin Grey, John Goodman as his best friend, and Jessica Lange as his wife. Quaid demonstrated the dangers of acting in football films when Tim Fox of the New England Patriots broke the actor's collarbone during filming of a scene for the movie.

One of the football players most deserving of the epithet "scholar-athlete" was Tim Green. Green was a Phi Beta Kappa scholar and co-valedictorian of his class at Syracuse who later earned a law degree from the university. He played defensive end and linebacker for the Atlanta Falcons from 1986 through 1993. Along with working as a commentator for National Public Radio and an NFL analyst for FOX Sports, he put his experience as a player and lawyer into his writing.

Green's nonfiction *The Dark Side of the Game: My Life in the* NFL elicited considerable excitement when it appeared in 1997. Green also has written twelve suspense novels as of 2007, in addition to *Football Genius* (2007), the first in a planned series of juvenile chapter books about football intended to encourage young readers.

The first five of Green's thrillers revolve around football: *Ruffians* (1993), *Titans* (1994), *Outlaws* (1996), *The Red Zone* (1998), and *Double Reverse* (1999). *Titans* introduces gambling and the mob into professional football, and in several of the novels Madison McCall, a top defense attorney who also happens to be quite beautiful, finds herself defending wrongfully accused individuals as well as facing personal dangers to herself. The novels offer exciting, fast-paced plots, interesting characters, and a lot of information about the world of football. Green's more recent books have turned away from football to rely more on story lines relating to the legal system.

Along with a worthy shelf of football novels, the sport has spawned many entertaining films in addition to those mentioned above. Some of the films have become classics. A separate entry in this volume extensively discusses those.

See also: Education; Films; Fitzgerald, F. Scott Key; Gifford, Frank Newton; Gridiron; Landry, Thomas Wade.

Additional Reading:

Deardorff, Donald L. *Hero and Anti-Hero in the American Football Novel: Changing Conceptions of Masculinity from the Nineteenth Century to the Twenty-First Century.* Lewiston NY: Edwin Mellon, 2006.

Dewey, Joseph. *Beyond Grief and Nothing: A Reading of Don DeLillo.* Columbia: University of South Carolina Press, 2006.

Gent, Peter. *The Last Magic Summer: A Season with My Son: A Memoir.* New York: W. Morrow, 1996.

Yardley, Jonathan. *Misfit: The Strange Life of Frederick Exley.* New York: Random House, 1997.

Little Rock Central Tigers

The students at Little Rock Central High School in Little Rock, Arkansas, in 1957 were not much different from high school students anywhere else in most respects. They attended classes, did homework, played sports, went on dates, and (if fortunate) experienced their first loves. However, two aspects of the school did set them off from many high school students in the United States. One was that their school had one of the greatest football teams in the history of secondary education. The Little Rock Central Tigers were the best team in the state and routinely beat top teams from Texas, Tennessee, Louisiana, and Kentucky as well.

By the time that the 1957 season ended, the Tigers had a winning streak of thirty-three games. They had demolished not only their Arkansas rivals but also Tilghman High of Paducah, Kentucky, the No. 1 team in Kentucky. The National Sports News Service of Minnesota named them the nation's top high school team, and the *Sporting News* chose Tigers running back Bruce Fullerton as the high school Player of the Year.

The second distinguishing characteristic of Little Rock Central, however, was that it was the place where Arkansas Gov. Orval Faubus chose to make his stand against integration. As nine African American students attempted to join the student body in the fall of 1957, Faubus ordered resistance and used the National Guard and the public to carry out his wishes against the plan for integrating Little Rock's schools worked out by the school superintendent, Virgil Blossom. Pres. Dwight D. Eisenhower sent in the army's Screaming Eagles of the 101st Airborne to replace the National Guard and protect the nine. They stayed, facing constant threats and harassment, and eventually the long, difficult school year ended.

Governor Faubus then decided that the only way he could avoid the continued advance of integration was to close the public high schools in Little Rock. Sacrificing football, however, was more than Faubus could accept, or at least more than what the public would accept, so the football season was permitted, but minus the academics and all other aspects of school life.

Not much about the football team in 1958 stayed the same. The high school's legendary football coach, Wilson Matthews, had left to become an assistant coach at the University of Arkansas. Some of the players had graduated, of course, and others transferred. The students with

their pep rallies were gone, and so were the busloads of fans that had regularly accompanied the team to away games. The Tigers, playing in something of a vacuum, struggled to victories in their first two games.

Then came the big test, in two ways. The team had to travel to Baton Rouge, Louisiana, to play an evening game against a formidable foe, Istrouma High School. At home the following day, the citizens of Little Rock faced a referendum on whether to integrate the schools. Little Rock lost twice: the Tigers, 42–0; and integration, by a 3–1 margin.

Eventually, of course, integration would come to Little Rock; and education (and sports) would return. But for a time in the 1950s, powerful social forces played out in Little Rock, Arkansas, around a legendary football program and a bunch of American teenagers.

See also: African Americans (College); African Americans (Professional).

Additional Reading:
Smith, Gary. "Blindsided by History." *Sports Illustrated*, April 9, 2007, 66–75.

Lombardi, Vincent Thomas (1913–1970)

It is a rare individual in the United States who has not heard of Vince Lombardi, who as coach of the Green Bay Packers so securely established the standard for coaching success that his name is now linked to the trophy presented annually to the team winning the Super Bowl: the Vince Lombardi Trophy. A hard taskmaster who nonetheless was loved by his players, Lombardi is credited with the single-minded saying, "Winning isn't everything, it's the only thing." No matter that Lombardi did not create the aphorism, the public has made it his.

Lombardi grew up in Brooklyn in an Italian Catholic family and remained a devout Catholic his whole life. He attended Cathedral Preparatory Seminary with the intention of becoming a priest but opted for a career in football instead. He attended Fordham University, a Catholic institution, where in the 1930s he was a member of the famous Seven Blocks of Granite offensive line under head coach Jim Crowley, one of the Four Horsemen of Notre Dame, and line coach Frank Leahy, a future Notre Dame coach.

After graduating in 1937, Lombardi worked at various uninspiring jobs, played for the semipro Brooklyn Eagles, and tried law school for one semester at Fordham. In 1939 he turned to coaching, at first as an assistant at St. Cecilia High School in Englewood, New Jersey, and then as the school's head coach, where he also taught chemistry, physics, and Latin. Lombardi cared a great deal about teaching and took courses at Seton Hall to improve his teaching methods. He quickly came to see coaching as being much like teaching, including fostering understanding and using repetition to reinforce learning, tactics that he would employ later with the Green Bay Packers.

In 1947 Lombardi returned to Fordham as the freshman coach and then as assistant varsity coach. After two years at Fordham, he moved to West Point, where during his five years under Col. Earl "Red" Blaik he absorbed the importance of organization and execution. His next stop was in the National Football League with the New York Giants in 1954. He coached the offense under Jim Lee Howell, with Tom Landry, another future coaching immortal, heading the defense.

The Giants won the NFL championship in 1956; in 1958, they won the Eastern Conference title but lost the championship game in overtime to the Baltimore Colts. Lombardi's many years of apprenticeship had paid off, though, and Green Bay offered him an opportunity to revive the moribund Packers. Lombardi was ready to become a legend.

At Green Bay, Lombardi preached hard work and discipline while endlessly repeating basic plays until they worked to perfection. He proved a perceptive judge of potential and a masterful teacher. He converted Paul Hornung from a former college quarterback to a Hall of Fame halfback. Bart Starr, an unprepossessing quarterback from the University of Alabama, became another Hall of Famer under Lombardi. Fullback Jim Taylor, great linemen such as Jerry Kramer and Fuzzy Thurston, the ultimate tough linebacker Ray Nitschke, defensive backs Willie Wood and Herb Adderley, and many other Packers blossomed under Lombardi's leadership and tutelage to write their names in football history as members of possibly the greatest NFL team ever. Hornung and Taylor mastered their coach's mantra of "running to daylight," which involved zone blocking by the offensive line and the back finding whatever hole was open.

In 1958, the year before Lombardi joined Green Bay, the Packers won one game. Under coach and general manager Lombardi, Green Bay went 7-5 in his first season. In 1960 the Packers finished first in their Western Conference but lost the title game to the Philadelphia Eagles. In 1961 the Packers went all the way, annihilating the Giants 37–0 in the championship game. In 1962 the Packers again defeated the Giants for the NFL championship.

Green Bay finished the 1963 season with an impressive 11-2-1 record but had one loss more than the Bears (11-1-2), the eventual NFL champions. The Packers slipped to 8-5-1 in 1964, finishing second to the Baltimore Colts.

To some onlookers, it might have appeared as if the Packers were in decline, but Lombardi would have none of that. After all, his football philosophy made losing unthinkable: "Winning isn't everything, it's the only thing." In one sense, of course, Lombardi did not believe that literally. Religion was certainly something that he valued above winning if winning is defined as scoring more points in a football game than the opponent. Nor did Lombardi believe in cheating or deliberately hurting an opponent in order to win. It was important to Lombardi to try to win, to make every appropriate effort to win, but to win the right way— to settle for nothing less than that type of effort.

The famous statement, as David Maraniss clarifies in his biography of Lombardi, *When Pride Still Mattered*, apparently originated with Melville Shavelson, screenwriter for the film *Trouble Along the Way* (1953), which starred John Wayne as a college football coach. The line in the film, however, is spoken by the coach's young daughter, who is quoting her father.

Lombardi returned the Packers to dominance in 1965 with a playoff victory over Baltimore and an outstanding defensive effort against running back Jim Brown to defeat Cleveland in the title game. Two more NFL championship years followed, including the famous Ice Bowl win over Dallas in the 1967 championship game. The 1966 and 1967 seasons were followed by the first two Super Bowls. The Packers won both of them, over the American Football League champion Kansas City Chiefs and Oakland Raiders. The 1967 season was all the more remarkable because it was a transitional year for Green Bay, as the longtime backfield mainstays Paul Hornung and Jim Taylor were gone, replaced by second-year players Donnie Anderson and Jim Grabowski.

Lombardi retired as coach after that season, having won six conference titles and five NFL titles in seven years, plus the first two Super Bowls. He remained as general manager, but finding that role boring he returned to coaching in 1969 with the Washington Redskins. Again Lombardi engineered a quick turnaround in a team's fortunes, transforming Washington from a team coming off thirteen consecutive seasons without a winning record to a challenger with a 7-5-2 record.

Unfortunately, Lombardi was diagnosed with anaplastic carcinoma of the colon in June 1970. Surgery removed part of the colon, but the cancer had already spread to his liver and lymph nodes. Little could be done for Lombardi as he finally faced an adversary he could not defeat. He died on September 3, 1970.

Lombardi's influence had been felt well beyond the football world. His dedication to winning, his extraordinary record of success, and the widespread respect accorded him impressed leaders of both political parties in the United States. Pres. John F. Kennedy had become a friend and admirer of Lombardi's, and David Carley of the Democratic National Committee mentioned Lombardi to Hubert Humphrey in 1968 as a viable running mate. Politics, however, could have done little to enhance the reputation of Vince Lombardi, who remains, decades after his death, the epitome of a winner.

See also: Films; Greatest Game; Hornung, Paul Vernon; Ice Bowl; Landry, Thomas Wade; Leahy, Francis William; Religion; Super Bowl.

Additional Reading:

Kramer, Jerry, ed. *Lombardi: Winning Is the Only Thing.* New York: Maddick Manuscripts, distributed by World Publishing, 1970.

Lombardi, Vince. *Run to Daylight!* With W. C. Heinz. Englewood Cliffs NJ: Prentice-Hall, 1963.

Maraniss, David. *When Pride Still Mattered: A Life of Vince Lombardi.* New York: Simon and Schuster, 1999.

Phillips, Donald T. *Run to Win: Vince Lombardi on Coaching and Leadership.* New York: St. Martin's, 2001.

Madden, John Earl (b. 1936)

John Madden is one of those rare individuals who can cut across the generations, appealing to new groups for different reasons. A Hall of Fame coach, a widely seen figure in commercial endorsements, a longtime football analyst on television, and the name on the most popular sports video game in America, Madden is one of the best known sports figures in the country.

Madden's professional playing career was cut short in his rookie season with the Philadelphia Eagles by a knee injury. He then turned to coaching, and after stints at Hancock Junior College in Santa Maria, California, and San Diego State University, he became linebackers coach for the Oakland Raiders in 1967. Two years later, at the age of thirty-two, he was named Oakland's head coach, one of the youngest professional head coaches in history.

In his ten seasons as head coach of the Raiders, Madden's teams won 103 regular-season games against thirty-two losses and seven ties for a winning percentage of .759, the highest by any NFL coach with 100 or more career victories. Madden never won fewer than eight games in a season, won his division seven times, and captured Super Bowl XI to conclude the 1976 season, accomplishments that led to his induction into the Pro Football Hall of Fame in 2006.

Madden left coaching when he was still in his early forties and began his long career in television. He joined NBC in 2006 on the Sunday night telecast, completing a sweep of all the major networks. He previously had worked for CBS, FOX, and ABC (including *Monday Night Football*). As of 2007 he had won fifteen Emmy Awards for his broadcasting.

For decades, Madden was seen regularly on television advertising a wide range of products, including Miller Lite beer, Ace Hardware, Tinactin, and Outback Steakhouse. Perhaps his most famous commercial depicted him smashing through the backdrop in a Miller Lite commercial yelling, "Hey, wait a minute!"

Young football and video fans, as well as young athletes, know Madden best for the video game that bears his name. A remarkably realistic football game, *Madden NFL 06*, the sixteenth edition of the game, sold approximately 1.7 million copies within a week of being released. *Madden NFL 07* was the top-selling video game in North America during 2006. So anticipated is each year's new version that stores open at midnight to meet the rush of shoppers. The culmination of the game is the Madden Bowl held just before the Super Bowl. Madden NFL also has spawned a popular Web site.

Madden also gives back, especially to youngsters. He started the John Madden Hall of Fame Education Foundation to help school and other youth groups with the cost of traveling to the Pro Football Hall of Fame. As of summer 2007 some 3,500 boys and girls had been able to visit the Hall with Madden's assistance.

Through career after career, Madden rolls on—by bus, of course. He may be the most famous fear-of-flying celebrity in the country, crisscrossing the land in his luxurious custom-designed bus, the *Outback Steakhouse Madden Cruiser*. As a result of his multiple points of entry into the nation's consciousness, Madden had achieved a Q score of 36 by 2005. The Q score is computed by Marketing Evaluations, which determines the public's familiarity with the individual and the person's appeal. With his 36, Madden ranked behind only Joe Montana (40) and Brett Favre (38) among NFL personalities. Successful, popular, likeable, Madden is firmly entrenched in America's popular culture.

See also: Commercials and Advertisements; Davis, Allen; *Monday Night Football*; Super Bowl; Television Broadcasting.

Additional Reading:
Madden, John. *All Madden: Hey, I'm Talking Pro Football*. With Dave Anderson. New York: HarperCollins, 1996.
———. *Hey, Wait a Minute, I Wrote a Book*. New York: Villard Books, 1984.
SportsGamer.com: Madden Web site. http://www.sportsgamer.com/games/madden07.

Magazines

Football fans can follow the sport in a number of periodicals readily available in bookstores or through subscriptions. They differ considerably in format, varying from glossy magazines to tabloid style, from pictures totally in color to primarily black-and-white. Some offer weekly coverage in depth while others focus more on feature articles. Whatever one's preference, there is something for just about everyone.

An old standby is *Sporting News*, a weekly previously known as *The Sporting News*. The publication was created in 1886 by Alfred H. Spink, a sportswriter for the *St. Louis Post-Dispatch* and secretary of the St. Louis Browns baseball team. For most of its life, the *Sporting News* was in newspaper format and known as the "bible of baseball," although it always carried stories about other sports as well. The Spink family owned the publication until 1977. During the 1980s and 1990s, it evolved into a modern, glossy magazine, and its focus broadened to include a variety of sports, including extensive coverage of professional and college football. It also publishes various annual magazines, including its *Complete Pro Football Draft Encyclopedia*.

Similar in appearance to the *Sporting News* is *Sports Illustrated*, also a weekly, the brainchild of *Time*'s Henry Luce. The first issue appeared on August 16, 1954, and included widespread use of color photographs. The magazine has employed an impressive roster of talented writers over the years including such figures as Frank Deford and Rick Reilly. During the fall, *Sports Illustrated* discusses not only professional and college football but also high school football. ESPN *The Magazine*, like *Sports Illustrated*, is highly visual and includes stories about football as well as a range of other sports. It is an oversized glossy magazine that began in 1998 and appears on a biweekly basis.

Pro Football Weekly, as the title indicates, is totally devoted to professional football. Since 1967 the tabloid newsmagazine has been offering pro news, currently including previews of NFL games, rosters and depth charts, statistics, fantasy football coverage, injury reports, photographs, and more. *Pro Football Weekly* also publishes several annual magazines, such as *Pro Football Weekly Preview*, *Fantasy Football Guide*, and *Pro Prospects Preview*, and airs a thirty-minute newsmagazine on television during the football season.

USA *Today Sports Weekly* is in tabloid format, primarily in black-and-white. It began as solely a baseball publication in 1991 but expanded its focus to include professional football in 2002 when it also changed its name from USA *Today Baseball Weekly*. Weekly football coverage began in 2007. During football season, *Sports Weekly* offers detailed matchup analyses of coming games with a recap of each team's previous contest and predictions regarding who will win and why. It also includes detailed statistics.

Other magazines, of course, carry occasional football stories. *Forbes*, for example, had an in-depth account of Robert Kraft and his New England Patriots in its September 19, 2005, issue. General-interest magazines, including some of the country's earliest, have looked at football from time to time, among them *Saturday Evening Post*, the former photojournals *Life* and *Look*, *Collier's* (with columns by Walter Camp and later Grantland Rice from the 1920s through the 1940s), and even the newsweeklies *Time* and *Newsweek*. Annual magazines have also been around for a long time, many of them published by Street and Smith, including its current *College Football* and *Pro Football*. Street and Smith and *Sporting News* are now owned by the same parent company.

Of all former magazines, perhaps *Sport* most deserves mentioning in connection with football. *Sport* appeared from 1946 until 2000. A monthly general-interest sports magazine, it pioneered full-page color photographs and emphasized human interest pieces. For example in its November 1961 issue, authors explore what the future might hold for Paul Hornung in light of past injuries that left him susceptible to future problems and what it is like being Ernie Davis, "the All-America show wherever Syracuse goes." The highly personalized writing by such authors as Grantland Rice and Roger Kahn helped generations of youngsters come to know a little better what their sports heroes were like as people.

See also: Davis, Ernie; Draft; Hornung, Paul Vernon; Internet; Literature; Newspapers; Rice, Grantland.

Additional Reading:

Fleder, Rob, ed. *Fifty Years of Great Writing: Sports Illustrated, 1954–2004.* New York: Sports Illustrated Books, 2003.

Mott, Frank Luther. *A History of American Magazines.* 5 vols. New York: Appleton; Cambridge MA: Harvard University Press, 1930–1968.

Manning, Peyton Williams (b. 1976)

Peyton Manning, named by *Sports Illustrated* in September 2007 as the best player in the National Football League, may be the greatest quarterback ever. What skepticism remained about his abilities appeared to dissolve when he led the Indianapolis Colts to victory in Super Bowl XLI on February 4, 2007, earning the Super Bowl Most Valuable Player award. In addition, Manning is one of the most socially conscious athletes in the United States, essentially adopting as his personal responsibility three locations: his hometown of New Orleans; Knoxville, Tennessee, where he played college ball for the University of Tennessee; and Indianapolis.

Manning's achievements with at least several years left in his career are extraordinary. At the conclusion of the 2008 regular season, Manning's eleventh in the NFL, he already had passed for 45,268 yards in regular-season play and thrown 333 touchdown passes. He had established several records, including most consecutive seasons of 4,000 or more passing yards (six), most total seasons surpassing 4,000 yards (nine), and most games with a perfect passer rating (four, including a playoff game). His most acclaimed record, however, was the standard for touchdown passes in one season, which he established in 2004 when he threw forty-nine touchdown passes, breaking Dan Marino's previous record of forty-eight. That record, however, fell to New England's Tom Brady in 2007.

Peyton's accomplishments are legion. In addition to those mentioned above, he was Louisiana High School Player of the Year (1993–94), made the All-America team at Tennessee, finished runner-up in the Heisman voting in 1998, won three of his four college bowl games, received the Davey O'Brien Award as top senior quarterback and the Johnny Unitas Award as the nation's top quarterback in 1997, was the first overall choice in the 1998 draft, earned the NFL co-Most Valuable Player award in 2003 and the award outright in 2004 and 2008, and was honored with the Walter Payton Man of the Year Award and the Byron "Whizzer" White Humanitarian Award in 2005.

Manning appears often in television commercials and is widely viewed as the NFL's most marketable player, largely because he not only is enormously talented but also is broadly liked and respected. His commercials and print advertisements for such businesses and charitable organizations as Gatorade, MasterCard, Sprint, Sony, the American Red Cross, St. Mary's Medical Center in Knoxville, and ESPN's *This Is SportsCenter* often include self-denigration. In a television spot for the latter, Peyton is visiting the SportsCenter studios with his parents and brothers (including father Archie, long-time quarterback for the New Orleans Saints, and brother Eli, current New York Giants quarterback). Peyton and Eli dawdle behind the rest of the family, engaging in horseplay typical of junior high boys, when Archie turns and gives them a dirty look. The commercials for MasterCard feature Manning, in a role reversal, as a fan of normal people, excited over meeting, for example, an accountant.

Manning has been very involved in recovery efforts after Hurricane Katrina, as early as September 2005 flying a planeload of supplies to Baton Rouge. He also has contributed funds in response to the Indian Ocean tsunami of December 26, 2004, and the terrorist attacks of September 11, 2001.

Manning serves as president of the PeyBack Foundation, the name a play on his own name and the concept of paying back to society. The foundation contributes money and arranges educational, social, and cultural events for youth in Indianapolis, Tennessee, and Louisiana. The PeyBack Foundation also hosts and pays the total costs of an annual PeyBack Classic for Indiana high school athletes. The 2006 event featured two high school football games at the RCA Dome in Indianapolis with eleven thousand fans attending. Part of the proceeds from the games went to the participating high schools.

With his football exploits, steady presence on television throughout the year, and major charitable efforts, Manning remains a household name. In addition, as he makes his way toward the college and professional halls of fame, he stands securely as one of the most respected athletes in the history of American sports.

See also: Brady, Thomas Edward, Jr.; Commercials and Advertisements; Forward Pass; Katrina (Hurricane); Super Bowl.

Additional Reading:
Hyams, Jimmy. *Peyton Manning: Primed and Ready.* Lenexa KS: Addax Publishing Group, 1998.
Manning, Peyton, and Archie Manning. *Manning.* With John Underwood. New York: HarperEntertainment, 2000.
Peyton Manning Web site (including links to the PeyBack Foundation). http://www.peytonmanning.com.

Marino, Daniel Constantine, Jr. (b. 1961)

Dan Marino was an All-American quarterback at the University of Pittsburgh, famed for his quick release and passing accuracy. He joined the Miami Dolphins in 1983, started the sixth game of his rookie season, and continued to fire touchdown passes for seventeen years.

When Marino finally retired following the 1999 season, he held a basket of records and was firmly established as one of football's all-time great quarterbacks. He became the first quarterback to throw for 5,000 yards in a season; established the single-season record, since broken by Peyton Manning and Tom Brady, for touchdown passes in a season (forty-eight);

and threw for more touchdowns (420) and yards (61,361) than anyone who ever played in the NFL. Brett Favre broke his career touchdown and passing yardage records in 2007, but that hardly diminished the stature of this member of the college and pro football halls of fame.

What is likely more regrettable from Marino's point of view than having his records broken is that despite those great personal accomplishments he never played on a Super Bowl winner. His only appearance in the big game was on January 20, 1985, in Super Bowl XIX, when Marino and the Dolphins lost to Joe Montana and the San Francisco 49ers 38–16. That was Marino's second season, and he surely expected to play in other championship games, but despite many playoff appearances he would never again appear in a Super Bowl.

Marino retired after the 1999 season and embarked on a career in broadcasting. He briefly returned to Miami in 2004 as senior vice president of football operations but resigned three weeks later. During his induction speech at Canton in 2005, he spotted his former receiver Mark Clayton in the audience and told him to go deep for a pass. He did, and Marino hit him once again for a completion.

Marino is currently part of The NFL Today show on CBS and HBO's Inside the NFL. His postplaying days have also included a number of endorsement contracts, such as commercials for NutriSystem, Papa John's pizzas, and Isotoner gloves. The latter seemed especially appropriate, given Marino's famous right hand.

In 1992 Marino and his wife, Claire, whose son, Michael, had been diagnosed with autism, established the Dan Marino Foundation to help children with autism and other neurodevelopment disabilities. A related project is the Dan Marino Center at the Miami Children's Hospital, which annually treats close to fifty thousand children with neurodevelopment problems. He also has worked with other athletes to help children with autism, including former quarterback Doug Flutie, who, like Marino, has a son with autism.

See also: Brady, Thomas Edward, Jr.; Commercials and Advertisements; Favre, Brett Lorenzo; Manning, Peyton Williams; Montana, Joseph Clifford; Super Bowl; Television Broadcasting.

Additional Reading:
Marino, Dan. Marino! With Steve Delsohn. Chicago: Contemporary Books, 1986.
———. Dan Marino: My Life in Football. With David Hyde. Chicago: Triumph Books, 2005.
Wilner, Barry. Dan Marino. New York: Chelsea House, 1996.

Marshall University Air Tragedy

Marshall University in Huntington, West Virginia, suffered the worst sports disaster in American sports history on a stormy night in 1970. The evening of November 14 the team was returning from a close defeat at the hands of East Carolina on a charter flight, the first time that the team had traveled by plane. Seventy-five people were aboard the Southern Airlines DC-9, including thirty-seven players, head coach Rick Tolley, Marshall broadcaster Gene Morehouse (whose son, Keith, later became play-by-play man for Marshall football games), and team physician Ray Hagley.

According to the official National Transportation Safety Board (NTSB) report, despite the mist and light rain all appeared normal with the plane when the crew contacted the Huntington Airport tower at 7:23 p.m. to receive clearance to land. However, the plane came in too low, below what is called the "minimum descent altitude," and struck trees about one mile short of the runway. The plane crashed and burned, all on board perishing. The crash may have been caused, according to the NTSB, by an error in using cockpit instrument data or by a malfunction in the altimetry system that determines altitude.

Freshmen, then ineligible for varsity competition, were safe at Marshall, as were a few other players who missed the game for injury-related or other reasons. Essentially, however, the team was destroyed. Many prominent Marshall citizens who regularly attended Marshall games died in the crash. Seventy minor-age children lost at least one parent; eighteen of them lost both.

The closeness between the university and the Huntington community made the tragedy even more devastating. In the aftermath of the crash, so many funerals were held that the university ran short of officials to represent the institution at them.

When the decision was made to continue the football program, aided by strong pressure from students and alumni not to give up, recruiting began for a new head coach. Marshall football had undergone a difficult period even before the crash, with the program suffering five straight losing seasons and being placed on a one-year probation by the NCAA for recruiting violations. Two coaches turned down the job, which was finally accepted by Jack Lengyel, who had coached at the College of Wooster in Ohio.

The NCAA permitted Marshall to play freshmen in 1971, but nothing was easy. With a few holdovers and a very young team, Marshall won only two games. The initial victory, though, on a last-second touchdown over Xavier, produced an extraordinarily emotional reaction from those in attendance. After the game, the team went into its locker room. An hour and a half later the players reemerged to find fifteen thousand people still in the stands.

Fortune would shine more sweetly on Marshall football in the future. The team started winning in the 1980s, and throughout the 1990s it was a powerhouse, featuring such stars as quarterback Chad Pennington and receiver Randy Moss. The team moved up from Division I-AA to I-A in 1997. In December 2006 *We Are Marshall*, an excellent, historically accurate, and sensitively produced film focusing on the immediate aftermath of the crash, was released. The film brought again before the nation a story of loss and perseverance that deserves to be remembered.

See also: Films; Moss, Randy Gene.

Additional Reading/Viewing:

Castro, James E. *Marshall University*. Chicago: Arcadia Publishing, 2005.

Keller, Julia. "It's Always with You." First published in the *Chicago Tribune*, September 5, 1999. http://members.aol.com/jeff1070/marshall2.html.

Memorial of the 1970 Marshall University Football Team Plane Crash Web site. http://www.marshall.edu/library/speccoll/virtualmuseum/memorial/default.asp.

We Are Marshall. Dir. McG (Joseph McGinty Nichol). Warner Brothers, 2006.

Mascots and Team Names

Mascots have elicited considerable controversy in recent decades, principally because of offensive imagery, nicknames, and symbols relating to American Indians.

Yet most sports mascots and names are not controversial; some even reflect interesting and imaginative traditions behind their selection. Many of the National Football League names, minus the highly offensive Washington Redskins, are cases in point. The Pro Football Hall of Fame offers considerable background to NFL names, demonstrating the varied approaches franchises have taken to naming their organizations. The Green Bay Packers and Pittsburgh Steelers offer a respectful nod to prominent types of work that once occupied many of their area residents: Green Bay's meatpacking industry (the Indian Packing Company having provided money for jerseys and a practice field for the new Green Bay team in 1919) and Pittsburgh's steel mills. The Baltimore (later Indianapolis) Colts chose their name because of the horse breeding and racing in the area.

In some cases, the team names have a history that a casual fan would be hardpressed to decipher without some assistance. The Buffalo Bills, for example, derived their name from Buffalo Bill Cody and the earlier history of professional football in Buffalo. The Buffalo team in the All-America Football Conference was initially called the Bisons, establishing a Western motif consistent with the team's owner, James Breuil of the Frontier Oil Company. The name was later changed to the Bills after William F. Cody, prominently associated (by later historians not very positively) with buffalo, which he helped almost to exterminate. The American Football League team kept the Bills name and continued to use it after shifting into the NFL.

The most literary name belongs to the Baltimore Ravens, the name coming from its most famous poetic son, Edgar Allan Poe, one of whose best-known poems is "The Raven." Animal names, of course, abound, each symbolizing some quality that team owners hoped to see in their teams: Bears, Lions, Panthers, Bengals, Broncos, and so forth. The Arizona Cardinals, however, despite exhibiting a bird logo, do not owe their name to the beautiful red bird of backyard fame. In fact, the name came from the reddish color. The team originally played in maroon jerseys bought from the University of Chicago. When someone criticized the color as being a faded red, Chris O'Brien, the owner of the then Chicago team, replied that the color instead was cardinal red.

Other teams exhibit various cultural and historical elements of their surroundings. The New England Patriots, for example, give homage to the birth of the American Revolution in the Boston area. The New Orleans Saints recall the famous New Orleans song "When the Saints Go Marching In" and less obviously the date of the franchise's birth, All Saints' Day (November 1), 1966. The original 49ers were brave folks heading westward to seek gold in 1849. The San Francisco 49ers have uncovered quite a bit of gold in their football history, although not so much recently.

Then there are the Redskins, the team that for many years resisted integrating. That ownership is long gone, but the nickname continues to offend people with even a smattering of historical knowledge and sensitivity. It is hard to imagine any name, except possibly "Savages," that would be more offensive regarding American Indians. Many people have pointed out that parallels to "Redskins" would be such terms as "Darkies" and "Palefaces." No team would offer the public those names, but Washington's management remains adamant against changing the name. Many media outlets, recognizing the complete impropriety of the term, in fact its completely

demeaning signification, have stopped using it. Newspaper listings of NFL games often cite teams' nicknames except for Washington, printing the city name instead. For the NFL team operating in our nation's capital to remain so obstinately insulting toward American Indians is especially reprehensible.

At the college level, most mascots and names are inoffensive if sometimes unclear in their reference. One can readily understand what a badger is, although few people outside Wisconsin might see the animal as particularly praiseworthy. A wolverine is a bit more feisty. But a Buckeye? Tree aficionados may recognize the name, but others who care enough to search will have to consult a handy dictionary. The Crimson Tide is a colorful name, and if images of a river of blood hurtling over the opposition arise, that probably is fine with Alabama supporters. The Trojan on horseback riding his charger around the field at Southern California games is surely one of the most memorable mascots. And if no one associated with Notre Dame objects to the "Fighting Irish" nickname with its stereotyping reference and the rather silly leprechaun mascot, others are not likely to complain.

Then there is the American Indian mascot controversy. Beginning in the 1960s, various individuals and organizations, including the National Congress of American Indians, began to oppose use of Indian mascots, names, and symbols by sports teams, from the elementary level to professional leagues. Although most people associated with their use undoubtedly did not intend to send insulting or harmful messages, and many proponents of Indian mascots and nicknames may have believed that they were honoring American Indian traditions, there clearly was a massive failure to recognize the implications of such practices. American Indian opponents pointed out that once again Euro-Americans were deciding for Indians what was in their best interest. Euro-Americans were appropriating what rightly belonged to a variety of Native American nations and using it as they saw fit. In addition, many of the depictions were inaccurate, such as Chief Illiniwek, the University of Illinois mascot (or symbol as the university preferred to call him). There never was such a chief, although that was perhaps the least of the offenses. Chief Illiniwek was portrayed by a series of Euro-American students from 1926 to February 2007, when he finally was retired. Although the figure was supposedly intended to reflect the Illiniwek, who once lived in what became the state of Illinois (which was named after them), the actor wore an Oglala Lakota costume. Nor was the dance he performed at all genuine.

The National Collegiate Athletic Association took a stand on the issue in August 2005, listing eighteen schools that used "hostile and abusive American Indian nicknames" and banning these schools from hosting postseason games until they removed all visual representations of the names. The University of Illinois, after unsuccessfully appealing the NCAA's inclusion of Chief Illiniwek on its proscribed list, finally retired him.

Some schools reacted quickly to concerns about their use of Indian mascots and nicknames, well before the NCAA issued its ban. Stanford, for example, switched its nickname from Indians to Cardinals in 1972. The Universities of Wisconsin and Minnesota instituted a policy of not scheduling games against teams with racist images and nicknames.

The NCAA accepted some institutions' use of American Indian nicknames, such as the Central Michigan Chippewas and the University of Utah Utes because the schools have a substantial relationship with the Saginaw Chippewa Indian Tribe of Michigan and the Northern Ute Tribe, respectively. Similar thinking lay behind the NCAA's decision to accept an appeal from Florida State University, which originally was among the eighteen listed schools. The university, with strong support from the Seminole Nation of Florida, insisted that its use of the Seminole name and its Chief Osceola mascot reflect a serious relationship with the Florida Seminoles through its Seminole Scholars scholarship program and other ties.

At the present time, Indian nicknames and mascots continue to be widespread, although not as common as they once were. Lists of schools still using them can be found at the American Indian Sports Team Mascots Web site.

See also: American Indians; Language.

Additional Reading:

American Indian Sports Team Mascots Web
site. http://www.aistm.org.

"Franchise Nicknames." The Pro Football Hall
of Fame Web site. http://www.profootball
hof.com/history/nicknames.jsp.

King, C. Richard, and Charles Fruehling Spring-
wood, eds. *Team Spirits: The Native American Mascot Controversy.* Lincoln: University of Nebraska Press, 2001.

Spindel, Carol. *Dancing at Halftime: Sports
and the Controversy Over American Indian Mascots.* New York: New York University Press, 2000.

McNally, John Victor (Johnny Blood, the Vagabond Halfback) (1903–1985)

Few players in the early years of the National Football League were the equal of
John McNally, better known as Johnny
Blood, and perhaps none were as colorful. Certainly no one else chose a name
off a movie marquee and then used it
throughout his professional career.

John McNally, who came from a
wealthy family involved in newspapers
and paper mills, did not need to worry about money. Nonetheless, when he
was still playing for St. John's College in
Minnesota, he decided to play professional ball as well, yet he did not want to
lose his college eligibility. So when he and
a pal, Ralph Hanson, were driving past
a movie house, McNally noticed the title of the film and decided to make use
of it. The film was a Rudolph Valentino
silent classic, *Blood and Sand.* McNally
took the first word for his last name and
suggested that Hanson adopt the latter.

They did so, and Johnny Blood (and less
famously and permanently, Ralph Sand)
was born.

Johnny Blood was a man of many talents. He starred in baseball and track as
well as football at St. John's, and he went
on to a sterling fourteen-year career as a
professional football player. He could do
it all: run with speed and power, block,
kick, pass, and tackle. Best of all, he could
catch passes. With the Green Bay Packers,
he played on four championship teams
(1929, 1930, 1931, 1936) and was possibly
the finest receiver in the game until the
arrival of his much younger Green Bay
teammate Don Hutson. For his football
accomplishments, he was named to the
Pro Football Hall of Fame in 1963.

A flamboyant character, Blood could
be counted on to do one outrageous thing
after another. After three years at St. John's
College, he decided that he wanted to
play for Knute Rockne at Notre Dame,
so he showed up there masquerading as
a freshman. When the freshman coach,
George Keogan, tried to make a tackle out
of him, he resisted and was thrown off the
team. Later with the Packers, Blood an-
tagonized a much larger teammate, La-
Vern Dilweg, who pursued him through
the train carrying the team back to Green
Bay. To elude his pursuer, Blood crawled
up on the roof of the caboose and then
made his way along the top from car to
car to the engine, where he regaled the
engineer and fireman with stories for the
rest of the trip. Another railroad esca-
pade involved Blood's missing the train

his team was taking, so he followed by car—on the tracks—until he caught up with his teammates.

Drinking and breaking curfew were common practices for the nonconformist Blood. Once when his Green Bay coach, Curly Lambeau, offered him a ten-dollar bonus per game to give up drinking, Blood declined but did agree not to drink after Wednesday evening. While serving as player-coach with the Pittsburgh Pirates (later the Steelers) in the late 1930s, Blood appeared in Los Angeles on a Sunday. Queried about his own team, he explained that they were not playing that Sunday. In fact, Pittsburgh *was* playing, and Blood had simply forgotten about the game.

A journalist bestowed the nickname "Vagabond Halfback" on Blood in response to his unpredictability and especially because of an incident in 1932 when he had to get back to Green Bay but had run out of money. He hopped a train and was discovered hiding in a baggage compartment. The trainman who discovered Blood recognized him and invited him into the baggage car for coffee and a bit of lunch. The trainman even leant Blood his razor so he could make himself more presentable.

As adept at football and showmanship as he was, Blood also was extremely bright. He graduated from high school at age fourteen. During his stint at Notre Dame, he hung around for a time after being dismissed from football, helping quarterback Harry Stuhldreher, one of

Notre Dame's Four Horsemen, with his poetry assignments. Blood later wrote a book. Most people assumed it would be about football, but instead it was about Malthusian economics. Nor, for all his devil-may-care attitude, was he anything other than thoroughly patriotic. When World War II arrived, Blood enrolled for that contest, too, serving as a cryptographer in India.

See also: Films; Four Horsemen of Notre Dame; Rockne, Knute Kenneth; World War II.

Additional Reading:

Gullickson, Denis J. *Vagabond Halfback: The Life and Times of Johnny Blood McNally.* Madison WI: Trail Books, 2006.

Hickok, Ralph. *Vagabond Halfback: The Sage of Johnny Blood McNally.* New Bedfort CT: n.p., 1991.

Middle Age

Football may be a young person's game, but middle-aged men like to keep on dreaming of scoring that winning touchdown, making the game-saving tackle, or driving the clinching field goal through the uprights. Of course, dreaming is always a little easier if there remains at least some basis in reality for those dreams.

Thus, if middle-aged men want to continue seeing themselves out on the football field, it helps to see real middle-aged football players still competing and getting the job done. That helps to explain the popularity of those players who have remained active and competitive into middle age.

The ultimate middle-aged role model was George Blanda, who continued playing until the age of forty-eight. Blanda was a quarterback and place-kicker for the Chicago Bears in the 1950s but seemingly had come to the end of his career with the 1958 season. However, the advent of the new American Football League in 1960 created a market for experienced players who might have a little something left.

In fact, Blanda, who began the 1960 season just short of his thirty-third birthday, had a great deal left. He starred as the starting quarterback with Houston through the 1966 season and also handled his team's kicking. Three times he led the AFL in pass completions and threw as many as thirty-six touchdown passes in a season. Then in 1967 he joined the Oakland Raiders and did some of his greatest kicking. For three consecutive seasons, 1967–69, he scored more than one hundred points. In 1973 he reached that point level again. He also served as a backup quarterback with the Raiders.

In 1970, at the age of forty-three, Blanda brought Oakland four victories and a tie in a five-game period with touchdown passes or field goals in the closing moments. When he finally hung up his cleats after the 1975 season, he had succeeded in playing through his forty-eighth year, and doing so productively, becoming the oldest player in the history of the National Football League. His second career, after being cut loose by Chicago, propelled him into the Pro Football Hall of Fame with a total of 2,002 points scored.

George Blanda was the oldest but not the only middle-aged football player to offer hope to millions of the over-forty crowd. Kicker Morten Andersen was still active in 2007 at the age of forty-seven. Several players performed at forty-five: kicker Ben Agajanian, kicker Gary Anderson, and two nineteenth-century players, end Bobby Marshall and guard-tackle John Nesser.

Three quarterbacks continued to play at forty-four, Steve DeBerg, Hall of Famer Warren Moon, and Vinny Testaverde, as well as kicker Eddie Murray. As of the 2006 season, at least forty-five NFL players had been active at the age of forty or older. It helped to be a kicker or quarterback, so middle-aged fans would do well to dream of themselves tossing a pass, making a field goal, or booming a punt. And definitely not carrying the ball. Not since 1906 (Ken Strong) has a running back survived into middle age.

So, middle-aged men, turn the lights down low, tune in the television, and get that cool drink and plate of munchies within reach. Then keep on dreaming. It can happen. After all, it happened to George, Morten, and a whole slew of others.

See also: Grandfathers.

Additional Reading:

Blanda, George. *Over Forty: Feeling Great and Looking Good!* With Mickey Herskowitz. New York: Simon and Schuster, 1978.

Pro Football Hall of Fame Web site. http://www.profootballhof.com/history/stats/40_and_over_club.jsp.

Twombly, Wells. *Blanda, Alive and Kicking: The Exclusive, Authorized Biography.* Los Angeles: Nash Publishing, 1972.

Monday Night Football

Prior to 1970 the world of football was neat and precise, each level in its place. High school teams played on Friday, college teams on Saturday, and the pros on Sunday. Occasionally, there was an exception, such as the professional games on Thanksgiving, but overall each football level kept to its appointed day. Mondays were decidedly not for football.

Mondays were for television viewers to get comfortable in front of their sets and join in the hilarity of *Rowan & Martin's Laugh-In.* Then later in the evening, they could prop up in bed and watch Johnny Carson on the *Tonight* show, with a much smaller number opting instead for the more cerebral *Dick Cavett Show.*

But National Football League Commissioner Pete Rozelle had an idea—prime-time football. The notion was revolutionary; prime time, as everyone knew, was not for sports. Had not boxing almost destroyed itself by trying to succeed in prime time? Not since the demise of *Friday Night Fights* in 1959 had any sport attempted on a regular basis to crack those posttwilight hours.

Yet Rozelle believed that he could see a bright future for professional football in the evening. He just had to convince one of the networks, but that proved difficult indeed. NBC was not about to give up the top-rated *Laugh-In.* CBS, like NBC, already was broadcasting NFL football on Sundays and said no thanks to Monday. That left ABC, and there Rozelle got a bite. Producer Roone Arledge enthusiastically bought into Rozelle's plan but then ran into opposition from his bosses. It took Rozelle's threat to join forces with the Sports Network, owned by the reclusive Howard Hughes, plus the positive response by a majority of the ABC affiliates to *Monday Night Football,* to bring ABC onboard.

The first Monday night game was broadcast from Cleveland on September 20, 1970, with the Browns hosting Joe Namath and the New York Jets, winners of Super Bowl III. Scheduled for the second week was a contest featuring Johnny Unitas and the Baltimore Colts against the Kansas City Chiefs, the defending NFL champion and winner of Super Bowl IV.

Beyond its position on the television schedule, *Monday Night Football* was like no other football telecast. In the booth were not two but three individuals. Keith Jackson did play-by-play, while Howard Cosell provided erudite commentary with a self-assured confidence (many would say arrogance) new to football television booths. Cosell had earned fame (and infamy in some quarters) by befriending and defending heavyweight champion Muhammad Ali when he changed his name from Cassius Clay and when he chose to yield his heavyweight championship rather than enter the military during the Vietnam War. Cosell took pride in his self-proclaimed honesty and frankness, assuring viewers that he was "telling it like it is." Rounding out the trio was Don Meredith, soon to be christened Dandy Don by Cosell. A former Dallas quarterback, Meredith brought down-home humor to the broadcast and proved a foil for Cosell, but able, with a quip, to puncture the eloquent one's bubble. Dandy Don also could tell it like it is. When a game was clearly decided, rather than maintain the pretence of uncertainty, he would signal the obvious outcome in song: "Turn out the lights, the party's over."

The next year, Frank Gifford, the Giffer, replaced Jackson, and the show was set. *Monday Night Football* was as much a show featuring the act of Cosell, Meredith, and Gifford as it was a sports event. About sixty million homes on the average tuned in to watch during the first season. ABC bumped Cavett from Monday nights, and viewers spurned shopping, going to the movies, and eating out, or any other endeavor that would take them away from their television screens.

In addition to the verbal repartee among the three stars of the booth, viewers marveled at the close-up depiction of the action, a focus that Arledge had pioneered in ABC's Olympics coverage. Nine cameras rather than the normal four or five provided a multitude of viewing angles, and instant replay and close-up shots gave the game an intimacy it had never enjoyed before. Halftime highlights brought the audience up to date on the games from the day before.

So quickly and thoroughly did *Monday Night Football* catch on that other sports followed suit. Major League Baseball offered prime-time World Series games in 1971, and in 1972 both the NCAA championship basketball game and the Summer Olympics were presented in prime time. The football program yielded a book about it, *Monday Night Mayhem* (1988), and a television film of the same title (2002).

The fabulous trio broke up in the 1980s, Cosell leaving after the 1983 season, Meredith a year later. Gifford stayed through 1997. Other big-name announcers replaced them. Al Michaels did play-by-play commentary from 1986 through 2005, the final year of *Monday Night Football* on ABC. John Madden, Joe Theisman, and a variety of others spent varying amounts of time in the broadcast booth for the games. The first woman joined the team in 1997 (Lesley Visser). No combination, however, equaled the magic of Cosell, Dandy Don, and the Giffer.

Many Monday night games proved historic. Cosell, who never saw football as isolated from the rest of American society, on December 8, 1980, broke the news to a shocked world of the murder of John Lennon. Three years later, on September 3, 1983, the incomparable Cosell called wide receiver Alvin Garrett a "little monkey." The outcry, accusing Cosell of racism, led to his departure from *Monday Night Football* after the season. It was an especially sad exit for Cosell, whose injudicious comment hardly reflected the kind of man he was. In fact, Cosell had been a longtime advocate for racial justice and one of the strongest supporters of Muhammed Ali when defending the great but highly controversial boxer was far from popular and certainly not a smart career move.

Joe Theisman suffered a broken leg during a Monday night game, November 20, 1985, one of the most gruesome football injuries in modern times. Just a few weeks later, on Monday night, December 2, the Miami Dolphins, the only NFL team to go through an entire season and postseason undefeated, stopped the Chicago Bears' attempt to equal that feat, beating the Bears, who came into the game with twelve straight victories, 38–24. Along the way, *Monday Night Football* became the longest running prime-time television sports series, bringing to the public 555 Monday night games over thirty-six seasons.

But all good things must eventually come to an end. The sports program that had led Ronald Reagan and Jimmy Carter to reschedule their 1980 debate away from a Monday, and that had risen in revenue value from $8.5 million a year for the NFL in 1970 to $555 million, also had slipped badly in the television ratings, from a high of 21.7 in 1981 to 10.9 in 2005. ESPN bought the rights to NFL football on Monday nights, starting with 2006, for $8.8 billion for eight years. With Al Michaels and Joe Theisman in the booth, football continued to be played on Monday nights, but, for those who had watched during the enchanted years of the 1970s

and early 1980s, it could never truly be *Monday Night Football* anymore.

See also: Cosell, Howard William; Gifford, Frank Newton; Namath, Joseph William; Television Broadcasting; Unitas, John Constantine.

Additional Reading/Viewing:

Gunther, Marc, and Bill Carter. *Monday Night Mayhem: The Inside Story of ABC's Monday Night Football.* New York: Beech Tree Books, 1988.

MacCambridge, Michael. *America's Game: The Epic Story of How Pro Football Captured a Nation.* New York: Random House, 2004.

Monday Night Mayhem. Dir. Ernest R. Dickerson. Turner Network Television, 2002.

Montana, Joseph Clifford (the Comeback Kid, Joe Cool) (b. 1956)

Joe Montana wrote some of the greatest comeback stories in football history while quarterbacking the University of Notre Dame football team and the San Francisco 49ers. With ice water seemingly in his veins, he was at his best when the game was on the line or even apparently lost. He achieved more than comebacks, though, during his career, leading Notre Dame to a national championship in 1977 and the 49ers to four Super Bowl wins.

Montana was recruited by Ara Parseghian but made his first appearances in a Notre Dame game for Dan Devine in 1975. An injury wiped out the 1976 season, but he won the starting quarterback job in 1977 after entering the Purdue game in the fourth quarter and throwing two touchdown passes to lead Notre Dame to a 31–24 victory. Notre Dame won the rest of its games, including a 38–10 victory over previously top-ranked Texas in the Cotton Bowl, to take the national championship.

Montana's most impressive victory at Notre Dame may have been his last. Playing against Houston in the Cotton Bowl on January 1, 1979, he led a fourth-quarter rally from a 34–12 deficit to win 35–34, throwing the winning touchdown pass with two seconds remaining. Making the comeback even more remarkable was Montana's absence from the contest during the third quarter as he fought hypothermia brought on by the frigid weather that included an ice storm. Notre Dame medical personnel fed Montana chicken bouillon and covered him with warm blankets until he was able to return. The game became immortalized as the "Chicken Soup Game."

Montana played for the 49ers from 1979 to 1992 but missed all of 1991 and most of 1992 with injuries. He finished his career with two seasons as quarterback of the Kansas City Chiefs.

Montana led the 49ers to victory in Super Bowls XVI, XIX, XXIII, and XXIV, earning Super Bowl Most Valuable Player honors in the first two as well as in his final Super Bowl appearance. Twice, in 1989 and 1990, the Associated Press named him the NFL Most Valuable Player.

He worked his "Montana Magic" many times with San Francisco, but two games especially stand out. In the National Football Conference championship game against the Dallas Cowboys on January 10, 1982, the 49ers trailed 27–21 with under five minutes remaining. Montana moved his team down the field, reaching the 6-yard line with about one minute left. Under pressure, Montana threw off-balance toward receiver Dwight Clark in the back of the end zone. Clark leaped and came down with the pass, giving the 49ers the victory and propelling them toward the organization's first Super Bowl win. The play became known simply as "the Catch."

San Francisco was in trouble again in Super Bowl XXIII, trailing the Cincinnati Bengals 16–13 with 3:10 left. Starting on the 49ers' 8-yard line, Montana moved his team quickly and effectively, completing eight of nine passes and, with thirty-four seconds remaining, connecting with receiver John Taylor for the winning touchdown.

During several of his years, beginning in 1985, Montana teamed with wide receiver Jerry Rice, possibly the greatest receiver in the history of the NFL. Against the Atlanta Falcons in 1990, Montana threw to Rice for five touchdowns. Through the 1988 season, including his first three Super Bowl games, Montana's coach was Bill Walsh, architect of the West Coast offense. Walsh called Montana the greatest quarterback of his time, maybe the best ever. A lot of people would agree with that assessment.

See also: Drive, The; Parseghian, Ara Raoul; Rice, Jerry Lee; Super Bowl; Walsh, William Ernest; Young, Jon Steven.

Additional Reading:
Montana, Joe. *Montana*. With Dick Schaap. Atlanta: Turner Publishing, 1995.

Montana, Joe, and Bob Raissman. *Audibles: My Life in Football*. New York: W. Morrow, 1986.

Walsh, Bill. *Building a Champion: On Football and the Making of the 49ers*. With Glenn Dickey. New York: St. Martin's, 1990.

Moss, Randy Gene (b. 1977)

Randy Moss has had a career filled with dichotomies: talented but troubled, capable of greatness but controversial, wanted yet unwanted by teams. By 2007 he had worn out his welcome with the Oakland Raiders and received what was widely viewed as his last chance to reestablish himself as a top player and perhaps claim Hall of Fame status. Ironically, that opportunity came from the professional organization probably least tolerant of individual egos and most committed to a team-first approach: the New England Patriots.

Moss's troubles began early and seriously affected his college plans. He signed a letter of intent in 1995 to attend the University of Notre Dame, but after he pleaded guilty to a charge of battery, which resulted in probation and a thirty-day suspended jail sentence, Notre Dame rescinded its offer. Next up was Florida State, but after smoking marijuana (a violation of his probation) he was out there as well and had to serve sixty days in jail.

Moss then transferred to Marshall University, at the time a Division I-AA school, which meant that he would not lose additional eligibility. At Marshall in 1996, Moss finally got to play college football and excelled. He gained 1,709 yards on seventy-eight passes, twenty-nine of them for touchdowns. Marshall was undefeated and moved up to Division I-A the following year. In 1997 Moss teamed with quarterback Chad Pennington as Marshall won the Mid-American Conference championship. Moss caught twenty-five touchdown passes, pulled in ninety-six receptions for 1,820 yards, and made first-team All-American. He also received the Fred Biletnikoff Award, given annually to the nation's best college receiver. Meanwhile he was quoted in a *Sports Illustrated* article saying that the tragic plane crash that killed most members of the Marshall football team in 1970 "wasn't nothing big," a statement that he claimed was misinterpreted.

Moss's brushes with the law bothered enough NFL teams that he was not drafted until the twenty-first pick, when the Minnesota Vikings took him. Once chosen, however, he wasted no time establishing himself as one of the most talented wide receivers ever to play in the NFL, catching a league-leading seventeen touchdown passes as a rookie. In each of his first six seasons, he gained more than 1,200 yards receiving and twice had more than 100 receptions. He reached highs of 111 receptions and 1,632 receiving yards in 2003 while equaling his highest total for touchdowns receptions, seventeen. In 2004, his final season with Minnesota, his receptions and yards dropped to forty-nine and 767 respectively, but he caught thirteen touchdown passes.

The extraordinary achievements on the football field unfortunately were accompanied by continuing legal and public relations problems. On September 24, 2002, a traffic control officer detected Moss preparing to make an illegal turn on a Minneapolis street and ordered him to stop. Instead, Moss slowly moved his vehicle ahead and bumped into her. Moss pleaded guilty to a traffic violation and received a $1,200 fine and forty hours of community service. Against the Green Bay Packers in a playoff game in January 2005, Moss scored a touchdown and then simulated pulling down his pants and mooning the crowd, for which the NFL fined him $10,000.

Moss was traded to the Oakland Raiders before the 2005 season. During the summer, he admitted in an interview with Bryant Gumbel that he had used marijuana. His first year with the Raiders was productive, but Moss's performance tailed off badly in 2006 and teammates criticized him for an apparent lack of effort. After nine years in the NFL, many observers thought that Moss's problems were not just attitudinal but also physical, that his once-mighty skills were eroding.

Moss suffered through physical ailments that curtailed his involvement in preseason games with his new team in 2007. Once the season started, though, he appeared to have lost little if any of his ability. A seemingly rejuvenated Moss made one sterling catch after another as Patriots quarterback Tom Brady found his new target capable of going up with two defenders and coming down with the ball, just as he had done during his early years with the Vikings. The player accused of caring more about himself than his team seemed to be working hard to demonstrate just the opposite, perhaps realizing that this truly was his last chance. Moss finished the regular season with twenty-three touchdown receptions, breaking by one the previous record set by Jerry Rice, and helping the Patriots finish their sixteen-game season undefeated.

See also: Brady, Thomas Edward, Jr.; Celebrations; Crime; Marshall University Air Tragedy; Perfection; Substance Abuse.

Additional Reading:
Bernstein, Ross. *Randy Moss: Star Wide Receiver.* Berkeley Heights NJ: Enslow, 2002.

Mr. Inside and Mr. Outside

Felix "Doc" Blanchard (1924–2009) and Glenn Davis (1924–2005) were backfield mates at the United States Military Academy at West Point, New York, from 1944 to 1946. Both Heisman Trophy winners, they comprised possibly the greatest tandem of running backs on the same team at the same time in the history of college football. They also symbolized for a nation the indomitable excellence of the United States during the final stages of World War II and in its immediate aftermath.

Blanchard, son of a Mississippi physician (hence his nickname), and Davis, son of a California bank manager, secured lasting fame on December 2, 1944, just days before the beginning of the Battle of the Bulge in Belgium. The game pitted

Army, ranked first in the nation in football, against its gridiron rival but partner in the war effort, the United States Naval Academy of Annapolis, Maryland, ranked second. Many college football programs had shut down during the war or were continuing with understaffed teams because so many young men were in Europe and the Pacific fighting Germany and Japan. Soldiers continued to be trained at West Point and Navy, however, where they also were available to play football, a condition that helped make the service academy teams national powerhouses.

The game stirred such interest that Pres. Franklin Delano Roosevelt ordered it moved to Baltimore's Municipal Stadium, which could hold sixty-five thousand spectators, and required that ticket buyers also purchase a war bond, a requirement of admission that raised $60 million. Concerned about Nazi submarines off the East Coast, a flotilla of warships, planes, and blimps patrolled the waters while a troop ship transported the Army team from the Hudson River into the Atlantic Ocean and Maryland's Chesapeake Bay.

The game lived up to its billing. Army led 9–7 at the beginning of the fourth quarter. Then Doc Blanchard, the powerful fullback, and Glenn Davis, the shifty speedster, put the game away. At a time when players still played both offense and defense, Davis intercepted a pass to stop a Navy drive at midfield. Blanchard then carried the ball six times in a row to set up a touchdown. Finally, from the 10-

yard line, Blanchard plowed into the end zone, a Navy defender hanging on to his back as he crossed the goal line.

Davis applied the finishing touch, a 50-yard touchdown run down the sideline. No Navy player even touched him. Army won that game 23–7, Blanchard and Davis immortalizing the nicknames that *New York Sun* sportswriter George Trevor had bestowed on them: Mr. Inside and Mr. Outside.

The nation knew that Army was good; after all, the team had already won eight games that year and defeated another powerhouse, Notre Dame, 59–0. The victory over Navy, though, signed and sealed the legend of the two players. Blanchard and Davis would always be remembered together, along with, but in public memory even more compellingly than, their also legendary coach, Earl "Red" Blaik. Perhaps sensing the unique tie that would bind his two players forever, Blaik almost always spoke of them at the same time and required that they be interviewed together. For an admiring nation, the two super backs symbolized all that was great about America: its fighting spirit, its refusal to give up, its invincibility, and its innate decency.

With the war ending in 1945, Blanchard and Davis continued to provide Army with victories. During their three years together, Army won twenty-seven games, lost none, and were tied once, an epic 0–0 battle with Notre Dame in 1946. Both players were selected as All-Americans each year. Blanchard won the Heisman

Trophy in 1945; Davis took the honors in 1946. Blanchard scored thirty-eight touchdowns in twenty-eight games, led the country in scoring in 1945, starred at linebacker as well, and handled the place-kicking and punting until an injury in his senior year required transferring the duty to Davis.

Davis, along with winning the 1946 Heisman after being the runner-up the previous two years, averaged 11.5 yards per carry in 1945 and 8.3 yards for his career, scored fifty-nine touchdowns, and was an excellent defensive back. Together the two scored ninety-seven touchdowns, a record for two teammates not broken until Reggie Bush and LenDale White scored ninety-nine for the University of Southern California almost sixty years later.

So famous did the duo become, and so representative of their country, that American soldiers began to identify enemy Germans posing as Americans by whispering "Blanchard" and waiting to see if they heard "Davis" in response. Songs were composed about them, they appeared on the covers of *Time, Life, The Saturday Evening Post*, and other magazines, and they acted in a film about their Army years, *The Spirit of West Point* (1947). During the filming, Davis hurt his knee, which seriously impeded his later short-lived professional football career.

Davis then served in Korea, completed his military obligation, and left the service prior to the outbreak of war on the Korean Peninsula. He joined the Los Angeles Rams for two seasons (1950–51), playing well his first year with 416 rushing yards, a 4.7 yards-per-carry average, forty-two pass receptions, and seven touchdowns. The next year his knee condition worsened, and he averaged just 3.1 yards per carry. He decided to retire rather than face uncertain surgical results.

Davis was engaged to Elizabeth Taylor for a time and married the actress Terry Moore. Long afterward as a widower, Davis married Yvonne Ameche, widow of another Heisman winner, the great University of Wisconsin and Baltimore Colts fullback Alan "the Horse" Ameche. In a growing family of Heismans, Cathy Ameche, Yvonne's daughter, married the brother of John Cappelletti, the 1973 Heisman winner.

Blanchard made his career in the military, became a pilot, and flew combat missions for the Army Air Corps and U.S. Air Force during the Korean and Vietnam wars. During the latter, he flew 113 missions over Vietnam and Thailand in a single year. Davis retired in 1971 as a brigadier general—and as a war hero.

See also: Films; Heisman Trophy; Magazines; World War II; Zero.

Additional Reading:

Blaik, Earl H. *The Red Blaik Story*. New Rochelle NY: Arlington House, 1974.

Cohane, Tim. *Gridiron Grenadiers: The Story of West Point Football*. New York: G.P. Putnam's Sons, 1948.

Pennington, Bill. "More Than a Game: Glenn Davis and Doc Blanchard." In *The Heisman: Great American Stories of the Men Who Won*. Edited by Bill Pennington, 52–79. New York: ReganBooks, 2004.

Music

Football music exists in conjunction with the professional game, as National Football League teams, for example, boast their own fight songs. Even diehard fans, however, often cannot recite a line of "Go! You Packers! Go!" or "Bear Down, Chicago Bears," demonstrating that for all practical purposes football music is an amateur phenomenon.

High school teams also have their fight songs, often modifications of college originals. Still, football music is principally known and venerated at the college level, where the most recognizable songs are the college fight songs, many of which have been around for much of their respective teams' history.

A fight song typically is a stirring, militaristic-sounding song designed to arouse the emotions of fan and player alike. Fight songs usually posit only one possible outcome: victory. Defeat is not an option, at least within the song's lyrics, even if the team may lose regularly. To some extent, therefore, the college fight song operates within its own world, both related to and apart from the reality of what is transpiring on the gridiron. It also can be interpreted as an expression of hope as much as a statement of projected victory.

The most famous college fight songs surely include "The Notre Dame Victory March" and "On Wisconsin" (the fight song of the University of Wisconsin at Madison). Both convey the certainty of success. Notre Dame will triumph over all opponents, and Wisconsin will inevitably roll to a touchdown on this particular possession. The original lyrics for the Notre Dame song refer only to sons of the university marching toward triumph, and this version remains the form usually available in print. However, the lyrics, if still suitable to football, no longer tell the whole story at a university that went coeducational long after the penning of the lyrics and now boasts some highly successful women's teams in other sports. Hence, the lyrics are occasionally expanded to include daughters as well as sons.

Other fight songs hearken back to the infancy of football and even encapsulate permanent rivalries within their lyrics. Thus, Yale's "Down the Field" refers specifically to Harvard, although vocalists may well substitute the opponent of the moment. Harvard's lyrics reciprocate by promising victory over Eli, the name borrowed from Elihu Yale, whose gift of books and other items in 1718 led to a new name for the college and a nickname for its students, the Elis. Navy's "Anchors Aweigh" promises something akin to doom and destruction for Army, but Army retains a sort of moral superiority by referring only to itself. The Michigan fight song, "The Victors," is another well-known martial ditty, possessing a broad enough appeal to appear, under the title "University of Michigan Song," as one of only two fight songs (along with "On Wisconsin") to make it into the recent *Fake Book of the World's Favorite Songs*.

Accompanying the fight songs are the kickoff chants, only marginally qualifying as music. As the team lines up for the kickoff, its fans utter—loudly and slowly, drawing out the enunciation until the decisive moment when the world, having held its collective breath, suddenly exhales—the initial word or words, and then scream the concluding portion. So from Irish fans will swell the word "Go . . . ," then, finally, will burst forth "Irish!"

Many football stadiums explode with similar chants: "Go . . . Dawgs!" (Georgia), "Go . . . Pack!" (North Carolina State), "Go . . . State!" (Penn State). A third element occurs in a number of the stadiums, Georgia fans, for example, following the kickoff with "Sic 'em! Woof, woof, woof!" Others prefer "O" to "Go," including Oklahoma, which follows with "U" for "University"; after the kickoff the crowd listens to the rousing rhythms of "The William Tell Overture."

Some football fans seem to prefer a wordless approach. At the University of Washington, football fans use a hand-chopping motion. At some stadiums, a combination of action and word is employed. Kansas State fans jingle their keys, followed by "Kaboom!" Washington State supporters pull out all the stops, rattling keys while yelling "Go," followed by "Cougs!"

A third type of song often sung at college football games is the school's official anthem, such as "Notre Dame, Our Mother," at the University of Notre Dame. The title of the university literally translates as "our lady," referring to Mary, the mother of Jesus, with the song thus celebrating both the university and its patroness. Singing the song at the conclusion of the game therefore is less a commemoration of the football team than a statement of community involving the team and the rest of the institution. Other universities have similar songs, although few, if any, are as well known as Notre Dame's.

Some popular songs about football also have survived, although far fewer than about baseball. A well-known example is "You Gotta Be a Football Hero," written by Al Sherman, Buddy Fields, and Al Lewis in 1933. Among the artists who have recorded the song are Ben Bernie, Fred Waring and his Pennsylvanians, and the Notre Dame Glee Club. In 1935 the song spawned a cartoon featuring Popeye the Sailor as a professional football player. The song also is heard in the films *The Longest Yard* (1974) and *The Cat in the Hat* (2003). The point of the song is that what truly excites girls is not wealth or a handsome face but the ability to make a crucial tackle or score a winning touchdown. It is the football hero who gets the beautiful girl.

Of course, few athletic contests, including football games, are complete without the stirring patriotic tune "The Star-Spangled Banner," written by Francis Scott Key during the War of 1812. Key published the lyrics in the *Baltimore American* in 1814, and the song quickly caught on with the American public. Congress declared it the national anthem of the

United States in 1931, but well before that date, while World War I was raging, the song became a staple of athletic contests and other events.

To have a football game, especially a college contest, without music would be like leaving home with one shoe off. It has become an essential ingredient, giving alumni something to hum long after they have forgotten where they packed away that college diploma.

See also: Films; Kickoffs; Language.

Additional Reading/Listening:
College Football Tradition Web site. http://www .1122productions.com/tradition/.
University of Michigan Band. *Touchdown, U.S.A.: The "Big Ten" and Other Great College Marches of the Gridiron.* Vanguard Records, 1991.
University of Notre Dame Marching Band. *The Band of the Fighting Irish.* University of Notre Dame, 1995.

Nagurski, Bronislaw (Bronko)
(1908–1990)

Bronko Nagurski was one of the most popular athletes of his time, rivaling Babe Ruth and Jack Dempsey in the public eye. Both an embodiment and symbol of raw power, Nagurski also was a great all-around athlete who excelled on offense and defense at the University of Minnesota and later with the professional Chicago Bears.

Nagurski, whose nickname was an easier-to-pronounce version of his first name but also represented the inability of his opponents to ride him to the ground, starred at both fullback on offense and tackle on defense from 1927 to 1929 at Minnesota, winning consensus All-America honors at tackle in 1929. As a runner, he was a bulldozing back almost impossible for a single defender to bring down. Weighing about 225 pounds, far more than most defensive linemen, contributed to his success.

Nagurski joined the Bears in 1930 and played with them through the 1937 season, returning in 1943 during World War II to help the war-depleted Bears for one final season. He excelled as a multipurpose back with the Bears, running, blocking, kicking an occasional extra point, and even throwing passes. As a back, he won All-Pro honors during 1932–34 and

1936–37, including a first-team selection on the Official NFL Team from 1932 to 1934.

Though known especially for his power, he achieved some of his most memorable moments as a passer. The jump pass seemed made for him. Defenders were understandably worried about his power running, so when he took a handoff and headed toward the line, only to stop, jump, and throw the ball, the defense tended to be caught flatfooted. Nagurski threw the winning touchdown, to another great Bears back, Red Grange, in the 1932 playoff game against the Portsmouth Spartans. In the first official NFL Championship Game, played in 1933, his passing produced two touchdowns in the Bears' 23–21 victory over the New York Giants.

Nagurski left the Bears in a contract dispute after the 1937 season to become a professional wrestler, winning three world heavyweight championships within different factions of the World Wrestling Association from 1937 to 1941. Yet when his old team called in 1943, he answered the summons. Then in his mid-thirties, he primarily played defensive tackle, but occasionally took the ball in clutch situations. His 3-yard touchdown run against Washington in the championship game put the Bears up 14–7 at the half, a lead they extended in the second half, winning 41–21.

Nagurski richly deserved his fame because of his on-field accomplishments, but legends also contributed to his stature. His Minnesota coach, Clarence Spears, for example, claimed that he discovered Nagurski while recruiting another player. Nagurski was plowing a field without a horse, just pushing the plow through the dirt. When Spears asked directions, the farm boy picked up the plow and pointed. An apocryphal story certainly, but for those who watched him play it was almost believable. While running a gas station during retirement, Nagurski was said to put gas caps back on with such force that a driver would need a wrench to remove the cap.

Nagurski's stature continued to grow after his second retirement from football. Grantland Rice named him the fullback on his all-time All-America team for the first half of the twentieth century. In an Associated Press poll in 1950 to select the greatest college players of all time, Nagurski ranked third, behind only Jim Thorpe and Red Grange. He became a charter member of the College Football Hall of Fame in 1951 and of the Pro Football Hall of Fame in 1963. Although Nagurski did not seek public acclaim, he was named Minnesotan of the Year in 1978. Two additional honors came in 1993. The Football Writers Association of America instituted the Bronko Nagurski Trophy, given to the college defensive player of the year, and Nagurski's fellow citizens

of International Falls, Minnesota, opened the Bronko Nagurski Museum as part of the Koochiching County Historical Society, the first museum dedicated to an individual football player. John Madden selected Nagurski for his All-Millennium Team in 1999, and the United States Postal Service issued a thirty-seven-cent stamp in his honor in 2003.

See also: Grange, Harold Edward; Halas, George Stanley; Madden, John Earl; Thorpe, James Francis.

Additional Reading:

Bronko Nagurski: The Greatest Football Player of All Time Web site. http://www.bronko nagurski.com/bronko.htm.

Collins, David R. *Football Running Backs: Three Ground Gainers.* Champaign IL: Garrard Publishing, 1976.

Dent, Jim. *Monster of the Midway: Bronko Nagurski, the 1943 Chicago Bears, and the Greatest Comeback Ever.* New York: Thomas Dunne Books, 2003.

Namath, Joseph William (Joe Willie, Broadway Joe) (b. 1943)

Joe Namath brought a strong right arm, supreme confidence, and an iconoclastic attitude to the football field and beyond, first with Bear Bryant's Alabama Crimson Tide and later with the New York Jets—as well as to some of the most famous commercials ever made by a football player. Much like the mischievous child adored for his talents, and whose misdeeds therefore are generally tolerated, even given some tongue-clicking approbation, Namath endeared himself to football fans throughout his career.

No one could have been more different

from Namath than the stern, godlike figure of Bear Bryant, who suspended his fun-living quarterback for the last two games of the 1963 season. Yet Namath led that same Alabama team to a national championship the next year, and Bryant later characterized Namath as the best athlete he ever coached. Bryant was a strong father figure for Namath, who like many young people pulling against the reins seemed subconsciously to crave someone who could impose, with affection, firm limits on him. Giving his induction speech at the Pro Football Hall of Fame ceremonies in 1985, Namath became extremely emotional while talking about his former coach, who had died two years earlier.

The New York Jets of the American Football League made Namath the league's first pick in the college draft in November 1964, and the St. Louis Cardinals of the National Football League also took him, as the league's twelfth pick. Namath opted for the Jets—for a then record salary of $400,000.

New York, the media capital of the country, was the right stage for Namath. He became the first professional quarterback to pass for more than 4,000 yards in a season (1967) and achieved greatness despite a career filled with knee injuries. Namath put himself squarely in the public eye—and on the national hot seat—by proclaiming publicly that his Jets would defeat the Baltimore Colts in Super Bowl III following the 1968 season. Namath had enjoyed another great season

and been named winner of the Hickok Belt as the year's top professional athlete, but the Colts were the champions of the long-established NFL. And, after all, the NFL champions, in the mighty persons of the Green Bay Packers, had demolished the AFL Super Bowl entries in each of the first two Super Bowls, so why should the third be any different?

Yet Namath backed up his boast with accurate passing (seventeen completions in twenty-eight attempts for 206 yards) and effective management of a well-balanced offense that produced ten rushing first downs and ten by passing. The victory established the AFL's parity with the older league. It also immortalized Namath and seemed to embolden him even more in his off-field exploits. He grew a Fu Manchu moustache and then shaved it off in a famous commercial for Remington electric razors. He also opened a New York bar that he called Bachelors III. When Commissioner Pete Rozelle tried to force him to sell the bar because of the disreputable clientele that frequented it, he retired from football. That applied considerable pressure to the commissioner to come up with a compromise, which he succeeded in doing, with Namath selling out but retaining rights to similar establishments in other cities.

Other television commercials also came Broadway Joe's way, most famously one for Beautymist pantyhose in 1974. The spot opened with the camera focused on an attractive pair of legs. It then moved slowly up to a pair of Jets shorts and then a Jets jersey, and finally to the face: Namath's. A beautiful woman then entered and kissed Namath lest any viewer question his masculinity. Namath is given credit for bringing many women into the fold as football fans with that ad, although his mischievous little-boy good looks and devil-may-care attitude likely had even more to do with that phenomenon.

Namath's playing career came to an end in 1977 after twelve years with the Jets and a thirteenth with the Los Angeles Rams, but he remained very much in the public eye. He appeared in television shows, including *The Brady Bunch, Rowan and Martin's Laugh-In, The Dean Martin Show, The Simpsons, The Love Boat, Fantasy Island,* and *The A-Team.* He even briefly hosted his own *Joe Namath Show* in 1969 and joined *Monday Night Football* for the 1985 season. It was longtime *Monday Night Football* regular Howard Cosell who popularized referring to Namath as Joe Willie.

Namath also acted in several films, including *C.C. and Company* (1970) and *Avalanche Express* (1979). He has worked on behalf of the March of Dimes for more than four decades, including hosting a golf tournament for the charity. He was interviewed on CBS's *60 Minutes* in 2006, the same year that his autobiography, *Namath,* appeared.

Some of his recent publicity, however, has been less positive. During a Jets game broadcast on ESPN in 2003, sideline interviewer Suzy Kolber asked Namath about Chad Pennington, the team's quarterback. After briefly responding, Namath frankly stated that he wanted to kiss Kolber. While not entirely at odds with his longtime public persona, the incident proved embarrassing for Namath, then sixty years old. Broadway Joe later admitted that he had imbibed too much champagne and that he had a drinking problem. Still, New York, along with much of the country, retains considerable affection for Broadway Joe, the swashbuckling quarterback who called the outcome of the Super Bowl and made it come true.

Namath achieved another milestone in December 2007 when he finally finished a game that had long been delayed—his college education. He received his diploma from the University of Alabama more than forty years after he had left the institution to become a household name. Namath had completed thirty credits through Alabama's External Degree Program over the previous five years to earn a bachelor of arts in interdisciplinary studies.

See also: American Football League (IV); Bryant, Paul William; Commercials and Advertisements; Cosell, Howard William; Education; Films; *Monday Night Football*; Substance Abuse; Super Bowl.

Additional Reading:
Kriegel, Mark. *Namath: A Biography.* New York: Viking, 2004.
Namath, Joe Willie. *Namath.* New York: Rugged Land, 2006.
———. *I Can't Wait Until Tomorrow . . . 'cause I Get Better-Looking Every Day.* With Dick Schaap. New York: Random House, 1969.

Newspapers

Newspapers are a major source of information about football from high school competition to the pros. Small local weeklies usually give extensive attention, often on the first page of the sports section, to the local high school team. The local games are described in detail, and large pictures capture pivotal moments of the contests. The hometown team is clearly favored, with no attempt to be impartial. If something bad has happened, such as player suspensions, the paper likely will report that, but with sorrow. There is nothing dishonest or improper about this. The local paper is part of the hometown community and, like the readers it serves, roots for the local boys.

Daily papers typically boost all local teams regardless of the level: high school teams, area colleges and universities, and, if a professional team is in the region, the pro team as well. Although accounts of nearby college and professional teams may be rendered with reasonable objectivity, they receive more extensive description than other teams, whose games are recounted much more succinctly. Local columnists in most dailies are easily perceived as fans rather than dispassionate analysts. Large urban dailies that have a national readership follow smaller dailies in giving local teams extensive coverage, but at least some of their columnists are likely to be less provincial in their approach.

Former Speaker of the United States House of Representatives Tip O'Neill once said that all politics is local. The same could be said, with only minor qualification, about football coverage. That reality mirrors the way newspapers conducted their business of reporting on football throughout the twentieth century.

By the beginning of the century, city dailies had developed sports sections several pages long for Sunday editions while allotting fewer pages, perhaps only one or two, to sports on other days. Sports coverage increased dramatically during the 1920s as the large daily sports section became a permanent fixture in urban papers throughout the week.

Accounts of most games (except for those played by local teams) usually were disseminated by the wire services, much as they are today. Other material, including columns by national figures such as Grantland Rice, was syndicated—yet another similarity to modern newspapers.

The inclusion of magazine sections in Sunday editions of urban papers extends back through much of the twentieth century with such inserts as *American Weekly* and *This Week*. A modern version is *Parade*, which although not primarily sports oriented does publish occasional sports stories, including its influential annual listing of high school football All-Americans.

From the first, newspaper editors and readers alike accepted a style of writing from football and other sports columnists that was markedly different from what most news reporters produced. Prior to World War II, columnists such as Rice were often self-consciously literary, leavening their prose with figurative language, classical allusions, considerable emotionalism, and even an occasional poem. Rice was a member of what has been called the "Gee Whiz!" school of journalism, often contrasted with the "Aw Nuts!" school (including such writers as Damon Runyon and Westbrook Pegler), which was less boosterish and more critical if not always less florid.

During the first half of the twentieth century, as immigrants poured in from Europe, newspapers arose to offer the new arrivals news in their own native languages as well as information about their new home, including its sports. Jewish newspapers chronicled the accomplishments of Jewish football players, and other papers did the same for members of their religious or ethnic readership groups. None equaled Polish newspapers, though, in extensive coverage of football. Sons of Polish immigrants and other ethnic groups quickly became part of the football world, especially at such Catholic institutions as Notre Dame (where the Fighting Irish were often not all that Irish), Fordham, Boston College, Marquette, Villanova, and Georgetown. Some of these universities later dropped football, but all were once attractive homes to Catholic immigrants who hoped to assimilate into and rise within American society.

African Americans—shut out of professional football until after World War II, excluded from southern universities even longer, and facing considerable racism even in many predominantly white northern schools—needed support and received it, if not often from the white newspapers, consistently from the black press.

Papers such as the *Chicago Defender*, *Pittsburgh Courier*, and *Baltimore Afro-American* reported in detail not only on football programs at historically black colleges but also on black players at predominantly white institutions. They argued steadily for racial justice and were an important element in the fight for equality during the civil rights movement of the 1950s and 1960s.

White newspapers in the North tended not to rock the boat and therefore generally sided with the status quo rather than with the struggle of football players to achieve a fuller measure of freedom and self-determination. That attitude applied not only to race but also to conflicts between players and management. During incidents such as the brief strike by San Francisco 49ers players in 1949 over their not being paid for a playoff game, or regarding such matters as rising player salaries during the 1940s as a result of the All-America Football Conference's competition with the National Football League, newspapers tended either to ignore players' rights or actively side with owners. A major exception was the *Daily Worker*, a Communist Party publication, which viewed players, both college and professional, as workers and hence deserving of the paper's support in what it perceived as a class struggle.

Support for the football power structure and the established traditions of the game also manifested itself in newspaper coverage during the football slush-fund scandals of the 1950s. As the public learned that several big-time football programs—Southern California, UCLA, Washington, and California—had channeled money to players in violation of NCAA regulations, most papers and their sportswriters and columnists continued to support the local teams. The *Los Angeles Daily News*, for example, strongly attacked Orlando Hollis, dean of the University of Oregon's law school, who also chaired the faculty committee that levied penalties against the offending institutions, including probation for USC, UCLA, and Washington.

Sometimes, however, newspapers broke with tradition and supported meaningful change, as with the Sugar Bowl controversy of 1956. Pittsburgh, with a black defensive back named Bobby Grier, was scheduled to play Georgia Tech. Many northern teams had generally followed an unwritten policy of allowing their African American players to participate when playing an all-white southern team in the North while sitting them down when playing in the South. The Sugar Bowl, situated in New Orleans, had never had a black player participate in the game before. Pittsburgh, however, made it clear that Grier would eat,

practice, live, and play with the rest of the team.

Georgia Tech raised no objections, but as the presence of Grier became public, Georgia's governor, Marvin Griffin, thinking that he was playing to a supportive public, balked at allowing Georgia Tech to play against an integrated team. The reaction was enormously negative both within and beyond Georgia. Georgia Tech students burned the governor in effigy, and the university Regents, while reaffirming segregation, also reaffirmed the university's contractual obligation to play the game. Ultimately, Georgia Tech prevailed on the field 7–0 when Grier was called for interference, which set up the game's lone touchdown. The interference call was highly controversial, with many observers believing that it was deliberately designed to harm Grier and the Panthers.

Most newspapers, including those in the South, strongly objected to Griffin's attempt to derail the Sugar Bowl. Northern newspapers attacked segregation and those who supported it. Others, especially in the South, objected to Griffin's violation of an agreement to play in the Sugar Bowl or because of perceived damage done to the sport.

Newspapers also have a long history of linking football with sex appeal, a connection blatantly obvious in professional football today with provocatively dressed cheerleaders but also evident at the college level, where cheerleaders are only marginally more covered than the

Dallas Cowboys Cheerleaders and their professional sisters.

In the years surrounding World War II, however, journalistic norms dictated a level of depiction quite modest by twenty-first-century standards but certainly titillating at that time. Paul Gallico explicitly noted the emphasis in a discussion of "S.A." (sex appeal) in his book *Farewell to Sport* (1938). Newspapers were obliged to avoid gratuitous sex, but, after all, pretty female swimmers, figure skaters, and, in football, majorettes and later cheerleaders naturally belonged in sports pages. The Kilgore Rangerettes from Texas—adorned in boots, short skirts, and cowboy hats—added considerable sparkle to the Sugar Bowl and a variety of other venues starting in the 1940s. From the late 1950s on, Purdue's Golden Girl majorette graced the pages of many newspapers and magazines. Accounts of games and a wealth of statistics were all well and good, but pictures of pretty girls made the sports pages really come alive over that morning cup of coffee.

Not a lot had changed by the twenty-first century regarding the relationship between newspapers and football except perhaps a greater willingness to explore the dark side of athletes when they seriously broke the law or violated standard norms of conduct. Day after day, O. J. Simpson, Michael Vick, and a variety of other offenders appeared in the sports pages and sometimes even on the front pages of the news sections, their actions scrutinized in minute detail. If newspaper journalists still generally evinced an attitude of protectiveness toward football, they were quite able to pull aside the protective curtain when individuals, even stars, egregiously betrayed the sport and their fans.

See also: African Americans (College); African Americans (Professional); Black College Football; Bowl Games; Crime; Dogfighting; Gambling; Magazines; Religion; Rice, Grantland; Sexuality; Simpson, Orenthal James; Ward, Arch.

Additional Reading:

Boyle, Raymond. *Sports Journalism: Context and Issues*. Thousand Oaks CA: Sage, 2006.

Fountain, Charles. *Sportswriter: The Life and Times of Grantland Rice*. New York: Oxford University Press, 1993.

Gallico, Paul. *Farewell to Sport*. New York: Alfred A. Knopf, 1938.

Oriard, Michael. *King Football: Sport and Spectacle in the Golden Age of Radio and Newsreels, Movies and Magazines, the Weekly and the Daily Press*. Chapel Hill: University of North Carolina Press, 2001.

———. *Reading Football: How the Popular Press Created an American Spectacle*. Chapel Hill: University of North Carolina Press, 1993.

Newsreels

From the beginning of the twentieth century until the rise of television in the 1960s, Americans received their nonprint visual news, including their information about football, from newsreels. The newsreel offered millions of viewers who never had a chance to attend a major college football game in person the opportunity to at least glimpse the Fighting Irish of Notre Dame battling Army as well as other great rivalries. Viewers also could experience the marching bands, pretty cheerleaders, and exuberant fans cheering on their favorites from the stands. No newsreel account of an Army game, for example, would be complete without seeing rows of cadets in uniform marching or cheering.

Newsreel football was usually college ball. The college game far outstripped professional football in popularity during the pretelevision era. Newsreels did cover the College All-Star Game and the National Football League Championship Game in the 1930s but did not routinely cover regular-season games until the late 1940s.

Along with cartoons, previews, and the feature film itself (sometimes double features), the newsreel was a staple of an afternoon or evening at the movie house. A typical newsreel was about ten minutes long divided into about six segments. Sports made up roughly 20 to 25 percent of the footage, with football dominating sports coverage in the fall. Sports usually comprised the final newsreel segment. Viewers could make their choice as to whether that placement categorized sports as the least significant or most important part of the newsreel.

Theaters received newsreels twice per week, enabling regular filmgoers to enjoy news that was reasonably new. By the late 1920s five major newsreels were available to the theaters: *American Pathé News, Movietone News, Paramount News, Universal News,* and Hearst's *International News.* All five, some under different names, lasted at least into the 1950s, with *Universal News* and Hearst's *News of the Day* surviving until 1967. Some of the country's most famous radio announcers also contributed their voices to newsreels, including Graham McNamee, Ted Husing, and Bill Stern.

The newsreels, like other media, reflected American society, both the good and the bad. Consequently, African Americans were usually absent from newsreel coverage of college football prior to World War II and, of course, totally absent from any coverage of professional football because the NFL was closed to black players. When a newsreel did venture into some measure of racial diversity, it usually did so in a demeaning way. Michael Oriard has pointed out in his *King Football* that newsreel stereotyping was common prior to the civil rights movement in the United States. The rare depiction of a black football player would likely be of a "flashy" halfback; in some newsreel accounts, African American players and cheerleaders appeared as comic figures if not out-and-out buffoons, with the football game little more than a minstrel show.

See also: African Americans (College); Films; Newspapers.

Additional Reading:

Fielding, Raymond. *The American Newsreel, 1911–1967.* Norman: University of Oklahoma Press, 1972.

Oriard, Michael. *King Football: Sport and Spectacle in the Golden Age of Radio and Newsreels, Movies and Magazines, the Weekly and the Daily Press.* Chapel Hill: University of North Carolina Press, 2001.

Smither, Roger, and Wolfgang Klaue, eds.

Newsreels in Film Archives: A Survey Based on the FIAF *Newsreel Symposium*. Wiltshire, England: Flicks Books; Madison: Fairleigh Dickinson University Press, 1996.

NFL Junior Player Development

The National Football League began its Junior Player Development (JPD) program to compensate for the declining number of junior high school football programs. The program in tackle football is designed for junior high school boys and girls ages twelve to fourteen.

The JPD curriculum is offered in three six-week courses. Participants progress through the three stages of development in consecutive seasons or years depending on how the program is administered locally. The Instructional and Competitive Concept Outline posted on the NFL Youth Football Web site notes that the three stages may be offered, for example, during three consecutive springs or in a spring/fall/spring sequence.

Each week has a life-skill focus developed by a sports psychologist: responsibility, goal setting, sportsmanship, self-control, smart moves, and teamwork. Along with these life skills, coaches teach fundamentals of football such as blocking and tackling in fifteen-minute segments. Participants practice at a number of positions in order to receive a comprehensive overview of the game, with execution rather than the outcome of a play emphasized.

The second stage of instruction includes improving basic skills, combining skills, and moving toward competition that more closely resembles an actual football game. The progression through the three stages also incorporates instruction on how positions work together. After completing the three six-week courses, the player advances into high school and will be more ready to play high school football. If the NFL planners are correct in their thinking, the students also will be better able to integrate sports, academics, and life skills.

Additional Reading:
NFL Youth Football Web site. http://www.nfl youthfootball.com.

Nicknames

The individual obviously is important within a football game as in every area of life. The television camera often focuses on an individual player, for example, the receiver catching a pass or a kick returner escaping one would-be tackler after another. Football, however, more than most team sports, is just that: a team sport. Although it is possible for a player to make a great play all by himself, it is uncommon. The pitcher in a baseball game can strike out a batter and, unless the catcher drops the third strike, he has essentially done that by himself. A batter without help from anyone can drive a pitch over the fence for a home run. In football, however, a player usually can do little without help.

The quarterback needs time, given by his offensive line, to throw the pass, and he needs a receiver to get sufficiently open to catch the pass. The running back needs people to open holes with their blocks. No matter how great a defensive player is, he is unlikely to make many tackles unless his teammates can hold up their end of the bargain or the offense will simply run plays away from him. That long punt return is not apt to occur without some well-thrown blocks, and the field goal will be batted back in the kicker's face without protection from his offensive line. The examples could go on and on.

So it is not surprising that this dependence on teammates has been noted with a long litany of special nicknames for units. The Four Horsemen of Notre Dame received their name from a sportswriter, Grantland Rice, in 1924. The name for the Irish backfield may have been primarily a bit of journalistic melodrama, as the famous photograph showing Harry Stuhldreher, Jim Crowley, Don Miller, and Elmer Layden astride four horses was an ingenuous publicity gimmick by the university, but the name revealed the teamwork that made each of the four a better player because of the presence of the other three.

In the mid-1940s Army boasted one of the greatest one-two running back tandems in the history of college football: fullback Doc Blanchard and halfback Glenn Davis. Each won a Heisman Trophy, but they have gone through history as a pair: Mr. Inside and Mr. Outside.

Fordham University featured an outstanding offensive line in the 1930s that proved at least close to immovable in the face of defensive charges. They were known as the Seven Blocks of Granite. The member best remembered today is Vince Lombardi, who went on to become the legendary Green Bay Packers coach.

In recent decades, defensive lines have especially been honored with nicknames, partly compensating for the tendency of linemen, except for the superstars, to be largely anonymous to all except close students of the game. Teamwork is of great importance for the defensive linemen, who must work together to plug holes against runners and find routes to the quarterback. The "Fearsome Foursome" has been applied to several defensive lines but most famously to the Los Angeles Rams of the 1960s, consisting of tackles Merlin Olsen and Roosevelt Grier and ends Lamar Lundy and Deacon Jones.

The defensive line of the Minnesota Vikings in the late 1960s and early 1970s earned the highly descriptive name the Purple People Eaters after the color of their uniforms. Swallowing up those offensive players were tackles Alan Page and Gary Larsen and ends Carl Eller and Jim Marshall. The Pittsburgh Steelers won four Super Bowls in the 1970s owing in no small amount to the Steel Curtain of defensive tackles Mean Joe Greene and Ernie Holmes and defensive ends L. C. Greenwood and Dwight White. The term was later extended to the entire defensive unit.

The Miami Dolphins went through the 1972 season undefeated, capturing the Super Bowl to conclude a perfect season. The team relied on a powerful running attack featuring Larry Csonka and Mercury Morris, a brilliant field general in quarterback Bob Griese, and an outstanding defense labeled the No-Name Defense because it supposedly lacked big-name stars but played brilliantly as a unit. Some of the defenders, however, did acquire substantial names for themselves, including linebacker Nick Buoniconti, tackle Manny Fernandez, and safety Jake Scott.

Nicknames for units seem to be less popular today, but the concept of teamwork is just as important. The top team during the first decade of the twenty-first century is one of the great examples of teamwork in the history of the NFL, exemplifying an approach in which individuals regularly subordinate themselves to a team-first philosophy. So thorough is this approach that the team's given name itself has come to designate teamwork: the Patriots.

See also: Four Horsemen of Notre Dame; Greene, Charles Edward Joseph; Lombardi, Vincent Thomas; Mr. Inside and Mr. Outside; Olsen, Merlin Jay; Page, Alan Cedric; Perfection; Rice, Grantland.

Additional Reading:

Aaseng, Nathan. *Football's Fierce Defenses*. Minneapolis: Lerner Publications, 1980.

Holley, Michael. *Patriot Reign: Bill Belichick, the Coaches, and the Players Who Built a Champion*. New York: William Morrow, 2004.

Levine, Al. *The Miami Dolphins: Football's Greatest Team*. Englewood Cliffs NJ: Prentice-Hall, 1973.

Peterson, James Andrew. *The Four Horsemen of Notre Dame*. Chicago: Hinckley and Schmitt, 1959.

Obesity

Obesity in professional football players has been widely recognized in recent years. Of course, those football players and their coaches prefer to think in terms of their merely developing the bulk and strength to stuff the run or block defensive linemen. Bulk means big bucks in the National Football League, although the health implications for the future of those players—heart disease, high blood pressure, diabetes, weight-related breathing problems such as sleep apnea, and other illnesses—are dire.

Not long ago, a three-hundred-pound lineman was an aberration. Now it is commonplace. More than six hundred NFL players weighed 295 pounds or more in 2005 summer training camps. A University of North Carolina study in 2003 found that 56 percent of NFL players were obese, which is to say almost every lineman, with obese players having a 52 percent greater chance of incurring fatal heart disease than the general public. An earlier study conducted for the National Institute for Occupational Safety and Health in 1994 stated that obese players are 3.7 times more likely than their non-obese teammates to die of heart disease. In other words, athletes usually are healthy but not if they weigh too much.

Of even greater concern is the increased obesity in recent years at the high school level, where only a tiny percentage of football players will ever become big-time college football players, let alone professional players. Yet large numbers of teenage players are putting their lives at risk by bulking up in order to pursue the dream of future football greatness and the financial rewards that come with it.

A 2007 study published in *The Journal of the American Medical Association* (*JAMA*) points out that adolescent overweight is a predictor of adult overweight. If the teen is obese, he is likely to remain so in later years. The study involved 3,683 linemen from Iowa high schools during the fall 2005 season, with at least two teams selected from each district in the state. The result: 45 percent were overweight, and 9 percent could already be classified with adult severe obesity. The condition was most pronounced at the 4A level, the highest class of football competition in Iowa, where presumably the potential for being seen by major college recruiters was highest, and therefore where there was the greatest motivation to bulk up.

Another 2007 study, published in *The Journal of Pediatrics*, also paints an ominous picture of youth obesity in football. The authors of this study examined 653 boys from 8.7 to 14.6 years old in Michigan youth football. Overweight criteria were borrowed from the International Obesity Task Force and the United States Centers for Disease Control and Prevention. According to these standards, 42.6 percent and 45 percent respectively of youth football players were found to be overweight or obese. Not surprisingly, overweight and obesity were most common among youthful offensive and defensive linemen.

Although obesity and overweight are serious problems among American youth in general, the problem, according to the Michigan study, is greater in football. Its authors also point out that obese teens tend to become obese adults.

Bulking up is not difficult to do, especially with encouragement by coaches or parents dreaming of football glory. Teens who want to gain weight can do so quite legally with dietary supplements. They also can often do so illegally with performance-enhancing drugs, since only three states (New Jersey, Texas, and Florida) have enacted statewide drug-testing programs.

One seemingly sensible answer is establishment of weight limits at every level of football from elementary-age teams to the NFL. This would save many lives, reduce injuries from mammoth humans colliding, and place a greater premium on talent and play execution.

See also: Substance Abuse.

Additional Reading:
Burniat, Walter, et al., eds. *Child and Adolescent Obesity: Causes and Consequences, Prevention and Management.* New York: Cambridge University Press, 2002.

Harp, Joyce B., and Lindsay Hecht. "Obesity in the National Football League." *JAMA* 293.9 (2005): 1061–62.

Laurson, Kelly R., and Joey C. Eisenmann. "Prevalence of Overweight Among High School Football Linemen." *JAMA* 297.4 (2007): 363–64.

Longman, Jeré. "Assuming an Unhealthy Burden in the Pursuit of Football Glory." *New York Times,* November 30, 2007.

Malina, Robert M., et al. "Overweight and Obesity Among Youth Participants in American Football." *Journal of Pediatrics* 151.4 (2007): 378–82.

Officials (Zebras)

While freedom is nice, too much freedom is anarchy—especially in sports. Given the violent nature of football, that sport in particular cries out for someone to exercise control, enforce the rules, prevent mayhem, and keep the whole process running in a reasonably coherent way. That is where the officials come in.

Football officials are often referred to as referees, although only one of the officials is officially a referee. That is the person in the striped shirt and the white cap. The other officials wear black caps, so everyone can easily spot the person in charge. The referee decides whether a team has scored and signals all penalties, requiring impeccable knowledge of not only the rules of the game but also all the signals for penalties.

The number of officials working high school games varies from state to state, even within a state. In southwestern

Maine, for example, the number is four: a referee positioned behind the offense, an umpire located behind the linebackers, and a line judge and linesman standing along the line of scrimmage and facing the action. Each has his or her specific roles to play and aspects of the game to keep watch over. A fifth official is added for playoff games and a sixth for the championship contest.

And it is "his or her," as women also can be found officiating football games. In some locales, they are fairly common at the high school level. During the 2007 season three women worked games in southwestern Maine.

The pay is not much. Those folks in Maine earn sixty dollars per game, and there is a lot of preparation: taking classes, learning the rulebook, passing an examination, and participating in weekly meetings.

Assisting the officials is a four-person chain gang. They handle the 10-yard chain marking first downs and the down marker and can be seen running onto the field when a first-down decision cannot be made with the eyes alone.

The higher the football rung, the less likely it is to find women officiating. Not until 2007 did a woman officiate at a Division I-A (now known as the Football Bowl Subdivision) game. Sarah Thomas, who for eleven years worked high school games, was part of the crew at a game between Memphis and Jacksonville State on September 15. Thomas was a star athlete in high school (five letters in softball, starting as an eighth grader) and college (basketball at the University of Mobile).

At both the college and professional levels, officiating crews include seven people. In addition to the four mentioned above, a back judge, field judge, and side judge help to keep the game orderly. These three are all positioned at least 20 yards down the field on the defensive side. With the increase in passing, the side judge was added in 1978. NFL officials typically have proven themselves over quite a few years at high school and college games before being hired.

The crew must work in close harmony to be effective, teamwork being as essential to good officiating as it is to successful playing of the game. Yet away from the football field, officials are just normal folks, the kind you live next to, work beside, and wheel your cart past in the grocery store. They may be in a little better shape than most in order to engage in the quick action necessitated by their game-time roles, but even most NFL officials pass their lives largely in anonymity. Yet those men and women who officiate the games are as essential to the sport of football as are those who play and coach it.

See also: Coin Toss; Women Players.

Additional Reading:

Brown, Chad, and Alan Eisenstock. *Inside the Meat Grinder: An NFL Official's Life in the Trenches.* New York: St. Martin's, 1999.

Jordan, Glenn. "They Earn Their Stripes." *Portland Press Herald,* September 21, 2007.

Long, Howie. *Football for Dummies.* 2nd ed. With John Czarnecki. Hoboken NJ: Wiley, 2003.

Markbreit, Jerry, and Alan Steinberg. *Born to Referee: My Life on the Gridiron.* New York: Morrow, 1988.

Ohio League

Early in the twentieth century, the seat of power for professional football shifted from Pennsylvania westward to Ohio, specifically Stark County, home to the towns of Canton and Massillon. The competition between the football teams from those two Stark County towns was fierce, and Massillon was tired of losing. So on September 3, 1903, a number of leading football-oriented citizens from Massillon held a meeting at the Hotel Sailor. When the meeting ended, they had a new team, the Tigers. Ed Stewart, a newspaperman, was named coach, and a lawyer, Jack Goodrich, became manager. Both also were important players, Stewart the quarterback and Goodrich a halfback. Perhaps the best player on the team, though, was Mully Miller, the fullback, by today's standards a diminutive 170 pounds.

The Tigers fulfilled their organizers' dreams by shutting out Canton 12–0. More than feeling their oats, the team then challenged powerhouse Akron to a contest. Just to make sure, however, the Tigers hired four veterans of the Pittsburgh Athletic Club, including two very talented brothers, Harry and Doc McChesney. Again the effort paid off, with Massillon winning 12–0 and claiming the state title.

Most people learn through imitation, and football teams are no exception. Several other Ohio teams started hiring players, with Shelby making history by signing the first African American professional football player in U.S. history, Charles Follis, a halfback. In 1904 the teams employing professional players formed the Ohio League, initially a rather loose association. Massillon again proved the best team in the region, perhaps in the country, as it continued to stockpile players from around the nation.

Canton had seen enough. The team signed a batch of players, including seven from the Akron squad and two from the University of Michigan. Canton started the season by annihilating six opponents by a combined 409–0 score. Then came a game against Latrobe, the top team in Pennsylvania. Canton lost 6–0, also losing player-coach Bill Laub to injury. "Blondy" Wallace was hired to replace Laub prior to the big game against Massillon. At 240 pounds, Wallace, a tackle, was enormous for his time. He decided to make radical changes in the team, restructuring the line and hiring former All-American halfback Willie Heston. The six hundred dollars paid to Heston made the new arrival the highest-paid per-game football player until the arrival of Red Grange in 1926. All the changes, however, proved too much too soon, and Canton lost to Massillon 14–4.

Before the start of the 1906 season, major rule changes occurred in football. The forward pass was legalized, the first-down distance was increased to 10 yards, a neutral zone was established between the offense and defense, and six men had to be on the line of scrimmage. The length of the game also was changed, reduced from seventy to sixty minutes. These rules were made for college ball, but professional teams followed college rules, so the changes affected them as well.

The upshot of the new rules was that teams had to do more in less time. The rules swung the pendulum from defense to offense by both requiring and facilitating an opening up of the game. The six-man-on-the-line-of-scrimmage rule effectively ended the wedge formation as a viable tactic, replacing it with outside runs and passes. The game became more exciting to watch and somewhat less dangerous to the players' health as strategy and speed made the game less dependent on physical force.

The latter effect helped to answer Pres. Theodore Roosevelt's strongly expressed concern about the eighteen deaths and 149 major injuries that had occurred in the single year of 1905. Another response to the president's threat to ban the game if it did not become safer was establishment of the Intercollegiate Athletic Association of the United States, which became the National College Athletic Association (NCAA) in 1910.

As the 1906 season began, Canton, now known as the Bulldogs, hoped to unseat Massillon. Both teams were strong, routinely shutting out their opponents and rolling up large margins of victory.

Along the way, Massillon established a historically important first when the Tigers took advantage of one of the new rules, George "Peggy" Parratt completing a forward pass to "Bullet" Dan Riley against the Benwood-Moundsville team. It remains the first documented forward pass in professional football.

Canton won the first game against Massillon, 10–5. In the rematch, however, Massillon won 13–6 for its fourth consecutive title. The victory was aided by use of a lighter football, the Victor ball, with punts regularly sailing over the head of the Bulldogs' safety to give Massillon excellent field position. The game also engendered another controversy when accusations of an attempted bribe surfaced. Ed Stewart claimed in the *Massillon Evening Independent* that Canton's Blondy Wallace had tried to fix the rematch in order to force a third, tie-breaking contest. A contract then was discovered showing that Massillon coach Sherburn Wightman had agreed to accept $4,000 to lose the second game. Wallace, long blamed for participating in a fix, was completely innocent. Wightman argued, at least in retrospect unconvincingly, that he had signed the contract to ferret out the evildoers.

Yet despite Wallace's innocence, the damage had been done in the public mind, and erstwhile fans stayed away in droves as Canton defeated Latrobe 16–0. As a result, the team went bankrupt. The expense of paying high salaries proved to be too much for not only Canton but also Massillon. Both the Bulldogs and the

Tigers came to an end with the 1906 season, but football in Ohio was far from dead.

Football continued, and by 1912 teams were proving profitable once again. Continued rule changes occurred. As of 1912 a touchdown counted for 6 points, teams had four downs rather than three to make 10 yards, and the field was shortened from 110 yards to 100. In 1915 a new Massillon team reclaimed the name Tigers, and Canton adopted its former name, the Bulldogs. In a move that would reverberate long into the future, Jack Cusack, manager of the Bulldogs, signed Jim Thorpe, the former Carlisle and Olympic star, paying him $250 per game. In the second meeting of the season between the old rivals, Thorpe kicked two field goals, dropkicking one and placekicking the other, to give Canton a 6–0 victory. The field goal had been changed from 4 to 3 points in 1909. Playing left end for the Tigers was future Notre Dame coaching legend Knute Rockne.

Thorpe proved to be a great draw, and attendance at Canton games rose dramatically. For the 1916 season Cusack signed Thorpe's former Carlisle teammate Pete Calac, who played fullback to Thorpe's halfback. Canton defeated Massillon 24–0 to win the state championship. The Bulldogs followed with another championship in 1917, but World War I and the influenza epidemic knocked out much of the football season, with neither Canton nor Massillon playing at all.

The 1919 season opened amid serious concerns about rising player salaries and players jumping from one team to another. By this time, Ralph Hay had replaced Cusack with the Bulldogs, Cusack having entered the oil business in Oklahoma. It would be in that same Ralph Hay's Hupmobile agency less than a year later that the National Football League would be born. Another important figure in the birth of the NFL, George Halas, also was involved in the 1919 Ohio League season, as an end for the Hammond, Indiana, team.

A third former Carlisle great, Joe Guyon, joined Thorpe and Calac to help defeat Massillon 23–0. A later victory over Hammond and a second decision over Massillon, the latter 3–0 on a Thorpe field goal, gave the Canton Bulldogs another state championship before the fabled Ohio League slipped into memory.

See also: Canton Bulldogs; Halas, George Stanley; Hay, Ralph E.; Professional Football Origins; Rockne, Knute Kenneth; Thorpe, James Francis; World War I.

Additional Reading:

Cusack, Jack. *Pioneer in Pro Football: Jack Cusack's Own Story of the Period from 1912 to 1917, inclusive, and the Year 1921.* Fort Worth TX: n.p., ca. 1963.

Maltby, Marc. *The Original Development of Professional Football, 1890–1920.* New York: Routledge, 1997.

Peterson, Robert W. *Pigskin: The Early Years of Pro Football.* New York: Oxford University Press, 1997.

Riffenburgh, Beau. "Pro Football Before the NFL." In *Total Football II: The Official Encyclopedia of the National Football League.* Ed. Bob Carroll et al., 5–13. New York: HarperCollins, 1999.

Olsen, Merlin Jay (b. 1940)

Merlin Olsen is widely recognized as one of the greatest defensive linemen of all time. His significance, however, goes far beyond that one accomplishment. He also established himself as a superior student, a universally recognized nice guy (despite being plenty tough on the football field), a skilled television broadcaster, and an effective and highly likable actor.

At Utah State University, Olsen earned All-America honors as a tackle and received the Outland Trophy in 1961 as the country's finest interior lineman. He also made Phi Beta Kappa and the Academic All-America team. In 1980 he became the first Academic All-American to be inducted into the College Football Hall of Fame.

Drafted by the Los Angeles Rams in the first round in 1962 as the third player taken overall, he earned Rookie of the Year honors and made the Pro Bowl squad. It was the first of fourteen consecutive years he was chosen for the Pro Bowl. Six times in his fifteen years in the NFL (all with the Rams) he was a first-team All-Pro. He played in a total of 208 games, the last 198 without missing a single one.

Olsen was as smart as he was strong and used both qualities to anchor the Fearsome Foursome defensive line of the Rams in the 1960s, which also included fellow tackle Roosevelt Grier and ends Deacon Jones and Lamar Lundy. The Foursome comprised one of the greatest defensive lines ever.

Olsen earned a master's degree in economics during his professional years. After retiring from football following the 1976 season, he turned to broadcasting, beginning a long partnership with Dick Enberg at NBC that would last from 1977 to 1988. He then spent one final year in the broadcast booth, with Charlie Jones. Along the way he also was inducted into the Pro Football Hall of Fame (1982).

Television viewers became accustomed to seeing Olsen doing much more than narrate football games as he represented FTD Florists and appeared in several television series. He had the lead roles in *Father Murphy* (1981–84) and *Aaron's Way* (1988). Television viewers may best remember Olsen for his role as Jonathan Garvey from 1977 to 1981 on the long-running *Little House on the Prairie* (1974–83). The series, with Michael Landon producing, directing, and starring, was set in the 1870s and presented as a domestic Western minus gunfights and battles with Indians but with a lot of family crises, love, and tears. Jonathan Garvey played a strong, faithful friend to Landon's Charles Ingalls in the series loosely based on the Laura Ingalls Wilder Little House books. During Olsen's years on the series, Jonathan lost his wife in a school fire, established a warehouse, and persuaded Charles to join him in a freight-hauling business along with a variety of other activities, such as trying to compete in a wrestling match against a champion wrestler. On reruns, Olsen continues to be an important member of the Little House world, as he remains one of college and professional football's immortals.

See also: Nicknames; Television Broadcasting.

Additional Reading:
Smith, Rick. *Stadium Stories: St. Louis Rams.* Guilford CT: Insiders' Guide, 2005.

Oorang Indians

The Oorang Indians were a short-lived (1922–23) all-Indian National Football League team that demonstrated both the popularity of Jim Thorpe and the general public's stereotyping of Indians that was common in the early twentieth century and would continue for many decades.

Walter Lingo, a wealthy breeder of Airedales, came up with the idea for the team, which he thought could help publicize his business. He bought an NFL franchise, named the team after his Oorang Dog Kennels in the small town of LaRue, Ohio, and hired Jim Thorpe as player-coach. Thorpe in turn recruited American Indians from about ten tribes to play for the Oorang Indians, including former teammates at the Carlisle Indian Industrial School. Next to Thorpe, who played sparingly in the team's games, Joe Guyon, an Ojibwa from Minnesota, was the best player on the squad. A running back, Guyon was later inducted into both the College Football Hall of Fame (1971) and the Pro Football Hall of Fame (1966).

Lingo believed that American Indians and his Airedales shared a closeness to nature and consequently believed it logical (as well as good business) to bring them together. Oorang players not only had to play football but also help care for and train Lingo's dogs. He advertised certain Airedales as Indian trained and sold them for higher prices.

Since the whole team was largely a marketing device, players and dogs alike performed before the game and at halftime. Player performances included Indian dances complete with Indian regalia, tomahawk-throwing contests, shooting exhibitions, and even bear wrestling. In the two years that the team existed, it played all but one game on the road, better to publicize Lingo's Airedales. Thorpe was paid well for his efforts, earning five hundred dollars weekly, but in retrospect his participation in this commercialization, even mockery, of Indian culture marks a regrettable period in his life.

The Oorang Indians were not a good team. They won only three games while losing sixteen during their two years and disbanded after the 1923 season, less because of their losing record than the public's gradual loss of interest in the team, which lessened its value to Lingo's Oorang Dog Kennels.

See also: American Indians; Mascots and Team Names; Thorpe, James Francis.

Additional Reading:
Whitman, Robert L. *Jim Thorpe and the Oorang Indians: The N.F.L.'s Most Colorful Franchise.* Mount Gilead OH: Robert Whitman and the Marion County Historical Society, 1984.

Page, Alan Cedric (b. 1945)

Alan Page was one of the greatest defensive players in football history, earning induction into both the college and professional football halls of fame. However, he enjoyed even greater success after his playing days as a justice on the Minnesota Supreme Court and a tireless worker for greater educational opportunities for inner-city youth.

A native of Canton, Ohio, birthplace of the National Football League, Page was a standout defensive end at the University of Notre Dame from 1964 to 1966, helping the Fighting Irish win the national title in his senior year when he was a consensus All-American. Extraordinarily fast and quick, Page once blocked a punt against Purdue and returned it 67 yards for a touchdown. The Minnesota Vikings drafted him in the first round in 1967 in the first combined NFL-AFL draft.

With the Vikings, Page switched to defensive tackle and played for Minnesota through part of the 1978 season when he was released. The Chicago Bears quickly signed him, and Page continued to star through 1981. He earned innumerable honors as a pro. He was named the NFL's Most Valuable Player in 1971 and made All-Pro nine years in a row (1969–77). Four times (1971, 1973–75) he was the NFC Defensive Player of the Year. He finished his professional career with twenty-three fumble recoveries, twenty-eight blocked kicks, and 173 sacks. Page was a vital member of Minnesota's famed Purple People Eaters defensive line that helped the Vikings go 104-35-1 while winning ten NFC Central division titles. In his final game, against the Denver Broncos, he recorded 3.5 sacks of quarterback Craig Morton.

Yet Page's postfootball accomplishments have been even more noteworthy. While playing for the Vikings, he attended law school at the University of Minnesota and turned to a legal career back in Minnesota after his retirement from the NFL. When he became Minnesota's assistant attorney general in 1987, he visited classrooms throughout the state urging youngsters to do their best academically in order to succeed in life.

After approximately five years as assistant attorney general, Page was elected to the Minnesota State Supreme Court, assuming his position as an associate justice in 1993. He thus became the first African American jurist ever to serve on Minnesota's Supreme Court. In addition, he formed the Page Education Foundation to help inner-city students advance to postsecondary education. The foundation enlists corporations and schools to provide matching grants for scholarships for minority students. Acceptance of a foundation scholarship obliges the recipient to give back to his or her community by returning to the inner city to work with young students. To emphasize the importance of education, he chose a school principal, Willarene Beasley, from a Minneapolis inner-city high school, to present him for induction into the Pro Football Hall of Fame in 1988.

As of 2009 Alan Page was still serving as a member of the Minnesota Supreme Court and continuing to help young people in his state find their way out of poverty through education. For this former football great, football became a means to helping many others achieve justice and a better way of life.

See also: Education; Nicknames.

Additional Reading:

Minnesota Supreme Court Web site. http:// www.courts.state.mn.us/?page=550.

Page Education Foundation Web site. http:// www.page-ed.org.

Parcells, Duane Charles (Bill, the Big Tuna) (b. 1941)

Bill Parcells coached the New York Giants to two Super Bowl victories and then embarked on a journey through several other teams, building winning clubs but falling short of the ultimate goal of another Super Bowl triumph. Like a reluctant lover, Parcells was wooed by a series of teams, yielded to some, withdrew periodically into retirement, but continued to tease. Despite retiring for a third time following the 2006 season, by midway through the 2007 season he was being talked about as a possible answer for the struggling Miami Dolphins.

Parcells became defensive coordinator of the Giants in 1979, left the following year for one season with the New England Patriots, and then returned to New York in 1981. It was supposedly during his year in New England that he received the nickname "the Big Tuna," an allusion to Charlie the Starkist Tuna in Starkist commercials. Parcells reportedly responded to an attempt by a player to con him about something with a statement to the effect that the player must have thought that Parcells was Charlie the Tuna, that is, a really naïve character.

By 1983 Parcells was head coach of the Giants, and after a horrible first year during which New York won only three games, he steadily improved the Giants until they won fourteen of sixteen games in 1986, followed by a Super Bowl win over the Denver Broncos. Quarterback Phil Simms and a stifling defense known as the "Big Blue" and featuring linebackers Lawrence Taylor, Harry Carson, and Carl Banks and end Leonard Marshall were among the team's top stars. Another Super Bowl victory followed the 1990 campaign, with backup quarterback Jeff Hostetler filling in for the injured Simms.

Parcells retired after his second Super Bowl victory and turned to television commentary for NBC before returning to coaching with the New England Patriots in 1993. By 1996 Parcells had the Patriots rolling all the way to the Super Bowl, only to lose to the Green Bay Packers.

Having fallen out with New England's owner, Robert Kraft, Parcells left after the season to assume the head coaching position with the New York Jets.

Considerable criticism came Parcell's way for allegedly focusing too much on securing the Jets job and too little on defeating the Packers. Commissioner Paul Tagliabue ruled that Parcells had violated his contract with New England and that New York would have to provide the Patriots with a first-round draft choice as compensation. Parcells coached the Jets for the next three years, enjoying his best season in 1998 when they went 12-4. He continued one more season as vice president of football operations, with his appointed successor, Bill Belichick, first accepting and then almost immediately resigning as head coach to take the coaching job with the New England Patriots.

A second retirement ended in 2003 when Parcells became coach of the Dallas Cowboys. His four seasons with Dallas were somewhat disappointing. The team made the playoffs twice but failed to win any postseason games. After the 2006 season Parcells retired from coaching for a third time, becoming an analyst for ESPN.

Few denied Parcells's ability as a coach, especially his considerable aptitude for taking a losing team and returning it to at least respectability (something he had accomplished in all of his head-coaching stops). Yet, many did question his long-term commitment to any particular or-

ganization. Still, as the Dolphins staggered through the 2007 season, Parcells's name surfaced as a possible coaching replacement—and if not Miami, then likely some other team somewhere, sometime, at least for the short term. If constancy were not Parcells's leading attribute, he at least retained his allure as a coach who could take a broken team and quickly make it better.

The curiosity regarding Parcells's future was finally satisfied in December 2007 when he accepted a position with Miami despite strong overtures from the Atlanta Falcons. However, Parcells was not returning to the sidelines. He became Miami's vice president of football operations and quickly took action, within weeks replacing both the general manager and the head coach of the team that had finished the season with a woeful 1-15 record. Parcells clearly was in charge, and in his first season, 2008, he already had the Dolphins in the playoffs.

See also: Belichick, William Stephen; Commercials and Advertisements; Super Bowl; Taylor, Lawrence Julius; Television Broadcasting.

Additional Reading:

Parcells, Bill. *Finding a Way to Win: The Principles of Leadership, Teamwork, and Motivation.* With Jeff Coplon. New York: Doubleday, 1995.

———. *Parcells: Autobiography of the Biggest Giant of Them All.* With Mike Lupica. Chicago: Bonus Books, 1987.

Shropshire, Mike. *When the Tuna Went Down to Texas: How Bill Parcells Led the Cowboys Back to the Promised Land.* New York: W. Morrow, 2004.

Parseghian, Ara Raoul (b. 1923)

Ara Parseghian is still remembered as the coach who returned the Notre Dame football program to glory in the 1960s, taking a team that went 2-7 in 1963 and turning it around to come within ninety-three seconds of an undefeated season and a national championship in his first season as coach in 1964. However, Parseghian is also known, and perhaps even more admired, for his efforts to defeat a deadly disease that afflicts children: Niemann-Pick Type C disease.

Parseghian came to Notre Dame with excellent qualifications. He had played professionally for the Cleveland Browns of the All-America Football Conference (1948–49), coached under Woody Hayes at Miami University in Ohio (1950), served as head coach at Miami (1951–55) with a record of 39-6-1, and coached at Northwestern (1956–63), where his record of 36-35-1 was achieved despite modest talent and included four straight wins over Notre Dame.

Parseghian's 1964 team won its first nine games and led Southern Cal in the season finale before losing the lead and the game with 1:33 remaining. The final score was 20–17. Parseghian led the Irish to an eleven-year record of 95-17-4 and national titles in 1966 and 1973, the period commonly referred to as the "Era of Ara." Those seasons included two of the most memorable games in college football history. Notre Dame fell behind Michigan State 10–0 in their 1966 meeting, but the Irish fought back to tie the score. With

possession of the ball and time running out, Parseghian chose to run out the clock and preserve the tie rather than attempt to score. The decision elicited considerable criticism, but Parseghian defended his decision as appropriate given the several players he had out with injuries and the heroic effort his team had made to tie the contest.

The 1973 season for Notre Dame concluded with a game against also undefeated Alabama in the Sugar Bowl. Parseghian had returned Notre Dame to postseason play in 1969 for the first time since January 1, 1925, when Notre Dame and the Four Horsemen defeated Stanford and Ernie Nevers 27–10 in the Rose Bowl. Now, four years later, the Irish were in a rugged seesaw battle. Notre Dame scored a field goal to take a 24–23 lead with 4:26 remaining in the game. Then the Irish got the ball back but faced a third down deep in their own territory. Choosing to gamble, Parseghian called a pass to a seldom-used tight end rather than run the ball and probably have to punt, thus giving Alabama a chance to come back and win. The play worked, and Notre Dame was able to hold on to the ball until time expired, ensuring itself the national crown.

Faced with health problems, Parseghian resigned after the 1974 season and went to work broadcasting football games for ABC (1975–81) and later CBS (1982–88). He was inducted into the College Football Hall of Fame in 1980.

Before long, tragedy began touching the Parseghian family. In 1994 three of

Parseghian's young grandchildren—Michael, Marcia, and Christa—were diagnosed with Niemann-Pick Type C disease, a genetic neurodegenerative disorder that usually strikes children and interferes with their ability to metabolize cholesterol. Cholesterol therefore accumulates in the brain, liver, and spleen, leading to death. All three of the Parseghian children died, Marcia last of the three, at the age of sixteen in 2005.

Parseghian helped to establish the Ara Parseghian Medical Research Foundation in 1994 to support research aimed at discovering the cause of the disease and its cure. As of 2009 scientists funded by the foundation had identified the gene that causes Niemann-Pick Type C, were carrying out therapeutic drug trials, and were seeking to understand the cell biology related to the disease—all steps toward finding a cure.

Parseghian writes on the foundation Web site, "The pain of losing our three youngest grandchildren is almost unbearable." The losses reflected in that simple but powerful sentence far transcend any football defeats, and no grandparent is likely to contemplate the Parseghian family's losses without thinking long and hard about his or her own grandchildren.

See also: All-America Football Conference; Bowl Games; Bryant, Paul William; Four Horsemen of Notre Dame; Hayes, Wayne Woodrow; Television Broadcasting.

Additional Reading:

Ara Parseghian Medical Research Foundation Web site. http://www.parseghian.org/apmrfweb.

Pagna, Tom. *Notre Dame's Era of Ara*. With Bob Best. South Bend IN: Hardwood, 1976.

Parseghian, Ara, and Tom Pagna. *Parseghian and Notre Dame Football*. Notre Dame IN: Men-In-Motion, 1971.

Paterno, Joseph Vincent (JoPa) (b. 1926)

Joe Paterno, affectionately known as JoPa, reminds us that a football coach really can be a lot like excellent wine. Age can enhance rather than dilute the quality. For more than half a century, Paterno has been molding young men into outstanding football players and, along the way, helping a lot of those young men become better people as well.

Paterno attended Brown University, where he was a quarterback for Coach Rip Engle. Engle left for Pennsylvania State University in 1950, taking along the recently graduated Paterno. The former quarterback expected his coaching to be a short-term job until he entered law school. The short term, as of 2009, had stretched to almost six decades.

Engle left Penn State after the 1965 season, and Paterno succeeded him as head coach. At the conclusion of the 2008 season, he had amassed an extraordinary list of achievements, including most years as head coach at one institution (forty-three), most bowl appearances (thirty-five), most bowl victories (twenty-three), most wins of any Football Bowl Subdivision coach (383), five undefeated and untied seasons, and two national championships. He also oversaw Penn State's transfer into the Big 10 (which remained the Big 10 even with an eleventh member). Penn State joined the conference in 1993, and the following season the Nittany Lions won the Big 10 title. In 2005 Penn State was cochampion of the Big 10. Over the years, Paterno won several coaching awards, including the Walter Camp Coach of the Year award in 2005, a year in which he overcame calls for his retirement by leading Penn State back from 3-9 and 4-7 seasons to go 11-1.

There is much more to JoPa than football, though, including his commitment to sound academics and the welfare of his institution. When he became head coach at Penn State, he announced a "grand experiment," a lofty-sounding term for trying to win both on the gridiron and in the classroom. Many people scoffed at his idealism, but Paterno pulled it off. By the end of the 2004 season, he had coached sixty-nine first-team All-Americans and twenty-three first-team Academic All-Americans. His players' graduation rate consistently has ranked among the highest in the country for football players.

He also has given generously of his time and money to help Penn State thrive as a top-rate academic institution. By 2007 he and his wife, Sue, had donated some $4 million to the university, including funds for the Pasquerilla Spiritual Center. He helped raise $13.5 million for the Pattee Library, an effort that led the university to name the library expansion in honor of the Paternos. Those who visit the Penn State Web site can take a tour of the Paterno Library as well as the Pattee Library. Paterno clearly stated his belief in the importance of a great library when, while being honored in 1983 after winning his first national championship, he emphasized to the university's Board of Trustees the importance of making Penn State No. 1 academically and stressed the value of a top library to both faculty and students. Under new selection rules that make an active coach eligible for the College Football Hall of Fame, Paterno was selected for induction in 2006. An injury that he incurred during a football game, however, prevented him from attending induction ceremonies, delaying his induction until December 2007.

Appreciation for JoPa extends even into Penn State Creamery, where a flavor of ice cream is named for him—Peachy Paterno. Having reached his eighty-first birthday while still patrolling the Penn State sidelines, Paterno may just keep going, accumulating wins, encouraging his players to excel academically, supporting his beloved university, and maybe even trying a bowl of that Peachy Paterno ice cream.

See also: Education; Hall of Fame (College).

Additional Reading:
Fitzpatrick, Frank. *The Lion in Autumn: A Season with Joe Paterno and Penn State Football.* New York: Gotham Books, 2005.
Newcombe, Jack. *Six Days to Saturday: Joe Paterno and Penn State.* New York: Farrar, Straus and Giroux, 1974.
Paterno, Joe. *Paterno: By the Book.* With Bernard Asbell. New York: Random House, 1989.
Pennsylvania State University Web site. http://www.psu.edu.

Payton, Walter Jerry
(Sweetness) (1954–1999)

Walter Payton was one of the most liked and admired of football players, earning the nickname "Sweetness" for his sunny disposition as well as his pleasing performance on the football field. He also was one of the best running backs ever, breaking Jim Brown's all-time record for career rushing yards and helping the Chicago Bears capture Super Bowl xx after the 1985 season.

Payton starred at Jackson State University, a historically black institution, where in both 1973 and 1974 he was voted Black College Player of the Year. Drafted in the first round by the Chicago Bears in 1975, he starred with Chicago through the 1987 season.

Payton broke O. J. Simpson's single-game rushing record on November 20, 1977, against the Minnesota Vikings when he ran for 275 yards despite having just recovered from the flu. The record would stand until 2000, when Cincinnati's Corey Dillon gained 278 yards against Denver. That season was Payton's best personally as he gained 1,852 yards rushing, scored sixteen touchdowns, and earned the NFL's Most Valuable Player award.

From a team standpoint, however, Payton's greatest accomplishment was leading the Bears to a remarkable 15-1 regular-season record in 1985 and then helping to crush the New England Patriots 46–10 in the Super Bowl. Having been instrumental in getting the Bears that far, though, Payton did not score

against New England. Coach Mike Ditka later expressed his regret at not making sure that Payton had a good scoring opportunity. For the second time, Payton was named his league's Most Valuable Player.

Payton broke Jim Brown's career rushing record in 1984 and retired after the 1987 season with 16,726 yards. That record would finally fall to Emmitt Smith of the Dallas Cowboys in 2002.

Walter Payton's story took a sad turn in 1999 when he announced that he had a rare liver disease, primary sclerosing cholangitis, which caused a cancerous tumor to develop on his liver. Payton used his illness through the Walter and Connie Payton Foundation to encourage organ donations but refused to use his celebrity status to push himself ahead on the waiting list for a liver transplant. Organ donations increased because of Payton's efforts, saving many lives, but not his. He died on November 1, 1999. Although the saying "The good die young" obviously is not always true, it seemed so in the case of Sweetness.

Honors flowed in. Chicago released a license plate and sticker featuring Payton, with proceeds going to organ donor programs in Illinois. A new Chicago high school was named Walter Payton College Prep. In addition, each year the best offensive player from a Division 1 FCS (formerly Division I-AA) football program receives the Walter Payton Award, and an NFL player receives the Walter Payton Man of the Year Award for distinguished community-service activities. Payton's son, Jarrett, honoring his father in a manner that likely would have brought the elder Payton considerable pleasure, wore his father's No. 34 at the University of Miami. Jarrett, also a running back, played professionally for Tennessee in 2005.

See also: Black College Football; Brown, James Nathaniel; Ditka, Michael Keller, Jr.; Perry, William Anthony; Simpson, Orenthal James; Super Bowl.

Additional Reading:
Payton, Connie, and Brittany Payton. *Payton.* New York: Rugged Land, 2005.
Payton, Walter. *Never Die Easy: The Autobiography of Walter Payton.* With Don Yaeger. New York: Villard, 2000.
———. *Sweetness.* With Jerry B. Jenkins. Chicago: Contemporary Books, 1978.
Towle, Mike. *Walter Payton: Football's Sweetest Superstar.* Nashville: Cumberland House, 2005.

Peanuts

The characters in Charles Schulz's long-running comic strip, *Peanuts,* played baseball more than any other sport, but football was far from absent. In fact, Charlie Brown became the most durable place-kicker in football history. He lasted even longer than Lou Groza (1946–59, 1961–67), George Blanda (1949–58, 1960–75), Gary Anderson (1982–2004), and Morten Andersen and John Carney (who began in 1982 and 1988 respectively and were still active in 2007), or any of the other gray-beards who booted field goals in the National Football League.

From 1952 to 1999 (Schulz died in 2000), Charlie annually (yes, once per year) attempted to kick the football. Each year except the last, Lucy held the ball, that is, until Charlie's toe was just about to make contact. Then she yanked the ball away, sending Charlie sprawling.

Somehow, Charlie always got suckered in again to trust Lucy—or maybe just to trust that somehow things would turn out right in the end. Football became a metaphysical experience for Charlie, even for Lucy, who in one strip noted that the experience was symbolic. Charlie seemed to have trouble with that concept, but whether he consciously understood or not what he was attempting year after year, he seemed to have what F. Scott Fitzgerald assigned to Gatsby, an "incorruptible dream." Gatsby's dream was to reclaim Daisy and then relive his life with her. Charlie's goal was more modest—to kick the football—but he was no less determined and persevering about it. One person's gullibility is another one's refusal to give up.

Even Lucy ultimately became bored with the routine, but not Charlie. In the last strip to feature Charlie as kicker, Rerun summons Lucy for lunch just as she is about to place the football. She goes because her mother has told her to, and Rerun (his name fitting the situation) is left as holder. Charlie has a new confidence, convinced that Rerun will never pull the ball away as Lucy had been doing for the better part of half a century. But is that once again his capacity for hope—and for disappointment?

We see Charlie approaching the ball,

but then Schulz switches to the lunch table where Lucy asks Rerun whether he pulled the ball away. Rerun, though, refuses to tell her—in fact, he says she will never know—and Lucy is left squalling in agony, as we are left in eternal uncertainty. Did Charlie finally get to kick the ball or not? Ultimately, we are left in the same place as Charlie, in a world dark at both ends, knowing the past imperfectly, uncertain about the future. Maybe Charlie finally got to kick the football, but we will never know.

See also: Fitzgerald, F. Scott Key; *Gil Thorp*; *Tank McNamara.*

Additional Reading:
Michaelis, David. *Schulz and* Peanuts: *A Biography.* New York: Harper, 2007.
Schulz, Charles M. *Charles M. Schulz: Conversations.* Ed. M. Thomas Inge. Jackson: University Press of Mississippi, 2000.
———. *Peanuts: A Golden Celebration: The Art and the Story of the World's Best-Loved Comic Strip.* Ed. David Larkin. New York: HarperCollins, 1999.

Perfection

Perfection is a goal that many strive toward but, of course, seldom if ever reach. To strive is sometimes to excel, even if the goal remains beyond our grasp. At other times, striving for an unreachable goal bears only fruits of disappointment and disillusionment. Theologians remind us that perfection comes only in the next life, at least in terms of personal spiritual development. In other ways, however, there may be such a state as perfection even in this mortal world.

In football, perfection is an elusive but not entirely impossible goal, at least as the football world defines perfection. Winning all games in a season without even a tie is the most obvious example of a defined state of perfection in football. That has happened many times at the high school and college levels, although playoff systems and the recent practice of pitting the two highest-ranked FBS teams against each other in the championship bowl game have reduced the number of teams that make it through the season unscathed.

No Football Bowl Subdivision team survived the 2007 season and its bowl undefeated. However, the national champions in 2000–02 and 2004–05 (Oklahoma, University of Miami in Florida, Ohio State, Southern California, and Texas) managed to do just that. They may be said to have achieved perfection, although undoubtedly not a single one of their coaches would claim perfection for his team. It is an absolute rule of coaching that no one is ever to be completely satisfied, for there is always room to improve. Thus, motivation runs up against the concept of perfection and, at least in the minds of coaches, always trumps it.

As of 2008 only one team in the long history of the National Football League stretching back to 1920 had gone through the season and postseason undefeated and untied. That single perfect team was the 1972 Miami Dolphins, which won all sixteen of its games, concluding with a Super Bowl victory over the Washington

Redskins, 14–7. Perfection, though, was not easy for Miami to achieve. Several of the games were close, with Miami winning one by 1 point, one by 2, and two by 4.

The New England Patriots, however, threatened to join Miami, winning all of its games during the 2007 regular season, the first undefeated and untied campaign by any NFL team since the league expanded its schedule to sixteen games. The Patriots made it all the way to the Super Bowl in their quest for perfection before succumbing to the New York Giants on a last-minute touchdown pass from Eli Manning to Plaxico Burress.

Other NFL teams have come close. The 1929 Green Bay Packers suffered one tie. The Chicago Bears were perfect in the regular season in 1934 and 1942 but lost in the championship game each year. The Cleveland Browns achieved perfection in 1948, winning fourteen games and then defeating Buffalo for the league championship, but they were in the All-America Football Conference, not the NFL.

So perfection, even when measurable, is hard to come by. In most ways, perfection cannot even be defined within football. What constitutes a perfect runner, pass receiver, or punter? Perhaps perfection may be determined for a field-goal kicker (never missing a kick) or for a blocker (never missing a block) and so forth, but such measures are clearly impossible to achieve over any significant length of time.

According to the NFL, an occasional quarterback has reached perfection in passing, Peyton Manning more than anyone else, though not by completing every pass, which many people might see as constituting perfection. Instead, according to NFL statistics, a rating of 158.3 is the highest established passer rating and thus constitutes perfection. Manning first reached that level on October 22, 2000, against the New England Patriots and has hit it again several times. Yet against the Patriots, he misfired four times, connecting on sixteen of twenty attempts. Consequently, that definition of perfection appears rather arbitrary, as if perfection for a student might be set at 98 percent rather than 100, or for an accountant making only one mathematical mistake per five hundred computations.

The upshot of this is that perfection in football is just as hard to reach (and define) as in any other area of life. Perhaps it is better to pin one's hopes for perfection on another sphere of existence, one in which no passes fall incomplete, no multiple-choice questions are marked incorrectly, and no mathematical figuring ever goes awry.

See also: Belichick, William Stephen; Brady, Thomas Edward, Jr.; Manning, Peyton Williams; Shula, Donald Francis.

Additional Reading:

Carroll, Bob, et al., eds. *Total Football II: The Official Encyclopedia of the National Football League.* New York: HarperCollins, 1999.

Foss, Martin. *The Idea of Perfection in the Western World.* Lincoln: University of Nebraska Press, 1946.

MacCambridge, Michael, ed. ESPN *College*

Football Encyclopedia: The Complete History of the Game. New York: ESPN Books, 2005.

Perry, William Anthony (the Refrigerator, the Fridge) (b. 1962)

During Super Bowl xx, on January 26, 1986, William Perry, commonly known as the Refrigerator or the Fridge because of his size (382 pounds on a 6-foot-1-inch frame), took a handoff and crashed into the end zone. The Bears won the game 46–10 over the New England Patriots, completing a season in which they had been defeated only once. Perry, who would play through the 1994 season, mainly for the Bears, became a household name and a beloved figure in Chicago.

Mike Ditka later regretted the decision to have Perry rather than Hall of Fame running back Walter Payton score the touchdown as Payton never got another chance to score in a Super Bowl. As for Perry, the carry was in some ways the highlight of his career, firmly establishing him in popular culture lore.

That 1985 season was a dream year for the Bears, their fans, and the rookie defensive tackle drafted in the first round out of Clemson. Perry not only played on the defensive line but at times also lined up at fullback, either as lead blocker or ball carrier. He rushed five times in goal-line situations during the regular season, scoring twice. Although the tactic was a legitimate power play, it likewise had a novelty effect: 382 pounds pounding against the defensive linemen. Perry also caught a 4-yard touchdown pass that year.

Nonetheless, Perry would get few opportunities with the football after that year. He had only three more rushing attempts in his career, caught no more passes, and scored no more touchdowns.

What remained was a reasonably effective defensive lineman with a mammoth frame, a Super Bowl ring sized 25 (the largest Super Bowl ring ever and approximately twice the size of most men's rings), and a future capitalizing on his fame as the Refrigerator.

Perry was immortalized by a G.I. Joe action figure in 1986 and had songs sung about him (Roq-In' Zoo's "Frig-O-Rator" and Hard Machine's "Refrigerator" shortly after his Super Bowl appearance). He and Payton recorded a song called "Together" as part of an antidrug effort.

In later years Perry participated in *WrestleMania 2* in Rosemont, Illinois; made Kentucky Fried Chicken commercials; appeared as a guest on Howard Stone's comedy talk show; and sponsored a line of Fridge Xone coolers and grills. He also has continued with speaking engagements and autograph signings.

In addition to his size, Perry was noticeable for his teeth: generally in bad shape with several missing (including a gap right in the front) thanks to inconsistent dental care, some collisions with football players, and a childhood encounter with pellets from a pellet gun. The gap-toothed smile, however, disappeared in 2007, replaced by a smile filled with beautiful white teeth, the result of a deal proffered by Sunrise Dental Care in Geneva, Illinois. The arrangement involved about $60,000 worth of free dental work in exchange for using Perry's fame in advertising. As those dentists know, there is nothing quite like a sparkling new refrigerator, especially one named William "the Refrigerator" Perry.

See also: Commercials and Advertisements; Ditka, Michael Keller, Jr.; Music; Payton, Walter Jerry; Super Bowl.

Additional Reading:
The Fridge: William Perry Web site. http://www .Fridge72.com.
Hewitt, Brian. *"The Refrigerator" and the Monsters of the Midway: William Perry and the Chicago Bears.* New York: New American Library, 1985.

Plimpton, George Ames (1927–2003)

George Plimpton was a prominent journalist, writer, and editor whose most acclaimed literary work may have been editing the highly regarded *Paris Review*. He also did some acting, appearing, for example, in the film *Good Will Hunting* (1997) and having a recurring role in the television series *ER* (1998, 2001). He also had the avocation of demonstrating that a regular guy really cannot compete athletically with professionals. Almost anyone could have told him that this is so, but few people wrote about the discovery with as much charm, humor, and insight.

Plimpton's most famous excursion into professional athletics came with the Detroit Lions of the National Football League in 1963 when, with knowledge of Detroit's coaches but not of the players,

he joined their preseason training camp. Plimpton, then thirty-six years old, was ostensibly competing for the third-string quarterback position, a somewhat credible rationale given that the role does not require extraordinary size or speed.

When Plimpton could not handle the snaps from center, however, the players quickly sensed something amiss. He did in fact get to play in a scrimmage but lost yards on each of his plays.

The experience did not net Plimpton any positive yardage, but it did produce a book, *Paper Lion*. The book, delving into the personalities of such Lions as quarterback Milt Plum, cornerback Dick "Night Train" Lane, and Hall of Fame linebacker Joe Schmidt, was well received by the public and in turn yielded a film starring Alan Alda (1968).

Plimpton had previously taken a turn pitching before a major league All-Star Game in 1960, writing about it in *Out of My League* (1961). He later had parallel experiences with a variety of other sports and also wrote two more books about football: *Mad Ducks and Bears* (after a brief encounter with the Baltimore Colts) and *One More July: A Football Dialogue with Bill Curry.*

See also: Films; Literature.

Additional Reading:
Plimpton, George. *Mad Ducks and Bears.* New York: Random House, 1973.
———. *One More July: A Football Dialogue with Bill Curry.* New York: Harper and Row, 1977.
———. *Paper Lion.* New York: Harper and Row, 1966.

Poe, Edgar Allan (1809–1849)

Edgar Allan Poe, one of the most famous of American authors, remains widely read. Some of his fiction (for example, "The Fall of the House of Usher," "The Masque of the Red Death," "The Tell-Tale Heart," and "The Pit and the Pendulum") still evokes chills for many a reader, and his "The Murders in the Rue Morgue" places him among the pioneers in detective fiction. Perhaps of all Poe's writings, however, his poem "The Raven" is best known.

It is through "The Raven" that Poe has his most direct, but not his only, link to football. Poe spent part of his life in Baltimore, a fact that still resonates with Baltimore residents. So when Cleveland Browns owner Art Modell moved the Browns to Baltimore prior to the 1996 season, and the team needed a new name, a *Baltimore Sun* telephone poll produced a huge outpouring of sentiment for the Ravens, after Poe's famous poem. Edgar Allan Poe's poem and preternatural bird thus live on not only in classrooms throughout the country but in the National Football League as well.

The poet, however, has additional links to football. His cousin John Prentiss Poe achieved a certain level of fame himself by serving as attorney general of Maryland and fathering six sons, all of whom followed their father to Princeton University. While there, they contributed, in most cases significantly, to Princeton's football fortunes.

One of the sons, the poet's namesake, Edgar Allan Poe, class of 1891, played quarterback and halfback, earning All-America honors. He later also followed his father into the position of Maryland's attorney general. Alexander Leitch points out in *A Princeton Companion* that such was his renown on campus that when someone asked whether he were related to the great Edgar Allan Poe, another responded that he *was* the great Edgar Allan Poe. Not least among the latter Poe's accomplishments was serving as an attorney for F. Scott Fitzgerald, himself a great aficionado of Princeton football.

See also: Fitzgerald, F. Scott Key; Ivy League; Literature; Mascots and Team Names.

Additional Reading:
Hutchisson, James M. *Poe*. Jackson: University Press of Mississippi, 2005.
Leitch, Alexander. *A Princeton Companion*. Princeton NJ: Princeton University Press, 1978.
Wagenknecht, Edward. *Edgar Allan Poe: The Man Behind the Legend*. New York: Oxford University Press, 1963.

Politicians

Several United States presidents have had connections to football and are discussed elsewhere in this book. In addition, others with strong backgrounds in football have used their athletic fame to help them enter politics in recent years and have had distinguished political careers.

Of all former players and coaches who entered the political arena, no one achieved so much success in both professions as Jack Kemp. A starting quarterback throughout the history of the American Football League, which spanned the decade of the 1960s, Kemp excelled for the Los Angeles/San Diego Chargers and the Buffalo Bills, making the AFL All-Star team seven times and winning the league's Most Valuable Player award in 1965. Kemp retired after the 1969 season as the all-time AFL leader in passes thrown, completions, and passing yardage.

Kemp was elected to the U.S. House of Representatives in 1971, representing the Buffalo region where he had played the final eight years of his football career. A nine-term congressman, Kemp sought the Republican presidential nomination in 1988. Although unsuccessful, he was named secretary of housing and urban development by the first President Bush. In 1996 Senator Robert Dole, the Republican presidential nominee, tapped Kemp to be his vice presidential running mate. Kemp acquitted himself well on the campaign trail and in debate that year, but he and Dole lost to the Democratic incumbents, Pres. Bill Clinton and V.P. Al Gore.

Steve Largent had an outstanding college career at the University of Tulsa, leading the nation in touchdowns his junior and senior years. However, viewed as undersized and not particularly fast, Largent was not chosen in the draft until the fourth round. Then the Houston Oilers released him. The Seattle Seahawks, however, gave him a chance, and Largent went on to enjoy a Hall of Fame career with Seattle.

A great possession receiver who worked tirelessly to improve and was always prepared, Largent made seven Pro Bowls and led the league in receiving yards twice. At retirement he held several records: most receptions (819); most receiving yards (13,089); most touchdown receptions (100); and, denoting his remarkable reliability, most consecutive games with at least one reception (177).

Largent, a Republican, ran successfully for Congress in 1994 and ended up representing the people of Oklahoma for eight years. He served on the Commerce Committee, was vice chairperson of the Energy and Air Quality Subcommittee, and, among several other assignments, was a member of the Telecommunications Subcommittee, the latter serving him well in his later position as CEO of a cell-phone industry lobby, the Cellular Telecommunications & Internet Association. Largent decided against a fifth congressional term, instead unsuccessfully running for the governorship of Oklahoma in 2002.

Two other former football greats recently lost bids to become their states' governors. Tom Osborne, a member of the College Football Hall of Fame and longtime coach of the University of Nebraska, sought the Republican nomination for governor of Nebraska in 2006. Despite his considerable popularity in the state, he lost in the Republican primary to the incumbent, Dave Heineman, taking 45 percent of the vote to Heineman's 49 percent.

Osborne had run successfully for the U.S. House of Representatives from Nebraska's Third Congressional District three times, serving in Congress from 2001 to 2007. He sat on committees dealing with agriculture, education, and workforce issues, matters important to him and to his state.

Prior to entering politics Osborne had established one of the greatest coaching records in college football history. In twenty-five years as Nebraska's football coach, he never won fewer than nine games and never failed to take his team to a bowl game. Three times he led the Cornhuskers to the national championship (1994, 1995, 1997). In his last five seasons, he won sixty games and lost just three.

Also in 2006, Lynn Swann ran for governor of Pennsylvania. The great receiver had starred for the University of Southern California and helped the Pittsburgh Steelers win four Super Bowls in the 1970s. His football exploits earned him induction into both the College Football Hall of Fame (1993) and the Pro Football Hall of Fame (2001). In addition, he had earned continuing name and face recognition through his work with ABC Sports from 1976 to 2005. Nonetheless, Swann faced a huge challenge running against the incumbent Democrat, Gov. Ed Rendell. Swann lost, taking just 40 percent of the vote to Rendell's 60 percent.

Two other former football stars recently elected to Congress were Republican J. C. (Julius Caesar) Watts and Democrat Heath Shuler. Watts quarterbacked the University of Oklahoma team to two consecutive Big 8 championships and two Orange Bowl victories. After graduating in 1981, he played for Ottawa and Toronto in the Canadian Football League.

Watts was elected to Congress in 1994 from Oklahoma's Fourth District, serving four terms. His committee assignments included the House Armed Services Committee and the House Select Committee on Homeland Security. In 1998 House Republicans elected him chair of the Republican Conference, the fourth-ranking leadership position in the House. After leaving Congress, Watts worked as a CNN analyst while also serving on the boards of several companies.

Heath Shuler entered the House of Representatives after a 2006 victory over eight-term Republican incumbent Charles Taylor in North Carolina's Eleventh Congressional District. A star quarterback at Tennessee where he was runner-up in the Heisman balloting in 1993, Shuler never reached the same level of success in the NFL. A combination of factors, including weak supporting casts with the Washington Redskins and New Orleans Saints and foot injuries, shortened his career, and he retired after another foot injury ended an attempted comeback with the Oakland Raiders in 1999.

Shuler returned to his home state to run for Congress and swept through the Democratic primary, winning 75 percent of the vote. He then defeated Taylor by a 54–46 percent margin. A member of the "Blue Dog Coalition" (a group of moderate Democrats), Shuler was named chair of the House Small Business Subcommittee on Rural and Urban Entrepreneurship.

As of 2007 Shuler was the only former professional football player still serving in Congress. If the past is any indication of what the future will bring, however, he is unlikely to be alone very long.

See also: American Football League (IV); Presidents of the United States.

Additional Reading:

Denton, Robert E., ed. *The 1996 Presidential Campaign: A Communication Perspective.* Westport CT: Praeger, 1998.

Osborn, Tom. *Faith in the Game: Lessons on Football, Work, and Life.* New York: Broadway Books; Colorado Springs: WaterBook Press, 1999.

Watts, J. C. *What Color Is a Conservative? My Life and My Politics.* With Chriss Winston. New York: HarperCollins, 2002.

Pollard, Frederick Douglass (Fritz) (1894–1986)

Frederick Douglass "Fritz" Pollard, named after the famous black abolitionist and journalist, was inducted into the Pro Football Hall of Fame with the class of 2005, more than a century after his birth and eighty years after his last game in the National Football League. The award brought a fitting reconsideration of a career that included not only a number of accomplishments as a football pioneer but also excellence as a player and coach.

Pollard attended Brown University where, following the 1915 season, he became the first African American to play in the Rose Bowl as his team lost to Washington State. During the 1916 season, the halfback was chosen as an All-American, only the second African American to be so honored; Bill Lewis was the first, with Harvard (1892–93). Pollard was inducted into the National Football Foundation College Football Hall of Fame in 1954, the second African American to be inducted, after Duke Slater of Iowa in 1951.

After serving in the army during World War I, Pollard entered professional football with the Akron Indians in 1919. The next year, Akron, now reorganized as the Pros, became a charter member of the new league that would come to be known as the National Football League. He not only starred for Akron, helping the team win the championship in 1920, but also became co-coach (with Elgie Tobin) in 1921. Pollard thus holds the distinction of being the first black head coach in NFL history. Among the players he recruited for Akron was the All-American from Rutgers, Paul Robeson, who later became a world-famous singer, actor, and political activist. Pollard later claimed that in essence he was Akron's head coach as early as 1919 as he instructed the team in a more open type of offense that he had experienced at Brown.

Pollard played and coached for several other NFL teams through 1925, organized an all-black All-Star team in 1928 that became the Chicago Black Hawks, and signed on as coach of the all-black Harlem Brown Bombers in 1935, a team named after boxer Joe Louis. Despite combining entertainment, including singing spirituals, with their play, the Brown Bombers became the most powerful black football team of its time. Pollard stayed with the Brown Bombers through the 1937 season.

In later years, Pollard coached football at Lincoln University, owned a Harlem music studio where bandleader Duke Ellington among others rehearsed, and published a New York newspaper. The music studio was a continuation of Pollard's lifelong love for music. Growing up in Chicago, Pollard learned to play several musical instruments and performed in his high school band. Recognizing Pollard's early success as a coach, the Black Coaches Association named its annual award given to an outstanding college or professional coach after him. In 2003 a group of coaches, scouts, and front-office staff created the Fritz Pollard Alliance to encourage minority hiring by the NFL.

See also: African Americans (College); African Americans (Professional); Professional Football Origins; Robeson, Paul Leroy Bustill.

Additional Reading:
Carroll, John M. *Fritz Pollard: Pioneer in Racial Advancement.* Urbana: University of Illinois Press, 1992.
Ross, Charles K. *Outside the Lines: African Americans and the Integration of the National Football League.* New York: New York University Press, 1999.
Willis, Chris. *Old Leather: An Oral History of Early Pro Football in Ohio, 1920–1935.* Lanham MD: Scarecrow Press, 2005.

Pop Warner Little Scholars

Pop Warner Little Scholars is a national nonprofit youth organization that sponsors football programs and cheerleading and dancing competitions for boys and girls ages five to sixteen. The organization had its origins in a problem that the owner of a Philadelphia factory was having in 1929 with youngsters throwing rocks through the factory windows. Joseph J. Tomlin (1902–88), a former athlete who was working as a stockbroker in New York and returning to Philadelphia on weekends, had an idea. He suggested that a number of factory owners, all of whom had the same problem, sponsor an athletic program that would give the young people something more constructive and enjoyable to do than break windows. With the support of the owners, Tomlin set up a four-team football league.

When the stock market crashed that fall, Tomlin lost his New York job and began devoting himself full time to youth athletics. The Junior Football Conference expanded to sixteen teams by 1933. The following April, Tomlin organized a football clinic, but because of inclement weather only one speaker, Glenn "Pop" Warner, showed up. Warner held his young audience of some eight hundred in thrall for two hours, and Tomlin persuaded Warner to lend his name to the organization, which became the Pop Warner Conference.

Tomlin believed strongly in a marriage of athletics and academics, and early on he arranged educational experiences for his young players, including speakers, reading materials, and tutors for children whose academic achievements were marginal.

At that time the organization included many young men beyond the current age limit of sixteen. During World War II a large percentage of these members departed for the war, and the number of teams declined sharply, reaching a low of forty-two teams.

After the war, the Pop Warner Conference rebounded, although the participants were generally younger than before. The first championship game, called the Santa Claus Bowl, occurred in bitter weather on December 27, 1947. In 1959 the name was changed to Pop Warner Little Scholars to highlight the academic focus of the organization. Today, children are required to meet certain academic requirements such as a grade point average of 2.0 (or 70 percent for grades based on percentages) to participate, although students who fail to meet the minimal grade requirement may become eligible if recommended by a school administrator.

Currently, approximately 360,000 boys and girls participate in football or cheerleading and dance. Although cheerleading was established for girls, boys may also participate and girls may play football. They compete in eight divisions based on age and weight limits ranging from Tiny-Mites (ages five to seven, weighing thirty-five to seventy-five pounds) to Bantams (ages thirteen to fifteen, 130–175 pounds, or sixteen with a weight between 130 and 160 pounds). There also are four classifications for flag football (a type of football that involves grabbing a flag from a player rather than tackling).

The age and weight matrix is hailed by Pop Warner officials as an important safety feature of the competition because youngsters are competing against other children of similar age and size. No individual statistics are kept in order to build a sense of community while avoiding depicting some participants as superstars and hurting others' self-esteem.

In recent years, the Pop Warner Super Bowl has been held in December at Disney's Wide World of Sports Complex in Lake Buena Vista, Florida. Sixty-four teams from two divisions with participants ranging from age eight to fifteen compete, with each team guaranteed at least two games. The cheer and dance competition occurs at the same time and place and features more than four hundred squads, also in four age ranges as well as in two squad sizes (large and small) and three competition categories based on experience.

Joseph Tomlin died in 1988 at the age of eighty-five. His legacy, however, endures in an organization that is the largest youth football, cheer, and dance program in the United States.

See also: Education; Warner, Glen Scobey; Women Players.

Additional Reading:
Balthaser, Joel D. *Pop Warner Little Scholars.* Mount Pleasant SC: Arcadia Publishing, 2004.

Pop Warner Little Scholars Web site. http://www
.popwarner.com.

Practice Squad

Members of the practice squad in the National Football League are sort of members of the team but not really. They are, one might say, practicing to become full-fledged NFL players when and if they are given the chance. In the meantime, they practice against the big guys, often simulating players that the team will be facing in the next game.

The very term *practice* connotes something less than genuine. College students preparing to become teachers were once referred to as doing "practice teaching" when they taught in high schools or elementary schools, usually as seniors. That idea of just practicing raised too many unpleasant ideas, for example, not really teaching (and perhaps therefore resulting in their students not really learning), practicing on youngsters (guinea pigs?). So for a variety of reasons, colleges and school systems turned to other terms, usually "student teaching." That has a nice ambivalent sense about it that is more comforting. After all, everyone involved (college student and learner alike) is a student.

Perhaps a nicer term can be found for the practice squad, but in the meantime members go on practicing and hoping that they will be moved up to the active roster. Some, of course, make it there, either for a genuine career or, a bit more commonly, for a cup of coffee (to borrow a baseball term), even up and down for many cups of coffee but never a full brunch.

Having a practice squad serves a useful purpose for the teams by providing instantly ready replacements in case an active player gets hurt. The number of players permitted on each team's practice squad currently stands at eight, up from five in 2004. A ninth is permitted if he comes from another country and the team is participating in the NFL's international program.

The current practice-squad program dates from 1989, but the practice of having practice (or replacement) players instantly available was one of many innovations by Paul Brown when he was coaching the Cleveland Browns in the All-America Football Conference from 1946 to 1949. Teams were permitted thirty-three players on the roster, but Brown had more than thirty-three good players and wanted to keep the extras. Consequently, he arranged for them to get jobs with the Zone/Yellow Cab Company in Cleveland so they were earning money and could still attend practices. Brown's players/taxi drivers were dubbed the "taxi squad," a name that remained in vogue for years. Old-time followers of football can still occasionally be heard using the term rather than "practice squad."

It may be hard to visualize a highly paid professional football player today driving a taxi, but members of the current practice squads have a most precarious existence—and their financial rewards can disappear in a heartbeat. If they are only one play away from becoming genuine NFL players, they also are one quick decision away from being dropped and having to find another line of work. In the meantime, they earn $5,200 weekly but have no guarantees about how many weeks they will be earning that sum. Nor are they eligible for long-term benefits or an NFL pension.

Many were in other types of jobs before being signed to the practice squad, and many will soon return permanently to nonfootball jobs. But some, like Jon Kitna, who went from Seattle's practice squad to a long and productive career as an NFL starting quarterback, will make it. That is the dream that drives the practice-squad players, and an occasional Kitna makes everyone wonder, "Maybe, just maybe."

See also: Brown, Paul Eugene.

Additional Reading:
Jenkins, Lee. "Shadow Warriors." *Sports Illustrated*, October 29, 2007, 66–70.

Presidents of the United States
Several United States presidents have been deeply involved with football, as players, as fans, or in their official capacities as president. Theodore Roosevelt may have had the greatest impact of all presidents, to some extent beyond what he intended. Roosevelt admired football as a means of helping young men become physically and mentally strong. A former Harvard student, he had strongly opposed Harvard Pres. Charles Eliot's efforts to drop

football in the 1890s. During that same time period, one of Roosevelt's presidential predecessors, Grover Cleveland, canceled the Army-Navy football game after receiving a report on the high number of football-related injuries and resulting lost workdays suffered by academy players.

By 1905 football injuries were rising again. According to a *Chicago Tribune* report, at least eighteen deaths and 159 serious injuries occurred that year as a result of football. Roosevelt was paying closer attention to the realities of football competition since he had two sons playing the game, Ted with the Harvard freshmen and Kermit at Groton.

A friend, journalist Henry Beach Needham, published two articles in *McClure's Magazine* attacking corruption in the sport occasioned by its growing status as big business (undermining the amateur ideal) and also slamming the increased lack of sportsmanship. Football violence, although not Needham's primary focus, dovetailed with his other concerns. Players, according to Needham, were often told to deliberately injure the other team's top player, a serious violation of normal standards of sportsmanlike behavior.

Endicott Peabody, headmaster at Groton, appealed to President Roosevelt to meet with the top three Eastern football powerhouses—Yale, Princeton, and Harvard—to address the declining commitment to sportsmanship. Roosevelt, thus facing complaints about football from a variety of sources, followed the advice of his son's headmaster and convened the meeting in the White House on October 10, 1905. The group, who included Walter Camp of Yale, obligingly prepared a statement affirming the commitment of their universities to appropriate standards of conduct and released the document, but in the meantime violent incidents ranging from the personal to the tragic continued. Son Ted incurred a bloody, broken nose against Yale as his opponents repeatedly attacked his position, either because he was the president's son or because he was the lightest player on the team, or perhaps for both reasons. And in a game between Union College and New York University, an NYU player suffered a cerebral hemorrhage and died a few hours later.

NYU Chancellor Henry MacCracken convened a meeting of representatives from twelve colleges on December 8. Later in December, a second meeting occurred, which led to the creation of the Intercollegiate Athletic Association. In 1911 the organization changed its name to the National Collegiate Athletic Association, which would continue into the twenty-first century to oversee football and initiate a variety of reforms.

Theodore Roosevelt had helped to set in motion a reform movement that would lead to many changes in football but also to a strong anti-football movement. President Roosevelt had no wish to see football harmed, despite later accounts, apparently inaccurate, of his having supposedly threatened to abolish the sport. In fact, he had no authority to do that and no desire to do so. What he did want, however, was a sport that would adhere to an honorable, amateur, sportsmanlike standard of conduct.

Woodrow Wilson was president of Princeton during the reform efforts of 1905 but refused to participate in the MacCracken meetings despite his serious concerns about football injuries and the direction in which he saw the sport moving. He wanted to make the game more appealing to spectators and also reduce violence by outlawing blocking in front of the ball carrier, in effect removing all mass-formation plays. That alteration he thought would radically alter the game, and he stood steadfastly by his goal.

Wilson viewed himself as a football expert and believed strongly, as did many others, that the game could build character. As a Princeton student, he wrote more than twenty articles for the *Daily Princetonian* in support of football; he also helped to coach football when he taught at Wesleyan University (1888–89) and during both his student and faculty days at Princeton (1878–79, and again in 1890). While a professor at Princeton, Wilson debated Prof. Burt Wilder of Cornell on the subject, "Ought the Game of Foot Ball to Be Encouraged?" Wilson argued in the affirmative.

A series of rule changes was finalized in 1910, Wilson's final year at Princeton before going on to become New Jersey's governor and later president of the United

States. These changes probably were not much influenced by Wilson directly but did correspond generally with his vision of the game. The new rules, among other changes, required seven men at the line of scrimmage, effectively ending the massed plays Wilson so strongly blamed for excessive violence in the game. Nor were pushing or pulling to be allowed, another anti-mass-formation change. Refinements in the passing game, including outlawing interfering with a receiver within certain areas of the field, further encouraged a more open (and appealing) type of contest.

Calvin Coolidge was an assistant football coach while a student at Amherst College in Massachusetts during the 1890s. An innovation of his was a set of plays that could be run in order without signals or words. "Silent Cal," as he later came to be known for his reluctance to say much in private (although he was an effective public speaker), apparently had been practicing the habit a long time. Many years later, Bill Walsh would use scripted plays at the beginning of a game to great effect with the San Francisco 49ers, a slight variation on Coolidge's plan.

Herbert Hoover was not a player, but he was the student manager of the football team at Stanford and a member of the first official Stanford class, which began studies as well as football in 1891. He also was a young man with definite ideas about money, a subject that he would do quite well with until he ran up against the stock market crash that ushered in the Great Depression. The University of California was perceived from the first as Stanford's main rival and therefore likely to draw a large audience for their football game. Hoover is usually credited with the idea of playing the contest in San Francisco, which promised a much bigger payday than on either school's own field. Some reports have at least one of the games played between 1891 and 1894 bringing in so much money in silver dollars that Hoover had to hire two wagons to transport it and six strong football players to guard the take from San Francisco ruffians.

Franklin D. Roosevelt, who followed Hoover into the White House, apparently took little notice of football during his presidency. Although he had explicitly suggested that major league baseball continue to operate during World War II in order to help keep people's morale high, he ignored football. In December 1944, however, he required that the Army-Navy game be moved to Baltimore's Municipal Stadium, which could accommodate sixty-five thousand spectators, and mandated that an admission ticket also include purchase of a war bond. The game netted $60 million, the most lucrative war-bond event of the war.

Roosevelt's successor, Harry Truman, became the first president since Coolidge to attend an Army-Navy game, when he witnessed Mr. Inside and Mr. Outside, Doc Blanchard and Glenn Davis, lead Army over Navy 32–13. The win capped off a national championship season for Army.

If Presidents Franklin Roosevelt and Harry Truman apparently did not focus a great deal on football, that surely could not be said for Dwight Eisenhower. As a cadet at West Point, Eisenhower was a talented football player. A running back on offense, as a linebacker on defense he had the unenviable task of trying to stop Jim Thorpe when Army played the Carlisle Indian Industrial School in 1912. It was in that game that Pop Warner introduced his double-wing formation, which helped to defeat Army 27–6. On one play, however, Eisenhower and Charles Benedict, another linebacker, hit Thorpe so hard that they knocked the great back almost unconscious. The next week, Eisenhower injured a knee severely, ending a promising football career.

Football remained important to Eisenhower, especially the fortunes of his old team. A few months after D-Day, General Eisenhower took time out from pushing the Nazis out of Europe to send his congratulations to Army's coach, Red Blaik, after the Blanchard-and-Davis-led team rolled past Navy 23–7.

During the period between his military career and his presidential service, Eisenhower served as president of Columbia University. The Ivy Group Agreement of 1945 had de-emphasized football, for example, tightening eligibility rules for playing and abandoning postseason play. Nonetheless, the old Army player could not resist urging his team to do better and bring him more victories for the university. As president of the United States, he was best known athletically as a golfer, but he retained his belief in athletics and physical fitness, establishing the President's Council on Youth Fitness in 1956.

The contrast between Eisenhower and his successor, John F. Kennedy, was remarkable. A new generation had come to power, and the youthful Kennedy, the youngest man ever elected president, conveyed an aura of physical well-being despite the fact that he had a variety of physical ailments, including a bad back. The Kennedy family was often photographed playing touch football, although the president's football-playing days were behind him by the time he arrived at the White House. The best football player in the family probably was the president's brother, Atty. Gen. Robert Kennedy, who had played end for Harvard in 1957.

President Kennedy had a genuine lifelong interest in the sport. When the Japanese attacked Pearl Harbor on December 7, 1941, Kennedy, then a young naval officer, was at Griffith Stadium in Washington DC, watching the Redskins play the Philadelphia Eagles.

When Kennedy was running for president in the Wisconsin primary, he met Green Bay Packers coach Vince Lombardi and developed great admiration for the no-nonsense coach. He maintained contact with Lombardi and sent a congratulatory telegram to Lombardi after his Packers defeated the New York Giants in the 1961 championship game.

In addition to his brother, Robert, President Kennedy's appointees had other football connections. Kennedy named former football great Byron "Whizzer" White to the Supreme Court. His secretary of the Interior, Stewart Udall, issued an ultimatum to Redskins owner George Preston Marshall in 1961 to integrate the Redskins, the last National Football League team to add African American players. Marshall followed through on his promise, integrating the team in 1962.

On September 30, 1961, President Kennedy signed the Sports Broadcasting legislation allowing the commissioner, through an antitrust exemption, to negotiate a television broadcasting deal on behalf of all NFL teams. The legislation thus permitted the league to implement its television-revenue-sharing plan, which was both to increase revenue and to keep all teams competitive by sharing the television money.

The president was an old Navy man and liked to drop in on the Navy team during its preseason training at the Quonset Point Naval Air Station in Rhode Island. The base was a landing spot for Air Force One, where Kennedy could transfer to a helicopter for the final leg of his trip to the Kennedy compound at Hyannisport on Cape Cod. While observing Navy's practices, Kennedy befriended a young quarterback named Roger Staubach, who, along with millions of other Americans, would be devastated by the assassination of the president on November 22, 1963.

Lyndon B. Johnson was sworn in as president after Kennedy's death. Like his predecessor, he was a great football fan and regularly had NFL highlight reels sent to the White House so he could catch up on Sunday's games. He also signed legislation approving the merger of the NFL and the AFL.

Probably the most ardent football fan of any president, however, was Richard Nixon. He had played football at Whittier College and loved to interact with football players and coaches. In 1959, for example, he visited the New York Giants locker room before the team's championship game, which they lost to the Baltimore Colts. The players marveled at his knowledge of their names and statistics. That same year, he presented the Heisman Trophy to Billy Cannon at the New York ceremony.

Vince Lombardi impressed Nixon as he had John Kennedy, perhaps even more so, as the presidential candidate at least briefly considered Lombardi as a vice presidential running mate in 1968. That idea died when Nixon learned that the Green Bay coach was a Democrat.

Nixon dropped in on Frank Gifford in the ABC booth during the preseason Hall of Fame game in 1971 and liked to visit Washington's practice sessions. George Allen, Washington's coach, became Nixon's closest football friend, and the president did not mind suggesting an occasional play for his friend to use. In 1971 he urged Allen to use a flanker reverse to

Roy Jefferson in a playoff game against the San Francisco 49ers. Allen obliged the president, but the play lost 13 yards. Washington also lost the game, 24–20. Nixon placed an early-morning call to Don Shula with a suggested play for Super Bowl VI the morning after Miami defeated Baltimore in the AFC title game. Shula, however, was less receptive than Allen to the president's suggestions.

One of Nixon's contributions to football tradition was the post–Super Bowl phone call to congratulate the winners. Quarterback Len Dawson was celebrating with his victorious Kansas City teammates immediately after Super Bowl IV when he was called to the phone. On the line was President Nixon.

Football was so much in Nixon's thoughts that he turned to football terminology many times to designate people and events. Henry Kissinger was his "quarterback" for the Paris Peace negotiations during the Vietnam War. He often spoke of having a "game plan" for efforts important to him. A bombing action against North Vietnam became "Operation Linebacker."

Nixon may have been the most ardent presidential football fan, but his successor, Gerald Ford, was probably the best player, likely even superior to Eisenhower. Ford was an outstanding student and athlete at South High School in Grand Rapids, Michigan, where he made the honor society, captained his football team, and made both all-city and all-state teams in football.

Advancing to the University of Michigan, Ford became an outstanding center and linebacker. He helped the Wolverines win the national championship in 1932 and 1933. The team slipped badly in 1934, winning only one game, but Ford was his team's Most Valuable Player. In a 1934 game against the University of Chicago, Ford tried to tackle Jay Berwanger, who would become the nation's first recipient of the Heisman Trophy. The result was a permanent scar on Ford's left cheek from Berwanger's shoe.

The Green Bay Packers and Detroit Lions came calling with professional football offers, but Gerald Ford had other plans. They included law school at Yale, where he also was an assistant football coach.

When Ford was a member of Congress in 1951, Ralph Furey, head of the NCAA television committee, instituted a partial ban on television broadcasts as a way to increase attendance at games. After refusing to permit a Michigan-Illinois game to be telecast, Furey rejected an application by a Detroit station to televise the upcoming meeting between Notre Dame and Michigan State. Constituents cried foul, and Congressman Ford intervened. Furey backed down and, now aware of political realities, also lifted the blackouts in Washington DC.

Ronald Reagan was neither the greatest football fan nor the most talented player among the presidents, but he was the best actor. Reagan's most famous film role may have been his portrayal of the legendary

Notre Dame star George Gipp in *Knute Rockne: All American* (1940). Gipp dies young, urging his coach, Knute Rockne, to ask the team someday when the going is especially tough to win one for him. Reagan had his nickname for life: the Gipper. He cultivated that title, even using it in reference to himself on occasion. When Paul Tagliabue was selected commissioner of the NFL, then former President Reagan placed a call to congratulate him. "Win one for the Gipper," Reagan urged.

Ronald Reagan had other football ties in addition to his acting. He played high school football in Illinois and continued to play at Eureka College. When he went into broadcasting, starting at a station in Davenport, Iowa, Reagan handled many football games and developed an impressive reputation in sports broadcasting. His communications skills led from there to films, and eventually to governor of California and president of the United States.

In something of a presidential slump, subsequent presidents have not been particular aficionados of the game. Perhaps that will change. One can hope.

See also: African Americans (Professional); Carlisle Indian Industrial School; Eliot, Charles William; Gipp, George; Ivy League; Kennedy, John F., Assassination of; Lombardi, Vincent Thomas; Mr. Inside and Mr. Outside; Politicians; September 11 Terrorist Attacks; Television Broadcasting; Thorpe, James Francis; Vietnam War; Walsh, William Ernest; White, Byron Raymond; World War II.

Additional Reading:

Falk, Gerhard. *Football and American Identity*. Binghamton NY: Haworth, 2005.

MacCambridge, Michael. *America's Game: The Epic Story of How Pro Football Captured a Nation*. New York: Random House, 2004.

Watterson, John Sayle. *College Football: History, Spectacle, Controversy*. Baltimore: Johns Hopkins University Press, 2000.

Professional Football Origins

Professional football in the United States grew out of amateur football, which itself developed from soccer and rugby, both long popular in Europe. The first college football game is believed to have been a contest between Princeton and Rutgers in 1869, although the rules governing that contest differed greatly from the way in which football is played today. Each team had twenty-five players, who moved the ball by kicking it or hitting it with their heads.

The American game began to evolve quickly, however, and in 1876, the year of the nation's centennial, rules were first codified at a meeting in Springfield, Massachusetts. Walter Camp entered Yale University that same year and quickly became a leading figure in further modifying the sport. The number of participants per side was reduced from fifteen to eleven in 1880, a center snapped the ball rather than the scrum opening of rugby, and the team with the ball had three plays to gain five yards and a first down.

Another rule change advocated by Camp was to permit tackling below the waist. This change in the late 1880s had a dramatic effect on the game, as tackling became much more violent. To offset the advantage that the rule gave the defense, offenses began to use wedge formations, which resulted in two large groups of players pushing and shoving each other. Injuries mounted, and even deaths occasionally occurred.

Within this extremely physical sport, men's athletic clubs began to sponsor teams, a step that quickly turned professional. Professional football arose in western Pennsylvania as a result of the ardent competition between teams such as the Allegheny Athletic Association (AAA), in what is now part of Pittsburgh, and the East End Gymnasium Club (EEGC), also in Pittsburgh. The EEGC relied on its club physical education instructor, William Kirschner, to both play and serve as something approaching a coach. By increasing his salary during football season and decreasing his other instructional responsibilities, the club in effect made Kirschner a football professional.

Determined to best its opponent, the AAA and the EEGC, the latter now renamed the Pittsburgh Athletic Club (PAC), started hiring outside players in 1892. Teams often played a ringer, that is, someone hiding his real identity, usually a college student who played under a pseudonym to maintain his amateur status. The PAC used A. C. Read, the Penn State captain, who played under the name "Stayer."

For a November 12 rematch between the teams, the AAA brought in three players from a Chicago club: William "Pudge" Heffelfinger, Ed Malley, and Ben "Sport" Donnelly. The first meeting had ended in a 6–6 tie, but this time the new arrivals,

especially Heffelfinger, made the difference. A three-time All-American at Yale (1889–91), Heffelfinger stripped the ball from the ball carrier and ran it back for a score, giving his team a 4–0 victory, a touchdown earning 4 points then.

The Allegheny Athletic Association's ledger book recorded a $500 one-game salary for Heffelfinger, making him the first player known to have been paid a salary in addition to expenses to play football. His former Chicago teammates were recorded as receiving expenses. Others almost certainly had been paid prior to this game, including Heffelfinger himself. It was not uncommon for a team to pay double the player's expenses as an inducement that also hid the reality that he was in fact being paid for his services, a practice that the AAA team followed with Donnelly and Malley. Sometimes a team gave expensive gifts such as a watch to the player, who then would pawn the item, receiving it anew after each game for further pawning. The former Yale star, however, is the first player for whom absolute evidence of payment exists, which makes him officially the first professional football player.

There was no turning back from the road of professionalism that football had started to travel. In 1893 the AAA hired the first full-time professional coach, Sport Donnelly, who had joined the team the previous year with Heffelfinger. By the mid-1890s, several Pennsylvania teams were paying players, and in 1896 the AAA became the first entirely professional team. Faced with a ban against playing other members of the Amateur Athletic Union because of its use of professionals, the AAA decided to go out with a bang by becoming totally professional. Donnelly coached the team, which included Heffelfinger and a number of other leading professional players, all of whom were paid $100 each, plus expenses, to play the team's final, two-game schedule.

The Duquesne Country and Athletic Club, also known as the Duquesnes, hired professional players in the late 1890s. When the team encountered financial trouble, the sportsman William C. Temple, who had provided the Temple Cup to the winner of an early version of the baseball World Series, assumed financial responsibility for the club, becoming the first owner of a professional football team. The Duquesnes were the cream of the professional football crop in the final years of the century, defeating even top college teams such as Penn State, Bucknell, and Washington and Jefferson, when college teams were still generally superior to the fledgling professional squads.

By 1902 the first professional league had formed, partly spurred on by the new competition in baseball between the young American League, which had begun play in 1901, and the National League. The two Philadelphia baseball teams, the Phillies and Athletics, moved their competition into the football arena with Phillies owner John Rogers starting a football team and Athletics owner Ben Shibe countering with one of his own. Thus was born the first professional football league, the National Football League. Not to be confused with the current NFL, this league did not last long. One of the most interesting footnotes to this league's brief existence, however, was the signing of New York Giants star pitcher Christy Mathewson to play linebacker for the Kanaweola Athletic Club, one of three clubs in the league. Mathewson demonstrated considerable talent at punting before the Giants insisted that he stop playing such a dangerous game.

Tom O'Rourke, manager of Madison Square Garden, originated a World Series of professional football in December 1902, but none of the NFL teams would play in it. O'Rourke then turned to the Syracuse Athletic Club, which swept three games to claim the series. By this time professional football was shifting its locus from Pennsylvania to Ohio, where professionalism would continue with the Ohio League, which in turn would yield to the long-running National Football League and a number of NFL competitors as professional football spread throughout the country.

See also: Camp, Walter Chauncey; Heffelfinger, William W.; Ivy League; Ohio League.

Additional Reading:

Carroll, Bob. Pro Football, From AAA to '03: The Original Development of Professional Football in Western Pennsylvania. North Huntingdon PA: Professional Football Researchers Association, 1991.

Finoli, David, and Tom Aikens. Birthplace of Professional Football: Southwestern Pennsylvania. Charleston SC: Arcadia, 2004.

Riffenburgh, Beau. "Pro Football Before the NFL." In *Total Football II: The Official Encyclopedia of the National Football League.* Ed. Bob Carroll et al., 5–13. New York: HarperCollins, 1999.

Punt, Pass & Kick

The Punt, Pass & Kick program, sponsored by the National Football League, was developed to help boys and girls improve their physical conditioning (especially important now with the serious obesity problem afflicting so many young people) and learn some of the fundamentals of football. The program also encourages teamwork among student-athletes. It is structured in four age divisions (8–9, 10–11, 12–13, and 14–15) and in separate competitions for boys and girls.

Participants are taught proper techniques of passing, punting, and kicking off a tee. Competition begins at the local level in August and September, with the top scorer in each age division for boys and girls advancing to sectional competition. The five boys and girls who scored highest in sectional competition then compete for the Team Championship. There may be several sectionals within a particular NFL team market. If there are more than five, then not every sectional winner will advance.

Each Team Championship occurs in November or December prior to the NFL game. In addition, a passing exhibition is featured either during pregame festivities or at halftime. Winning at this level, however, does not guarantee advancement. Only the four boys and four girls with the highest Team Championship scores in each age division (a total of thirty-two) move on to the Finals at a January NFL game.

Points throughout the competition levels are awarded according to the distance that the football is thrown or kicked. Although it is possible to win overall without actually winning in one of the three skill areas, that is unlikely. Typically, a winner has finished first in at least one, and often two, of the areas. More than four million youngsters compete in the Punt, Pass & Kick program annually. Graduates of the program include such NFL stars as Troy Aikman, Brett Favre, and Dan Marino.

See also: Favre, Brett Lorenzo; Marino, Daniel Constantine, Jr.; Women Players.

Additional Reading:
NFL Youth Football Web site. http://www.nfl youthfootball.com.

Purdue's Golden Girl

Perhaps the best-known twirler (also known as a majorette) is Purdue University's Golden Girl. The tradition of the Golden Girl was born in 1954 when Juanita Carpenter donned her costume (much like a one-piece, skin-tight, gold lamé swimsuit bedecked with gold sequins) to lead the marching band. The costume is now among the many historic artifacts at the National Football Foundation's College Football Hall of Fame in South Bend, Indiana.

The "Golden Girl" title was a take-off on the common reference to Purdue quarterback Len Dawson as the Golden Boy. Gladys Wright, wife of Al Wright, the Purdue band director, suggested the name to her husband, and he made it permanent. Both the name and the role survived Dawson's departure, with the Golden Girl continuing today to lead the Purdue Marching Band. The present Golden Girl, as of 2009, is the twenty-seventh to hold that position, Merrie Beth Cox.

The Golden Girl of 1958, Addie Darling, probably did more than anyone to bring the position to national prominence. Darling was to perform a half-time dance on a piece of plywood placed on top of a drum at the Purdue–Notre Dame game at South Bend. As the band played "Hawaiian War Chant," she began to dance but, given the small space on which she was standing, had to keep her feet together. The inevitable result was a considerable amount of wiggling, which caught the attention of the television cameraman and therefore a wide viewing public. An Associated Press article noted that some people had accused her of wiggling too much, a complaint, it should be noted, that came from Purdue coeds and not from any of the males in attendance.

The next week, during the Purdue-Illinois game, so many photographers followed her that she was instructed to stay away from the Purdue bench so there would be room to conduct football business. A large photo spread soon appeared in *Look* magazine. The publicity did not harm her position as Golden Girl, but her marriage in November 1960 made her ineligible to continue. Tragically, a cerebral hemorrhage ended her life less than one year later, in February 1961.

In 2004, Purdue celebrated its fiftieth year of the Golden Girls with a gala, and quite golden, event. Director Emeritus Wright and many of the Golden Girls, as well as other alumni, attended. The Golden Girl had long before achieved iconic status. For years, Indiana state maps distributed at Shell gas stations noted Purdue's location with a Golden Girl image. So valued was the role that a Texas oil millionaire once offered band director Wright a blank check and a promise to outfit his daughter completely in gold, including a gold Cadillac, if she were made Purdue's Golden Girl. Wright declined the offer.

See also: Cheerleaders; Music; Sexuality.

Additional Reading:

Oriard, Michael. *King Football: Sport and Spectacle in the Golden Age of Radio and Newsreels, Movies and Magazines, the Weekly and the Daily Press*. Chapel Hill: University of North Carolina Press, 2001.

"Twirlers, Dancers and Flags." Purdue University Web site. http://www.purdue.edu/BANDS/aamb/auxiliaries.html.

Quarterback

Quarterbacks are discussed throughout this volume, in entries devoted to individual players (Tom Brady, Peyton Manning, Brett Favre, Joe Namath, Joe Montana, and others) and in discussions of quarterback-related topics, such as the forward pass. Quarterbacks occupy an especially large number of pages because they occupy a special place not only in fans' consciousness but also in the general public eye. Even people not particularly fond of football tend to know quarterbacks better than most other players.

This notoriety is because the quarterback has a central role in almost every play, with the exception of special-teams plays such as kickoffs, punts, extra points, and field goals. The television camera focuses on the quarterback, who takes the snap from center and then does something with the ball. Whether he hands it off, passes, runs with the football himself, or even fumbles the ball or is sacked, he is the center of attention, at least until he disposes of the ball.

If the quarterback makes a miscue, there is little chance of the play succeeding. He is the field general, the leader, in former times also the play-caller. Now he usually receives the play from the coach but retains the freedom to change the play if he wishes. He also must manage the clock, making sure that the play gets started before the play clock expires.

The quarterback is a romantic figure, especially if he is talented and handsome. In recent decades the pass has become increasingly common, with some teams relying on the short pass as a sort of pseudo–running game, making the quarterback even more visible.

Much rests on the shoulders of the quarterback, and when his team comes from behind to win the game in the closing moments, it is usually the quarterback who receives the credit. The winning drive is remembered chiefly for the quarterback who managed it, although the other players must also play a crucial role in the comeback, for example, the linemen by giving the quarterback time to pass and the receivers by getting open and making the catch.

So it is the quarterback whose name is often seen gracing the backs of fans attired in a facsimile of their favorite's jersey. It is the quarterback who regularly vies for the Heisman Trophy, the NFL's Most Valuable Player award, and other honors not explicitly designated for other positions. It is the quarterback, of course, who also runs the risk of becoming the goat in defeat by throwing a critical interception or fumbling the ball when a defensive lineman crashes into him. Yet

without such risks, the rewards would
be less. A hero who does not face danger
cannot truly be a hero, not even on the
football field.

See also: Drive, The; Forward Pass; Greatest Game; and individual entries allotted to
quarterbacks.

Additional Reading:

Maxymuk, John. *Strong Arm Tactics: A History and Statistical Analysis of the Professional Quarterback.* Jefferson NC: McFarland, 2007.

Schaap, Dick. *Quarterbacks Have All the Fun: The
Good Life and Hard Times of Bart, Johnny,
Joe, Francis, and Other Great Quarterbacks.*
Rev. ed. Chicago: Playboy, 1975.

R

Radio

Radio once was high tech—as high as one could get. In those early days of the twentieth century, college football and radio came of age together, as professional football and television would later do. Radio, of course, also was used to broadcast the pro games and still is, but now more on a local or regional level rather than nationally. In recent decades, college football, like the professional game, also has become a staple of television network broadcasting, leaving high school football largely to be followed by radio or— more commonly yet—in person.

The real story of football and radio, though, is the story of college football. An experimental station at the University of Minnesota attempted to broadcast a football game as early as 1912 with a spark transmitter and telegraphic signals. The first licensed radio station, KDKA in Pittsburgh, began broadcasting on November 2, 1920. The presidential election results were its first broadcast, but sports were not far behind. KDKA carried its first game on October 8, 1921, with Harold Arlin at the microphone. Pop Warner's University of Pittsburgh team edged West Virginia 21–14.

The first coast-to-coast broadcast of a football game occurred on October 28, 1922, on New York's WEAF. Princeton defeated the University of Chicago 21–18. High school football appeared on KDKA on December 9, 1921, with Robert "Buzz" Klingensmith calling Wilkinsburg's 7–6 victory over Washington High.

Quin Ryan helped WGN in Chicago become a prominent radio station that continues today as a television station viewed throughout much of the country. Owned by the Tribune Company, the station boasted a name that stood for "World's Greatest Newspaper." Ryan announced one of the most famous games of the 1920s, Notre Dame and the Four Horsemen's 27–10 triumph over Ernie Nevers and Stanford in the Rose Bowl on New Year's Day, 1925. He later broadcast Knute Rockne's funeral in 1931. No less a broadcasting authority than Ronald Reagan called Ryan the father of sports broadcasting.

The decade of the 1920s is often referred to as a golden age of sports, and college football was one of the nation's most popular sports. The same decade was also a golden age of radio, with the new device spreading from 60,000 households in 1922 to 12 million by the end of the decade (over one-third of American homes). Licensed stations also proliferated, both cause and effect of the growing fascination with radio. From three in August of 1921, the number of stations increased to thirty by the end of the year and approximately two hundred during 1922. By the end of the Roaring Twenties, 618 stations were broadcasting throughout the country.

In addition, broadcasting networks were linking stations across the country. The National Broadcasting Company (NBC) actually operated two networks, the Red and the Blue, starting in 1926. The Columbia Broadcasting System (CBS) started up in 1927, and the Mutual Broadcasting System began in 1934. The Federal Communications Commission forced NBC to divest itself of one of its networks in 1943, with the Blue network becoming the American Broadcasting Company (ABC).

As early as 1923, magazines began carrying advertisements for radios that explicitly linked the new device with football. The *Saturday Evening Post*, for example, carried an ad selling the Music Master Radio Reproducer, a bell-like speaker attached to a radio that promised to bring the sounds of the college football game right into your living room: the band playing, the crowds cheering and singing, the announcer's vivid descriptions. The ad visually depicted football players emerging from the Music Master.

Early announcers quickly earned fame, some becoming the new superstars of radio. *Time* magazine appeared on the newsstands on October 3, 1927, with announcer Graham McNamee on the cover speaking into a microphone. McNamee was among the popular early announcers often cited as the Big Three of sports radio. A former aspiring singer, McNamee joined Station WEAF in New York in 1923 and became the star of the new NBC network throughout the 1930s. His signature greeting was "Good evening, ladies and gentlemen of the radio audience." Criticized by some listeners for lack of accuracy, he saw his role primarily as one of storyteller and entertainer.

McNamee did the first national broadcast of the Rose Bowl in 1927 on the NBC network, a 7–7 tie between Stanford and Alabama. He also was at the mike during the 1929 Rose Bowl when Roy "Wrong Way" Riegals of the University of California recovered a Georgia Tech fumble and dashed 83 yards the wrong way before a teammate could stop him at his own 1-yard line. Backed up near their own end zone, California punted but had the kick blocked, leading to a safety and an 8–7 win for Georgia Tech.

Edward Britt "Ted" Husing supplanted McNamee as the No. 1 sports announcer in the 1930s. Working for CBS, Husing far excelled McNamee in accuracy and detailed descriptions of the action. A former high school football player himself, Husing knew the game from firsthand experience, which served him well during broadcasts. He announced the first-ever football games on CBS, the Army-Stanford and East-West games in 1929.

Announcing football games in the 1920s and early 1930s was an enormous challenge. The microphone was primitive, and multiple mikes had to be set up to catch music and crowd noises throughout the stadium. The radio announcer, initially treated as a poor cousin of the newspaper reporters, was kept out of the press box and often had to broadcast high above the action with little protection from the elements. Football uniforms typically did not include numbers on the front of the jerseys, so identifying players was especially difficult, requiring the hiring of a spotter to work with the announcer.

Husing devised a clever instrument to help with player identification. He used apartment house doorbell panels that had slots for twenty-two names. The "annunciator," as he called it, had a small white light under each slot. The device was covered with glass and connected to a separate keyboard that had twenty-two buttons. The spotter would watch the action and hit the correct buttons to identify players. In addition, Husing used combinations of lights to designate specific plays. Husing then could just watch the annunciator and announce the game without even looking at the field.

Husing finally left CBS to become radio's top-paid disc jockey at an annual salary of $250,000 on *Ted Husing's Bandstand*, which aired on WMGM. A brain tumor necessitated a series of operations in the 1950s, leaving him blind and temporarily unable to speak. During this period of his illness, he was featured on the popular television show *This Is Your Life* hosted by Ralph Edwards. Husing recounted his early career as a broadcaster in his memoir *Ten Years Before the Mike* (1935).

The third member of the Big Three was William Chenault Munday, a 1925 University of Georgia graduate who never really left his beloved state behind. He brought to his announcing a Southern drawl and homespun idiom that included such expressions as "the land of milk and honey" and "Beulah land" for the end zone. According to Munday, a player who was tackled was "brought down to terra firma." He routinely greeted his listeners with "How do you do, ladies and gentlemen of the loud speaker ensemble."

Munday joined NBC in 1929 to announce football games. He was working with McNamee at the 1929 Rose Bowl during the Roy Riegels wrong-way run and announced Knute Rockne's last game, the 1930 27–0 Notre Dame victory over Southern California that gave the Fighting Irish the national championship. He also announced the University of Georgia games. Munday's career declined in the late 1930s because of his alcoholism, although he overcame his addiction and made a strong comeback to announcing in the 1950s.

The Big Three of McNamee, Husing, and Munday were followed by many other broadcasters who brought games to their audiences and fame to themselves— nationally or locally—as radio continued to spread throughout the country. Wives ironed clothes and husbands watered their lawns to the sounds of Notre Dame, Army, Michigan, Southern

California, Alabama, and a welter of other teams on Saturday's pigskin afternoons. The games were brought to them by the likes of Bill Stern, Harry Wismer (who later became owner of the New York Titans of the American Football League), Ty Tyson, Tom Manning, Halsey Hall, and a multitude of others.

One of those others for a short while, until he went on to bigger things, was Ronald "Dutch" Reagan. The future president earned his spurs as the "Great Communicator" broadcasting sporting events, including football games. On November 2, 1935, much of the football world was listening to Tom Manning broadcast Notre Dame's 18–13 comeback victory over Ohio State on a touchdown toss in the closing seconds of the game by halfback Bill Shakespeare (not related, so far as anyone has determined, to the playwright of the same name). On that same day in Iowa, however, at least some football fans were following the Iowa-Indiana game, narrated by Dutch Reagan, who regularly updated his audience on the Notre Dame contest as well. Reagan made a major error, though, when he saw the Buckeyes ahead 13–0 in the fourth quarter and then, a few minutes later, received a Western Union message giving the final score. Assuming it was a misprint, he did not share the outcome with his audience. The Iowa-Indiana game also had its excitement as the two teams battled to a 6–6 tie.

The National Football League was not entirely absent from radio. Fans of the Rams, for example, could follow their team on WGAR with Bob Kelley before the team's move from Cleveland to Los Angeles after the 1945 season and on KMPC out West after the move. In Chicago and New York, broadcasts of professional games began even earlier, in 1926 and 1928 respectively. Yet pro football continued to play second fiddle to the college game until the rise of television in the late 1950s and 1960s. Not until 1940, for example, was the NFL Championship Game broadcast on network radio.

As programming expanded on radio in the 1930s, several popular programs involved football. Grantland Rice's *Sports Stories* (1943–45) featured short stories that had previously been published in magazines. Fictional football heroes who also proved their abilities in a variety of other venues included the protagonists on *The Adventures of Frank Merriwell* (1934, 1946–49) and *Jack Armstrong, the All-American Boy* (1933–50). Armstrong even took on cattle rustlers out West and Nazi spies while helping to make Wheaties the Breakfast of Champions and box tops a currency of exchange (for rings, pedometers, and a variety of other objects).

By the 1960s the great age of radio had passed, with football fans increasingly turning to the new visual medium. Over the following decades, radio retreated to its local and regional origins, although many of the most famous television broadcasters also broadcast on radio, a boon for mobile Americans who could follow at least a local game while driving.

Jack Buck, Ken Coleman, Dick Enberg, Curt Gowdy, Keith Jackson, and Lindsey Nelson are among those who handled radio duties while becoming even more famous, and certainly more recognizable, on television. Some broadcasters even preferred radio. Keith Jackson, who as a young announcer called a high school game from a third-floor classroom across the street from the football field and later became famous, among other reasons, for his trademark "Whoa Nellie!" expression, has noted that radio requires more of the announcer than does television. The radio announcer must re-create and tell a story with all of the descriptive and narrative skills involved in doing so rather than play a secondary role to pictures. For many years, many announcers did just that, and they helped millions of Americans experience the thrill of football games that they could see, not through pictures on a screen, but through the words of the radio announcer.

See also: Magazines; Presidents of the United States; Rice, Grantland; Television Broadcasting.

Additional Reading:

Husing, Ted. Ten Years Before the Mike. New York: Farrar and Rinehart, 1935.

McNamee, Graham. You're on the Air. New York: Harper and Brothers, 1926.

Oriard, Michael. King Football: Sport and Spectacle in the Golden Age of Radio and Newsreels, Movies and Magazines, the Weekly and the Daily Press. Chapel Hill: University of North Carolina Press, 2001.

Patterson, Ted. The Golden Voices of Football. Champaign IL: Sports Publishing, 2004.

Radio Helmet

Football shares with the broader American society an interest in technological advances that contribute to improved communications. Perhaps no relationship within football is more important than that between the coach and the quarterback, so a clear line of communication between the two is a must.

One of the more interesting early technological experiments was designed to enhance precisely that relationship, especially during games. Back in 1956, John Campbell and George Sarles, both from Ohio, contacted Paul Brown, coach of the Cleveland Browns, regarding a device they were trying to perfect. It was a small radio receiver designed to be placed within a player's helmet. The idea was that the coach could talk directly to the quarterback during the heat of battle, instructing his field general regarding play selection without having to send in a substitute player to relay the directive.

Brown, an innovative coach, was, as it were, all ears. He liked the idea but instructed the two inventors to work in secret so that no one else would catch on to what they were trying to do. The men therefore experimented in the woods behind Campbell's house.

When the device appeared to be working as intended, it was tried out in an exhibition game between the Browns and the Detroit Lions. Backup quarterback George Ratterman had the receiver within his helmet and listened to his coach convey orders. The Lions coaches, however, were bright enough to figure out that something unusual was happening when Brown failed to send in his usual messengers. A sharp-eyed coach spied the receiver in Ratterman's helmet, and the secret was out. The Browns used the receiver for three more games until Commissioner Bert Bell ruled the device illegal.

Radio helmets would finally take their place on the football field in 1994 when they were legalized. Meanwhile the receiver used by Ratterman ultimately made its way into the Pro Football Hall of Fame where the quarterback's technologically enhanced helmet is on display.

See also: Brown, Paul Eugene; Hall of Fame (Professional).

Additional Reading:
Brown, Paul. *PB: The Paul Brown Story.* With Jack Clary. New York: Atheneum, 1979.
Eckhouse, Morris. *Day by Day in Cleveland Browns History.* New York: Leisure Press, 1984.

Religion

In the summer of 2000 the United States Supreme Court ruled on a case that had been making its way through the judicial system since 1995. Down in Texas, four students and their parents sued the Santa Fe Independent School District of Galveston County to try to stop the district's practice of having its student body elect a student as "chaplain" to lead a prayer prior to the start of the high school team's football games.

The legal issue revolved around the First Amendment of the U.S. Constitution, which mandates that "Congress shall make no law respecting an establishment of religion, or prohibiting the free exercise thereof." The Supreme Court in 1962 had outlawed school-sponsored prayer in public schools and thirty years later extended the prohibition to public school graduation ceremonies.

The Fifth U.S. Circuit Court of Appeals ruled in 1999 that the Texas school district was in violation of the Constitution. Then in 2000, in a 6–3 decision, the Supreme Court declared that those prayers at football games did indeed violate the First Amendment. Delivering a prayer over the school public address system by someone representing the student body and under school supervision constituted a school-sponsored prayer and violated the required separation of religion and government.

Santa Fe Independent School District v. Doe was not the first time that religion and football had come together. In fact, the two important areas of American life had cohabited, divorced, rejoined, and separated over and over again throughout the history of football.

During the late nineteenth century and early years of the twentieth, while football was blossoming in Eastern universities such as Yale, Princeton, and Harvard, all of which originated with religious affiliations, Southern evangelicals were attacking football as comparable to the violent spectacles once witnessed in the Roman Coliseum. The organ for disseminating strong anti-football religious arguments was the *Christian Advocate,* a

Methodist weekly edited by J. M. Buckley. Both Methodists and Baptists urged colleges to abandon their football programs, which, they argued, induced animalistic behavior in their students, and some institutions complied. Emory College, a Methodist institution, dropped football, adding the sport to a list of banned activities that included drinking alcohol, gambling, dancing, taking up with ladies of ill repute, and attending plays and cockfights.

Trinity College, a Methodist school in Durham, North Carolina, later to be known as Duke University, forced out its pro-football president, John Franklin Crowell, in 1894 and abolished the sport altogether by 1895. Twenty-five years later, football would resurface at Duke. The Baptist Wake Forest dropped football after a one-game season in 1895 and did not bring intercollegiate football back until 1908. Wofford College, in the Methodist tradition, abandoned football in 1897, resuming play in 1914; Furman, a Baptist university, dropped the game in 1903 for ten years. Baylor University attempted to ban football in 1906, but student protest, including a mock funeral complete with a tombstone, persuaded officials at the Baptist school to resuscitate the sport.

Members of the Church of Jesus Christ of Latter-day Saints, more commonly referred to as Mormons, began a small academy in Provo, Utah, in 1876. It grew to become Brigham Young University in 1903, with athletics promoted. Football, though, was an exception. Church officials disliked the violence of the game itself and the drinking and general rowdiness that the games seemed to encourage. When a player died because of his football injuries in the late 1890s, it was time to act. The church banned football in 1900 and did not lift the ban until 1919.

The ban on football meant that Mormon communities that sent students to the university were not sponsoring football either, so it took years for the sport to make a strong comeback. The team resumed intercollegiate competition in 1922 and did not have a winning season until 1929. In later decades, football became part of the missionary work that is part of university life. Along with students, football coaches traveled to far corners of the world, including the South Pacific, with a lot of football recruits from that area arriving from the 1950s on.

To firm up the recruiting process in the region, head coach LaVell Edwards added the University of Hawaii to his team's schedule in the 1970s. Under Edwards, Brigham Young became an offensive powerhouse and won the national championship in 1984.

Jewish athletes thrived in football as in other sports. The major Jewish institution associated with the sport was Brandeis University. The institution, however, also was welcoming to members of other faiths and offered three campus chapels, for Jewish, Protestant, and Catholic students. Founded in 1948, the university was named after Louis D. Brandeis, the first Jewish Supreme Court Justice.

Abram Sachar, a historian who had taught at the University of Illinois, was hired as president.

Sachar, a football enthusiast who had taught Red Grange when the Galloping Ghost was a student at Illinois, hired former college and professional star Benny Friedman to head up the athletics program. Friedman appointed himself football coach and enjoyed early success at Brandeis, losing only one game in 1957. As Brandeis faced financial pressure relating to its athletics program, it began to cut football's budget. The team's on-field fortunes declined quickly, and intercollegiate football was dropped after 1959.

Islam until recently has not had a large presence in the United States, but as the Muslim community has grown in size so has its involvement with football. Dearborn, Michigan, has an especially large Muslim community, in excess of 250,000. As William Baker points out in his book *Playing with God*, Muslims made up one-third of the student body at Dearborn High School by 2005, including twenty-five members of the football team.

Baker recounts the challenge for the players that the holy month of Ramadan presents. The month occurs during the football season, and prescribed rituals include fasting from sunrise to sunset, not an easy thing for high school athletes to do while playing such a physically demanding game as football. The solution included having snacks and drinks on the sideline during games for the players to consume after sunset, and to begin practices late in the afternoon so that by the conclusion of practice players would be able to eat the food that the school had ready for them.

Some of the most honored football programs have occurred at Catholic colleges. The University of Notre Dame has a long and revered football tradition. Although many of the Fighting Irish are neither Catholic nor Irish, the team attends mass together before each game. As the game progresses, the mural of Jesus on the side of the library towers above the stadium walls. With Jesus' arms upraised in a gesture resembling the referee's after a score, the mural has long been known as "Touchdown Jesus." In recent years, Boston College has come to challenge Notre Dame for the role of top football program at a Catholic institution.

Professional football, primarily played on Sundays, competes with church attendance for the allegiance of many football fans. It can be argued that football is the primary Sunday religious ritual for many devotees of the sport.

The conflict between church attendance and football did not go unrecognized by the National Football League. Religion has played an important role in the lives of many people associated with professional football, including some of its most successful coaches. Vince Lombardi, a devout Catholic, insisted that his players focus on the three essentials: religion, family, and the Green Bay Packers. Some of his players questioned whether that order truly reflected the coach's priorities.

Tom Landry, longtime coach of the Dallas Cowboys, was a born-again Christian who became a strong supporter of the Fellowship of Christian Athletes, an organization started in the 1950s by Don McClanen, a high school coach in Oklahoma. Landry made many appearances on behalf of evangelist Billy Graham, promulgated fealty to the same trio that Lombardi championed (God, family, and football), and encouraged attendance at weekly Bible study gatherings created for players and their spouses.

Given the difficulty of squeezing in church attendance before a game, Lombardi established nondenominational services in the team hotel before games. By 1970 most NFL teams sponsored game-day services, and before long teams were adding chaplains to minister to the players' spiritual needs.

Sunday, of course, has become cemented in people's consciousness as the day when the Super Bowl is played. Something of Christmas and New Year's (and perhaps Thanksgiving) for those who prefer their religious liturgy to consist of pigskins and goal posts, the game is the most watched event on television. Few individuals, regardless of their religious devotion, would dare to schedule a religious service opposite the Super Bowl. Fortunately, the game is played in the evening, long after most people have attended their Sunday services, during which more than a few likely cast upward a prayer that their favorite team might prevail.

See also: Falwell, Jerry Lamon; "Hail Mary" Pass; Holy Roller; Immaculate Reception; Landry, Thomas Wade; Lombardi, Vincent Thomas; Touchdown Jesus.

Additional Reading:

Baker, William J. *Playing with God: Religion and Modern Sport.* Cambridge MA: Harvard University Press, 2007.

Forney, Craig A. *The Holy Trinity of American Sports: Civil Religion in Football, Baseball, and Basketball.* Macon GA: Mercer University Press, 2007.

Graf, Gary. *And God Said, "It's Good!": Amusing and Thought-Provoking Parallels Between the Bible and Football.* Liguori MO: Liguori/Triumph, 2007.

Irons, Peter H. *God on Trial: Dispatches from America's Religious Battlefields.* New York: Viking, 2007.

Retirement

Retirement for many Americans is a time to live out long-deferred dreams: a time to travel, play golf, sleep late, develop long-desired hobbies. Yet for many people, retirement is vastly different as they struggle to scrape by financially, deal with encroaching disabilities, or combat loneliness. So it is with retired football players.

Many former professional players have it just fine, enjoying the fruits of their hard-won salaries and luxuriating in retirement's golden age. But not so for many others, especially those who played before the huge salaries of recent years. For many of them, including once household names, retirement is as great a struggle as it is for any other American. In some cases, the struggle is intensified by physical disabilities brought on by the constant collisions of body against body that characterize professional football, in their cases collisions that occurred prior to the more recently developed understanding of the physical and mental toll that football can exact on participants.

In recent years, the National Football League and especially the National Football League Players Association have come in for considerable criticism regarding the level of support offered retirees. Accounts of former players living in poverty, some even homeless, many facing astronomical medical expenses for disabilities that appeared to be football caused, increasingly brought retirees and their families into conflict with a union that, in their opinion, gave short shrift to former players. Contrasts with the more generous Major League Baseball retirement pensions exacerbated the relationship between retiree and union.

Willie Wood, the Hall of Fame safety and punt returner for Vince Lombardi's Green Bay Packers in the 1960s, became a much-publicized example. By 2007 Wood had endured two knee-replacement surgeries, a hip replacement, and multiple back surgeries. Largely confined to a wheelchair, he faced estimated medical expenses of $100,000 with a $2,000 monthly football pension. At that, his pension dwarfed what his longtime partner in the Green Bay secondary, Herb Adderley, received: $126.85 per month as of July 2007. The low figure was partly caused by Adderly's decision to start collecting his pension early, in his case at age forty-five. Some retirees have found themselves in a difficult bind, having to start receiving the pension early because of disabilities that make working difficult and having inadequate financial resources to handle their medical expenses.

Overall, as retirees have often pointed out, the differences between football and baseball pensions were huge as of 2007. The average annual Major League Baseball pension stood at $36,700, three times the average professional football pension of $12,165; this despite the large margin between the NFL's $7.1 billion gross revenues and MLB's $4.3 billion.

Accusations of inadequate pension and disability support led to a congressional hearing in June 2007 before a subcommittee considering commercial and administrative law. Among those appearing before the panel was Brent Boyd, a guard with the Minnesota Vikings in the 1980s, who recalled being homeless and continuing to suffer from post-concussion syndrome (symptoms such as dizziness, headaches, and depression). Boyd testified that he received the minimum non-football-related disability support from the NFL and argued that the NFL was refusing to acknowledge any liability for such injuries. Mike Ditka, the former Chicago Bears player and coach, also testified, pleading for a process that cuts through red tape. Ditka created the Mike Ditka Hall of Fame Assistance Fund in 2004 to help retired players with severe medical and financial problems. In late 2007, however, he dissolved the fund amid complaints that it had actually distributed only a small portion of its funds to needy players. Ditka announced that the remaining money would be distributed to an Illinois facility for developmentally challenged youth and the Gridiron Greats Assistance Fund.

Part of the problem, according to those testifying as well as other critics of the current NFL pension and disability system, is that NFL claim decisions are made by a group of individuals chosen by the NFL and the NFLPA. No one representing retirees is part of the process. Nor are any independent medical personnel involved.

The congressional subcommittee was clearly disturbed by the current situation. Rep. Tom Feeney of Florida noted that the former players should be protected under the NFL pension plan but are not protected. Rep. Linda Sanchez of California added, "What is even more troubling is that through projects such as NFL Films, the NFL continues to profit off those very same players who are denied benefits." Following the subcommittee's action, the Senate Committee on Commerce, Science, and Transportation decided to hold a hearing regarding compensation for retired players. Among those testifying before the committee were Ditka, former Dallas fullback Daryl "Moose" Johnston, and legendary Chicago Bears running back Gale Sayers, all of whom accused the NFL and the players union

of neglecting former players. Among the cases they cited was that of "Iron" Mike Webster, who retired in 1990 after seventeen years as an NFL center, fifteen of them with the Pittsburgh Steelers. Webster died in 2002, his final years spent ill and sometimes destitute; at one point, according to his son, Garrett, he was found in a decrepit, rat-infested hotel. The issue of how former players are treated was not going away.

Representatives from the NFL and the NFLPA, including the union's executive director, former player Gene Upshaw, defended their commitment to retired players. They pointed out that 317 retired players, as of June 2007, were receiving disability benefits and that the most recent bargaining agreement, concluded in 2006, raised the pension 25 percent for players retired before 1982 and 10 percent for post-1982 retirees.

A number of recent initiatives have begun to address the problem of retirees living in poverty or with severe disabilities. In addition to the Ditka program, Jerry Kramer, who played guard for Lombardi's Green Bay Packers, started the Gridiron Greats Assistance Fund mentioned above. A nonprofit organization, Gridiron Greats raises money through a variety of avenues, including auctions and donation drives. It then dispenses the money to former players who are in great need and who have inadequate pension and disability support. Grants address medical costs as well as basic living expenses, such as food, housing, clothing, and transportation. The organization even supplies an individual to help the applicant fill out the necessary forms in order to avoid the "hoops" that many critics have accused the NFL of setting up.

Sylvia Mackey, wife of former Baltimore Colts great tight end John Mackey, is responsible for getting the ball rolling on a new, NFL-supported program called the 88 Plan after Mackey's uniform number. Individuals experiencing dementia (which afflicts Mackey), Alzheimer's, or related neurological problems are eligible to receive up to $88,000 annually to support in-patient care, or up to $50,000 for home custodial care. Gene Upshaw promised to avoid the so-called red tape with this new program that, by summer 2007, had thirty-five approved applications and nineteen more being processed without any retirees having been turned down.

In another effort to make applications easier, Commissioner Roger Goodell and Upshaw agreed that any former player who qualifies for Social Security disabilities will automatically qualify for NFL disability benefits. As of July 2007, meetings also had started among the commissioner, Upshaw, and retired players to consider disability pay and health care for retired players. The league and union announced in December 2007 further streamlining of the disability plan to take effect immediately.

In October 2007 the NFL added an additional $10 million to its medical fund for retired players, earmarking the money to support joint replacement surgery and cardiovascular screening, as well as to help with assisted living expenses.

It appears as if finally there is a consensus among the NFL, the NFLPA, retirees and their families, and Congress that more must be done to treat retired players fairly. For fans who watched their football heroes perform on Sunday afternoons, the image of a disabled great in a wheelchair lacking the funds to secure the medical help and basic dignity that he needs and deserves should be a troubling vision. Retirement should be dignified and as happy and pain free as possible, for both the general public and those who played the game of football.

See also: Commissioners; Disabilities; Ditka, Michael Keller, Jr.; Labor-Management Relations; Upshaw, Eugene Thurman, Jr.

Additional Reading:
Colston, Chris. "NFL's Retirees Feeling Forgotten" and "Super Scars of the NFL." *USA Today Sports Weekly*, June 27–July 3, 2007, 34–39.
Jerry Kramer.com, Home of the Gridiron Greats Web site. http://www.jerrykramer.com/ggaf factsheet.html.
NFL Players Association Web site. http://www.nflpa.org.

Rice, Grantland (1880–1954)

Grantland Rice was an enthusiastic and self-consciously literary sportswriter whose view of sports was idealistic, and he expressed his viewpoint in inspirational writing that helped elevate sports figures to heroic status. He also liked to leaven his journalistic pieces with heavily descriptive writing and often with poetry.

One of his best-known poems, "Alumnus Football," advances his strong sense of sportsmanship as part of the heroic ideal. It ends with the observation that what will matter most when the "One Great Scorer" judges you is not whether "you won or lost," but "how you played the game"—a line that has moved securely into the English language as a moral principle widely recognized, if few can identify the source.

The most famous Rice passage remains his account of the Notre Dame backfield of 1924 known, after his account of their triumph over Army and a subsequent photograph taken by a Notre Dame publicity aide, as the Four Horsemen of Notre Dame. Knute Rockne and Red Grange were among the figures he saw as heroic, along with stars in a variety of other sports, including Babe Ruth, Bobby Jones, Jack Dempsey, and Bill Tilden.

Rice attended Vanderbilt University in Nashville, Tennessee, where a sportswriting scholarship named for Rice and another Vanderbilt alumnus, Fred Russell, is given annually to a freshman planning a sportswriting career. Positions at the *Atlanta Journal* and *Cleveland News* led to a variety of positions in the East, including his work for the New York *Herald Tribune*, where his famous piece on the Four Horsemen appeared. Starting in 1925, Rice succeeded Walter Camp as selector of college football All-America teams. His columns were nationally syndicated after 1930, helping Rice become known as the "Dean of American Sportswriters."

See also: Four Horsemen of Notre Dame; Grange, Harold Edward; Literature; Newspapers; Rockne, Knute Kenneth.

Additional Reading:

Fountain, Charles. *Sportswriter: The Life and Times of Grantland Rice.* New York: Oxford University Press, 1993.

Rice, Grantland. *Only the Brave and Other Poems.* New York: Barnes, 1941.

———. *The Tumult and the Shouting: My Life in Sport.* New York: Barnes, 1954.

Rice, Jerry Lee (World) (b. 1962)

Jerry Rice earned the nickname "World" at Mississippi Valley State University because there was no pass in the world he was not able to catch. That was only a slight exaggeration, and even that all-encompassing name did not account for the miles he picked up after his catches.

The consensus pick as the greatest receiver ever, Rice went to Mississippi Valley, a historically black university, because no Division I-A school would offer him a scholarship. There, at a school with a long history of football futility, in the tiny town of Ita Bene, Mississippi (population about 2,200), Rice teamed with quarterback Willie "Satellite" Totten to form the "Satellite Express" and implement Coach Archie "Gunslinger" Cooley's run-and-shoot offense.

In his college years, Rice accounted for 301 receptions, 4,693 receiving yards, and fifty touchdowns, twenty-seven coming in his senior season of 1984. His team put up some extraordinary scores, especially in 1984, when Mississippi Valley averaged 60.9 points per game. The team beat Kentucky State 86–0, scored 65 or more points six times, and twice exceeded 80. Rice was selected not only Division I-AA All-American but Division I-A All-American as well by some organizations despite his not playing at that level. Both quarterback and receiver scored their ways into the College Football Hall of Fame.

Yet the pros were not sold on Rice. Not fast enough, many of them thought. The San Francisco 49ers, however, traded up in the 1985 draft to ensure that they would get Rice. The rest, as the saying goes, is history.

Rice broke virtually every career receiving record by the time he played his last professional game in 2004, leaving some so shattered that they will likely never be exceeded. To name just a few: most pass receptions (1,549), most seasons with fifty or more receptions (seventeen), most yards receiving (22,895), most seasons with 1,000 or more yards receiving (fourteen), most games with 100 or more receiving yards (seventy-six), most touchdown receptions (197). He also holds the single-season record for most receiving yards (1,848). In 2007 Randy Moss broke his single-season record for most touchdowns receiving, scoring one more than Rice's twenty-two. Rice also scored the most total touchdowns in a career (208).

Rice played most of his career with San Francisco (1985–2000) and finished with four seasons split between the Oakland Raiders and the Seattle Seahawks. He reported to training camp with the Denver Broncos in 2005 but did not make the team and retired. Teammates, opponents, and observers alike noted not only Rice's enormous talent but also his work ethic. He followed a strenuous off-season training schedule and was a model of consistent effort in practice.

Rice especially came through in the big games. He played on three Super Bowl winners in San Francisco and excelled in each of those contests. In Super Bowl XXIII against the Cincinnati Bengals, Rice caught eleven passes for 215 yards and a touchdown. The following year against Denver he caught seven passes for 148 yards and three touchdowns. In Super Bowl XXIX against the San Diego Chargers, this time with Steve Young rather than Joe Montana at quarterback, he had ten receptions for 149 yards and three scores.

More recently, television viewers have been able to see different kinds of moves from Rice. Bringing his quickness, grace, and work ethic to the dance floor, he participated in *Dancing with the Stars*. Although a dancing novice, he teamed with his partner to finish second in the competition. Football fans uninterested in dancing could instead listen to Rice on his *Late Hits* radio show on Sirius Satellite Radio's NFL channel or watch his performance as an NFL analyst on KNTV in the Bay Area.

See also: Black College Football; Montana, Joseph Clifford; Moss, Randy Gene; Radio;

Super Bowl; Walsh, William Ernest; Young, Jon Steven.

Additional Reading:
Rice, Jerry. *Go Long!: My Journey Beyond the Game and the Fame.* With Brian Curtis. New York: Ballantine Books, 2007.
Rice, Jerry, and Michael Silver. *Rice.* New York: St. Martin's, 1996.

Rivalries

Rivalry and competition go together, as the song says about another pair of passionate experiences, like a horse and carriage. All the better if the teams have a long history of confronting each other with bragging rights, if not a championship, on the line.

The list of rivalries in football is extensive. Virtually every high school, college, university, and professional team has at least one important rivalry. Many have multiple rivalries. The author of this book grew up in southwestern Wisconsin and attended a small-town high school named Darlington High School. Football was the primary sport in Darlington in those days, and the most important game was against another small-town team some ten miles away, Mineral Point High School. Proximity played an important role in that rivalry. So did the fact that we just did not like each other very much.

National Football League teams also have rivalries, none more enduring than that between the Green Bay Packers and the Chicago Bears, who have been rivals since 1921. The two teams have had their ups and downs, with one or another at times successful, sometimes neither, and occasionally both. Whatever their particular records in a given season, however, the game mattered.

When the NFL divided into two divisions in 1933 (renamed conferences in 1950), the Bears and Packers remained together in the Western Division. When in 1967 the league formed four divisions, the Bears and Packers again were together, in the Central Division. In 1970 the NFL and the American Football League merged, forming two conferences and a total of six divisions. Once again the Bears and Packers retained their rivalry, within the Central Division of the National Football Conference. In 2002 the NFL again was reorganized, this time into eight divisions within the two conferences. Gone was the Central Division of the National Conference, with each division named for one of the four cardinal points. For the Bears and Packers, only the name of the division changed, to the North Division, as they remained united as they had been for more than eighty years.

Other teams have been moving along with them for many years, and the Minnesota Vikings have developed their own rivalry with the Packers. Other NFL teams also have had serious rivalries over the years. New England, for example, is locked in current rivalries with Miami and the New York Jets, both of whom compete against the Patriots in the East Division of the American Conference. Sharing the same division and state, Cincinnati and

Cleveland have a special rivalry. On the whole, though, the proliferation of divisions and other factors have reduced, if not eliminated, the intensity of some traditional rivalries. The San Francisco 49ers and the Rams (when they were in Los Angeles) offered fans one of the NFL's most important rivalries, partly because of their common state. With the Rams now in St. Louis, and the teams in recent years having been less consistently successful, that competitive relationship has diminished even though they remain in the same division.

Then there is the college scene, awash in rivalries, some in their third century. The strength of the alumni movement in American colleges and universities helps to explain the endurance of rivalries in higher-education football. For many, college loyalty supersedes high school bonding, creating a lifelong following.

Thus, fans (many of them true fanatics) continue to follow with passionate intensity the battles between Yale and Harvard, Michigan and Ohio State, Nebraska and Oklahoma, Army and Navy, Grambling and Southern (Baton Rouge), Texas and Texas Tech, Miami and Florida State, Notre Dame and Southern California, Alabama and Auburn, Indiana and Purdue, Washington and Washington State, and on and on, including the longest-running football rivalry of them all—Lafayette and Lehigh, who have been competing against each other since 1884. In many cases, the outcome of the game between traditional rivals helps to determine a conference title, even a national championship.

Often, college rivalries involve a trophy, some of them quite unusual. The Michigan-Minnesota winner gets to keep the Little Brown Jug until the other team wins a future contest between them. The history of the jug demonstrates how a lasting tradition can grow out of a most trivial matter. It all began with the Michigan coach, Fielding Yost, bringing his own water supply to Minnesota for the 1903 contest. Unfortunately, the five-gallon jug was left behind after the two teams fought to a 6–6 tie; maybe Yost was distracted by Michigan's twenty-eight-game winning streak coming to an end. The Minnesota athletics director, L. J. Moore, told Yost that he would have to win it back, thus beginning the tradition of the Little Brown Jug. In addition, Minnesota plays Wisconsin for the Paul Bunyan Axe (also for the Slab of Bacon), Iowa for a bronze pig statue called the Floyd of Rosedale, and Penn State for the Governor's Victory Bell.

A few more memorable trophies, among the vast number of them, include the Old Oaken Bucket (Purdue and Indiana), the Shillelagh (Purdue and, of course, the Fighting Irish of Notre Dame), the Golden Egg (the irreverent name for a statue of an early football, competed for by Mississippi and Mississippi State), and the Little Brown Stein (Montana and Idaho).

Certain factors are common among these rivals. A long history of competition already has been mentioned, but that competition must have involved, at least over the long haul, a real competitive balance. After all, how can two teams be rivals if one always wins? There should be a strong emotional dimension to the game as well, based on some tangible or intangible factor, such as sharing a geographical location or simply having a visceral distaste for each other. If the teams and their fans do not care about their meeting any more than they care about any other contest, how can they be true rivals? They also must maintain that competition. A lengthy break in scheduling each other, even if competition is later resumed, will surely break the chain that links them together as rivals. So there are rational reasons for rivalries, but reason can take one only so far. Much about a rivalry remains irrational, passionate, inexplicable. And true fans would have it no other way.

See also: American Football League (IV); Yost, Fielding Harris.

Additional Reading:
Bradley, Michael. *Big Games: College Football's Greatest Rivalries.* Washington DC: Potomac Books, 2006.
College Football Rivalries Web site. http://www.1122productions.com/rivalries.
Michael MacCambridge, ed. *ESPN College Football Encyclopedia: The Complete History of the Game.* New York: ESPN Books, 2005.
Wilner, Barry, and Ken Rappoport. *Gridiron Glory: The Story of the Army-Navy Football Rivalry.* Lanham MD: Taylor Trade Publishing, 2005.

Robeson, Paul Leroy Bustill (1898–1976)

Paul Robeson was a great football player at Rutgers College (later Rutgers University). An end, he played from 1915 to 1918, earning All-America honors in both 1917 and 1918. He was named to the Frank Menke All-America list in both seasons, and in 1918 he made the All-America team named by Walter Camp, who did not pick a team in 1917. His accomplishments at Rutgers led to his induction into the College Football Hall of Fame in 1995.

After Rutgers, Robeson played professional football from 1920 to 1922. In 1921 he played for the great African American halfback and coach Fritz Pollard at Akron and moved with Pollard to Milwaukee the following year. Robeson left professional football after just three years, having earned enough money to help put himself through law school at Columbia, where he was a classmate of future Supreme Court Justice William O. Douglas.

If Robeson had done nothing except play football, he would not be much remembered today, but in fact he was one of the most brilliant, multitalented, socially conscious, and controversial figures of the twentieth century.

Robeson grew up in New Jersey, son of a former slave who became a Presbyterian minister and a mother who came from an abolitionist Quaker family. A brilliant student, Robeson, only the third African American to attend Rutgers and the first to play football there, was named a Phi Beta Kappa scholar and graduated as valedictorian of his class in addition to earning All-America honors in football.

After graduating with a law degree from Columbia in 1923, Robeson worked for a Wall Street law firm but quickly turned to the stage. He became a world-famous stage and screen actor as well as a renowned singer. Among many other acting vehicles, he starred in Shakespeare's *Othello* on Broadway (1943–45), establishing a record for the longest Broadway run of any Shakespeare play that, as of 2009, had still not been equaled. His rendition of "Ol' Man River" from *Show Boat* became one of his most famous songs. Robeson performed in concert throughout the world and could sing in approximately twenty languages and converse in twelve.

Above all, however, Paul Robeson cared for the cause of social justice and equal rights. He committed himself to the cause of African Americans and other minorities, as well as working people and disadvantaged groups throughout the world. His political views led the State Department to revoke his passport in 1950, and the House Un-American Activities Committee called him to testify about his supposed sympathy for Communism. He also suffered from blacklisting as a performer, and his recordings and films became almost impossible to acquire.

A gala celebration of his seventy-fifth birthday in Carnegie Hall, produced by Harry Belafonte, began to turn a more appreciative and balanced spotlight back on him. Since Robeson's death in 1976, he has continued to undergo renewed analysis and appreciation for his many talents and accomplishments, including, of course, his skill at football.

See also: African Americans (College); African Americans (Professional); Films; Pollard, Frederick Douglass.

Additional Reading:
Boyle, Sheila, and Andrew Bunie. *Paul Robeson: The Years of Promise and Achievement.* Amherst: University of Massachusetts Press, 2001.
Robeson, Paul. *Here I Stand.* 1958. Boston: Beacon, 1971.
Stewart, Jeffrey C., ed. *Paul Robeson: Artist and Citizen.* New Brunswick NJ: Rutgers University Press, 1998.

Robinson, Eddie Gay (1919–2007)

Eddie Robinson, the most famous coach in the history of black college football, also was one of the most successful coaches at any level of the sport. When he retired from coaching in 1997, he held the record for most victories ever by a college coach: 408. That record has since been surpassed, but Robinson's contributions to Grambling State University and college football remain legendary.

Robinson was born in Jackson, Louisiana, on February 13, 1919, the son of a cotton sharecropper father and a mother who worked as a domestic. He attended Leland College, where he quarterbacked his team to a two-year record of 18-1. In 1941, a year after graduating from Leland, he became head football coach at Grambling State University, then known as the

Louisiana Negro Normal and Industrial Institute.

At first, there was virtually no money for the football program. Robinson had to do just about everything himself. He lined the field, fixed sandwiches for his players to take on trips to away games, mowed the grass on the football field, taped players' ankles, and wrote reports on the games for the local newspaper.

By his second season, Robinson had built a team that went undefeated and untied in nine games without another team even scoring on it. The institution changed its name to Grambling College in 1946, and the names "Robinson" and "Grambling" soon became almost synonymous. For fifty-five years, from 1941 to 1997, minus the 1943–44 war years when the football program was suspended, Robinson coached the Grambling Tigers. He compiled an overall record of 408 victories against just 165 losses and fifteen ties. His teams won seventeen conference championships, compiled twenty-seven consecutive winning seasons (1960–86), and were Black College National Champions or Co-Champions nine times. During the two years when the football program was on hiatus, Robinson coached the Grambling High School team and won a high school championship.

Grambling earned the unofficial title of the Cradle of the Pros during Robinson's tenure as more than two hundred players went on to play professionally, seven of them taken in the first round of the draft. Five members of the All-Time Black College Football Team chosen by the Sheridan Broadcasting Network in 1993 were products of Robinson's coaching, including Doug Williams, who became the first African American quarterback to win a Super Bowl when he led Washington over Denver in Super Bowl XXII on January 31, 1988. Williams also succeeded Robinson as football coach at Grambling in 1998. The others were running back Tank Younger (in 1949 the first African American from a black college to make the NFL), wide receiver Charlie Joiner, defensive lineman Willie Davis, and defensive back Everson Walls. Buck Buchanan, a defensive lineman for Grambling, could just as well have made the team. He became the first player from a black institution to be the overall No. 1 draft pick when the Kansas City Chiefs selected him in 1963.

At the end of Robinson's career, victories came with greater difficulty. His final three seasons (1995–97) were all losing campaigns, the first time that Grambling had suffered consecutive losing seasons in almost fifty years. By that time, though, Robinson's legacy was so secure that it would have taken much more than a few losses to tarnish it.

The honors had been coming for years and continued to arrive. In 1968 Howard Cosell and Jerry Izenberg produced a documentary called *Grambling College: 100 Yards to Glory*. It could just as accurately have been entitled *The Accomplishments of Eddie Robinson*. Grambling's new football stadium built in the 1980s was named Eddie G. Robinson Stadium. The town of Grambling and Baton Rouge both named streets after him. *Sports Illustrated* on October 14, 1985, made Robinson the first black college coach ever featured on its cover when he passed Bear Bryant for career wins. In 1992 Robinson received an award from the National Football Foundation for his contributions to amateur football. Several awards are given in his name: the Eddie Robinson Award for coach of the year in Subdivision FCS, the Football Writers Association Robinson Award for national coach of the year, and the Robinson Award for the top player in black college football. In addition, he was inducted into the College Football Hall of Fame in 1997.

Grambling apparently was planning to fire Robinson prior to the 1997 season. The outcry was so great, including from Louisiana State officials, that Grambling kept him for that final season. Shortly after retiring, Robinson was diagnosed with Alzheimer's. He died ten years later, on April 3, 2007.

See also: African Americans (College); African Americans (Professional); Black College Football; Bryant, Paul William; Grambling State University.

Additional Reading:

Davis, O. K. *Grambling's Gridiron Glory: Eddie Robinson and the Tigers' Success Story: Complete with Photographs from the Author's Collection.* Ruston LA: O. K. Davis, 1983.
Hurd, Michael. *Black College Football, 1892–1992: One Hundred Years of History, Education, and Pride.* Virginia Beach VA: Donning, 1993.
Robinson, Eddie. *Never Before, Never Again: The Stirring Autobiography of Eddie Robinson, the Winningest Coach in the History of College Football.* With Richard Lapchick. New York: St. Martin's, 1999.

Rockne, Knute Kenneth (1888–1931)

Knute Rockne may be the most famous coach yet, approximately eighty years after his death at the age of forty-three in a plane crash in 1931. Rockne made the University of Notre Dame football team the first truly national team, established a still unequaled record for winning, and helped to elevate college football during the Roaring Twenties to one of America's greatest sports.

Rockne's story could have been right out of a movie, and ultimately it would be portrayed on the silver screen. An immigrant from Norway and son of a carriage maker, Rockne went to work for the Chicago Post Office after high school in order to earn enough money to attend college. Finally, four years after high school, he boarded a train for South Bend, enrolled at Notre Dame at the age of twenty-two, and entered on a path that would rewrite sports history.

At Notre Dame from 1910 to 1914, Rockne took full advantage of what college life had to offer. He was an outstanding student, graduating magna cum laude and earning a graduate assistantship at Notre Dame in chemistry. He wrote for the school newspaper, was active in the campus theater group, played the flute in the orchestra, picked up some money boxing, and set a school record in the indoor pole vault. He also played football.

Rockne starred at left end for Notre Dame, becoming captain as a senior in 1913. That year, he teamed with quarterback Gus Dorais to work on passing, and they put their expertise on display in an upset of mighty Army, 35–13. Notre Dame finished undefeated, and although Rockne and Dorais had not invented the forward pass, their use of it against Army crystallized the pass as an effective football weapon. The game was brought before the public again in the 1955 film *The Long Gray Line* about longtime U.S. Military Academy instructor Marty Maher.

After graduating, Rockne stayed at Notre Dame to study chemistry and assist football coach Jesse Harper. When Harper retired after the 1917 season, Rockne was named to replace him.

Over thirteen seasons, Rockne's teams won 105 games against just twelve losses and five ties, a winning percentage of .881 that no major college or professional coach has ever equaled. He won three consensus national championships (in 1924, 1929, and 1930) and also finished first in one or more polls in 1919, 1920, and 1927. Five of his teams went undefeated (1919, 1920, 1924, 1929, and 1930). Among the many great players he coached were George Gipp and the Four Horsemen (Harry Stuhldreher, Jim Crowley, Don Miller, and Elmer Layden).

Rockne took his team across the country, playing Army and Princeton in the East, Georgia Tech in the South, Southern California in the West, and Stanford in the 1925 Rose Bowl, in the process making Notre Dame the first university with a truly national football program.

In addition to publicizing his team, Rockne proved to be an innovative and inspiring coach. He installed a box formation that involved considerable motion (the "Notre Dame Shift," which often had all four members of the backfield shifting from one place to another just before the snap), made effective use of the forward pass, and used substitutes much more than was customary at the time. He even designed his team's uniforms and pads to help his players move more quickly.

Rockne's final team was one of his best, concluding its unbeaten, untied season with a 27–0 shutout of Southern California. Rockne agreed to assist with the film *The Spirit of Notre Dame* that was being made in Los Angeles during the off-season. To that end, on March 31, 1931, he boarded Transcontinental-Western's flight 599 in Kansas City, Missouri, where he had stopped off to visit his sons, Bill and Knute Jr., who were in school there. Soon after takeoff, one of the wings on the Fokker Trimotor plane broke away, apparently the result of fatigue cracks. The plane crashed in a wheat field near Bazaar, Kansas, killing all aboard.

Rockne's death shocked the United States. The newspaper headlines screamed "ROCKNE DEAD" throughout the country. Pres. Herbert Hoover, Gen. Douglas MacArthur, the king of Norway (Rockne's birthplace), scores of rival coaches, and multitudes of others, famous and commonplace, paid tribute to the fallen coach. Six of Rockne's players carried the coffin out of Sacred Heart Church after the funeral. The coach who had embraced so much of Notre Dame over the years had also become a Catholic. He was buried in Highland Cemetery on the edge of the campus he had helped to make world famous. Today fans of Notre Dame football pass by Rockne's resting place on each Saturday of home games on their way to the football stadium erected in 1930, truly the House That Rockne Built.

Rockne's fame would endure and become the stuff of legend. A 1940 film, *Knute Rockne: All American,* starred Pat O'Brien as Rockne and a young actor named Ronald Reagan as George Gipp. The film immortalized the dying Gipp's request of Rockne that someday, when the going was especially tough, Rockne would ask his team to win one for the Gipper. That day came against Army in 1928 and produced a 12–6 come-from-behind win. It came repeatedly over the following decades for the actor-turned-politician who as president of the United States regularly referred to himself as the Gipper. Shortly before the conclusion of his second term, in 1988, President Reagan went to Notre Dame to unveil a new U.S. stamp honoring Rockne. After Reagan's death, Pres. George W. Bush, speaking at the 2004 Republican National Convention, called on listeners to win one more for the Gipper. Politics aside, it is unlikely that the name and fame of

Knute Rockne will fade away as long as football is played.

See also: Bowl Games; Forward Pass; Four Horsemen of Notre Dame; Gipp, George; Presidents of the United States; Religion; Trick Plays.

Additional Reading:

Brondfield, Jerry. *Rockne: The Coach, the Man, the Legend.* New York: Random House, 1976.

Robinson, Ray. *Rockne of Notre Dame: The Making of a Football Legend.* New York: Oxford University Press, 1999.

Rockne, Knute. *The Autobiography of Knute K. Rockne.* Ed. Bonnie Skiles Rockne (Mrs. Knute K. Rockne). South Bend IN: Distributed by The Book Shop, 1931.

Steele, Michael R. *Knute Rockne: A Bio-bibliography.* Westport CT: Greenwood, 1983.

Rooney Rule

Few people have rules named after them, especially a positive, idealistic rule that contributes toward a more just society—rather than a rule forever emblazoning one's name with a serious misdeed, something shameful that one carries into eternity.

So it is with the Rooney Rule, named for Dan Rooney, owner of the Pittsburgh Steelers and chairperson of a National Football League committee charged with increasing workplace diversity. The Rooney Rule requires NFL teams to at least interview one minority candidate for each coaching vacancy. One might argue that the rule bloomed only in response to a lawsuit by the late famous lawyer Johnnie Cochran and Cyrus Mehri charging the NFL with discriminating against minorities in its hiring practices. Yet the rule did come into being, and its goal of increasing coaching opportunities for minorities is laudable regardless of the precipitating cause.

The rule, implemented in 2002, imposes a fine of up to $200,000 if a team neglects to interview a minority candidate. In 2003 the Detroit Lions incurred the maximum penalty when the team moved immediately to hire Steve Mariucci as head coach once the position became open. Rooney backed up his talk with action by hiring an African American coach, Mike Tomlin, to replace Bill Cowher, who retired after the 2006 season.

The greatest strength of the Rooney Rule lies not merely in the letter of the law that it establishes, but in the way that it changes attitudes. Professional sports tend to be highly traditional, with people doing things the way they always did them. The small number of African American coaches in recent years probably reflected an implicit bias more than conscious and deliberate racial discrimination. Owners had always hired white coaches and therefore, when an opening developed, naturally thought in terms of hiring a white coach.

The Rooney Rule requires owners to stop and think about the hiring process. That period of reflection can lead to the realization that, indeed, a black candidate may be just as good a fit for the team as a white candidate. Gradually, the mind-set changes so that owners and team officials no longer automatically think white. The rule seems to be working, as the number of African American coaches had increased to six by the year 2007, and both coaches in the Super Bowl following the 2006 season were African Americans: Tony Dungy of the triumphant Indianapolis Colts and Lovie Smith of the Chicago Bears. Having this particular rule named after him should be, for Dan Rooney, a real medal of distinction that he can wear with pride.

See also: African Americans (Professional).

Additional Reading:
Blumenkrantz, Adam P., and Raphael Rajendra. "NFL Rule Combats Discrimination in Hiring." NorthJersey.com, February 9, 2007. http://www.northjersey.com.
Brock, Timothy C., and Melanie C. Green, eds. *Persuasion: Psychological Insights and Perspectives*. 2nd ed. Thousand Oaks CA: Sage Publications, 2005.

Rugby

Rugby is an ancestor of both American and Canadian football. Transported to the United States from Europe, it appeared among secondary and college students in North America by the middle of the nineteenth century. During the second half of the century, rule changes gradually transformed rugby and rugbylike contests into what has become known as American football.

Rugby itself has never been monolithic with just one set of rules. Its essence, as with football, is to move a ball across the goal line with the defense attempting to prevent that from happening. In some versions, players had to move the ball by kicking or dribbling it. Another approach to the sport permitted carrying the ball and allowed tackling or tripping the runner.

Rugby derives its name from Rugby School, one of England's oldest public schools (what in the United States would be termed private schools), which is located in Warwickshire, England. The school was founded in 1567 with funds left for that purpose by a man named Lawrence Sheriff, who made his money by supplying Queen Elizabeth I with food. Thomas Hughes's autobiographical novel *Tom Brown's Schooldays*, first published in 1857, brought the institution into the realm of American popular culture.

Legend has it that rugby was created by William Webb Ellis at Rugby in 1823, a story as mythic as the supposed invention of baseball by Abner Doubleday at Cooperstown. Ellis, supposedly disregarding prior rules of the game, lifted the ball into his arms and ran with it, a fine story immortalized on a plaque at Rugby School. Not until 1845 was a set of rules governing rugby written down, although some version of the game had likely been played at Rugby since the seventeenth century.

Rugby began to diverge along two avenues in the 1860s. The Football Association, formed in London in 1863, outlawed running with the ball and hacking (that is, kicking a runner in the shins and thus causing him to fall down). Many teams rejected these changes, believing that they removed courage and spirit from the game. Many of those who supported the more traditional sport met in January 1871 in London to form a rival Rugby Football Union. The evolution of rugby also involved differences in number of players, some rules establishing thirteen, others fifteen.

Regardless of the precise set of rules, rugby players wear little or no padding, making the game quite dangerous to the health of the participants. Rules therefore are usually enforced strictly, and sportsmanlike behavior is expected.

Rugby remains widespread in England, but in the United States, football (as it is known here) has almost totally supplanted rugby. The other form of "football" popular in the United States is no longer rugby but soccer.

See also: Camp, Walter Chauncey; Ivy League.

Additional Reading:

Creek, Frederick Norman Smith. *Rugby Football.* London: English Universities Press, 1963.

Hughes, Thomas. *Tom Brown's Schooldays.* 1857. New York: Dutton, 1972.

Powell, John Talbot. *Inside Rugby: The Team Game.* Chicago: Regnery, 1976.

Saban, Nick Lou (b. 1951)

Nick Saban is the Four-Million-Dollar Man, the first college coach to sign a contract for $4 million per year. The University of Alabama Trustees approved an eight-year $32 million contract for Saban in June 2007, although he actually had been named coach in January. The unprecedented contract represents Alabama's determination to return its football program to the level of success that it enjoyed under the legendary Paul "Bear" Bryant, who as Alabama's head football coach from 1958 through 1982 led the Crimson Tide to thirteen Southeastern Conference championships and six national titles.

Saban appeared well qualified for that attempt. In eleven years as a college head coach (at Toledo, Michigan State, and LSU), he compiled a record of 91-42-1, with a national championship at LSU in 2003 when the Associated Press named him Coach of the Year. He also had been a successful assistant coach at both the college and professional levels, including four seasons (1991–94) as defensive coordinator under Bill Belichick with the Cleveland Browns. Saban brought to Alabama not only an impressive record of wins and losses but also a reputation for instilling discipline in his players and encouraging in them a commitment to academic success and engagement in community service.

Nonetheless, his appointment was controversial, primarily for two reasons. Before accepting the Alabama position, Saban had been coach of the Miami Dolphins in the National Football League, where he had been less successful than at the college level, going 15-17 in his two seasons with Miami. Still, few if any observers doubted his ability as a college coach, but many did look askance at his adamant proclamations that he was not leaving Miami for the Alabama job—until he did precisely that. In addition, many viewed his salary as extravagant, inappropriately high, and another example of the excessive emphasis placed on big-time college sports.

Saban's contract calls for him to receive an annual base salary of $225,000, with most of the $32 million coming through a personal services fee that rises annually from $3,275,000 the first year. There also are incentives for reaching certain goals, among them the SEC championship, selection as SEC or national Coach of the Year, and graduated benchmarks for his players' graduation rate. Saban also receives two cars, a country club membership, and flight time in noncommercial planes.

The University of Alabama expects a

lot for its money, namely a return to the golden days of Bear Bryant and assorted conference and national championships. Whether Saban, as skilled as he is, can produce enough for the university administration and Crimson Tide faithful to be satisfied, only the future will tell.

See also: Belichick, William Stephen; Bryant, Paul William.

Additional Reading:

Bragg, Rick. "In the Nick of Time." *Sports Illustrated*, August 27, 2007, 53–58.

Saban, Nick. *Nick Saban's Tiger Triumph: The Remarkable Story of LSU's Rise to No. 1*. Chicago: Triumph Books, 2004.

———. *How Good Do You Want to Be?: A Champion's Tips on How to Lead and Succeed at Work and in Life*. With Brian Curtis. New York: Ballantine Books, 2005.

Sanders, Barry David (b. 1968)

Barry Sanders followed one of the greatest seasons in college football history with an extraordinary career as a Detroit Lion. One of the most elusive running backs ever to step on a football field, he piled up rushing yards at a record-breaking pace with Detroit. Then, after gaining almost 1,500 yards in his tenth season, and with the all-time rushing record within reach, he retired.

Sanders backed up future Buffalo Bills great Thurman Thomas at Oklahoma State University for two years before becoming the regular in his junior year after Thomas's departure for the pros. During his one year as a starter (1988), he led the nation in rushing yards (2,628), all-purpose yards (3,250), and scoring (234

points, the result of thirty-nine touchdowns). Overall, he set thirty-four NCAA records and captured the Heisman Trophy as well as the Camp and Maxwell awards as the top college player in the country.

Forgoing his final year at Oklahoma State, Sanders was taken in the first round of the 1989 draft by the Lions. He gained 1,470 yards rushing as a rookie and proceeded to gain more than 1,000 yards during each of his ten seasons, reaching a high of 2,053 yards in 1997. Three times he led the NFL in rushing, and he gained more than 1,500 yards five times, including a record four years in succession. His honors included Rookie of the Year in 1989, Most Valuable Player in 1997 (shared with Green Bay quarterback Brett Favre), and ten selections to the Pro Bowl.

During Sanders's years with Detroit, however, the Lions had only modest success, winning just one playoff game. That apparently figured into his decision to walk away from the game while still at his peak. When he retired, he had rushed for 15,269 yards, second to Walter Payton, whom he trailed by just 1,457 yards, fewer yards than Sanders had gained in his final year.

His retirement was not without controversy. Sanders had signed a new contract two years before and still had several years remaining. Consequently, the Lions attempted to recoup part of his $11 million signing bonus. Ultimately, an arbitrator ruled that Sanders would have to return part of the money.

The controversy was ironic in that for all the excitement that his running style generated on the field, Sanders avoided the limelight and seldom even celebrated after a touchdown, eschewing the dancing and other antics so common today. His electrifying running style led to many carries for loss as he often would retreat behind the line of scrimmage looking for a way to break free. More often than not, of course, he succeeded. That success resulted in Sanders's induction into the College Football Hall of Fame in 2003 and the Pro Football Hall of Fame the following year.

See also: Favre, Brett Lorenzo; Payton, Walter Jerry.

Additional Reading:
Sanders, Barry. *Barry Sanders Now You See Him: His Story in His Own Words*. With Mark E. McCormich. Indianapolis: B. Sanders, Inc., with Emmis Books, 2003.
Knapp, Ron. *Sports Great Barry Sanders*. Rev. ed. Springfield NJ: Enslow, 1999.

Sanders, Deion Luwynn
(Neon Deion, Prime Time) (b. 1967)

Deion Sanders, befitting one of his nicknames (Neon Deion), is one of the most colorful individuals to have played football, from his stylish clothing and expensive jewelry to his effervescent personality and extraordinary speed as a cornerback. At the same time, his other popular nickname (Prime Time) also says much about him, especially Sanders's desire to be at the center of attention, although he actually received the name from a college teammate because they often played basketball together during the prime-time television period. As a player, he often was at the center of things, usually because of his playing ability.

Colorful and prominent, Sanders also was one of the most multitalented athletes of his time. He starred both as a great cornerback and at returning kickoffs and punts while also being an excellent major league baseball player. On the diamond, he performed for the New York Yankees, Atlanta Braves, Cincinnati Reds, and San Francisco Giants for nine seasons (1989–95, 1997, 2001). A good defensive outfielder, he fit his baseball career around his football schedule and therefore usually played fewer than one hundred games per year. A dangerous base stealer and an effective though not very powerful hitter, Sanders enjoyed his finest season in 1992 when he batted .304 in ninety-seven games for the Atlanta Braves and led the league with fourteen triples. He became the only person to play in both a World Series (with the 1992 Braves) and a Super Bowl (Super Bowls XXIX with San Francisco and XXX with Dallas).

Sanders won the Jim Thorpe Award in 1988 at Florida State, an award given annually to the top college defensive back. That year he also led the nation in punt-return average. In his final two seasons with the Seminoles, he was a consensus All-American.

Sanders joined the NFL in 1989 with the Atlanta Falcons and later played with the San Francisco 49ers, Dallas Cowboys, Washington Redskins, and Baltimore

Ravens. His accomplishments were many. In 1992 he led the NFL in kick-return yardage (1,067), average yards per return (26.7), and kicks returned for touchdowns (two). Equally adept at returning punts, he led the league in 1998 with an average of 15.6 yards per return and two touchdowns.

As a cornerback, Sanders was outstanding at covering even the fastest receivers, although he incurred criticism for sometimes less than stellar tackling. In his fourteen seasons he intercepted fifty-three passes. In 1994 he intercepted six, which he returned for 303 yards (a 50.5-yard average) and three touchdowns. Sanders also occasionally played on offense as a receiver, and in 1996 he became a regular two-way player while Michael Irvin was serving a suspension. He ended up catching thirty-six passes.

Sanders for a time was reportedly the highest-paid defensive player after signing a seven-year contract with Dallas in 1995. He retired after the 2000 season but returned to play for the Baltimore Ravens during 2004–05. His nineteen defensive and return touchdowns are the most ever, and he scored touchdowns five different ways in the regular season: on interceptions, punt returns, kickoff returns, passes caught, and a fumble recovery. In the postseason, he added a rushing touchdown—the six methods of scoring touchdowns also a record.

Sanders brought considerable attention to himself with his high-stepping, "Deion shuffle" celebrations after scoring touchdowns and helped to establish the tradition of exuberant end zone celebrations so common in the NFL today. After his playing career, he turned to television with *The NFL Today* on CBS. Since then he has also appeared on ESPN and the NFL Network and made commercials for such products as Nike, Pepsi, Pizza Hut, Burger King, and American Express. In July 2007 he generated some criticism by the manner in which he supported Michael Vick when the Atlanta Falcons quarterback was arrested for his participation in a dogfighting enterprise. Sanders seemed less than sensitive to the severity of Vick's actions by likening his passion for dogfighting to his own passion for jewelry. In Sanders's own memoir, however, he acknowledged the temptations of a fast lifestyle that almost destroyed his own life.

See also: Celebrations; Commercials and Advertisements; Dogfighting;; Super Bowl; Television Broadcasting.

Additional Reading:
Sanders, Deion. *Power, Money & Sex: How Success Almost Ruined My Life*. With Jim Nelson Black. Nashville: Word, 1998.

Sayers, Gale Eugene (b. 1943)

Gale Sayers was known as the Kansas Comet, a nickname that proved applicable not only to his dazzling speed but unfortunately also to his brief race through the football sky. Drafted by the Chicago Bears in the first round in 1965, the Kansas native scored a record-setting twenty-two touchdowns in his rookie year using his eye-popping speed and ability to change directions on the proverbial dime. The twenty-two touchdowns remain a record for rookies.

Sayers joined the Bears with his fellow 1965 first-round selection Dick Butkus, who would become a Hall of Fame linebacker for Chicago. On a muddy Wrigley Field against the San Francisco 49ers in December, Sayers tied the all-time record for most touchdowns in a single game when he scored six times. He began the scoring with an 80-yard pass reception and run. Later he recorded touchdowns on runs of 21, 7, 50, and 1 yards. Then in the fourth quarter, he added an 85-yard punt return for a touchdown.

Earlier in that rookie year, Sayers had scored four touchdowns against the Minnesota Vikings, including one on a 96-yard kickoff return. His touchdowns that year included fourteen rushing, six receiving, and a punt and kickoff return each. The next year, Sayers led the NFL in rushing with 1,231 yards. His fourth season was cut short by a right-knee injury when he was hit by 49ers cornerback Kermit Alexander while attempting a sharp cut. After surgery and rehabilitation, he returned in 1969 to lead the league in rushing again, this time with 1,032 yards, despite his team's horrific 1-13 record. For the fifth year in a row, he made All-Pro.

Unfortunately, Sayers suffered a serious injury to his other knee in 1970 and carried the ball only twenty-three times; he suffered yet another knee injury in 1971 and managed just thirteen carries that year. An attempted comeback in 1972 failed, and he was through, having played five years with the Bears, not counting his 1970–71 abbreviated seasons. Nonetheless, his extraordinary achievements during those five years—including an overall average of 5.0 yards per carry and the still-standing record of 30.56 yards per kickoff return—earned him membership in the Pro Football Hall of Fame in 1977 at the age of thirty-four, making him the youngest person ever inducted. That same year he also became a member of the College Football Hall of Fame.

Gale Sayers is also remembered for the remarkable friendship between him and teammate Brian Piccolo. During Sayers's rehabilitation from his first knee injury, Piccolo strongly supported Sayers on his road to recovery. The two men also were roommates at a time when the NFL generally did not have interracial roommates. In 1967 George Halas made the Bears the first NFL team to integrate rooming assignments. The friendship blossomed, but tragedy struck when Piccolo was diagnosed with testicular cancer during the 1969 season. Piccolo had surgery in November and again in April 1970, this time to remove his left lung. By June it was clear that the cancer had spread to other organs, and he died on June 16, 1970.

The Sayers-Piccolo relationship was made into an extremely moving and popular television film, *Brian's Song* (1971), starring Billy Dee Williams as Sayers and James Caan as Piccolo. The film took some liberties with the facts, for example, portraying Sayers as being in the hospital as his friend was dying, but overall it effectively conveyed the friendship between the two teammates. An unusual movie in that it was both highly emotional and made for men, *Brian's Song* was brought to another generation of football fans in 2001 in a remake (for ABC's *The Wonderful World of Disney*) starring Mekhi Phifer and Sean Maher.

After football, Sayers achieved great success in sports management, business, and technology. He completed a master's degree in educational administration at his alma mater, the University of Kansas, and served Kansas as an assistant athletics director. He then spent five years as athletics director at Southern Illinois University before moving to Chicago and beginning Sayers and Sayers Enterprises, a sports marketing and public relations firm. Sayers later established a computer company providing technology products and services. In 1999 he was inducted into another hall of fame to go along with his football inductions—the Chicago Entrepreneurship Hall of Fame. The University of Kansas honored Sayers's achievements and contributions to both the university and the broader society with the Gale Sayers Microcomputer Center. Sayers also has devoted considerable time and effort to promoting a variety of worthwhile organizations, including the Boys and Girls Clubs of America, the Boy Scouts of America, the American Cancer Society, and the Cradle Adoption Agency.

See also: Films; Halas, George Stanley.

Additional Reading:

Blinn, William. *Brian's Song.* New York: Bantam Books, 1972.

Morris, Jeannie. *Brian Piccolo: A Short Season.* 1972. Chicago: Bonus Books, 1995.

Sayers, Gale. *I Am Third.* With Al Silverman. New York: Viking, 1970.

———. *Sayers: My Life and Times.* With Fred Mitchell. Chicago: Triumph Books, 2007.

Scouts

Sport is not the only area of American society in which scouts search out future employees (or unpaid participants in the case of amateur athletics). Employment agencies, commonly referred to as "headhunters," exist for many professions, although the scout actively traveling about to observe future members of his or her client's organization is primarily part of athletics and the broader entertainment industry.

There actually are two types of scouting on behalf of a football team. Many scouts are headhunters, but others scout future opponents. The latter attend games played by teams on their team's schedule and look closely at both team and individual tendencies. Much film study also is part of the scouting process. A team committed to winning would no more face an opponent without extensively scouting the team than show up without helmets and shoulder pads.

Still, the scouting that draws most of the public's interest is the former type, geared toward bringing skilled players into the fold. In football, scouting is itself big business, serving the larger business that is football. Scouting starts early. In areas where high school football is taken quite seriously, which is a good chunk of the country, coaches, concerned parents, and team boosters already are following youth football games looking for future high school stars.

College recruiting picks up the pace considerably, with top recruiters essential to the success of a major college program. A variety of publications chart the success and failure of colleges' recruiting efforts and rank the top recruiting classes. Newspapers and sports magazines record high school players' college commitments, including nonbinding verbal commitments made by second-semester juniors. Even one bad recruiting year can undermine a team's future success for several seasons.

The scouting/recruiting process at the college level has long been fraught with potential dangers, especially the use of inappropriate inducements to bring in championship-caliber players. Young athletes have been bribed in a variety of ways, including use of sex to entice them into making a commitment to a particular football program. Money, of course, has been a common medium of bribery.

One of the most famous recruiting scandals involved Southern Methodist University, which after a long history of allegedly paying players in violation of NCAA rules received the so-called death penalty in February 1987. What that meant was that the entire football program was suspended. Although technically the suspension was for only the 1987 season, in effect the penalty turned into a two-year suspension because the NCAA prohibited all home games and all football scholarships for the second season.

National Football League teams put considerable time and money into scouting college players leading up to the annual college draft. Scouts tour schools, observe games and practices, interview players' coaches and the players themselves, and look at any factors that might affect the team's return on its investment, such as a player's attitude, drug use, legal problems, and academic performance. When considering its top picks, a team will often receive reports from multiple scouts.

NFL teams also participate in the annual Scouting Combine during which top pro prospects exhibit their wares. They are timed and examined while undergoing various tests involving speed, strength, and position-related skills (for example, passing accuracy). The player's performance at the combine can impact his position on draft day, and that can mean a lot of money gained or lost by the player. Higher draft choices obviously command much more money than players who are taken in a lower round, or even later in the same round.

One of the skills that pro scouts especially measure is the individual's speed in the 40-yard dash. Since Paul Brown focused on his players' speed running 40 yards with the Cleveland Browns in the 1940s, that measurement has been codified if not deified. Scouts and coaches never trust any other person's measurement, so everyone carries a stopwatch.

Speed parameters for players at specific positions are taken quite seriously. A wide receiver who fails to run the 40 in 4.4 seconds or less is suspect. Perhaps the most famous example of a receiver coming up short in the 40-yard dash is Jerry Rice. Rice was consistently timed at about 4.6, although he always seemed to play faster than his actual time. As a result of being too slow, Rice dropped to the sixteenth spot in the first round of the 1985 draft, was taken by the San Francisco 49ers, and became probably the greatest receiver in the history of the NFL.

Some coaches never joined the 40-yard crowd. Vince Lombardi, for example, was once asked how fast Hornung ran the 40. His reply, according to Ivan Maisel, was, "What the hell difference does it make? He gets to the end zone, doesn't he?"

There will always be a Vince Lombardi who defies scouting norms and a Jerry Rice who overcomes them, but scouting will continue at a furious pace. Football is about competition, and finding the best players gives a team a decided competitive edge—whether the game involves high school, college, or professional teams.

See also: Agents; Brown, Paul Eugene; Lombardi, Vincent Thomas; Rice, Jerry Lee.

Additional Reading:
Belichick, Steve. *Football Scouting Methods.* Mansfield Center CT: Martino, 2008.
Lemming, Tom, and Taylor Bell. *Football's Second Season: Scouting High School Game Breakers.* Champaign IL: Sports Publishing, 2007.
Maisel, Ivan. "Mad Dash." In *The Football Book.* Ed. Rob Fleder, 168. New York: Sports Illustrated, 2005.

September 11 Terrorist Attacks

The terrorist attacks of Tuesday, September 11, 2001, changed the lives of everyone in the United States, including, of course, those associated with football. The attacks demanded an immediate response from the football community. Even during world wars, football and other sports have continued, with the blessings of United States presidents, to offer Americans respite from contemplating war and to demonstrate that an enemy cannot completely disrupt the American way of life. Yet at the same time, it was important to pay respect to those who had died on that terrible day. It could not be business as usual, even as the need to continue with business seemed apparent.

College games scheduled for Thursday, September 13, such as the Penn State–Virginia and Ohio University–North Carolina State contests, were not played. Nor were games scheduled for the next Saturday, September 15. Some of the games thus affected were dropped permanently because of the difficulty of rescheduling them. Some were rescheduled at the end of the season. In other cases, teams found new opponents, adding games that could fit into both teams' schedules.

The impact on the National Football League was in some respects more complex. The games that were to have occurred on Sunday, September 16, and the *Monday Night Football* telecast planned for September 17 were postponed. An immediate question was whether those games could be rescheduled at the end of the season or would have to be canceled. Adding another week of regular-season games at the end was difficult because of the playoff schedule leading to the Super Bowl, which was set for January 27, 2002.

The NFL made several decisions to accommodate adding that extra week to play the postponed games. Both the playoffs and the Super Bowl were moved one week later, the latter occurring on February 3 rather than January 27.

With much of the planning already completed in light of the original January 27 date, one obstacle after another had to be faced in rescheduling the Super Bowl, including dealing with a scheduling conflict occasioned by the new date. A convention was already scheduled for the New Orleans Superdome on February 3. NFL officials considered shortening the playoffs or moving the game to another venue, but they eventually were able to negotiate a solution with the Superdome officials and the organization planning the convention that kept the game at its scheduled site.

Considerable quick planning occurred to transform the festivities surrounding the game itself in light of the death and devastation that occurred on September 11. A new Super Bowl logo was designed suggesting the shape of the United States to reflect American patriotism and pride.

Prior to the game, a contingent of singers, including Barry Manilow, sang Manilow's "Let Freedom Ring," and in a video, current and former NFL players read from the Declaration of Independence. Another video presented a message from former Presidents Gerald Ford, Jimmy Carter, George H. W. Bush, and Bill Clinton, as well as from Nancy Reagan substituting for her husband, Ronald Reagan, who was suffering from Alzheimer's disease and was unable to participate. In addition, the pregame show featured singers Mary J. Blige and Marc Anthony accompanying the Boston Pops Orchestra in a performance of "America the Beautiful" and Paul McCartney singing "Freedom," which he had written in response to the events of September 11.

The Boston Pops played and Mariah Carey sang the traditional opening song for sports events, "The Star-Spangled Banner." Pres. George W. Bush and former Naval Academy and NFL great Roger Staubach then presided at the coin toss.

The halftime show also recalled September 11 with such performances as "Beautiful Day" and "MLK" by the Irish rock group U2. The group concluded its three-song set with a moving rendition of "Where the Streets Have No Name," during which two large backdrops listed the names of victims of the terrorist attacks. Bono wore an American flag sewn into the lining of his coat, which he revealed to the audience, symbolizing his closeness to the American people and especially those affected by the attacks.

In a continuing reminder of September 11 as well as the threat of additional terrorism, especially at large facilities or events attended by large numbers of Americans, the Super Bowl is annually designated a National Special Security Event. The game received that designation from the Department of Homeland Security and thus is subject to heightened security measures.

Oh, yes, the New England Patriots won that Super Bowl, 20–17, over the St. Louis Rams on a game-ending field goal by Adam Vinatieri. It was appropriate that those in attendance and those watching on television had an especially dramatic and entertaining game to view. Life would go on, often very well, but with those terrible hours of September 11, 2001, never far removed from America's consciousness.

See also: Presidents of the United States; Super Bowl; Tillman, Patrick Daniel.

Additional Reading:
Calhoun, Craig, Paul Price, and Ashley Timmer, eds. *Understanding September 11.* New York: New Press; Distributed by Norton, 2002.
Casil, Amy Sterling. *Coping with Terrorism.* New York: Rosen, 2004.

Sexuality

Football has long been viewed as an especially masculine activity despite the emergence of several leagues of women football players in recent years. Football is a violent game in which men, especially in the NFL, routinely strut about, literally beating their chests (as well as kicking, dancing, and engaging in other physical antics) to convey the rush of conquest after laying a crushing tackle on another player or scoring a touchdown. One imagines primitive man might have acted similarly after bringing down an animal with a club or big rock.

Men want to prove that they are real men in football, which is one reason why they traditionally have put their health in jeopardy by playing with injuries, including concussions. Many football players (as well as other men) also define themselves at least partly through sexual conquest, seeing it as a further proof of their masculinity. It should be pointed out, however, that these tendencies are by no means universal, and plenty of football players are as moral and faithful to their wives or girlfriends as individuals in any other line of work.

The world of football, however, has included many persons noted (or self-styled) as "ladies' men," with such famous examples as Jim Brown, Paul Hornung, and Joe Namath. Hornung, in his memoir *Golden Boy,* openly talks about his sexual exploits, often perpetrated in tandem with his close friend, the Packers' wide receiver Max McGee. Football players do not necessarily have to try hard to find women, as groupies regularly hang out in hotel bars frequented by players. Having sexual intercourse is referred to as "scoring," a term no longer confined to athletes, and women with whom players have been intimate are "trophies" or "conquests."

Far more troubling than consensual

sex between willing partners is the reality that violence against women has long been a serious problem with football players. The offenses range from sexual abuse and sexual assault to murder. Rae Carruth, for example, was sentenced in 2001 to eighteen years in prison for plotting the murder of his fiancée. The case of O. J. Simpson is discussed elsewhere in this book.

Sex is also institutionalized within football. Sex appeal has been part of the game throughout most of its history. In the 1920s the big man on campus (recognized as the ultimate prize for young ladies) was the football star. Once cheerleading became primarily a feminine function, attractive girls were regularly seen as part of the game's allure. In recent decades, cheerleaders for professional teams have become overtly sexual in their costuming and routines, and at the college level cheerleaders are often only marginally more modest in their clothing than their professional counterparts.

Sex has also become part of the recruiting process at some institutions, with high school seniors entertained during campus visits by friendly females lined up for the occasion. At other times, women quite innocently have found themselves in threatening situations they did not anticipate. The University of Colorado experienced a major scandal after two women charged that they were raped in 2001 at an off-campus party for players and recruits. The university finally agreed in 2007 to settle the lawsuit. A separate inquiry supported by the university's Board of Regents found that alcohol, drugs, and sex were being used to entice top football players to join the Colorado football program. Although few if any universities would actually sanction such practices, there clearly has been a serious lack of oversight and perhaps, especially on the part of coaches, more than a little of simply not wanting to know what zealous boosters might be arranging.

Another serious incident at Colorado involved Katie Hnida, who in 2002, after transferring to the University of New Mexico, became the first woman to play in a Division I-A football game. Hnida had been invited to join the football program at Colorado in 1999 and spent one season with the team before being cut. She alleges that during her time at Colorado she was sexually harassed and raped by teammates.

With masculinity and sexuality so intertwined within football, it is not surprising to find that the subject of homosexuality in football is not much discussed by players, at least not openly. Certainly many gay players have been members of college and professional teams, but few have openly admitted they were gay because of the supercharged masculine culture of football.

The first NFL player to "come out of the closet" was David Kopay, a running back with five teams from 1964 to 1972. Three years after leaving the NFL, he admitted his sexual orientation in an interview with the *Washington Star*. He later published an account of his life, *The David Kopay Story*. Only a few other football players, and always after the conclusion of their football careers, have said that they are gay. Roy Simmons, an offensive lineman for the Giants and Redskins from 1979 to 1983, discussed his orientation on *The Phil Donahue Show* in 1992. In his memoir *Out of Bounds* he recounts the heavy toll that concealing his homosexuality took on his personal and professional life. Simmons also has acknowledged being HIV-positive. Esera Tuaolo, a defensive lineman who spent five of his nine NFL seasons with Minnesota, published his memoir, *Alone in the Trenches*, in 2006. The title succinctly states the feeling of isolation that has consistently afflicted gays in football.

Jerry Smith was an outstanding tight end with Washington between 1965 and 1977 who caught 421 passes for 5,496 yards and sixty touchdowns. An All-Pro, Smith's sixty receiving touchdowns were a record for tight ends at the time. Kopay writes in his memoir about his sexual relationship with Smith, who less than ten years after his final game died of AIDS complications, having hidden his homosexuality to the end.

See also: Brown, James Nathaniel; Cheerleaders; Crime; Dallas Cowboys Cheerleaders; Hnida, Katharine Anne; Hornung, Paul Vernon; Namath, Joseph William; Sanders, Deion Luwynn; Scouts.

Additional Reading:

Benedict, Jeff, and Don Yaeger. *Pros and Cons: The Criminals Who Play in the NFL*. New York: Warner Books, 1998.

Hornung, Paul, told to William F. Reed. *Golden Boy*. New York: Simon and Schuster, 2004.

Kopay, David, and Perry Deane Young. *The David Kopay Story: The Coming-Out Story That Made Football History*. 1977. Los Angeles: Advocate Books, 2001.

Nelson, Mariah Burton. *The Stronger Women Get, the More Men Love Football: Sexism and the American Culture of Sports*. New York: Harcourt Brace, 1994.

Sanders, Deion. *Power, Money & Sex: How Success Almost Ruined My Life*. With Jim Nelson Black. Nashville: Word Publishing, 1998.

Simmons, Roy, and Damon DiMarco. *Out of Bounds: Coming out of Sexual Abuse, Addiction, and My Life of Lies in the NFL Closet*. New York: Carroll and Graf, 2006.

Tuaolo, Esera. *Alone in the Trenches: My Life as a Gay Man in the NFL*. With John Rosengren. Naperville IL: Sourcebooks, 2006.

Shotgun Formation

The shotgun has yielded its name to many objects and situations, such as the shotgun house or the shotgun seat. The gun is favored by a lot of hunters because, although they usually will not admit it, the area covered by the shot makes it easier to hit something with a shotgun than with a rifle. The shotgun thus can compensate for a deficient aim and has kept that sense of making up for deficiencies in some of its metaphoric applications. The shotgun wedding, for example, compensates for the groom's presumed premarital liberties and apparent reluctance to marry the object of his unseemly desires. He therefore must, as the old tradition holds, be marched at the barrel of a shotgun to the church.

The shotgun formation shares this

sense of compensation. In this case, what is compensated for is usually a strong pass rush. Positioning the quarterback 5 to 7 yards behind the center gives the passer a clearer vision of the field and more time to locate his receivers as well as the enemy rushers and defenders. "Shotgun" refers to the quarterback's wide field of vision before he lets the pass fly, paralleling the wider target area that a shotgun shell hits.

Although the shotgun owes something to earlier tactics, including the short-punt formation, the modern version appeared in 1960. Red Hickey, coach of the San Francisco 49ers, devised it to counter the rugged pass rush of the Baltimore Colts and used it against them on November 27, 1960. John Brodie, filling in for the injured Y. A. Tittle, was himself injured early in the contest and was replaced by the third-string quarterback, Bob Waters. Waters worked the shotgun effectively against the surprised Colts, with San Francisco winning 30–22.

The 49ers, with Brodie returning at quarterback, won three of their final four games and looked forward to a successful 1961. San Francisco drafted Billy Kilmer, who could run well, an important attribute for a quarterback in the shotgun formation because he usually has to run with the ball when his receivers are covered. With Hickey rotating Brodie, Waters, and Kilmer, the 49ers won four of their first five games. Then the Chicago Bears figured out that by moving a linebacker to the line of scrimmage, they could get enough pressure on the quarterback to disrupt the play. The result was a 31–0 victory for the Bears.

Hickey gave up on the shotgun formation, but Tom Landry brought it back with the Dallas Cowboys, and other teams followed suit. Today many teams use the formation, usually when they need a lot of yardage for a first down. Since the defense knows a pass is probably coming anyway, the shotgun formation is not giving anything away. Teams can, of course, run out of the formation and sometimes do just to keep the defense guessing a bit. Some teams will use the formation even when they have effective offensive lines in order to allow the quarterback to be completely focused on what is happening beyond the line of scrimmage.

See also: Forward Pass; Landry, Thomas Wade; Tittle, Yelberton Abraham.

Additional Reading:
American Football Coaches Association. *The Football Coaching Bible.* Champaign IL: Human Kinetics Publishers, 2002.
———. *Offensive Football Strategies.* Champaign IL: Human Kinetics Publishers, 2000.

Shula, Donald Francis (b. 1930)

Don Shula reached two remarkable goals in his coaching career: single-season perfection and the most career wins of any professional football coach in history. Then, in retirement from football, he encouraged people along seemingly contradictory roads: eating at the series of restaurants that bears his name and losing weight.

Don Shula played football at John

Carroll University and for the Cleveland Browns, the latter trading him in 1953 to the Baltimore Colts in a fifteen-player trade, at the time the largest trade in NFL history. He finished his playing career with the Washington Redskins in 1957. Primarily a cornerback, he intercepted twenty-one passes in his career.

Shula turned to coaching after his playing days, serving as a college assistant at Virginia and Kentucky, and then with the Detroit Lions in the NFL. He started his thirty-three-year career as a head coach with the Colts in 1963 at the age of thirty-three. He compiled an impressive 71-23-4 record in seven seasons with Baltimore, making it to Super Bowl III after the 1968 season only to lose to the New York Jets in a game that Joe Namath promised to win and then did precisely that.

Shula accepted an offer from Miami Dolphins owner Joe Robbie to coach Miami starting in 1970. Although he had only two losing seasons in his long tenure with Miami, his peak years came from 1971 to 1973 when the Dolphins appeared in three consecutive Super Bowls, winning the final two. The 1972 team went undefeated and untied, winning all fourteen regular-season games and stretching the streak to seventeen with a victory over Washington in Super Bowl VII. The next year, Miami lost two games in the regular season and defeated Minnesota in the Super Bowl, giving Shula's Dolphins a two-year record, including postseason games, of 32-2. Those early 1970s teams featured

quarterback Bob Griese, running backs Larry Csonka and Mercury Morris, receiver Paul Warfield, and a strong and cohesive defensive unit known as the "No-Name Defense."

Shula led Miami back to Super Bowls XVII and XIX after the 1982 and 1984 seasons, the latter with a young Dan Marino at quarterback, but lost both games. Shula passed George Halas of the Chicago Bears in career wins and retired with a regular-season record of 328-156-6. His postseason appearances increased the totals to 347-173-6. Shula holds the distinction of being the only coach to take his teams to six Super Bowls. Two sons followed Shula into coaching and served as head coaches: Mike at the University of Alabama and Dave with the Cincinnati Bengals.

Shula has remained in the public eye since retirement. He founded the Don Shula Foundation prior to his first wife's death from cancer. The foundation attempts to discover a cure for breast cancer. A series of restaurants bears his name: Shula's Steakhouse. He appears often on television with his second wife, Mary Anne, in NutriSystem commercials to comment on their weight loss, presumably in part from not eating too often at his steakhouses, and encourage other senior citizens to try NutriSystem. On November 15, 2005, Shula was featured in a public awareness campaign as the first person signing up for the new Medicare Part D prescription drug plan. Many of these appearances are aimed at generations who watched Shula lead the Colts and Dolphins to victory and along the way become one of the greatest and most respected coaches in football history.

See also: Commercials and Advertisements; Halas, George Stanley; Nicknames; Marino, Daniel Constantine, Jr.; Namath, Joseph William; Perfection.

Additional Reading:

Brown, Jody. *Don Shula: Countdown to Supremacy: A Game-by-Game Review and Yearly Highlights of Don Shula's Twenty Years as a Head Coach in the National Football League.* New York: Leisure Press, 1983.

Perkins, Steve, and Bill Braucher. *The Miami Dolphins: Winning Them All.* New York: Grosset and Dunlap, 1973.

Shula, Don. *The Winning Edge.* With Lou Sahadi. New York: Dutton, 1973.

Shula, Don, and Ken Blanchard. *The Little Book of Coaching: Motivating People to be Winners.* New York: HarperBusiness, 2001.

Simpson, Orenthal James (O.J., the Juice) (b. 1947)

Probably no one associated with football has ever dropped so precipitously from fame to infamy as O. J. Simpson. For a long time Simpson (a member of the college and professional football halls of fame) was on top of the world. He set the junior college career rushing record at San Francisco City College (1965–66) with 2,552 yards and fifty-four touchdowns. Then he dominated college ball at the University of Southern California. In 1967 he led the country in rushing with 1,451 yards as USC won the national championship. He repeated as an All-American in 1968, carrying the ball 355 times for 1,709

yards and twenty-two touchdowns. He also earned the Heisman Trophy and the Maxwell Award as the outstanding collegiate football player.

The Buffalo Bills made Simpson the first player chosen in the 1969 draft. He went on to lead the NFL in rushing four times, with his greatest seasons occurring in 1973 and 1975. In the former, he became the first back ever to rush for 2,000 yards, finishing with 2,003. He averaged 6.0 yards per carry and rushed for twelve touchdowns. In 1975 he gained 1,817 yards, caught passes for 426 yards, and scored twenty-three touchdowns. Simpson was limited by injury to seven games in 1977 and completed his playing career with two seasons for the San Francisco 49ers.

Possessor of fame, good looks, an engaging personality, and a "nice guy" image, Simpson moved easily into television, film, and advertising. He was part of the *Monday Night Football* broadcasting team, first as an occasional replacement in 1983 and then as a regular for the next two years. He also worked on *The NFL on NBC*, hosted an episode of *Saturday Night Live*, and appeared in the extremely popular ABC miniseries *Roots*. Simpson acted in a number of movies, including *The Towering Inferno* (1974), *The Cassandra Crossing* (1976), *Back to the Beach* (1987), and the *Naked Gun* trilogy (1988, 1991, 1994). Television viewers watched him race through airports for Hertz in a famous series of television commercials as the magazine *Advertising*

Age named Simpson its Spokesman of the Year in 1976.

The public on the whole viewed Simpson as a fine family man (married to Marguerite Whitley in 1967 and father of three children) and sympathized with him over the death of his youngest child, Aaren, who drowned in the family swimming pool in 1979 just before her second birthday. The breakup of Simpson's first marriage and his divorce from his second wife, Nicole Brown, did not appear to alter significantly the public's perception of Simpson.

All of that changed dramatically in the summer of 1994. On June 12 Nicole Brown and a friend of hers, Ronald Goldman, were found murdered outside her condominium. Evidence quickly led the Los Angeles Police Department to identify Simpson as the primary suspect in the murders, but he was allowed to turn himself in to the police. That was to occur on June 17.

The surrender turned into a bizarre television event as viewers throughout the country watched spellbound as police cars followed a white Ford Bronco carrying Simpson and driven by his friend Al Cowlings. A Los Angeles news service helicopter filmed the low-speed pursuit, which meandered along Interstate 405 while fascinated fans gathered at overpasses, many holding up signs containing messages for Simpson. Finally, Simpson ended the strange parade after former USC football coach John McKay urged him to turn himself in.

The "Trial of the Century" began on January 25, 1995. The participants—witnesses, prosecutors, and Simpson's "Dream Team" of defense attorneys—became national celebrities as Court TV carried the trial live. Pieces of evidence—such as a glove that, apparently having shrunk after being soaked, frozen, and thawed, and therefore no longer fit Simpson as he dramatically attempted to force it onto his hand—became permanently fixed in the public's consciousness.

The trial heightened racial tensions, as whites and African Americans, according to polls taken at the time, sharply diverged in their opinions of Simpson's guilt or innocence. In addition, defense attorney Johnnie Cochran was accused of playing the "race card" as he tried to paint the trial as racially motivated in order to persuade the primarily African American jury to acquit.

The jury found Simpson not guilty on October 3, 1995, after only three hours of deliberation. Although Simpson remains legally not guilty of the murders, the aftermath ended the great public love affair with the Juice, and trial-related issues continued to make the news.

Fred Goldman, Ronald's father, brought a wrongful death suit against Simpson and won, a civil jury in Santa Monica, California, finding Simpson responsible for Goldman's death and guilty of battery against both victims. The court ordered Simpson to pay $33.5 million in damages. Simpson was forced to sell his Heisman Trophy and some other possessions, but he retained his NFL pension under California law that protects an individual's pension against being seized to pay a debt. He also retained his Florida home under similar Florida State law. As a result, Simpson was able to continue a lifestyle seemingly similar to what he had earlier enjoyed.

The next major chapter in the story took place over a book that Simpson planned to publish with ReganBooks. Entitled *If I Did It*, the book, ghostwritten by Pablo Fenjves, was to be an account by Simpson of what he would have done if he had planned to commit the murders. Judith Regan, the publisher, acknowledged that she considered the account to be essentially a confession. Amid public opposition to Simpson's benefiting financially from the case, Rupert Murdoch, CEO of the company that owned ReganBooks, withdrew the book from publication.

Fred Goldman again took legal action, seeking rights to the book as a way to collect a portion of the money Simpson had earlier been ordered to pay in the wrongful death judgment. A federal bankruptcy judge ruled in Goldman's favor in June 2007, and the book was published with the altered title *If I Did It: Confessions of the Killer* and some additions to the text.

Then came another bizarre chapter in Simpson's life. Apparently attempting to reclaim memorabilia that he claimed was stolen from him, Simpson, accompanied by several other men, burst into a casino hotel room in September 13, 2007,

allegedly with a gun. Three days later, police arrested Simpson, who initially was held without bail before being released on $125,000 bail, having surrendered his passport and facing charges that included assault and robbery with a deadly weapon and kidnapping.

Simpson claimed innocence, arguing that he was attempting a "sting" operation to reclaim his objects and that he had not used a weapon in the attempt. On November 28, 2007, he was arraigned on kidnapping and armed robbery charges and entered a "not guilty" plea. A trial date of April 7, 2008, was set, but the trial was later delayed until September 8, 2008, to allow the defense sufficient time to prepare. On October 3, 2008, Simpson was found guilty of twelve charges, including kidnapping and armed robbery. On December 5 he was sentenced to thirty-three years in prison with the possibility of parole after nine years.

See also: Commercials and Advertisements; Crime; Films; Heisman Trophy; *Monday Night Football*; Television Broadcasting.

Additional Reading:

Bugliosi, Vincent. *Outrage: The Five Reasons O.J. Simpson Got Away with Murder*. New York: W.W. Norton, 1996.

Dershowitz, Alan. *Reasonable Doubts: The O.J. Simpson Case and the Criminal Justice System*. New York: Simon and Schuster, 1996.

Fox, Larry. *The O.J. Simpson Story: Born to Run*. New York: Dodd, Mead, 1974.

Fuhrman, Mark. *Murder in Brentwood*. Washington DC: Regnery, 1997.

Simpson, O.J. *If I Did It: Confessions of the Killer; with Exclusive Commentary "He Did It" by the Goldman Family*. New York: Beaufort Books, 2007.

―――. *O.J.: The Education of a Rich Rookie*. With Pete Axthelm. New York: Macmillan, 1970.

Six-Man (Eight- and Nine-Man) Football

Perhaps the type of football closest to small-town America is six-man football. The game is played at small high schools, usually those with under one hundred students, primarily rural schools far from any town of significant size.

Six-man football was the brainchild of a Nebraska educator named Stephen Epler. Epler was a teacher and coach at the high school in Chester, Nebraska, in the 1930s when he envisioned an approach to football that would permit boys from small schools to play a sport heretofore denied them.

Epler dramatically revised football rules to accommodate the limited number of players and the reality that there would be great differences in ability among the teams. Although rules for the six-man version of the sport vary somewhat from state to state, a basic pattern includes a team with three linemen and three backs. All of the players are eligible to catch passes, but the quarterback must hand off the ball, lateral it, or throw a pass before the ball may cross the line of scrimmage. Quarterback sneaks or keeper plays are illegal because with everyone eligible to catch a pass and therefore needing to be covered, it would be almost impossible to defend against the quarterback carrying the ball.

The wide-open nature of the game and the limited number of defenders permit a lot of high-scoring games, hence the rule extending the yardage necessary for a first down to 15 yards from the 10 yards typical of other forms of American football. Because of the wide disparity in talent levels among small schools, six-man football has a "mercy rule." If a team is ahead by 45 points at any time during the second half, the game is ruled over.

The likelihood that the small body of players will not include a skilled kicker is reflected in the allotment of 2 points for an extra point that is kicked versus just 1 point for an extra point by running or passing. A field goal is worth 4, not 3, points. The reduced number of players explains the reduction in the size of the playing field from the usual 50 by 100 yards to 40 by 80 yards. There are just not enough players to cover the standard-size field.

The game caught on quickly, spreading throughout the Midwest and Plains states. By 1938 it had reached Texas, where today it remains common after disappearing from most other states. According to Carlton Stowers, author of *Where Dreams Die Hard*, an account of one season with a Texas six-man team, about 30,000 schools were playing six-man football in 1953, but by the twenty-first century, the number had dropped to between 225 and 250, more than half of them in Texas.

The culprit behind the drop in six-man teams is the same one behind the virtual disappearance of one-room schools—school consolidation. In addition, many towns that once featured their own schools have disappeared completely or have shrunk to one or two stores surrounded by pastures.

Six-man football offered dreams of football stardom to many thousands of high school boys, even if few would advance to big-time college sports, and even fewer to professional ball. Jack Pardee, however, was an exception. Pardee attended little Christoval High School in Texas, where he accounted for nine touchdowns in a regional championship game against Fort Davis in 1952. He then played for Paul "Bear" Bryant at Texas A&M and, after earning All-America honors, went on to become an outstanding linebacker in the National Football League with the Los Angeles Rams and Washington Redskins (1957–72). Pardee later was head coach with the Chicago Bears, Washington, and Houston Oilers (now the Tennessee Titans).

Six-man football may one day become extinct, which would be unfortunate. Its survival helps to keep alive a tradition of rural community where almost everyone comes together to root for the home team because the boys playing the game are neighbors, and neighbors care about neighbors.

The larger versions of six-man football—eight-man and nine-man teams—share most of the characteristics of the smaller squad but with a shade less intimacy and a bit less of the small-town closeness. High school teams that feature eight or nine players also often play on smaller fields, tend toward high scores, exhibit considerable disparity in talent levels (hence a "mercy" rule), and align in modified versions of the eleven-man formations. Eight-man teams typically have a quarterback, two running backs, a center, two guards, and two ends either split or tight. The defense is likely to be aligned with three linemen, three linebackers, and two backs.

Eight-man teams still can be found in a number of states, including Wyoming, Oklahoma, Nebraska, and Iowa. Nine-man teams, most commonly located in the Dakotas, usually add a fourth lineman on defense and a fourth player in the offensive backfield who may flank out as a receiver. Like their smaller counterparts, the nine-player squads demonstrate that love for football can be accommodated if people just employ a little ingenuity.

Additional Reading:
Nebraska Eightman Football Coaches Association Web site. http://www.webspawner.com/users/ne8man.
Sixmanfootball.com: The Bible of Six-Man Football in Texas Website. http://www.sixmanfootball.com.
Stowers, Carlton. *Where Dreams Die Hard: A Small American Town and Its Six-Man Football Team.* Cambridge MA: Da Capo, 2005.

Stagg, Amos Alonzo (the Grand Old Man of the Midway) (1862–1965)

Amos Alonzo Stagg lived to the age of 102, his career stretching from the birth of American football to the television age and the great surge in popularity of the professional game. He spent essentially a whole career coaching football at the

University of Chicago (1892–1932) and still sandwiched that period within other careers. He was called the Grand Old Man of the Midway, a term referring to Chicago, but was really the grand old man of college football overall. Few if any participants in the game had a greater impact on it than did Stagg.

Amos Alonzo Stagg matriculated at Yale University in 1885 as a divinity student and became an outstanding end for the university's football team. He probably was better at baseball, though, excelling as a pitcher and receiving offers to play professionally. He also was a basketball pioneer, popularizing the sport at the University of Chicago while he was also coaching football. During his first year at Chicago, he introduced the new sport and later coached the first five-man game (against the University of Iowa on January 16, 1896) and organized the University of Chicago National Interscholastic Basketball Tournament (1917). Stagg, who coached his Chicago basketball team to seven Big 10 titles, was enshrined in the Basketball Hall of Fame in 1959, eight years after his induction as a charter member of the College Football Hall of Fame as both a player and a coach.

But it is football for which Stagg is best remembered. He helped Yale post a 53-2-1 record in five seasons as a player (1885–89) and was a member in 1889 of the first All-America football team. Among his teammates on that honorary squad were quarterback Edgar Allan Poe of Princeton, a relative of the poet after whom he was named and later an attorney for the famed novelist F. Scott Fitzgerald; and Pudge Heffelfinger of Yale, usually credited with becoming the first professional football player three years later.

Stagg began his coaching career at Springfield College in Massachusetts in 1890, moved to the University of Chicago in 1892, and after being pushed out there when he turned seventy signed on with the College of the Pacific in Stockton, California, in 1933, continuing until 1946. He accumulated 314 victories, at the time a record. Although eighty-four years old when he left Pacific, he still was not ready to retire and became an assistant coach under his son, Amos Alonzo Stagg Jr., at Susquehanna University (1947–52). When his wife's health started declining, he returned with her to Stockton where he coached kicking at Stockton Junior College (1953–58), finally retiring at the age of ninety-six.

Stagg was a great innovator. The College Football Hall of Fame gives him credit for a wide range of inventions, including the end-around, hidden-ball trick, quick-kick, double reverse, Statue of Liberty play, and man-in-motion, as well as the practice of huddling between plays. He also devised the first batting cage for baseball and a trough for the overflow in swimming pools.

In a strange balancing of the old and the new, the Manhattan Project scientists working to develop the first atomic bomb during World War II carried out one of their most crucial projects beneath the University of Chicago's Stagg Field, which was no longer in use for sports. There they created the first successfully sustained nuclear chain reaction. Students of Stagg's life and work may consult the Amos Alonzo Stagg Collection at the University of the Pacific Library.

See also: Fitzgerald, F. Scott Key; Heffelfinger, William W.; Ivy League; Poe, Edgar Allan; Trick Plays.

Additional Reading:

Considine, Bob. *The Unreconstructed Amateur: A Pictorial Biography of Amos Alonzo Stagg*. Ed. Ralph Cahn. San Francisco: Amos Alonzo Stagg Foundation, 1962.

Lester, Robin. *Stagg's University: The Rise, Decline, and Fall of Big-Time Football at Chicago*. Urbana: University of Illinois Press, 1995.

Stagg, Amos Alonzo, and Henry L. Williams. *A Scientific and Practical Treatise on American Football for Schools and Colleges*. Hartford CT: Press of the Case, Lockwood and Brainard, 1893.

Substance Abuse

Substance abuse takes many forms and applies to all levels of football at least from high school through the professional ranks. Steroid use at the professional level has received much of the attention, but it and other performance-enhancing substances are prevalent among college and high school students as well. In addition, alcohol continues to be a widespread problem.

The National Football League and the NFL Players Association have agreed on a plan to combat the use of performance-enhancing substances that are illegal or otherwise prohibited. These substances—which can increase size, strength, and speed—include anabolic/androgenic steroids and human and animal growth hormones. Also prohibited are many related substances including masking agents that can prevent detection of steroids.

The NFL is concerned about these substances for three primary reasons. First, they threaten the integrity of the game by giving users unfair advantage, which may also encourage other players to begin using the substances in order to catch up. Second, the NFL recognizes the dangerous health effects of steroids and other performance-enhancing substances, which have been linked to a wide variety of illnesses, including various cancers, as well as sexual dysfunction and extreme mood swings. "Roid rage" has become an all-too-common condition. Finally, the use of such substances sends a dangerous message to young athletes, encouraging them to place their own health and lives at risk by following the lead of players they admire.

The NFL and the Players Association agreed to a system of testing that includes preemployment, preseason, and regular-season testing as well as postseason testing for teams that make the playoffs. In addition, random testing occurs during the off-season, with additional testing for players who have failed previous tests or otherwise have given the NFL reasonable cause to believe that they have been violating the substance-abuse policy.

Penalties build in intensity. The first infraction, such as a failed drug test, leads to a four-game suspension without pay. The second violation elicits an eight-game suspension, and a third failure leads to a suspension for a full season with the suspended player required to petition the commissioner for reinstatement.

The NFL took another important step toward combating performance-enhancing substances when in January 2008, accompanied by Major League Baseball, it joined in a large-scale research effort led by the United States Olympic Committee (USOC) and the United States Anti-Doping Agency (USADA). The NFL agreed to contribute $3 million to a collaborative effort that will fund research through the new Partnership for Clean Competition. One of the major goals of this effort is to develop an effective test to detect the presence of human growth hormone. The NFL in October 2007 had contributed $1.2 million to the Atlas and Athena program, which tries to direct high school students away from steroids and HGH toward healthy eating and exercise practices. USOC chairman Peter Ueberroth noted at the time of the alliance with the NFL and MLB that he hoped the collaborative effort would also lead to developing effective and inexpensive tests that could be used with high school athletes.

The National Collegiate Athletic Association's drug policy mandates a one-year loss of eligibility for a player who tests positive for steroids or other banned substances. The second positive test leads to a permanent ban.

Little testing occurs at the high school level, however, with just three states (New Jersey, Texas, and Florida) requiring statewide testing as of 2007. The penalties vary widely: a positive test yielding a thirty-day suspension in Texas, a ninety-day suspension in Florida, and a one-year suspension in New Jersey. Texas ratchets up the penalty considerably for repeat offenders: a one-year suspension for a second offense and a permanent ban for a third.

One of the impediments to extensive high school testing is the cost, which recently led Florida to drop its statewide program. A test for one athlete usually runs from $100 to $150. Still, Illinois and New Mexico are considering statewide testing of high school athletes. California's legislature mandated testing in 2004, but Gov. Arnold Schwarzenegger vetoed the bill. Some states prefer to rely on educational programs, but probably a combination of education and testing (with penalties and treatment) is the best answer.

The old source of substance abuse, alcohol, remains a huge problem throughout football and may sometimes be overlooked in light of the seriousness accorded steroid use. In fact, alcohol and football have long gone together, with serious health ramifications and loss of life. A Harvard School of Public Health study in 2002 found that more than half (53 percent) of sports fans engage in binge drinking as opposed to 39 percent of nonfans.

In an experiment conducted by Virginia Tech's College Alcohol Abuse Prevention Center, researchers using breathalyzers tested tailgaters prior to four football games. They found that 86 percent of the individuals they tested had drunk alcohol, and about 46 percent had blood-alcohol levels that reached or exceeded the state's standard for intoxication. And that was before the games, during which surely many would have continued drinking. About one-third of those who said that they planned to drive after the game already were intoxicated.

Some universities have taken steps to address the drinking problem. Florida, Kentucky, and Ohio State have prohibited alcohol advertising on radio and television broadcasts that come under their jurisdiction. Some schools, such as Ohio State, prohibit alcohol advertising on stadium signs or in game programs. University of Miami in Florida has dropped Coors and Bacardi as sponsors and eliminated selling beer in the stands. The University of Wisconsin decided to continue its relationship with Miller and Anheuser-Busch as sponsors but prohibits advertising in Camp Randall Stadium and does not allow the beer companies to use the Wisconsin logo in posters or promotions.

Alcohol also continues to be a problem at the professional level, where many athletes in recent years have incurred disciplinary action by the NFL and/or the legal system. Chris Henry of the Cincinnati Bengals, for example, was charged with driving under the influence in June 2006 and pleaded guilty to a reduced charge of recklessly operating his vehicle. A few months later, he spent two days in jail for permitting minors to drink in his hotel room. Wide receiver Koren Robinson pleaded guilty in October 2006 to drunken driving and fleeing police. Shortly afterward, the NFL suspended him for one year. Robinson's history of alcohol-related problems led Seattle and Minnesota to sever their ties with him. During the 2007 season, however, he returned to action with the Packers and appeared to be turning his life around.

These are just two of many recent examples of NFL players suffering the consequences of their abuse of alcohol. Commissioner Roger Goodell, who has taken a firm stand against inappropriate behavior by players and other league personnel, issued a May 2007 ban on alcohol on team buses and flights as well as at team functions in addition to the previous ban on alcohol in locker rooms. The prohibition extends to all team personnel and team guests. To its credit, the NFL Players Association agreed with the policy change.

What happens at the professional and college levels impacts the behavior of high school students. Drinking is likely to remain a serious problem at the high school level, but proper modeling by players who have succeeded at the collegiate or professional level can only help high school players resist alcohol. Alcohol abuse must be addressed at all levels, with appropriate preventive and disciplinary action directed toward high school athletes. A comprehensive approach that includes modeling of good behavior by professional and college players, punishment for dangerous behavior, and a conscientious effort to lessen the presence of steroids, alcohol, and other dangerous substances can positively impact the behavior of America's youth.

See also: Commercials and Advertising; Commissioners; Crime; Labor-Management Relations.

Additional Reading:

Committee on the Judiciary, United States Senate. *Steroids in Amateur and Professional Sports: The Medical and Social Costs of Steroid Abuse.* Washington DC: U.S. Government Printing Office, 1990.

Jendrick, Nathan. *Dunks, Doubles, Doping: How Steroids Are Killing American Athletics.* Guilford CT: Lyons, 2006.

"National Football League Policy on Anabolic Steroids and Related Substances, 2007." NFL Players Association Web site. http://www.nflpa.org/RulesandRegs/SteroidPolicy.aspx.

Stainback, Robert D. *Alcohol and Sport.* Champaign IL: Human Kinetics, 1997.

Wieberg, Steve. "Colleges Are Reaching Their Limit on Alcohol." *USA Today,* November 16 and 21, 2005. http://www.usatoday.com/sports/college/2005-11-16-colleges-alcohol_x.htm.

Subway Alumni

The term *subway alumni* refers to fans of a sports team, originally a college football team, who are neither students nor alumni of the institution. Such fans may ride a subway to the game instead of just walking across campus, but in most cases, despite the name, they find another mode of transportation. Even when the term *subway alumni* first came into use, in the 1920s, most of the subway alumni were actually driving cars to the game.

No one can say with absolute certainty who invented the term. A line of thinking posits its origins with subway riders who read the sports page en route to their destinations. The famous sportswriter Grantland Rice claimed the term as his own. However, primary credit appears to belong with another writer, Paul Gallico, sports-page editor of the New York *Daily News*, who, while likely not coining the expression, was the first to use it regularly during the 1920s.

Gallico, although no fan of Notre Dame football, applied the term to the large numbers of people who attended the annual Notre Dame–Army football game played in New York. After using Ebbets Field and the Polo Grounds (the homes of the baseball Dodgers and Giants) in 1923 and 1924, the contest shifted to Yankee Stadium in 1925 and continued to be played there, with only occasional interruptions, through 1944.

The rise of Notre Dame football in prominence in the 1920s, when the team became the first truly national program, thus gave rise to the concept of subway alumni. As other college teams grew in prominence, the concept became more widespread, until today many institutions have a national following that includes support for their football programs, even if few of those supporters actually ride the subway lines to the big game.

See also: Newspapers; Rice, Grantland.

Additional Reading:

Eden, Scott. *Touchdown Jesus: Faith and Fandom at Notre Dame.* New York: Simon and Schuster, 2005.

Sperber, Murray. *Shake Down the Thunder: The Creation of Notre Dame Football.* New York: Henry Holt, 1993.

Suicide

Suicides are certainly not the province of football alone. In fact, there is some indication that a football player or other athlete may be less likely to commit suicide than other individuals, perhaps because they feel committed to something and are part of a cohesive group. However, the bad news about suicide and football players is that other data indicate they also are at serious risk.

According to the Centers for Disease Control and Prevention, almost four thousand people aged fifteen to twenty-four committed suicide in 2001. That is precisely the age range of high school and college students (including the ages at which most people play football). In addition, concussions, a serious problem in football, are now recognized as a cause of depression, which in turn is a serious element in most suicides. Finally, an athlete who attempts suicide is more likely than a nonathlete to succeed in seriously hurting or killing himself or herself.

Suicide clustering is a documented but little understood phenomenon. Five current or former members of the high school football team of Winthrop, Maine, committed suicide within a space of twenty-six months between 2003 and 2005. Although it was generally agreed that blame did not rest on anything connected to the football program, the numbers also seemed to rule out mere coincidence.

Kyle Ambrogi, a twenty-one-year-old student at the University of Pennsylvania, ran for two touchdowns against Bucknell on October 8, 2005. Suffering from depression, he returned to his mother's house two days later and shot himself to death in the basement.

In December 2005, James Dungy, whose father, Tony, recently coached the Indianapolis Colts, died by suicide. He had been a defensive end in high school and a frequent visitor to his father's practices and games when he coached the Tampa Bay Buccaneers. After graduating from high school, the younger Dungy returned to Tampa Bay to attend Hillsborough Community College. Friends described him as friendly and easygoing.

Andre Waters, who played professionally with Philadelphia and later Arizona from 1984 to 1995, suffered numerous concussions, more than fifteen by his own count. In November 2006, he committed suicide. An autopsy report stated that his brain exhibited considerable damage and resembled the brain of an eighty-five-year-old man suffering from Alzheimer's.

The stories go on and on, each with its own tragic dimensions. Certainly steps can be taken to prevent suicide, including, in football, watching carefully for concussions and ensuring that a player does not return to action until he is completely healed. It is easy to misdiagnose a concussion, especially within an environment that has traditionally encouraged players to "suck it up" and play through injuries. In addition, coaches and others associated with football need to be aware of the warning signs for suicide. With resources (including printed materials, online information, and workshops) literally at people's fingertips, there is no excuse for not being aware of the danger.

See also: Concussions.

Additional Reading:

Coleman, Loren. *Suicide Clusters*. Boston: Faber and Faber, 1987.

Drehs, Wayne. "A Tragic Turn." ESPN.com E-Ticket, http://sports.espn.go.com/espn/eticket/story?page=ambrogi.

Joiner, Thomas E. *Why People Die by Suicide*. Cambridge MA: Harvard University Press, 2005.

"Suicide Prevention." Centers for Disease Control and Prevention. http://www.cdc.gov/ncipc/dvp/suicide.

"Suicide Prevention, Awareness, and Support." Suicide.org. http://www.suicide.org/concussions-can-lead-to-suicide.html.

Super Bowl

Today no organization would be so foolhardy as to schedule a meeting or any social gathering during the Super Bowl—except for a Super Bowl–watching party. Plenty of those occur, with the football game offering another reason to celebrate during the winter months. In fact, a huge chunk of the U.S. population hunkers down with plenty of snacks to watch the game as well as its pregame and halftime festivities.

The Super Bowl—attracting football devotees, casual fans, and people who normally could not care less about football—has become the most-watched program on television in the United States. The all-time U.S. record (as of 2007) for a television audience (for any sort of program, sports related or not) was set on February 1, 2004, when approximately 144.4 million viewers watched Super Bowl XXXVIII according to A. C. Nielsen figures based on individuals who tuned in for at least part of the broadcast. The viewing audience remained huge for subsequent games, with the Super Bowls in 2006 and 2007 the second and third most-watched programs in U.S. television history.

Then came Super Bowl XLII on February 3, 2008. Enticed by the New England Patriots' effort to become the first team since inauguration of the sixteen-game regular season to go undefeated throughout both the regular season and the postseason, a new record number of viewers, 148.3 million, watched at least a portion of the broadcast. Many may have been disappointed by the outcome but surely not by the excitement that the closely fought contest generated. With thirty-five seconds left in the game, Giants quarterback Eli Manning hit Plaxico Burress with a touchdown pass to give New York a 17–14 upset win over the Patriots, dashing New England's hopes for a perfect season. It should be noted, however, that Super Bowl XLII, by another

Nielsen measure—the average number of viewers throughout the broadcast—is just in second place, behind the final episode of *M*A*S*H* in 1983 (97.5 million to 106 million).

However, it was not always this way. The Super Bowl started rather modestly by today's standards. In fact, it was not even called a Super Bowl then. Instead, the agreement to merge the National Football League and the American Football League, to become completed in 1970, consisted of certain preliminary steps, including a game between the two league champions. That game was called the AFL-NFL World Championship Game and featured Vince Lombardi's Green Bay Packers defeating the Kansas City Chiefs 35–10 on January 15, 1967.

The game appeared on both CBS and NBC with thirty-second commercials selling for $85,000. Played in Los Angeles' huge Memorial Coliseum, the game did not come close to selling out and therefore was blacked out in the Los Angeles area.

By Super Bowl III, the game was being officially called the Super Bowl. Kansas City Chiefs owner Lamar Hunt derived the name from a toy called the Super Ball, which he noticed bounced unusually high when his daughter threw it against something, and the long tradition of college football bowls.

What really distinguished the third game, however, was not so much the name, as iconic as that would become, but the outcome. The New York Jets of the upstart AFL, quarterbacked by Joe Namath, who had predicted a win, upset the NFL champion Baltimore Colts 16–7. The Super Bowl had arrived, and after the merger it continued with the champions of the National and American Football Conferences playing each other for the NFL championship.

The last Super Bowl that did not sell out and therefore had to be blacked out in its own region was Super Bowl VII, which, like the first game, was played in the Los Angeles Coliseum. With television becoming a potent marketing tool and advertisers wanting exposure for the big money they were paying to air commercials during the game, a blackout would never again be allowed.

Super Bowl XLI, on February 4, 2007, featured the Indianapolis Colts defeating the Chicago Bears 29–17. It was an exciting game that ended the mark against quarterback Peyton Manning that he never won the big one. The following year, it was brother Eli's turn to prove that he could win the big one. However, in these contests as in other Super Bowls there was much more to the game than just the game itself.

The Super Bowl has become a huge American festival lasting for two weeks or more. The pregame hype builds toward the game like an avalanche cascading down a mountain—except everyone survives and a lot of people get richer, especially those folks associated with the NFL, television, and the companies that advertise during the broadcast.

There seems to be no shortage of businesses vying to sell their products during the game, even at the heady price of $2.6 million per thirty-second spot, the price of doing business at Super Bowl XLI. In fact, the Super Bowl commercial has become an advertising genre in itself, a sort of event within the main event, previewed and reviewed in the media and discussed at length around the water cooler.

The roster of memorable Super Bowl commercials is lengthy, but few if any can take dramatic precedence over the "1984" Apple commercial during Super Bowl XVIII on January 22, 1984. In the commercial, an athletic-looking young woman enters a gathering of people and flings a hammer at a large image of Big Brother on a screen in front of the crowd, smashing the screen. The commercial coincided with the year denoted in the title of George Orwell's classic novel. The commercial helped Apple sell fifty thousand Macintosh computers over the following one hundred days. One of the more memorable recent Super Bowl commercials is of a linebacker racing through a company office and tackling every employee who is breaking an office rule. That spot, "Terry Tate Office Linebacker" (2003), was done on behalf of Reebok. This and many other Super Bowl commercials do not necessarily focus primarily on the product, instead striving to ensure that viewers will remember the commercial itself and, therefore, also by association whatever is being sold.

As Super Bowl commercials can help to sell the products they advertise, they also can help to make a career. Model Cindy Crawford's career, for example, took flight after her Pepsi commercial during the 1992 Super Bowl. The "Hare Jordan" commercial in 1992, during which Michael "Air" Jordan and Bugs "Hare Jordan" Bunny defeat four other players in a basketball game on behalf of Nike led to the film *Space Jam* (1996).

A new commercial twist was introduced for Super Bowl XLI, a commercial-making contest sponsored by the NFL. Approximately 1,700 people auditioned ideas for commercials at NFL stadiums during the 2006 season. The winner was Gino Bona, the business-development director of a marketing firm in Portland, Maine. His concept dealt with the sorrow fans feel when the pro season has finally ended and included such images as a bunch of fans receiving their end-of-season bar tab, a No. 1 finger being put away in a closet, and a Patriots fan washing off his face paint. Joe Pytka, who had directed dozens of Super Bowl ads, helped transform Bona's vision into a commercial that then aired during the game.

The popularity of commercials makes it difficult for viewers to find a good moment to rush to the bathroom. It has long been a common statement, although actually an urban myth, that large numbers of people flushing toilets at the same time seriously reduce local water pressure during Super Bowl breaks in the action.

The Super Bowl also means food— lots of it. In fact, the American Institute of Food Distribution reports that only Thanksgiving exceeds Super Bowl Sunday for quantity of food consumed. The biggest single portion of that food consists of snack items, especially suitable for folks who do not want to push away from the game long enough to push into a formal dining table.

The game and commercials are by no means the only entertainment that the Super Bowl offers. Halftime is a major showcase for famous entertainers. Paul McCartney, formerly of the Beatles, was the halftime headliner at Super Bowl xxxix on February 6, 2005. McCartney, sixty-two years old at the time, sang four songs, concluding with "Hey Jude."

Viewers, especially those music fans old enough to remember when McCartney was a mop-haired Beatle, were able to take comfort in the knowledge that he was unlikely to lose any of his clothing, although he did remove his jacket at one point. That was quite different from the "wardrobe malfunction" (a new term, proving that the Super Bowl even adds to people's vocabulary) at the previous Super Bowl. At halftime of Super Bowl xxxviii, Janet Jackson was performing a medley of songs with Justin Timberlake along with a variety of suggestive moves as they headed into their final line, which warned that she would be naked by the end of the song. Janet Jackson did not suddenly become naked, but a portion of her top flopped open when Timberlake pulled at it. Supposedly that was not to

happen when he yanked, but it did and out came Jackson's right breast.

cbs switched to an aerial view of the stadium, collectively averting the nation's eyes, but a bit too late. Multitudes complained to the Federal Communications Commission, and many (perhaps most) viewers assumed that the incident at the mtv-produced halftime show was deliberate. The nfl promised that mtv would never again be allowed anywhere near a Super Bowl halftime. The fcc fined Viacom, at the time owner of both cbs and mtv, $27,500 (at the time the largest individual fine allowed) for each of the twenty television stations owned by cbs. The United States Congress raised the maximum fine per violation to $325,000 in order to help guard against future wardrobe malfunctions and other acts of television indecency. Jackson's wardrobe malfunction and its aftermath quickly became a staple for comedians, including David Letterman and Jay Leno.

The Jackson-Timberlake event prompted networks to mute or remove a variety of sexually suggestive moments from their programming, including some lyrics from songs that the Rolling Stones sang at halftime of Super Bowl xl. Some viewers, perhaps looking overly hard for violations, complained that Prince, who performed at halftime of Super Bowl xli, positioned his guitar so that it would resemble a huge phallus.

Despite wardrobe malfunctions and excessive eating of junk food, the Super Bowl remains one of the nation's most popular events—and the most watched television program of the year. Its presence on Sundays has the practical advantage of maximizing the size of the audience but also helps stamp the event as something of a secular holy day. If sport has become almost a religion for many millions, then Super Bowl Sunday is their ultimate ritual. Along with all of its other benefits, the Super Bowl has served the educational function of helping generations of Americans learn their Roman numerals. And, yes, it also continues to decide the NFL's championship team.

See also: American Football League (IV); Commercials and Advertisements; Commissioners; Jewelry; Lombardi, Vincent Thomas; Manning, Peyton Williams; Namath, Joseph William; September 11 Terrorist Attacks; Television Broadcasting.

Additional Reading:

Harline, Craig. *Sunday: A History of the First Day from Babylonia to the Super Bowl.* New York: Doubleday, 2007.

Kanner, Bernice. *The Super Bowl of Advertising: How the Commercials Won the Game.* Princeton NJ: Bloomberg, 2004.

Leiker, Ken, and Craig Ellenport, eds. *The Super Bowl: An Official Retrospective.* New York: Ballantine Books, 2005.

Weiss, Don. *The Making of the Super Bowl: The Inside Story of the World's Greatest Sporting Event.* With Chuck Day. Chicago: Contemporary Books, 2003.

Tailgating

Tailgating is a popular custom at football games, usually occurring prior to the game but also sometimes continuing after the contest. The term arose around 1965 and is a variation on the picnic that had long accompanied sporting events as well as other activities. Essentially, tailgating means having a picnic, but usually not on a soft lawn under an apple tree. Tailgating now usually occurs in a parking lot and may or may not actually involve a tailgate. Its origins predate American football and include such memorable historical moments as the gathering of Washington's social elite to picnic and observe the first major battle of the Civil War at Bull Run in 1861.

The term *tailgate* came into fashion with the popularity of station wagons in the 1960s. The back door of station wagons or trucks that can be let down to provide a table is, as Stephen Linn observes in *The Ultimate Tailgater's Travel Guide*, a descendant of the chuck wagon of cattle-drive fame. Charles Goodnight, a prominent nineteenth-century cattleman, is usually given credit for inventing the chuck wagon. It carried the food and supplies needed to feed and clothe the cowboys during roundup and on the drive. A box at the back was used to store dishes, pots, and pans. Its lid would fold back and down, and with a leg inserted underneath made a table that the cook used in preparing food. The chuck wagon, quickly copied by cattlemen throughout the West, provided the original tailgate.

The custom of having a meal prior to a football game, however, arose in the East, apparently at Harvard-Yale games as the nineteenth century was yielding to the twentieth. The practice permitted alumni to socialize and do business, with good food and drink. For Ivy League grads, it was an elitist mixing of business and pleasure.

As the decades passed, tailgating bridged the social classes. Today, tailgating varies in complexity, cuisine, and beverages. It often is a family venture, either in isolation or as part of a football community. Many tailgaters may eat and drink together from a communal tailgate (often a folding table). Gas grills and other modern amenities make the event almost like dining in one's backyard, except for all those other vehicles surrounding the diners.

The food may be traditional fare: hot dogs, hamburgers, bratwursts, and beer. Or it may tend to the more exotic. A tailgating Web site, Tailgating America, lists such tailgating delicacies as beer-boiled shrimp, Jamaican jerk chicken, deer roast, stuffed banana pepper surprise, and Kentucky burgoo, along with many other dishes. The site also includes checklists for would-be tailgaters to make sure they remember everything they will need. Vital supplies include extra ice, sunblock lotion, rain gear (just in case), toilet paper, and, to avoid having to stay longer than planned, jumper cables. Suggestions for making the experience thoroughly enjoyable range from dressing in team colors to planning the menu carefully to arriving several hours before game time in order to secure a good parking spot to cleaning up carefully afterward. The good tailgater, after all, is also a courteous tailgater.

Additional Reading:

Linn, Stephen. *The Ultimate Tailgater's Travel Guide: More than 20 Great Road Trips.* Nashville: Rutledge Hill Press, 2006.

Tailgating America Web site. http://www.tailgating.com.

Tank McNamara

Tank McNamara, distributed by Universal Press Syndicate, is the most widely read football-related daily comic strip. The protagonist, Tank McNamara, a burly individual befitting his name, is a local sports television reporter who previously had starred for the Enormous State University Sandcrabs and played professionally in the National Football League. Since 1974 Tank has been reporting on a variety of stories that although usually sports related often have broader societal implications.

Tank was something of a bumbler when he first appeared on the scene, the creation of writer Jeff Millar and artist Bill Hinds. He had trouble speaking intelligently and was prone to absurd actions such as leaping on anything that fell to the floor as if it were a fumbled football.

Over the years, however, Tank matured, developing greater facility as a sports reporter while the comic strip turned to a range of serious issues, emphasizing social comment and satire while de-emphasizing its earlier broad humor. Steroids, greed, gambling, and crime are some of the issues that the strip has portrayed. Being topical became an important goal. In late November 2007, for example, *Tank McNamara* featured the financial tug of war between the National Football League and cable television regarding whether the NFL Network should be on basic cable or extra-cost packages, a conflict that kept the network off television for many millions of football fans. This occurred at a time when the NFL Network was the only television source for a game between Green Bay and Dallas, each 10-1 at the time, and the final game of the season for the New England Patriots, who were attempting to complete their season undefeated. Just days before the Patriots' season-ending game against the New York Giants, however, the NFL did agree to allow simulcasts of the contest on CBS and NBC. The strip also brought the presidential race into the conflict by having Senator Hillary Clinton supposedly planning to hold Senate hearings on the matter.

At the same time, Tank has become

more multidimensional and appealing. He developed a long-running relationship with a colleague at his television station, Angela, whose son Tank treats as if he were his own.

An annual highlight of the strip is its "Sports Jerk of the Year" award, with readers invited to vote for the top jerk. Several sports have been represented in this balloting, with star receiver Terrell Owens twice winning the dubious honor.

As of 2007 *Tank McNamara* was still popular, appearing in approximately three hundred newspapers, usually in the sports section. And with football and other sports steadily offering so many controversial stories, Tank is unlikely to run out of topical issues anytime soon.

See also: Gil Thorp; Peanuts; Television Broadcasting.

Additional Reading:
Millar, Jeff, and Bill Hinds. *God Intended Blond Boys to Be Quarterbacks!* Mission KS: Sheed Andrews and McMeel, 1977.
———. *The Tank McNamara Chronicles.* Kansas City KS: Sheed, Andrews, and McMeel, 1978.

Taylor, Lawrence Julius (b. 1959)

Lawrence Taylor was one of the most ferocious and effective linebackers ever to play the game. In fact, he may have been the best linebacker ever. He was such a force on defense that he single-handedly compelled coaches to alter their offensive schemes. He also spent years as a serious drug abuser, battled back to overcome his drug problems, and embarked on an acting career.

Taylor, an All-American at North Carolina, was a first-round draft choice of the New York Giants, the second player chosen overall in the 1981 draft. Seldom if ever has a rookie had such an immediate impact as Taylor. He made 133 tackles, recorded 9.5 sacks, and made first-team All-Pro, an honor that he would earn in each of the following eight seasons.

Extremely fast, strong, and intense, Taylor was dominating as an outside linebacker. He rejected the traditional way of playing the position, which was to identify and then react to the play, instead adopting an aggressive, proactive approach. In 1986 he became the first defensive player in fifteen years to be named the NFL's Most Valuable Player. That year he had 105 tackles and 20.5 sacks.

In a memorable game against the New Orleans Saints in 1988, he played wearing a harness to hold his damaged shoulder in place and still made seven tackles and three sacks while also forcing two fumbles. Taylor teamed with fellow linebackers Carl Banks and Harry Carson to give the Giants possibly the greatest linebacking tandem in history.

Taylor also was controversial from the start. He and his agent demanded a rookie contract of $250,000, an astronomical figure at the time. Giants players threatened not to play if the rookie were paid more than they, although most later modified their objections. Once Taylor joined the team, they quickly came to admire his talent.

After the 1983 season, Taylor entered

into an agreement with Donald Trump, owner of the New Jersey Generals of the United States Football League, to play for the Generals. As part of the deal, Taylor received a $1 million interest-free loan. Taylor quickly regretted his decision, and the Giants were forced to buy him out of the agreement. They also tendered Taylor a new six-year contract averaging slightly more than $1 million per year.

Taylor was instrumental in the Giants' Super Bowl victories under Bill Parcells following the 1986 and 1990 seasons. However, Taylor's career was far from smooth. He held out for three weeks during the 1982 preseason, inadvertently broke Redskins quarterback Joe Theismann's right leg on *Monday Night Football* in 1985 (ending Theismann's career), tested positive for cocaine and was suspended for thirty days in 1988, and was fined heavily during a lengthy preseason holdout in 1990. A ruptured Achilles tendon in 1992 put Taylor out of action for almost half the season, but he returned the following year for a final campaign before retiring.

Taylor was so dominating and aggressive as a linebacker that Washington coach Joe Gibbs played two tight ends and an H-back to try to keep Taylor out of the offensive backfield. The H-back, a second back in an essentially one-back offensive formation, usually lined up close to the line of scrimmage to help with blocking. Bill Walsh of the San Francisco 49ers employed another strategy against Taylor, using an offensive guard to block him.

When the defense began to exploit the hole left by the designated guard, Walsh and other coaches used the left tackle instead to try to stop Taylor. All of these defensive maneuvers were designed to put someone stronger than a running back on the powerful linebacker. Quarterbacks always had to be aware of the onrushing Taylor, not only to avoid being sacked, but also because of his skill at chopping at the ball to knock it out of the quarterback's hands.

After retirement Taylor turned increasingly to drugs. Arrests and drug-rehab efforts followed over the years. In his first autobiography and during an infamous interview with Mike Wallace on CBS's *60 Minutes* in November 2003, Taylor publicly acknowledged his misdeeds: his widespread drug use dating back to his second year with the Giants, the exorbitant expense of his habit (up to thousands of dollars daily), his substitution of teammates' urine to cheat drug tests, his sexual escapades with women, and his practice of hiring prostitutes to visit opponents' hotel rooms prior to a game. Despite his fear that his lifestyle might keep him out of Canton, he was elected to the Pro Football Hall of Fame in 1999.

Taylor's confession to Wallace, however, along with his rejection of his earlier drug-filled lifestyle, began to reshape his image. He started referring to his earlier self as "L.T." and his current, drug-free existence as "Lawrence Taylor."

The "new" Lawrence Taylor has become involved in acting. He appeared in the film *Any Given Sunday*, directed by Oliver Stone (1999); played himself on the award-winning HBO television series *The Sopranos*; and was one of the speakers in the video games *Grand Theft Auto: Vice City* and *Blitz: The League*.

While Lawrence Taylor, neither the former nor the latter, will ever be mistaken for "Mr. Nice Guy," he appears to have pulled himself back from the precipice over which for years he seemed destined to plummet. The progression of titles for his autobiographies is illuminating: *Living on the Edge*, then *Over the Edge*, and finally, just *Taylor*, as if at last he did indeed find his real self.

See also: Films; Gibbs, Joe Jackson; Parcells, Duane Charles; *Monday Night Football*; Substance Abuse.

Additional Reading:
Taylor, Lawrence. *Taylor*. New York: Rugged Land, 2006.
———. LT: *Living on the Edge*. With David Falkner. New York: Times Books, 1987.
———. LT *Over the Edge: Tackling Quarterbacks, Drugs, and a World Beyond Football*. With Steve Serby. New York: HarperCollins, 2003.

Television Broadcasting

There was a time not so long ago when football was confined to certain days of the week: high school football on Friday, college football on Saturday, and professional football on Sunday. That clear demarcation as well as the confinement of the sport to just three days of the week has long since passed into history. Now, throughout the fall, football can be seen virtually every night and from the comfort of one's living room. In addition, viewers have a wealth of games to choose from.

On a typical Saturday (November 10, 2007) in the Portland, Maine, viewing area, for example, viewers were able to choose from among fifteen college games, fourteen of them live, along with a replay on ESPN Classic. The games started at noon and continued well past midnight, with a wide assortment of networks getting in on the action: ESPN, ESPN2, NESN, WPME (a local affiliate of MYNetwork), CSN, VERSUS, NBC, ABC, and CBS. College games, however, had been occurring throughout the week: on SCNE, NESN, and ESPN on the previous Tuesday; ESPN2 on Wednesday (along with taped replays of games on ESPN and ESPN2 early Wednesday morning); ESPN on Thursday (along with a high school game on SCNE); a taped replay on ESPN Friday morning; and a taped game early Saturday morning on ESPN2. Clearly, there is plenty of college football available for everyone, including insomniacs. Devotees of high school football, however, with some regional exceptions, have to get their football fill in person or through the radio.

The National Football League appears throughout the afternoon and evening on Sundays, thanks to CBS, FOX, and NBC. In addition, ESPN broadcasts a Monday night game, and when the season really heats up about halfway through (starting on November 22 in 2007), the NFL Network televises an eight-game Thursday and Saturday schedule. The NFL Network, however, is not currently available in those areas (including Portland, Maine) served by Time Warner.

The professional season ends with what has become the most watched program on television in the United States: the Super Bowl.

But it was not always this way. In the early days of television when there was little money to be made from television broadcasts, both college and professional football officials were terrified that the new medium would seriously harm game attendance and decrease football-generated revenue.

The first televised college game saw Fordham defeating Waynesburg of Pennsylvania 34–7 on September 30, 1939. Early telecasts took place in either New York or Philadelphia, but even in those cities there were relatively few television sets prior to World War II, and the telecasts, using just one camera stationed around midfield, were not especially compelling. In addition, the black-and-white telecasts made it difficult to distinguish one team's members from another's.

By 1949 televisions were spreading and attendance at college games was dropping, phenomena that led the NCAA to establish a television committee to explore the relationship between these two changes and determine the likely effect of television on football attendance in the future. The NCAA hired the National Opinion Research Center (NORC) to conduct a study of viewing habits. NORC reported back in 1950 that in areas where

television was widely available, significant numbers of football fans had stopped going to games in favor of watching football telecasts. Where television was less common (the Southwest, Plains, and Rocky Mountain areas), attendance at games had increased. Small colleges were especially hard hit by declining attendance.

The NCAA then moved to limit television broadcasts. Among the institutions opposed to the limitations was the University of Notre Dame, which had a national following and had been using its unrestricted telecasts on the Du Mont network to publicize its educational programs along with pulling in substantial money ($160,000 in 1950). Ultimately, Notre Dame complied despite suffering significant financial losses.

The blackouts of football games quickly became a major political issue, with politicians responding to their constituents' complaints about not being able to see their favorite teams on television. Future Pres. Gerald Ford, a former football star with the University of Michigan and then a congressman from Michigan, became involved in 1951 when the NCAA refused to allow the Michigan-Illinois game to be telecast and then followed with a ban on the upcoming Notre Dame game at Michigan State. Ford complained to Ralph Furey, head of the NCAA's television committee, and the organization lifted its ban on the Fighting Irish and Spartans, supposedly because the game was already sold out. The response, however, was an attempt to avoid a political battle, and the NCAA followed by lifting its blackout of games in Washington DC in a further attempt to forestall political opposition.

Attendance at college games actually dropped in 1951 after the institution of the blackout policy. Nonetheless, the NCAA stepped up its efforts to limit telecasts, dropping regional broadcasts and allowing one national game per week, the fewer games also meaning that fewer schools would be affected. With attendance holding up reasonably well in the Midwest and the West, the Big 10 and Pacific Coast (PAC) conferences began to argue for a more liberal approach to football telecasts. They were joined in their opposition to the NCAA policy by legislators in a number of states and, of course, Notre Dame.

In response, the TV committee modified its approach for 1955, identifying five Saturdays when regional broadcasts would be permitted. At the same time, the NCAA began to use television as a weapon to enforce its regulations. When several universities were found guilty of recruiting violations, including channeling money to players, their access to television was stripped away. The NCAA Council banned the University of Washington, UCLA, and Southern California football teams from appearing on television. The scandal led to the demise of the PAC and the creation of a new conference in 1960, the Athletic Association of Western Universities, also known as the PAC-8 and later the PAC-10.

By the mid-1970s large football schools had grown tired of being outvoted by the greater number of smaller institutions within the NCAA, and many of them banded together into what would soon become known as the College Football Association (CFA). By the early 1980s the CFA was focusing strongly on opening up television for more broadcasts of their games and thereby increasing not only their visibility throughout the country but also their television revenue. Under pressure from the CFA, the NCAA negotiated television contracts with CBS, ABC, and TBS (Turner Broadcasting Sports) in July 1981.

A Supreme Court ruling in 1984 found that the NCAA television plan constituted a "classic cartel" in restraint of trade by limiting the number of games available to the consumer. The decision freed universities to offer their games to the networks, and the result was quick and dramatic. The number of games available on television jumped from eighty-nine in 1983 to almost two hundred. Individual conferences cut their own network deals, with even the Ivy League signing on with, appropriately, public television. The University of Notre Dame entered into an arrangement with NBC in 1990 to televise all of its games. In the mid-1990s, the CFA, so successful that it no longer needed to exist, announced that it would go out of business. The business of college football, though, was thriving and would continue to thrive, in no small measure because of television.

Professional football, like college football, made its television debut in 1939. The Brooklyn Dodgers defeated the Philadelphia Eagles 23–14 on October 22. Not until after World War II, however, did television become much of a factor in the NFL. At that time, teams worked out their own deals, the revenue depending on the size of the local market. Only road games were televised. When the local team was at home, the contest was blacked out locally in order not to hurt attendance at the games. Nor were other games broadcast into the region when the local team was playing at home for fear too many people would stay in their living rooms to watch that game on television rather than go out to the local stadium.

A turning point in the rising popularity of the NFL and the subsequent increase in television visibility came in 1958 when the Baltimore Colts defeated the New York Giants in New York in overtime to win the league championship. NBC broadcast the game nationally, and the audience got to see the exciting, sudden-death contest featuring one of the league's first superstars, Johnny Unitas. The battle would be billed as the "Greatest Game Ever Played."

The 1958 championship game whetted people's appetite for more, and congressional action facilitated the league's marriage with television. To avoid antitrust violations, Congress approved a single-network contract for the NFL, and Pres. John F. Kennedy signed the bill into law on September 30, 1961. The following January 10, owners approved a contract with CBS for the network to broadcast all regular-season games for $4.65 million per year. That was just the beginning, for the television revenue stream would soon grow from its early trickle to a rushing flood.

A number of developments over the years helped to raise the floodgates. Technology brought to the games a variety of user-friendly innovations that gave the fan at home a far closer view of the action than would be possible in the stadium, including instant replay, slow motion, and split-screen views. In later years, much more would be added, such as on-screen score updates and a colored line to show where the offense must reach for a first down.

The agreement to merge the NFL and the American Football League was probably inevitable once the AFL signed a television contract with ABC, which gave the new league the public visibility and financial support to compete with the established NFL. That agreement included a championship game between the two leagues, starting in January 1967. The contest would later become known as the Super Bowl and set all-time records for television watching, not just for sports events but for all programming. *Monday Night Football* brought the game to prime time in 1970 and proved a huge success. In 1973 Congress passed, at the strong urging of Pres. Richard Nixon, legislation lifting the NFL's blackout if a game were sold out seventy-two hours prior to game time. The impetus for the legislation was the popularity among Washington lawmakers of the revitalized Washington Redskins under Coach George Allen. The rise of cable networks in the 1980s, especially ESPN, continued the proliferation of professional football on television.

The NFL itself got into broadcasting in November 2003 with the launch of its own NFL Network. The network, supported by ad revenue, is available on some cable and satellite systems and likely will become available just about everywhere in the future.

NFL Network operates twenty-four hours a day, 365 days per year. The network broadcasts eight regular-season games on Thursdays and Saturdays in addition to preseason games, replays, and classic games from the past. As of 2007 Cris Collinsworth and Bryant Gumbel were handling analysis and play-by-play for the Thursday and Saturday games. NFL GameDay presents discussions of the weekend's games with highlights, interviews, and postgame press conferences. NFL Films is an important resource, its holdings offering extensive programming possibilities. NFL Network also includes many other football-related programs, including extensive coverage of Hall of Fame ceremonies, the Super Bowl, and the NFL Draft.

Television revenue reached $420 million annually from 1982 to 1986 and then continued to escalate. The 1998–2005 agreement with CBS and ESPN brought in $2.2 billion per year, an eight-year total of $17.6 billion. Even that paled next to the subsequent package, which included six-year contract extensions with CBS and FOX, finalized in 2004, to run through the 2011 season, and 2005 agreements with NBC and ESPN to broadcast Sunday and Monday night games through 2011 and 2013 respectively. The total package reportedly is worth about $3.8 billion annually. With thirty-second ads for the Super Bowl selling for $2.6 million in February 2007, football is increasingly about big money and television as much as it is about touchdowns and quarterback sacks. At the same time, the experience of watching the game has evolved considerably, generally along positive directions. At the moment, everyone seems to be winning.

See also: American Football League (IV); Cheating; Commissioners; Greatest Game; *Monday Night Football*; Politicians; Presidents of the United States; Super Bowl; *Tank McNamara*.

Additional Reading:

Barnidge, Tom. "The NFL on TV." In *Total Football II: The Official Encyclopedia of the National Football League.* Ed. Bob Carroll et al., 511–13. New York: HarperCollins, 1999.

MacCambridge, Michael. *America's Game: The Epic Story of How Pro Football Captured a Nation.* New York: Random House, 2004.

NFL Network Web site. http://www.nfl.com/nflnetwork.

Patton, Phil. *Razzle Dazzle: The Curious Marriage of Television and Professional Football.* Garden City NY: Dial, 1984.

Watterson, John Sayle. *College Football: History, Spectacle, Controversy.* Baltimore: Johns Hopkins University Press, 2000.

Text Messaging/Instant Messaging

Text messaging may be all the rage with teens and college students, and popular as well with a lot of adults. Not, however, with the National Collegiate Athletic Association.

The NCAA said a forceful no to coaches communicating with prospective student-athletes as part of the recruiting process. Then, when some Division I coaches objected and the Eastern College Athletic Conference brought forward a proposal to overturn the ban, the NCAA stood firm. In response, the conference's commissioner, Joe D'Antonio, withdrew his league's proposal to approve instant messaging.

The NCAA reaffirmed its ban on text and instant messaging at a Division I business meeting on January 12, 2008. Kerry Kenny, vice chair of the division's Student-Athlete Advisory Committee, labeled such messaging unprofessional and unduly intrusive. One would not apply for a job that way or inform an applicant of his or her getting a job, he explained, so similarly, the recruiting process should be conducted in a dignified, professional manner.

Some coaches argued that high school students are comfortable with text messaging and that the medium helps colleges with limited budgets to compete for student-athletes. Apparently, however, many students had complained that they were being flooded with text messages that were taking up too much of their time and sending their cell phone bills skyrocketing.

In the end, the ban seemed to be a victory for the right of students to their privacy as well as an attempt to control a form of communication by coaches that, if permitted, would be virtually impossible to monitor.

Additional Reading:
O'Neil, Dana. "NCAA Opts to Uphold Ban on Text Messaging Recruits." ESPN.com. January 12, 2008. http://sports.espn.go.com/ncaa/news/story?id=3193796.
"The Use of Technology in the Recruiting Process." NCAA Web Site. http://www.ncaa.org/wps/ncaa?ContentID=505.

Thanksgiving

The first Thanksgiving did not include football, but it might seem that way. Since early in the twentieth century, football has been as much a part of Thanksgiving as turkey, pumpkin pie, and cranberry sauce.

Many high school teams have managed to get in a good game of football, usually against a traditional rival, before heading home to the dinner table. In recent years, the traditional turkey game has faded from many locales, although it persists in some places. Portland, Maine, is a continuing example of the tradition.

Since 1911 Portland High School and Deering High School (also in Portland) have faced each other in football. The rivalry remains very much alive, with Deering scoring a 39–14 victory in the 2008 contest. Despite the impressive victory, though, Portland High continued to lead the series by a significant margin, with fifty-three wins to Deering's thirty-six, and seven ties. If one wonders who is counting, the answer is probably just about every Portland and Deering alumnus.

Thanksgiving used to be an important day on college teams' schedules, as with high schools, especially reserved for prime rivals such as Oklahoma and Nebraska. One of the most memorable Thanksgiving Day college games occurred between those two teams in 1971. Defending national champion Nebraska, winner of twenty-nine straight games, was ranked No. 1 in the country and also had the best defense. Unbeaten Oklahoma, ranked second, had the nation's top-rated offense.

Johnny Rodgers returned a punt 72 yards for a touchdown to put Nebraska ahead. The game then turned into a see-saw battle, with Oklahoma twice coming from behind to take the lead. In the final minutes, Nebraska drove for the winning touchdown, with Jeff Kinney scoring with just 1:38 left. Nebraska went on to conquer previously undefeated Alabama in the Orange Bowl and repeat as national champions.

At the professional level, Thanksgiving games have continued to be part of the holiday festivities. A new league, soon to be called the National Football League, played Thanksgiving Day games in its inaugural year of 1920. Akron beat Canton 7–0 but had to share the day with five other contests.

The game that really marked Thanksgiving football as an institution and also energized the new league with the general population occurred five years later. On Thanksgiving Day, 1925, the Chicago Bears unveiled their new player, the first NFL superstar, Harold "Red" Grange, also known as "the Galloping Ghost." Grange already was a legend from his football heroics at the University of Illinois. Grange had a good game against the hometown rival Chicago Cardinals despite not scoring any touchdowns. Grange picked up 92 yards from scrimmage, made 56 yards on punt returns, tossed six passes, and intercepted a pass to stop the Cardinals' most serious scoring threat as the contest ended in a scoreless tie. Fans came out in record numbers for an NFL game—thirty-six thousand. If there were any doubt about the reason for the huge turnout, one had only to glance at the game's official program, which featured Red Grange on the cover. The new Bear received an astronomical salary of $12,000 for playing, but the expense was worth it for the Bears. George Halas then took his team on a barnstorming tour across the country to capitalize on Grange's fame and drawing power.

The NFL continued to play Thanksgiving games with a hiatus of a few years during World War II. Once G. A. Richards, a radio executive, purchased the Portsmouth (Ohio) Spartans, moved them to Detroit, and rechristened them the Lions in 1934, Thanksgiving came to be permanently associated with the Detroit club, although other teams continued to play on Thanksgiving from time to time through 1952. Those first Thanksgiving Day games in Detroit were especially appealing, as they involved contests against the Chicago Bears, both NFL powers. Chicago won the 1934 game, but Detroit got revenge the following year, a triumph that propelled the Lions to the NFL championship.

Contributing to the popularity of the Detroit games was Richards's creation of the first NFL national radio network in 1934. Fans throughout the country could follow the game on whichever of the network's ninety-four stations came in the clearest.

Throughout the 1950s and early 1960s, the Lions faced off against the Green Bay Packers. Then Detroit started to vary its opponent but continued with the Thanksgiving tradition. The NFL had a new league rival during the 1960s in the American Football League, and that rivalry carried over to Thanksgiving as the AFL regularly scheduled at least one game for the holiday. By 1966 Detroit was joined on Thanksgiving by the Dallas Cowboys, who, like Detroit, has continued to put Thanksgiving on its schedule. In 2006 a third game was added, Kansas City against Denver.

With colleges and many high schools having decided to take the holiday off, it now remains for the NFL to carry most of the responsibility for keeping football on the platter with the turkey, the pigskin next to the drumstick.

See also: American Football League (IV); Grange, Harold Edward.

Additional Reading:
Harvey, Walter. *Football's Most Wanted II: The Top 10 Book of More Bruising Backs, Savage Sacks, and Gridiron Oddities.* Washington DC: Potomac Books, 2006.
Murray, Mike, ed. *Lions Pride: 60 Years of Detroit Lions Football.* Dallas: Taylor Publishing, 1993.

Thorpe, James Francis (Wa-Tho-Huk) (1888–1953)

Upon entering the Pro Football Hall of Fame at Canton, Ohio, visitors immediately encounter a tall statue of Jim Thorpe. The statue towers above anyone who ventures near, befitting the accomplishments of the man who was named best all-around athlete of the first half of the twentieth century in a poll conducted by about four hundred sportswriters and broadcasters in 1950.

What earned Thorpe that accolade? Certainly heading the list was his performance at the 1912 Olympics in Stockholm, Sweden, where he won both the pentathlon and the decathlon. Even the subsequent scandal surrounding his performance (that he had previously played semipro baseball, surely a mild scandal by modern standards), which resulted in his gold medals being withdrawn, could not dull the luster of his athletic skill. In fact, replicas of the gold medals were restored to Thorpe, although after his death, in 1983.

Thorpe's athletic accomplishments began young, when he was a student at the Carlisle Indian Industrial School in Carlisle, Pennsylvania. Thorpe, whose American Indian name was Wa-Tho-Huk, appropriately meaning Bright Path, was born of a part Sac and Fox father, Hiram Thorpe, and a mother, Charlotte, whose heritage included Potawatomi, Menominee, and Kickapoo. His father sent him to Carlisle shortly before he turned sixteen. There he became an All-American halfback and performed skillfully in archery, baseball, basketball, field hockey, lacrosse, swimming, tennis, and track and field. In 1912 he scored twenty-nine touchdowns for Carlisle, leading the team to a victory over the powerhouse Army squad and earning Carlisle recognition as perhaps the finest team in the country.

Thorpe played major league baseball, primarily with the New York Giants, from 1913 to 1919. A good defensive outfielder with, of course, exceptional speed, Thorpe had trouble hitting the curve ball, which resulted in a modest career batting average of .252.

In football, though, he shone more brightly. Thorpe began his professional football career with the Canton Bulldogs in 1915, the fame from his Olympic triumphs helping to give professional football an important push forward. The $250 per game that Jack Cusack, general manager of the Bulldogs, gave Thorpe, for the time an extremely high salary, paid big dividends in on-field performance, publicity, and attendance figures. Thorpe was outstanding at rushing, passing, catching passes, punting, placekicking, dropkicking, blocking, and tackling. He also coached the Bulldogs, leading them to Ohio League championships (the closest

to a national championship that existed then) in 1916, 1917, and 1919.

Thorpe was named the first president of the American Professional Football Association (later renamed the National Football League) in 1920. The following year, he returned to the field, retiring in 1928 after playing with the Cleveland Indians, Oorang Indians, Rock Island Independents, New York Giants, Canton Bulldogs again, and Chicago Cardinals.

Honors accumulated for Thorpe in later years. In addition to being named top athlete of the first half of the twentieth century, he was inducted into the College Football Hall of Fame (1951) and the Pro Football Hall of Fame (1963), in the inaugural sets of inductees. Burt Lancaster starred in a film about his life, *Jim Thorpe: All-American* (1951); a town, Jim Thorpe, Pennsylvania, was named after him; and the U.S. Postal Service issued Jim Thorpe stamps in 1984 and 1998. The legacy of Jim Thorpe also continues to live in the award named after him that goes annually to the outstanding defensive back in college football. In 2000, in the dawning of a new century, the Associated Press and ABC's *Wide World of Sports* named James Thorpe the greatest athlete of the twentieth century.

See also: American Indians; Canton Bulldogs; Carlisle Indian Industrial School; Commissioners; Hall of Fame (Professional); Oorang Indians; Professional Football Origins.

Additional Reading:

Crawford, Bill. *All American: The Rise and Fall of Jim Thorpe*. Hoboken NJ: John Wiley and Sons, 2005.

Jenkins, Sally. *The Real All Americans: The Team That Changed a Game, a People, a Nation.* New York: Doubleday, 2007.

Peterson, James A. *Thorpe of Carlisle.* Chicago: Hinckley and Schmitt, ca. 1920.

Schoor, Gene. *The Jim Thorpe Story: America's Greatest Athlete.* 1951. New York: Washington Square Press, 1968.

Tillman, Patrick Daniel (1976–2004)

Pat Tillman set a new standard for patriotism among American athletes when he turned down a lucrative contract to continue playing safety for the Arizona Cardinals and enlisted in the U.S. Army along with his brother Kevin. The move came after the terrorist attacks of September 11, 2001, which motivated Tillman to join the effort to protect his country against international terrorism. The decision hearkened back to an earlier era when famous athletes willingly exchanged their sports uniforms for military ones to fight on behalf of their country.

Tillman was an enormously accomplished individual with a bright future. He starred as a linebacker at Arizona State University, three times making the All-PAC-10 team, and in 1997 he received his conference's Defensive Player of the Year award. Tillman was just as successful academically, making the PAC-10 All-Academic Football Team three times and earning an NCAA postgraduate scholarship for his accomplishments in the classroom and on the football field.

Tillman was drafted by the Arizona Cardinals in 1998 and steadily improved as a professional. Switched from linebacker to safety, he became a starter in his first season. His 224 tackles in 2000 set a single-season franchise record. At the same time, he started work toward a master's degree in history at Arizona State and volunteered with the Boys and Girls Club of Arizona and the March of Dimes. In 2002 he married his high school sweetheart.

Following the terrorist attacks of September 11, 2001, Tillman set aside a $3.6 million contract to enlist. It was an act of great patriotism and self-sacrifice, although the greater sacrifice would come later. Pat and Kevin completed training at the Army Ranger school in late 2002 and were sent to Iraq in 2003 and Afghanistan in 2004. On April 22, 2004, Pat Tillman was killed in Paktia Province near the Pakistani border. The first reports indicated a heroic death with Tillman giving his life to provide cover for his fellow soldiers. The military announced that he would be awarded posthumously the Silver Star and Purple Heart and promoted to corporal.

About five weeks after Tillman's death, his family learned that the military suspected that he had been killed by friendly fire, that is, by his fellow soldiers. That by itself would have made the death even more tragic, but the truth was even worse. It quickly became clear that the military had known within hours of Tillman's death that he had not been killed by the enemy and had kept that knowledge secret from his family and the media. Even the awards were accompanied by wording that referred to enemy fire despite the military's knowledge of the actual cause of death.

Details regarding the friendly fire shooting became known when Brig. Gen. Gary M. Jones released his report on the incident in early May 2005. The family learned, for example, that Tillman's body armor and uniform were burned shortly after his death, apparently in an attempt to destroy evidence of the cause of death. Phone and Internet connections were locked down and a guard was placed on another soldier wounded in the incident to prevent information from leaking out.

A week later, Lt. Gen. Stanley McChrystal sent several generals a memo suggesting that Tillman had died from friendly fire and that someone should warn President Bush. Whether the president ever received that warning, he did not mention the cause of Tillman's death in his comments about him at a White House correspondents' dinner several weeks before the truth became public. Tillman's parents accused the military of covering up and deliberately lying about the manner of their son's death for public relations reasons.

A series of congressional and other investigations looked into Tillman's death and the actions taken by members of the military afterward. Subsequent information revealed that Tillman's platoon had been divided into two groups so that they could move more quickly toward their destination after a Humvee had broken down and delayed the unit. Tillman was in the first group. The second apparently came under fire. Tillman and his fellow soldiers prepared to offer support and fired on the enemy position. Members of the second group then apparently thought that the first group was the enemy and fired. Tillman waved his arms and called out, frantically identifying himself, but he was shot three times in the forehead.

The multiple investigations have led to modest disciplinary action. Lt. Gen. Philip Kensinger, a three-star general who headed army special operations at the time of the incident, was censured for violating army procedure and faced a possible demotion. According to an army report, Kensinger should have informed the Tillman family or his superiors that Tillman's death was being investigated as a friendly fire shooting. Several other officers received reprimands.

In the meantime, Tillman has received additional honors. The Arizona Cardinals inducted him into the stadium's Ring of Honor, dedicated a stadium walkway as Pat Tillman Freedom Plaza, and erected a statue of him. Both the Cardinals and the Arizona State Sun Devils retired the numbers he wore for them (40 and 42). In addition, the Pat Tillman Foundation was established to inspire people to bring about positive changes in themselves and in society through the Leadership Through Action program. In 2008 Tillman's mother, Mary, published a book about her son and the family's attempt to discover the truth about his death and its aftermath. Despite the apparent duplicity surrounding the military's immediate reaction to Pat Tillman's death, the young man who gave so much for his country will long stand as a model of excellence, generosity, and courage.

See also: September 11 Terrorist Attacks; World War I.

Additional Reading:

Tillman, Mary. *Boots on the Ground by Dusk: My Tribute to Pat Tillman.* With Narda Zacchino. New York: Modern Times, 2008.

Towle, Mike. *I've Got Things to Do with My Life: Pat Tillman: The Making of an American Hero.* Chicago: Triumph Books, 2004.

United States Dept. of Defense. Office of the Inspector General. *Review of Matters Related to the Death of Corporal Patrick Tillman, U.S. Army* [electronic resource]. Alexandria va: Inspector General, Dept. of Defense, 2007. http://purl.access.gpo.gov/GPO/LPS80334.

Title ix

Title ix of the Education Amendments Act of 1972 requires publicly funded schools to make equal opportunities available to male and female students in a variety of areas, including access to higher education, career education, science and mathematics, and many other aspects of college life, including athletics. It is in athletics, however, that Title ix has received the most attention and ignited the most controversy.

Title ix offers three ways in which colleges and universities can establish compliance. The school may demonstrate (1) that the percentages of male and female athletes are substantially proportionate to the percentages of male and female students attending the school; (2) that the school, although it has not achieved proportionality, has steadily been expanding athletic opportunities for the underrepresented group (male or female); or (3) that the athletics programs at the school accommodate the interests of students of both sexes. Title ix was written for both sexes, although, since women had relatively few athletic opportunities in higher education prior to its enactment, its impact has been especially great on women's programs.

In the 1960s there were no national championship competitions or athletic scholarships for women. By the early 1970s, prior to enactment of Title ix, athletic scholarships for women totaled approximately $100,000. The total by 2007 had reached about $421 million. Prior to 1972 about 32,000 women participated in intercollegiate sports; by 2007 the number had risen to more than 150,000. Clearly, Title ix has dramatically opened athletic doors for women as well as other doors that often follow athletics: a stronger sense of self-worth, enhanced understanding of teamwork, better preparation for professional careers, and, for many, an opportunity to earn a college degree that they otherwise might not be able to afford. There also is some opportunity, for a small percentage of women athletes, to continue in their sport professionally, for example, in basketball.

A continuing criticism is that the increased budget for women's sports has led to dropping some men's sports. That has occurred, but Title IX defenders respond by pointing out that colleges and universities have made the choice to put increasing funds into football and basketball rather than maintain some less expensive men's sports.

So how has Title IX affected football specifically? The answer is that it has not had much impact, certainly not an adverse effect overall. Since 1993, when Santa Clara University dropped its football program, approximately forty higher education institutions have added football as of 2007. Despite occasional cries of poverty by athletics directors, spending on football programs has continued to rise. Coaches' salaries have skyrocketed at some universities, reaching as high in 2007 as $3.45 million (Bob Stoops at Oklahoma) and $4 million (Nick Saban at Alabama).

Division I-A (FBS) football rosters routinely number 120 players or more, with the attendant costs for each player, including insurance, equipment, tutors, transportation, and housing. Kansas State University reported, for example, that even a walk-on, that is, a student-athlete not on an athletic scholarship, costs the program about $3,816 annually. A study reported by the National Women's Law Center in Washington DC notes that between 1996 and 2000 there was an annual increase of $3.57 million in expenditures for men's Division I-A sports, with 68 percent of the total ($2,463,000) going to football.

Defenders of big-budget football programs regularly argue that football programs help to fund other, low-revenue sports. Yet a 1999 study showed that 58 percent of Division I-A and I-AA (FBS and FCS) football programs did not even break even, let alone help fund other sports. The average annual deficits in these programs were approximately $1 million and $630,000 respectively.

The obvious conclusion is that Title IX, regardless of its impact on other sports, has done nothing to harm football programs, which collectively continue to thrive.

See also: Women Players.

Additional Reading:

Hogshead-Makar, Nancy, and Andrew Zimbalist, eds. *Equal Play: Title IX and Social Change*. Philadelphia: Temple University Press, 2007.

McDonagh, Eileen, and Laura Pappano. *Playing with the Boys: Why Separate Is Not Equal in Sports*. New York: Oxford University Press, 2008.

Mitchell, Nicole, and Lisa A. Ennis. *Encyclopedia of Title IX and Sports*. Westport CT: Greenwood, 2007.

"Title IX and Men's 'Minor' Sports: A False Conflict." National Women's Law Center Web site. http://www.nwlc.org/details.cfm?id=2735&section=athletics#rat.

NCAA Title IX Resource Center Web site. http://www.ncaa.org/wps/ncaa?ContentID=1488.

Tittle, Yelberton Abraham (Y.A.) (b. 1926)

Y. A. Tittle appears in the photograph kneeling in front of goalposts, bloodied and exhausted. Blood streams down his forehead and the side of his face, and he looks too lost in exhaustion and frustration to rise. He is almost bald, an old man who has finally reached the end of the football road. It is a moving spectacle. This incident, caught on film by Morris Berman after a Giants defeat by Pittsburgh in Tittle's final season and often noted as a visual depiction of the phenomenon referred to as "the agony of defeat," could represent the signature moment in the career of Tittle. But the fact is that it offers a misleading portrait of his career.

In fact, Tittle was an enormously talented and successful quarterback. He joined the Baltimore Colts of the All-America Football Conference out of Louisiana State University in 1948 and immediately made his presence felt, winning the Rookie of the Year award. Tittle then joined the National Football League with the Colts when the leagues merged in 1950. The Colts dissolved after the 1950 season, and Tittle moved on to the San Francisco 49ers. He made the Pro Bowl with San Francisco in 1953, 1954, 1957, and 1959.

After the 1960 season, San Francisco traded Tittle to the New York Giants, and the veteran quarterback went on to have his greatest seasons. He led his team to the Eastern Conference championship in each of his first three years with the Giants. In 1961 he completed more than 57 percent of his passes and received the NFL's Most Valuable Player award. The next year, he passed for 3,224 yards and thirty-three touchdowns. In 1963 he completed 60.2

percent of his passes while throwing for 3,145 yards and thirty-six touchdowns, earning another Most Valuable Player selection. The thirty-six touchdown passes remained the NFL record until Dan Marino threw for 48 touchdowns in 1984. Tittle also became the first quarterback to throw thirty or more touchdown passes two years in a row.

Unfortunately for Tittle, despite the strong supporting cast around him, the Giants could not quite get to the finish line. In each of those remarkable seasons from 1961 to 1963, New York lost in the championship game. The Packers intercepted Tittle four times in the 1961 title game and rolled over the Giants 37–0. The same teams met again the next year. The contest this time was much closer, but the Packers prevailed 16–7. In 1963 the Giants had a different opponent, the Chicago Bears, but the outcome was similar: a 14–10 defeat, with Tittle having perhaps the worst day of his career, throwing five interceptions. In 1964 the Giants stumbled to a 2-10-2 regular-season record, and Tittle, who turned thirty-eight during the season, saw his skills deteriorate. He threw only ten touchdown passes while being intercepted twenty-two times. After that disappointing season, he retired.

Tittle went into the insurance business and was inducted into the Pro Football Hall of Fame in 1971. In 1995 his daughter made him a focus of her study of the nature of heroism in her book *Giants and Heroes: A Daughter's Memoir of Y.A. Tittle.*

Apparently with the old quarterback's career highs and lows in mind, and seeing him as a genuine representative of his time, David Halberstam planned to interview Tittle for a new book he was writing about the Baltimore–New York championship game of 1958. On his way to the interview on April 23, 2007, Halberstam was involved in a fatal automobile accident, making Tittle an ironic ancillary to the circumstances surrounding the death of one of the twentieth century's most important journalists.

Additional Reading:

De Laet, Dianne Tittle. *Giants and Heroes: A Daughter's Memoir of Y.A. Tittle.* South Royalton VT: Steerforth, 1995.

Eskenazi, Gerald. *There Were Giants in Those Days.* New York: Grosset and Dunlap, 1976.

Tomlinson, LaDainian (LT) (b. 1979)

LaDainian Tomlinson established new NFL records in 2006 for most touchdowns and most points scored in a single season. Having overcome a variety of difficulties in his personal life, Tomlinson continued his remarkable path toward football immortality with widespread respect from players and fans alike. That respect came not only from his on-field accomplishments but also from his extensive charitable work.

Born in Rosebud, Texas, LaDainian Tomlinson had a childhood filled with struggles. While he was still a youth he lost a brother and his grandfather to death. His father, who imparted his love for football to his son, became disabled with a back injury. A divorce left LaDainian's mother, Loreane, with the task of caring for her remaining children by herself. Her efforts imparted to young LaDainian a passion for helping others that he would later manifest through his Touching Lives Foundation.

Despite these early difficulties, Tomlinson earned an athletic scholarship to Texas Christian University in Fort Worth, Texas, where he starred as a junior and senior (1998–99) after playing part-time during his first two years. Once given the starting job at running back, Tomlinson began to put up huge numbers. He rushed for 1,850 yards and eighteen touchdowns in 1998 and set a new NCAA single-game rushing record with 406 yards against the University of Texas at El Paso. The next year he led the nation with 2,158 rushing yards and scored twenty-two touchdowns, earning the Doak Walker Award as the best running back in the country.

The San Diego Chargers drafted Tomlinson in the first round in 2001, and the rookie picked up where he left off in college. In each of his seasons through 2007 he rushed for at least 1,200 yards and caught more than fifty passes. Also a threat with the option pass, he completed eight of eleven passes during those years, seven for touchdowns. By the end of 2007, he had amassed 129 touchdowns, 115 of them by rushing.

Tomlinson caught 100 passes in 2003 and scored twenty touchdowns in 2005, but he had his best overall season in 2006.

He led the league in rushing with 1,815 yards and earned well-deserved accolades for his record-setting scoring. He ran for twenty-eight touchdowns and caught passes for three more, the thirty-one total touchdowns breaking Shaun Alexander's record of twenty-eight, which he had set the previous year. Tomlinson's total of 186 points broke a much older record, set by Paul Hornung of the Green Bay Packers in 1960, when he scored 176 points with a combination of touchdowns, field goals, and extra points. Tomlinson also holds a variety of other records, including most consecutive games rushing for a touchdown (eighteen) and most games in one season with four or more touchdowns (three). He shares with former Baltimore Colts great Lenny Moore the mark for most consecutive games scoring a touchdown by any means (eighteen). The season brought Tomlinson the NFL's Most Valuable Player award and the ESPY Award for Male Athlete of the Year as well as a number of other awards from individual publications and organizations. Shortly after the conclusion of the season, however, his personal life received another difficult blow when his father and a brother-in-law were killed in an automobile accident.

Tomlinson (with Drew Brees) also was named corecipient of the Walter Payton Man of the Year Award for his humanitarian efforts as well as his on-field accomplishments. Tomlinson and his wife, LaTorsha, have organized a wide range of activities through their Touching Lives Foundation to help people in San Diego and their home state of Texas. The foundation organizes such events as youth football camps and a fishing trip for youngsters from the Monarch School in San Diego, which is a residence for homeless and at-risk teens. The foundation provides Thanksgiving dinners to more than one thousand San Diego families and Christmas gifts to young patients at San Diego Children's Hospital and Health Center. Through the "21 Club" project, the foundation invites twenty-one youngsters from San Diego youth groups to attend a Chargers game, complete with photographs of themselves on the field and gifts. The School Is Cool Scholarship Fund awards thirty college scholarships annually to high school students from San Diego and Tomlinson's own former high school, University High in Waco, Texas.

Tomlinson's efforts on and off the football field led the CBS television series *60 Minutes* to film a segment about his life, airing in the fall of 2007. It is clear that LaDainian Tomlinson believes not only in being very good on the gridiron but also in doing good.

See also: Education; Hornung, Paul Vernon.

Additional Reading:

Ellenport, Craig. *LaDainian Tomlinson: All-Pro On and Off the Field*. Berkeley Heights NJ: Enslow, 2006.

LaDainian Tomlinson Web site (with a link to the Touching Lives Foundation). http://ladainiantomlinson.com/home.htm.

Touch Football

Touch football is a version of American football that substitutes touching the ball carrier with either one or two hands rather than tackling the person. Consequently, as with flag football, touch football is a much less hazardous game than tackle football and can be played safely by a more heterogeneous group of players.

Touch football can be played by varying numbers of individuals at a time, often in a park or yard. Without yard markings or goal posts, improvisation often is necessary to determine how a team makes a first down or scores. Kicking and punting may be discarded out of necessity. In some cases, an individual plays for both teams, perhaps centering the ball or acting as quarterback.

Although often a playground sport, touch football also has been recognized as an effective way for more organized football teams to practice with minimal risk of injuries. Consequently, many college and high school teams play touch football during practice, especially to work on certain plays. Credit for developing touch football has been given to the United States Navy during the 1940s, although it is impossible to know precisely where or when the first game of touch football was actually played.

Various organizations have formalized touch football. Among them is the United States Flag & Touch Football League (USFTL), a nonprofit organization developed in Cleveland, Ohio, in 1988. The organization has promulgated standard rules, conducts clinics, trains and certifies officials, and produces educational aids such as videotapes and manuals. Under its auspices, a variety of state, sectional, regional, and national tournaments are held.

See also: Flag Football.

Additional Reading:
Unites States Flag & Touch Football League Web site. http://www.usftl.com.

Touchdown Jesus

At least where football is concerned, the most famous image of a deity is the mosaic of Jesus on the south side of the Theodore M. Hesburgh Library at the University of Notre Dame. The image is known as the *Word of Life* mural to those few observers who are not football fans.

Within the world of football, though, which at Notre Dame seems to be most of the world, observers fondly, if a bit irreverently, call the mural Touchdown Jesus, as the mural depicts Jesus with both arms raised in the traditional touchdown gesture. What has cemented the unofficial name in Notre Dame football is that the image is readily visible to game spectators over the walls of the stadium.

The mural is based on a commissioned painting by Millard Sheets. Sheets shows Jesus teaching a group of apostles and scholars, befitting the building to which the mural is affixed. The point is that Jesus is the ultimate teacher, and his gesture is meant to highlight his instruction while perhaps also elevating his students' eyes and thoughts to heaven. The impressive mural was constructed from eighty-one different types of stones from sixteen countries.

For football fans, however, Jesus appears to be signaling another touchdown for the Fighting Irish. That his arms are permanently raised merely symbolizes the eternal hope that fills the hearts of Notre Dame fans, even in down seasons. Perhaps the mural also signals to the Irish faithful that Jesus, after all, really is on their side.

See also: Golden Dome; "Hail Mary" Pass; Holy Roller; Immaculate Reception; Religion

Additional Reading:
Eden, Scott. *Touchdown Jesus: Faith and Fandom at Notre Dame.* New York: Simon and Schuster, 2005.

Trades

Trades are an important part of many professional team sports. They are one way in which teams attempt to improve, engineering player exchanges to shore up weak positions on the team while trading players no longer considered essential. For fans, trades help fill in the long off-season. Fans think about possible trades, concoct trades in their own minds, and debate the wisdom of accomplished trades. Some trades bring sadness because they remove a favorite player; others induce rejoicing as they promise better times ahead for the hometown team.

Yet those same fans that revel in sports trades never experience being traded in any other profession. A business does not trade three entry-level workers for a midlevel management figure; a high school does not trade a Latin teacher and a librarian for a Social Studies instructor. If an employer actually tried that, most employees would be quick to sue. An employee may be transferred within a company, but that is hardly the same thing. Americans pride themselves on freedom, and freedom to choose or not to choose a place of employment is one of those important freedoms—even if many people, from a practical standpoint, do not have a lot of employment options.

So professional football has long practiced that most un-American, but American-loved (within sports), practice of making trades. General managers, of course, refer to it as trading contracts, not people, but that is a fine point that has no impact on the final result. Most daily newspapers, in fact, have a special section devoted to listing transactions.

Some trades work out; others fail. Some are small, even inconsequential (except to the individual or individuals traded); others involve a welter of players. The largest trade in National Football League history occurred on October 13, 1989. Eighteen players (some of them draft choices, later fleshed out with actual players) moved between the Dallas Cowboys and Minnesota Vikings. The key to the trade was running back Herschel Walker, whom Minnesota coveted. During the previous season, Walker's third in the NFL, he had carried 361 times for 1,514 yards and caught fifty-three passes for another 505 yards. He looked like one of the greatest running backs ever, and Vikings officials saw in him a path to the Super Bowl.

Accompanying Walker to Minnesota were four draft choices (three immediately and a fourth following an ancillary deal between Dallas and the San Diego Chargers). None of the draft picks were higher than the third round. In return, Dallas received five players and eight draft choices, including first- and second-round picks in 1990, 1991, and 1992. Analysts usually consider the trade disastrous for Minnesota. Walker never approached his 1988 level with the Vikings. His most productive year with Minnesota was his first, actually split between the Cowboys and Vikings, when he rushed for 915 yards. After two disappointing seasons, he was on his way to a new team, the Philadelphia Eagles, where he surpassed the thousand-yard mark in 1992 but then steadily slipped, ending his career in 1997. In the meantime, the Vikings traded away much of their future with the high draft choices that they sent to Dallas.

What was bad for Minnesota, however, was good for Dallas, which having loaded up on high draft choices was ready for a successful run through the 1990s. Dallas won one game in 1989, the year of the trade. The Cowboys improved to 7-9 the following year and made the playoffs in 1991 with an 11-5 record. In 1992, 1993, and 1995, Dallas won the Super Bowl. The Vikings should have heeded the old saying: "Be careful what you wish for; you may get it."

The ideal trade, football people will say, is one that benefits both sides, as a trade that turns out to be too lopsided may inhibit a general manager from making a future deal. For that reason, teams tend not to make trades with divisional rivals. Helping another team is all right if you help yourself at the same time, but helping a direct rival always threatens to be counterproductive. So if trading ever moves into other realms of American society, no trade is likely to be consummated with a rival selling the same product or that nearby high school trying to attract the same students.

Additional Reading:

Bruton, James. *A Tradition of Purple: An Inside Look at the Minnesota Vikings.* Champaign IL: Sports Publishing, 2007.

Donovan, Jim, Ken Sims, and Frank Coffey. *The Dallas Cowboys Encyclopedia: The Ultimate Guide to America's Team.* Rev. ed. Secaucus NJ: Carol Publishing Group, 1999.

Trading Cards

Football cards made their first appearance in the late nineteenth century, usually as inserts in packages of cigarettes. What is usually recognized as the first football card was produced around 1887 and distributed within packs of Old Judge and Gypsy Queen cigarettes from Goodwin & Company. The company offered smokers fifty cards, but only one was of a football player—Henry "Harry" W. Beecher, a Yale star as well as the grandson of the famous clergyman and newspaper editor Henry Ward Beecher and grandnephew of Harriet Beecher Stowe, author of the abolitionist novel *Uncle Tom's Cabin.*

The Mayo Cut Plug Tobacco Company in the early 1890s distributed thirty-five cards of top players from what would come to be known as the Ivy League. Although football fans today may wonder why players from Princeton, Yale, and their ilk would merit such attention, in fact, college football grew up on those Eastern campuses, and the Eastern football teams were some of the early powerhouses.

One of the most valuable football cards is from this Mayo set. Through a printing error, one card lacks the player's name and college affiliation, but the player has been identified as John Dunlop of Harvard, who helped to develop the flying wedge formation. According to FootballCardShop.com, fewer than ten of these cards are known to exist, and the price of one in excellent to mint condition is about $18,000.

From the late nineteenth century through the first half of the twentieth, multisport sets of cards were common. These typically included some football players, usually college stars, with Red Grange seemingly the most popular subject. Not all of the sets, though, were designed to sell tobacco products. The sporting goods giant A.G. Spalding issued a set in 1926 under its Sports Company of America imprint that included Red Grange, in this case wearing a Bears uniform, and Ernie Nevers.

By the 1930s other products were being marketed with the aid of trading cards, including football cards. These included Dixie Cup ice cream (with the picture on the underside of the lid), boxes of candy, doughnuts, Kellogg's cereal, and packages of gum. In some cases, as with the boxes of doughnuts, the cards had to be cut out of the surrounding cardboard that comprised the container. A 1933 set of cards, the Goudey Sport Kings, included athletes from a variety of sports, among them the football immortals Red Grange, Knute Rockne, and Jim Thorpe. The Sport Kings set foreshadowed the alliance of gum and trading cards that would firmly shove tobacco products aside and become the dominant product relationship for several decades after World War II.

Topps got into the football card business in 1948 with its Hocus-Focus Magic set, which included football stars. The cards came in packages of bubble gum but had to be developed by the buyer. When a youngster held the card up to the light, as if by magic the picture appeared—at least most of the time. In that same year, both Bowman and Leaf packaged football cards with bubble gum, a marketing device that would continue for decades, supplying youngsters with squares of pink gum that, if the child happened to leave the package out in the sun, would leach into the cards.

Topps temporarily dropped out of the football-card business after 1948, leaving the field to its competitors, but returned to football cards in 1955 with an "All-American" set. The next year, Topps purchased Bowman and stood alone in the business for the rest of the decade.

During the 1960s the American Football League arose to challenge the National Football League. Fleer produced a set of cards depicting AFL players in 1960 and continued to do so (adding NFL players for one year, in 1961) until Philadelphia Gum bought the right to issue NFL cards in 1964, shoving Topps into the AFL and pushing Fleer completely out of the football (as well as baseball) card business. In 1968 Topps secured the right to issue cards with both NFL and AFL players and continued to be the primary producer of football cards after the merger of the two leagues. Topps even produced cards for the United States Football League during its short life (1983–85).

Topps enjoyed a monopoly of the football-card business until 1989, at which time competitors began to arrive in droves. By 1992 twenty nationally distributed sets of football cards were available.

As with baseball cards, football cards, especially after World War II, were primarily the province of youngsters who collected and sometimes traded them. By the latter decades of the twentieth century, however, collecting had become a business with young entrepreneurs buying sets and maintaining them in mint condition toward a future when they hoped to sell them for a substantial profit. With money to be made, large numbers of adults returned to their childhood practice of buying cards or embarked upon the practice for the first time. Card shows proliferated, as did shops buying and selling cards. Collectors, young and old, found plenty of magazines informing them of the value of their possessions. Not all boys and girls turned into businesspeople, of course, some traditionalists continuing to approach cards the way their grandfathers had. Along with the rise of trading-card finances, the old partner, bubble gum, disappeared. Not much hurts the value of a card more than a big pink stain.

Many of the cards today far outpace their earlier versions in quality, the photographs sharp, the colors vibrant, the surfaces glossy, and in some sets the images almost three-dimensional. One pays for the visual effects, of course, a recent package of Bowman's 2007 NFL cards selling for $3.00 for ten cards, a 2007 package of Upper Deck supplying fifteen cards for $5.00, and Topps offering nine cards for $1.75.

See also: Commercials and Advertisements; Grange, Harold Edward; Rockne, Knute Kenneth; Thorpe, James Francis.

Additional Reading:
Beckett, James. *Beckett Official Price Guide: Football Cards.* 27th ed. New York: Random House, 2008.
Bonner, Mike. *Collecting Football Cards: A Complete Guide with Prices.* Radnor PA: Wallace-Homestead, 1995.
Bonner, Mike, and Carl Lamendola. *Collecting Vintage Football Cards: A Complete Guide with Checklists.* Bangor ME: BookLocker.com, 2007.
Clary, Jack. *Topps Football Cards: The Complete Picture Collection: A History, 1956–1986.* Ed. L. Kirshbaum. Statistical index by William F. Himmelman and Larry Schwartz. New York: Warner Books, 1986.

Trick Plays

Football has always had its trick plays, forcing football officials, like people in other walks of life, to try to determine what is within the rules and what is not. What constitutes ingenuity, and what is simple dishonesty? It is good to be imaginative, most people would say, but bad to take advantage of others, yet into which category does a particular action fall? Innovation is commendable, but unsportsmanlike conduct is dishonorable. Most people decry loopholes that permit compliance with the letter of the law while shoving aside the spirit of the law, yet many of those same people will take advantage of any opportunity that arises.

Over the course of football's history, rule after rule has been introduced to try to encourage innovation but contain out-and-out trickery. The vast accumulation of these regulations has removed the most egregious tricks, but not, of course, the defect in human nature that leads people to peering into every nook and cranny of the law to find an opening.

One of the most entertaining trick plays, in retrospect, although assuredly not to those who suffered its consequences, was the hidden-ball trick. All fans can admire a quarterback's deft ball handling, a quick and graceful reach to one back while he then hands off to another. That clearly is clever but not overtly deceitful. A particularly clear-sighted defender has a reasonable chance to follow the motions. Not so, however, when Glenn "Pop" Warner had his Carlisle Indians

hide the football under a jersey, especially when all of those jerseys had a football-shaped patch sewn on. When Carlisle played Harvard in 1903, the Harvard coach, Percy Haughton, would have none of the patches and demanded they be removed. However, under the rules of the time, he could not prevent stuffing the ball under a jersey.

As the second half opened, Warner pulled out the trick play. Jimmy Johnson caught the ball and was immediately encircled by his teammates who formed a V wedge. Johnson, hidden from sight of the Harvard players, stuffed the ball under guard Charlie Dillon's jersey. Most of the players removed their helmets and carried them like footballs. Dillon, however, ran with arms flapping as if to block, clearly not carrying anything under his arm. Appropriately, the game was played on October 31, yet Harvard ultimately earned the Halloween treat, winning 12–11. Finally, in 1911, the rules caught up to Warner's ingenuity (or unsportsmanlike trickery), outlawing the hidden-ball play.

Another great coach, Fielding Yost of Michigan, devised a remarkable trick pass play and used it against the University of Pennsylvania on November 16, 1907. Yost devised a formation with the center actually playing right end and snapping the ball from there. The rest of the players were at least 5 yards from the snapper because, under 1907 rules, a pass could not be thrown from a point less than 5 yards laterally from the center. In a complicated maneuver that involved the snap and two passes, Michigan scored, apparently tying the game at 6 all. The play also appeared to conform to the requirement that a pass be caught at a point at least 12 yards to the side of the center, in this case to the left of the center. In fact, the center (or snapper) was far to the right in this formation. Yet the referee ruled the play illegal, claiming that the ball was not caught 12 yards to the left, apparently thinking of the usual position of the center rather than where the center had actually lined up on the play. Nonetheless, those who abhor deceit can consider justice to have been done. Pennsylvania defeated Michigan 6–0.

The great coaches seemed the most likely to push the ethical limits of the game through trick plays. The reason may lie in their greater creativity and their burning desire to find ways to win, qualities that helped make them great and sometimes sent them a bit off the track. Other coaching immortals who stand accused of this sort of extreme creativity include the fabled Notre Dame coaches Knute Rockne and Frank Leahy and Michigan's Bo Schembechler.

Rockne developed the Notre Dame shift, which involved quick movement of the offense at the line of scrimmage to prevent the defense from getting set. By 1927 the rules-makers had caught up with that trick, requiring a full-second stop before snapping the ball and increasing the penalty for an illegal shift from 5 to 15 yards. Leahy specialized in feigned injuries when he had run out of timeouts and needed to stop the clock. A ruling in 1948 that faking injuries was unethical had not proved sufficient to deter the practice, as in Notre Dame's 14–14 tie against Iowa in 1953 that saved the team's unbeaten record. Leahy had players fake injuries in each half, leading to scores, the latter coming with two seconds left in the game. Leahy also refined Rockne's shift, employing what was called a "sucker shift" to help defeat Southern California 9–0 in 1952. The false-start rule was strengthened to include any movement that would trigger the play to start, but the American Football Coaches Association asked to handle the problem of fake injuries. It did so with considerable success, bringing the moral judgment of all the coaches to bear on potential misdeeds by individual members. No one seemingly wanted to be called a cheater by his peers.

Bo Schembechler's Wolverines were playing on the natural grass surface at Purdue in 1979, and he was concerned about the footing. He consequently used his ingenuity to circumvent without breaking the rules (at least the letter of the law). His opposing coach, Jim Young, who had served as a Michigan assistant and consequently was aware of Bo's trickery, informed the officials that Michigan players were wearing cleats that exceeded the half-inch limit.

Schembechler, when accosted by one of the officials, quickly took off one of the cleats to show that, in fact, it was not longer than the limit. However, a washer added to the shoe extended the distance from shoe to grass, achieving the same effect of a longer cleat. Players were permitted to keep their cleats and washers for the nonce, but the rules were changed to establish a maximum length from "tip of cleat to sole of shoe."

Perhaps the two most audacious trick plays occurred in 1913, a year in which the demons of trickery were especially active. The Iowa offense approached the line of scrimmage in a game against Northwestern, and Hawkeye linemen started pointing at the defense, claiming that Northwestern should be penalized. Quarterback Sammy Gross brazenly picked up the ball and announced that he would mark off the penalty. While the defenders stared in amazement at Gross's effrontery, he marched off the 15 yards and then broke into a run. The play led to still another new rule, this one prohibiting the ball being put into play except through a legal snap.

That same year, a new kind of teamwork developed during pass plays, the so-called Mutt and Jeff play. A tall individual would hoist a shorter one onto his shoulders, with the rider, stretching far above the heads of the defenders, able to snare a pass with little chance of an interception. Such a play was good for a laugh, although laughter was not deemed a primary goal of the game. Naturally, another rule entered the rule book.

"Honesty is the best policy," many a wise adult has cautioned children. That has not always been the case in football or in life. Cheating, deceiving, or tricking in order to gain an advantage has been the practice of many a footballer, including some of the sport's most revered coaches. In recent years the game appears to have improved its honesty quotient. One is unlikely to see a player today riding astride another or a running back crossing the goal line with a football-shaped bulge under his jersey. However, that may have more to do with the thickness of the rule book than with the depth of coaches' and players' integrity.

See also: Carlisle Indian Industrial School; Cheating; Leahy, Francis William; Rockne, Knute Kenneth; Warner, Glen Scobey; Yost, Fielding Harris.

Additional Reading:
Nelson, David M. *Anatomy of a Game: Football, the Rules, and the Men Who Made the Game.* Newark: University of Delaware Press, 1994.

Triple Crown

American society places great value on both specialization and versatility. Given the complexity of our society, efficiency at performing challenging tasks usually is best achieved by someone who performs that task repeatedly. Yet at the same time, we still admire the Renaissance person, the individual who seems to know so much about so many things and can accomplish a wide range of tasks.

Football is an enormously complex team sport, with each player needing to perform his specialized function well or the play will break down. The finest passer and receiver are nothing if a lineman misses a block, permitting a defensive lineman or linebacker to get to the quarterback before he has time to pass. Or everyone can block brilliantly, but if the halfback cuts the wrong way, the play is a bust. So each player must perform his specialized role as perfectly as possible.

But in football as in the wider society, specialization coexists with versatility. Less so, to be sure, than when players played both offense and defense, but versatility still counts. We admire, for example, and reward with a big contract, the complete back who can run, catch passes, and block.

So the player who can lead in more than one category is especially admirable—and rare. Leading the league in multiple categories is more difficult in football than in baseball, perhaps because the specialization-versatility pendulum has swung more toward specialization in football than in baseball (even in the American League with the designated hitter and pitchers who never have to hoist a bat).

The triple crown exists in both sports, but in baseball the three categories are fixed: batting average, home runs, and runs batted in. Limiting the accomplishment to those three categories makes winning baseball's triple crown especially difficult. In football, the triple crown has historically referred to leading the league in any three major areas. Yet even during the both-ways heyday of versatility in football, a player seldom won the triple crown; and since defensive and offensive players became strictly delineated, no one has managed the feat.

Only three players have managed the triple crown in football, and strangely enough, all three did it within a space of four seasons. In 1943 Slingin' Sammy Baugh, the great Washington Redskins quarterback (and defensive back), led the National Football League in passing (133 completions, which netted 1,754 yards and twenty-three touchdowns), punting (fifty punts, which produced 2,295 yards for a 45.9-yard average), and interceptions (eleven).

Steve Van Buren, a running back with the Philadelphia Eagles, achieved the triple crown in 1945 by rushing for 832 yards, scoring 110 points (on eighteen touchdowns and two extra points), and kickoff returns (thirteen for 373 yards and an average of 28.7 yards per return). Then just one year later, Bill Dudley of the Pittsburgh Steelers led the league with 604 yards rushing, ten interceptions for 242 yards, and a punt-return record of twenty-seven for 385 yards.

So in football, specialization seems to be the wave of the present and of the future. Even place-kickers, who used to do other things (such as Lou Groza, the Cleveland Browns lineman; Paul Hornung, the Green Bay Packers halfback; and George Blanda, the ageless Bears and Raiders quarterback), now usually only line up and kick. We will continue to value the player who can do multiple tasks well, but he will remain something of an

aberration in football and a reminder of
what used to be.

See also: Baugh, Samuel Adrian; Hornung, Paul
Vernon.

Additional Reading:

Carroll, Bob, et al., eds. *Total Football II: The Of-
ficial Encyclopedia of the National Football
League.* New York: HarperCollins, 1999.
Coenen, Craig R. *From Sandlots to the Super
Bowl: The National Football League, 1920–
1967.* Knoxville: University of Tennessee
Press, 2005.

Unitas, John Constantine (Johnny U, the Golden Arm) (1933–2002)

Johnny Unitas is as close to being Mr. Quarterback as anyone who ever played the game. A "rags to riches" story, Unitas overcame humble beginnings and initial failures to set the standard for professional quarterbacks.

Born in Pittsburgh in 1933, Unitas was only five years old when his father died; he was raised by his Lithuanian immigrant mother. Finding a college proved difficult. A tryout at Notre Dame did not elicit an invitation, and Indiana University also turned him down. Then after the University of Pittsburgh offered Unitas an athletic scholarship, he failed the entrance exam. Louisville, however, accepted him, and Unitas played well but not spectacularly for weak Louisville teams.

His hometown Pittsburgh Steelers drafted him in the ninth round in 1955 but cut him, leaving Unitas to work construction while playing for the Bloomfield Rams semipro team for six dollars per game. In 1956 Unitas secured a tryout with the Baltimore Colts and was signed as a backup. But when starting quarterback George Shaw was injured against the Chicago Bears in the fourth game of the season, Unitas was pressed into service. His first pass was into the right flat. Cornerback J. C. Caroline intercepted it and raced 59 yards for a touchdown. The rest of the game went badly as Unitas and his running backs had trouble with handoffs and fumbles. The Colts lost 58–27.

The rest of Unitas's professional story, however, would be much brighter. He played effectively in the next game, a 28–21 win over Green Bay, and by the end of the season had completed 55.6 percent of his passes, at the time the best completion percentage ever by a rookie quarterback. By 1958 Baltimore was champion of the NFL with an overtime victory over the New York Giants in the title game—a contest often called the greatest professional game ever. Unitas led his team downfield against the Giants, a drive that commenced with two minutes left in the game and concluded with a tying field goal with seven seconds on the clock. In overtime, Unitas led an 80-yard drive, mixing clutch passes to receivers Raymond Berry and Jim Mutscheller with runs by L. G. "Long Gone" Dupre and Alan "the Horse" Ameche. From the 1-yard line, Ameche scored the winning touchdown.

The Colts repeated as NFL champions in 1959. Unitas was sidelined by an injury for most of the Colts' 1968 regular season and Super Bowl. During the Super Bowl game, however, he was put in during the second half and led his team's only touchdown drive in the loss to Joe Namath and the New York Jets. Two years later, the Colts, with Unitas quarterbacking, returned to the Super Bowl, winning 16–13 over Dallas.

Unitas played with Baltimore through 1972 and spent one final season with the San Diego Chargers. When he retired, he held most important passing records, many of which have since been broken. One record that may well endure forever, though, is Unitas's feat of throwing at least one touchdown pass in forty-seven consecutive games, stretching from December 9, 1956 (his rookie season), until the next-to-last game of 1960 when Los Angeles defeated Baltimore 10–3. During his career, Unitas was named the NFL's Player of the Year three times: in 1959, 1964, and 1967.

Unitas cut a memorable figure in his crewcut and his high-top shoes. After he died of a heart attack on September 11, 2002, Indianapolis Colts quarterback Peyton Manning wanted to wear the Unitas style of cleats but was refused by the NFL. Ravens quarterback Chris Redman wore the high-tops without asking permission and was fined $5,000.

Many honors have come Unitas's way, including induction into the Pro Football Hall of Fame in 1979. In a fifty-year celebration of the NFL, Unitas was voted the league's all-time greatest player. Statues of Unitas stand in Unitas Plaza in front of the Baltimore Ravens stadium and in the north end zone of the University of Louisville stadium. Some students at Louisville enjoy the privilege of rooming in Unitas Tower. The Johnny Unitas Golden Arm Award goes annually to the top senior college quarterback.

At Unitas's funeral, Raymond Berry, who had caught so many touchdown passes from him, gave the eulogy. He spoke of many of the qualities that made Unitas great, including his leadership, toughness, and team concept. He also spoke of the love that he and other teammates had for Unitas. When Jim Parker, the great offensive lineman, for example, heard of Unitas's death, he pulled his car over to the side of the road and wept because, after protecting him so long against defensive linemen, he was not there at the end to protect him.

See also: Drive, The; Greatest Game; Namath, Joseph William.

Additional Reading:

Callahan, Tom. *Johnny U: The Life and Times of John Unitas.* New York: Crown Publishers, 2006.

Sahadi, Lou. *Johnny Unitas: America's Quarterback.* Chicago: Triumph Books, 2004.

Towle, Mike. *Johnny Unitas: Mister Quarterback.* Nashville: Cumberland House, 2003.

Unitas, John. *Playing Pro Football to Win.* With Harold Rosenthal. Garden City NY: Doubleday, 1968.

Unitas, John, and Ed Fitzgerald. *Pro Quarterback, My Own Story.* New York: Simon and Schuster, 1965.

United States Football League

The United States Football League featured some of the all-time football greats (Jim Kelly, Steve Young, and Reggie White, among others), three Heisman winners

(Herschel Walker, Mike Rozier, Doug Flutie), some excellent coaches such as George Allen and Jim Mora, major media deals with ABC and ESPN, good television ratings, a February to July season that eliminated football competition, a commissioner (former ESPN president Chet Simmons) who knew both sports and the media, and the incomparable Donald Trump. Yet the league still failed after three years, proving that nothing succeeds in producing failure like bad decisions.

Simmons suggested two guidelines to all owners: that each team limit its player payroll to approximately $1.2 million and that teams not sign players who had college eligibility remaining. Within a few months of that directive, the New Jersey Generals signed Heisman Trophy winner and outstanding running back Herschel Walker of the University of Georgia for $5 million over three years. So much for the guidelines, which were designed to avoid bidding wars and keep the teams fiscally viable.

The USFL began play in 1983 with twelve teams arranged in three divisions. Walker led the league in rushing with 1,812 yards while the Generals' attendance averaged 33,822. Nonetheless, the team finished a disappointing 6-12. The Philadelphia Stars, which would be the top team during the league's short history, finished 15-3 but lost the championship game to the Michigan Panthers 24–22. Good television ratings and attendance figures that largely lived up to expectations could not overcome the excessive

spending of the teams, which averaged a $3.3 million deficit for the year.

The Generals had a new owner, Donald Trump, in 1984, and the team improved to 14-4 as expansion increased the number of teams from twelve to eighteen, now in four divisions. Jim Kelly, who would become a Pro Football Hall of Fame quarterback with the Buffalo Bills in the National Football League, mastered the run-and-shoot offense while making the Houston Gamblers (a fitting name) both exciting and successful (13-5). Kelly passed for 5,219 yards and forty-four touchdowns, winning the USFL's Most Valuable Player award.

George Allen, who had led outstanding NFL teams in Los Angeles and Washington, fashioned a strong defense with the Arizona Wranglers that was just good enough (10-8) to sneak into the playoffs. A playoff loss to eventual champion Philadelphia was his final game as a professional head coach. For the second straight year, however, league losses totaled about $40 million.

Then came two decisions that would contribute to the demise of the USFL. One was to switch to a fall schedule in 1986, which had immediate ramifications for teams that would have to go head-to-head with NFL teams. Some teams quit; others moved to non-NFL cities, the Stars among them. The USFL champions switched from Philadelphia, where the NFL Eagles were well established, to Baltimore, which had lost the Colts to Indianapolis prior to the 1984 season. Despite the change in locale and a mediocre regular-season record (10-7-1), the Stars repeated as champions in 1985. Overall, the league dropped from eighteen to fourteen teams for its third season and restructured into two conferences without divisions.

The second ominous decision was to sue the NFL in October 1984, charging the older league with violating antitrust law by pressuring television networks not to broadcast USFL games in the fall. The USFL asked for monetary damages, which would be tripled under antitrust law, and an injunction to prevent the NFL from entering into contracts with the networks. The case went before a federal court in New York. With the league losing money and attendance and television ratings generally down in 1985, and several teams disbanding after the season, the USFL was increasingly dependent on winning in the courts in order to continue playing on the field.

A decision was rendered in July 1986, finding that the NFL had violated antitrust law. The jury, however, apparently believed that the real reasons for the USFL's financial difficulties lay with the league itself. Consequently, the jury awarded the sum of one dollar, tripled to three dollars. Commissioner Harry Usher, who had replaced Simmons shortly after the lawsuit was filed, announced on August 4, 1986, that the league was suspending operations, including cancellation of the 1986 season, pending an appeal. Most players who were able to do so joined the NFL, and when a federal appeals court in New York upheld the original judgment on March 10, 1988, the USFL was no more.

See also: Young, Jon Steven; White, Reginald Howard.

Additional Reading:
Byrne, Jim. *The $1 League: The Rise and Fall of the USFL.* New York: Prentice Hall, [1987].
USFL Web site. http://www.oursportscentral.com/usfl/index.php.

Upshaw, Eugene Thurman, Jr. (1945–2008)

Gene Upshaw was a Hall of Fame guard with the Oakland Raiders for fifteen years, the first player who spent most of his time at guard to earn induction into the Hall. His second career was as a labor leader, including serving as executive director of the National Football League Players Association (NFLPA) from 1983 to 2008. In recent years, after securing relative peace with league management, he came under strong criticism from retired players accusing the league and the union of failing to offer enough help to needy former players.

Upshaw attended Texas A&I (now Texas A&M–Kingsville), earning NAIA All-America honors while playing center, tackle, and end. Taken in the first round of the 1967 draft, the first joint NFL-AFL draft, he played his entire career with Oakland. At one point, he started 207 consecutive games. Upshaw—an intelligent, strong, and fast lineman—was especially effective leading the sweep. He made all-league seven times and played in Super Bowls II, XI, and XV, the last two winning efforts. The appearances made him the only person to play in Super Bowls in three different decades. He was inducted into the Pro Football Hall of Fame in 1987.

Upshaw had been involved with the NFLPA while playing with Oakland—as a player representative, member of the executive committee, and president. In 1983 he was named executive director. In his various union roles, he was intimately involved with the Collective Bargaining Agreements of 1977, 1982, and 1993, as well as the extensions negotiated in 1996, 1998, 2002, and 2006.

While helping to win considerable advancements for the players in salaries, benefits, and, of special significance, free agency, he also increasingly faced criticism from former players who felt left out of the riches. Their complaints focused on inadequate assistance for veterans suffering health and financial problems as well as unfair sharing of revenue from the union's licensing program, National Football League Players Incorporated (also known as Players Inc.). Upshaw defended his record and that of the NFLPA in appearances before Congress and elsewhere while committing himself to further address the needs of those who helped make the NFL the popular and lucrative sport that it has become.

Upshaw received the Byron "Whizzer" White Humanitarian Award in 1980 for service to the sport, the community, and the country. In 1982 the A. Phillip Randolph Award was bestowed on him for his accomplishments as a black leader. The NCAA Division II sports information directors annually present the Gene Upshaw Division II Lineman of the Year Award.

On August 20, 2008, Gene Upshaw died unexpectedly of pancreatic cancer after being diagnosed with the illness only days earlier.

See also: Commissioners; Davis, Allen; Labor-Management Relations; Retirement; Super Bowl.

Additional Reading:
LaMarre, Tom. *Stadium Stories: Oakland Raiders.* Guilford CT: Globe Pequot Press, 2003.
NFL Players Association Web site. http://www.nflpa.org.

Vietnam War

The Vietnam War did not have the impact on football and other sports of earlier wars, especially World War II. Yet football players and fans alike, as members of American society, could not totally escape a war that came close to ripping the country apart. It is also true that each death, to those closely associated with the person who has died, is huge.

So it would be unfair to minimize the effects of the Vietnam War because, for example, only seven active professional athletes (six of them football players) served in the Vietnam War, or because just one active professional athlete died in the war. Altogether, about twenty-eight NFL players at some point, in most cases before playing professional ball, served in the military during the war. Most athletes, however, chose the reserves as a safer and less professionally disruptive military alternative. College deferments kept most college players on campus and away from the jungles and rice paddies of Vietnam, at least until they graduated. Then Pres. Richard Nixon ended the draft in January 1973, freeing athletes as well as other potentially draft-eligible individuals from having to enter military service.

Still, powerful examples of heroism and dedication link the world of football with the Vietnam War, such as the story of a professional athlete who did lose his life in the war: Lt. Robert Kalsu. Bob Kalsu was born in Oklahoma in 1945, starred as a high school athlete, was recruited to play football at the University of Oklahoma, and earned All-America honors as an offensive lineman as a senior in 1967. He also was team captain that year as Oklahoma swept through its season with just one loss, 9–7, to Texas. A seemingly natural leader, Kalsu was a cadet colonel in the Reserve Officers' Training Corps (ROTC) on campus. Oklahoma capped its season by edging Tennessee 26–24 on January 1, 1968, and later that month Bob Kalsu married his sweetheart, Jan Darrow.

Kalsu's military obligation apparently scared away some professional teams, but the Buffalo Bills of the American Football League drafted him in the eighth round. Kalsu was commissioned a second lieutenant after graduation and also embarked on a professional football career. He resisted efforts by friends to persuade him to enter the reserves, arguing that he was no better than anyone else and that he had made a commitment to serve on active duty. Meanwhile, he earned a starting job at right guard for the Bills in 1968 and was named their Rookie of the Year. That season, however, would be his only one.

By July 21, 1970, Bob Kalsu was at Firebase Ripcord on top of a hill more than three thousand feet above sea level in northern South Vietnam northeast of A Shau Valley and northwest of Hue, not far from the demilitarized zone. An injury to his commanding officer had put Kalsu in charge of a battery of six howitzers. The North Vietnamese regularly pounded the Ripcord position with mortars, sometimes adding a round of tear gas.

Kalsu, though, was feeling good. He had a wife he loved, a twenty-month-old daughter, and another baby due that very day. His men respected him because he was both brave and gentle, and because he would not ask his men to do anything he would not do, such as unload artillery shells from the supply helicopters.

However, the tear gas that day made breathing difficult in Kalsu's bunker, so he stepped out to get some air. Just then another round hit, instantly killing the young soldier, husband, father, and football star. Two days later, in the early morning of July 23, Bob Kalsu's wife gave birth to their son.

Don Steinbrunner, whose death in the war has only recently come to light, shares with Kalsu the sad distinction of being the only men with NFL experience who died in Vietnam. A former Cleveland Browns tackle who played in eight games in 1953, Steinbrunner served in the air force as a navigator and died when his plane was shot down in 1967.

Rocky Bleier's Vietnam story was much less tragic. He played for three years at Notre Dame, starting at halfback as a junior for the 1966 national champions and serving as team captain as a senior. The Pittsburgh Steelers took Bleier in the sixteenth round of the 1968 NFL Draft. He played sparingly that first season with Pittsburgh and was then drafted again, this time into military service.

On August 20, 1969, Private Bleier was carrying a grenade launcher when his platoon came under fire in Hiep Duc Valley, which was about forty miles below Da Nang and the location of major fighting between the North Vietnamese and Americans that summer. A wound to Bleier's left thigh knocked him down, and after he crawled about two hundred yards, a grenade exploded nearby, sending shrapnel into both of his legs.

The wound seriously threatened Bleier's career, but he made a remarkable physical comeback and returned to the Steelers in 1971. He helped his team win the Super Bowl after the 1974, 1975, 1978, and 1979 seasons and gained more than a thousand yards rushing in 1976.

Bleier chronicled his experiences in a memoir, *Fighting Back: The Rocky Bleier Story*. In 2007 he received the Distinguished American Award from the NFL, given to an individual who applies character-building traits inculcated through amateur football—such as leadership qualities—to other aspects of the individual's personal and professional life.

Not surprisingly, many of the former college football players who served in Vietnam were service-academy graduates. One of the most famous of these was Pete Dawkins. Overcoming polio, Dawkins starred as a halfback at Army in the late 1950s and won the Heisman Trophy as a senior in 1958. He also was a Rhodes Scholar, president of his class at West Point, top cadet officer, and an All-East hockey player, along with many other honors that he received. In 1975 he was named to the National Football Foundation College Football Hall of Fame.

During his tours in Vietnam during the 1960s, Dawkins served with great distinction, earning the Combat Infantry Badge, two Bronze Stars with "V" for valor, the Air Medal, and the Joint Services Commendation Medal. When he left Vietnam, the soldier who succeeded him at his post was Bill Carpenter, the "Lonely End," who had been Dawkins's teammate at Army. Dawkins later earned a doctorate from Princeton University and climbed steadily through the military ranks, becoming a brigadier general in 1981. In 2002 the Association of Graduates of the United States Military Academy of West Point awarded Dawkins its Distinguished Graduate Award.

Although the immediate impact of the Vietnam War on football was markedly less than that of World War II, those former (or future) football players who served in Vietnam generally did so with distinction. If they were relatively few in contrast with earlier wars, they certainly were not inconsequential.

See also: Heisman Trophy; Super Bowl; World War II.

Additional Reading:

Bleier, Rocky. *Fighting Back.* Rev. ed. New York: Stein and Day, 1980.

Nack, William. "A Name on the Wall." *Sports Illustrated,* July 23, 2001, 60–73.

Pennington, Bill. "Fundamental Principles: Pete Dawkins, 1958." In *The Heisman: Great American Stories of the Men Who Won.* Ed. Bill Pennington, 140–57. New York: ReganBooks, 2004.

W

Walker, Ewell Doak, Jr. (the Doaker, Dynamite Doak, Dauntless Doak) (1927–1998)

Doak Walker virtually defined versatility. As a three-time All-American at Southern Methodist University in the 1940s, he carried the ball, caught passes, threw passes, returned kickoffs and punts, and kicked field goals and extra points. His ability as a defensive back was sufficient that when he turned pro with the Detroit Lions he occasionally filled in on defense while continuing to do just about everything else as well.

Walker played football as a freshman in 1945, then served in the U.S. Army and returned for three more years with Southern Methodist (1947–49). He received the Maxwell Award in 1947 as the nation's top player and added the Heisman in 1948. His exploits led to naming of the award given annually to the best college running back after him—the Doak Walker Award.

Walker was selected by Detroit in the first round of the 1950 football draft (the third player chosen), and earned Rookie of the Year honors. In his six-year professional career, he made All-NFL five times and twice led the league in scoring. During his years with the Lions, they won three divisional titles and twice captured the league championship by defeating the mighty Cleveland Browns quarterbacked by Otto Graham.

Walker excelled despite weighing just 173 pounds, small by NFL standards, even in his day. Many people thought that he was too light to make it in professional football. He not only succeeded but also earned induction into both the College Football Hall of Fame (1959) and the Pro Football Hall of Fame (1986).

Walker remained an athlete to the end. He was skiing on January 30, 1998, in Colorado when he suffered an accident that left him paralyzed. He never recovered from his injuries and died on September 27.

See also: Heisman Trophy; Williams, Errick Lynne, Jr.

Additional Reading:
Parker, Raymond K. *We Play to Win! The Inside Story of the Fabulous Detroit Lions.* Englewood Cliffs NJ: Prentice-Hall, 1955.
Walker, Doak, told to Dorothy Kendall Bracken. *Doak Walker, Three-Time All-American.* Austin TX: Steck, 1950.

Walsh, William Ernest (the Genius) (1931–2007)

Bill Walsh earned the nickname "the Genius" for his innovative approach to offense as an assistant coach with the Oakland Raiders, Cincinnati Bengals, and San Diego Chargers (1966–76), and even more so for his achievements as head coach of the San Francisco 49ers (1979–88). His success with San Francisco included a ten-year record of 102-63-1, six NFC Western Division titles, and victories in Super Bowls XVI, XIX, and XXIII. Walsh was named National Football League Coach of the Year in 1981 and NFC Coach of the Year in 1984. With only ten years of head coaching behind him, he was inducted into the Pro Football Hall of Fame in 1993.

Walsh changed professional football enormously and in doing so gave the American public one of the most exciting and popular teams in sports history. He took over a 49ers team that had gone 2-14 in 1978. Although the team had the same record during his first season, within three years of his becoming head coach San Francisco was the Super Bowl winner.

The key to his success and to the 49ers' fame was his introduction of the West Coast offense. The approach was new, and defenses had great trouble dealing with it. In Walsh's offensive philosophy, much depended on the accuracy and decision making of the quarterback, and few coaches have been more adept at developing quarterbacks than Walsh. As an assistant, he helped Ken Anderson of the Bengals and Dan Fouts of the Chargers become outstanding quarterbacks, and he worked his magic in San Francisco with Joe Montana and later Steve Young.

The West Coast offense featured ball-control offense through short- and medium-range passing rather than rushing with a constant big-strike capability. A finesse and speed offense, it began with carefully developed and complex schemes and angle blocking by the line. Receivers ran a lot of crossing routes and slants that, with a receiver like Jerry Rice, could turn a short pass into a touchdown. The tight end was a prominent receiver rather than primarily a blocker, and running backs were used extensively as receivers. The quarterback had to make quick reads and often threw to a second or even third choice. The complex patterns and use of backs often created mismatches, a back, for example, covered by a much slower linebacker.

Famed for his offensive genius and development of quarterbacks, Walsh also trained his assistant coaches well. Large numbers of them went on to become head coaches and in turn passed on Walsh's innovations and techniques to their assistants, who in turn became head coaches. The coaching tree descending from Walsh included on the first-generation branch, as of 2007, George Seifert (who succeeded Walsh at San Francisco and won two more Super Bowls), Mike Holmgren (a Super Bowl winner with Green Bay), Bruce Coslet, Dennis Green, Ray Rhodes, and Sam Wyche. The second-generation branch featured Brian Billick, Pete Carroll, Jeff Fisher, Jon Gruden, Gary Kubiak, Steve Mariucci, Andy Reid, and Mike Shanahan, with the tree certain to grow even more. While all coaches make their own contributions, influence means much, and Walsh's influence is likely to endure for a long time.

Walsh's influence also included establishing the Minority Coaching Fellowship program in 1987 to help minority coaches advance up the coaching ladder. Here as in other areas, Walsh was an innovative pioneer, and his legacy in this area was established when the NFL made his mission its own.

Even after retiring as coach of the 49ers, Walsh never left football far behind. He worked as a television analyst for NBC-TV and served stints as head coach at Stanford; administrative assistant (essentially a consultant) to the San Francisco coaching staff; general manager of the 49ers; consultant to his successor as general manager, Terry Donahue; and a member of the athletics director's staff at Stanford, including the role of interim athletics director. In addition, he gave motivational speeches, wrote two books, and did some teaching in the Stanford Graduate School of Business.

See also: Montana, Joseph Clifford; Rice, Jerry Lee; Rooney Rule; Super Bowl; Young, Jon Steven.

Additional Reading:
Dickey, Glenn. America Has a Better Team: The Story of Bill Walsh and San Francisco's World Champion 49ers. San Francisco: Harbor, 1982.
Harris, David. The Genius: How Bill Walsh Reinvented Football and Created an NFL Dynasty. New York: Random House, 2008.
Walsh, Bill. Building a Champion: On Football and the Making of the 49ers. With Glenn Dickey. New York: St. Martin's Press, 1990.

———. Finding the Winning Edge. With Brian Billick and James A. Peterson. Champaign IL: Sports Publishing, 1998

Ward, Arch (the Cecil B. de Mille of Sports) (1896–1955)

Arch Ward was one of the most influential sports journalists ever. As sports editor of the Chicago Tribune from 1930 until his death in 1955, Ward not only wrote about sports but also contributed to the popularity of several of them.

A graduate of the University of Notre Dame, Ward entered journalism as a publicity writer for Knute Rockne. He later moved to the Rockford Star and joined the Chicago Tribune in 1925, entering a pantheon of such nationally famous sportswriters as Damon Runyon, Westbrook Pegler, Paul Gallico, Ring Lardner, and Heywood Broun.

Ward, also known as the Cecil B. de Mille of sports, helped to develop the amateur Golden Gloves in boxing and created the baseball All-Star Game, which premiered in 1933 in conjunction with the Chicago Century of Progress World Fair. His impact on football took two tangible forms: a football contest between college stars and the National Football League champions and a new professional football league. The first College All-Star Game, in 1934, resulted in a scoreless tie between the college All-Stars and the Chicago Bears. Then in 1946, the All-America Football Conference began play. Ward is usually credited with being the inspiring force behind the new league. Although the league lasted just four years, some of its teams merged with the NFL and contributed to the spread of professional football across the country.

The College All-Star Game was played annually in Chicago at Soldier Field as a fund-raiser for Chicago charities. At the time of its inception, college football was more popular than the professional game. Its stars generally shone more brightly than their professional counterparts, and, because the professional game lacked the status of college football, its top players did not automatically enter the NFL.

The College All-Star Game continued through 1976 as part of the NFL preseason. For about half of the game's history, the college team was competitive, winning twice in the 1930s, three times in the 1940s, three more times in the 1950s, and a final, ninth time in 1963 against Vince Lombardi's Green Bay Packers. At the conclusion of the series, the NFL teams held a sizable advantage of thirty-one wins against nine losses and two ties.

Even while the college team was losing every year from 1964 to 1976 (with the exception of 1974 when due to the professional players' strike there was no game), many of the games were close. Salaries of players, however, had increased by the 1970s to a level where players were reluctant to risk injury and, in the case of college players, possibly risk careers that were just beginning.

The College All-Star Game served important purposes, though, including raising considerable money for worthwhile causes and helping to popularize professional football. By the 1970s, partly through the spread of television, the NFL had risen so far in public esteem that it no longer needed the college game's shirttails. Having become a sports adult, it was ready to move off on its own. Some of that increase in popularity must also be credited to Arch Ward because of the annual contest that he created.

See also: All-America Football Conference; Newspapers; Rockne, Knute Kenneth.

Additional Reading:
Littlewood, Thomas B. *Arch: A Promoter, Not a Poet: The Story of Arch Ward.* Ames: Iowa State University Press, 1990.

Warner, Glen Scobey (Pop) (1871–1954)

Glen "Pop" Warner is perhaps best known today for the youth organization that still carries his name, the Pop Warner Little Scholars, which sponsors Pop Warner football competition as well as cheerleading and dance competition. However, Pop Warner was one of the greatest and most innovative coaches in college football history.

Warner was born in Springville, New York, in 1871. He attended Cornell University, where he starred at guard and served as captain of the football team and earned a law degree. There he also earned his lifelong nickname because he was older than most players.

After graduation Pop Warner decided to use his football rather than legal knowledge and signed on as football coach at the University of Georgia, a position that in 1895 lacked the glamour it would have today. In fact, the university had no athletic facilities at all except for a bare field. Nor was the university much of a university by modern standards, enrolling fewer than 250 students, 13 of whom went out for football.

Warner, though, succeeded in building a winning team at Georgia before returning to coach at his alma mater. Later coaching stops included the Carlisle Indian School in Pennsylvania, Cornell again, a second tour at Carlisle (where he coached Jim Thorpe), the University of Pittsburgh (where he was undefeated 1915–17 and won the university's first national championship in 1916), Stanford (in 1926 winning Stanford's only national title), and Temple. At Temple, he met Joseph Tomlin, founder of what later became the Pop Warner Little Scholars, and lent his name to the organization.

Warner's football innovations included the single- and double-wing formations, the screen pass, the naked reverse, the spiral punt, and the three-point stance. He also introduced numbers for players' jerseys, shoulder and thigh pads, and the huddle. When he retired after forty-four years of coaching (1895–1938), he had accumulated 319 wins against just 106 losses and thirty-two ties. Warner was inducted into the College Football Hall of Fame in 1951, three years before his death.

See also: Carlisle Indian Industrial School; Pop Warner Little Scholars; Thorpe, James Francis.

Additional Reading:
Anderson, Lars. Carlisle vs. Army: Jim Thorpe,
Dwight Eisenhower, Pop Warner, and the Forgotten Story of Football's Greatest Battle. New York: Random House, 2007.
Bynum, Mike, ed. Pop Warner: Football's Greatest Teacher: The Epic Autobiography of Major College Football's Winningest Coach, Glenn S. (Pop) Warner. Birmingham AL: Gridiron Football Properties Corporation, 1993.
Warner, Glenn S. Pop Warner's Book for Boys. New York: Dodd, Mead, 1945.

Wheaties

Wheaties, the Breakfast of Champions, was created by accident in 1921 when a health clinician in Minneapolis happened to drop some wheat-bran gruel on a stove. The heat converted the gruel into wheat flakes that, the clinician noted, tasted quite good. The head miller at Washburn Crosby Company (later General Mills) agreed, and a new cereal was born. Initially called Washburn's Gold Medal Whole Wheat Flakes, when the cereal was ready to be marketed in 1924 it was renamed Wheaties so that the food itself rather than its name would be the mouthful.

By 1933 General Mills hooked the cereal up with sports, sponsoring the Minneapolis Millers minor league baseball team on radio and putting up a large advertising sign in left field at Nicollet Park. Knox Reeves, who ran an advertising agency in Minneapolis, sketched the contents of the sign, settling on a depiction of the cereal box and the sports-appropriate slogan, "Wheaties—The Breakfast of Champions."

From then on, if a man—or later a boy when the cereal got seriously into the children's cereal market in the 1950s—wanted to become athletic, he needed to be sure to eat Wheaties and exercise. Wheaties was marketed as an accompaniment to physical exercise (if not the other way around) leading to the goal of physical fitness. Most early Wheaties champions were men, with the swimmer Esther Williams a notable exception in 1959. As American society came to recognize the value of women also achieving athletic success, Wheaties expanded its scope as well. Gymnast Mary Lou Retton became a Wheaties spokesperson in 1984, the same year she won a gold medal in the Olympics.

Although Wheaties' original sports association was with baseball, the cereal quickly was pegged to a wide variety of sports. Sports stars began showing up on Wheaties boxes in the 1930s and have continued to do so down to the present day. The Chicago Bears' Bronko Nagurski appeared in 1937. Wheaties football stars included Tom Fears, Otto Graham, and Johnny Lujack in 1951, and Glenn Davis and Bob Waterfield in 1952. Bobby Layne appeared in a 1956 series of Wheaties "Invisible Color" pictures that required only the application of water to bring out the colors "like magic."

Even whole football teams, both college and pro, made Wheaties boxes in the early years of the twenty-first century, among them the University of Michigan and the University of Notre Dame in 2006 and the New England Patriots in 2002.

Selected exemplary athletes have been chosen over the years as Wheaties spokespeople. The first was Olympic champion Bob Richards in 1958. Of the seven chosen as of 2007, one, Walter Payton, was a football player. Each spokesperson is not only an embodiment of athletic excellence but an inspirational role model and a leader in community, especially charitable, activities.

Many other food products and beverages have sponsored football over the years, with beer perhaps the most obvious product in the twenty-first century for pro games. Yet Wheaties continues to occupy an important place in the popular history of American sports, including football, as a proponent of physical fitness and community responsibility, with a special focus on the welfare of children and adolescents.

See also: Mr. Inside and Mr. Outside; Nagurski, Bronislaw; Payton, Walter Jerry.

Additional Reading:

Bruce, Scott. *Cereal Box Bonanza: The 1950's: Identification and Values.* Paducah ky: Collector Books, 1995.

———. *Cerealizing America: The Unsweetened Story of American Breakfast Cereal.* Boston: Faber and Faber, 1995.

Wheaties Web site. http://www.wheaties.com.

White, Byron Raymond (Whizzer) (1917–2002)

Among the many college and professional football players who have trod the gridiron during the game's history, few have risen higher than Byron "Whizzer" White. Nor have few (if any) so consistently come in first in area after area of endeavor.

In high school at Wellington, Colorado, White starred in football, baseball, and basketball. He was student body president as a senior and graduated first in his class. He earned an academic scholarship to the University of Colorado, where he made Phi Beta Kappa, again graduated first in his class, and was selected as a Rhodes Scholar.

White also excelled athletically at Colorado, becoming a first-team All-American and finishing runner-up in the Heisman balloting to Clinton Frank of Yale in 1937. In his final season, as a quarterback and tailback, White led the nation in rushing, scoring, total offense, and all-purpose running. At this time, a journalist bestowed on White the nickname "Whizzer," reflecting his speed and skill.

So promising as a football player was Whizzer White that Art Rooney, owner of the Pittsburgh Pirates (later renamed the Steelers), offered the academically and athletically brilliant graduate the extraordinary salary of $15,800 to play for him. However, White had been chosen as a Rhodes Scholar and wanted to pursue that opportunity. When he received a one-year postponement from the Rhodes officials, he took Rooney's offer and led the National Football League in rushing with 567 yards in 1938.

Then White went to England, where he met future Pres. John F. Kennedy, son of the U.S. Ambassador to the Court of St. James, Joseph P. Kennedy. The two became friends, a friendship that would last and bring the two men together again in a variety of ways.

When war broke out, both White and Kennedy returned to the United States, White resuming his football career with the Detroit Lions and entering law school at Yale. Again in 1940 he led the NFL in rushing (514 yards). After a second season with Detroit (during which the multitalented player punted for more yards than anyone else), he joined the military, serving in the Pacific as a naval intelligence officer and earning two Bronze Stars. Among his duties was writing the formal report on John Kennedy's heroism when his PT 109 boat sank.

White entered a career in law after the war, working in a Denver law firm. In 1960 he joined in his friend's presidential campaign and was appointed deputy attorney general under Robert F. Kennedy. When an opening on the Supreme Court developed in 1962, President Kennedy named White to the highest court in the land, where he served for thirty-one years, one of the longest tenures on the court in history.

As a member of the Supreme Court, White was both highly respected and sincerely liked by his colleagues. His legal philosophy, however, came in for criticism as he took some controversial positions. While in the Justice Department, White had strongly supported integration efforts in education and public accommodations and was at the forefront of trying to protect the Freedom Riders, young blacks and whites opposing segregation in the South.

On the Supreme Court, White voted for federal affirmative action, voting rights, and to expand the federal government's power over the states. However, he also took a number of conservative positions. He opposed, for example, the so-called Miranda rights, which are required to be read to suspects who are placed under arrest, famous today from countless television shows. He also was in the minority on *Roe v. Wade* in 1973, which legalized abortion. Perhaps his most controversial ruling was to uphold the state of Georgia's ban on consensual homosexual acts.

Whizzer White retired from the Supreme Court in 1993. His life showed that he cared much about football but even more about service to his country. He demonstrated that service in the navy during World War II, as a strong proponent of integration in the Kennedy administration, and as a dedicated Supreme Court justice.

See also: Presidents of the United States; World War II.

Additional Reading:
Hutchinson, Dennis J. *The Man Who Once Was Whizzer White: A Portrait of Justice Byron R. White.* New York: Free Press, 1998.

White, Reginald Howard (Reggie, the Minister of Defense) (1961–2004)

Reggie White was one of the greatest defensive ends in football history. Nicknamed the Minister of Defense, he earned the title not only for his outstanding accomplishments on the gridiron, including his record-setting sacks, but also his devotion to his religious ministry, a calling that led him into considerable controversy at the end of his career. On the day after Christmas, 2004, White died at the age of forty-three, apparently, according to the medical examiner, from cardiac and pulmonary sarcoidosis complicated by sleep apnea.

After an All-American career at the University of Tennessee, White joined the Memphis Showboats of the United States Football League in 1984. In 1985 he signed with the Philadelphia Eagles after the USFL folded, playing thirty-one games that year between the two leagues. White starred with the Eagles through 1992 and then signed as a free agent with the Green Bay Packers, becoming the first major star to switch teams through unrestricted free agency.

White provided the defensive leadership that enabled the Packers to make the Super Bowl after the 1996 and 1997 seasons, winning Super Bowl XXXI in January 1997 as White achieved a Super Bowl record three sacks. He retired from the Packers following the 1998 season but returned with Carolina in 2000.

White recorded 124 sacks in 121 games with Philadelphia and later also became the Packers' all-time sacks leader with 66.5. He made first-team All-Pro ten times and was named the NFL's Defensive Player of the Year by one or more organizations in 1987, 1991, 1995, and 1998. At his retirement, he held the record for most career sacks (198) and most consecutive seasons with ten or more sacks (1985–1993). Bruce Smith eclipsed White's record for career sacks, retiring in 2003 with an even 200.

Ordained as a minister at the age of seventeen, White was deeply religious. During his playing years, he also served as associate pastor of the Inner City Church in Knoxville, Tennessee, which was burned down in 1996, one of several African American churches struck by arsonists during the middle of the decade.

White remained enormously popular throughout his career, but that popularity was somewhat undermined by social and religious statements he made in his later years. White appeared before the Wisconsin legislature in March of 1998 and made comments that evoked stereotypes about racial groups. At the same time, however, he also emphasized that everyone is made in God's image. He later spoke out strongly against homosexuality and appeared in an advertising campaign urging gays and lesbians to reject their sexual orientation as if it were something they could choose to accept or reject. The campaign especially upset the NFL and the Packers because he appeared in his Packers uniform in the advertisements, although he stopped wearing his NFL uniform in the campaign after the league objected. White also began studying the Torah and Messianic theology, leading some observers to wonder whether he was abandoning his commitment to fundamentalist Christianity.

White's untimely death, however, appeared to erase any lingering ill will. The Packers retired his No. 92 jersey during a halftime ceremony in 2005. Later that season, the Eagles followed suit. White's induction into the College Football Hall of Fame had occurred in 2002, but his entry into the Pro Football Hall came posthumously, on August 5, 2006. White's son, Jeremy, introduced his mother, Sara White, who gave the acceptance speech on behalf of her late husband.

See also: Religion; Sexuality; Super Bowl; United States Football League.

Additional Reading:

White, Reggie. *Fighting the Good Fight: America's "Minister of Defense" Stands Firm on What It Takes to Win God's Way*. With Andrew Peyton Thomas. Nashville: T. Nelson Publishers, 1999.

———. *God's Playbook: The Bible's Game Plan for Life*. With Steve Hubbard. Nashville: T. Nelson Publishers, 1998.

———. *Reggie White in the Trenches: The Autobiography of Reggie White*. With Jim Denney. Nashville: T. Nelson Publishers, 1996.

Wild Card

The wild card in football refers to inclusion of a nondivisional winner in postseason playoffs. Within the National Football League, the term simply means that the wild-card team has qualified to be in the playoffs despite its failure to finish in first place. The point is to give more teams a chance to win the championship, thus increasing fan interest (especially the fans of the wild-card team or teams) and also boosting television revenue by adding additional playoff games.

After the National Football League and American Football League merged in 1970, the teams were aligned in two conferences with three divisions per conference. In each conference the team with the best winning percentage among those clubs that did not win a divisional title became a wild-card team.

Since then, additional aligning has occurred with subsequent revisions in the structure of postseason competition and alterations in the number of wild-card teams.

The NFL expanded to thirty-two teams in 2002 and was restructured into eight four-team divisions—four divisions per conference. In each conference, the four divisional winners and two wild-card teams qualify for the postseason. Within each conference, the two divisional winners with the best records receive a first-round bye while the other two winners play the two wild cards.

It might appear as if the wild-card teams, obviously not the best teams during the entire year, would have little chance to win the ultimate prize, the Super Bowl. However, some teams get hot at the end, so the teams that make it to the Super Bowl sometimes are the hottest teams, not necessarily the teams that have been the best throughout the season.

In fact, five wild-card teams have won the Super Bowl as of 2008: the 1980 Oakland Raiders, the 1997 Denver Broncos, the 2000 Baltimore Ravens, the 2005 Pittsburgh Steelers, and the 2007 New York Giants. The fact that wild-card teams do sometimes win it all gives hope to teams (and their fans) who find themselves out of the race for a divisional title. "If we can just make the playoffs, anything can happen," they think. And they are right. In a way, life is like that for most people. It is not so important where a person is at the moment but where he or she ends up.

See also: Super Bowl.

Additional Reading:

Carroll, Bob, et al., eds. *Total Football II: The Official Encyclopedia of the National Football League.* New York: HarperCollins, 1999.

Wildfires

Wildfires struck Southern California during October 2007, burning more than half a million acres, destroying or damaging more than 3,300 buildings, and causing at least seven deaths. Tens of thousands of people had to flee their homes in the face of raging fires that struck seven counties, doing their greatest damage in San Diego County where more than five hundred homes and one hundred businesses were destroyed.

Qualcomm Stadium, home to the San Diego Chargers of the National Football League, became a temporary shelter for approximately ten thousand people driven from their homes. In contrast to the dreadful experiences of evacuees at the Superdome in New Orleans during Hurricane Katrina, the Qualcomm experience was festive and reasonably comfortable despite the fears of many temporary residents that they might return to homes no longer standing.

Tents were set up for many of the evacuees while others slept under the stars on cots, as the stadium does not have a roof. Some of the elderly were given more privacy and comfort in stadium club boxes. Well-stocked buffets, rock-and-roll bands, televisions, and visits from Gov. Arnold Schwarzenegger helped to distract people temporarily from their fears. To ensure that none of the lawlessness that prevailed at the Superdome would surface at Qualcomm, heavily armed police and National Guard troops stood guard.

The Chargers made room for their guests by moving their practices to Tempe, Arizona, the home of the Arizona Cardinals, who had a bye week. By game time, October 28, however, the Chargers were able to return home to host Houston. The team enjoyed considerable good fortune in that although about forty members of the organization were forced to leave their personal residences, all were able to return.

The game against Houston, which San Diego won 35–10, included a pregame ceremony honoring firefighters and safety officers. A fire relief collection netted more than $72,500, which was given to the Salvation Army and families of injured firefighters.

Chargers owner Alex Spanos and president/CEO Dean Spanos contributed $1 million to help victims of the wildfires, the same sum they contributed to help after wildfires in 2003. The NFL and the NFL Players Association contributed $250,000 through their Disaster Relief Fund to the San Diego relief effort. Opening up their football home as well as their purse to help their neighbors, and sharing in the same uncertainty over the fate of their own homes, the San Diego Chargers proved that they were not merely a football team but a part of the San Diego community.

See also: Katrina (Hurricane).

Additional Reading:
Carle, David. *Introduction to Fire in California.* Berkeley: University of California Press, 2008.
Cottrell, William H. *The Book of Fire.* 2nd ed. Missoula MT: Mountain Press, 2004.
Rothman, Hal. *A Test of Adversity and Strength: Wildland Fire in the National Park System.* Washington DC: U.S. National Park Service, 2005.

Williams, Errick Lynne, Jr. (Ricky) (b. 1977)

Ricky Williams established himself as one of college football's greatest running backs while playing for the University of Texas from 1995 to 1998. He set a long list of records, including most rushing yards (6,279) and rushing touchdowns (seventy-two), and won the Heisman Trophy in 1998, a season in which he rushed for 2,124 yards and twenty-seven touchdowns. In addition to the Heisman, he received the Walter Camp Foundation Player of the Year Award and the Maxwell Award, among other honors. He also became the first person to win the Doak

Walker Award (given annually to the nation's best running back) in consecutive seasons (1997–98). Although some of his records, including those for career rushing yardage and touchdown totals, would be broken, he left behind a remarkable college career.

Williams's Texas years seemed to mark him as a can't-miss prospect, and Mike Ditka, coach of the New Orleans Saints, agreed, trading all of his team's 1999 draft choices plus the first and third picks the following year for the right to choose him. That led to a photograph on the cover of ESPN *The Magazine* of the new player and his coach dressed as bride and groom, with Williams decked out in a white bridal gown.

The marriage, however, went sour quickly, as ultimately did Williams's NFL career when he repeatedly violated the NFL's drug policy. The Saints went 3-13 in 1999, Williams had a so-so rookie year, picking up 884 yards but averaging just 3.5 yards per carry and scoring only two touchdowns, and Ditka was fired. The next year, Williams improved, rushing for 1,000 yards in ten games before breaking an ankle. He gained 1,245 yards the next year but was traded to the Miami Dolphins.

With Miami, Williams seemed to realize his enormous potential as he led the NFL in rushing with 1,853 yards and scored seventeen touchdowns. He had another good, if not as spectacular a season in 2003, gaining 1,372 yards on the ground, catching fifty passes, and scoring ten touchdowns. However, in December he tested positive for marijuana. It turned out that he had previously tested positive for the same drug not long after joining Miami.

Amid rumors that Williams had failed still another drug test, and facing suspension, he announced his retirement just before the opening of training camp in July 2004. Williams did not play at all that year but returned in 2005, completed his four-game suspension for violating the league's substance-abuse policy, and played in the final twelve games of the season, rushing for 743 yards.

Then came another drug violation in early 2006, resulting in a suspension for the entire year. With the Dolphins' permission, Williams played for the Toronto Argonauts in the Canadian Football League, the league at the time having no policy against signing players suspended by the NFL (an oversight since rectified).

Still another apparent drug-test failure in the spring of 2007 delayed his return to the Dolphins. On October 1 Williams applied for reinstatement by the NFL, and with the Dolphins attempting to avoid suffering a winless season, the team agreed to take him back. Commissioner Roger Goodell reinstated Williams on November 14, and Williams made his first appearance on the field for Miami on November 26, in the team's eleventh game of the season. His return, though, was short-lived, but not this time for drug-related reasons. After carrying the ball six times for 15 yards, he suffered a tear of his right pectoral muscle, underwent surgery, and missed the rest of the season.

Williams, shy, seemingly introverted, but clearly highly intelligent, had rejected the opportunity to turn pro after his junior season in order to complete both his degree and his football commitment to the team. Sporting dreadlocks, tattoos, and body piercings, Williams may have looked as if he wanted nothing to do with conventional people, yet he has proven himself to be a sensitive individual with a deep capacity for compassion and loyalty. A case in point was his relationship with Doak Walker. After Williams met Walker following the 1997 season, he quickly developed great empathy with the much older man who in many ways was his opposite. On January 30, 1998, Walker suffered a terrible, paralyzing accident while skiing. While he lay in a hospital attempting to recover, approximately every ten days he received a letter from Ricky Williams. After Walker died on September 27, Williams posted a picture of the former football great in his locker and received permission to switch his jersey to No. 37, which Walker wore at Southern Methodist.

Williams's contract with Miami ran through 2008, a season in which he helped the Dolphins make the playoffs. Perhaps he finally is conveying to football fans precisely who he really is.

See also: Canadian Football League; Ditka, Michael Keller, Jr.; Heisman Trophy; Substance Abuse; Walker, Ewell Doak, Jr.

Additional Reading:

Pennington, Bill. "'Kindred Spirits': Ricky Williams and Doak Walker." In *The Heisman: Great American Stories of the Men Who Won.* Ed. Bill Pennington, 314–29. New York: ReganBooks, 2004.

Richardson, Steve. *Ricky Williams: From Dreadlocks to Ditka.* Champaign IL: Sports Publishing, 1999.

"Ricky Williams Profile." Miami Dolphins Web site, December 15, 2007, http://www.miami dolphins.com/newsite/team/roster/player Bio.asp?docid=9631

Wine

Wine and football may seem incongruous to many people. Yes, beer probably remains the dominant beverage of choice for the pigskin crowd, but wine is coming on strong, especially with football players. Large salaries often lead to cultural enhancements such as good restaurants, and good restaurants usually mean good wine, hence the growing popularity of the fruit of the vine.

In fact, football is spawning more than a few oenophiles. Chris Hinton may be best remembered as a bruising and highly effective offensive lineman with the Colts, Falcons, and Vikings in the 1980s and 1990s, but he is now the owner of a large and successful enterprise in Alpharetta, Georgia, about twenty-five miles from Atlanta, known as Hinton's Wine Store. In addition to selling a wide variety of quality wines, he sponsors such nonfootball-sounding activities as wine tastings, a Wine of the Month Club, and a Connoisseur Wine Club.

Hinton's love and considerable knowledge of wine developed out of his appreciation for good food when he was a player. Before long, he became a real wine expert. One of the highlights of his football career came off the field when he shared a $3,000 bottle of Chateau Latour with Chicago Bears safety Dave Duerson.

Hinton sells wine, but other football figures now are making it. Terry Hoage, a standout safety with several teams between 1984 and 1996, has begun his own winery in Paso Robles, California. A small, boutique winemaker, Hoage runs a family business, doing just about everything by hand. His products include the highly respected Hedge Syrah.

Another winemaker is former coach Dick Vermeil, who took the Philadelphia Eagles to the Super Bowl in 1980 and returned, this time victoriously, in 1999 with the Los Angeles Rams. He since has partnered with OnTheEdge Winery in the Napa Valley near Calistoga, where he has his own family roots, to produce the Jean Louis Vermeil Cabernet Sauvignon. The wine honors his ancestors Jean Louis Vermeil and Garibaldi Iaccheri, who once owned the vineyard lands, now the property of the Frediani Vineyards, that produce the grapes used in their famous descendant's wine. The most famous wine story involving Vermeil comes out of his coaching days when he promised kicker Morten Andersen of the Kansas City Chiefs, also an oenophile, a bottle of an especially exquisite wine if he made a field goal. Anderson made the kick but could not collect when the NFL ruled that the wine was a performance-based bonus not part of the kicker's contract. Given the changing taste of today's players, supplying a favorite wine may soon be a common provision of players' contracts.

Additional Reading:
Duerson, Adam. "Chris Hinton: A Big, Bold Finish." *Sports Illustrated*, July 2, 2007, 84–87.
Hinton's Wine Store Web site. http://www.hintonswinestore.com.
Terry Hoage Vineyards Web site. http://terryhoagevineyards.com.

Women Players

Throughout much of the twentieth century, women watched football games and, from the 1920s on, but especially after World War II, served as cheerleaders. They did not often play football, for the game was viewed as strictly a masculine endeavor. In fact, football was widely perceived as the ultimate male sport, and therefore to allow women to play the game would be to destroy women's femininity, emasculate the sport, and overturn the natural gender roles.

From time to time, however, women did play football, but so long as it was all done in fun with no serious intent, everyone could have a good laugh about it. The so-called powder bowl games typically featured high school or college females playing a game of touch football for a charitable cause. Michael Oriard in his book *King Football* cites a number of these powder bowls: Wellesley coeds in 1922, students at the exclusive Woodberry School in Atlanta in 1927 and 1928, Carnegie Tech students in 1938, a contest at Western State College in Colorado in 1939, Ohio University students in 1954, University of Iowa coeds in 1958, and a variety of other contests.

Newsreels prepared for theater showing brought several of these games before the public in the 1920s and 1930s. Consistently, however, no one took these games seriously as attempts to undermine natural masculine and feminine gender roles. The female players were seen fixing their hair, applying makeup, and looking appropriately feminine and attractive, lest they be mistaken for male wannabes. To further the joke, males sometimes would assume the role of cheerleaders at these contests, the "powder boys" hamming it up by, for example, racing onto the field during a timeout to deliver combs and compacts to the players.

Even a real female athlete, such as the great Babe Didrikson, had to reassure the public that, athletics aside, she was a real woman. Although she was filmed playing football with the Southern Methodist team in 1947, the photograph of her in *Life* appeared with a story entitled "Babe Is a Lady Now." The article described how much Didrikson loved cooking and dressing up for her husband.

While American society was ready to enjoy powder bowl games but not real efforts at coed football, it also appreciated the occasional sexually oriented image of an attractive woman in an abbreviated football uniform. Film and pulp magazines featured women in revealing attire punting, passing, or, in perhaps the most provocative of the poses, bending over to hike a football back between her quite bare legs (the viewers, of course, behind her).

Attitudes could turn quickly if a female actually tried seriously to enter the male world of football. One might get away with it if she were just kicking, especially if she were photographed showing off her shapely legs in a kick that might warrant membership in a chorus line. There appeared to be no great backlash, for example, against Helen Bilyeu trying to make the San Diego State team, especially when a photograph showed her in shorts kicking high to show off her legs. She did not actually play, but a high school student in Atmore, Alabama, did. Luverne Wise kicked for her team, converting six extra points in 1939, but was also recognized in the press for how pretty she looked running along the sidelines to warm up.

Kicking, of course, was not viewed as truly playing the game. In fact, many football players and fans still feel that way about kickers, an attitude that benefited the aforementioned young women. Frankie Grove, though, was a tackle for Stinnett High School in Texas, one of the most ardent football states in the country. She got into a game against rival Groom High School for eight plays during her team's final game of the 1947 season and took pride in getting her face covered with mud. Neither the school nor the rest of the Alabama football world was amused. The school board fired Coach Truman

Johnson, and the state outlawed girls playing football in the schools.

Slowly the opportunities for females in football increased, to a great extent because of the passage of Title IX of the Education Amendments Act in 1972. With the weight of law on the side of females who wanted to play sports in school and federal funding dependent on schools making opportunities for them to do just that, girls gradually began to break down the barriers to playing football in secondary schools across the country.

Dugan Wiess was a pioneer place-kicker for Walton High in Defuniak Springs, Florida, in 1973, and recounted her experiences in an article for *Seventeen* magazine. After California in 1973 allowed girls to play on previously all-male teams, Toni Ihler played on both the offensive and defensive lines for Portola High School, and Diane Thompson performed as a split end for Live Oak High.

The gender barrier steadily fell from state to state during the 1970s and 1980s. Sally Gutierrez at Quemado High in 1975 became the first girl to play high school football in New Mexico. In 1977 Massachusetts joined the coed world when Anne Babson played for the Ipswich Junior High School team. Donna Wilborn made the Mount Horeb, Wisconsin, high school team in 1978. In 1982 Beth Bates kicked for Williamsburg High School in Kentucky. Many other high school girls also became football pioneers across the country.

As more girls played secondary football, increasing numbers of them achieved considerable gridiron success. Lisa Mims averaged 40 yards per punt at Louisville High School in Alabama in 1977. Katie Tribble was not only the first girl to score in an Arizona high school game but also made the *Arizona Republic's* Class 4A All-State team as a kicker. That same year, Jennifer Brezinski ran 4 yards for a touchdown for the Indiana School for the Deaf against Edinburgh High School, becoming the first girl to score in an Indiana varsity high school game.

By 1983 girls playing high school football had evoked enough interest to yield a popular film on the subject. Helen Hunt starred in *Quarterback Princess*, about real-life Tami Maida, who played quarterback for the Philamath High School team in Oregon. By 2005, according to former college player Katie Hnida in her memoir *Still Kicking*, more than 2,700 high school girls were playing football on high school teams.

The National Football League also had entered the arena of female high school football, sponsoring clinics. An NFL-sponsored clinic held in York, Maine, in August 2007, for example, helped about thirty girls from Maine and New Hampshire to develop both basic football skills and related life skills such as responsibility, sportsmanship, teamwork, decision making, and leadership. The weekend clinic also included forty-five-minute flag football games. Among those participating was Christine Newcomb, who had started at safety the previous year for her Winnacunnet (New Hampshire) High School freshman football team.

Title ix also had an impact on college football, although the numbers of females playing at that level remained much lower, partly because of the level of competition and partly because the college game more firmly retained its adamantine masculinity. Not until 1995 did a woman dress for a Division i-a game: Kathy Klobe with the University of Louisville. The first to play in a college game was Liz Heaston, with Willamette University in Salem, Oregon, in 1997. She also became the first to score, kicking two extra points. In 2001 Ashley Martin also scored, kicking three extra points for Jacksonville State University in Alabama.

Katie Hnida achieved three important firsts in college football. At the University of Colorado, she became the second female to dress for a Division i game (as a freshman against Kansas on September 18, 1999) and the first to dress for a bowl game (against Boston College in the Insight.com Bowl on December 31, 1999). At the University of New Mexico, on December 25, 2002, she became the first woman to play in a Division i game when she attempted an extra point in the Las Vegas Bowl against UCLA, although the kick was blocked. The following year, she became the first woman to score in a Division i game when she kicked two extra points against Texas State on August 30, 2003.

The increased number of high school girls playing football likely will translate eventually into more women competing for football positions at the college level. When that occurs, the quality of professional women's football will rise as well.

Women have been participating in professional or semiprofessional football for decades. Early efforts to establish semiprofessional women's leagues occurred in Ohio (1934), Los Angeles (1939), and Chicago (1941). *Life* magazine and the wire services carried stories about a game between the Hollywood (Chet Relph) Stars and Los Angeles (Marshall Clampett) Amazons, two of the 1939 teams that went by dual names referring alternately to locale or sponsor. Cleveland talent agent Sid Friedman started the Women's Professional Football League in the mid-1960s. The National Women's Football League originated in 1974. Still later, the Women's American Football League (2001) and American Football Women's League (2002) formed. None of these leagues still operates.

Three women's leagues, as of 2007, were in existence, all three featuring full-contact, tackle football. The Women's Professional Football League (WPFL) began in 1999 with two teams, the Lake Michigan Minx and Minnesota Vixens, playing six exhibition games. The first full season was 2000 with eleven teams. Financial and managerial problems led to the shortening of that initial season, but the WPFL resumed in 2001. Fifteen teams competed in 2006, with the Dallas Diamonds defeating the Houston

Energy 34–27 in the championship game, the third consecutive WPFL title for Dallas. The WPFL is the only one of the three leagues to play a fall schedule, the others opting for a spring-summer season to avoid direct competition with college and NFL games.

The National Women's Football Association (NWFA) started in 2000 as the National Women's Football League but was compelled by the NFL to change its name in order to avoid implying a link to the NFL. As with the WPFL, the NWFA started with two teams playing an exhibition schedule of six games. It began regular-season play in 2001 with eight teams and expanded to its recent number of more than forty. The Pittsburgh Passion defeated the Columbus Comets 32–0 for the 2007 championship, with the season ending in July. The NWFA had enhanced its chances for survival by developing considerable television and marketing savvy. It concluded an agreement with CoLours TV, a network on the Dish Network, to televise some of its games. The league partnered with Brainpads, maker of a new mouthpiece that supposedly decreases the likelihood of concussions, and the Phenom Factory, which manufactures a compression suit designed to minimize the effect of strong hits. The NWFA also initiated an annual Gender Bowl pitting NWFA All-Stars against a team of middle-aged males and, to emphasize its contributions to women's advances in American society, began using the slogan "Baby, Look at Us Now," a follow-up to the once common "You've Come a Long Way, Baby."

The Independent Women's Football League (IWFL) began play in 2001. It is organized as a nonprofit corporation based in Texas but with teams throughout the United States and in Montreal. The IWFL included twenty-eight teams as of 2007, with the Detroit Demolition triumphing over the Atlanta Xplosion 17–7 for the league championship.

Many WPFL and NWFA teams jumped to a new Women's Football Alliance in 2009. Such consolidation is necessary if women's professional football is to reach the type of position currently enjoyed by the Women's National Basketball Association. That status also will probably require some relationship with the NFL. For the men's league to enter into any sort of relationship with a women's league, however, the NFL will have to accept a change in traditional attitudes about football as a strictly masculine sport. That will be a challenge, but the attitudinal change also seems ultimately inevitable.

See also: Hnida, Katharine Anne; Magazines; Newsreels; Pop Warner Little Scholars; Punt, Pass & Kick; Sexuality; Television Broadcasting; Title IX.

Additional Reading:

Hnida, Katie. *Still Kicking: My Journey as the First Woman to Play Division I College Football*. New York: Scribner, 2006.

National Women's Football Association Web site. http://www.womensfootballcentral.homestead.com.

The Official Site of the Independent Women's Football League. http://www.iwflsports.com.

Oriard, Michael. *King Football: Sport and Spectacle in the Golden Age of Radio and Newsreels, Movies and Magazines, the Weekly and the Daily Press.* Chapel Hill: University of North Carolina Press, 2001.

Princesses of the Gridiron: Girls in Tackle Football Web site. http://www.fortunecity.com/wembley/mueller/641/princesses/girls.html.

Women's Professional Football League Web site. http://www.womensprofootball.com.

World Football League

The World Football League originated in 1974 as an ambitious effort to bring football to the world. It fell far short of that goal, succumbing after its second season without making it beyond the borders of the United States. What it is best remembered for is the raid on the Miami Dolphins that brought three of the best-known Dolphins—fullback Larry Csonka, halfback Jim Kiick, and receiver Paul Warfield—to the Memphis Southmen.

Certain strategic decisions were supposed to bring the league success—for example, beginning in July, well before the NFL started play; and playing on Wednesday nights to avoid conflicts with NFL and college games—but the league suffered financial problems from the start. The Detroit Wheels and Jacksonville Sharks failed to last the initial season, and the New York Stars and Houston Texans relocated during the first year to Charlotte, North Carolina, and Shreveport, Louisiana, respectively.

During the second season, the league changed its name to the New World Football League and adopted a new financial plan referred to as the Hemmeter Plan after the new commissioner, Chris Hemmeter. The supposed salvation of the league was to come about through profit-sharing by the players with a minimum salary of five hundred dollars per game. However, the new financial plan applied only to most of the players, not to the big-name stars, such as the three former Dolphins who joined Memphis for the 1975 season. They earned $3.5 million among them, but their greatest seasons already were in the past, and Memphis did worse with them than in the previous season, slipping from 17-3 to 7-4. However, the three did help their new team draw substantial crowds, unlike most of the franchises.

Twelve games into the second season, Hemmeter drew down the curtain on the league, leaving its players to scramble for new jobs. Some returned to the NFL, as did the three former Dolphins, although not to their previous team.

One of the effects of the World Football League was to help derail the Miami Dolphins, who had won four consecutive divisional championships (and two Super Bowls) before the departure of the trio. Miami failed to make the playoffs in 1975 and dropped to 6-8 by 1976.

The other effect was to give several coaches valuable experience and position them on a path toward future head coaching jobs in the NFL. The list included Lindy Infante, Jack Pardee, and Marty Schottenheimer. In addition, John McVay, as general manager and vice president of the San Francisco 49ers, helped capture five Super Bowls.

See also: Perfection; Super Bowl.

Additional Reading:
Gluck, Herb. *While the Gettin's Good: Inside the World Football League.* Indianapolis: Bobbs-Merrill, 1975.
Maher, Tod, and Mark Speck. *World Football Encyclopedia.* Haworth nj: St. Johann, 2006.

World War I

Pres. Woodrow Wilson signed the United States Congress's resolutions of war on April 16, 1917, formally taking the United States into World War I. Within a month, Congress passed the Selective Service Act providing for the selective draft of young men into the army. Relying on both enlistment and the new military draft, the United States set about building an army that could bring the war to a successful conclusion. By the end of the year, approximately two million recruits were preparing for combat.

An immediate effect of this recruiting effort was to reduce dramatically the number of men available to play football at either the college or professional level, the latter still in its infancy. Large numbers of young men marched off to wage the war that in President Wilson's words would make the world "safe for democracy," or, as H. G. Wells expressed it, the "war that will end war" (words that resonate naïvely today these many wars later). This exodus caused football programs to shrink in size or disappear completely. Yale, for example, played just three games in 1917 and completely canceled its 1918 season. Harvard played seven games, mainly by competing against service teams, but played just three games the next year. Princeton played two games in 1917 and three in 1918, all against military squads. In some parts of the country, such as the Midwest, many teams maintained at least close to a normal number of games, although with depleted rosters.

Football, however, did not die. To a great extent, it just shifted its residence from college campuses to military bases. Military camps fielded teams that competed against each other as well as against collegiate teams. Many of the players on these squads just a short time before had been helping their college or even professional teams to victory. These military games often came complete with the usual trappings of college, such as large audiences, hearty cheering, and bands (typically military) playing rousing halftime songs.

Football was also used as part of the training to get soldiers in shape. John Sayle Watterson describes a particular regimen borrowed from football in which two platoons of soldiers lined up against each other, one line attempting to push through the other group, and then the two exchanging roles—mimicking line play in football.

Prior to World War I, collegiate football had endured much criticism and many attempts at reform, especially because the game was seen as overly violent. However, with young men dying in the trenches of Europe, the sport quickly began to look relatively tame. As a result, much of the impetus for reforming football died away with the war.

Teams in the professional Ohio League struggled to play in 1917 as team members left to join the war effort. The Youngstown Patricians started the season as one of the stronger teams in the league but finally had to disband after losing so many players. Many of the Youngstown players who were still around joined the Massillon Tigers, improving that team, but not quite enough. In the first meeting of the season between Massillon and their traditional rival, the Canton Bulldogs, Canton prevailed 14–3. The following week, however, Massillon won 6–0, handing Canton its first defeat of the year. Canton nonetheless claimed the league title with a 9-1 record while Massillon finished with three losses.

The Ohio League teams lost considerable money that year because of canceled games. Things got even worse for the league in 1918. Canton and Massillon did not play at all, and the Columbus Panhandles played just one game—against Dayton. The Dayton Triangles were the only team to finish a full schedule, and they managed that by arranging contests with weaker Indiana teams. In fact, the only Ohio game for Dayton was its contest with Columbus. Primarily because no other league team came even as close as Dayton to approaching a complete season, the Triangles claimed a largely meaningless league title.

The Ohio League resumed full competition in 1919, but it would be the league's final season. By 1920 a new league had taken the field, one that would soon be known as the National Football League.

The war ended with the signing of an armistice by German delegates on November 11, 1918, known thereafter as Armistice Day. Gradually, those young men who had not paid the ultimate price for victory started returning home. Among them were many football players, a sizable number of whom resumed their football careers.

Among those who did not live to make that return trip was one of America's greatest athletic heroes, Hobey Baker. His name still lives today on the trophy awarded annually to the nation's best college hockey player, the hockey equivalent of the Heisman Trophy.

Baker was a student and football player (as well as a hockey star) at Princeton from 1910 to 1914. When he was a senior, one of his many hero-worshipers was a Princeton freshman and future novelist named F. Scott Fitzgerald.

Baker may have been as talented in football as in hockey, but the conservative nature of football in those days kept him from exhibiting his skills freely, although he showed enough to be inducted later into the College Football Hall of Fame as well as the Hockey Hall of Fame. In a game dominated by kicking, he made quite a name for himself as a punt returner, arguably the most important role on the team. As a sophomore in 1911, his skilled handling of punts helped preserve a 6–3 victory over Yale and give Princeton the national championship.

As a junior, Baker developed a new strategy for returning punts. He would gauge where the ball was going to land and stand about 5 yards back of that spot. Then as the ball soared in his direction and the defenders converged on him, he would start running and catch the ball in full motion, an exciting daredevil tactic that at times allowed him to gain more yards on punt returns in a game than the entire offense would generate. He also did his team's dropkicking. One of his most memorable kicking feats occurred against Harvard in 1912 when he booted two field goals in a titanic 6–6 tie. Baker was named to two All-America teams that year. That Baker was strikingly handsome with yellow hair (which he refused to cover with a helmet) added to his heroic stature.

Baker's final collegiate game was against Yale in 1913. The game ended in a 3–3 tie, Princeton's lone score coming from a Hobey Baker field goal. Yale had a chance for victory when one of its players broke loose on a long run, only to be caught and tackled by Baker at the 6-yard line. Princeton held, and the game remained tied.

The dashing Baker took flying lessons after graduation and willingly joined the war effort, flying with Eddie Rickenbacker. Baker shot down several German planes, probably three, although newspaper accounts credited him with as many as fourteen, certainly a highly inflated total. He was promoted to captain, survived the war, and received his orders to return to the United States on December 21, 1918. He decided, though, to take one final flight before leaving. Then he learned that a green recruit had refused to take a newly repaired plane on a test flight. Baker decided to test fly the plane himself instead of taking his own plane on a farewell flight. His men urged him not to go up in the repaired machine, even rolling his own plane out of the hangar.

But no one could dissuade Baker from substituting himself for the scared newcomer. He took the plane with its repaired carburetor up, and about a quarter of a mile out the engine stalled. Even then, Baker likely could have saved himself by picking out a good spot and crash-landing the plane. Instead, he determined to fly it back to the field and land the plane rather than destroy it. The plane, however, started to lose altitude. It crashed, and when Baker's men got to him, they found him bleeding from the right side of his head and his right foot caught in a loop attached to the rudder bar. They extracted Baker from the wreckage, but he died in the ambulance, his death recorded in newspapers throughout the country.

For the nation, Hobey Baker became the personification of heroic youth lost too quickly to death, but in that death never growing old. If there has been a recent parallel to Hobey Baker, it probably would be Pat Tillman, a former football star dead far too early in Afghanistan. Football came out of World War I even stronger than it was before, but as with every war, the most serious effect was the loss of young lives.

See also: Fitzgerald, F. Scott Key; Ivy League; Ohio League; Tillman, Patrick Daniel.

Additional Reading:
Davies, John. *The Legend of Hobey Baker.* Boston: Little, Brown, 1966.
Maltby, Marc. *The Original Development of Professional Football, 1890–1920.* New York: Routledge, 1997.
Mennell, James. "The Service Program in World War I: Its Impact on the Popularity of the Game." *Journal of Sport History* 16, 3 (Winter 1989): 248–60.
Watterson, John Sayle. *College Football: History, Spectacle, Controversy.* Baltimore: Johns Hopkins University Press, 2000.

World War II

On Sunday, December 7, 1941, many Americans were listening to National Football League games on radio. A good number were also at games. At 12:55 p.m., Eastern Time, the "day that will live in infamy," as Pres. Franklin D. Roosevelt termed it, was being born amid great bloodshed and devastation in Hawaii. The Japanese were attacking Pearl Harbor, propelling the United States, despite its previous strong isolationist sentiment, into World War II.

As Americans were dying in the surprise attack on Pearl Harbor, the Chicago Bears were defeating their Windy City rivals, the Chicago Cardinals, 34–24, in Comiskey Park. In New York's Polo Grounds, the Brooklyn Dodgers were pummeling the Giants 21–7. And in the nation's capital, the Washington Redskins were edging the Philadelphia Eagles 20–14 in Griffith Stadium.

At these three games taking place at that historic moment, public address announcers in Chicago and New York instructed servicemen to report to their units. At Griffith Stadium, the announcement was more circumspect, paging top government and military personnel but not yet informing the public of what was happening.

What was happening, of course, would transform not only the United States but also the world. It would have a major impact on football as well. When the United States declared war the following day, football players, like men from all other walks of life, signed on to the struggle against tyranny. Women also signed on, some serving the military effort directly, many others taking men's places in factories that quickly began spewing out planes, ships, bombs, guns, and bullets.

Almost one thousand men associated with the National Football League answered their nation's call during World War II. The number included several owners. George Halas of the Bears (having also served during World War I) entered the U.S. Navy. Co-owners of the Cleveland Rams, Dan Reeves and Fred Levy Jr., enlisted in the Army Air Corps. Also serving in the armed forces were Dan Topping of the Dodgers (marines), Wellington Mara of the Giants (navy), and Alexis Thompson of the Eagles (army).

Tom Landry, future coach of the Dallas Cowboys, left the University of Texas to join the Army Air Corps, ultimately flying thirty missions as a B-17 copilot. On one of his bombing raids, he crashed in Belgium on his return from a raid over Czechoslovakia. Andy Robustelli, who would become a Hall of Fame defensive end for the Los Angeles Rams and New York Giants, served as a 20-millimeter gunner on the U.S.S. *William C. Cole*, a destroyer escort ship. Chuck Bednarik was a gunner on a B-24 Liberator during thirty bombing runs over Germany. He returned after the war to become a two-way star at center and linebacker for the Philadelphia Eagles for fourteen years and make the Pro Football Hall of Fame. Long before his induction into Canton in 1967, he had earned even more noteworthy honors: the Air Medal, four Oak Leaf Clusters, the European Theater Operations Medal, four Battle Stars, and a Good Conduct Medal.

One of the most remarkable war stories is that of Mario "Motts" Tonelli. A two-hundred-pound fullback and defensive back out of the University of Notre Dame, Tonelli was drafted by the New York Giants in 1939 and played for the Chicago Cardinals in 1940. Along with so many other players, he joined the war effort in 1941 and, the following year, was on Bataan when the Allied forces on the Philippines surrendered to the Japanese. Tonelli was forced to march two hundred miles over seven days on the infamous Bataan Death March. Of the approximately 75,000 Americans and Filipinos forced to make that deadly trek, some 7,000 to 10,000 died along the way. Tonelli was then sent to Japan on one of the so-called Japanese hell boats and kept as a prisoner of war for three and a half years. By the time he was freed at the end of the war, Tonelli was down to ninety pounds. He recovered, however, and returned to the Cardinals for a final season. In a bizarre coincidence, Tonelli's number at one of the POW camps was 58, the same number he wore with both the Fighting Irish and the Cardinals.

Tonelli finally returned, but at least twenty-one men associated with the NFL, nineteen of them players, did not. Al Blozis, an All-Pro tackle for the Giants (1942–44), died on January 31, 1945, in Colmar, France. Just six weeks beyond playing for the Giants in the NFL Championship Game, he was searching for members of his platoon in the Vosges Mountains when an enemy machine-gunner shot and killed him.

Another of those who did not return alive earned the Medal of Honor. Jack Lummus was an offensive and defensive end for the Giants in 1941. He got into nine games that rookie year and caught one pass, for 5 yards. He would not catch another. On March 8, 1945, he died on Iwo Jima. Having gone two days and nights without rest, First Lieutenant Lummus led his rifle platoon of marines against a network of enemy positions. Felled by a grenade, Lummus got up, attacked, and destroyed the Japanese emplacement. Wounded by a second grenade, he continued fighting, destroyed another pillbox, and resumed leading his men forward. Finally, the wounded Lummus stepped on a land mine, losing both of his legs. Before dying, he urged his men forward. Carried to a field hospital, he died a few hours later.

Among the other former football players who died on Iwo Jima were Howard "Smiley" Johnson and Jack Chevigny. Johnson starred as a guard and fullback at the University of Georgia and then joined the Green Bay Packers, for whom he was a guard in 1940 and 1941. Shortly after Pearl Harbor, Johnson enlisted, rising to the rank of captain. He earned a Silver Star for his actions during the 1944 battle for Saipan, but during the 1945 assault on Iwo Jima he was fatally hit. He ordered a corpsman to assist other wounded soldiers instead of him and died while they were being helped. His widow wrote of the difficulty of rearing a child without a father in her book *Roads and Crossroads*. Each year the outstanding lineman in the Peach Bowl is given the Smiley Johnson Award.

Jack Chevigny never played in the NFL but was a running back for the University of Notre Dame in the 1920s and a coach with the Chicago Cardinals in the NFL and the University of Texas. His most famous football moment came in 1928 when he scored the tying touchdown for Notre Dame after Knute Rockne's famous

"win one for the Gipper" pep talk during halftime of the Army game, which Notre Dame won 12–6. Chevigny was in the first waves of marines storming the beaches of Iwo Jima. Accounts variously attribute his death to a sniper or a shell that struck as he used a bomb crater as a foxhole. A story, possibly apocryphal, has been told about Chevigny and the formal Japanese surrender aboard the *Missouri*. While coaching Texas, he defeated his alma mater and in turn received a pen inscribed "To a Notre Dame boy who beat Notre Dame" (or, according to another account, "To an old Notre Damer who beat Notre Dame"). He supposedly carried that pen with him, and after his death, according to the account, it was found by the Japanese and somehow made its way to a Japanese officer who used it to sign the surrender papers—the pen ultimately being reclaimed and returned to the United States.

Maurice Britt, of the Detroit Lions, also an offensive and defensive end in 1941, like Lummus caught just one pass his rookie season, which also proved to be his sole year in the NFL. His reception resulted in a 45-yard touchdown. After Pearl Harbor, he enlisted in the army as a second lieutenant and fought in Morocco, Sicily, and Italy. On October 10, 1943, he brazenly performed calisthenics in the open to draw German fire at Mignano, Italy, which his fellow soldiers henceforth referred to as "Britt's Junction." He and his men repelled the Germans, but in the battle Britt lost an arm.

Britt received the Medal of Honor for his bravery. After the war, his football career over, he entered business and politics, serving as lieutenant governor of Arkansas in the 1960s. He also served as district director of the Small Business Administration, a post to which Pres. Richard Nixon appointed him in 1971 and which he held until 1985.

Altogether, three NFL figures earned the Medal of Honor in World War II. Joe Foss was the third. He entered the Marine Reserves in order to join the Naval Aviation Cadet program in 1940, prior to Pearl Harbor. His marine squadron was transferred to the South Pacific in October 1942, with Foss as the executive officer, and led a flight of eight Wildcat fighters on missions, the group earning the nickname "Foss's Flying Circus." By January 1943 his Flying Circus had shot down seventy-two Japanese planes, with Foss, a celebrated "ace," himself downing twenty-six. Later that year, he received his Medal of Honor at a White House ceremony. A planned film about Foss starring John Wayne failed when Foss would not allow a fictitious love story to be added. He later served (as a colonel) as director of operations and training for the Central Air Defense Command during the Korean War. In the mid-1950s he embarked on a political career, serving two terms as governor of South Dakota and losing a race for the U.S. House of Representatives to future senator and U.S. presidential nominee George McGovern. Foss served as commissioner of the American

Football League in the 1960s, hosted the television programs *The American Sportsman* and *The Outdoorsman*, and served from 1988 to 1990 as president of the National Rifle Association.

While the war was being waged abroad, some football players were working the home front to raise funds to prosecute the war. NFL personnel played important roles in selling war bonds, three Green Bay Packers—quarterback Cecil Isbell, end Don Hutson, and coach Curly Lambeau—for example, selling $2.1 million of war bonds in one night at a Milwaukee rally.

Some even continued to play football, as the NFL limped along during the war years, relying heavily on former NFL players such as Bronko Nagurski who came out of retirement and individuals who would not under normal circumstances have been able to make a pro team. Some players were able to get weekend leave from their military assignments to play. The shortage of qualified players obviously hurt the quality of play and forced some teams to take drastic measures to survive.

The Cleveland Rams, in fact, suspended play for the 1943 season. That same year, two teams—the Pittsburgh Steelers and Philadelphia Eagles—merged temporarily as the Steagles, splitting home games between the two cities. The teams dissolved their union in 1944, but the Steelers immediately joined with the Chicago Cardinals as the Card-Pitt Combine. The combination lost all ten games, earning the pejorative nickname "the Carpets." That union mercifully ended after one season, with the two teams resuming their individual ways in 1945. The Boston Yanks and Brooklyn Tigers (previously known as the Dodgers) combined in 1945 as the Yanks and played without an official home city. After that season, Dan Topping switched his Brooklyn franchise into the All-America Football Conference.

On America's campuses, World War II also had a large impact on football, as young men interrupted their college careers to join the war effort. College football teams, themselves depleted in personnel, played against other colleges similarly reduced, but also against military-base teams that typically included players who shortly before had been playing college ball, sometimes for the same team against which they were now competing.

The Navy V-5 preflight training program, which stressed physical conditioning and exercise and which encouraged development of football teams, included coaches who would earn lasting fame after the war, among them Woody Hayes, Bud Wilkinson, and Paul "Bear" Bryant. Earl "Red" Blaik, Army's football coach, had especially powerful teams during the war years.

Congress passed the GI Bill of Rights during the war to help veterans afford college. After the war, large numbers of men somewhat beyond the typical college age enrolled in colleges and universities throughout the country, also swelling the ranks of college football players. With the U.S. government paying fifty dollars per month for school expenses, increasing numbers of men showed up for classes and for football practice. The growing numbers of football players helped to usher in two-platoon football and, on the professional level, make the new All-America Football Conference more feasible and more talented than previous NFL competitors. World War II had changed the world, not only in large geopolitical terms but also in a myriad of smaller ways, including the future of football.

See also: Bednarik, Charles Philip; Bryant, Paul William; Halas, George Stanley; Hayes, Wayne Woodrow; Landry, Thomas Wade; Nagurski, Bronislaw; Rockne, Knute Kenneth.

Additional Reading:
Algeo, Matthew. *Last Team Standing: How the Steelers and the Eagles—"the Steagles"— Saved Pro Football During World War II*. Cambridge MA: Da Capo, 2006.
Andrew Jackson Lummus Jr. Web site. http://www.jacklummus.com.
"Football and America: World War II." The Pro Football Hall of Fame Web site. http://www.profootballhof.com/history/general/war/worldwar2.
Foss, Joe. *A Proud American: The Autobiography of Joe Foss*. With Donna Wild Foss. New York: Pocket Books, 1992.
Johnson-Stovall, Arie. *Roads and Crossroads*. Cedar Falls: Association for Textual Study and Production, University of Northern Iowa, 1997.
Watterson, John Sayle. *College Football: History, Spectacle, Controversy*. Baltimore: Johns Hopkins University Press, 2000.
"We Salute the NFL's War Dead." Cold Hard Football Facts Web site, May 24, 2007. http://www.coldhardfootballfacts.com/Article.php?Page=824.

X

X's and O's

Football strategy consists of plenty of X's and O's, referring to the diagramming of plays by a coach using the two letters to designate offensive and defensive players. Strategy requires considerable knowledge of football history (for in football there really is little that is completely new), detailed awareness of what current opponents tend to do, and an understanding of the capabilities of one's own team. It also demands creativity and ingenuity on the part of the coaching staff, as the head coach is hardly a lone scientist creating recipes for victory out of his own personal memory and imagination. He uses scouting reports, frequency charts of what opponents tend to do in certain situations, game film, input by assistant coaches and players, and up- to-date technology.

All of this is similar to the sort of planning that anyone running a business must do, except that in business the competitor and customer are the people whose tendencies are scrutinized rather than opposing quarterbacks and linebackers. A game plan is like a business plan in that both are crafted carefully, consider all likely variables, and chart a path that leads to a desired outcome. As employees need to be familiar with the business plan, players must study the playbook, with its X's and O's in a multitude of configurations. Not surprisingly, individuals throughout the business community talk about game plans, teamwork, and scoring big. Being proactive is vital, and recognition that the "best defense is a good offense" has become standard throughout American society.

Strategy in all walks of life must be limited to the possible, and strategic patterns are not infinite. Rich Korch, writing in *Total Football*, states that with eleven players there are about five hundred possible plays. An actual playbook may have far fewer than one hundred. A casual fan probably would have trouble memorizing more than a handful. Football players must feel that they really are back in school as they pore over their playbooks—and guard them with their lives. A team would no more want an opponent to get his hands on a copy of the playbook than any business would wish its chief competitors to know all of its future plans.

Additional Reading:

Dolan, Edward F. *Basic Football Strategy: An Introduction for Young Players.* Garden City NY: Doubleday, 1976.

Korch, Rick. "The Playbook." In *Total Football II: The Official Encyclopedia of the National Football League.* Ed. Bob Carroll et al., 474–90. New York: HarperCollins, 1999.

Lamb, Kevin. "The Evolution of Strategy." In *Total Football II: The Official Encyclopedia*

of the National Football League. Ed. Bob
Carroll et al., 459–73. New York: Harper-
Collins, 1999.

Long, Howie. *Football for Dummies.* 2nd ed.
With John Czarnecki. Hoboken NJ: Wiley, 2003.

Y

Yost, Fielding Harris
(Hurry Up) (1871–1946)

"Hurry Up" Yost had one of the most memorable football nicknames, as did his Michigan Wolverines—the "Point-a-Minute" teams—that he coached during his long tenure at Michigan (1901–21, 1925–26). The team designation especially referred to his early squads, which seemed to opponents to be scoring a point a minute while dominating the nation in football.

After four one-year stints as football coach at Ohio Wesleyan, Nebraska, Kansas, and Stanford (with a combined record of 32-6-2), he took over the Michigan program and instantly led a good team to even greater heights. During his first four years there, Michigan won forty-three games with one tie and no losses, claiming the national title each year. The 1901 season ended with a 49–0 victory over Stanford on January 1, 1902, in the first-ever Rose Bowl.

Yost was facing his former team, which still included many players that he had coached the year before. Michigan came in not only undefeated and untied but also without having given up a single point. The victories included a 128–0 demolishing of Buffalo and an 89–0 romp over Beloit. The easy win over Stanford gave Michigan a season advantage of 550 points to 0. It perhaps should be pointed out that the Point-a-Minute moniker was not quite literally accurate. Michigan would have needed to score 660 points that year to truly equal a point every minute. Even Hurry Up Yost could not get his team to do that.

Only a 6–6 tie with Minnesota marred Yost's otherwise perfect record during those first four years. As 1905 progressed, it was more of the same, with Michigan entering its final game of the season undefeated and untied, a string of fifty-six straight games without losing. At the University of Chicago, however, the streak and the Point-a-Minute offense ground to a halt. Chicago, under its own legendary coach, Amos Alonzo Stagg, won 2–0.

Michigan continued to be a very good team, although there were some bumps in the road. Michigan dropped out of the Big 10 after the 1906 season (and after winning the conference title five times in Yost's first six years) because of the conference rules limiting the number of games to five and the number of years a student could play to three. Michigan returned to the conference in 1917.

Yost won another national championship in 1918 and again in 1923. Despite being out of the conference for ten years, his teams captured the Big 10 title ten times, including Yost's final four seasons as Michigan's coach. He continued as athletics director until 1941, having taken on that responsibility as well as coaching in 1921.

Under Yost's leadership, Michigan constructed its Michigan Stadium, the first intramural sports building in the country, and the country's first multipurpose field house. The latter is now called Yost Ice Arena. He also earned a law degree from the University of West Virginia, furthered religious toleration by adding Jewish athletes to his team (including the great Benny Friedman), popularized the principle that football builds character, created the linebacker position, inaugurated the practice of a man in motion in order to deceive the defense, and established the position of the football coach as a true professional. Yost received a salary commensurate with what Michigan professors were paid. Today, of course, football coaches at leading football programs are paid many times what most professors receive.

Yost endeared himself to fans with his special pronunciation of his school: "Meeshegan." He also was in the habit of urging his players to "hurry up" and do whatever he was asking them to accomplish, hence the origin of his nickname. Players heard that phrase a lot and apparently took it to heart judging by Yost's win-loss record. In 1951 the new College Football Hall of Fame hurried up and made Yost a posthumous member of the first class of inductees.

See also: Stagg, Amos Alonzo; Zero.

Additional Reading:

Behee, John Richard. *Fielding Yost's Legacy to the University of Michigan.* Ann Arbor MI: Uhlrich's Books, 1971.

Yost, Fielding. *Football for Player and Spectator.* With Wayne DeNeff. 1905. Ann Arbor MI: Sarah Jennings, 1992.

Young, Jon Steven (Steve) (b. 1961)

Few players have brought more natural intelligence to the game of football than Steve Young. He also demonstrated the truth of the poet John Milton's seventeenth-century admonition in his Sonnet XIX: "They also serve who only stand and wait."

Young was that much-talked-about but actually quite rare individual, the complete student. An outstanding athlete in high school in football, baseball, and basketball, he also earned a 4.0 GPA and was a National Merit Scholar. Committed to his faith as a member of The Church of Jesus Christ of Latter-day Saints, he rose early in the mornings to attend a religious class before continuing with his regular high school studies.

Young then attended Brigham Young University, a fitting choice given his religion and his status as a descendant of Brigham Young, who after the assassination of Joseph Smith, the founder of the Latter-day Saints (also known as Mormons), led his religious group from Illinois into Utah in the 1840s. In college Young became an outstanding quarterback. In his senior season, in 1983, he was selected All-American and won both the

Davey O'Brien Award and Sammy Baugh Award as the top quarterback in the country. The National Football Foundation and College Football Hall of Fame, the NCAA, and the Western Athletic Conference all honored him for his academic as well as athletic accomplishments. He later continued his education, earning a law degree from Brigham Young in 1994. When he was taking snaps from San Francisco 49ers center Bart Oates (also a lawyer) in the mid-1990s, the two formed the only all-lawyer quarterback-center tandem in NFL history.

Young's path to eventual greatness in the pros, however, was not an easy one. He signed with the fledgling United States Football League, which scheduled its games in the spring, playing for the Los Angeles Express during their 1984 and 1985 seasons. The league ceased operating after 1985, and the Tampa Bay Buccaneers selected Young in a supplemental draft. His two seasons with Tampa Bay (1985 and 1986) were unsuccessful for both Young and the team. When Tampa Bay selected Heisman-winning quarterback Vinny Testaverde in 1987, the club traded Young to the San Francisco 49ers.

The 49ers, however, had one of the greatest quarterbacks ever to play the game, Joe Montana, so Young sat and waited. When he did get to play, he showed considerable ability, for example, throwing ten touchdown passes with only thirty-seven completions in 1987, and without a single interception.

With Montana injured for all of 1991 and most of 1992, Young finally got his chance to start. He played so well that San Francisco traded Montana to the Kansas City Chiefs after the 1992 season. Young continued as his team's quarterback until a concussion sidelined him early in the 1999 season. After that year, he retired.

During Young's years with San Francisco, he led his team regularly into the postseason, winning Super Bowl XXIX on January 29, 1995. Young set a Super Bowl record by throwing six touchdown passes, earning the game's Most Valuable Player award. In the 1992 and 1994 seasons he was named the Most Valuable Player in the NFL. In addition, he won six passing titles to tie Sammy Baugh for the most ever. A great running quarterback as well as an accurate passer, Young averaged 5.9 yards per carry, gained 4,239 yards, and scored forty-three touchdowns in his NFL career. In Super Bowl XXIX, he not only dominated San Diego with his passing but also was the game's leading rusher with 49 yards. As of 2007 he owned the third highest single-season passer rating in NFL history (112.8 in 1994), trailing only Peyton Manning (121.1 in 2004) and Tom Brady (117.7 in 2007).

After retiring from the NFL, Young remained active in a variety of areas. He has worked as a television analyst for ESPN on the network's *Sunday NFL Countdown*, addressed the Republican National Convention in 2000, worked with the Salt Lake Organizing Committed to help plan the 2002 Winter Olympic Games, represented

a wide variety of companies (among them
Toyota, Marriott, Visa, and Nike), and
served on Pres. George W. Bush's President's Council on Service and Civic
Participation.

Most impressive of Young's postplaying activities has been his heavy involvement in service organizations. He created
and chairs the Forever Young Foundation, a name reflecting its founder and
the children it helps. The foundation, as
its Web site states, "serves children who
face significant physical, emotional, and
financial challenges by providing academic, athletic, and therapeutic opportunities unavailable to them." Forever Young
works with a variety of charities in order to provide these services, especially in
Northern California, Arizona, and Utah.
Prominent among the foundation's efforts is the establishment, in partnership
with the NFL, of "Forever Young Zones"
that include technology labs in "Y.E.T.
Centers." Among the recent recipients
of these "zones" are the Lucille Packard
Children's Hospital at Stanford University and the Primary Children's Hospital in Salt Lake City.

See also: Education; Montana, Joseph Clifford; Religion; Super Bowl; Television Broadcasting; United States Football League; Walsh,
William Ernest.

Additional Reading:
Christopher, Matt. In the Huddle with . . . Steve
    Young. Boston: Little, Brown, 1996.
Forever Young Foundation Web site. http://
    www.foreveryoung.org.
Livsey, Laury. The Steve Young Story. Rocklin
    CA: Prima, 1996.

Zero

The word *zero* comes into English from Latin through Italian and means "nothing." The concept usually is negative, even overwhelmingly negative. In football, though, as in most areas of human endeavor, it all depends on one's point of view. Zero may connote absolute dominance or utter futility. When Fielding "Hurry Up" Yost's 1901 Michigan football team outscored its collective opponents 550 to 0, certainly Michigan dominated about as much as any team can, racking up scores so quickly as to earn its "Point-a-Minute" nickname. On the other hand, Michigan's opponents could hardly be exempt from earning a booby prize for futility.

To be shut out is the ultimate embarrassment in a football game. With the game hopelessly lost, the loser still tries mightily to score something, if only a field goal, to avoid the dreaded zero. The defense, though, smelling the blood of a whitewashing, will play feverishly to prevent the score.

When a team loses, the score is usually cited as "60 to nothing," for example, the word *zero* yielding to its historical meaning. The loser has done nothing good, has accomplished nothing positive, has gained nothing to show for its efforts. It is as if the team did not even show up, the players mere shadows of some reality that knew better than to waste its time trying to score, let alone win the game.

Once in a great while, however, the zero takes on a different connotation, as in a titanic struggle between powerhouses Notre Dame and Army on November 9, 1946. Playing at New York's Yankee Stadium in front of more than seventy-four thousand spectators, the top-ranked Army squad featuring the immortal running back combo of Doc Blanchard and Glenn Davis faced the second-ranked Fighting Irish. Neither team scored, the zero-to-zero contest leaving Army undefeated, but Notre Dame tore through the remainder of its schedule and passed Army to win the national championship. Was the set of zeroes a reflection of nothing in that game, or the result of two massive talents dueling each other to a draw? History chooses the latter interpretation.

So sometimes nothing really can be a lot, even in football. But probably no one could have told that to those 1901 teams on the zero side of that 550–0 score.

See also: Mr. Inside and Mr. Outside; Yost, Fielding Harris.

Additional Reading:
Kaplan, Robert. *The Nothing That Is: A Natural History of Zero.* New York: Oxford University Press, 2000.
Seife, Charles. *Zero: The Biography of a Dangerous Idea.* New York: Viking, 2000.

Index

Page numbers in italic indicate references to a main entry.

Aaron's Way, 258
Abbott, Cleve, 35
ABC (American Broadcasting Company), 229, 230, 293, 350, 352, 353
abortion, 391
Adams, Bud, 15
Adderley, Herb, 213, 301
The Adventures of Frank Merriwell, 295
advertising. *See* commercials and advertisements
Advertising Age, 67
Aethlon: The Journal of Sport Literature, 208
Afghanistan, 359, 406
African Americans: All-America Football Conference and, 7–8, 11, 12; in coaching, 1, 4–5, 6, 9, 35, 38, 84, 171–72, 181, 275, 276, 309–11, 313–14, 386; in college football, 1–5, 34–36, 38, 84–85, 102, 181, 246, 275; NFL exclusion of, xi, 2, 5, 7, 245, 248; and NFL integration, xi–xii, 5, 6–9, 11, 12, 47, 196, 320; in Ohio League, 5, 255, 275–76; in pro football, 5–9; as quarterbacks, 9, 84; racial stereotyping of, 7, 9, 76, 171, 230, 245, 248; and segregation in South, 3–4, 34, 49, 84–85, 212, 246. *See also* black college football
Against the Grain, 128
Agajanian, Ben, 228
agents, player, 9–10, 13, 200
Aiello, Greg, 74
Aikman, Troy, 95, 288
Akron East Ends, 255
Akron Pros, 1, 6, 275
Alabama, University of, 224, 263, 307, 316–17; national championship teams, 39, 49, 50, 242, 316, 317; in 1926 Rose Bowl, 45; and segregation, 3, 4, 50
Alaska, 23
Albany Firebirds, 25
Albert, Frankie, 142
alcoholism, 114, 243, 294, 337–39
Alda, Alan, 271
Alexander, Kermit, 320
Alexander, Shaun, 365
Ali, Muhammad, 75, 229, 231
All-America Football Conference, 11–13, 46, 69, 142, 159, 410; and African American players, 7–8, 11, 12;

competition of with NFL, 11, 70, 245, 410; dissolution and NFL merger, 8, 13, 15, 47, 70, 196, 386–87; founding of, 7–8, 11, 70; impact of, 11, 12, 13, 386–87; and West Coast expansion, 12, 70, 119
Allegheny Athletic Association, 162, 286–87
Allen, George, 283–84, 354, 378
Allen, Rex, 46
Allen, Woody, 76
All-Star Game, College, 7–8, 11, 12, 69, 166, 197, 386–87
All the Right Moves, 120–21
Alone in the Trenches (Tuaolo), 327
Ambrogi, Kyle, 340
Ameche, Alan, 131, 149, 236, 376
Ameche, Don, 11
Amer-I-Can, 44
American Basketball Association, 68
American Bowl, 139
American Cheerleader Magazine, 64
American Football Coaches Association, 99
American Football League (AFL) (1926), 13–14, 147
American Football League (AFL) (1936–37), 14
American Football League (AFL) (1940–41), 14–15
American Football League (AFL) (1960–70), 15–17, 83, 159, 192; merger with NFL, 16–17, 70–71, 83, 283, 306, 342, 353; rivalry with NFL, 16, 83, 353, 357, 370; and Super Bowl III, 16, 242, 342
American Football Women's League, 400
American Indians: in football, xii, 17–21, 57–59, 259, 357–58; and mascots and team names, xii, 20, 223, 224–25; stereotyping of, 21, 259. *See also* Carlisle Indian Industrial School; Thorpe, Jim
American Professional Football Association, 6, 69, 155, 157, 404; Jim Thorpe and, 18, 56, 68, 160, 358. *See also* National Football League (NFL)
The American Sportsman, 409
American Weekly, 244
Amherst College, 281
Andersen, Morton, 228, 267, 397
Anderson, Donnie, 175, 214
Anderson, Gary, 228, 267
Anderson, Hunk, 20
Anderson, Ken, 29, 385
Andrews, Dana, 167
Andrie, George, 174